BIOGRAPHICAL SKETCHES

OF THE

BENCH AND BAR

OF

South Carolina:

BY

JOHN BELTON O'NEALL, LL. D.,

PRESIDENT OF THE LAW COURT OF APPEALS AND THE COURT OF ERRORS.

To which is added,

THE ORIGINAL FEE BILL OF 1791.

WITH THE SIGNATURES IN FAC-SIMILE.

THE ROLLS OF ATTORNEYS ADMITTED TO PRACTICE,

FROM THE RECORDS AT CHARLESTON AND COLUMBIA, ETC., ETC.

IN TWO VOLUMES.

VOL. II.

CHARLESTON, S. C.

S. G. COURTENAY & CO., PUBLISHERS.

No. 9 Broad Street.

1859.

CONTENTS VOLUME TWO.

ATTORNEY GENERALS:

Bailey, Henry.................. 38
Hayne, Robert Y.............. 11
Letters written at his death... 18
Legaré, Hugh S............... 34
Pringle, J. J.................. 3

U. S. DISTRICT ATTORNEYS:

Gadsden, John................ 51
Parker, Thomas............... 47

SOLICITORS:

Clarke, Caleb.................. 76
Davis, W. R.................. 81
Evans, D. R.................. 59
Ervin, James.................. 63
Elmore, F. H.................. 85
Proceedings in the U. S. Senate and House of Representatives... 86
Edwards, J. D................102
Hanna, W. J..................105
Jeter, J. Speed................ 83
McIver, A. M..................104
Pearson, P. H................. 99
Player, T. T...................101
Saxon, B. H.................. 74
Stark, Robert................. 66

MEMBERS OF THE BAR:

Bowie, George.................207
Bacon, Edmund................222
Blanding, Abraham.............236
Letters illustrative of his character.........................243
Bowie, Alexander..............420
Butler, George.................476
Brooks, Whitfield..............473

MEMBERS OF THE BAR:

Carnes, Peter..................148
Creswell, Robert...............173
Cogdell, John S................215
Chappell, J. J.................250
Cross, G. Warren..............258
Clifton, W. C. C................270
Calhoun, J. C..................283
A memoir, by B. F. Porter, of Alabama.........................289
Crafts, William, Jr.............345
Extract from Rev. S. Gilman's memoir.........................351
Eulogy by E. S. Courtenay...357
Caldwell, John.................368
Crenshaw, A...................371
Cuningham, R.................395
Clendenen, R..................423
Courtenay, E. S...............536
Caston, W. Thurlow...........587
Dunlap, John..................175
Dozier, A. Giles...............211
Dellett, James.................426
Dawson, L. E..................518
Egan, Thomas.................231
Ervin, J. R....................374
Elliott, Benjamin..............402
Elmore, B. T...................501
Elliott, Benjamin, Jr............581
Ford, Timothy..................150
Farrow, Samuel................159
Fraser, Charles................313
Felder, John M................325
Incidents in the early history of Orangeburg...............337
Falconer, William 343
Farrow, Patillo.................503

MEMBERS OF THE BAR:

Goodwin, Charles....................146
Griggs, Isaac....................176
Geddes, John....................209
Gibbes, W. Hasell....................213
Gist, Joseph....................219
Grimké, T. Smith....................378
Glascock, John S....................408
Gregg, James....................430
Grimké, Henry....................542
Griffin, N. L....................546
Hagood, Johnson....................163
Hooker, John....................247
Hanford, Enock....................317
Hunt, B. F....................436
Herndon, Z. P....................482
Henry, James E....................522
Harrison, Thomas....................544
James, Benjamin....................171
James, J. Stobo....................516
Lowndes, William....................260
Levy, Chapman....................281
Lomax, William....................419
McCready, John....................178
McKibben, James....................263
Miller, John B....................272
Miller, Stephen D....................410
Murphy, John.................... 416
McDuffie, George....................463
McCraven, John....................487
McCord, D. J....................509
McWillie, William....................505
May, P. H....................514
Nibbs, William....................156
Noble, Patrick....................390
Nott, Henry J....................512
Pinckney, Thomas....................111
Pinckney, C. C....................130
Pinckney, Charles....................138
Patterson, Angus....................441
Pepoon, B. F....................477
Preston, W. C....................531

MEMBERS OF THE BAR:

Porter, B. F....................549
Pope, Thomas H....................556
Rutledge, Edward....................115
  Letter of John Rutledge....................120
Rhett, A. M....................569
Simons, K. L....................182
  Letters, &c....................186
  Eulogy by John Gadsden....................192
Simkins, Eldred....................276
Simons, E. P....................488
  Tribute of Rev. S. Gilman....................498
Sims, Alexander D....................560
  Dr. Zimmerman's Eulogy....................561
Singleton, R. W....................567
Siegling, John Jr....................589
Taylor, Robert A....................469
Taylor, John....................168
Tillinghast, R. L....................585
Witherspoon, I. D....................558
Wilson, John Lyde....................319
Ward, Henry Dana....................394
Williams, Thomas....................459
Witherspoon, John D....................233
Walker, J. Murdoch....................574
  Letter from Hon. W. D. Porter, 576
Yancey, B. C....................322

Roll of Chief Justices....................597
" " Law Judges.................... *ib.*
" " Chancellors.................... *ib.*
" " Recorders....................598
" " Attorney Generals.................... *ib.*
" " Solicitors.................... *ib.*
" " Adm. Judges for the District of South Carolina.................... *ib.*
" " U. S. Attorneys for the District of South Carolina..599
" " Attorneys admitted at Charleston.................... *ib.*
" " Attorneys admitted at Columbia....................605

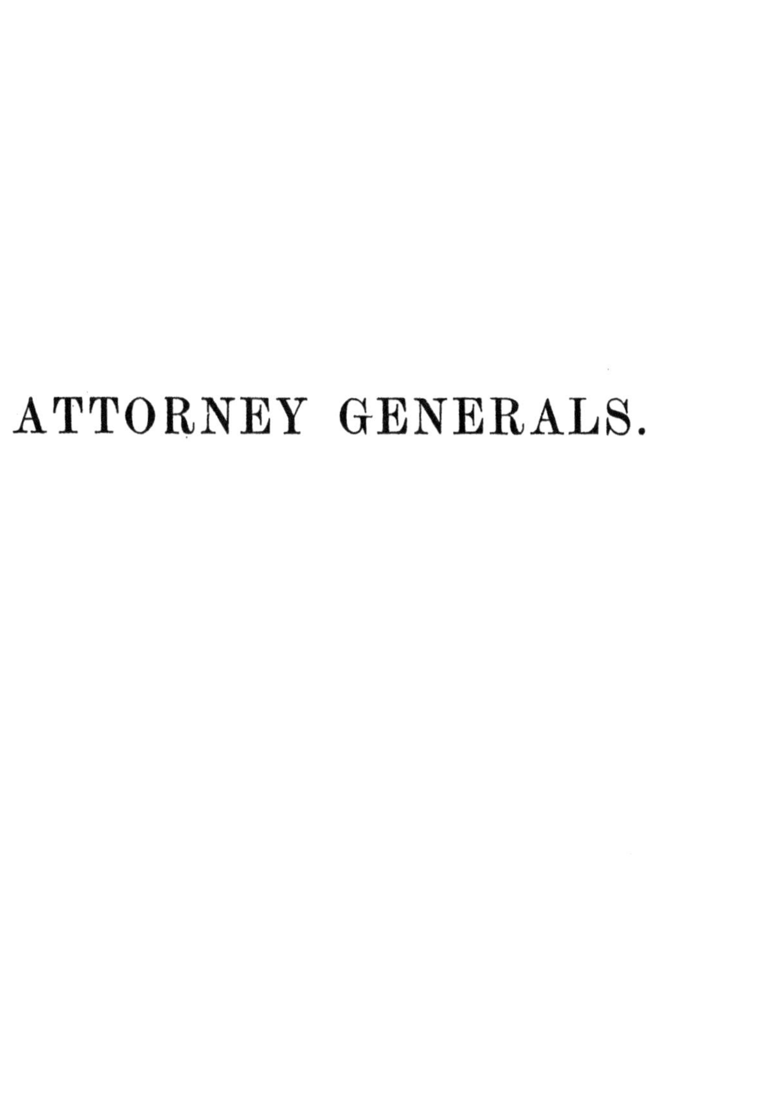

ATTORNEY GENERALS.

JOHN JULIUS PRINGLE.

John Julius Pringle, an eminent lawyer of South Carolina, for sixteen years Attorney General of that State, was born in Charleston on 22d July, 1753. His classical education was begun there, and completed in the then recently chartered College of Philadelphia, under the auspices of the Rev. William Smith, where he acquired the elements of a scholarship for which he was remarked through life. After completing his collegiate course, he returned to Charleston, and commenced reading law in the office of Chief Justice John Rutledge, in the year 1772. After remaining there some time, he went to England, and became a student in the Temple. In the choice of his profession, he may have been influenced by the fact of his father's having served as Associate Judge of the Common Pleas, in the province of South Carolina, under appointments received respectively in 1760 and 1762.

Whilst engaged in his studies at the Temple, where he laid the foundation of his future eminence at the Bar, the great question of the subjugation of the colonies was the leading topic of discussion both in and out of Parliament, and he engaged his pen in the cause of his country. An article, published by him in one of the daily papers, was written with so much ability and displayed such correctness of information on American affairs, that the Duke of Richmond, an active and prominent opponent of the Ministry, in the House of Lords, solicited, through the editor, an interview with its author.

Having kept the requisite number of terms at the Temple, he might have been called to the Bar but for the oaths of allegiance which he would have been compelled to subscribe.

The Revolutionary war breaking out, he went over to the Continent, and remained some time in France. Whilst there, in 1778, he became the Secretary of Mr. Ralph Izard, who had been appointed by Congress a Commissioner to the Court of Tuscany. We find in Sparks' Life of Franklin, that Mr. Izard, upon some real or imaginary grievance, addressed a letter to Dr. Franklin, requesting an explanation. Mr. Pringle, who was the bearer of it, was instructed to submit to Dr. Franklin the particular grounds of Mr. Izard's complaint, which he did, and furnished Mr. Izard with a written statement of his interview and conversation with Dr. Franklin, which is reported by Mr. Sparks. The ability displayed in his account of this interview would show to the inquiring reader the maturity of his mind. There was no interruption, however, of his friendly visits to Passy.

The difficulty of obtaining a safe passage homeward, compelled him to go to Holland, from which he returned by way of the West Indies, in one of the islands of which he was detained some time by illness. Having reached his native city, he was admitted to the Bar in 1781, and thenceforward applied himself most diligently to the practice of the law.

In 1787 he was chosen Speaker of the House of Assembly, and served in that capacity for two years. His fellow-citizens manifested their high confidence in him by offering to send him a delegate to the Convention at Philadelphia, which he declined, on account of the absence which it would necessarily require from professional duties, to which he had determined exclusively to devote himself. But he consented to serve in the Convention which formed the Constitution of the State.

Having now acquired a standing of eminence at our Bar, he received from General Washington the appointment of District Attorney in the United States Court for South Carolina. His commission, which bore date 20th September, 1789, being accompanied by a request from the President that he would not decline its acceptance, as it was desirable that there should be no refusal of office by any one to whom an appointment was tendered under the new government. He therefore accepted it, and served until, by his special recommendation, the late Mr. Thomas Parker was put in his place, who filled the office ably and honorably until his death, in 1820.

It must be known to all acquainted with our history that

the treaty of peace between the United States and Great Britain was followed by difficulties that threatened its speedy interruption. Infractions of its provisions were mutually charged by the parties. Those alleged against the United States related to the payment of debts, the confiscation of property, and the prosecution of persons for their conduct during the war. It being important that the government should be informed of the truth, a letter was addressed to Mr. Pringle by Mr. Jefferson, then Secretary of State, 12th August, 1800, "with the special approbation of the President," requesting him to obtain and transmit information of all proceedings and decisions whatsoever in this State, which might be considered infractions of the treaty, and also of all acts and circumstances which might enter into the justification or explanation of them.

On the 20th of December, 1792, he was appointed Attorney General of South Carolina, which office he filled with distinguished ability and untiring industry for sixteen years; attending annually, under the existing arrangements of the Courts, two terms of four different circuits. During that interval, several important offices were tendered to him by the General Government, which he uniformly declined, in pursuance of his determination to make his native State and City the scene of his labors.

Being temporarily absent at Philadelphia, early in 1796, to argue a case before the Supreme Court; whilst there, an offer was indirectly made to him to appoint him a commissioner under Mr. Jay's treaty. But his preference of home prevailed, and he returned to Charleston early in March of that year. The spell that bound him to his native city was too strong to be broken. It fortified him against every attraction of office and honor that would force him from its sphere. Of this he gave the most striking proof in resisting the inducements offered to him in the following letter:

"WASHINGTON, JUNE 15, 1805.

Sir: The office of the Attorney General of the United States being vacant, it would be extremely pleasing to me if I could avail the public of your services in that station; I therefore take the liberty of proposing the commission to you. Though the circumstances which may principally influence your decision are unknown to me, it may not be improper to state some which lie more immediately under my view than your own. The practice in the Supreme Court of the United States, held here, and the District Courts of Columbia, held here and at Alexandria, is said to be easy and profitable. The higher Courts of Maryland and of the United States, within that State, are within half a day's ride, to wit: at Anapolis and Baltimore. The recess, which the administration is in the practice of taking in the months of August and September, would enable them to dispense with your attendance till October or November, although it will be acceptable at any earlier moment convenient to yourself. So soon as you shall signify to me your acceptance, a commission shall be forwarded to you. And should we be not so fortunate as to obtain your aid, an early notice of that is desirable.

Accept my salutations and assurances of great respect,

TH. JEFFERSON.

To John Julius Pringle, Esq.

Amongst the private reasons of Mr. Pringle for declining this honor, was one (known to the writer of this memoir, too characteristic of his heart not to be mentioned). He had an aged and infirm parent, to whose brief remnant of life his presence imparted its chief earthly solace. To quit her, was impossible.

Being conspicuous and leading at the Bar in the early history of our State, it is not too much to say that no one has made a deeper impression upon the principles of our jurisprudence. His learning was various and profound, and his arguments remarkable for their ingenuity. An instance of this singular ingenuity, which attracted, at the time, the general admiration of his brethren of the Bar, may be found in his reasoning in the amicable suit of J. R. Pringle and wife *vs.* Exors. of McPherson, reported in 2 DeS. Eq. Rep. 524. Another of his arguments may be found in Lindsay's case, 2 Bay, 38. Judge Richardson, accounting, in a dissenting opinion, for the successful impression left by Lindsay's case, says, in The State *vs.* Dawson, 2 Hill's Law Rep. 114, "The City, too, employed the Telamonian Ajax of the day, and he held his broad shield over the city claim for extension, and put his strong hand over the pages of Bynkershock and Vattel," &c.

He was as remarkable for his modesty as he was for his ability, so that it was said of him, as it was of the distinguished Sir Matthew Hale, that he was as remarkable for declining honors as others are for seeking them.

After relinquishing the office of the Attorney General of the State, he seldom appeared in Court, except as counsel in some leading case. Very few of the lawyers of the present day have brought into the heat and dust of the Forum so much of classical attainment and refined literary taste.

And when his professional labors were ended, the attainments, which had been ornaments before, became the solace of his declining years.

Among the sources of pleasure accompanying him in retirement was that of having seen four of the former students of his office elevated to the Bench of his native State—Chancellors Marshall and Waties, and Judges Lee and Richardson. The early election of Judge Waties to the Common Pleas Bench, 1789, was mainly owing to the friendly exertions of Mr. Pringle. And it is but due to him to say, that he always manifested an affectionate interest in the advancement of those who had received their legal education under his auspices, at the same time extending the greatest kindness and indulgence to all the younger members of the Bar, whom he was ever willing to assist with friendly counsel and gratuitous professional services.

Whilst invariably declining offices that would remove him from the endearments of domestic life, and whose competitions and responsibilities were correspondent to their elevation, he was not unwilling to be useful to his fellow-citizens at home, and served them in several capacities. He was President for four years of the Board of Trustees of the College of Charleston; also, for a like term, President of the Charleston Library Society. For several years he was Chairman of the Vestry of St. Michael's, and, upon his resignation, presented to the church the large chandelier that now adorns its interior. Withdrawn from all worldly employments at the approach of old age, and receiving its warnings and admonitions with that tranquillity which is the concomitant of virtue, he sought and enjoyed no other society than that of his own family. His mind had been disciplined by affliction, and its fruits were patience.

Reading, to the last, was his chief employment; Providence, in its kindness, having left to him this resource, by the unimpaired preservation of his sight. Though familiar with classic and English literature, the branch of the latter in which he appeared most to delight was the writings of the great divines. The sermons of Barrow and Atterbury were almost his inseparable companions. He also greatly admired the gigantic intellect of Bishop Horseley, whose sermons on the "Lord's Resurrection," contained, as he said, as able and triumphant an exposition of evidence as he had ever read. The highest reward of a virtuous life is peace at the last.

> "Nulla recordanti lux est ingrata gravisque;
> Nulla subit, cujus non meminisse velit."

In this happy repose of conscience he was gathered to his fathers.

[Extract from the Charleston Courier of 20th March, 1843.]

DEATH OF THE HON. JOHN JULIUS PRINGLE.

This venerable and distinguished civilian closed his long and honorable pilgrimage on earth on Friday last, having nearly reached his ninetieth year. He was born in this city about the year 1754, and was the son of the Hon. Robert Pringle, who was appointed Assistant Judge of the then province of South Carolina, on the 3d March, 1760, and held that office during the successive Chief Justiceships of James Michee, William Simpson and Charles Skinner. He received the rudiments of an excellent classical education in this city and in Philadelphia, and afterwards studied law in the

Temple, in London. Returning to his native city soon after the Revolution, he commenced the practice of the law with eminent success and ability. He bore a prominent part in the early legislation of our State, and on the 8th March, 1787, he was elected Speaker of the House of Representatives, succeeding Judge Grimké in that office. On the 20th December, 1792, he was appointed Attorney General of the State, and continued to fill that office with eminent ability until he resigned, and was succeeded by Langdon Cheves on the 17th December, 1808.

For many years before his death, Mr. Pringle had retired from public life and professional engagements, enjoying *otium cum dignitate*, and embellishing private life by the practice of social virtues, and giving grace to old age by indulgence in literary pursuits.

As a gentleman, he was a model of courtesy and refinement; as a lawyer, he was one of the most profound and eminent that ever illustrated our jurisprudence or adorned our Bar; and we are gratified to learn that a sketch of his life may be expected from one who knew him well, and who will do justice to his unsullied purity of character, his eminence in learning, and his soundness of judgment—all combined with a diffidence that instinctively shrank from display, but never from duty.

The funeral of the venerable subject of this inadequate tribute took place on Saturday last, and the several Courts of justice then in session adjourned for the day, in order to do honor to his obsequies.

The Court of General Sessions and Common Pleas, Judge Evans presiding, adjourned on motion of H. Bailey, Esq., Attorney General.

The Court of Equity, Chancellor D. Johnson, presiding, adjourned on motion of the Hon. M. King; and the Chancellor ordered the following entry to be made on the journal: The Court, having met this morning according to appointment, immediately adjourned to attend the funeral of the venerable John Julius Pringle, one of the last survivors of the men of the Revolution, and formerly Speaker of the House of Representatives and Attorney General of the State, and ordered that this adjournment be entered on the minutes and no farther business be done this day.

The District Court of the United States, Judge Gilchrist presiding, adjourned on motion of E. McCrady, Esq., District Attorney. On the presentation of the motion, his Honor said: The Court agrees with the gentlemen of the Bar, in the propriety of paying every respect and honor to the memory of their deceased brother, submitted in their behalf. This testimony of respect is due to Mr. Pringle, not only as a member of a profession which he adorned and illustrated by his practice in the days of the Rutledges and the Pinckneys, but as a man distinguished for his virtues in public and private life. Let the Court be adjourned.

The following entry was ordered to be made on the journal: On motion of the United States Attorney, in behalf of the Bar, it is ordered that, in consideration of the death, and in token of the respect of the Bench and the Bar for the memory of the late John Julius Pringle, this Court do now adjourn; and it is ordered that this rule be entered upon the journals of the Court.

ROBERT Y. HAYNE.

This gentleman, who filled every walk of life well, and even with distinguished success, passed away not quite twenty years ago, amid the tears and praises of his native State, and yet the monument to perpetuate his name has not been erected,* and I have seen no just biography of his life and actions. To place him properly before the people of South Carolina would be a grateful office to an old friend and fellow-laborer in many of the fields of life.

Robert Y. Hayne was born the 10th day of November, 1791. He was reared in the country, near Charleston, and his education was scarcely beyond academic, but he seems to have stored his own mind with knowledge. He studied law with Judge Cheves, and was admitted to the Bar 2d November, 1812, just eight days before he was of age. This precedent, which was then set, has been repudiated by the Judges since; and each and every young man, who happens now to want a few days of age, at the examination day, is obliged to wait for months after, before he can be examined.

---

* CITY COUNCIL, Tuesday, Oct. 8, 1839.

The Mayor reported to Council the proceedings of the public meeting of citizens on the 2d instant, in relation to the death of the Hon. Robert Y. Hayne, in connection with which he offered the following resolutions for the consideration of Council, viz:

Whereas, The citizens, at their meeting on the 2d instant, in relation to the lamented death of the Hon. Robert Y. Hayne, adopted, among others, the following resolution, viz:

Resolved, That in further testimony of our admiration and gratitude for the character and services of the deceased, we cordially concur in the suggestion of the Honorable the City Council, that a monument be erected to his memory in the centre of the City Square, and that the City Council be, and they are hereby authorized and requested to erect the same in the name of the City of Charleston, and the Neck, &c., &c., &c.

Be it therefore *Resolved*, 1st, That a monument shall be erected to the memory of the Hon. Robert Y. Hayne, in the centre of the City Square, &c., &c.

The resolutions were *unanimously* agreed to by the *Citizens of Charleston, and by the City Council.*

Knowing the importance to the young and needy of a short time, I confess such a harsh rule has never met my approbation.

His first wife was the daughter of Gov. Chas. Pinckney, by whom he had three children—two sons and one daughter—the former are dead, the latter is still living; his second wife was the daughter of the late Col. Wm. Alston, by whom he had two sons, both of whom are still living.

Robert Y. Hayne succeeded to most of the business of his great master; who had, in 1810, been elected to Congress. His advice to his pupil, "never distrust yourself," strengthened him for his work then and ever afterwards.

His career at the Charleston Bar was success and reputation at every step. Much of it he owed to his unrivalled statement of his cases: he understood them well, and he presented the clear image of them in his own mind as in a mirror to his auditors.

He was the captain of an uniform volunteer company, and protected one of his men with fearless intrepidity from the outrages of a mob, in consequence of some inconsiderate foolish expression.

In 1814, he was elected to the House of Representatives from St. Philip's and St. Michael's; and here began the development of his talent as a legislator—acute, fearless, wise, and laborious. On the election of Gov. Williams,* he was appointed one of his aids, and thereby obtained the title of Col. Hayne,

*In December, 1814, the Legislature seemed not to be satisfied to elect either of the avowed candidates for Governor. The mess at Mrs. McGowen's consisted of a large number of the upper country members; among whom were Col. Starling, Major Robert Wood, and others, with whom I was well acquainted. I was then a little beyond 21, had been admitted to the Bar in May, and had been in service with Col. Tucker and Maj. Wood at Camp Alston. I had, therefore, some of the presumption of youth with the privilege of acquaintance with these eminent men. I had seen by the papers that Gen'l. David M. Williams, of Society Hill, had resigned his commission in the United States service, and was at home. I took the liberty of suggesting to the gentlemen of Mrs. McGowen's mess Gen'l. Williams, as a fit person to be Governor. It met with unanimous approbation, and on consulting his friend, Timothy Dargan, of Darlington, who said he knew the General did not desire the office, but he knew he had never refused to serve when elected, he was put in nomination before the Senate and House of Representatives, and was elected by an overwhelming vote. A messenger was despatched to inform him of his election. The messenger met him driving his own wagon near Society Hill, and inquired if Gen'l. Williams was at home; he was

by which he was long distinguished. In 1816, I first entered the State House as a member from Newberry. There I first met Col. Hayne, although I had frequently seen him, and admired him as a young and active member. He was, I found, not only intelligent, but a useful member in the preparation and prosecution of business. In December, 1817, the Judges, to obtain the increased salary, resigned. Colonel Hayne was put in nomination against Judge James, and from the indications of the first ballot, would have been elected on the second. Col. Hayne sought the advice of Gen'l. Huger, and after a conference with him, announced to the House that he was not a candidate, and would not accept the office. This saved the Judge for a time.

In 1818, Col. Hayne was elected Speaker on the promotion of Mr. Speaker Bennett to the Governor's office. I was not then a member, but, I have no doubt, he performed the duties of the Chair admirably well. I see it is stated in Gen. McDuffie's eulogy, that he had never looked into a book of Parliamentary rules before he was elected Speaker.

He had served four years as a member, and, with his constant opportunity of seeing and observing the course of

---

answered that he was not, but that the driver was the man. The messenger could hardly believe the fact. He, however, delivered the written message. The General read it, and swore he regarded it as the greatest misfortune of his life. He, however, said to the messenger go home with me, and I will send an answer in the morning. He accordingly wrote that he would be in Columbia on the proper day, and take the oath of office. The day rolled around—few had ever seen Gen'l. Williams—an immense crowd was in attendance. Gen'l. Williams rode on horseback, dismounted, hitched his horse at a rack, which once stood near the wall before the State House. Gen'l. Williams was introduced by a committee of the Senate and House, and stood in front of the Speaker. I saw him then from the gallery, for the first time. He was in a blue broadcloth dress-coat, buff pants and vest. His face was a stern florid one. He was not more than five feet eight in height, of a full habit, inclining to corpulency. His portrait in the College Library, by John S. Cogdell, Esq., is a good likeness, as he stood before me that day. His speech was one which went home to the hearts of every hearer. As soon as he had taken the oath, his commission had been read in the Senate chamber, and he had been proclaimed by the Sheriff of Richland, from the eastern portico of the State House, I, with Capt. John Henderson, Col. James Williams, and Capt. Geo. McCreless, three of the members from Newberry, started to walk to our lodgings, at Capt. John Caldwell's. Henderson said to Williams, "that is none of your little d—d racoon Governors."

business, it was hardly necessary for such a prompt and ready man to look into Jefferson's Manual. My experience is very much that of Col. Hayne—"*good sense and a firm purpose*," with competent general education, to qualify a man for any thing.

He was elected Attorney General on the election of J. S. Richardson to the Bench. It is stated in the preface of 1st N. & McC. that he was elected on the 22d of December; but there is some mistake in this respect, for he signed all the Acts ratified on the 16th of December; and his successor, Patrick Noble, signed those ratified on the 18th of December, which was the close of the session: so that he must have been elected on the 17th or 18th of the month.

He held this office for nearly four years, and discharged its various and complicated duties with signal success and reputation. About, or possibly before, his election as Attorney General, his first wife, the daughter of Gov. Pinckney, died; and, during his Attorney Generalship, he married his second wife, Miss Alston, the daughter of Col. William Alston.

In December, 1822, Col. Hayne, who had been by successive promotions, made Major-General, was elected Senator in Congress, beating Judge William Smith by a few votes. This was a great triumph for so young a man to be elected over a veteran in the service of the country. Judge Smith was a Radical, and in favor of Wm. H. Crawford for President. Gen'l. Hayne was an anti-Radical, and opposed to Mr. Crawford. These were then Mr. Calhoun's political views.

My purpose is not to follow Gen. Hayne through his success in Congress. He discharged his duties as Senator with his characteristic energy and ability. He was the Chairman of the Committee on Naval Affairs, and so discharged the duties that he was, on the election of General Jackson to the Presidency, favorably spoken of for the office of Secretary of the Navy.

In the Senate he was the leading antagonist to the Tariff, and fairly competed with Webster on that question. In January, 1832, in opposition to a resolution offered by Mr. Clay, Gen. Hayne made an appeal for conciliation, which would have been fortunate if it had been adopted. He said,

"I call upon gentlemen on all sides of the House to meet us in the true spirit of conciliation and concession. Remove, I earnestly beseech you, from among us this never-failing source of contention. Restore that harmony which has been disturbed, that mutual affection and confidence which have been impaired. Dry up at its source this fountain of the waters of bitterness. It is in your power to do it this day, by doing equal justice to all. And be assured that he to whom this country shall be indebted for this blessing, will be considered the second founder of the Republic. He will be regarded in all aftertimes as the ministering angel, visiting the troubled waters of political dissension, and restoring to the element its healing virtues."

This eloquent appeal was in vain.

On the 26th of October, 1832, an Act was passed to call a Convention of the people of South Carolina, the object of which was to consider the laws levying duties and imposts for the purpose of encouraging domestic manufactures. This was the avowed purpose, but really and truly the purpose was to nullify the then Tariff.

The Convention assembled the 19th of November, 1832, and with Gen. Hamilton, the Governor, at its head, passed the Ordinance of Nullification. Such of the members as believed in its doctrines signed it. I was a member of the Convention, and with Judges Huger and Richardson, Gov. Manning, and many others, refused to sign it. Gen. Hayne was a member, and signed it. I do not question his motives. I always believed him as honest as any other man in the country.

In December, 1832, Gen. Hayne was elected Governor and Commander-in-Chief in and over the State. He entered upon the duties of his office in a most critical moment of time. One false step would have involved the State in the horrors of a domestic civil war: for a large portion of her citizens were in open and avowed hostility to her measures.

The President of the United States, Gen. Jackson, issued a proclamation denouncing the proceeding of the State. It was met by a counter proclamation by Gov. Hayne. In this paper war I do not mean to decide who had the advantage.

I only say that I am thankful, and so I presume is every other citizen, that it ended in paper pellets instead of iron hail.

On the 11th March, 1833, the Convention reassembled to consider the interposition of Virginia and the Act of Congress then recently passed, "for such a reduction and modification of the duties on foreign imports as will ultimately reduce them to the medium standard." At the commencement Gen'l. Hamilton resigned his place as President, so that his successor as Governor might be placed at the head of the Convention. This was done, and the Convention, on the 15th March, 1833, rescinded the Ordinance of Nullification, and happy had it been for the people had no further action taken place. It was proposed early to nullify the "Force Bill." This was regarded by many as a "Brutum Fulmen," and would have attracted no particular opposition. I was a member of the committee of twenty-one, to whom the revision of the Ordinance of Nullification, the interposition of Virginia and the Force Bill, were referred.

In the course of its deliberations Judge Harper proposed to nullify the Force Bill; Gen. McDuffie sneeringly said, "I should like to see you nullify the army provisions of that bill."

In the course of the proceedings of the Convention, came up the allegiance question. Myself and other members were violently opposed to the proposed oath, declaring that primary and paramount allegiance was due to the State. We thought that the Convention, called for another purpose, had now completed that, and had no right to touch that matter. We were willing to leave the change of the Constitution in that behalf to the regular course pointed out in that instrument. The Convention receded from business and went into caucus on that question, and substituted for the oath before the Convention, the "second section of the ordinance to nullify the Force Bill," 1st Stat. 400. This, as Gov. Miller affirmed on the floor of the Convention, was giving the force of truth to the allegation which had been made, that Disunion was the real meaning of the action of the Convention. He moved to strike it out; and if the members of the Union party, who were members of the Convention, had been in their places it would have been struck out, and the years of painful State strife on that subject would have been spared. But they were absent, and the section was retained by a majority of very few votes. Often have I regretted this unfortunate circumstance, although the bill to alter the Fourth Article of the Constitution—making the oath of office to be an oath of allegiance to the State, so long as a citizen thereof, in addition to the former oath, as required by the Constitution of 1790, finally passed 6th December, 1834, after the decision by the Court of Appeals, in the State *ex relatione* McCrady *vs.* Hunt, 2 Hill, 1—was satisfactory to the entire Union party of South Carolina.

Gov. Hayne was, I think, in September, 1835, elected Intendant of the City of Charleston, with a salary of $4.000. In December, 1836, the style of the corporation of the city was changed from Intendant and Wardens to Mayor and Aldermen. Whether Gov. Hayne was the Mayor of the city or not, I am not sure, though I think he was. While exercising the chief authority of the city, he contributed much to its prosperity and welfare.

In 1836, was originated by Dr. Drake and E. S. Thomas, of Cincinnati, the project of the great Louisville, Cincinnati and Charleston Rail-road. The Act incorporating the Company to build the same, was passed by South Carolina on 21st December, 1836. No project ever met with such unanimous approbation. Nullifiers and Union men, in South Carolina, vied with each other in the support of it. The Convention of Delegates from Ohio, Kentucky, Tennessee, Georgia, North Carolina, Virginia, and South Carolina, at Knoxville, in July '36, exceeded any body which I ever saw for numbers and respectability. Gov. Hayne was the president of that body, and certainly gave direction, energy, and wisdom to most of its plans. When the Company was organized in '36–'37, he was elected president, and for a while this great work was magnificently projected and carried out. The great commercial revulsion of May, 1837, like the worm which cut down Jonah's gourd, in like manner cut down the pros-

2

pects of this mighty enterprize. Still, the President was not one to succumb while anything could be done. The Hamburgh Rail-road was purchased; it was embanked from end to end. The road from Branchville to Columbia was laid out and let to contractors. I well recollect the great procession—in the Spring of 1838—from Columbia to Col. Chappell's land, just east of and beyond Columbia, where the president, Gov. Hayne, threw out the first spade-full of earth.

Through all difficulties he pressed the work until September, 1839. Then he met the board for the last time at Ashville, North Carolina; and in a few days Robert Y. Hayne ceased to be numbered among the sons of earth. He left his second wife and several children surviving him.

Few greater or better men have ever lived. He was a statesman of great wisdom; a patriot of undoubted honesty and purity of purpose.

He was a lawyer in every respect worthy of imitation. By the force of his own genius and efforts, he stood, in a few years, at the head of the Charleston Bar; then, as always, remarkable for a constellation of eminent lawyers.

In all the relations of private and domestic life he was a model of excellence. Life was a short period of probation to him. Forty-eight years, lacking a few months, were all which he was permitted to illustrate. But they accomplished more than three score and ten would with most men. He was, we are to believe, ripe for the harvest, and was therefore gathered to his fathers.

We append the following notices as illustrative of the talents and public life of Gov. Robert Y. Hayne. They were addressed to his brother, Colonel Arthur P. Hayne, (a distinguished soldier of the war of 1812, and the friend and companion in arms of Andrew Jackson,) shortly after the death of Governor Hayne, by his cotemporaries. The first was written by a distinguished statesman and orator; the second by a learned and eminent jurist; and the third by an able theologian of exalted piety:

"When I commenced life here, General Hayne was in the Senate of the United States, and shortly after his return to our State, I went into that body, which limited the pleasure of my personal intercourse with him to a very short period.

I had, therefore, but little opportunity of observing those minute and striking particulars in his conduct and character, which would be most interesting in the detail, and which, in the aggregate, composed the shining and useful life, the premature termination of which has occasioned a general mourning. Perhaps, too, there was something in his character which naturally exempted his career from the occurrence of frequent striking incidents, and tended rather to produce an important general result, than conspicuous insulated events; for his nature was made up of the higher, graver, and more sedate qualities and virtues—wisdom, fortitude, prudence, perseverance, industry—cardinal qualities—in short, those upon the exercise of which, the well-being of society depends; upon which mankind repose with an instinctive feeling of safety, while they bring a willing tribute of respect and admiration. It is the peculiar and distinctive property of one thus endowed, to be, in every circumstance of life, equal to the occasion—meeting every emergency with a power which could not be overtasked, and with a discretion which would not over-act. This was my own estimate of your brother; and when I went into, shortly after he had left, the Senate, I found the members of that body entertained the same sentiments in regard to him. He had left upon their minds a feeling of profound respect, and many of its wisest and best members regarded him with love and admiration. Judge White especially, often spoke of him with enthusiasm, and declared that he had known no man more fit for the Presidency of the United States—a sentiment in which very many concurred.

When, towards the close of General Hamilton's administration, the progress of the South Carolina controversy with the General Government seemed to lead to a dangerous collision, all those in the State who were actively engaged in it, with one accord, turned their eyes to General Hayne as the leader in the approaching crisis. There was no division of sentiment, no balancing between him and others. His superior, indeed, his perfect fitness for the occasion, left us no choice, and compelled him to resign a situation suited to his taste, adapted to his habits, for which he had peculiar talents, and in which he was, in the midst of circumstances, promising the highest gratifications to the loftiest ambition, for one full of difficulties and dangers, of labors and uncertainties; but which necessity involved, at least, a temporary sacrifice of a wide field of national glory for a circumscribed sphere of State duty. His long and exclusive occupation in public affairs, to the entire neglect of his private, had made it inconvenient for him to encounter the increased expenses which our peculiar condition exacted from the Governor. All the difficulties and peculiarities of his position, were fully present to his mind, and were the subject of a free and confidential conversation between him and several of his friends. The interview was protracted until a late hour of the night, and concluded by this declaration from General Hayne, "Gentlemen, you think my services are needed by the State?—she shall have them: I acquiesce from a sense of duty. You must give me a liberal support, and we will do the best we can."

At this conversation I remember Judge Harper and Governor Hamilton were present.

All the State knows with what assiduity, firmness, wisdom and success, he passed through the most critical and eventful executive term that our history presents.

There was a remarkable instance of that entire readiness for each emergency, as it occurred, in the manner in which he met the proclamation of General Jackson against South Carolina.

That document, which spread terror with its progress through the Union, arrived in the morning in Columbia, where the Legislature was then in session; and was, at ten o'clock, laid before the Committee of Federal Relations. While that Committee had it under consideration, the chairman stepped into the Executive Chamber and inquired of the Governor whether he would undertake a prompt and official reply to the proclamation. The Governor said, 'I will undertake it if the Legislature so desire.'

At the meeting of the House the committee reported the

proclamation with a set of resolutions, amongst which was one requesting the Governor to issue his counter-proclamation. Two days afterwards, in as little time as was necessary for the mere penmanship, was issued a document, whose elegance of composition, elaborate and conclusive argument, just and clear constitutional exposition, confuted all the show of argument in the President's proclamation, tearing away all the subtle disguises of its labored sophistry, and rousing by its tone of proud defiance, devoted patriotism and spirited rebuke, all the highest feelings of the country. No performance could have been more perfect for the occasion, and I doubt whether such a document has ever been thrown off in the same space of time.

His inaugural address to the Legislature upon being elected Governor, was the most successful display of eloquence I have ever heard. It inspired the hearers with irrepressible enthusiasm, which burst forth in involuntary plaudits. I was agitated and subdued under its influence; many wept from excitement, and all of all parties, were borne away entranced by the magic powers of the speaker. I never read the address, which was afterwards published, for I was unwilling to confuse the images which the speaking of it had left upon my mind.

In lamenting his death, in common with the whole country, I also mourn it, as the extinguishment of hopes which I have cherished of his future and much more extended usefulness in the highest sphere of our country; for I indulged myself in looking forward to a period when the country, wearied out with the contest of heated parties waging a war of wild and selfish expedients for power, would call for some citizen of wisdom and virtue, to preside over it; and I firmly believed, as I ardently desired, that call would be directed to General Hayne.

I understood from General Hayne, that he was collecting materials for the history of the South Carolina contest, which at some future time, he intended to digest and publish; and I inferred from what he said, that the outlines had been written. Whatever he did upon this subject, would be very interesting, and the documents collected by him would be of great value and interest."

"In the fall of 1809 or 1810, I had first the pleasure of forming the acquaintance of the late most deeply and deservedly lamented Hon. Robert Y. Hayne. He was then a very young man, a student of law in the office of the Hon. Langdon Cheves. We were members of a debating society that met every week in Queen street, in the school-room of Michael O'Donovan, a well-educated and respectable Irish gentleman. In that society he took a leading part, and seldom failed to speak on every question chosen for discussion. He was generally well prepared. His views were so well arranged and to the point, as to have much weight in the appointed debate; and if any unexpected question was started in it, which claimed a prompt consideration, he seemed as ready to meet it as if it had formed the subject of inquiry. In truth, he, at that early day, and in these preparatory exercises, gave evidence of the ability and eloquence for which he was afterwards distinguished.

When Mr. Cheves went to Congress in, I believe, the fall of 1810, Mr. Hayne remained in the office of Mr. A. B. Northrop, until his death in, I think, 1812, when he was soon after called to the Bar. My impression is, that he was examined for admission before he was of age, and that he was admitted by the unanimous vote of the whole Bench, with the understanding—perhaps with the special order—that his commission should be delivered to him on the day that he reached twenty-one years of age.

A considerable time—certainly several months—had elapsed between the death of Mr. Northrop and the call to the Bar of Mr. Hayne; time enough surely to have permitted a large portion of the business which had been created by Mr. Cheves, and left to Mr. Northrop, to pass into the hands of the professional gentlemen then in full practice. But he had no sooner appeared in Court, and given public proof of his remarkable talents, than the majority and most valuable of the clients of Messrs. Cheves and Northrop attached themselves to him, and remained with him as long as he remained in the profession. It was indeed surprising to see how soon he took his place among the leaders at the Bar, and the ability and courtesy with which he maintained his position. His manner of examining witnesses was entitled to the highest praise. He had the happy faculty of conciliating the good-will of the person under examination—even though prejudiced against his client—accommodated his questions with his character and capacity—and put them to him with exquisite tact and discretion. No attempt was ever made to browbeat, bully, or intimidate. Every inquiry was clear and explicit, and seldom or never admitted of an equivocating answer. It was not to be misunderstood, and was put with the utmost urbanity. The witness might see its aim and object; but whatever his predispositions may have been, he could not easily avoid a substantive reply, so that the accomplished advocate very seldom failed to draw from him, ho reluctantly soever, all thht he knew that could benefit the cause of the advocate's client. He well knew, too, when and where to stop in an examination, and never harrassed and worried a witness by endless repetitions, after he had obtained all that was necessary in his case.

No advocate that I have known excelled, I may fairly say none equalled, Mr. Hayne in the fullness, precision and clearness of the statement of his cases to the Court. Indeed, I have always considered this as his most distinguished characteristic. The most experienced lawyers at the Bar, when counsel with him, usually pressed on him this part of their common duty. He studied the facts and circumstances with much care. His powerful memory enabled him to retain them accurately; his admirably good sense weighed with great sagacity their respective weight and importance, and his ready, and copious, and earnest eloquence presented them with the utmost effect. Nothing was overlooked or omitted that affected the merits of the matter in hand; or that could aid or influence the Court in forming its judgment. To the views of his antagonists he was courteous and just. Often have I listened to his strictures on the statements and arguments of his opponents, and heard him put them more fully and strongly than these opponents had themselves done, and then showed that the conclusions from them to which they desired to bring the Court could not be sustained. Indeed, his statement of a case generally was so admirably managed, made with so much earnestness and sincerity, with so strict a regard to truth, and so thorough a conviction of its justice, that it was in reality, and in addition to its conveying a full and clear view of the facts, a very able argument, and almost necessarily and involuntarily led the Court to take a favorable view of it, and to listen attentively to anything that might afterwards be urged in its support.

In arguing a point of law it was not Mr. Hayne's usage to fill his brief with an array of analogous cases, or to make a parade of legal learning. He carefully collected, and never failed to procure, the leading authorities directly applicable to the matter at issue. He enforced them with great discrimination and effect. In reply, he was scarcely less distinguished than he was in his original statements. He suffered no opposing authority to pass without examination and comment. He was exceedingly felicitous in detecting the difference in fact or circumstances between the cases quoted against him, and the one before the Court; and he seldom failed to invalidate, or at least to diminish, their authority. He followed his antagonist from argument to argument, leaving none unnoticed and, in his best manner, unanswered, with so much ingenuity and candor of manner, and so much clearness and force, as would sometimes, I fear, make the worse appear the better reason, and modify or influence the previously formed opinion of the Court.

As an advocate, he was preëminently successful. During his whole legal practice he never, at the Bar, for one moment exhibited the slightest impatience of temper. With great energy of manner and rapid and earnest eloquence, he always displayed the highest self-possession and control. He was always master of himself and of his subject. He never seemed, even in the least degree, embarrassed or disconcerted when any fact or point, apparently unexpected, arose in the progress of a cause, but met it with the same calmness and spirit as if he had anticipated it, and was perfectly prepared for it. On every occasion, and under all the circumstances in his professional career that fell under my—not very limited—observation, he ever bore himself with the candor, firmness and courtesy of the gentleman.

In writing these brief reminiscences of my ever-lamented friend, your brother, Robert Y. Hayne, I have, my dear Col. Hayne, confined myself to my recollections of his professional life. No man with whom I have ever been intimate, better deserved an affectionate, earnest and copious biographer. Were his life truthfully and fully written, as I believe it deserves, it would hold out to the youth of our country an example of industry, perseverance, integrity, powerful and well-directed talents, and stainless honor, worthy of their highest admiration and their most earnest emulation."

"I regard it as one of the happiest circumstances attendant on my social intercourse in Charleston, that I enjoyed the immediate neighborhood and confidence of your lamented brother. My admiration of him began when I was a student in college, with his earliest notoriety as a public character; and the subsequent intimate familiarity enjoyed during the seven years in which I was his next-door neighbor, only tended to increase and confirm it every day. The intelligence of his death was a shock which I shall never forget. It had never occurred to me that Robert Y. Hayne *could die* in middle life; and when my wife sent for me to direct my attention to the mournful paragraph in our Charleston paper, I had a feeling (a wrong one I know) of violated propriety, as if death had invaded a territory not committed to him yet, and had shot aside of his proper mark at an object not intended to die. May God forgive all the reluctance and rebellion with which my fond heart has met this stroke, and yielded to Heaven's inscrutable, yet wise dispensation! The circumstances of our intercourse would, doubtless, have furnished many incidents of the kind you now require of me, had they been marked and noted at the time. But my mind was unconsciously under a sort of delusion, that neither death, nor separation, nor forgetfulness, could ever remove these facts from my sight, or prevent their continued multiplication. Alas! how much might I have learned from that great, that good, that estimable man, had I anticipated in time the course of events. Lately, and before the receipt of your letter, my attention had been recalled to the facts of my past intercourse with my friend by the action of the two societies, in our University, with regard to his death. Our students (an admirable body of young men) had cherished the most devoted admiration of Gen. Hayne. His public speeches were eagerly caught up in fragments, for the purposes of declamation and exercises in elocution; and our spacious rotunda echoed every week his gallant and glowing sentiments. When he died, a sensation was produced in college, as if they had lost a father, and both societies united in an urgent request to me to deliver an eulogium on his memory. To this I could but reply, that the selection of such a man as *McDuffie* to be the eulogist of a such a man as *Hayne*, seemed to me to preclude all minor arrangements, and ought to be enough for *the whole country.* Not satisfied with this, they reiterated their request, alleging that my intimacy with their beloved *honorary member* would enable me to supply a *home* view of him, which to them would be far more interesting and useful than an eulogy upon his splendid public career. I am, therefore, driven to this answer, that I must comply with their request before the *retired audience* of the college body, if *I can command the time.* Amid an unusual press of other duties crowding upon me, just before our commencement, I am trying to recall such facts as might enable me to meet the call of our young men. A few of these facts may possibly suit your purpose, and with a mournful pleasure I proceed to record them. On a ride which I took with Gen. Hayne, in his barouche, to his plantation on Goose Creek, our conversation took a turn the most familiar and unreserved. The circumstances and scenery around us recalled the early associations of our lives: each was led to speak of his being brought up amid rural scenes and labors, and of the effect thus produced upon subsequent characters. The conversation was more than usually interesting to me, because his experience and observation accorded so well with my own. He said that he owed the chief excellencies of his character, and his success in life, in a high degree, to the training which he had unconsciously received in the country during his boyhood. Rural labors and rural sports had contributed to physical strength and mental energy so efficiently and obviously, that the power of patient endurance, the habit of application, the feeling individual responsibility and care, the practical turn, the disposition to finish what he had begun—the unconquerable purpose—had been early and insensibly incorporated into the very elements of his character; that if he had any distinction among his fellow-men, it was to be traced, under Providence, to these causes. He illustrated the effect on his body and mind by an incident of his boyhood, which I can but briefly advert to. During the Christmas holidays, some friends from town were spending their leisure at the family mansion. His taste was to take a deer hunt. The weather was exceedingly cold and inclement. A deer was found and pursued into a pond, then deep, (in some places to the arm-pits,) and wholly frozen over; the other parties in the hunt were glad of this excuse to retire from the bitter cold to enjoy their Christmas dinner. They endeavored to induce him to accompany them, but without effect. Irrespective of privation, or sufferings, or danger, he must pursue the enterprise to its close; and he actually waded into the pond, (his clothes, on every little exposure to air, freezing upon him,) followed the deer from place to place, without attendant, without dog, without dinner, until a late hour of the night, and rested not until he had secured his game. His return, and his triumph, were not known to the family until the next morning. During the summer, previous to the election of Mr. Barnwell as President of the South Carolina College, Gen. Hayne was pleased, in a very confidential conversation, to urge that post on my attention. I replied, by alleging the fact, (which he very well knew,) that my studies had all been directed into a channel very different from that which the preparation for such a post would require. He replied, very decidedly, 'that is of no consequence; I have always found that *good sense* and a firm purpose, with competent general education, qualify a man for anything.' He then related an anecdote of Bishop Watson. Some of his friends, appreciating his talents, and anxious for his promotion, had him appointed to the Chair of Chemistry, which he afterwards filled with so much honor and usefulness in one of the English Universities. When he received news of this appointment, he remarked that of the whole circle of science, he knew least about this subject. But, having great confidence in his own resolution, he consented to accept the office, on condition that the authorities of the University would allow him to spend a year in France to collect apparatns, and to avail himself of the improvements in that department on the Continent. This was agreed to; he went to France, procured an able master, applied himself with unquenchable energy, and in a year returned, well furnished for his new and arduous employment. He illustrated his position by a fact in his own life. Soon after he made his appearance in the Legislature of South Carolina, very young and inexperienced, he was most unexpectedly elected Speaker of the House of Representatives. He knew *just nothing* of parliamentary rules, had never seen a book on the subject, and knew not a dozen Members of the House, beyond the Charleston Delegation: what was he to do? To recede would be disgraceful. Undismayed by the appalling and critical responsibility which had fallen on the very threshold of his career, he determined to see what energy could do. From a friend, he borrowed a copy of Jefferson's Manual, and retired to his room to open it, for the first time in his life. That night he slept not, nor relaxed his application for one moment. He thoroughly mastered its contents, digested and arranged in his own mind all its rules and principles, and, at noon next day, went into the House, fully prepared for any question of order or contingency that might arise. His most intimate friends at the time knew nothing of his difficulty, or of the manner in which he had surmounted it. His next difficulty—that of not knowing the names of the members, he surmounted to the surprise of everybody. When any member rose, he had the Clerk of the House, in an under tone, to call his name. He then fixed his attention so closely and exclusively on him for a moment, surveying him from head to foot, that he became master of his identity, and never forget it. In this manner, he learned the names of all the speakers in the House, in a few hours; and, before the first week was gone, he had learned all, so that he could instantly call any man's name. To any one who has seen Gen. Hayne, and observed *the penetrating glance of his eye*, the operation of ascertaining the names of the members will be perfectly intelligible. It will be remembered, by many in Charleston, that soon after the destruction of Abolition pamphlets and papers, taken from the post-office, at night, by persons unknown, a meeting of the citizens was called, and, under the auspices and efforts of John Lide Wilson, and other unquiet spirits, an effort was made to sanction that lawless invasion of the post-office by a public vote. Feeling a great concern for the honor of the city and the public tranquillity, I departed from my usual course of neutrality, and attended the meeting. I occupied a position near your brother, and not far from the long table in the City Hall. The tide of popular feeling ran high; it was even thought and said that the progress of the mail must be arrested until its contents should be duly scrutinized by State officers, and pronounced harmless as to the exciting subject. It seemed like a perfect waste of effort, if not an utter self-sacrifice, to oppose violent measures at such a crisis. What was the particular course of proceedings, I cannot now recollect; that is of no consequence, as you can possess yourself of the facts on the spot. But, I well remember, that on some new and decided demonstration of popular excitement and meditated excesses, Gen. Hayne, with the rapidity of thought, mounted on a bench, elevated his person, and, in his most full and audible tones, addressed a motion to the chair in favor of order. His manner was more characterized by strength and determination than I ever witnessed from any man on any occasion. He had labored, in a style of conversation, on the floor, for some time before that, with the advocates of violent counsels; now perceiving them grow more confident, encouraged by every demonstration around them, and seeming secure of triumph, he instantly mounted his extemporaneous rostrum. His form, voice and manner, commanded universal and instant silence and attention. He took a comprehensive, yet highly condensed view of all the topics involved in the question and issue, and obtained a complete triumph of reason, law and order. It satisfied me, and I think all present, that his devotion to the cause of good order was such, as to make him willing to encounter popular odium in its support.

Of that critical and fearful period, when he was Governor of the State, I could state many things. Many others saw him, even more intimately than I did at that time, and I will, therefore, speak only of two conversations which we had alone. I had rendered to him, as Chief Magistrate of the State my public services, in case of any emergency to command me as he might choose. I used, therefore, a freedom of remark to him respecting existing facts and prospects, which I did not indulge, to any one else.

In one of our conversations, happening at the time of the arrival of the vessel in the harbor, which was freighted with arms and munitions of war, for the use of the State, he told me that he had been awaked out of sleep, at a dead hour of night, by several of his friends, who came to inform him that a company of the Union party (as it was called) was then forming to go on board the vessel, and throw the property of the State into the dock. They urged him to order out a volunteer company instanter, to go on board the vessel and guard the public property. His reply was decided: that he would do no such thing: that he did not believe, in the first place, that any would be fool-hardy enough to do what was talked of. But suppose they are, and the arms of the State are thrown into the dock, the State can buy more: the loss of property will be trifling, compared with the importance of maintaining our position and principles with a perfectly pacific bearing. 'Suppose,' continued he, 'I were to do as you desire, and order out a company, the families of their neighborhood would know it—the inhabitants of the streets through which they would pass must know it—our opponents. would hear of it—they would say, "they are arming to butcher us," and would fly to arms themselves. In the present state of excitement, nothing could prevent a bloody collision between armed parties meeting at night in the streets. No, gentlemen! I am determined that if, in this controversy, blood must be shed, the first drop must be shed by our opponents.' I always regarded this incident as furnishing complete evidence of his unusual self-possession, his clear, cool decision and unequaled moderation, in the most exciting and difficult circumstances. Upon every review of the events of that fearful crisis, I am convinced that Robert Y. Hayne was an instrument *prepared by Heaven,* to save the country from the horrors of a civil war. No other human being but he alone could have controlled those angry elements, and guided the State through that stormy period without a collision of arms. Every day of my life I thanked God for such a man, and supplicated the throne of mercy in his behalf until the danger was past. He, too, seemed to feel the need of wisdom, power and resources, superior to human, for that momentous occasion. He attended worship in my church, during all that time, with the regularity of a member; and ever seemed to feel when there, or in private, when the subject was adverted to, his responsibility and dependence on Heaven. His usual habits, however, at church, were those of reverence for Christian institutions and of attention to the preacher—so marked and fixed that I have never seen it exceeded. I speak, of course, only of what I saw, which was in my own place of worship. I often saw his eyes filled with tears, of which he seemed to be so far unconscious as to keep them still fixed on the preacher. I have an humble hope that the thousand prayers that have been offered for him were heard, and that God has taken him to rest. The whole impression of his character, left after a long, close, intimate observation, is that he was the *purest public man* I ever knew.

Your brother once gave me an account of his habits of preparation for debate, which was to me exceedingly interesting. With this, however, both yourself and our mutual friend, Gov. McDuffie, must be more familiar than I. In what I have written of your brother's conversations, I do not pretend, in all cases, to give his precise words, but only the substance. Sometimes there was a force, and a fire, which I could not convey. If I have occasionally spoken of myself in connection with him, forgive it. I did it only to refer to the occasions on which he spoke, that the force of his remarks might be better understood. I am conscious, after all, that my account is meagre, and that it very inadequately presents that great, good man, even in the points of which it professes to treat. Your kindness will accept it, dear sir, as the best tribute I can offer to departed worth, amid the multiplied and responsible duties that now hang upon me."

We conclude this just tribute to "distinguished worth" by appending some extracts from a letter from the brother of Governor Hayne to Gen. George McDuffie, dated at Charleston, 1st November, 1837:

"I place before you an account of the last interview that ever took place between that *great and good man, General Jackson*, and Governor Robert Y. Hayne. In the autumn of 1837, by the direction of the State of South Carolina, my brother repaired to Nashville, for the purpose of obtaining the concert of the State of Tennessee to the granting of a 'Charter with Banking principles, to the Louisville, Cincinnati and Charleston Rail-road Company.' General Jackson, being informed of General Hayne's arrival at Nashville, he directed his private secretary, Major A. J. Donaldson, to wait on him, with his kind regards, requesting him, before he left the State, to do him the favor to pass a day with him at the 'Hermitage.' The invitation was accepted, and as soon as he had finished the public business, he rode out to the 'Hermitage,' and remained with General Jackson during the day. He found his host very feeble, and much changed in appearance, but his mind was strong and vigorous, his memory good, his manner calm, courteous, gifted, as when he first became acquainted with him, in 1820, at the same place. The day passed pleasantly in the company of the 'Hero of Orleans,' the right-hand man of God, to save that city, the State of Louisiana, and those bordering on the Mississippi, and the Gulf, from plunder and ruin.

"The day was gone............the parting hour had arrived, and not one word had been uttered in relation to their former antagonistic positions. My brother rose to go; standing before the General, he seized his hand, and said, 'General, it is more than probable, we shall never meet again in this world, and, as we are about to part, I would say to you, with perfect frankness and sincerity, that, if in the discharge of official duties, circumstances have occurred, and many such, we both know, have occurred, to shake our friendship, on my part, they are now, and ever will be, forgotten.' General Jackson rose from his seat, hardly able to stand, and, taking the hand of his guest, said, in reply, 'Governor Hayne, the kind, frank, and noble sentiment, you have just given utterance to, are those I truly feel, and, from the bottom of my heart, I sincerely reciprocate all you say. And now, my dear sir, I rejoice that our mutual friendship is restored; and that we stand together, *as of old.* The purity of your character—the virtues which adorn your spotless life, as a public man, and, in the social and domestic circle—won my friendship in our first interview, in 1820, at this place. I say it now, and I say it with pleasure, and in sincerity, that, in that great record of your country, which belongs to history, your name will stand conspicuous on the roll of her illustrious sons, as an able jurist, an elegant orator, a wise counsellor, a sagacious and honest statesman.'

"This last meeting reflected honor on both parties, and most happily illustrated their high and exalted characters. I have supposed that so touching an account might find a place in your forthcoming eulogium on the character and public services of Governor Hayne. 'They parted, for the last time, as friends—never again to meet in this world.'"

HUGH SWINTON LEGARÉ

The biographical notice of this eminent scholar, by his sister, would, if it were accessible to every one, supersede the necessity of any further remarks about him, except in reference to his character as a lawyer. But as that accompanies his writings, and will be in the hands of few, I propose to give a brief sketch of his life and character, in connection with the Bar and Bench of South Carolina. In doing so, I shall avail myself not only of the biographical notice by his sister, but also of my own knowledge of Mr. Legaré. I knew him from his entrance in the College of South Carolina to his death, and mingled with him in the Legislature, and heard him often at the Bar of South Carolina.

He was born in the City of Charleston, on the 2d January, 1797. His parents were Solomon Legaré and Mary Swinton. In him were, therefore, blended two distinct races of people—the Huguenots on the part of his father, and the heroic Swintons, of the Scottish Border, on the part of his mother. Hugh seems to have been a well-formed and proper child, until his fourth year, when the small pox fell upon his joints, and dwarfed his limbs; leaving, however, his trunk and head in their proper proportions. This defect annoyed him much in life, and caused him to resort to various devices, to hide the defects of his person. He gave early evidence of the genius which his after-life displayed. From his mother, he caught that love of reading, which made him the scholar of after-life. To Mr. Ward, Dr. Gallagher, and Judge King, he was indebted for the fine developments of his mind, in his acquirement of English and the classics, until about the close of his thirteenth year. He was then sent to Willington. It seems, in the beginning, there was mutual dislike between him and his teacher, Dr. Waddell; but before he left for the South Carolina College, this had vanished. He entered the sophomore class, about commencement December, 1811, but did not, I presume, join his class until after the Christmas vacation, January, 1812. He was then fifteen years of age. was then in the senior class, and recollect Hugh perfectly; his under-size, and his fine attainments, attracted the attention of every one. He joined the Clariosophic Society, and soon became a regular speaker in the debates. It was very unusual for a sophomore to partake in the debates, and measure swords with the juniors and seniors. His course, at first, was regarded as presumptuous; but as acquaintance ripened, and it was seen that his knowledge was beyond his years, he was not repulsed from the higher position which he was seeking.

He graduated, with the first distinction of his class, in December, 1814. I have no recollection of his valedictory speech; and, therefore, presume that I was not present. He was then not quite eighteen. He returned to his mother, in his native city, and pursued the study of the law under the direction of Judge King, and was proposed for admission, when he attained full age. But he had formed a wish to visit Europe, and in May, 1818, he sailed for France, and spent near two years in France, Germany, and Edinburgh, Scotland—very much to his advantage, both as a scholar and a speaker.

In the early part of 1820, he returned to Charleston, and set about the work of retrieving his mother's affairs, which had suffered much from the want of proper management. To this occupation, he united his final preparation for admission to the Bar. He was admitted 12th January, 1821. In October, 1820, he was returned, from one of the parishes, a Member of the House of Representatives, and served two years—making very little public impression. In 1824, he was returned to the House of Representatives, from St. Philip's and St. Michael's, and continued, by successive elections, until 1830, when he became Attorney General. During this time, I had the opportunity of often hearing Mr. Legaré. His speeches were, beyond all doubt, fine specimens of oratory; and yet they wanted that practical force and application, which other less finished speakers gave, and, therefore, he was never regarded *as the greatest among the great men of the South Carolina Legislature.*

During a part of this time, and until 1832, he was the principal writer of the Southern Review: his writings there, as elsewhere, are as finished and perfect as scholarship and genius could make them.

The office of Attorney General did not suit him; and it was unfortunate for him that he followed so able an Attorney General as Mr. Petigru. The division in politics in South Carolina, which was beginning, in 1830, to assume an angry and threatening aspect, and which grew more and more violent, until 1832, when the Convention and the Ordinance of Nullification seemed to rend asunder all past associations, and arrayed parents, children, brothers, and friends, on opposite sides. These various matters prepared him to accept the office of Charge d'Affaires, at Brussels, which was offered to him by the United States Government, in 1832. He imme diately repaired to his post, and remained abroad until 1836. He thus escaped all the difficulties and pain attending the contest which grew out of Nullification.

Immediately on his return, in October, 1836, he was elected to Congress, and served two years with great *eclât.* But he was too much a Whig to suit parties at home; he was, therefore, thrown out at the election, in October, 1838.

He returned to the Bar; and, by the aid of Mr. Petigru, was placed in prominent positions in the great cases argued from 1837 to 1841. Pell and Ball, in the Court of Equity, is one in which Mr. Legaré had a fine opportunity of display. I did not have the opportunity of hearing Mr. Legaré in that case, and, therefore, speak from public opinion. In the State *vs.* The Bank of Charleston, Dud. 187, which was heard before me, May Term, 1837, Mr. Legaré was for the *quo warranto,* and, therefore, on the popular side. His speech was an excellent one, but could not be compared to the fine legal argument of his friend, Petigru, on the other side.

In 1841, he was appointed, by Mr. Tyler, Attorney General of the United States. He was here on the theatre which suited him. He had to deal with great questions. Here, too, his consummate knowledge of Civil Law stood him in great stead. He was winning fame, and marching steadily on to greatness, when the fatal messenger came; and, on the 20th June, 1841, in the City of Boston, he closed his life, and was interred, with public honors, at Mount Auburn. Hence, the friendly zeal of one of South Carolina's generous and talented sons, (Mr. Richard Yeadon,) by the consent of his sister, removed his remains to the Magnolia Cemetery, near Charleston, and a suitable monument erected to his memory.

This sketch was not intended to present his merits, as they should be, as a scholar, or statesman, but simply to place his name among his brethren of the South Carolina Bar; and to say of him, that he was, indeed, as a lawyer and a man, one to whose memory the respect, which attends on greatness, should be paid.

HENRY BAILEY.

Henry Bailey, Esq., was born 7th July, 1799.

What were his opportunities of education, I do not certainly know; he, however, showed, in his different offices, that he had received a good substantial education. He wrote a beautiful hand, and had a perfect knowledge of the English language He was a merchant, but had the misfortune to fail in business Whether he was married before, or after this, I do not know. He married the daughter of Rene Godard, Esq., to whose memory and virtues, I can pay no higher compliment than by saying, she was a *model wife*.

He studied law with James L. Petigru, Esq., and was admitted to the Bar, in Columbia, in 1823. He settled in Coosawhatchie. I first saw him at Barnwell, Spring Term, 1829, when he arranged the case of Bourdeaux *vs.* Cave, 1 Bail. 250. The verdict in that case was for the defendant. He appealed and carried it to the Court of Appeals, in Columbia, his argument will be found 1st Bail. 253. It induced the Court to depart from former decisions, and adopt a new rule, which, however, has been since, uniformly followed.

He was elected State Reporter, November, 1829, and continued in that office until November, 1832, when he declined to serve longer, and Mr. Hill succeeded him. Mr. Bailey removed to Charleston, as soon as he was elected reporter. His first and second Law Reports, and his Equity Volume, have certainly never been surpassed, for accuracy, and manner. Indeed, they cannot be read by any one, who will not award the meed of praise to him, which he so well merited, as being then, and until now, the very best of our reporters. He was elected Attorney-General, November, 1836, and by successive elections at the end of every four years, he was continued until November, 1848, when he declined to serve longer. In this high and responsible office he discharged his duties admirably well. In the fall of 1840, he was opposed by a gentleman, who now fills, with so much credit to himself, and advantage to the country, the office of District Judge, for South Carolina. There was a serious objection to the habits of Mr. Bailey, in one respect, yet Mr. Bailey's eminent fitness for the office enabled him to triumph. A friend said to the author, whose sympathy, and perhaps influence, had been for Mr. Bailey, at the termination of the election: "You have done the deed." Yet, the same gentleman, whose moral, legal, and intellectual standing will compare with any man in the State, said to the author, spring of 1841: "You were right, Mr. Bailey is the man for us." He had prepared the pleading in the State *vs.* The Bank of South Carolina, 1st Spears, 433. His argument, in that case, was certainly equal to any which the most accomplished jurist ever delivered. In May, 1847, he managed, with consummate skill, the defence in the Union Bank *vs.* Sollee, 2d Strob. 390; and he, and Mr. Petigru, literally snatched their client from ruin, both of means and character, and his surety from heavy loss, notwithstanding, they were opposed by the clearness and acumen of such lawyers as Memminger and Hayne. Their respective arguments will be found from page 396 to 403. Mr. Bailey's argument on the circuit was certainly his *chef-d'ouvre.* He spoke for more than three hours—and that with good sense—producing strong and effective arguments. This was in 1847 and 1848, and this case was, probably, the last of his brilliant efforts. For he died at 2 P. M., on Saturday, 2d April, 1849. His latter days (indeed, from December, 1848), were of suffering. His mind and body were alike sufferers. His wife preceded him to the tomb, and from her death, his friends knew, that that which did occur, would likely happen. He left three sons, Godard, William, and John.

Henry Bailey had his failings, but all who knew him will concede, he was kind, benevolent, and honest. As a friend, he was sincere and devoted; as a husband and father he was most attached; as a master, he was, perhaps, too indulgent; as a citizen, he knew and did his duties; as a lawyer, he was surpassed by few. His instructor, Mr. Petigru, Judge King, and Mr. Memminger, were possibly his superiors. None others, of the excellent Bar of Charleston, excelled him. Not quite fifty years of life were awarded to him—they were in most respects, years of virtuous usefulness.

On his tomb, in the first Baptist church-yard, is inscribed: "*Quis desiderio sit pudor, aut modus, tam cari capitis.*"

The notices, of the Charleston Mercury and Courier, of his death, are appended:

[From the Charleston Mercury, April 30, 1849.]

"DEATH OF THE HON. HENRY BAILEY.

"It is with unfeigned regret that we announce the death of the Hon. Henry Bailey, which took place at 2 o'clock, P. M., on Saturday last, at his residence in this city.

Mr. Bailey had but just returned from the Island of Cuba, whither he had gone for the benefit of his health, which had been seriously affected by recent illness. In the death of this distinguished gentleman the public generally has sustained no ordinary loss, and the profession to which he belonged has been deprived of one of its brightest ornaments. Indeed, as a lawyer, Mr. Bailey had few, if any, superiors. His knowledge of the law was profound, and his practice characterized equally by great fairness and liberality, and by the most zealous fidelity to the interests of his client. He was, in fact, remarkable for the devotedness with which he identified himself with whatever cause he was called upon to advocate; and yet, as was once remarked to us by his most distinguished professional cotemporary, 'he was never known to use his great legal attainments for the purpose of oppressing others, or securing personal advantage to himself.'

Mr. Bailey entered upon the practice of the law at a somewhat advanced period of life, and the Legislature very soon manifested its appreciation of his eminent abilities, by electing him, in 1836, Attorney-General of the State—a position which he continued to fill until the session of 1848, at which time he declined a re-election.

His remains will be interred in the cemetery of the Baptist Church, at 4 o'clock, this afternoon."

[From the Charleston Mercury, of May 9, 1849.]

"MEETING OF THE CHARLESTON BAR.

"A meeting of the Charleston Bar was held at 9 o'clock, A. M., on Tuesday, 8th May, inst., at the Bar Library. Mr. Henry A. DeSaussure was called to the chair, on motion of Mr. J. Phillips; and Mr. DeSaussure requested Mr. James Simons to act as secretary of the meeting.

On assuming the chair, Mr. DeSaussure, in brief, stated, that the object in calling together the Bar was, to express their sense of the distinguished ability, great attainments, amiability, and worth, of the late lamented Henry Bailey, Esq., former Attorney General of the State.

Mr. James L. Petigru then arose, and, under evident sensations of deep feeling, said, that he had desired that the expression of feeling of the Bar of Charleston should have come from some other member than himself, who, having been so closely associated with the deceased, might be supposed to have his opinion of his merits biassed by the regard and attachment he entertained for him; but that he had undertaken it, because he believed, that all present would concur with him in what he was about to say, and that the recent sad funeral ceremonies of his friend had manifested the deep sense of the loss which the community, as well as the Bar and the social circle, had experienced in the death of Henry Bailey.

Mr. Petigru then read the following preamble and resolutions:

Among the vicissitudes of human life, the loss of friends is that which most frequently reminds us of the dark side of the picture—the prevalence of evil, and the vanity of human hopes—and seldom have we received a more impressive lesson of that melancholy strain, than in the event which has caused this meeting of the Charleston Bar. In the demise of Henry Bailey, we have lost an ornament of the profession, and a familiar friend. It was impossible to know him intimately, to see him daily in the discharge of social duties, and hear him as often as any grave question engaged the attention of the Courts in the public, without feeling the effect of his superior intellect and amiable disposition. The respect paid to his talents was as sincere as the confidence which his integrity and candor inspired. The law was studied by him as a profession, and his practice was aloof from the contagion of any sordid art. His mind had no sympathy with evasion or deceit; and his ideas of the law were elevated by the purest conceptions of justice and equity. To his clients, a safe and able adviser; to all who came in reach of his active benevolence, a sincere and faithful friend, he has been followed to the grave by many painful feelings of regret. In him, the country has lost a son, whose heart was filled with devotion to the public good. The city of his birth mourns the extinction of the hopes that reposed on him; the Courts of Justice are deprived of a counsellor, and the members of the Bar of a friend who lived in their affections. Long will it be before his place is filled. The memory of that voice, upon which persuasion so often hung; of those gentle and manly features, so often lighted up by beams of approving kindness, will long be retained by those to whom they were known; and the name of Henry Bailey, while it revives the recollection of many great and noble qualities, will excite the emotions of a deep and tender feeling of regret. To mark our sense of the merit of our departed friend and brother, we would surround his memory with some memorial of our esteem, therefore:

Resolved, That we deplore the loss which our fraternity, and the public, have sustained in the removal from the sphere of his usefulness of our deceased brother and friend, Henry Bailey; and we tender to his family the assurance of our sympathy in their grief.

Resolved, That, as a testimony of our deep respect for the memory of one so much esteemed, the Charleston Bar will wear the crape of mourning for one month."

The preamble and resolutions were seconded by Mr. Brewster, and unanimously adopted.

On motion of Mr. Phillips, Mr. Issac W. Hayne, Attorney General, was requested to present the preamble and resolutions in the Court of Common Pleas and General Sessions, now sitting, with the request, that they be entered on the journal of the Court.

On motion of Mr. Brewster, it was ordered that a copy of these proceedings be transmitted to the family of the deceased, and also be published in the newspapers of the city.

On motion of the Attorney General, the meeting then adjourned.

HENRY A. DeSAUSSURE,
Chairman.

James Simons, *Secretary.*"

[From the Charleston Courier, April 30, 1849.]

"DEATH OF HENRY BAILEY.

"We are at a loss to know in what terms to announce the decease of this gentleman to our readers. He departed this life, in this city, on Saturday last, 28th inst., having but a few days previously returned from Cuba, where he went with a view of restoring a broken constitution; but it was the decree of Providence that the hoped-for restoration of health should prove falacious, and he only returned to be sepulchred in the native soil he loved so well and so faithfully.

Mr. Bailey had filled, for a series of years, the high, honorable, and distinguished post of Attorney-General, of the State; and not only in that character, but in every other position, where talent and ability were required—whether at the bar, as a practitioner, in political matters, or when called on to represent his fellow-citizens, generally on public occasions—he ever proved himself equal to the task, and in all cases, even exceeded the expectations of his most ardent admirers.

He has departed from among us. He has gone to that bourne from whence no traveller returns. That voice that has often enchained and enlightened public assemblies, in our city, is hushed in death. That manly form, whose very step was dignity—that placid, firm, and thinking countenance, that commanded respect, even before his eloquent language reached the ears of an audience, is now rigid and inanimate, and it will be long before the recollection of his power, as a debater, either at the Bar, or in a popular assemblage, will be effaced from the memory of those who have listened to his oratorical bursts.

It is not our province to eulogize the deceased—it should be confided, as it doubtless will be, to other and abler pens. But we may be permitted to say, what none will deny, that in the decease of Mr. Bailey, the Charleston Bar has lost a member, who, in legal knowledge, had but few equals, and the community an advocate, ever faithful to what he conceived to be their best interests."

U. S. DISTRICT ATTORNEYS

FOR SOUTH CAROLINA.

THOMAS PARKER.

This eminent lawyer descended to the tomb before I had the opportunity of knowing him. Hence, all I can say is from the information of others.

It seems he was born in Goose Creek, about the year 1760, and was the son of John Parker, whose wife was a Miss Hervey.

What were his opportunities of education, cannot now be ascertained; but from his great eminence, it is probable that they were ample.

He married Miss Mary Drayton, the only daughter of that eminent man, Chief Justice William Henry Drayton, and the sister of Governor John Drayton.

I am informed, he was enrolled in the Charleston Militia, and was present at the siege of Savannah, and at the unfortunate assault on the 9th of October, 1779. He also bore a part in the partizan warfare of the low country; but I have been unable to ascertain particulars.

He was admitted to the Bar of South Carolina on the 10th February, 1784, and to the practice of the United States Courts on 26th October, 1790. He was appointed United States District Attorney for the State of South Carolina, in 1792, by President Washington, and held this very important position, with the most distinguished success, for the period of twenty-eight years. He was an active member of the Bar of South Carolina for thirty-six years.

He died on Friday, 25th of August, 1820, in the sixtieth year of his age, having numerous descendants.

From the character given of him, by the Charleston Bar, at their meeting of the 29th of August, he must have been well entitled "to be recognized as their leader." For, he was, according to their showing, a courteous, kind, honorable gentleman, and an old and experienced, and well-informed lawyer.

Tradition is, that his word was *law*. Whatever Tom Parker declared to be law, was at once conceded.

I had hoped that his distinguished pupil, Judge Edward Frost, would have sketched the character of his great preceptor; but so it is, his arduous duty, in directing the ascent of the iron horse over the Blue Ridge, prevents him from undertaking to do that which he could have done more satisfactorily than any living man.

The testimony of the Bar of Charleston, however, with Col. William Drayton at their head, is surely enough to show forth the character of Thomas Parker, Esq., for all time to come. In closing this short sketch, I must refer the reader to the proceedings of the Bar of Charleston, which is appended:

[From the Courier of August 31, 1820.]

"MEETING OF THE CHARLESTON BAR.

"At an adjourned meeting of the members of the Charleston Bar, held at the Court-House, on the 29th of August, 1820, Mr. William Drayton was called to the Chair, when the following preamble and resolutions were unanimously approved and adopted:

It having pleased Divine Providence, by the recent death of Thomas Parker, Esq., to remove from the Bar of this State, and from the society of its members, one of the oldest and most respectable of its practitioners. We, the survivors, cannot silently commit to the tomb, one whom we have so long proudly recognized as our head—whom we have so long venerated for his profound learning in the law—esteemed for his amiable liberality and exemplary candor as a practitioner, and admired for those very eminent forensic talents which have distinguished him through life. We have witnessed in him, not only the qualities of an accomplished advocate, but have seen those qualities enriched by great integrity, a scrupulous sense of honor and duty, a high regard for the rights of justice, and a lenient dispensation of its final process, when left to the exercise of his own feelings and discretion. To intellectual talents of the first order, peculiarly manifested by a deep and thorough investigation of every subject connected with his profession, a close and logical mode of reasoning, and conclusions drawn with clearness and demonstration, he united a habitual candor in stating and examining objections, or the arguments of his opponents, and appeared no less solicitous that his reasoning should be just, than that his cause should be gained. He was remarkably decorous in his addresses to the Court, and in his competitions with the Bar.

All the Judges who have, in succession, occupied the Bench during the long course of his practice, have habitually given to his opinions the greatest weight, to his arguments, in Court, the profoundest attention, and to his rank, as counsel, the highest consideration. In the year 1792, General Washington, who, among his great and transcendant qualities, was peculiarly happy in discerning and selecting fit characters for public offices, appointed our departed friend to the office of District Attorney, in this State. The prudence, diligence, integrity and ability, with which he exercised its diversified duties, have secured to him the confidence of each succeeding administration, and often drawn forth the most honorable encomiums from the heads of the Executive Department. To some of us, he hath been known at an earlier period of his life, when,. like ourselves, being occupied only by the duties of a practitioner, he was more at liberty to indulge in the private intercourses of society. Here he often mingled with his early associates; and it was here that a cheerful and benign disposition, a lofty, but unobtrusive independence of character, and a remarkable amenity of manners attracted a large circle of intimate friends, whose attachments have remained, though latterly, the freedom of such intercourse hath unavoidably been abridged by the arduous duties of his public office. To others of us, he has been known only in his later career, when, almost overwhelmed with those duties he devoted himself to, in a course of incessant exertion; and although our intercourse was chiefly on professional occasions, we could easily discern and appreciate the excellence of his native character, and admire with it, that honorable sense of public duty which seemed to engross his whole attention, to the exclusion of those gratifications of leisure and amusement for which he had a taste, and which contribute to mitigate the asperities of human life. By all of us, he hath been sufficiently known, esteemed and venerated, to call forth this public, but imperfect testimonial of *our regret* for the loss which we and society have sustained, and of our affection for a member who, for upwards of thirty-six years, hath maintained at our Bar, a standing no less honorable to the profession, than to this country that gave him birth and education; and which may boast that, among the earliest tokens he gave of manhood, was the buckling on of his armor in defence of her liberty and independence. Therefore,

Resolved, That the members of the Bar, in Charleston, will wear crape on the left arm for the space of thirty days, as a badge of mourning for the death of Thomas Parker, Esq.

Resolved, That the foregoing preamble and resolution be published in the gazettes of this city, and that a copy of them, signed by the Chairman of the meeting, be transmitted to Mr. Thomas Parker, the eldest son of the deceased.

WILLIAM DRAYTON, *Chairman*."

JOHN GADSDEN.

John Gadsden was the second son of Catharine and Philip Gadsden, and was born on the 4th of March, 1787. His brother, the Bishop of the Diocese of the Protestant Episcopal Church, in South Carolina, preceded him, by birth, a year or more. James Gadsden, our recent Minister to Mexico, was the next junior to both. In his untiring energies, and in the footsteps of his grandfather, he has not overlooked the fame which links his name with his progenitor. He is the eldest surviving brother of a once numerous family, equally divided between eight sons and eight daughters, of whom there remain one sister and six brothers.

With this brief episode we pass on to the narrative:

By the paternal and maternal side, these "*tria juncta in uno*" inherited the good name of distinguished and venerated patriots of the Revolution.

Gen. Christopher Gadsden, and John Edwards—the cavalier and the Puritan, eminent merchants, of spotless integrity, in the province of South Carolina—have left to their posterity, a part from their Revolutionary prestige, an imperishable name. In their devotion to the cause of American Independence, they were not surpassed, and need no cenotaph to embalm their memories. The inscription stands in bold relief, on the page of history: of indomitable spirits, inflexible perseverance, steadiness of purpose, enduring firmness, their pledges were those of "fortune, life and honor," redeemed in the success of the struggle, which secured the independence of the colonies. Subsequent to the siege and surrender of Charleston, in 1780, they, with other defenders of the commonwealth, were transferred to prison-ships, or transported, as rebels, to St. Augustine. It was thought dangerous to leave them on parole, in their abiding city, or to exchange them as prisoners of war.

Such an ancestry, the subject of this memoir, in all the vicissitudes of life, cherished and honored as an unappreciable inheritance. Trained in the wholesome discipline of a devoted, pious, affectionate, beloved mother, and under the unremitting devotion, assiduous, exemplary care of a maiden aunt, whose counsel, encouragement, and solicitude for their welfare, proved the beacon lights through the conflict and pilgrimage of life. They were early initiated in elementary and classic lore, at the Associated Academy, in our city—an institute founded and reared by individuals, who felt sensibly the importance and necessity, in our midst, of a well organized and judiciously ordered seminary.

The chairs of instruction were efficiently and adequately filled. Ripe scholars, from the Universities of Edinburgh and Dublin, occupied prominent stations, and in their discipline rivaled the unenviable reputation of Dr. Busby, to whom the use of the birch was considered ancillary, if not an indispensable acquisition of learning. To such arbitrary power, or ruffian violence, the subject of this notice was never amenable. From the academy, he (with his two brothers,) was transferred to Yale College, New Haven, Connecticut; the celebrity of which was then in its infancy, and under the presidency of Dr. Dwight—a divine of rare excellence, profound learning, and an eloquence, that brooked no rivalry. It attained a rank among the literary institutions of the day which it has never lost. Some of the best-educated men in our State, claim her as their Alma Mater; among whom, we need only mention Stephen Elliott and John C. Calhoun—both of whom were proudly awarded the same grade of distinction, that of L.L. D. In 1804, John Gadsden graduated, and at the annual commencement was awarded *one* of the honors of his class. The part assigned him at commencement, though the youngest, was a merited distinction and mark of his superiority. He wrote the dialogue for the occasion; and its acceptance by the Faculty was an evidence of its high appreciation. He took his share in the performance, and in the exhibition found favor in a gratified audience.

His acquaintance with books, and the literature of the day, commenced *here;* and, in after-life, was cultivated and improved with an ardor irrepressible. Still, in his minority, "an age too soon," he entered on the profession of the law, and at the legal time assumed its robe of office. Deprived of the resources of an ancestral estate, he was stimulated to greater diligence and the more intense study; thus giving unsubdued energies to the attainment of what had been achieved by the greater lights of the Revolution and of the Forum, aspiring with no unholy ambition to the professional fame of the Pinckneys, Rutledges, Watieses, and others of kindred eminence.

He did not think his legal education complete, without the mastery of the Civil and Common Law.

Yet, under the pressure of adverse circumstances, he found a hinderance, which a too early admission to the Bar thrust upon him. Other than that, in his depressed (pecuniary) condition, he would willingly, with one of the ablest jurists of England, have given "*vigenti annos*" to its prosecution.

The knowledge, however, of both, was not inconsiderable, and had their bearing in all the important cases in which he was engaged. As a dialectician, he was, in no way, inferior to his competitors. He held with Blackstone, that he "would not derogate from the study of the Civil Law, as a collection of written reason," yet he did not carry his "veneration so far as to sacrifice Alfred and Edward to the manes of Theodocius and Justinian." Success at the Bar, is of slow growth; his progress was, *therefore*, *very* gradual. In the absence of clients, he increased and added to his reputation, and laid up a store which, in succeeding years, was to be his pabulum.

He estimated his profession at the highest standard. No remunerative fees were ever tendered to him, which he did not merit; and many were withheld where his services were onerous and gratuitous. The widow never tendered nor was asked a recompense. The poor had his advice, and in their consultation with him, left only their gratitude. His reward—the stimulus to the greater mastery of his profession—the ripened fruit of what he had chiefly coveted—a knowledge of the law. His soul was in his profession. He cared not for its emoluments. With the divine Hooker, he believed a thorough knowledge of it a link in the chain which unites earth with heaven—an inspiration from above. In the affairs of the State, though not an indifferent looker-on, he may be said to have taken no part.

In no sense was he a politician; yet, ever ready to obey the calls of his State, and those of his native city. He represented the former in a half session of the Legislature, and successively filled the place of *Intendant* of our city, when its honors were considered an ample return for personal services. He was, unsolicited, appointed District Attorney of the United States. As successor to Thomas Parker, he filled, with like integrity, ability and learning, the position to which he was called; and in the discharge of its duties, he closed his life.

A consistent member of St. Philip's Church, he uniformly worshipped there—occupied the old family pew, and as it were, in the midst of a paternal ancestry, bowed his knee. With no love for religious polemics, he *abhorred* its controversies. He maintained his own opinions, yet never interfered with those of others. He was free from everything like cant and dogmatism, and considered that, in spiritual matters, it was an issue between every man and his Maker. His knowledge of his profession was profound. He gave himself wholly to its study. In the interval between professional duties, he hung over his books with an intensity which, if I may so speak, rapped up his very being. He never returned to his home at the usual dinner hour. His frugal meal was taken at his office; and at night, when his family had retired, he would, of a winter's evening, re-kindle his grate and renew his studies to midnight. Few men had so many resources within himself. He knew what was "due to his birth, though fortune threw him short of it." In all his transactions with mankind, he was not otherwise than just. In "his pretensions," he desired no other return than distant "intrusiveness." With no love for disputation, no pedantry, and no sourness of temper, there was an enviable complacency about him, that never tired. His conversation was pleasant and agreeable—in keeping with a ripe judgment, and a rich felicitous imagination. He gave to his *closet*, not the public, many of his best fugitive pieces, in poetry and prose. He had a keen perception of the beautiful in nature and art. In a tour embracing all the celebrated springs in Virginia—its mountains, valleys and streams—he would, around his own hearth, often entertain his friends with graphic delineations and exquisite pencillings.

In October, 1830, his health began to decline, and the solicitude of his relatives became painfully intense.

The angry controversy on the subject of State Rights, was then in its incipiency; its rancor and ill-feeling found no response in his bosom. He escaped, by his early demise, arraying himself on either side of the foreshadowing crisis.

He was zealously interested in Jackson's first election, and, as a strong adherent to the Constitution of the United States, to which he had devoted his earliest consideration, it was his good fortune to have escaped the unprofitable strifes and collisions in our State, which, it would appear, have led to no advantageous result. He occupied at his decease, the ancient residence of his maternal grandfather, where he dispensed, with an elegance his own, the hospitalities of the educated and refined gentleman. On the 31st of January, 1831, after a lingering illness, and in his forty-fourth year, he entered on the unseen world.

> Foe to loud praise and friend to learned ease,
> Content with science in the vale of peace,
> Calmly he looked on either life, and here
> Saw nothing to regret, or there to fear.
> From nature's temperate feast, rose satisfied,
> Thanked Heaven that he lived, and that he died.

He died prematurely, but not without achieving an enviable reputation, and a position at the Bar which ranked him among its highest aspirants.

He thought for himself—was slow to come to conclusions, which to others, seemed inevitable. His opinions once formed, were the abiding convictions of his life.

With an enviable and commendable gravity, he lived unobtrusively: neither seeking, claiming nor declining the honors of public station—accepting them when tendered, and caring nothing for them when withheld.

As a Member of the Legislature, Intendant of the City, and

District Attorney of the United States, he had the confidence, respect, and regards of a generous community.

His manners were thought to be stern and repulsive, but it was the sternness of unyielding integrity, and unwillingness to encounter the every-day instability of public life.

His charities were those which exempted his "right hand from a knowledge of his left." His recipients found no "clutched gift," and were never made to feel the degradations of poverty.

He lived and died "*integer vitæ*," leaving a bereaved widow, the granddaughter of his maternal grandfather, John Edwards, who soon followed him to his spiritual inheritance; and an infant son, claiming the intellect and virtues of his gifted sire, and who, with high promise, is now ripening into usefulness and distinction in the pious calling to which he has dedicated his mission on earth.

SOLICITORS.

DAVID R. EVANS.

He was a native of Great Britain, and was born at Westminster, 20th February, 1769. His father, David Evans, came to America, with his family, and settled in Fairfield, at Winnsboro', in 1784. It appears from the records of the first County Court, in 1785,—"Present, Richard Winn, John Winn, John Buchanan and Thomas Craig, Justices; John Milling was elected clerk, and David Evans deputy clerk. He afterwards became clerk, in the place of Mr. Milling, who resigned to make room for him."

David Evans was appointed, in 1795, as successor to Major John Winn, Commissioner of Taxations, for Camden District—a very lucrative office.

David R. Evans was educated at Mount Zion College. The Rev. Thomas McCall was then the president of this ancient and valuable institution of learning. He studied law with Jacob and Daniel Brown, of Camden, who had an office at Winnsboro', and were the first lawyers who practiced at that place. Robert Stark, of Columbia—whose first wife was a Winn—and William Smith, of York, soon followed them. Mr. Evans studied four years, applied, and was rejected. After an interval of a year he applied again, and was admitted. This was in 1796. He was very wild and dissipated in early life, which accounts for his rejection.

Although Mr. Evans studied law with Daniel Brown, yet, in 1800, he acted in an affair of honor between him and Thomas Baker, as the second of the latter. In a lawsuit against Baker, who was a farmer, living near Winnsboro', Brown had said or did something, which was offensive. Baker, in retaliation, called him a d—d saddle-bag lawyer. Brown challenged Baker to fight a duel. Baker was anxious to settle the difficulty by an affair of *fisticuffs*. Mr. Evans, his second, insisted he should accept the challenge, which he did. The parties met on the Wateree River, were placed back to back, walked five paces, wheeled and fired; both fell and died. Baker lingered for a few minutes, and said: "Evans, are all men like me on the field of honor?" This, perhaps, showed the heroism of the man. The whole transaction was one of unrelenting ferocity, and was part and parcel of the wickedness of the times. In after-life it must have been, to Mr. Evans, a subject of grief, that he had been the instigator of the duel, on the part of Mr. Baker, instead of being, as he ought to have been, a pacificator.

In 1799, he married a daughter of Gen. Richard Winn. In 1800, he was elected to the Legislature (the House of Representatives) of South Carolina. Before the election his popularity was much affected by his connection with Minor Winn, a very unpopular man; but a speech, which he delivered on the 4th of July, and which was republican in its sentiments, secured his election. Col. McCreight says, that he visited Camden soon after this speech, and that Capt. Carter, a Revolutionary soldier, congratulated him on having such a republican in Winnsboro'. A Mr. Lee had delivered, at the same time, a 4th of July speech, which was very displeasing to Capt. Carter. He obtained Mr. Evans' speech, published and circulated it widely. This old soldier said that he commanded a company on the extreme left of Gates' line, at the battle of Gum Swamp, near Camden, and, at the first fire, all his men fled: left alone, he went to the captain, next to him, whose men had also abandoned him, and asked what was to be done? He received no satisfactory answer. Whereupon he said to his neighbor: "I'll be d—d if I am here to be shot down." He jumped on his pony, which he had fastened in the bushes, left the field, and said he, "I suppose I was the first man out of the reach of danger."

Mr. Evans was probably continued in the Legislature until he was elected Solicitor of the Middle Circuit, in 1804. He continued in this office until 1811, when he resigned, and David Johnson, of Union, was elected in his place.

Mr. Evans early distinguished himself as a lawyer, in his management of the case of the State *vs.* Golding, indicted for a rape. Col. McCreight, who knew Mr. Evans from his beginning to his death, thinks him the ablest lawyer whom he ever heard in a Court House. He ranks him as superior to Judge Smith, as an argumentative speaker. He was, perhaps, too *severely* logical. His sentences were short and pointed; this gave clearness and effectiveness to his speeches. The melody of his voice added much to the pleasure of hearing him.

From 1800 to 1812, Mr. Evans had a very large and lucrative practice. During this time he met at Winnsboro', on his circuit, the most eminent lawyers of the time—Smith, Brevard, Nott, Stark, Blanding, Hooker, and Gist—and he was not regarded as inferior to any of them.

In 1805, he lost the wife of his youth. She died childless. In December, of this year, he was elected a trustee of the South Carolina College, for four years. In 1809, he was again elected for another term. In this year he was married to Miss Nancy Yongue, the daughter of the Rev. S. W. Yongue, of Winnsboro'.

In 1812, he was elected to Congress, as a Representative from Laurens, Newberry, and Fairfield. On this occasion he triumphed over Robert Creswell, Esq., of Laurens—a good and virtuous man, and a lawyer of considerable celebrity. He served only one term. On his way to Washington, in 1814, travelling in his own carriage, he was near enough to hear and did hear, the firing at Bladensburgh, which preceded the burning of the capitol. He accounted for the disgraceful, cowardly flight of our militia, on that occasion, by the fact that great numbers of people, men, women, and children, were gathered together from curiosity to see the British soldiers. They, of course, fled at the approach of danger, and thus created a panic among the militia, who were in arms.

Mr. Evans found his health unequal to the duties of a Representative in Congress; he therefore, declined being a candidate in 1814, and retired to the privacy and enjoyment of domestic life, on his plantation, near Winns' Bridge, on Little River.

In 1818, he was elected Senator, from Fairfield District, and again, in 1822. He could not be induced to serve again in 1826. His hearing was becoming more and more indistinct, and his general health was much impaired. He, therefore, abandoned, public life.

In 1818, he was elected President of the Fairfield Bible Society, at its organization. He was the President of Mount Zion Society from 1836 to 1841. He was a ruling Elder in Lebanon Church, (Jackson's Creek,) and in the Presbyterian Church, at Winnsboro', for thirty years before his death.

His second wife died also childless, and preceded him to the tomb.

He died 8th March, 1843, being 74 years and 16 days old.

Out of his estate, of $100,000, he gave $8,000 to benevolent societies, of which $5,000 was given to the Tract Society. The balance he bequeathed to his nephews and nieces.

Thus, in the fullness of time, a good and great man was gathered to his everlasting rest.

In his intercourse with men Mr. Evans was plain and unpretending. His life was one of unostentatious usefulness. He had the reputation, with the Bar and Bench, of a profound lawyer. His long service at the Bar, as a lawyer and solicitor, gave him a position far above any other lawyer of his circuit.

As a legislator, he was characterized by honesty and faithfulness more than show. He commanded respect, both in the Legislature and Congress. He was a Christian, and in his life and conversation, for more than forty years, showed that he feared God, and worked the works of righteousness; and in all the relations of life was an example of purity and faithfulness.

JAMES ERVIN.

He was the son of Hugh Ervin, who lived about five miles from Indian Town, Williamsburgh District, and was born in October, 1778. His mother was a Cooper or James; my informant, the venerable John D. Witherspoon, does not remember which. By an unfortunate accident, at his birth, one of his feet was dislocated in the middle, turning the toes at a right angle to the heel. No surgeon living, in that section of the country, his foot was suffered to remain so. This foot, eg and thigh, were somewhat smaller and shorter. The other leg and thigh were longer than usual. He was a hearty boy, strong and active. His lameness excited the pity of his father and relations, and they determined to send him to college. His father died when he was nine years old, but his friends remembered and carried out his parent's purpose. When he was eleven or twelve years of age, they sent him to a grammar school, kept by the Rev. Thomas Reese, in Salem County, part of Sumter District. He remained in that school about two years, until Mr. Reese broke up his academy. About 1792, he was sent to the grammar school at the Long Bluff, (now Society Hill,) kept by Thomas Park, afterwards Professor of Languages in the South Carolina College, where he was prepared for college.

He went to the Rode Island College, now Brown University, and entered the sophomore class, in May '95. Whilst in college, he conducted himself orderly and correctly. He early distinguished himself as an orator, and was considered the best speaker in the college. This faculty and his correct deportment procured for him the salutatory oration and the second honor of his class. He graduated in September, 1797, and soon entered the office of W. D. James, Esq., as a law student. He was admitted to the Bar, in Columbia, November Term of the Constitutional Court, 1800. In the summer of that year, he was started as a candidate for the House of Representatives, from Marion District, and was elected. He thus became a law-maker before he was a law-expounder. Such an instance of early popularity, is of rare occurrence. He was elected a second time in 1802. In December, 1804, when Solicitor Wilds was elected a Judge, Mr. Ervin was elected Solicitor of the Northern Circuit. He remained in office until 1816. In December, 1809, he was elected for four years a member of the Board of Trustees of the South Carolina College. In December, 1813, he was again elected for four years. In October, 1816, he was elected to the House of Representatives, in Congress, against Mr. Benjamin Huger, and was returned a second time, without opposition. He was the only member from this State, who adhered to the original policy to encourage domestic manufactures. He voted for Mr. Clay's Tariff Bill. He introduced, and eloquently advocated resolutions, calling upon Congress to do what they had promised in honor of General Washington's memory. But his eloquence was wasted on the empty air. Congress, if they had not forgotten the Father of his Country, were too busily engaged in the pursuit of factious projects, to honor him who had advised against all such things.

Mr. Ervin's health failed in Congress. He retired to private life after 1820, and so remained until 1841, when he died.

He was a very popular boy and man, and had a better start in life, than any young man in the Pee Dee Country. He never took a very high stand as a lawyer, not from the want of talent—for, in this behalf, he was very respectably endowed—but his mind was devoted more to the acquisition of property—in trading in lands and negroes—than in the pursuit of legal knowledge. He had a fine constitution, and was killed by a fall from his horse.

The foregoing statement is from my venerable friend, John D. Witherspoon, Esq., of Society Hill. I have seen Mr. Ervin, but I had no such knowledge as enabled me to give such a life-like description as is above.

His name recalls two Bar anecdotes, which I have often heard, and which may amuse some one:

A woman was indicted for an assault and battery on a boy; the little fellow was the witness. He said that he and the son of the defendant—near to her house—had quarrelled and fought; that he whipped her son, who ran crying to her. She came out with a rope in her hand, and, said he, "she penned me up in a corner of the fence." He stopped, supposing that everybody knew what followed. The Judge, Mr. Justice Bay, said, "what then, what then, my little man?" "Maybe she did not pour into me about right," was the reply. Mr. Ervin asked, "what was the woman's name?" The little boy said, "Mr. Ervin, you know her as well as I do; she has been *at your still-house* a hundred times. She is called Big Sall and Fighting Sall!" The woman was, of course, convicted. The venerable, and usually kind Judge, was so much outraged by the account given of the woman, that, on sentence day, he told her, "her conduct was very unmatron-like, that she had been at still-houses, and was called "Big Sall and Fighting Sall." "I therefore," said he, "will lay you in jail one month"—"stop, stop, Mr. Clerk," said he, "add another month to her imprisonment."

In another criminal case, it was important to prove that the defendant had ran away. The Solicitor put up a rather quizical sort of witness, and asked, "did not the defendant elope?" The witness replied, "she pulled string." "Pull, pulled string," said the Judge, "what do you mean by that?" "She cut dirt," was the witness's reply. "Cut, cut dirt—pull, pull string"—"what do you mean?" said the Judge. "I mean," said the witness, "she puffed the gravel." "Pull, pull string—cut, cut dirt—puff, puff the gravel," said the Judge—"the man is crazy; take him out of Court, Mr. Sheriff." The Solicitor said, he means that she eloped. "Well, well, my man, why could you not say so?" The witness replied, "every man to his notion, as the woman said when she kissed her cow." This startled the Judge, as a monstrous thing; and he said, in his most emphatic, stammering way, "this woman kiss a cow—take him out of Court, Mr. Sheriff."

ROBERT STARK.

Robert Stark was born near Petersburgh, Virginia, 10th January, 1762. His parents must have removed, when he was very young, to South Carolina, probably to the Bridge, Edgefield District. At the age of sixteen, he entered the service of his country, as a soldier, and was in the battles of "Blackstocks," "Cowpens," and "Eutaw Springs." At the battle of Eutaw, he belonged to a company commanded, as I understood him to say, by Captain Richard Johnson, of Edgefield District. I see he is called Lieut. Johnson, in a correspondence between Judge William Johnston and Col. Hammond. In a charge made by that company, they drove the artillerists from the gun, before the Brick House. Captain Johnson leaped off his horse, and took from his pocket a twenty-penny nail, and, placing it in the touch-hole, with the hilt of his heavy dragoon sabre, drove it as far as he could, saying, as he did so, "you have plagued us all day, and you shall do so no more." Mr. Stark told me, that Capt. Johnson, when he entered upon that battle, was dressed with a white vest and pantaloons; and, when he left it, he was covered with blood from his breast to his boots. Before the close of the war, Mr. Stark became the adjutant of the regiment commanded by Colonel Hammond.

On the 11th September, 1785, he married Mary Winn, of Fairfield, South Carolina, who was the mother of nine children, all of whom are dead, except Elizabeth, the youngest, now Mrs. Heriot, of Georgetown. Mrs. Stark died 10th December, 1801.

He was admitted to the Bar, in the County Court, at Orangeburgh, on the 22d October, 1787, on the condition that he should produce credentials, according to law, at the next Court. The law, then, was, that an applicant for admission to the Bar, who was not a graduate, but who had studied four years, might, if competent, be admitted by the Judges of the

Court of Common Pleas. P. L. 363. Hence, I suppose, he was admitted, in the Circuit Court at Orangeburgh, in the November following.

The scene in the County Court between Carnes and himself is worth repeating. Mr. Stark was a rather unpromising beginner at the law. Carnes was the County Attorney. Stark was engaged in the defence of an assault and battery case. In the course of the controversy, Carnes said, "may it please your worships, I don't believe the young gentleman knows what an assault and battery is." Stark, shaking his fist in Carnes' face, said, "that is an assault," and, following it with a full blow above the eye, said, "that is battery." Carnes, rubbing his forehead, sat down, exclaiming, "I did not think the fellow had so much sense."

In 1796, he was elected to the House of Representatives, from Saxe-Gotha—now Lexington District—and, I presume, he was reëlected, and served until 1804. On the 18th July, 1802, he was married to Mary Hay, by whom he had eleven children, eight of whom survive.

On the 24th of November, 1802, he was elected Speaker of the House of Representatives, and served two sessions, 1802 and 1803. As Speaker, he became, *ex-officio*, a member of the Board of Trustees of the South Carolina College. In the spring of 1804, he removed to Columbia. In December, 1805, he was elected a member of the Board of Trustees of the South Carolina College, and continued, by successive elections every four years, until December, 1821.

On the 5th day of December, 1806, he was elected Solicitor of the Southern Circuit, and was continued until December, 1820, when, strange to say, his Revolutionary services, faithful discharge of duty, and his numerous family, were overlooked, and another was placed in his stead. He had acted as Mr. Solicitor Colcock's deputy, on a large part of the circuit, before he was elected.

In the office of Solicitor, he was a terror to *evil doers;* his pursuit of crime was unwearied, and generally successful He prepared his indictments with great care, and seldom was the most astute able to pick a flaw in them. He arranged and embodied his facts in such a way, that he brought out his whole case. His voice was capable of being heard at a great distance, and when he began his argument, he generally gathered all the people lagging around the Court-House into it, and the prisoner would literally be said to tremble before the judgment-seat.

At Barnwell, on one occasion, a party had committed some heinous offence; he fled the State; his death was subsequently announced in the newspapers; his wife administered on his estate, and at Court she appeared in her mourning weeds. Mr. Stark disregarded all this matter, and at Court was seen swearing his witnesses, and sending the bill to the Grand Jury. The late Colonel Haigood said to him, "surely, Mr. Stark, you are not indicting *a dead man?*" "Dead or alive, I'll have him," was the reply. And sure enough, at the next Court, the supposed dead man was in Court, to answer to the indictment.

The spring of 1815 was the first Court which I attended at Edgefield: there had been no Fall Term, owing to the sickness of Judge Brevard. Mr. Stark gave out forty bills of indictment, of which thirty-nine were found "true," for every grade of offence, from assault to murder. The late Judge Grimké presided. He was, like Mr. Stark, a terror to *evil doers.* In the course of the Term, one of the Edgefield rowdies, looking on, said, "this is no place for me—Stark holds, and Grimké skins."

I knew Mr. Stark well, and had much to do with him as Solicitor; and I have no hesitation in saying, that the objection, which was urged against him, that he was "*too severe*" was altogether untrue. He was a firm, just man, in the discharge of his duty; but there was no one who sooner yielded to the just claims of mercy than he did.

In 1814, Mr. Stark and myself defended Colonel Starling Tucker, before the Court Martial ordered to try him, on charges preferred against him by the Commander-in-chief, Governor Allston, in relation to the service of the first class of the militia, ordered into service from the brigade, then ranked as the second, now the tenth. As few survive, who were connected with that service, it will, perhaps, not be inappropriate, that a survivor should here write some account of it.

By the order of the Commander-in-chief, the militia was arranged in four classes; those charged with the execution of the order in the second brigade, included all under the age of forty-five, and over eighteen, whether they were liable to ordinary militia duty or not; inasmuch, as those not liable to militia duty were regarded as alarm-men. In consequence of this, clergymen, public officers, former officers who had served more than seven years, were subjected to the classification. The Newberry Artillery, to which I belonged, commanded by Captain George McCreless, offered themselves as a company for the first class, and were accepted. Among those in Newberry who were not liable to duty, but who were classed, were the Rev. Dr. M. W. Moore and Major Frederick Nance; the former entered upon the tour of duty in person; the latter sent his son, Robert R. Nance, as a substitute. The detachment, under the command of Colonel Starling Tucker, Majors Robert Wood and Samuel Cannon, were mustered into service on the 1st, 2d and 3d of March, 1814, by the Brigade-Major, Thomas Wright, at Newberry Court-House, and commenced their march on the 4th, for the point to which they were ordered—Camp Allston, two miles below Sheldon Hill, in Beaufort District. I was appointed the Judge-Advocate of the regiment, but was allowed to remain, as a private in Captain McCreless's company. On the way down, the regiment, below Barnwell, began to meet the discharged soldiers of Colonel Carter's regiment, to the relief of which we were marching. Those first met had been discharged on account of sickness; they were the most squalid, emaciated creatures and were hardly able to walk. They depicted to the soldiers of Tucker's regiment the unnecessary hardships to which Colonel Youngblood, who had obtained the command, in place of Colonel Carter, had subjected them. As might have been expected, it created a feeling of indignation, which could not be well allayed. I remember, on one occasion, when some of Carter's regiment were met, and their narration of hardships, ascribed to Colonel

Youngblood, had been listened to, that John Toubs, of Edgefield, who belonged to Caldwell's troop of cavalry, but who was the Acting Forage-Master of the regiment, said to Colonel Tucker, "the day you give up the command of your regiment, *I will shoot you.*"

At Pocotaligo, the regiment was met by Captain Benjamin Frazier, of Edgefield, and he said to Colonel Tucker, "you are marching right into ——." Yesterday, an order was published requiring a detail of two companies, to throw up a *tête du pont* on Port Royal Island, under the direction of Colonel Youngblood." Said he, "the object is thus, by companies detailed, to take your command from you." The regiment did not immediately take possession of the ground occupied by Carter's regiment, an old field just beyond a Road leading from Garden's Corner, and a mile from Bull's Point. They encamped in a wood to the left of the Beaufort road, below Mr. Fuller's. The guard in charge of the magazine was relieved by a guard detailed from Tucker's regiment.* Immediately after the regiment encamped, a council of all the officers of the line assembled, to consult as to what should be done, as to the detailed order to throw up the *tête du pont*, and they unanimously advised that it should be disobeyed; and every one, from the highest to the lowest, so pledged themselves. This was not only disobedience, but mutiny, and might have been visited with serious consequences; but there was a great palliation in the excited state of the men's minds, and their belief that the duty demanded was to be done under a stern disciplinarian, and would probably be at the sacrifice of many lives, who were unaccustomed to the climate.

Colonel Tucker, however, managed the thing with great skill. From day to day, he parried Colonel Youngblood's demand for this detail; and never gave a positive refusal. The regiment was ordered to be discharged, about the 5th of April, in consequence, I have no doubt, of Dr. Moon's spirited personal remonstrance as to the inutility of the service, and the

---

*The order before-mentioned, when communicated, proved to be an order promulgated by an extra aid, who had not been announced in general orders, or, in anywise, before known in that character.

danger to the health of the soldiers from the position. In his order directing the discharge, the Commander-in-chief required the Colonel to state what progress had been made in the *tête du pont;* and if none, what had prevented it. Col. Tucker was advised by his officers to state to the Governor, that, owing to the short period of service, and the probable sickness of the troops, and the excited state of their feelings from representations made to them, no progress had been made. Colonel Tucker, unfortunately, returned no answer to the Governor, and this, I have always believed, was the cause of his arrest.

Soon after, the regiment encamped in the woods, below Fuller's—probably the second night—Colonel Youngblood, Captain John King, and Captain John Miller, at about twelve o'clock, mounted their horses at Garden's Corner, and rode, as Youngblood stated on the Court Martial, to the centre of Colonel Tucker's encampment, without being hailed. They then rode to the magazine guard, and were probably brought to by the sentinel on duty, to whom Youngblood stated who they were, and that they were on their way to Bull's Point, to look after the schooner Live Oak, which was expected, with provisions for the regiment. He called for the officer of the guard, who came, and to whom the same explanation was given, and he foolishly permitted them to proceed. After riding to the Point, and returning as soon as they reached the road leading to Garden's Corner, Youngblood said, "there is so much remissness, let us try what an alarm can do." Accordingly, each fired a pistol, which, under an old Act, constituted *an alarm.* The effect was that the whole camp was roused, and a state of confusion rarely seen ensued.

Some notion might be conceived by comparing it to a bee-hive suddenly overturned. Col. Tucker mounted and rode to the right of the encampment, dismounted, tied his horse to a tree, and ordered a scout from the company of cavalry. Capt. Wm. Caldwell detailed three of his best-mounted and most fearless men, John Toubs, George Caldwell, and Westley Brooks. They galloped to the magazine guard, and were there told of Youngblood's visit. Toubs said, "boys put your horses to the top of their speed, and we will overhaul them before they reach Garden's Corner." This was done, and the saddles were scarcely removed from Youngblood's horses until the scout was present. It was fortunate that Youngblood and his party had reached their quarters, for they were pursued by fearless and enraged men, and I have often heard Toubs swear, "if he had overtaken them, he would have made Youngblood a head shorter!" In the pursuit the scout were joined by the Colonel, Capt. Caldwell, and two privates of the cavalry, James Gillam, and Henry Gray.

Before he joined the scout, Tucker had gone among the regiment on foot to aid in the formation: he was heard inquiring "where is my horse?" Some member of the artillery company, which was next on the right to the cavalry, pointed him out. The regiment was formed by Capt. Wm. Irby, the adjutant, who was an old soldier of '76, after much difficulty. On the return of the scout, the soldiers were permitted to retire. The next day, however, told many a ludicrous anecdote. Lieut. R. said that one of Capt. B.'s men being much alarmed, fled to a tree, which he had selected, to climb; he was seen to look up, and heard to exclaim, "Captain is that your tree?"

The regiment, in a day or two, took possession of the ground previously occupied by Carter's regiment, except the artillery company, which was stationed at Bull's Point.

As I have already said, the regiment was ordered to be discharged about the 5th April. The night after the discharge was one of riot and wild confusion in the camp: I presume every cartridge in the possession of the soldiers was fired.

The Colonel was arrested and tried on, I think, fourteen charges—most of them were not proved. Indeed, the real facts were never known to those who prepared the charges. The Court, as far as I remember, were composed of Col. John J. Chappell, president; Col. Adam McWillie, Col. Evan Benbow, Major Abram Blanding, Major Joseph Mickle, and Major Benoni Robinson. James Dillett, Judge Advocate. Mr. Stark advised a plea in abatement, or bar, be prepared against the argument: the plea was overruled. The defence was prepared and read by myself. The Court convicted the Colonel of the charge of disobedience of orders, and sentenced him to be suspended ten months from his command. This lenient sentence from such men, showed that Tucker had much to excuse him.

Indeed, the whole affair made Starling Tucker subsequently, the Brigadier of the Tenth Brigade, Major-General Fifth Division, and a Member of Congress.

On the 4th of July, 1819, Solicitor Stark had the misfortune to lose his wife. He remained a widower near six years. On the 4th of June, 1825, he married a third time. The lady who then became Mrs. Stark, was Grace H. Baker.

On the 2d day of December, 1826, the Legislature elected him to the office of Secretary of State. Thus they, in some degree, removed the charge of ingratitude, which was incurred in 1820, by depriving him of the office of Solicitor.

He died the 4th day of September, 1830. As a lawyer, Mr. Stark occupied a high position in his day. He had not the advantages which many lawyers have since enjoyed. He was schooled in the camps of the Revolution. He overcame his want of education by diligent and patient study. His arguments, both on law and fact, were lucid and convincing. He had extraordinary powers before a Jury, for they believed and knew *he was honest.*

In all the relations of life, he fulfilled every duty which he could be expected to perform. He was an honest, just, and good man, and I know no higher panegyric which can be bestowed.

In person, he was about five feet eight inches high; very corpulent: his legs were enormous—one, I think, was twenty-eight inches around, and the other was either twenty-six or twenty-seven; his complexion was swarthy; his face was the index of the man—cheerful, frank and bold.

BENJAMIN H. SAXON.

This gentleman's name appears on the roll of Attorneys in Charleston, but the date of admission is not given. He was a practicing lawyer at Laurens, 1st January, 1800; he studied with Robert Goodloe Harper, Esq.

He was elected Clerk of the Senate before 1805, and continued in that office until 1810. He was an accomplished clerk, so far as the manual portion of the duties was concerned, but his disposition was unaccommodating, and, in consequence of the too frequent exhibition of this imperfection, he lost his office.

In 1811, he was elected Solicitor of the Western Circuit; in 1818, Warren R. Davis succeeded him. From 1822, he filled various State offices—such as Surveyor-General, Treasurer of the Upper Division, and, finally, Book-keeper in the Branch Bank, until, perhaps, 1850.

He then removed to Georgia. He was united to the Baptist Church when he was more than eighty.

He married a Miss Walton, of Georgia, and removed from Laurens to Abbeville District, and lived *there* many years. He had a family of several children. His wife lost her reason many years before her death, and died an incurable lunatic, in the asylum, at Columbia. He has told me that he was advised to use the hickory as a means of cure. He was very reluctant to resort to such a measure. He, however, on one occasion, when returning home, cut a switch; as he entered the house, she met him, in one of her wildest frenzies; he struck her a single blow with the switch: she stopped, looked at him in perfect amazement, and said, "Mr. Saxon do you strike me?" He threw down the switch, and bore as best he could this saddest affliction—the insanity of his wife. For years he supported her in the asylum, at Columbia.

He died at the house of his son, Robert, in Georgia, after he was more than four-score. He was a well-informed lawyer; he possessed an easy and graceful elocution. He was for years, when at the Bar, afflicted with tertian ague: this made him more irascible than he otherwise would have been. The difference between him and Solicitor Taylor, his predecessor, was striking in this respect. Solicitor Taylor was a man of perfect good humor. The most worrying part of a country lawyer's life, in time of Court, is the constant inquiry of witnesses, "mayn't I go home?" To Mr. Taylor, the State witnesses constantly addressed this question? "Oh, yes, go home," was his reply.

To Mr. Solicitor Saxon, as the evening rolled on, a witness would address an inquiry, "Mr. Saxon mayn't I go home?" "Yes, go home," was impatiently answered. Another—"Mr. Saxon mayn't I go home?" "Yes, go home," with a furious blasphemous expletive, was the answer. Another—"Mr. Saxon mayn't I go home?" "Yes, go home," with a superlative blasphemous expletive, following!

Mr. Saxon was a strictly honest man. He was a kind husband and father. In the insanity of his wife, and the death of many of his children, he suffered much. Still he bore up with unflinching fortitude, and, at last, with the consolations of religion, he triumphed over the last great enemy of man!

CALEB CLARKE.

Solicitor Clarke was born in St. Mary's County, Maryland, 1st July, 1777.

He received a common-school education *only*. He came to Charleston in 1800, and lived for a time with his brother Robert, a merchant of that city.

He began the study of the law with Henry Bailey, Esq., the father of Attorney General Bailey, in the City of Charleston; but subsequently came to Columbia, and studied law with Thos. Henry Egan, Esq. He was admitted, I presume, to the Bar in 1805; his name, however, does not appear on the rolls of Attorneys at Columbia or Charleston.

He settled, and commenced the practice of law at Winnsboro', the same year.

In 1812, he married Julia Harrison, of Chester District. Her father, two or three years before, came from Virginia, and settled on the Catawba River, where he died.

Mr. Clarke was elected (it is stated) repeatedly to the House of Representatives of South Carolina. I recollect seeing him in the House of Representatives in 1811, and hearing him make a speech against the union of Laurens, Newberry, and Fairfield, in the same Congressional District. The intercourse between Fairfield and Laurens, he said, was so little, that the people scarcely knew one another, and hence ought not to be united in the same Congressional District. As an illustration of this, he affirmed that he did not know a man from Laurens District, "except this *here* man," (pointing at a member from Laurens,) "old Mr. Burnside."

In 1815, in the place of Mr. Solicitor Johnson, who was elected a Judge, he was a candidate for the office of Solicitor of the Middle Circuit: after repeated ballotings, the Legislature failed to make an election between him and his opponent, Richard Post Johnson. The Governor appointed Mr. Clarke Solicitor *pro tem.* In November, 1816, he was elected over John Wood Farrow, Esq., of Spartanburgh. He was again elected in 1820. In 1824, he declined being a candidate.

In 1814, he was appointed aid to Brigadier General Turner Starke, with the rank of captain.

He lost his wife, and after several years of widowhood, he married Mrs. McKelvy. He died 29th December, 1849: his second wife died before him. He left four children of his first marriage surviving him, to wit: Dr. Henry Clarke; Anna, now the wife of Wm. A. Latta; Caroline, the widow of Henry J. Neill; and Julia, the wife of Wm. A. Moore, and the children of his son Matthias, who died before him.

Mr. Clarke abounded in anecdotes, which he always told with spirit and humor. He enjoyed the company of his friends. He was often depressed in spirits, but when not under a gloom, he, in general, was a man of the most buoyant and lively disposition.

He prepared his cases with great labor and care, and generally managed and argued them well. He understood the Machiavelian policy too common at the Bar, to take all advantages, and he pursued it.

Fairfield was once very much divided, and two parties, the English or Virginian, and the Irish, were known and acknowledged. Mr. Clarke belonged to the Irish party. He often told me that if he could get his cases before his own party, he was sure of a verdict, and that he always endeavored to carry his cases before such a Jury!

When the great case of Liles *vs.* Liles was tried, Judge Huger presided, and Clarke had made a similar statement to him. It was the first case tried the second week of the term, and, as was usual, was expected to go before Jury No. 1; but, the Judge discovering, as he thought, Mr. Clarke's anxiety to go before that Jury, turned his chair round and ordered it to Jury No. 2. Whether this had any effect, I do not know, but Mr. Clarke's client lost the case.

Mr. Clarke had a large practice in Fairfield, and he had a very respectable practice in Chester and Lancaster.

He was a bold impassioned speaker, with a great deal of

repetition, and very little order in his speeches. This arose from his imperfect education, and the style which too much pervaded Bar speaking, when Mr. Clarke came to the Bar. The length of a speech was more looked at than the matter, and the notion of Sergeant Scarlett had also its weight, that it was necessary to repeat, in order to hammer an idea into the heads of ignorant jurymen.

Mr. Clarke was quick to resent an insult, and as prompt to strike in a quarrel as any one can be. The following anecdote may illustrate this:

A Mr. Ferguson, from Chester District, was quite provoked at not being able to borrow a razor at the tavern where he was stopping. The tavern-keeper petulantly pointed to Clarke's office, and asked why he did not go over there and get shaved? Mr. Clarke had just come out of the Court House into his office, in a hurry to get a paper, when Ferguson stepped in, and began to pull off his coat; Clarke observing him all the time very suspiciously. As soon as he laid off his coat, he took a seat, and said to Clarke "*shave me.*" Clarke seized a stick, and said "I'll shave you," accompanied by a strong imprecation, and rushed upon Ferguson, who did not wait to be *thus shaved*, and fled before the outraged attorney could even *lather* him.

NOTE.—The annexed description by a friend, of a scene in the Court of Equity, in which Mr. Clarke was one of the actors, may amuse. It ought to be known that Col. Gregg was very deaf:

In July, 1846, at Winnsboro', the case of Johnson *vs.* Lewis (2 Strob. Eq. 157) was tried, Chancellor David Johnson presiding: Clarke and Gregg, counsel for plaintiff; McCall and DeSaussure for defendants. The case had then been on the docket for fifteen or sixteen years, "under reference" most of the time. As will always happen, under such circumstances, counsel themselves had forgotten many of the facts with which they had once been familiar; and the hearing, "like a wounded snake, dragged its slow length along." The trial occupied two or three days—much time being consumed in search for papers and documents, continually wanted and mislaid in the accumulated mass.

But "the longest day will ha'e its e'en," and about half-past two P. M. of the third day, both sides announced that they had "closed." The weather was intensely hot; the thermometer at ninety-seven degrees, and the Chancellor had left the Bench and taken a chair in the aisle, near the clerk's desk, where, *on theory*, there *shined* in a draught of air. He had his coat off, and although his bulk doubtless caused him to suffer greatly, he never for a moment betrayed the slightest impatience.

After a pause, the Chancellor observed, "proceed with the argument, gentlemen. How many will argue this cause?"

Col. Gregg perceiving the stop, and not understanding the cause, leaned over to Mr. Clarke, and *whispered very low*, "what is the matter now, Mr. Clarke?"

Mr. Clarke, (at the top of his voice.) "the Chancellor says we must go on with the argument."

Gregg—"What! go on with the argument *now!* Why you have not closed—have you?"

Clarke—"Oh yes, and you must go on."

Col. Gregg touched Mr. Clarke on the shoulder, and beckoned him to withdraw to a conference, intended to be *private*, near the window, and about ten to fifteen feet from where the Chancellor was seated. Being thus *in private*, and out of *hearing*, if not out of sight, the conference was continued *without a whisper*, in a tone which might readily be heard in the Court-yard below, as distinctly as in the Court-House.

Gregg—"You don't mean to say that I have to argue this case *now!* Why, I wanted to look over the papers; I do not understand as clearly as I would wish what you have been doing to day, [and no wonder,] and I wanted to take the evening to look it over."

Chancellor, (taking part, from his seat, in this *private* conversation)—"Tell him, Mr. Clarke, that the argument *must* proceed. This trial has taken far too much time already?"

Clarke—"The Chancellor says we *must* go on."

Gregg—"Oh no! that will never do, Mr. Clarke. At what time does the old gentleman adjourn Court?"

Chancellor—"Tell him three o'clock."

Clarke—"The Chancellor says three o'clock."

Gregg—"And what is the time now?"

Chancellor, (taking out his watch)—"Tell him half-past two!"

Gregg—"Oh, then, you see it is no use, because if he *forces* me, I don't expect to *touch* the case in that time; so he will gain nothing."

(By this time, the dignity of the Court and Sheriff following the audience, began to give way, and the smiling to become audible.) "Look here, Mr. Clarke, (in Col. G.'s *bland* style,) now, you say it is only a half-hour before he goes to dinner, and as I do not expect to go on, *can't* you or some one else, find something to amuse the old gentleman until then, as he won't adjourn now, which he ought to do." (Explosion from the audience.)

Chancellor—"Well, Mr. Clarke, as Mr. Gregg *won't* go on, tell him I will try and find some amusement until three o'clock."

Clarke—"He says, very well, he will do something else until three, and you can go on in the morning."

Col. Gregg's grave features relapsed into a smile, and laying his hands kindly on Mr. Clarke's shoulder, in the same *confidential whisper*, observed, "He did, did he? Well, that was clever in him. The fact is, Mr. Clarke, the old man is always accommodating *if you manage him right*," and walked to his seat with a gravity, which indicated his innocence of having given any information as to the subject of his late private conference with his associate. But the audience, and especially the Bar, yielded to the ludicrousness of the scene, and the Chancellor, finding the Court in no condition to go on—fifteen minutes more having elapsed—kindly observed, "Well, gentlemen, as we seem to have more of the amusement than even Col. Gregg expected, we may as well adjourn at once. Mr. Sheriff, adjourn the Court until to-morrow morning, at ten o'clock."

WARREN RANSOM DAVIS.

Solicitor Davis was born, as I believe, about May, 1793. He graduated in the South Carolina College in the Class of 1810. He studied law in Columbia, where his mother resided, and was admitted to the Bar in Charleston, in May, 1814, but received his license in Columbia, where he signed the roll of Attorneys.

He settled at Pendleton, to practice law, where Mr. McDuffie, at the same time also settled. Mr. Davis succeeded and got business; Mr. McDuffie had none; and it was left to his partnership with Col. Simkins, at Edgefield, to introduce him to the splendid career which he afterwards ran.

In 1818, Mr. Davis succeeded Benjamin H. Saxon as Solicitor. The duties of this office he admirably performed, and secured for him a large practice out of it, in the whole of his circuit—the Western.

Mr. Davis' ambition was not for distinction atthe Bar. It was in political life, that he wished to shine. He anxiously sought a seat in Congress. He was elected from Pendleton and Greenville, in 1824, and continued, by successive elections, to his death, in 1834.

His life was a short, and I had almost said, a "*merry one.*" Every company in which he mingled, experienced the joy of his wit. Indeed, humor was his nature, he rioted always in its wild luxuriance.

At the Bar he was a highly respectable lawyer. I have listened to his arguments, both on the circuit and in the Constitutional Court, with pleasure and instruction. The case of Young *vs.* The Commissioners of Roads for Edgefield, presented a new question, which he argued with great zeal and ability.

In Congress he did not win that high distinction, which his friend, Mr. McDuffie, seized at the instant when his foot crossed the threshold of Congress, and afterwards so well maintained. Mr. Davis' stand was very respectable, and he often did more to drive an adversary from the field, by his playful wit, than he could have done with all the thunders of McDuffie's eloquence. He died, as he wished to die, "*gracefully.*" He rests in the Congressional Cemetery. Neither wife nor child dropped a tear to his memory, for he died as he lived, a bachelor.

JOHN SPEED JETER.

John Speed Jeter was born about seven miles south of Edgefield Court-House, 20th June, 1779. It is believed that he received his classical education at Dr. Waddell's school, and that he read law in the office of Abraham G. Dozier, Esq., at Cambridge, Abbeville District, South Carolina. He was admitted to the Bar in the fall or winter of 1811, at Columbia, and commenced practising law at Edgefield Court-House. He had little elocution, though he could, and did, make short, plain, and sensible speeches. He was a good collection lawyer—by which I mean that he collected the debts placed in his hands for suit, as soon as he could; and when collected, he paid over the same to the parties entitled to receive the same.

On the 8th September, 1814, he married Sabra Simkins, the daughter of John Simkins, Esq. He was a staff officer in the militia, and thus obtained the title of Major.

In December, 1820, he was elected solicitor of the Southern Circuit, over the head of the Revolutionary soldier, Robert Stark, who had been solicitor from 1806, first under a commission "*quamdiu bene se gesserit.*" In 1812, the tenure of the office was changed, by Act, to four years. Mr. Stark was elected in 1816, and in 1820 his office, according to the Act of 1812, terminated.

Mr. Stark contended that he was still in office, under his commission of 1816, and sued out a rule against Mr. Jeter, to show cause why, an information in the nature of a *quo warranto*, should not be filed to ascertain by what authority he exercised the office of Solicitor? On the circuit the rule was made absolute. In the Constitutional Court the circuit decision was reversed, and Mr. Jeter confirmed in his office, (1st McC. 233.) In 1824, he was re-elected. In December, 1828, the State was divided into five, instead of six circuits, and Edgefield and Newberry, of the Southern Circuit, were thrown into the Western, Mr. Solicitor Earle's circuit; and

Mr. Jeter, was thus legislatively deprived of the chance of being any longer Solicitor.

Mr. Jeter, I think, performed the duties of Solicitor very well. He was prompt in his business, and tried his cases in the shortest possible time. He indulged in no parade, made use of no unnecessary words, and the result was that the criminal business, under his rule, was speedily dispatched.

Mr. Jeter was, I think, a Member of the House of Representatives, when he was elected Solicitor. He was elected Senator for Edgefield, in 1838, and was again re-elected in 1841. In 1846, he was not a candidate. N. L. Griffin, Esq., succeeded him in office.

Mr. Jeter was partially blind for some time. He died 14th April, 1847, leaving two daughters surviving him—Sarah, the wife of Mr. Harris, and Caroline, the wife of the Rev. Mr. Walker.

Mr. Jeter was a kind-hearted, companionable man. He was honest, faithful, and firm in all the relations of life. There may have been, and may be many greater men than John S. Jeter, yet there have been, and will be few who have been, and will be, more respected for purity of intention.

FRANKLIN H. ELMORE.

Colonel Elmore was born in Laurens District, about 1799. He was the second son of General John A. Elmore, a soldier of the Revolution. After the usual academic education, he entered the South Carolina College, where he graduated in the Class of 1819. He studied law at Laurens Court House. He was elected the Captain of a beautiful Light Infantry Company, and soon afterwards became involved in a sharp controversy with Col. Turner Richardson, as to the right of his company to the right of the line. This being refused, he marched his company off the ground, at a regimental review. For this, he was arrested and tried in August, 1821, by a General Court Martial, who sustained his right, and acquitted him.

In the Fall of 1821, he was admitted to the Bar, and settled at Walterborough. In December, 1822, he was elected Solicitor of the South-eastern Circuit, which, in 1828, was changed to the Southern. In 1824, he was appointed by Governor Manning, one of his aids, with the rank of Colonel. He was part of the Governor's brilliant cortege, which received Gen. LaFayette, in March, 1825, and escorted him through the State. He married, in Columbia, Harriet Taylor, the second daughter of General Taylor. In 1825, he was elected a Trustee of the South Carolina College. He was re-elected in 1829 and 1833. He continued to be the Solicitor until, I presume, 1834, when, in October, he was elected to Congress, and took his seat in December, 1835. He remained in Congress until he was elected, in December, 1839, President of the Bank of the State of South Carolina, in the place of Judge Colcock, who had died the January preceding. To this office he was annually elected until May, 1850, when he was appointed by Governor Seabrook, Senator in Congress, in place of Mr. Calhoun. In a very short time after he reached Washington, in May or June, 1850, he closed his useful and honored life, leaving his widow and several children, who still survive.

Col. Elmore was a singular instance of uninterrupted popularity, beginning early and never deserting him till his death. He was a man of undoubted, though not showy talents. He was an excellent lawyer, and had a fine practice, at Walterborough, and on his entire circuit. He argued his cases with good sense and great legal acumen.

He was regarded as a first-rate politician, and was an intimate friend of President Polk, who, it is said, offered to him a foreign mission.

As President of the Bank, he sustained it, in its most difficult and trying times. He encountered successfully, all the attacks of his eminent classmate, Christopher Gustavus Memminger. He published a most triumphant defence of the bank in the winter of 1849.

Col. Elmore was an excellent man, true and faithful to his friends. He was a kind husband and father, and was a faithful unswerving public officer.

His death was universally lamented, both at Washington and in this State. A new career of usefulness was just opening to him, when death cut short his life.

His body was conducted, by Congressional Committees, to Columbia, and there deposited in the Presbyterian Churchyard.

We append the proceedings in the United States Senate and House of Representatives, on the announcement of his death:

Obituary Addresses delivered on the occasion of the death of the Hon. Franklin H. Elmore, in the Senate and House of Representatives of the United States. May 30 *and* 31, 1850.

OBITUARY ADDRESSES.

In Senate, Thursday, May 30th, 1850.

On motion by Mr. Hunter, the reading of the Journal was dispensed with.

DEATH OF HON. F. H. ELMORE.

Mr. Butler rose, and said: Mr. President, my heart sinks under the melancholy duty which misfortune and affliction have imposed upon it.

Within less than three years, it has fallen to my lot to announce the deaths of two colleagues of the other House; and it was but the other day, that I communicated to the Senate the death of the lamented Calhoun. We have scarcely divested ourselves of the badges of mourning to his memory, before we are called on to replace them on the occasion of his successor's death, whose place in the Senate was but as a transit to a common tomb. Such is human existence! It is as a shadow that fleeth, and continueth not!

My friend and colleague, the late Franklin Harper Elmore, breathed his last at his lodgings, in this city, last night, at half-past eight o'clock. For several years, the state of his health has been a source of solicitude and anxiety to his friends. His mind had been tasked by many cares and responsibilities; and it was thought, that even a change of excitement and employment would afford him relief. It was with reluctance that he accepted the distinguished compliment implied in the appointment that was tendered him by the Governor of South Carolina, to fill, for a time, the vacancy in the Senate occasioned by the death of his illustrious predecessor. He took his seat in this body on the 6th of this month, and, for a week or ten days, the hearts of his family and friends were gladdened by the prospects and hopes of returning health. These delusive hopes were excited only to make disappointment the more poignant and afflictive. A new form of disease—a neuralgia that pervaded the whole system—was as the hand of death upon him. His sufferings were very great, and from the time of his attack were incessant. It is a source of consolation that he retained his mind until the actual invasion of death. His physicians, distinguished for their skill and knowledge, gave his case uncommon attention, and did all in their power to afford him relief. It was his happiness to have with him a being—the nearest to him by all the ties of this earth, the partner of his bosom, and the mother of his children—a devoted wife, who poured out upon him all that an affectionate heart could bestow. There were alleviations and sources of solace in an hour of awful trial; but they could not arrest the demands of the inexorable messenger.

In witnessing my friend's exit from this earth, I hope I have not had a lesson without its mournful instruction.

Mr. Elmore, from the time he entered upon the arena of life till his death, has acted no ordinary part in public affairs. He has filled many employments and trusts of honor and responsibility; and the confidence of his fellow-citizens, to the last, was an honorable commentary on the manner in which he discharged these duties.

Mr. Elmore was a native of Laurens District, South Carolina, and died in the fifty-first year of his age. His father, General Elmore, was a native of Virginia, and was an active soldier of the Revolution, serving under General Greene, in his celebrated Southern campaign of 1781. His mother was a Miss Saxon, a name distinguished in the partisan war of the Revolution. After passing through the ordinary academical course, my friend entered the South Carolina College, in November, 1817, and graduated, two years afterwards, with honor, and with a reputation that at once presented him to the favorable consideration of the public. He read law in my office, in the Town of Columbia, and in 1821 was admitted to the Bar.

Such was the impression that he had already made on society, that in the year 1822, the year after his admission to practice, he had conferred on him one of the highest honors of his profession. He was elected Solicitor (a public prosecuting officer) of the Southern Circuit—an office that involved high responsibility and important public duties. His energy, industry, and ability, soon confirmed the sanguine expectations of his friends.

He continued to be successively elected to this office, until he was called, by his fellow-citizens, to fill a new sphere of action, and one for which I have always thought him eminently qualified, both from taste and ambition. He took his seat in the House of Representatives, in December, 1836, to fill a vacancy occasioned by the resignation of General Hammond; he was again elected, and served throughout the twenty-fifth Congress. During this time, he won a high reputation for parliamentary address and ability. The impression which he made on his colleagues and cotemporaries was such as to flatter the pride and gratify the ambition of any public man.

In December, 1839, Mr. Elmore was elected President of the Bank of the State of South Carolina. This was a position of real difficulty, that required financial talents of a high order. Its labors and responsibilities were great, and almost overwhelming. My friend continued to be elected to this office until his late nomination to the Senate. Such testimonials of merit are higher and more abiding than verbal eulogy.

Shortly after Mr. Polk came into office, he tendered to Col. Elmore the most distinguished mission in his gift—a mission to the Court of St. James. His own modest distrust of his qualifications to equal public expectation, as well as his duties and obligations at home, induced him to decline the honor. Mr. Polk's opinion had been formed of Mr. Elmore whilst they were Members of Congress, and was a flattering tribute to his character.

As a public man, Colonel Elmore showed great sagacity in his opinions of men. Whilst he was prudent in taking his course, he showed great tenacity of purpose, and exhibited uncommon perseverance in the attainment of contemplated ends. His private relations presented his life in a view that his friends may well love to look upon. His habits were temperate, his deportment modest, and his disposition amiable. As a husband and father, he loved, and was loved, with deep and tender affection. Although this place would not seem to allow of such an indulgence, I hope my friendship for their venerable and venerated grandmother's family will be a pardon for saying a word, that may be of service to the bereaved children of a deceased friend. You have a father's example to guide you, and a father's reputation to preserve. These, with an affectionate mother's care, may inculcate on you the virtues that will carry you through the temptations of life to honor and respect. God grant, that a friend's remark may have a beneficial influence on your future destiny!

Mr. President, I offer the following resolutions:

"*Resolved, unanimously*, That a committee be appointed

by the Vice-President, to take orders for superintending the funeral of the Hon. Franklin H. Elmore, which will take place, to-morrow, at twelve o'clock, meridian, and that the Senate will attend the same.

"*Resolved, unanimously*, That the members of the Senate, from a sincere desire of showing every mark of respect due to the memory of the Hon. Franklin H. Elmore, deceased, late a Member thereof, will go into mourning for him one month, by the usual mode of wearing crape on the left arm.

"*Resolved, unanimously*, That, as an additional mark of respect for the memory of the Hon. Franklin H. Elmore, the Senate do now adjourn."

Mr. Hunter.—I cannot permit the occasion to pass, without offering my tribute of respect to the memory of the dead. I, too, knew him, and knew him as a friend. We entered Congress together, and for the first time, as I had supposed, in 1837, when there was, perhaps, more bitterness in party divisions, than I have known before or since. I have counselled with him, I have acted with him, and can truly say, that I found him wise in counsel, firm and energetic in action. I have seen him under circumstances, and exposed to trials, which test most severely the qualities of the head and the heart; and, under all circumstances, and in all emergencies, he so bore himself as to win the confidence of friends and the respect of adversaries. I say adversaries, because if he had an enemy, I did not know or see him. His was the high capacity and rare excellence of pursuing his own ends with ability and firmness; but in a manner so kindly, so gentle and persuasive, as to disarm political opposition of all personal bitterness.

Mr. President, I speak not in the extravagance of eulogy, but from observation and experience, when I say, that his was, indeed, a rare and beautiful character, in which the stronger and gentler elements were mingled in the happiest proportions. He could command your confidence by the means which won your love. When I heard he was to be sent to this place, Mr. President, there was no man who rejoiced more in the prospect of his coming than myself. I thought he was the very man to be useful in the troubled scene upon which he was about to enter. His wisdom, his firmness, his known moderation and patriotism, all fitted him for the time and the place; and I anticipated, with pleasure, the display of his powers here in all the fullness of their maturity. I had heard that he was sick, but I did not know that the hand of death was upon him, and had hoped that a change of scene and circumstances would restore him, and that long and useful years were before him. Alas, sir, how delusive was that hope; and, indeed, of how many human hopes may not the same be said? The hopes—nay,

> "The glories of our mortal state
> Are shadows, not substantial things."

Yes, sir, the light of that eye is quenched, which I have so often seen kindled under the influence of high and generous emotion. Those lips are sealed, that tongue is mute, from which I have heard the words of wisdom, of eloquence, and truth. But the loss is ours more than his. It is the loss of the country which he would have served so faithfully—of the family which mourns him so deeply.

Mr. President, into the sacred circle of that domestic grief, I do not venture to intrude. These are blows which none can heal but He who dealt them. But, sir, it is a satisfaction to his friends to know that he has left a name which will be long cherished and respected, and an example whose light, living and radiant above even the darkness of the tomb, will shed a guiding ray upon those who may succeed him.

Mr. Yulee.—Much attached to him whose worth has just been faithfully told, I ask to offer a tribute to his memory. Gentle and benevolent, generous and frank, affectionate and true, were the emotions of his heart. A clear and well-poised mind, and firm and well-ordered principles of action, made him wise in judgment and just in purpose. The high qualities that composed his noble character, gave him, through all his life, a leading influence in the social and political concerns of the community he belonged to, and would probably have placed him very soon, if spared to act in the present juncture of public affairs, among the distinguished few who, by notable wisdom, integrity, patriotism, and usefulness, attract the especial regards of their country, and mark their memory in its history.

Mr. Webster.—Mr. President, I sincerely sympathize with the honorable Member from South Carolina, whose painful duty it has been, within so short a period, to announce the death of another colleague. I sympathize, sir, with all the people of South Carolina, by whom, as I know, the gentleman now deceased was greatly respected and loved. I sympathize with that domestic circle to whom his death will be a loss never to be repaired. And, sir, I feel that the Senate may well be the object of condolence on the death of a gentleman so well known in the other branch of the Legislature, of so much experience in the various duties of public and official life in his own State, and who has so recently come into this body with every qualification to render here important public service, and with every prospect of a usefulness—except so far as that prospect may have been dimmed by serious apprehensions in regard to his health.

Sir, I had the good fortune to become acquainted with Mr. Elmore ten or twelve years ago, when he was a Member, and I may say a leading Member of the House of Representatives. I had formed a very favorable opinion of his character as a man of integrity and uprightness, of great respectability, and great talent. I regretted his departure from the councils of the nation, because a person with his qualifications, and with his habits of business, grows every day more useful in our political circles, so long as he remains in the possession of his faculties, and in the active performance of his duties. It happened to me, sir, some years afterwards, and not now many years since, to form a personal and more private acquaintance with the deceased. I had the pleasure of seeing him among his own friends, of cultivating his acquaintance in the midst of those circles of social life in which he was regarded as a treasure and an ornament. I owe, sir, to him, whatever is due for kindness and hospitality, for generous welcome, and for an extension of the civilities and courtesies of life.

I shall cherish his memory with sincere regard as a valuable and able public man, and a gentleman entitled to high estimation in all the relations of life.

Mr. Davis, of Mississippi.—Mr. President, the close personal friendship, subsisting between myself and the deceased, constitutes at once a disqualification on my part for speaking of him, and an impelling power which will not permit me to remain in silence. My acquaintance with him commenced some twelve years ago; during a part of that time I have been on intimate terms with him, and may be permitted to express my concurrence in what has been said of him on this occasion. He has been truly portrayed as one in whose character was blended firmness and gentleness, wisdom and modesty. These were his characteristics; and above all, directing and controlling all, there was that stern devotion to duty, that single appliance to whatever was the task before him, which constitutes one of the great elements of every public character, distinguished for virtue and public usefulness. It was this devotion to duty in the sphere alluded to by his colleague which, no doubt, shattered his constitution, and thus terminated his life. On the bed from which he never rose, when wasted by disease and racked by pain, that principle which caused him to devote head and heart to his duty still ruled supreme over physical suffering and exhaustion. I saw him but a short time before his death. His first words to me then were those which pointed to the current business of the Senate, and to those interests of which he felt himself to be more immediately the representative, and of which we know he was so true, so able, and so faithful an advocate. The country loses much in losing such a citizen; the Senate loses much in losing such a Member; his State loses much in losing such a Representative. But there is a deeper grief, a greater loss, a darker pall spread over his bereaved family. The veil which excludes that sacred grief from public contemplation, yet permits us to offer our hearts' best sympathy with the mourners' affliction.

I feel, Mr. President, that I am utterly disqualified for the purpose of justly describing his many endearing and radical virtues; still more for the set phrase of formal eulogy. I shall not attempt either one or the other. I will leave to other tongues and to other times whatever it may be becoming and proper to say. I cordially second the resolutions presented by the colleague of the deceased.

After a pause—

Mr. Davis, of Mississippi, moved that when the Senate adjourns, it adjourn to meet to-morrow at eleven o'clock.

The motion was unanimously agreed to.

The resolutions offered by Mr. Butler were agreed to.

The Vice-President oppointed the following gentlemen the committee under the resolutions:

Messrs. Yulee, Clemens, Badger, Jones, Corwin and Norris.

And the Senate then adjourned.

HOUSE OF REPRESENTATIVES.

FRIDAY, May 31, 1850.

The Journal was read and approved.

Mr. Jones.—In pursuance of the understanding of the House on Wednesday morning that we would on yesterday adjourn to Monday, I now move that when the House adjourns to-day, it adjourn to meet on Monday next.

The question being taken, the motion was agreed to.

A pause of a few moments ensued.

DEATH OF MR. ELMORE.

A message was received from the Senate, by the hands of Asbury Dickins, Esq., their Secretary, informing the House of the decease of Hon. F. H. Elmore, a Senator from the State of South Carolina, and communicating the proceedings of the Senate with respect thereto.

The message having been read—

Mr. Woodward rose and addressed the House as follows:

MR. SPEAKER—It is not only expected, but desired, by every one present, that we should spend a few moments in enlivening our remembrance of the distinguished person whose much-lamented and untimely death is the subject of the resolutions just received from the Senate. Not that the solemnities about to be entered upon can add anything to the reputation of the deceased, or increase the estimation in which he was, and is to be, held by the country. No eulogy of mine could add to a fame from which aspersion could never be able to detract. I have not risen, therefore, to do justice to the dead. The dead has done full justice to the dead. The death of Franklin H. Elmore holds no claim upon his life uncancelled. I rise to discharge a debt due to you, to ourselves, and the country—due to the proprieties growing out of the relations under which we stood to the deceased, when living, and the relations under which we stand to those, who, in his death, have suffered bereavement. It is not necessary that any one should here, on this occasion, bear testimony to his uncommon intellectual endowments, or his pure and elevated character. The knowledge of these, and the deep impression they have made on the public mind, will impart much greater interest to an unadorned narrative of his life, than any elaborate eulogium could possess.

Franklin Harper Elmore was born in the year 1799, in the District of Laurens, State of South Carolina. He was the second son of Gen. John Elmore, who served in the war of the Revolution, under Gen. Greene. He received his education in his native State, and was graduated at the South Carolina College, in the year 1819. In 1821, he was admitted to the Bar, and the year after was elected by the Legislature Solicitor, or State's-Attorney, for the judicial circuit, which included Columbia, the seat of government. The duties of this office he continued to discharge with ability and distinction for fourteen years, having been successively re-elected, at periods of four years. From this office he was, in December, 1836, transferred to the House of Representatives of the United States, to fill the vacancy occasioned by the resignation of the Hon. James H. Hammond, subsequently a distinguished Governor of South Carolina. He was again chosen Representative at the next regular election. The whole period of his service in this body was three years. He was here known and marked as the man of thought, and counsel, and action. He but seldom mingled in debate, though he was gifted with parliamentary powers. He was, however, destined to pass to a different sphere.

In 1839, the Presidency of the Bank of the State of South Carolina became vacant. This bank, owning a large capital, and being the fiscal agent of the State, holds a responsible position relative to neighboring monetary institutions. The weight of this responsibility had been increased by the general crash and derangement of 1837–8. Circumstances made it peculiarly necessary to place at its head a man of deep and comprehensive mind, capable of discipline and system—of complex combinations, and full of circumspection and forecast. Col. Elmore was the individual fixed upon. For upwards of ten years he continued at the head of the institution, unceasing in assiduity, and indefatigable in labor. It was mainly during this period that he achieved his reputation as a financier and commercialist. And if results were not altogether as favorable as could have been desired, the explanation, doubtless, will be found in the reflection that there are conditions which impose a limit upon possible success in all affairs, and no degree of human talent or effort is capable of transcending this limit. It is confidently believed that the laborious career just referred to undermined his constitution, disabling it to withstand the assaults of an accidental malady. He is believed to have died of erysipelas.

It would hardly seem appropriate to detail the circumstances, so recently commemorated, under which he appeared amongst us as a Senator from his native State. I cannot, however, refrain from remarking, how striking and impressive is the thought, that, having been called so unexpectedly to take the post of his great predecessor, he should also have been called so speedily to follow his footsteps to the grave; as if drawn by some strong affinity for the one who had gone before him; as though he had been beckoned still onward to a happier state by the friendly spirit of a just man made perfect. I believe that Mr. Elmore's voice was heard but once in the Senate, and that was, in answering to his name when called by the Secretary.

The intellectual endowments of Col. Elmore, his mental culture and acquirements, his elevated character, the purity of his morals, his unexceptionable good breeding, and the perfection of his social qualities, all conspired to bind his fellow-man to him; some by one law of human sympathy, some by another.

Not unfrequently engaged in the honorable competitions of life, he was, of course, sometimes the object of those irritations of feeling which rivalries are apt to engender. These heart-burnings, however, could scarcely ever survive a social interchange of ten minutes, or even a transitory greeting upon the street. And, strange as the verbal contradiction may seem, I speak with perfect sincerity when I say, that his enemies—if he had an enemy—were also his friends. And yet his popularity was not of an intense character: it was too universal to be intense. It did not meet with sufficient resistance to give it the highest degree of compactness. It seemed to exist, or rather live by a gentle law of nervous connection with the community; and there is no portion of the community, whose sensibilities will not be touched by his death.

Upon the nearer socialities that have been broken, I choose not to make any remarks. The disconsolate heart shrinks from the gaze of the world; and what our eyes may not look at, let our lips forbear to mention.

Mr. W., at the close of his remarks, submitted the following resolutions:

"*Resolved*, That this House has heard with deep sensibility the announcement of the death of the Hon. Franklin H. Elmore, a Senator in Congress, from the State of South Carolina.

"*Resolved*, That, as a testimony of respect for the memory of the deceased, the Members and officers of this House will wear the usual badge of mourning for thirty days.

"*Resolved*, That the proceedings of this House in relation to the death of the Hon. Franklin H Elmore, be communicated to the family of the deceased by the Clerk.

"*Resolved*, That this House will, as a body, forthwith repair to the Senate Chamber, to attend the funeral of the deceased."

The resolutions were unanimously adopted.

After a pause—

The Speaker stated, that in compliance with the resolutions

just adopted, the House would now proceed to the Senate Chamber.

And thereupon, the Members of the House, preceded by their Speaker and Clerk, repaired to the Senate Chamber, to attend the funeral proceedings.

After having deposited the corpse in the Congressional burying-ground, the officers and Members returned to the House.

And then the House adjourned to Monday.

PHILIP EDWARD PEARSON.

Philip Edward Pearson was born in Fairfield District, near Montecello, in 1786. His father, Philip Pearson, was an eminent surveyor. He was educated at the Rev. James Rogers's Academy, Montecello, and studied law at Columbia, Newberry, and Winnsboro'. He was in the office of Thomas Henry Egan, in Columbia, probably in 1803. I recollect seeing him, and his brother, William, often, at Newberry, in 1804, and was told they were studying law with Samuel Thee, Esq. He finished, I presume, his reading with Caleb Clarke, Esq., at Winnsboro', in 1805 and 1806, and was admitted to the Bar, at Columbia, in 1807.

He settled and practiced law, at Winnsboro', as soon as he was admitted. In 1809, he married Miss Rachel Yongue, the daughter of the Rev. S. W. Yongue.

He was elected to the Legislature both before 1824 and after 1832. In 1824, he was elected Solicitor of the Middle Circuit, in the place of Mr. Solicitor Clarke, for four years; and, in 1832, he was elected again for another term.

In 1830, he was elected, by the Board of Trustees, a Trustee of the South Carolina College; and, in 1833, he was elected, by the Legislature, a Trustee for four years.

In 1814, just before the declaration of peace, Mr. Pearson was appointed Aid to Major-General William Strother, with the rank of Major. Mr. Caleb Clarke, at the same time, was appointed Aid to General Starke. Pearson, after receiving his commission, came up to a crowd, cursing England, and boasting of his appointment. Capt. Clarke, who was present, said, "Major Pearson, do you know the reason peace was declared? The Prince Regent, hearing that we had received military commissions, became alarmed, and concluded peace hastily."

In 1838, Mr. Pearson removed to Alabama, and, after some years, to the neighborhood of Matagorda, Texas, where he died, a few years ago; leaving his wife and three children—Dr. Adolphus Pearson, Texas, Mrs. John Woodward, and Mrs. Samuel F. Price, of Alabama.

Mr. Pearson was a man of various acquirements; more by his own industry than by education. He was fond of antiquarian researches, and preserving legendary lore. He wrote the article in Mills's Statistics on Fairfield, and a letter on witchcraft, published in first Statistics. Before his death, he was preparing, as he informed me by letter, an account of the Broad River Section of Fairfield District. I hope he lived to complete it, and that it will yet see the light.

He was a pleasant, companionable man—abounding in anecdote. He was a good lawyer—preparing and arguing his cases well. His arguments were generally clear and to the point; never very long, *which was, then and is now, most commendable.*

THOMPSON T. PLAYER.

Thompson T. Player, was the son of Major Joshua Player, of Fairfield. He was his son by his first wife, and graduated in the South Carolina College, in the Class of 1822. He studied law, at Newberry, in the office of Judge O'Neall, for perhaps, two years, then visited Litchfield, Connecticut, to attend the law school there. He soon became dissatisfied, and wrote to Judge O'Neall, requesting to resume his place in his office, which was granted with pleasure. He returned, and there finished his course. In 1827, he was admitted to the Bar, and settled at Winnsboro'. He was elected to the House of Representatives, in the General Assembly, in 1830, and again in 1832. He married the youngest daughter of General Hampton, who died in, perhaps, a year after marriage. He was elected Solicitor of the Middle Circuit in 1833, and was continued until 1841. In 1833 and 1837, Mr. Player was elected a Trustee of the South Carolina College. In 1841 Mr. Thomas M. Dawkins succeeded Mr. Player as Solicitor. The latter, after he ceased to be Solicitor, devoted himself to the acquisition of wealth, first, at New Orleans, and subsequently, he married a fair lady in Tennessee, by whom I have understood, he acquired an estate. He lived in Nashville, where he died, within the last five or six years.

Mr. Player was a gentleman, of good education and soft manners. He had respectable talents, spoke well, except when he resorted to art. He was, however, too artificial, and too much of a copyist, to be an orator. He was a good lawyer, and when he left my office, he was better prepared for success at the Bar, than any one, out of more than twenty students, who had passed out of it.

In his Solicitorship he did his duty well. In the case against Fleming, for the murder of Barkley Shipp, of Fairfield, notwithstanding he was opposed by Col. Preston, he so managed and argued the case, that no advantage was obtained over him. His argument in the case, *ex parte* McCrady *vs.* Hunt, 2 Hill, 1, can be read in the report of that case, and an opinion can be formed of him as a lawyer.

JOHN D. EDWARDS.

This gentleman was born, as I believe, in 1797. He was in the sophomore class of the South Carolina College, when I was Senior, in the year 1812; he was then a mere boy. He graduated in the class of 1814, of which Hugh S. Legaré was the leading member. I did not see Mr. Edwards after my graduation, until 1824, when I was Speaker of the House of Representatives. He then stood before me, with a head white as snow. Twelve years had raised him to manhood. An unfortunate event had blanched his locks, and had made such an alteration in his appearance, that I should never have known him, had he not said, "I was in college with you, I am John D. Edwards."

He studied law, was admitted to the Bar, in the City of Charleston, on the 7th May, 1818. He settled first at Walterboro', and practiced with William Singleton, as his partner. After the death of his partner, he removed to Barnwell, where he lived and practiced law several years. He returned then to Walterboro', and was the partner of Franklin H. Elmore, both before and after 1829. He was several times a Member of the House of Representatives of this State.

On the election of Mr. Elmore, to Congress, in 1836, Mr. Edwards was elected Solicitor of the Southern Circuit, and was continued, by successive elections, to 1848, when he was superseded by the Honorable M. L. Bonham.

He married a beautiful and accomplished lady, Miss Abigail Swift, in the City of Charleston. He was utterly ruined by an imprudent indorsement for a friend. His lovely wife died shortly before, or soon after, leaving an interesting family of two daughters and three sons. The kindness of a brother lawyer, who never saw want without sharing his loaf with it, provided the means whereby a home was secured to him and his children. Mr. Edwards, in his past kindness to an orphan, was richly entitled to the sympathizing friendship of friends. He died about 1857.

As a lawyer, he was zealous and indefatigable. His impulsive disposition made him sometimes overshoot the mark.

As Solicitor, he was diligent, attentive, and persevering, and although not a profound lawyer, yet he rarely failed to attain the ends of justice.

He spoke easily and fluently, and had many of the graces of oratory, in style and manner; yet, he never could be called an *orator.*

Col. Edwards was one of the kindest, and most attached, and devoted husbands and fathers with whom I was acquainted.

He was hospitable to a fault; for his kindness, in this respect, trenched deeply on his limited means.

He was a nephew of Chancellor DeSaussure, and like him, he cultivated *hospitality and kindness*, as a household virtue.

He was a gentleman of the old school. His faults, whatever they were, are buried with him. Let his virtues be remembered, and let his children never want a friend to protect them, as he did Richard W. Singleton.

ALEXANDER MARKLAND McIVER.

Alexander Markland McIver was born 21st February, 1799, in Darlington District. His mother was the sister of General David R. Williams. She was, therefore, of Welsh descent. His father, judging from the name, was descended from the great family of McIver, in the Highlands of Scotland, so much distinguished by Flora McIver, who succeeded in securing the escape of the Pretender in his flight from Scotland.

He graduated in the class 1817, in the South Carolina College, and studied law with Judge Evans, then at the Bar, and was admitted to the Bar of the Law Court, 27th April, 1820, and to that of the Court of Equity, 17th January, 1828. He was married to Mary Hanford, the eldest daughter of Enoch Hanford, Esq., 23d January, 1822.

He was a Member of the House of Representatives of South Carolina, between 1830 and 1833. He was elected Solicitor of the Northern, now the Eastern Circuit, in the place of Thomas J. Withers, now Judge Withers, on the 13th of December, 1841. He was thrice elected, and died in his third term, on the 10th of July, 1850. His friend, General Hanna, succeeded him. His early death, in October, 1853, opened the way to Mr. McIver's son, Henry McIver, who was appointed by the Governor *pro tem.*, and who was, in December succeeding, elected, and has most worthily since fulfilled the duties of this great law office.

Alexander M. McIver left at his death, surviving him, his widow, six sons and three daughters. Mr. McIver was a member of the Baptist Church. He was an excellent man, devoted to his family. He possessed very good talents, and a fine elocution; and if he had improved the powers with which God had endowed him, he must have been eminent in any walk of life. But he felt not that necessity which makes a man use his mind, as a means of living. The result was, that he never rose above mediocrity in his profession, which, it seemed to me, he never liked.

WILLIAM J. HANNA.

This gentlemen I first met at Chesterfield, in October, 1830, when I was exceedingly sick, and from him I then received such attentions as endeared him to me in all his subsequent life. He was admitted to the Bar in 1829, and had not long been a resident at Chesterfield. He was born on the 13th Decembor, 1806, in York District. He was the son of James Hanna, and was called after his grand-father, Col. William Hanna, of the Revolution. His mother was Violet Barry, the niece of Gen. Thos. Moore, and sister of Andrew Barry, of Spartanburgh District. He began practice at Chesterfield, as the partner of his relation, Minor Clinton, Esq.

He had an academic education. Soon after settling at Chesterfield, he married Dorothy, the daughter of John Craig, Esq., very much against the wishes of her father; but she, fortunately, though acting against her father's wishes, made a better match for herself than her father could have done for her. The old gentleman was afterwards not only reconciled, but also *gloried* in his son-in-law as an honor to him and his household.

Gen. Hanna was a remarkable man: *he was self-made.* As a lawyer, he was well informed; his preparation of his business and cases was admirable: everything was in order. Every matter, in his cases, he knew, and knew how to bring it out properly and in its proper place. His statements and arguments were as clear as *a sun-beam.* The consequence was that he was never tedious, and most generally successful. As a Member of the Legislature, he was always in his place, prompt, and ready, and useful in business. He was a pure patriot; very possibly, however, like many other good men in Carolina, he was mistaken in his politics.

In a few years, he became the leading lawyer at Chesterfield, and occupied a commanding position on the circuit. His wife died on 23d June, 1841, leaving three children.

He was regularly promoted through all the military grades to that of Brigadier-General, and I have often heard him commended as an excellent officer. He was three times elected to the State Senate—first, in 1842, and again in 1846 and '50. On the 16th February, 1842, he married his second wife, Eliza A. Chapman, who died in April, 1843, leaving one child, who still survives. In 1844, he married Margaret C. Chapman, the cousin of his first wife. He succeeded Alexander McIver, as Solicitor of the Northern, now the Eastern Circuit, in 1850, which position, however, he held but for a short time for, on 22d March, 1853, he died, and was succeeded in office by Henry, the son of his friend, the late Alexander McIver, leaving a widow and three children, who still survive him.

He presented an example of purity, and lived a life, of which his descendants should be proud. In every relation of life he was without reproach, and the tears of love and affection of all who knew him, fell upon his early but honored grave.

CHARLESTON, S. C., 21st September, 1859.

Dear Sir,—Yours of the 9th inst., relative to the late Gen. Hanna, was duly received.

I have only delayed replying until I could see some of the family to get definite information.

William Jefferson Hanna, was born 13th December, 1806, in York District, South Carolina. He never received a collegiate education. He was admitted to practice in the Courts of Law 25th November, 1829, and in the Court of Equity 3d December, 1836. He was married to Dorothy C. Craig, 21st March, 1833; she died 23d June, 1841, leaving three children, who still survive. He was married a second time to Eliza A. Chapman, 16th February, 1842; she died 15th April, 1843, leaving one child who is still living.

He was married a third time to Margaret C. Chapman, 24th July, 1844, who bore him three children, all of whom, with the widow, still survive.

He was commissioned Brigadier-General 9th May, 1839, which office he held until about the last of September, 1845. He was elected to the Senate of South Carolina in 1842, 1846, and 1850. He never was a Member of the House of Representatives. He was elected Solicitor in December, 1850, and died at Chesterfield Court House, 22d March, 1853.

So far from regarding your letters as troublesome, I can assure you that it gives me great pleasure to be of any service to you, and shall be glad for you to call on me whenever you may think I can be of service.

Yours, very respectfully,

HENRY McIVER.

Hon. John Belton O'Neall,
Newberry, S. C.

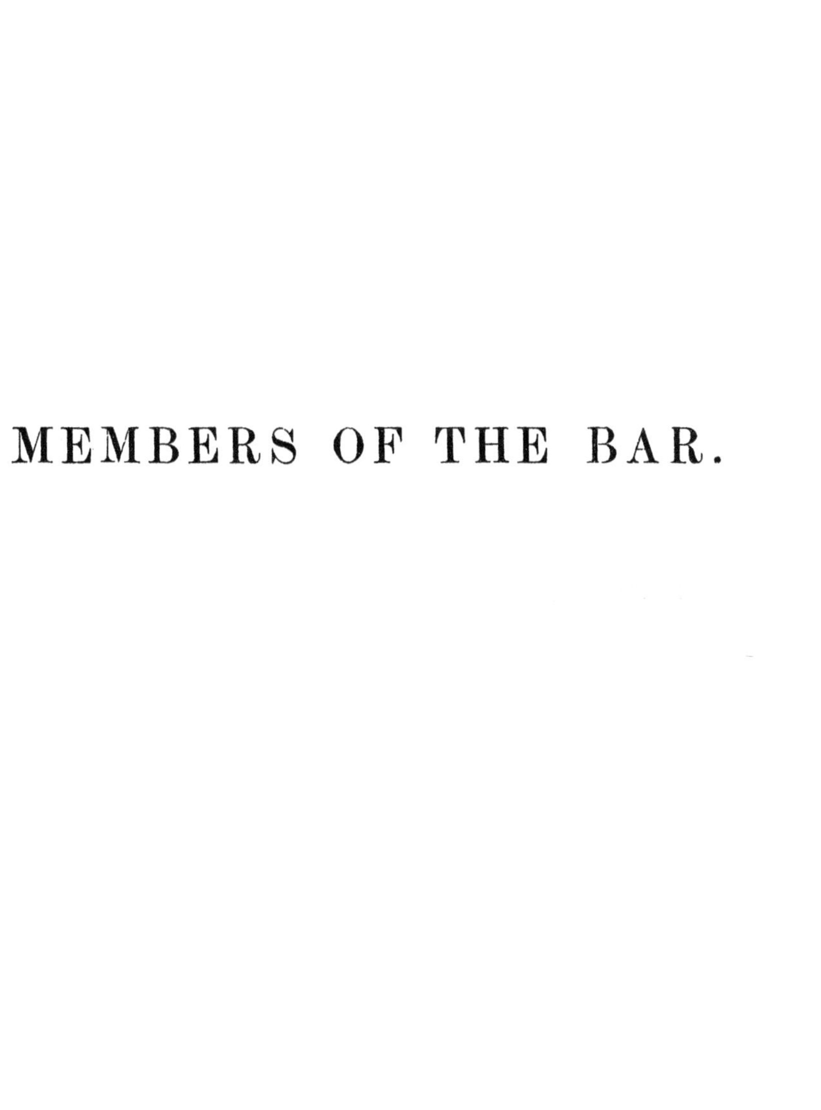

MEMBERS OF THE BAR.

THOMAS PINCKNEY.

General Thomas Pinckney, the second son of Chief Justice Charles Pinckney, and Eliza Lucas, the daughter of Col. Lucas, the Governor of Antigua, was born 23d October, 1750, and in 1753, was carried with his brother, Charles Cotesworth Pinckney, by their father, to England, to be educated. In 1758, Chief Justice Pinckney, in consequence of the French war, returned to South Carolina, and soon after died. His will directed that his sons should receive the best education, "were it even necessary to sell part of his estate for that purpose."

Thomas Pinckney was educated at Westminster and Oxford, studied law at the Temple, and was admitted as a Barrister.

When he returned to Charleston, about the year 1772 or 1773, the dispute between the mother country and colonies, was drawing rapidly to a head.

On the 7th June, 1775, Thomas Pinckney was appointed 1st Lieutenant of one of the regiments ordered to be raised by South Carolina.

I see it is stated in Lieber's American Encyclopedia, that "Thomas Pinckney rose to the rank of Major." This may be so, in the continual change of officers in those regiments before and after they were placed on the Continental establishment.

It seems that he was the aid of General Lincoln, who took the command of the Southern Army, 7th December, 1778, and that he acted in that capacity, with Count DeEstaing, in the siege and disastrous attack on the town of Savannah, 9th October, 1779.

Whether Thomas Pinckney was present and surrendered at Charleston, on the 12th of May, 1780, I am unable to say. It is possible he was, and that, with General Lincoln, as a part of his suite, went to Philadelphia, in a vessel which was there furnished. If so, he must have been exchanged, for he was the aid of General Gates, in his unfortunate defeat at Gum Swamp, near Camden, in August, 1780. In that affair he bore a gallant part. He was wounded and taken prisoner, and was sent, as a prisoner of war, to Philadelphia. He had, I presume, no further opportunity of service in the Revolution.

In 1789, he was offered by President Washington, the office of District Judge of the United States for South Carolina, but he thought his private interest forbade his acceptance.

He was a Member of the Legislature in 1791, and drew the Act to establish a Court of Equity within this State.—1 Faust, 29.

In 1789, he was elected as the successor of Governor Moultrie. The duty of Governor now consists more in granting pardons, reviewing the militia, giving big dinners at the session of the Legislature, in Columbia, than anything else Then it was a very different thing: the State was to be recovered from the disorders of the Revolution—the law was to be enforced, and order everywhere established. This was done by Governor Pinckney.

Soon after the termination of his office, 16th January, 1792, he was appointed by President Washington, Minister to the Court of St. James. This highly responsible office, he accepted, and discharged its various duties much to the satisfaction of his government.

He was afterwards employed on a mission to the Court of Spain. He there negotiated the treaty of St. Ildefonso, which secured the free navigation of the Mississippi.

The situation of his estate made him feel the necessity of a return home; he, therefore, solicited his own recall. He returned to America, and Charleston, in 1796.

Soon after his return, he was elected to Congress. He acted in that body generally, in support of the measures of President Adams. The Federal party, which was then in power, soon lost it, and Mr. Pinckney retired from public life, and devoted himself to the care of his estate and the education of his children.

The Federalists of South Carolina, were, generally, good men. A large body were soldiers of the Revolution, or men born in its storms—they feared the excesses of anarchy—they looked upon the horrors of the French Revolution, as the plain results of unrestrained Democracy. They were, therefore, in favor of a strong government, and desired to strengthen instead of weakening, the Federal Government.

They were mistaken in their opposition to the Republican principles, which, in 1801, obtained the ascendancy, with Jefferson as President. But such men as the Pinckneys, Daniel E. Huger, Judge Nott, Judge DeSaussure, and many others, were too good, too virtuous and pure, to be *ostracised.* They were, therefore, as the opportunity served, called into the service of the State. Differences in political opinions have never, to the honor of the State be it said, *long* excluded good men from her service.

At the commencement of the war of 1812, Thomas Pinckney was, by President Madison, appointed a Major-General, and had charge of the Southern Division or Sixth Military District. There was in it little opportunity of distinction. The Creek war was waged within it. Subordinate generals, such as Floyd, in Georgia, and General Jackson, in the Creek Nation, fought the battles, and brought the war to a conclusion. General Pinckney was in the field when the battle of the Horse Shoe, by General Jackson, satisfied the Creeks that they were beaten, and when Weatherford surrendered himself.

General Pinckney advised the War Department to divide his military district, (extending from North Carolina to the Mississippi.) This was done, and General Jackson, at his recommendation, appointed to the South-western Division. In it General Jackson gathered the imperishable laurels of the repulse of the British from before New Orleans.

At the return of peace, General Pinckney resigned his commission, and sought in the retirement of private life, the blessings of his family and home, from which he had been long deprived.

Such a man could not do otherwise than adorn private life.

8

His life had been almost an epitome of his country's history. He had borne a part in the war which accompanied the birth of his country, and in that which maintained and asserted her rights. He had lived to see the uncovered bones of his countrymen, slain in the Revolution, gathered to peaceful graves, and the desert places produced by that war, to blossom like the rose. He had lived to see the whitening sails of his country's commerce on every sea, and her agriculture feeding and clothing the nations of the world.

In private life, he did all he could to encourage the further development of his country, and to crown her with the garlands, not only of commerce and agriculture, but of science.

The life of this eminent statesman and soldier, was closed 2d November, 1828, in the seventy-eighth year of his age.

EDWARD RUTLEDGE.

Here again, I have paused and reflected much, before I put my pen in motion. The difficulty of doing full justice, to the great name to which I have come, is fully appreciated. Not quite sixty years have passed away since the muffled drum, the solemn tread of the soldiery, the tolling bell, and the regular platoon firing, proclaimed to the State that Gov. Rutledge was—is not—and in St. Philip's Church-yard mingles with his mother earth; yet, it is difficult to obtain the means of giving a sketch of his life.

He was born 23d November, 1749, and was the youngest child of Dr. John Rutledge. He received his classical education in the City of Charleston, under David Smith, A. M., of New Jersey College, who, as Dr. Ramsay says, "was an able instructor in the learned languages." He studied law with his brother, John Rutledge, but that not being then regarded as enough, he was, in 1769, entered a student in the Temple, London. His brother's letter of advice to him soon after his arrival, is appended, as a note to this memoir, and is recommended to students and lawyers, of the present day, as worthy of frequent perusal. He, after four years' absence, returned to Charleston *a Barrister*, and, in 1773, began to practice law.

In 1774, he, with his brother John, Henry Middleton, Christopher Gadsden, and Thomas Lynch, were appointed Delegates to the General Congress, which met at Philadelphia, in September. "He and John Jay, of New York, were nearly of an age, and the two youngest members of that honorable body."

For three successive years he was a member, and on the 4th of July, 1776, with Thomas Heyward, Jr., Thomas Lynch, and Arthur Middleton, signed the Declaration of Independence. This, of itself, is a record of immortality, and places the name of Edward Rutledge where it must ever be surrounded with the sun-light of glory.

In the Congress of 1774, '75, '76, and '77, he had great influence. He was always at his post, and in every way devoted himself to the service of the country. On the 12th of June, 1776, he was with John Adams, Sherman, Harrison, and Wilson, appointed on the first board of war.—3 Washington's writings, 429. The arduous duties of directing and providing for the defence of the country was discharged by these eminent men, entirely to the satisfaction of the General-in-chief. On the 11th of September of the same year, he, with Dr. Franklin, and John Adams, under the appointment of Congress, had an interview with Lord Howe on his propositions for peace, on Staten Island, in which they maintained that nothing short of Independence would satisfy the United States.—4 Washington's writings, 88. Dr. Ramsay, in his Second Volume of the History of South Carolina, at page 521, says of Mr. Rutledge: "His protracted absence from home, and continued attention to public business, was no small sacrifice. His talents and popularity would have commanded the first practice at the Bar; but he loved his country too well to be influenced by pecuniary considerations to neglect its interests."

"In 1779, he was again appointed a Member of Congress, but on his way was seized with an obstinate and tedious fever, which prevented him from proceeding to the seat of their deliberation."

It seems, too, that Edward Rutledge held a commission in the militia when it was something more than "fuss and feathers." He rose through "all the grades of rank in the Charleston Battalion of Artillery, to that of its Lieutenant-Colonel. In 1779—when the British were defeated and driven from Port Royal Island—he commanded a company of artillerists, which earned its full share of the glory of that victory."—2d Ram. 522.

In the year 1780, after the fall of Charleston, in May, "he became a prisoner of war, and was sent to St. Augustine, where he was confined eleven months, and on his exchange, *delivered* above eight hundred miles from home and friends."

In, I presume, September, 1781, Mr. Rutledge, from Philadelphia—soon after his exchange, and before his return home—wrote to Gen. Washington, suggesting and urging a combined attack by the French fleet and the land troops, on the City of Charleston, about which he said he had consulted the Chevalier De la Luzerne, and who had promised to use his influence with the Count DeGrasse, to effect the object. To this Gen. Washington, from his camp before York, on the 6th October, 1781, politely replied, speaking of Mr. Rutledge's plan as a "very desirable" one, and uses this strong sentence: "Of this, however, you may be assured, that, after the present operation is closed—and I hope it will terminate well—everything, which depends upon me, and all the influence I can exert, shall be used towards exterminating the British from the Southern States."—8 Washington's writings, 174.

Mr. Rutledge returned to South Carolina, and was elected a member of the Jacksonborough General Assembly, which met 8th January, 1782. He served in that body, and afterwards in the Council, and as Dr. Ramsay says: "in both rendered essential service to his country."

But, until the 14th of December, 1782, he was not permitted to set his foot within his native city. On that glad day, however, he was one among the gentlemen welcomed home, by their mothers, wives, sisters and daughters.

He resumed his practice, and devoted himself unceasingly to that pursuit and the home concerns of South Carolina. He was a member of the Convention which framed the Constitution of 1790.

He was a member of what may be properly called the Organic Legislature of 1791. He drew "the Act for the abolition of the rights of Primogeniture, and for the giving an equitable distribution of the real estate of intestates, and for other purposes," passed the 19th of February, 1791. Such a law was, I suppose, suggested by Pendleton, Burke, and Grimké, in 1789, in their contemplated digest, but it was left for the skill and wisdom of Edward Rutledge to prepare that wisest and best measure, required by Fifth Section, Tenth Art. of the Constitution of 1790, "for the abolition of the rights of Primogeniture, and for giving an equitable distribution of the real estate of intestates." If he had done no other act, I should think it was enough of glory for any single man. For it has broken up the aristocractic feature of property, which had before prevailed in South Carolina, and has given equality—practical equality—which never otherwise could have existed.

In 1794, (24th May,) when his brother John had, on assuming the Chief Justiceship of South Carolina, declined the office of Associate Judge in the United States Supreme Court, Gen. Washington addressed a joint letter to Gen. Charles Cotesworth Pinckney, and Edward Rutledge, asking: "Will either of you gentlemen accept it?" They both declined, mainly for the reason, that in the Legislature of South Carolina, of which they were Members, they could be of more service to the General Government.—10 Washington's writings, 164 and 165.

On the 15th October, 1798, Gen. Washington, writing to the Secretary of War, James McHenry, and speaking of officers for the expected French war, mentioned Edward Rutledge in reference to the artillery.—11 Washington's writings, 322.

For seventeen years this great and good man pursued his profession and served in the Legislature. In December, 1798, he was elected Governor and Commander-in-chief in and over South Carolina; and on the 23d of January, 1800, he closed his valuable life. It thus seemed that the State which he had loved, served, and honored, reserved this highest honor, as a fitting testimonial of love and honor to be last bestowed on him. The inscription on his tomb, in St. Philip's Church-yard, is so remarkable for its simplicity that I transcribe it: "Beneath this stone are deposited the remains of his Excellency, Edward Rutledge, late Governor of this State, whom it has pleased the Almighty to take from this life, January 23d, 1800, at the age of fifty years and two months. The virtues of this eminent statesman require not the aid of an inscription here, to recall them to our recollection: it is believed that they are engraved on the hearts, and will long live in the remembrance of his countrymen."

His wife survived him for thirty-six years. He left, at least, one son, Henry Middleton Rutledge, who removed to Tennessee, and there died, leaving many descendants—amongst whom was Mrs. Daniel Blake, whose admirable fugitive poetry, published after her death, privately for her husband, Daniel Blake, and styled "Reliques," will long live and show that she had, indeed, the fire of her noble grandfather.

To the young I would commend her "Life's Duty." In it she admirably says:

"Steadfast fix thy soul—thine eye;
Secret power shall them assuage,
Hand unseen shall still their rage,
Enter then the thunder cloud.
There is light beyond its shroud,
Dark though darker grows thy lot,
Light and calm, oh! doubt it not;
To the steadfast will be given,
The mysterious boon of heaven."

To Dr. Ramsay, the gifted historian of South Carolina, I appeal for a sketch of Edward Rutledge, as an orator, a lawyer, a legislator and a man. Speaking of Edward Rutledge, he says: "His eloquence was great, but not precisely in the same line with his brothers. Demosthenes seemed to be the model of the one; Cicero of the other. The eloquence of the elder, like a torrent, bore down all opposition, and controlled the passions of the hearers; that of the younger was soothing, persuasive, and made willing proselytes.

"In the practice of law, Edward Rutledge was directed by the most upright and generous principles. To advance his personal interest was a secondary object; to do good, to promote peace, to heal breaches, to advance justice, was a primary one. His powers of persuasion were not to be purchased to shield oppression, or to support iniquity. When he thought his client had justice on his side, he would go all lengths in vindicating his claims; but would not support any man, however liberal, in prosecuting unfounded claims, or resisting those that were substantially just. *He abhorred the principle, that an advocate should take all advantages for his client, and gain for him whatever he could, whether right or wrong; or, on the other hand, to assist him with quirks and quibbles, which ingenuity can contrive, or the forms of law permit, for defeating or delaying the claims of substantial justice.*

"For the seventeen succeeding years after '82, he followed his profession, and, at the same time, served in the Legislature. Though a private member, he, by his persuasive eloquence, directed most of the important measures adopted in that period for the improvement of the country. Many were the points which his eloquence either carried through, or defeated in, the Legislature. For the good obtained, and the evil prevented, his memory will be long respected by his countrymen."

When it is remembered that Dr. Ramsay was President of the Senate from 1791 to the close of 1797, it will be, at once, seen, that the praise bestowed is no general indiscriminate praise:

"In moderating those collisions which, in Carolina, too often produced *duels*, Mr. Edward Rutledge had great address. His opinions, as a man of honor, were appreciated by all parties, and, being impartial, seldom failed of bringing round those explanations, which, without degrading, were satisfactory. As a lawyer, and a gentleman, he was justly entitled to the honorable appellation of a peace-maker. He was eminently the friend of the distressed, and thought nothing too much for their accommodation and relief. The talents of few were estimated equally high. The virtues of none attracted a greater portion of love and esteem."

I append Governor John Rutledge's letter to his brother, and extracts from the city papers, on the death of Governor Edward Rutledge:

"CHARLESTON, July 30th, 1769.

"*Dear Edward*,—As I had not leisure, before you went, to reduce to writing some observations, which I mentioned verbally to you, concerning your studies in England, I take this first opportunity (per Curling) of doing it, lest you may forget any of them. This, I hope, will find you well, in London, after the fatigues of a voyage; and, having had time to look about you, and see what strangers are generally desirous of viewing, I expect you will be sitting down seriously to business. The very first thing with which you should be thoroughly acquainted is, the writing short-hand, which you will find of infinite advantage in your profession, and which will give you the means of great superiority over others who do not write it. I need not enlarge on the advantages of it, but say, I think you will find it absolutely necessary; therefore, be master of it, as soon as you possibly can learn it; and when you can once write it, take notes of everything at Court. I would even write down, in short-hand, cases you hear, which are not worth transcribing fair. Your time may as well be employed in writing, as hearing, them. If they are not worth transcribing, no time is lost; and the writing it on every occasion will soon make you perfect, and able to keep up with the speakers, which is the chief end of writing in this manner. I would take down every public discourse, either at the Bar or pulpit, which you hear, for this very purpose. And, now, I mention the latter, by no means fall into the too common practice of not frequenting a place of worship. This you may do, I think, every Sunday. There is generally a good preacher at the Temple Church, and it will be more to your credit to spend a few hours of that day there, than as it is generally spent, in London especially, by the Templars.

"Be constant in attending the sittings in Chancery, out of terms, and when there are no sittings at Nisi Prius, in London or Westminster; for I would prefer attending the King's Bench, and sittings of the Chief Justice of that Court, at Nisi Prius, when they are held. And remember what I hinted to you, of attending, alternately, in the different Courts, by agreement between you and some of your intimate fellow-students, and then of comparing and exchanging notes every evening; by which means, if you select proper acquaintance, in whose judgment you can confide, you will have the same advantage as if you attended all the Courts in person. Don't pass too slightly over cases, and not note them, because you think they are trifling. Many cases appear so, at a cursory overlooking, and, indeed, may be not very material, and yet you will find use for them.

"But you must exert yourself to the utmost, in being able, by some means or other, to attend the House of Commons constantly, or, at least, whenever anything of consequence is to come on. There, I believe, you will not be suffered to take notes; however, you will soon know that. You must get introduced to Mr. Garth, and probably, by his means, you may always get in. Don't say, that they have come to a resolution not to admit any strangers into the gallery, and by that means you could not get in, as Hugh did. I know it is a common order, to clear the galleries, but that people there generally fall back, and no notice is taken then of them; for you must, at all events, get admittance there, and make yourself well-acquainted with the speakers. Reading lectures upon oratory will never make you an orator. This must be obtained by hearing and observation of those who are allowed to be good speakers—not of every conceited chap who may pretend to be so. I would, also, have you attend the House of Lords, upon every occasion worth it. You will find you may easily get introduced to some lord, who will take you in with him; and, by no means, spare a few guineas, at Christmas, among the door-keepers, &c., for that, I warrant, will do the business. I would not have this make you a dabbler in politics. What I intend by it is, that you may have opportunities of seeing and hearing the best speakers, and of acquiring a good manner and proper address, and of being able, on occasion, of giving your sentiments, when necessary, upon what you have seen and heard there. I believe Sheridan is the only lecturer, in England, upon oratory; and, I think, it would be advisable to attend him, and mark well his observations. He reads with propriety, though he is much too stiff, and his voice exceeding bad. I would go a short circuit, just before you come out; but it should be to a place where you might have something worth seeing, besides the mode of conducting business there, which is soon understood, *i. e.*, to Oxford, or some other place generally visited by travelers. The Circuit Bill goes with Lord Charles.—(Montague, *ed.*) If it is confirmed at home, (England, *ed.*) you should make yourself acquainted, from experience, of the method of doing business upon the circuit, in England. If you stick close to French, and converse generally in that language, you will soon be master of it; and I would not have you attempt it, unless you are resolved to speak it as well and as fluently as you do English; for I have no notion of being such a Frenchman as most of our Carolinians are, who have been taught that language, who can seldom do more than translate it, after much difficulty. I think you may, only by attending to it occasionally, make yourself perfectly master of it; and so as to be able to read it, or speak it, off-hand, fluently, and not as if you took your words out of a vocabulary. Whatever you attempt, make yourself completely master of; for nothing makes a person so ridiculous, as to pretend to things he does not understand; and it will not be sufficient for a man, in such case, to rest satisfied, because he may pass as a complete scholar amongst those with whom he may have to do in general, who, perhaps, may know little about the matter—such a one may meet sometimes with his superiors, and in what situation will he then be? I know nothing more entertaining, and likely to give you a graceful manner of speaking, than seeing a good play well acted. Garrick is inimitable; the other actors not worth seeing, after him, in the same characters. Mark him well, and you will profit by him.

"You must not neglect the classics; but rather go through them from beginning to end. I think you had better get a private tutor, who will point out their beauties to you, and make you, in six months, at your age, better acquainted with them than a boy, in school, generally is in seven or eight years. Read Latin authors, and the best, frequently, so as to be as well-acquainted with Latin as French. I have often thought, were I to begin the world again, I would do what I am sure one would after find of use: make a book, and in it note down the remarkable expressions and sayings of wise and great men, whenever I met with them—not to serve as Joe Miller's Jests, or a collection of *bon-mots*, to make one pass for a merry fellow, or rather a maker of fun for a pack of fools—but often to embellish your arguments or writings. Indeed, amongst wits, it would be useful, and show that a man had not confined himself entirely to dry law. You see that Lord Bacon did not think this beneath him: read his collection of apothegms. However, I would not confine this to the sayings of the ancient generals, poets, and heathen philosophers, (though amongst them there are many good things,) but bring it down to the present times; and, in it, I would insert the beautiful passages I met with, such as were striking, nervous, or pathetic, in the different authors I read in the different languages. Horace, Juvenal, and Virgil, would add not a little to this collection. Now is your time to begin, and go through a good deal of this business; when you enter upon the practice of the law, it will be too late to begin this. I would have you read occasionally the purest English authors, to acquire an elegant style and expression. What different impressions do the same sentiments make, when conveyed in different modes of expression; but for a man who speaks in public, whose business it is not to be content with barely proving a thing, by, perhaps, a dull argument, after having wearied out his hearers with bad language, and a deal of tautology—and if he has said some good things, has buried them in rubbish—but to engage the constant attention of his hearers, to command it, and to carry immediate conviction along with him. The history of England should be read with great care and attention—all the different writers of that history read and compared together, and your own observations made upon them all together—showing wherein they agree, disagree, &c., and in which credit is to be placed. It will be necessary, for your own use, to make a compendium of this history, which no man can carry in his head.

"Don't neglect to learn surveying, that is the principal branch of mathematics which you will have occasion for, and I would be thoroughly acquainted with it; not only to work a problem upon paper, but with the practical part also. Consult Corbet upon every matter, with regard to your studies, in which you are in any doubt. And now, with regard to particular law books—Coke's Institutes seem to be almost the foundation of our law. These you must read over and over, with the greatest attention, and not quit him till you understand him thoroughly, and have made your own everything in him, which is worth taking out. A good deal of his law is now obsolete, and, altered by Acts of Parliament; however, it is necessary to know what the law was before so altered. Blackstone, I think, useful. The reports are too tedious to be all read through; at least, whilst you are in England, I would give the preference to the most modern, as there you will find doctrines in the old books often corrected or exploded, and it will be of no use to stock your common-place book (which I hope to find very copious and well stored) with what is not law, and, perhaps, never was. I look upon it, that if you go through all the cases reported since the Revolution, when the Constitution seems to have been re-established upon its true and proper principles, and, since which time, by the alteration of the Judges' commissions, and their increasing independence to what it is at this day, the law has been in its greatest perfection, and not encroaching either upon the people's liberties, or the prerogative; I say if you do this, you will have a collection of the very best cases. The old ones, which either agree with the modern, or are contradictory to these, you will see confirmed or exploded; and, by always turning to examining, and marking them when reading your new cases, you will, by this occasional reading them, have read them as effectually, and, indeed, much more so, than if you had set out with them at first, but I would read every case reported from that time to the present. Distinguish between your readings of law and equity, and don't confound the two matters—they are kept very distinct in the Courts in England, though here blended together very often, and very ridiculously. And the same method of reading cases should be followed, also, with regard to the equity books. I would have you, also, read the Statute Laws throughout, to know when a thing is allowed to be law—whether it be by common or statute law, which we are often very ignorant of. The recitals of these laws should be particularly noticed, which are the best authority to know what the law was before making the Act. Vast numbers of them you will find of no manner of use, except, indeed, as matter of history, in which light they will afford you some assistance; but this thing, I think, in the main, will be of vast service to you. When I say you should read such a book, I do not mean just to run cursorily through it, as you would a newspaper but to read it carefully and deliberately, and transcribe what you find useful in it. If this method was taken, one would seldom read any book without reaping some advantage from it. Stock yourself with a good collection of law maxims, both Latin and English—they are of great use. Don't omit any that you come across, and the authorities for them, which may often be of service in the application of them. Make yourself thoroughly acquainted with all the terms of the law, which you easily may, now when they are so polished and modernized as they are at present, and free from the old Frenchified, uncouth words, in which they were formerly couched. However, you must understand the terms, to understand the authors that use them. The little book called *Termes de le Ley* or terms of the law, will help you. 'Doctor and Student' is a good book, though a little one, and good authority. Bacon, you know, is my favorite, and where authors seem to differ, I think he will best reconcile them. Be well acquainted with the Crown Law, Hale's Hankins, and Judge Foster; and what other Crown Law books there are, read carefully.

"You should not confine yourself to the securing men's properties, without regard to their liberties and lives, which are the most preferable. Don't confound these branches of study, for they are distinct. 1. The Common Law, which regards civil affairs, and the Statute Law on the same subject. 2. The Crown Law and Statute Law on that head. 3. Matters of Equity. The Ecclesiastical, and Marine, or Admiralty Law, are soon known, so far, at least, as will be of use here. But you should go now and then to Doctor's Commons, where these Courts are held, and get a little insight into the precedents and manner of proceeding there. I believe you will think I have cut out work enough for you while in England, and, indeed, though it is a long time to look forward, if you mind your business, you will have not too much time to spare. However, I hope you will not fail to do this; your own reputation is at stake. You must either establish it when young, or it will be very difficult to acquire it. I am persuaded you need no argument to urge you to it, and should be most heartily vexed, and disappointed, if you do not answer my expectations when you return. One word with regard to your deportment: Let your dress be plain always, in the city, and elsewhere, except where it is necesssary it should be otherwise, and your behaviour rather grave. Remember the old man's advice to his son; think twice before you speak once. I have written much more than I thought of doing when I first sat down, and, with great freedom. I have no other motive but your welfare, which I sincerely wish; and, therefore, I would not omit anything, which there is a chance of being any way useful to you. Farewell, my dear brother; let me hear from you by every opportunity, and believe me yours, affectionately,

"J. RUTLEDGE.

"P. S.—I have not so high an opinion of logic, as to think no man can speak well without being a good logician; yet I think it will be of great service. It will enable you to reason closely, and with propriety, to establsh your principles and deduce the consequences much better than many, who, being unacquainted with it, say many good things which are not to the purpose, and frequently fall off from the point, which occasions tiresome repetitions, and is painful to the hearers. I would, therefore, recommend to you to get yourself well instructed in logic by a private tutor. Since writing the above, I have got from H. R. the directions which I gave him when going to England, some of which are of little use What others there are in it, which do not contradict the general scheme above laid down, you will take proper notice of."

[City Gazette and Daily Advertiser.]

"Charleston, Saturday, January 25th, 1800.

"We announce to the public, with infinite concern, the decease of our valuable fellow-citizen, His Excellency Edward Rutledge, Esq., Governor and Commander-in-Chief of the State, who closed, on Thursday night, a life of 50 years, devoted to the cause of philanthropy and the interests of his country. Amongst the patriots of 1776, this excellent character held a distinguished situation; and his integrity, his zeal and his exertions in our Revolutionary war, aided by uncommon talent, ranked him amongst those great political pillars, by which the fabric of American Independence might be said to be supported. His eloquence, which shone forth in the Senate, and at the Bar, was brilliant and impressive; it pleased the ear and went home to the heart. Rich in ideas, and happy in his manner of expressing them, he was accustomed to command attention, to delight as well as to persuade his audience. The many important services rendered by this virtuous man to the United States, and particularly to this, his native land, are faithfully recorded in the pages of history. They are engraven on the hearts of his countrymen, and the recollection of them shall not die.

"If we view his conduct in the walks of private life, there is an abundant scope for the most heartfelt eulogium. As the husband, the parent and the relative, he may sometimes be equalled, but he will never be surpassed. Mild and endearing in his deportment, with the accomplished manners of the gentleman, he diffused on all around him the rays of his own good humor and urbanity. He delighted to do good, and to relieve the widow, or to wipe away the tear of the orphan, was to his mind of sensibility a feast indeed. In the midst of the exercise of every virtue which makes man amiable, he is taken from us. Carolinians, ye have just wept for the loss of your Washington, and ye will not be sparing of your tears over the urn of your Rutledge."

"MONDAY, January 27th, 1800.

"On Saturday last, the inhabitants of this city paid the last honors they had in their power to show, to the remains of their late most worthy and beloved Chief Magistrate, Gov. Rutledge. The regiment of horse, the regiment of artillery, and the uniform companies of the 28th and 29th Regiments of Militia, formed in procession, and preceded the corpse from the house of the deceased, with their colors in mourning, their arms reversed, and the music playing a dead march.

After the military came the clergy, then the body, which was followed by the horse of the deceased in military mourning: Major Rutledge attended as chief mourner, then other relatives, friends and domestics. The procession was closed by citizens, all of whom evinced the grief they felt, and the loss they, and the State at large, had sustained in being deprived of this excellent man. His body was deposited, with military honors, in the family burying-ground, in St. Philip's Churchyard. During the procession minute guns were fired by a detachment of artillery, and the vessels in the harbor displayed their colors at half-mast during the day.

CHARLES COTESWORTH PINCKNEY.

General Charles Cotesworth Pinckney was the eldest son of Chief Justice Charles Pinckney and Eliza Lucas. He is to be regarded as one of the founders of the Republic, and was alike renowned for his civic, as for his military virtues. Never having had the opportunity of seeing the great Carolinian, increases ten-fold the difficulty of perfectly sketching his life. Difficult as is the task, still it must be performed.

He was born in the City of Charleston, 25th February 1746. At the early age of seven years, his father, Charles Pinckney, the late Chief Justice of South Carolina, carried him to England, where he was subsequently educated. He studied law in the Temple, and returned to Charleston a barrister, in 1769. The dispute between the mother country and the colonies had then begun, and afterwards progressed, so that the first general Congress met in Philadelphia on the first Monday in September, 1774. Delegates were appointed from South Carolina, by a meeting held in Charleston, at a Tavern, N. E. corner of Broad and Church streets, called the Corner. The first Provincial Congress, (as it was called,) of South Carolina, met 11th January, 1775. Of this body, Charles C. Pinckney was a member from St. John's Colleton.

The Declaration of the Bill of Rights, and the association adopted by the General Congress at Philadelphia, were considered by the Provincial Congress of South Carolina, and adopted. Sundry other measures were adopted, both of sympathy and relief, for Boston, Massachusetts, and for general protection and domestic relief, as will be seen by referring to 1st Moul. from p. 19 to 56. The Congress appointed the 17th of February, as a day of fasting, humiliation and prayer. The scene as described on that day, by Gen. Moultrie, is worth preserving: "Every place of worship in Charleston was crowded with the inhabitants ; and Congress went in a body to St. Phillip's, from the State-House, agreeably to their resolve, and most of them in their military array. On their entering the church, the organ began a solemn piece of music, and continued playing until they were seated. It was an affecting scene; as every one knew the occasion, and all joined in fervent prayer to the Lord to support and defend us in our great struggle in the cause of Liberty and our Country, and the Rev. Dr. Smith, (at the request of the Provincial Congress,) delivered an excellent and suitable discouse on the occasion, which very much animated the men ; whilst the female part of the congregation were affected in quite a different manner: floods of tears rolled down their cheeks, from the sad reflection of their nearest and dearest friends and relations entering into a *dreadful civil war—the worst of wars*, and what was most to be lamented, it could not be avoided."

On the 2d June, 1775, the Provincial Congress which had been called to meet, in consequence of the battle of Lexington, directed two Regiments of Infantry and one of Rangers to be raised. Charles Cotesworth Pinckney was appointed a captain.

These regiments were rappidly filled. On the 14th September, 1775, three companies of the 2d Regiment,(Col. Moultrie's,) were detailed under the command of Col. Mott, to capture the British fort on James' Island. The companies were commanded by Capts. Pinckney, Elliott and Marion. The garrison, on learning the intended attack, fled to their shipping, and the South Carolina troops took possession without firing a gun. Before the 9th December, 1775, Capt. Pinckney became a major, and in that capacity was detailed with four companies to "ford over from Haddrell's Point to Sullivan's Island, and there surprise, seize and apprehend a number of negroes who were supposed to have gone over to the enemy." Major Pinckney, on reaching Haddrell's Point, found that there was no ford where a body of men could be passed. This being reported to Col. Moultrie by the major, he and his command were recalled. On the 19th, he was detailed with four companies to throw up, at Haddrell's Point, a battery, to command the Cove at the back of Sullivan's Island, and thus to drive off the British ships, the Cherokee and Tower, which were blocking up the harbor. Capt. Bakeman, of the Artillery, was also detailed for the service, and ordered to provide stores and amunition for four 18-pounders. Col. Moultrie and a great many gentlemen volunteers accompanied the expedition, on a very dark and cold night, and by daylight were carried in, and in a few hours more laid their platforms and mounted some guns, and opened their embrazures. The ships moved their stations—a few long shot paid them a morning salutation. This battery gave free access to Sullivan's Island. On the 10th of January, '76, a detail of two companies from the 2d Regiment was ordered to Sullivan's Island, to protect the men who were employed in building a fascine battery. This movement drove the British ships entirely off.

On the 2d March, 1776, Col. Moultrie was ordered to take command of the fort which was erecting on Sullivan's Island. It is probable that the whole of the 2d Regiment accompanied him. Major Pinckney, however, did not take part in the gallant defence of Fort Moultrie, on the 28th June, '76. He was on some other service.

On the 20th of September, '76, the State assented to the resolution of Congress, placing their regiments on the Continental establishment. On the promotion of Col. Moultrie to Brigadier General, Major Pinckney became Colonel of the 2d Regiment. This was before January, '77. In April '78, Gen. Howe, who had command after Lee, was recalled from Charleston, owing to the embodying of the Schopelites, and their passage into Georgia below Augusta. This, with some movements of the enemy in Florida, indicating an attack on Georgia, he ordered 200 men to be in readiness to move, and soon after directed their march to be expedited. This was, I suppose, the beginning of the invasion of Florida, for on the 24th of May, Col. Pinckney writes from Fort Howe, on the Altamaha, in which he describes the route to St. Mary's and the attack of Fort Tonga, St. Augustine. The division of the enemy's forces, at Fort Tonga, on the St. Mary's River, at St. John's, St. Augustine, and southwards of that post, was pointed out as very fortunate for the invading force. From Fort

Tonga, owing to sickness and the assertion of the right to command their respective contingents, by Gov. Houston of Georgia, Col. Williamson of South Carolina, and Commodore Bouler of the Navy, the expedition was abandoned in July, '78. In January, '79, Col. Pinckney was President of the Senate of South Carolina, which was then in session in Charleston. Gen. Moultrie, who was, at that time, under the orders of Gen. Lincoln, opened a correspondence with him. Their several letters from the 10th January, '79, to the 1st February, ' 9, shows the unfortunate lethargy which pervaded South Carolina, and the sad want of discipline in the militia.—1st Moul. 258—276. Notwithstanding this, Gen. Moultrie managed to defeat the British at Beaufort.

What part Col. Pinckney bore in repelling the invasion of Prevost, or in the subsequent battle of Stono, or the siege of Savannah, do not appear. Whether he was, in that time, engaged as the aid of Washington, does not appear. It seems from Lieber's American Encyclopedia, he belonged to the military family of the Commander-in-Chief. He must have returned to South Carolina in 1779 or 1780; for it seems that Col. C. C. Pinckney, before 22d March 1780, had the command of Fort Moultrie. He was withdrawn from that command after the ships had passed Sullivan's Island, and his successor, on the 6th May, surrendered without firing a gun. On the 28th March, 1780, the enemy crossed the Ashley River, above the ferry, and soon invested the city, which, on the 12th of May, was surrendered. It is stated in Lieber's American Encyclopedia, that Col. Pinckney was for continuing hostilities to the last extremity—not that he thought they could repel the enemy, "but because," said he, "we shall so cripple the army before us, that, although we may not live to enjoy the benefits ourselves, yet to the United States they will prove incalculably great." This noble, self-sacrificing sentiment, was exactly in character with the noble, chivalric South Carolinian. It was, however, fortunately not acted on. He became a prisoner of war, and so remained with his gallant friend Gen. Moultrie, till 9th February, 1782, when they, with many others, were exchanged for Gen. Burgoyne. In the meantime, however, after remaining for nearly a year in Christ's Church Parish prisoners, they had been permitted to go to Philadelphia on parole. Gen. Moultrie says, "early in April he left Philadelphia, and arrived in Waccamaw in June, where he remained till September, when he paid a visit to Gen. Greene." He says: "It was the most dull, melancholy, dreary ride, that any one could possibly take, of about one hundred miles, through the woods of that country which I had been accustomed to see abound with live stock and wild fowl of every kind, *was now destitute of all.* It had been so completely chequered by the different parties, that not one part of it had been left unexplored; consequently, not the vestige of horses, cattle, hogs or deer, &c., was to be found. The squirrels and birds of every kind were totally destroyed. The dragoons told me that, on their scouts, no living creature was to be seen, except now and then a few camp scavengers, (turkey-buzzards,) picking the bones of some unfortunate fellows who had been shot or cut down, and left in the woods above ground."

To obtain an escort, Gen. Moultrie went a circuitous route to Gen. Marion's camp on Santee. On his way from Marion's to Greene's camp, he says: "My plantation was in the direct road, where I called and stayed a night. *On my entering the place, as soon as the negroes discovered that I was of the party, there was immediately a general alarm and outcry through the plantation, that 'Massa was come, Massa was come!' and they were running from every part to see me. I stood in the piazza to receive them; they gazed at me with astonishment, and every one came and took me by the hand, saying: 'God bless you Massa! we glad for see you, Massa!' and every now and then some one would come out with 'a Ky,' and the old Africans joined in a war-song in their own language,* 'welcome the war home.'" The good old General remarks: "it was an affecting meeting between the slaves and the master. The tears stole from my eyes and ran down my cheeks." He says: "I then possessed about two hundred slaves, and not one of them left me during the war, although they had had great offers; nay, some were carried down to work on the

British lines, yet they always contrived to make their escape and return home. My plantation I found to be a desolate place—stock of every kind taken off, the productions carried away, and my estate had been under sequestration.—2d Moul., 354, '5, '6. I have cited these passages with a two-fold purpose: first, to show the desolation produced by the Revolutionary war, and second, the fidelity and devotion of slaves to their masters. I intend the last more for the contemplation of Abolitionists, than any one else; and I would say to them, read and at last know the sacred tie which binds the slave to his master.

After the evacuation of Charleston, on the 14th of December, 1782, Col. Charles Cotesworth Pinckney returned and devoted himself to his profession and his private affairs. From that time to 1788, he was actively employed in retrieving his affairs and in following out the business of a lawyer. In that respect he earned a great reputation, and realized large profits.

He was a member of the Convention which, in '88, framed the Constitution of the United States, and of that which ratified it on the part of South Carolina, and of the Convention which, in 1790, gave us the Constitution of the State.

On the 24th May 1791, he was offered, with Edward Rutledge, the place of an Associate Judge of the United States, when John Rutledge declined that office. Both declined the acceptance, saying, amongst other reasons, that they could be of more service to the United States in the State Legislature. On 22d January, 1784, the contemplated resignation of Gen. Knox, the first Secretary of War, being made known to the President, Col. Pinckney was offered, by Gen. Washington, that post; and, again, on 24th August, 1795, on the resignation of Edward Randolph as Secretary of State, he was tendered that appointment by the President; he declined both, on the ground that his private affairs required his constant attention. At the reörganization of the Militia, he was appointed Major General. He was offered, by Gen. Washington, on the 8th day of July, 1796, the office of Minister to France. He accepted this great trust, resigned his commission as a military officer, and soon after sailed for France. The French Directory were very hostile to the United States, and assumed a most dictatorial authority. In reply to some of their high pretensions, he uttered the sentiment which has made his name immortal: "Millions for defence, but not a cent for tribute." All the conciliatory propositions from the United States were rejected with scorn and insult, and the Minister ordered out of the territories of France. Gen. Pinckney communicated to his Government the indignities offered to him, and retired to Holland. He was joined by Gen. Marshall, afterwards Chief Justice Marshall, and Mr. Gerry, with fresh instructions of pacification, but all was vain; the French Directory were mad with success. Gen. Pinckney returned home, and found that he had been appointed 2d Major General of the Army of the United States, in the contemplated war with France. Gen. Hamilton, his superior in rank in the war of the Revolution, had been, at the instance of Gen. Washington, appointed 1st Major General. Gen. Pinckney did not imitate Knox, and refuse to serve in consequence of such preference. He said that he was satisfied that Gen. Washington had sufficient reasons for it. "Let us," he continued, "first dispose of our enemies, we shall then have leisure to settle the question of rank." Indeed, before he knew of Knox's refusal to serve as 3d Major General, he was willing, if that would satisfy him, to let him rank as second.

Fortunately, however, the rulers of France listened at last to the propositions of peace on the part of the United States, and the sword which had been partially drawn, was returned to its scabbard.

In 1800 he was voted for as an opponent to Mr. Jefferson. He failed! That was the death-struggle of his party, (the Federal.) In 1801 he was elected at the head of the first Board of Trustees of the South Carolina College. He never sought office afterwards. For more than fifteen years before his death, he was the President of the Bible Society of Charleston, to which office he was appointed by the unanimous voice of the Christian community of Charleston.

He died 16th August, 1825, in his eightieth year. Full of years, glory and usefulness, he was gathered to his fathers.

We append the epitaph inscribed to the memory of this illustrious citizen, which is on an entabliture in the interior of St. Michael's Church, Charleston, S. C. The design of this memorial, as well as the inscription, are by Charles Fraser, Esq.:

TO THE MEMORY OF
GENERAL CHARLES COTESWORTH PINCKNEY,
ONE OF THE FOUNDERS OF
THE AMERICAN REPUBLIC.
IN WAR,
HE WAS THE COMPANION IN ARMS
AND THE FRIEND OF WASHINGTON:
IN PEACE,
HE ENJOYED HIS UNCHANGING CONFIDENCE,
AND MAINTAINED WITH ENLIGHTNED ZEAL
THE PRINCIPLES OF HIS ADMINISTRATION,
AND OF THE CONSTITUTION.
AS A STATESMAN,
HE BEQUEATHED TO HIS COUNTRY THE SENTIMENT,
MILLIONS FOR DEFENCE,
NOT A CENT FOR TRIBUTE.
AS A LAWYER,
HIS LEARNING WAS VARIOUS AND PROFOUND;
HIS PRINCIPLES PURE, HIS PRACTICE LIBERAL.
WITH ALL THE ACCOMPLISHMENTS
OF THE GENTLEMAN,
HE COMBINED THE VIRTUES OF THE PATRIOT
AND THE PIETY OF THE CHRISTIAN.
HIS NAME
IS RECORDED IN THE HISTORY OF HIS COUNTRY,
INSCRIBED ON THE CHARTER OF HER LIBERTIES,
AND CHERISHED IN THE AFFECTIONS OF HER CITIZENS.
OBIIT XVI. AUGUST. MDCCCXXV.
ÆTATIS, LXXIX.

CHARLES PINCKNEY.

Having undertaken to write a sketch of the life and services of this eminent man, I deeply regret that I have not in my possession, a number of papers and documents relating to him, which would have enabled me to have written much more fully and satisfactorily than I can from memory alone. As it is, however, I will endeavor so to arrange the incidents and circumstances of his highly distinguished and eventful life, as will convey some idea to the reader of who and what he was, and to what extent he was identified with the political history of his country.

Charles Pinckney was the eldest son of Col. Charles Pinckney, an eminent lawyer—one of the most decided Whigs and patriots of the American Revolution, who was President of the Convention of South Carolina, in January, 1775, President of the Senate in 1779, and President of the Council 1780. He was born in Charleston, in the year 1758. He was educated by Dr. Oliphant, who was, at that time, the principal schoolmaster in the city. His entire education was received in Charleston, which, considering that he was a highly accomplished classical scholar, and subsequently, became a lawyer and civilian of the very highest distinction, certainly reflects no small credit upon the literary institutions of our city at that early day. He studied law, under his father, who was an ornament of the profession, and, like his father, he became, in early manhood, a decided Whig, and did all in his power to aid his State in her resistance to the tyranny and oppressions of North and Bute.

In 1779, when but of age, he was elected a Member of the Provincial Legislature, to represent Christ Church Parish.

In 1780, he was taken prisoner by the British, and sent, in the schooner Pack Horse, with a large number of other prisoners, amongst whom were some of the most respectable and distinguished citizens of Charleston, to St. Augustine, where they were detained for a considerable time on board that prison ship. He was appointed by his fellow-prisoners, in conjunction with General John Barnwell, to protest against this act of perfidy and outrage. He penned the communication to the British authorities, so that his first essay in political life, was from a prison ship, an incident of which a republican most justly might be proud. The remonstrance drawn up by him on that occasion, is preserved in Ramsay's History of the Revolution in South Carolina.

In 1785, he was appointed one of our delegation to the old Congress, being then in his 27th year.

In 1786, he united with Mr. Monroe, in opposing the relinquishment of the Mississippi, and, in that year, he was also appointed by Congress, one of a committee to the Legislature of New Jersey, to urge that State to comply with the requisition of Congress, which it had refused to do, respecting the contribution of its quota for the support of Government. The embassy succeeded. The committee requested him to address the Legislature, which he did; and his speech is preserved in Carey's Museum, vol. 2, pp. 153-4.

In 1787, being then twenty-nine years old, he was appointed by the Legislature, one of four delegates to the Federal Convention—that august body, which was composed of the most eminent men from every part of the Union—and whose important office it was to revise the Articles of the Old Confederation, and to devise and recommend an entire new Constitution for the future government of the United States. He submitted and advocated a plan of government, prepared by himself, the greatest part of which was adopted by the Convention, and is incorporated in the present Constitution—so much so, that he has always been considered as entitled to the high and honorable designation of the Father of the Constitution. Sketches of his speeches in the Convention are preserved in "The Madison Papers." Some of them are also preserved in "Elliott's Debates," in the Federal Convention.

Young as he was, and surrounded, too, as he was, by the most eminent sages and statesmen of the country, to have assumed and maintained such a position, in such a body, as to have caused their work literally and emphatically, to be identified with him, as his, is certainly an honor of no ordinary character; and it would have been a source of great gratification to the writer to have been able to exhibit, in a condensed form, the principles and policy by which he was governed in the composition of his plan. Suffice it, however, to say, that though our ancestors had just emerged from the colonial state, and were, necessarily, much imbued with British principles and habits of thought and action, yet, it is evident that Mr. Pinckney very widely departed from the monarchical, and made large advances to the republican form of government, from the fact that, since the adoption of the Constitution, amidst all the changes that the country has undergone, and the decided spirit of democracy that almost everywhere prevails, not a single political feature of that instrument has been altered, nor has any fault been ever found by the people with the general tone and spirit by which it is pervaded. Nor indeed, would it be easy for human ingenuity to devise a plan more admirably adapted to a country like ours, embodying, as it does, the beautiful two-fold principle of State Rights and Popular Sovereignty—one branch of the Legislature representing the people in their sovereign capacity, the other representing the States in their federative union, and the Executive Department representing both. Such a system was intended to endure forever, and so it would, but for the bad passions of men, who, rather than not rule, would ride to power upon the ruins of their country, and the fanatical ignorance of the masses, who suffer themselves to be led blindfolded, by the wily arts of political aspirants. In reference to this part of his life, Mr. Pinckney frequently spoke of the deep diffidence and solemnity which he felt, being the youngest member of the body, whenever he addressed the Federal Convention.

In 1788, he was appointed a delegate to the State Convention, by which the Federal Constitution was ratified. His speeches in that body, in favor of adopting the Constitution, are preserved in "The Debates in the State Convention," as arranged and published by the late Benjamin Elliott, Esq.

In 1789, he was elected Governor of South Carolina, for the first time.

1790, he was elected President of the State Convention by which the present Constitution of the State of South Carolina was adopted.

1791, he was re-elected Governor, without opposition.

In 1795, he delivered a very able and eloquent speech, in St. Michael's Church, in opposition to Jay's treaty with England. There was a very large popular meeting on that occasion, and a great contest between the old Republican and Federal parties. A number of eloquent speeches were made on both sides. Mr. Pinckney's speech is preserved in the American Remembrancer.

In 1796, he was a third time elected Governor of the State. In this election he was opposed by General Pickens.

In 1798, he was elected a Senator to the Congress of the United States, in which election, he was again opposed by General Pickens. During his service in the Senate, he delivered a number of speeches upon different subjects, especially two, very able, in relation to the proper organization of the Judiciary Department of the Government.

During the year 1800, he was very active and efficient in promoting Mr. Jefferson's election to the Presidency of the Union. He wrote and published a series of political addresses to the people of the State, under the signature "A Republican," strongly advocating the support of Mr. Jefferson. He also, during the same year, wrote and published a series of papers, under the signature of "A Planter," in especial opposition to, and denunciation of, the memorable "Alien and Sedition Laws," which were enacted during the administration of the elder Adams.

In 1802, he was appointed by Mr. Jefferson, Ambassador to Spain, in which service he continued until 1806. Mr. Pinckney had the high honor, while Minister to Spain, of having negotiated the treaty, by which, not only Louisiana was acquired by the United States, but also all that vast territory which now constitutes the State of Texas; an acquisition, not only highly advantageous, in a military and commercial point of view, to the Union generally, but of inestimable value in relation to the Southern and slave-holding States.

Immediately upon his return from this embassy, he was again elected to the Legislature from Christ Church Parish—the very parish by which he had first been introduced into public life in 1779, and at the first session of the Legislature, in December, 1806, he was again, and for the fourth time, elected Governor of the State.

In 1810, he was elected a member of the Legislature, from St. Philip and St. Michael.

In 1812, he was re-elected to the Legislature, from St. Philip and St. Michael. At that time politics ran very high in Charleston. Our country was then at war with Britain. Mr. P. was a very decided and powerful advocate of that war. The federal party made every effort in their power to defeat him. But they were unable to succeed.

In 1814, he retired from active political life, but, notwithstanding his unwillingness to be further engaged in politics, he was again compelled to come forth, in 1818, as a candidate for Congress, from Charleston District. The field had been, for some time, occupied by two distinguished gentlemen—in the election of either of whom Charleston District would have been represented by a Federalist. The Republican party at length became excited, and having determined, if possible, that such an issue should not take place, they nominated Mr. Pinckney, went vigorously to work in his support, and he was elected by a large majority.

In 1820, he made a very able and admirable speech in Congress, on the celebrated Missouri Compromise Bill. To his honor be it said, he was opposed to that compromise—one of the very few Southern men that were. His opposition showed equally his firmness, his foresight, and sagacity. He distinctly foresaw the effects of the measure, and earnestly warned the South against them.* The Missouri Compromise has since (a few years ago) been repealed. Its repeal was hailed with great gratification by the slave-holding States, from whom an

*This speech is preserved in Niles' Register, 18th volume, pages 349 and 350.

oppression and a stigma were thus removed. And its repeal would still have continued to be a just subject of rejoicing to the South, if the oppression and the stigma, which it inflicted, had not been revived and enforced in another, more insidious, and more effectual form, by the passage of an Act, (the Kansas Nebraska Act,) and the propagation of the new-fangled doctrine connected with it, known by the name of Squatter Sovereignty, of which the practical effect is, and was, doubtless, intended to be, under the pretended garb of equal rights and non-intervention by Congress—to deny protection, by the Federal Government, to the persons and property of slaveholders in the common Territories of the Union, and thus, literally and forever to exclude them from regions bought by their treasure and their blood, and thus enable the enemies of the South to execute their threat—their disorganizing, treasonble, and destructive threat—that not another slave State shall ever be admitted into this Confederacy. But it is not my purpose to dilate upon this subject, though I cannot help feeling that we have arrived at a crisis, in which the South is literally placed between Scylla and Charybdis—in which its only means of preventing the success of the great Abolition party of the North, seems to be by uniting with and supporting that Free-soil Democratic party of the North—whose success would constitute, by the votes of the slave States themselves, not only a virtual surrender of their rights, but even a distinct and absolute acknowledgment, on the part of those States, that they had no right in the Territories for which to contend.

His speech on the Missouri question was the last act of Mr. Pinckney's public life. After that he retired again to private life. Having suffered very heavy pecuniary misfortunes, by which his large and opulent estate had departed from him, he secluded himself much from the world. But he retained his cheerfulness and love of employment. He was constantly occupied in reading or writing—principally in the latter. He wrote a pamphlet of some two hundred pages in support of Mr. Monroe's election to the Presidency, when he was opposed by Mr. Crawford. He also wrote an account of his travels in Europe—having traveled extensively through Spain, and Italy, and Germany, and France. For a long period of his life, he was engaged in correspondence with Mr. Jefferson, Mr. Madison, Mr. Monroe, and other eminent Americans. He left amongst his papers numerous letters received from them—all of the most friendly character, and also others from Dr. Franklin and the Marquis LaFayette. Mr. P. was constantly employed, and, indeed, indefatigably, as a writer. As a public speaker, he was dignified, commanding, and impressive. His eminent ability was accompanied and recommended by the remarkable persuasiveness and courtesy of his manner, and the invariable fairness of his arguments, and the justice which he never failed to render to opponents. His voice was uncommonly clear, and musical, and sonorous. There were oftentimes when he was very ardent and impassioned, and his speaking rose to the very highest order of eloquence. Hence his powerful influence as a public man. He was emphatically the founder, and for a long time the leader, of the old Republican party of South Carolina. The people had unbounded confidence in his integrity, his sincerity, and his high character, as well as in the purity and soundness of his political principles. He commenced his political career as a Republican, a lover of popular liberty, and a devoted champion of the great doctrine of State-Rights; and he maintained his principles, with unswerving fidelity and consistency, to the close of his existence. No man ever charged him with political tergiversation. As, in the beginning, he was a firm coadjutor of Jefferson, so, in his very last effort, that on the Missouri Compromise, he made as fine an exhibition of the relative rights and powers of the General and State Governments, and as powerful and conclusive a demonstration of the political equality of the States, and of the right of citizens of the slaveholding States to occupy the common territory of the Union, and to carry their slave property with them, and of the duty of the General Government to protect them and their property there, until the territory should become a State, and, as such, determine its own political and social institutions for itself, as was ever delivered by any statesman on the floor of Congress. He was a man of very enlarged and liberal views, and always earnestly desirous to sustain the principles of free government, and to maintain the equal rights and privileges of all classes of our citizens. He warmly advocated the abolition of the Primogeniture laws. It was principally owing to his influence and exertions, in the Convention which formed our State Constitution, that the civil and political disabilities, which had all along previously been imposed upon Hebrews, were removed, and no longer suffered to disgrace our Government. He it was, as Governor, who first recommended the establishment of free schools, in a message to the Legislature, in which he eloquently depicted the advantages of a general system of popular education. Nor was there any project or enterprize, generally speaking, of a patriotic or public-spirited description, calculated to reflect honor on the State, or to promote the welfare of the people, which did not find in him an enlightened friend and firm supporter. He was a man of great personal dignity. He was a delightful convivial companion. His conversational powers were perhaps never excelled. There was a charm about him, which arose partly from his fascinating manners, and his sweet musical voice, but principally, perhaps, from the vast fund of knowledge, information, and anecdote, which he possessed, of almost every kind and character; and from the remarkable readiness, and ease, and power, with which he could either impart instruction, enter into argument, or contribute to amusement. In conclusion, it is almost unnecessary to add, that he was a man of high-toned sentiment and sterling integrity, loved and admired by his friends, bitterly opposed and impugned by his enemies, and one whom his country always delighted to honor, through all the vicissitudes of his varied and eventful life.

Mr. Pinckney died in 1824, aged sixty-six years. He had three children—Frances Henrietta, who married the late Hon. Robert Y. Hayne; Mary Eleanor, who married the late David Ramsay; and Henry Laurens, who is the sole survivor of his family.

CHARLES GOODWYN.

This gentleman was in the "sere and yellow leaf" when I first saw him. He had a great reputation, as a lawyer, in the early administration of justice in South Carolina; was a native of England, and was admitted to the Bar, in Charleston, on 28th May, 1784.

I have heard it said, that, after the conclusion of Jay's treaty, when the excitement was very high, and public meetings were held in Charleston on the subject, Mr. Goodwyn, who was then a stranger, at a meeting in Charleston, sprang upon the stage, and made a speech against the treaty, which electrified the whole audience, thenceforward he was favorably known.

He, after his admission, settled at Ninety-Six, and practiced much in the County Courts. It is said, that, on one occasion, he was making a speech to the Jury, before their worships, the County Circuit Judges, at Laurens; the president, who had taken a drop too much, was very drowsy, and dropped off into a comfortable nap. Mr. Goodwyn elevated his voice, as he became excited, so as to awaken his worship, he exclaimed, "take care, Goodwyn, don't do that again," he dropped off into another unconscious state. While Goodwyn's case grew more and more interesting, as his argument and his speech grew louder and louder, so much so as to arouse the Justice, who arose in great wrath, threatening to trounce the lawyer for disturbing his rest.

Mr. Goodwyn married a daughter of General Andrew Williamson—the "Cow-Driver," as the children designated him. Judge Ramsay married the other daughter; together, they bought Silver Bluff, now the property of Senator Hammond. The debt thus contracted caused ruin to both.

I do not remember to have heard Mr. Goodwyn make more than one speech, and that was in the Court of Appeals, in one of the jury-land cases, when he was for the defendant.

Patrick Duncan, the plaintiff, was present with his land-papers, in a tin-box. Mr. Goodwyn, in allusion to it, said, "Patrick Duncan's tin-box is worse than Pandora's box—in the bottom of that, *there* was hope, but in Patrick Duncan's box there is no *hope*." This, said in his indescribable rage and manner, was irresistibly ludicrous.

When I first knew the old gentleman, in the spring of 1815, at Edgefield, he still represented many cases; but he uniformly moved for a continuance, and generally succeeded. This carried out a former practice, *a retainer*, to begin, and then *a refresher* for each continuance.

Mr. Goodwyn died many years since, leaving descendants in Edgefield. His style of speaking had more of the English accent than suited American hearers. It was too pompous—depending more upon words than matter. He was a fluent speaker, and, when young, was, I presume, entitled to the reputation of which I have already spoken.

PETER CARNES.

This gentleman is better known for his humor than anything else. He was a native of Maryland. I know that his wife was Elizabeth Wirt, from the fact of seeing a copy of his will, made by my grandfather, at whose house, "Springfield," he was once dangerously ill. I see from the rolls of Attorneys in Charleston, he was admitted to the Bar on 8th March, 1785.

To Chief Justice Rutledge, and other boon companions, at Ninety-Six, he described his life. He said, that he began first, as a house-carpenter—that this did not at all answer his purposes. He next tried his hand as a mill-wright, then as the manufacturer of balloons. Neither of these prospering, he became a Methodist exhorter. Here again he failed, *which drove him to the Bar.* As a lawyer, he said he had succeeded wonderfully. Chief Justice Rutledge said to him, "Brother Carnes, how much would your balloon carry up?" Carnes, looking round and espying Shaw, who was an Englishman—(he was admitted to the Bar, in Charleston, 10th August, 1784)—and a very diminutive man, walked up to him, slapped his hand upon his shoulder, and said, "it would carry on a good, stout chunk of a boy, as big as brother *Pop Corn.*" Shaw was very excitable; this observation filled him brimfull of wrath. Carnes said, "brother Shaw often provokes me until I am ready to knock him down, but when I look at him, he looks so much like a pretty little gal, that I feel like kissing him." At this moment, William Tate, a lawyer, remarkable for a frizzly head, entered the room, Carnes, wheeling round and facing him, said, "enter frizzly." Tate, who, like Shaw, was irascible, said, "Mr. Carnes, I should like to know what you mean?" Carnes said, "Tate, you look like the fragments of a hail storm borne upon a whirlwind."

The Chief Justice's shield was all which saved Carnes from the wrath of the two subjects of his wit.

William Tate was admitted to the Bar, in Charleston, 20th February, 1787. He was one of the government recruits for the Revolution in France. He went to France, received a commission as Chef de Brigade or Demi-Brigade. He was landed as a part of the invading army of Ireland—captured—and after many years' absence—I think, about 1819—returned to this State. I remember seeing him once—a very venerable grey-headed gentleman. What became of him I do not know. His brother, Robert, once owned the plantation north of Saluda, in Newberry, opposite to Saluda Old Town, which, at the time I speak of seeing William Tate, was the property of Major William Dunlap, and was claimed in a bill in equity, by William Tate and others. They failed.

In a case of trespass for assault and battery, tried at Ninety-Six, William Shaw, above spoken of, was the defendant's Attorney. Peter Carnes was for the plaintiff. Mr. Shaw pleaded, "*molletur manus imposuit.*" The case turned out, in proof, to be a very aggravated assault and battery. Carnes said to the Judge, when, in his turn, he had the opportunity to address them, "Gentlemen, you all know I am no Latin scholar, but I think I can translate the gentleman's plea, '*molletur*,' he mauled, '*manus*,' the man, '*imposuit*,' and imposed upon him. Now, gentlemen, did you ever hear of such impudence—to shamefully abuse my client, and then to come into Court and brag of it?" The argument was irresistible. Other anecdotes of this great humorist, will be found in the Annals of Newberry, at pages 12, 20, 21, 22.

If I have been correctly informed, he realized a large fortune at the Bar, and died in Augusta, Georgia, in consequence of over-exerting himself at the defence of a man for murder.

TIMOTHY FORD.

Timothy Ford was born in 1762, and died 7th December, 1830, aged 68 years. He was "venerable from age, but more venerable for the character and usefulness of his life."

Mr. Ford was a native of Morristown, New Jersey, and received his preparatory education in the vicinity of that place. He then entered Princeton College, at which he graduated with one of the honors of the institution. The period of his youth was, however, that of the Revolution, and his studies were, consequently, subjected to interruptions, which, in one of less constancy of purpose, would materially have impaired his habits and checked his progress. But, notwithstanding the excitements and difficulties of the times, a foundation was laid, upon which, in maturer life, he reared a superstructure of various and useful knowledge.

Mr. Ford was between thirteen and fourteen years old at the commencement of the Revolutionary war; and an attachment to the principles of the Revolution, grew with his growth and strengthened with his strength. Circumstances, too, aided to promote and elevate his devotion to these principles. The head-quarters of General Washington were, for a considerable time, at Morristown, and he occupied a part of a house, the property and residence of Mr. Ford's mother. Opportunities and occasions of intercourse were thus enjoyed, from which juster views of the character of the contest were derived, and its spirit more thoroughly imbibed. During this period, in the severe winter of 1780, the expedition to Staten Island was undertaken; and anxious to participate in the dangers and toils of the army, he was one of the detachment on this service. In a subsequent part of the same year, a body of American troops was sent to meet a portion of the British forces, which had been marched from New York to the neighborhood of the Connecticut farms in New Jersey. A short, but sharp conflict, took place at Springfield. The attack being made by a company of Washington's body-guards, commanded by Captain Coalfax, whom Mr. Ford accompanied as a volunteer, he was wounded in the leg by a musket ball and disabled. While sitting and endeavoring to staunch the blood with his handkerchief, he received a second wound in the same limb. After fainting from loss of blood, and reviving, he was recognized by Col. Livingston—an aid to the officer in command—who had been sent to order a retreat, and was returning. The Colonel dismounted, and, with the aid of a soldier, placed Mr. Ford upon the horse, and mounting behind him, carried him off from the field, but not without great risk of further injury: for the horse, while they were on him, was shot through the body. As soon as practicable Mr. Ford was removed to Morristown, to be greeted by a mother, who, like other matrons of the Revolution, felt the spirit, though tenderness may have checked the expression of the Spartan exhortation, "on your shields, or with them." To her care, under a Providence, is to be attributed his recovery from a six weeks' confinement to his bed. During his sufferings, however, he was cheered by the consciousness of having done his duty, and by the approbation of the distinguished persons around him. Soon after he had been placed upon his bed, he received a visit from Col. Hamilton, who, taking him by the hand, "congratulated him on having received, what he himself had long sought without success—a wound in the cause of his country."

Mr. Ford studied the law in New York, and soon after the close of the war, settled in South Carolina. His legal learning was profound, his discernment clear, his judgment good, and his practice liberal. He continued his useful services in this profession to the time of his death; for many years, however, confining his practice to the Court of Equity. The recent expression of the feelings of the Bar on his death, testify the elevated rank he held in his profession.

"At a numerous meeting of the members of the Charleston Bar, held on Saturday last, (December 11, 1830,) for the purpose of testifying their respect for the memory of their deceased brother, Timothy Ford, Esq., Mr. G. W. Cross was requested to act as Chairman, and Mr. Gregorie as Secretary of the meeting. The following preamble and resolutions were then presented by Hon. Mitchell King, and unanimously adopted:

The members of the Charleston Bar have met to express their feelings and regret at the loss which they, in common with this community, have sustained by the death of their venerable brother, Mr. Timothy Ford, and to pay a tribute of respect to his memory. They have causes of regret peculiar to themselves. They leave to others the duty of commemorating his services—to the Union, as a soldier of the Revolution—to the State, as a Member of the Legislature—to the City, as a member of the Council—to Literature, as a Trustee of the Charleston College, as President of Library, and Literary and Philosophical Societies—to the cause of Religion, as a member of the Bible Society. But they will speak of him as one of their own body, whose memory and character they cherish and respect.

Mr. Ford was a native of New Jersey. Soon after the Revolution, he settled in this State, and was admitted to our Bar. It was then filled by very eminent men—the Rutledges, the Pinckneys, and others—models of all that was profound in wisdom, firm in purpose, polished in manners, and distinguished in honor, who had conducted their country in triumph through the war of Independence, and then cultivated and adorned the arts of peace.

With these gentlemen, Mr. Ford entered the lists of honorable and successful competition, and soon held a very respectable rank among them. He had been prepared for the profession by severe and diligent study, and brought to it a mind stored with legal learning and general knowledge. He devoted himself to it, with great zeal and indefatigable perseverance. He seemed to think nothing done while anything remained undone that could insure success. No pains were spared, no investigation too tedious or laborious, that promoted the ends of justice. His opinions were formed with the utmost caution, and the extent of his knowledge, and the clearness and soundness of his judgment, generally, led him to accurate conclusions. Indeed, he almost exhausted every legal question submitted to his deliberate consideration, and brought every relevant authority to bear upon it, that the most careful research and patient industry could accommodate. The lawyer must have been diligent and inventive indeed, who could find much that was new and important to say on a subject discussed by Mr. Ford. But, while he strove to insure success, he disdained to use any merely technical advantage, or to exert his abilities for the perversion of justice to promote the interest of the most favored client.

In his intercourse with his professional brethren, he exhibited great kindness and courtesy. With all, he was sociable and communicative—to his juniors he was uniformly attentive and polite. The arguments of the youngest of the members, when opposed to him, were treated with every respect—no sneer or sarcasm, or depreciating remark from him, ever wounded their feelings. Under the most urgent circumtances, and in the ardor of legal contention, no excitements ruffled his temper or prompted him to overstep the boundaries of generous competition. Imbued with a nice sense of honor, he shrunk almost intuitively, from the slightest infringements of its laws, and he maintained among us, in the most arduous and spirit-trying duties of the profession, the same self-command and politeness that distinguished him in private life. In conducting his cases in Court, he observed the utmost comity to the Bench. He was, as he deserved to be, always heard with much respect. He broached no crude or half-formed notions: his opinions were weighed and adopted with great care, and always received consideration from the Court. There was nothing light or frivolous in his habits of thought, nothing gaudy or meretricious in the style of his elocution; it was clear, logical, comprehensive and dispassionate—better calculated to elicit truth and promote the ends of justice, than to please the fancy and rouse the feelings. His whole professional career was marked with high integrity and honor. He has closed a long and useful life, amid the mourning of his friends and the regret of the community. He has left to his associates and his successors at the Bar, the grateful recollection of his many virtues, the example of his attainments and his unsullied and excellent character.

Resolved therefore, That we sincerely lament the death of our venerable brother, and, as a token of his worth and our regret, we do wear the usual mourning for him, for one month.

That we do deeply sympathise with his bereaved family in the loss which they have sustained, and we earnestly wish them all those consolations which the memory of his talents, his usefulness, his pure character, and his unaffected piety, is so well calculated to afford.

That a copy of this preamble and these resolutions, be communicated, by the Chairman of this meeting, to the family of Mr. Ford, and be published in the Gazettes of the city.

GEO. WARREN CROSS, *Chairman.*"

J. LADSON GREGORIE, *Secretary.*

As a Member of the Legislature, and of the City Council, his services were highly valued by his colleagues, and by the community at large. In all the departments of practical duty, which, during a long life, he had been selected to fill, his course was marked by that firm and enlightened prudence, which has been justly said to be the result of a combination of virtues.

Industry and close attention to whatever he undertook, were habitual to him. He devoted as much time to books as his professional and social duties permitted. His attainments in general literature were, therefore, considerable, and the accuracy of his information remarkable. He was, at all times, ready to promote, by every means in his power, the cause of learning and science. He was many years a Trustee of the College of Charleston, and, at the time of his death, President of the Charleston Library Society, and of the Literary and Philosophical Societies of South Carolina. Mr. Ford was always deeply interested in questions connected with the constitution, welfare, and policy of the country. Devoted to the principles of the Federal Charter, he was their zealous defender and advocate, and, at different periods of his life, he contributed, by the judicious efforts of his pen, to their elucidation and support. Nor was the ardor of his patriotism diminished by age. He was to the last, alive to everything that concerned the honor, the interests, and the destinies of the Union. He took pleasure in commending the annals of the Revolution, as the source of pure and elevated devotion to our country; for he considered the spirit of the Revolution the safeguard of our institutions. But it is most gratifying to his friends, to recall that part of his character which, as it best comports with the condition of man, adorns him most—his religious feelings.

In early youth he lived in the house, and under the care of his grandfather, the Rev. Dr. Jones, of New Jersey, from whom we may reasonably infer he received that direction of character, which, in subsequent life, was more and more developed. He had long been a student of the Bible. His attachment to other reading, never diverted him from the reading of the Scriptures; and it was his high honor to add to his attainments in polite literature, the rich knowledge of the Word of Life. Interested in the pure and unostentatious charity of distributing the holy volume, he was one of the founders of the Bible Society of Charleston—the first institution of the kind established in this State—was one of its original officers, and died a member of the Board of Managers. Let not the example of a life like his be lost on the community. Let all learn from it, that practical usefulness is a title to respect and esteem, and religion the crown of gray hairs.

WILLIAM NIBBS.

William Nibbs was one of those lawyers who could accurately prepare a record according to the forms, in Lillie's Modern Entries, but was utterly inadequate to manage properly a case in Court. He was, therefore, always dependent on a co-partner, or on some friendly lawyer.

He was a Roman Catholic in religion, a native of one of the West India Islands, and had been an office clerk *there* before he came to South Carolina. It is probable that he served an apprenticeship in Ramsay & Goodwyn's office. He was, I see from the roll, admitted to the Bar, in Charleston, 23d January, 1792.

I recollect Mr. Nibbs as far back as 1804. He always boarded, in time of Court, at my grandmother's, Hannah Holly, at Springfield. He was a singular character, eccentric, simple as a child, always imposed upon by the designing. He lives, therefore, more in the laughable incidents attending his professional life, than in anything useful, which he ever performed.

He was the partner of Judge Gantt, when I first recollect him. He always carried his immense book of precedents, which he had written out, and the records of cases (in which he had been concerned) pending, or which had been disposed of in any other way than by judgment, stuffed into a pair of saddle-bags, which, when placed upon his saddle, was straight as a log. He rode a tall horse, and when Nibbs, who was rather of short stature, was mounted, saddle-bags and all, he cut rather an odd figure.

Between Springfield and Newberry, on the old road, which was a few hundred yards below the present one, the creek (Scott's) was crossed at a ford below a cotton gin, which belonged to Moses Evans, (the ford now used was in the midst of the pond.) Nibbs, riding from Newberry, after night, instead of following the turn of the road to the left, to the ford, rode straight on, plunged into the pond, and, of course, encountered a cold bath, and had a short swim. When he reached Springfield, his ample saddle-bags, containing clothing, precedents, and records, had to be unpacked, and the contents dried. He generally walked on foot from Springfield to Court, with his partner, Gantt, and my uncle, John Holly, Sen., who was a bachelor. Nibbs was, also, a bachelor, and was very garrulous. My uncle was a very taciturn man. After many years, Nibbs, who was then alone as a lawyer, and lived at Ninety-Six, Cambridge, (I should say between 1808 and 1812,) married; and then at every Court he was loud in his assertions, to his old bachelor friend, of the delights of matrimony. He ceased to attend at Newberry about the era of my admission to the Bar, 1814.

I fell heir to one of his notable cases—John Gooch and wife *vs.* John Demony. It was in his favorite line, dower. Mrs. Gooch was the widow of Michael Sanders, and claimed dower out of the land devised to his adopted son, John Demony. The case was defended by Anderson Crenshaw; and he had exhausted all his talents, as his pleader, to Nibbs' great annoyance. I found, after a Term or two, that both demandant and her husband, and the respondent, were insolvent, and, upon the death of the demandant, the case quietly went to rest.

Nibbs afterwards practiced mostly in Abbeville, in the bounds of which District his dwelling was situated. My friend, Chancellor Bowie, says: "He was poor," and as a lawyer, "barely made a decent subsistence for his family." "On one occasion," says the Chancellor, "he had managed a case successfully, for the Rev. Mr. Lilly. He called for his fee." Mr. Lilly jestingly replied: "Why, Mr. Nibbs, I thought you gentlemen of the Bar were not in the habit of charging us ministers for your services." "Ah! with regard to that," said Mr. Nibbs, "you look for your reward in the next world; we lawyers expect ours in this!" This was nigher an approach to wit than I ever heard ascribed to my poor friend on any other occasion.

He was admitted, late in life, to the Equity Forum. He was employed in a case which he tried, and lost, before Chancellor

Thompson. He was in an agony of distress, and said in the hearing of the Judge, "how can I go home and tell my client that I have lost his case?" The witty Judge said: "Nibbs, go home and tell your client you had a good case, but the Judge was a d—d fool, did not understand your case, and therefore you lost it."

The last time I saw him, was in the Equity Court of Appeals, between 1818 and 1820. He was the Solicitor on record in a very important case. I think B. F. Whitner, Esq., was his associate. The decree on the Circuit was in their favor. Mr. McDuffie was on the other side, and had appealed. It was his duty to prepare the briefs and bring up the Circuit Decree. Nibbs, who had never before appeared in the Appeal Court, prepared the briefs. When the case was called, on a very warm day in December, some difficulty was made by Mr. McDuffie, that the Circuit Decree was not present. Mr. Nibbs sprang to his feet and said: "In regard to that, may it please your Honors, I know where it is." And before anybody could say anything he was off in a run, to the College, a mile distant, in chase of his friend and colleague, Whitner, who had a copy. He found him and the copy, and in haste returned. The heat of the day caused him to perspire so freely, as to wet the black lining of his hat; the coloring matter in streaks had run down his face. Utterly unconscious of his streaked condition, he made his first and last speech in that Court, gained his case and went on his way rejoicing.

He soon after removed to Florida, died there, leaving his wife and only son surviving him. The latter, I have heard, did not do well, and is now, perhaps, also dead.

SAMUEL FARROW.

Samuel Farrow, who was one of the hardy, pioneer lawyers of the upper country, and who, notwithstanding the want of an early liberal education, toiled on through difficulties, until he won honor, and fame, both at the Bar, and in the halls of Legislation, National and State, was born in the State of Virginia, in 1759 or '60. His mother was Rosannah, the sister of the veteran soldier of liberty, Col. Philemon Waters, whose memoir will be found in O'Neall's Annals of Newberry, at page 218. His father, John, about 1764 or '65, removed to South Carolina, and settled in the then Ninety-Six, now Spartanburgh District, on the Enoree, about five miles above Musgrove's Mills. His father, about the commencement of the Revolutionary war, returned to Virginia, to settle his unfinished business; on his way home he was taken with the small pox, and died in North Carolina. He left five sons and three daughters, Thomas, John, Landon, Samuel, and William; Sarah, Mary and Jane.

Samuel Farrow and his three elder brothers were Whigs, in the Revolutionary struggle. They belonged to a company commanded by Ford, and were mostly engaged in the scouting and skirmishing affairs, with which the country abounded. In some one of these affairs, which very often were severe battles, on a small scale, Samuel Farrow was wounded by a blow with a sword, on his face. The scar is shown on a portrait, in the possession of his niece and hor husband, T. F. Murphy, Salem, Alabama.

Samuel Farrow was in the battle of Musgrove's Mills, on the 18th of August, 1781. Before or after this brilliant affair, he and two of his brothers, John and Landon, were taken prisoners, and confined in Ninety-Six goal. Their mother, who, like her brother, Col. Waters, was endowed with unconquerable courage and perseverance, obtained their release, by delivering to Col. Cruger, *six British prisoners.* She remarked to him that "*it was the best trade she had ever made; for,*" said she, "*I can now whip you four to one.*"

After the close of the Revolutionary war, Mr. Farrow studied law with Robert Goodloe Harper, Esq., and was admitted to the Bar, in the City of Charleston, on the 28th of January, 1793. He practiced in the Circuit Court of Ninety-Six, and in the County Courts of Newberry, Laurens, Union and Spartanburgh. I have often heard two anecdotes in connection with his name. When a young man he made a speech before Judge Burke, (who it seems had no great liking for the young lawyer,) in which he spoke of the necessity of the law being strong. "Yes," said Burke, "the law should be like a wall, through which the lions, bears and wolves cannot break; but now," he said, "it is so weak that the *raccoons* and *squirrels* slip through with ease."

At Newberry, in the County Court, Mr. Farrow had brought a suit against Major Thomas Willoughby Waters, who insisted on defending his own case, and made a speech to the Jury. Mr. Farrow said, "he would not condescend to answer the defendant standing: he would do so by lying down." He accordingly lay down, according to the tradition, and made his speech to the Jury.

In '94 or '95, Mr. Farrow married Miss Elizabeth Herndon, the daughter of Col. Benjamin Herndon, of Newberry, who had, while he resided in North Carolina, performed the part of a soldier of liberty, in the battle of King's Mountain.

When the Circuit Court System of '99 went into operation, Mr. Farrow was a leading lawyer at Union, Spartanburgh, Laurens and Newberry. He was endowed with indomitable perseverance, and never knew the word despair. Like Robert Bruce of Scotland, he arose from every defeat, fresher and stronger. The case of Garey and wife *vs.* the Executors of James, 4th Des., is an instance of that kind.

He and Judge Grimké, from being intimate friends, became bitter enemies. He was, perhaps, often the subject of the Judge's vindictiveness, while he, beyond all doubt, pursued the venerable Judge with unrelenting hatred, until the attempt was made, in 1810, to impeach him, and which failed in 1811.

Mr. Farrow was elected Lieutenant Governor in 1810; this was a deserved compliment to an old soldier and an eminent lawyer.

Mr. Farrow was elected to Congress from Pinckney District, in October, 1812, and took his seat in 1813. He continued in Congress until 4th of March, 1816. In that time the war of 1812 was waged to a successful termination. Mr. Farrow was a firm supporter of the administration of Mr. Madison. After the Capitol was burned in 1814, at the session of Congress which ensued, it was proposed to adjourn to some other place. This Mr. Farrow indignantly repelled, saying, he "would sooner sit under a canvas awning, than remove."

He was elected to the House of Representatives, of South Carolina, in October, 1816. I sat by his side during the sessions of 1816 and 1817, and never have I seen a more zealous and indefatigable member. I remember when a Revolutionary claim was presented, to which objection was made that it was barred by lapse of time, he indignantly replied that he "hoped never to live to see the day when an old soldier's claim would be barred by the statute of limitations."

His experience and wisdom bore him safely over the rocks on which, for some time, I was ship-wrecked. He was returned to the Legislature and served in the House in 1818, 1819, 1820 and 1821.

In 1821, he, with William Crafts, succeeded in obtaining an appropriation of $70,000, for the erection of the Lunatic Asylum, and a School for the Deaf and Dumb, in Columbia. The Asylum was built, and has blest many a one. It originated with Mr. Farrow, from seeing by the road-side, on his way to Columbia, a poor woman from Greenville, who, at the sessions of the Legislature, visited Columbia for many years. The School for the Deaf and Dumb was long postponed, but has at last been carried out, and appropriately located at the Cedar Spring—a Revolutionary battle-ground of Spartanburgh District.—Acts of '21, p. 36.

He then declined public honors, and on the 18th of November, 1824, closed his useful life in Columbia, at the house of Major Clifton. His remains lie at his residence, Spartanburgh District, near Head's Ford, on the Enoree River. His widow survived him, but has since passed away.

Mr. Farrow was an honest conscientious man, in all the affairs of life. As a lawyer, he was devoted to his client—his cause was as his own. His arguments at the Bar often showed his want of education; but when one looked on his face, and saw the scar, inflicted by the sword of the enemy, his incorrectness of speech was forgotten, and his auditors were borne irresistibly to his conclusion.

As a Legislator, he knew nothing save what he felt to be for the interest of his country. *He was a Patriot of* '76, and what more need be said ?

In all the relations of home, he was the kind husband, the devoted son and brother; and his niece, whom he raised, will say he was *uncle and father !* His slaves miss the kind "*massa*," who cherished and protected them.

His neighbors and friends mourned after him with the feeling that they might not again be blessed with another such companion.

The people of Spartanburgh long mourned his death ; he was a son by adoption for more than sixty years—by the almost unanimous votes, with which she had always inducted him into office. His life's example may, and I hope will be, a beacon light to many of her young sons to guide them to honor and usefulness.

JOHNSON HAGOOD.

William Hagood, the father of the subject of this sketch, was a native of Western Virginia, of English parentage. He married, early in life, Sarah Johnson, of that State, who, upon the maternal side, was of French descent; and, after the birth of several of his children, about the year 1776, removed to the neighborhood of Ninety-Six, in South Carolina. Johnson Hagood was then four years old. The neighborhood of Ninety-Six had already been the theatre of important events in the contest with the mother country, then pending, and was destined, at a later period, to witness some of the most stirring events of the war in the South. He often spoke of having a distinct recollection of such incidents of the war as would impress themselves upon a child's remembrance. Upon one occasion, being sent, after night, for medical assistance in his father's family, he passed the scene of one of those guerilla skirmishes, which so especially marked the later years of the war in that section of the State. Several corpses were lying unburied upon the field, and wolves were feeding upon them—a spectacle well calculated to try the nerves of a lad of six or seven years. At another time, he was present, with his father's family, in the piazza, after supper, together with some neighbors, who had called, when the group were fired upon by a skulking Tory, and one of the number wounded. His father embraced the popular cause, and bore his share in the trials of the times. He was a man of the pioneer type, with but little of education or refinement; but possessed of many of the simple and hardy virtues, which are the especial growth of the frontier.

The subject of our memoir acquired the knowledge of reading and writing from his parents, and early betrayed a fondness for books. When the war was over, and civil order restored, many distinguished lawyers, from various parts of the State, were accustomed to attend the Courts held at

Ninety-Six; and, in the absence of sufficient public entertainment, were often thrown upon the private hospitality of the vicinity. Among these lawyers, was Robert Goodloe Harper, then rapidly rising into distinction in South Carolina. His attention, while staying with William Hagood, during one of the terms of the Court, was attracted by the avidity with which his son devoured everything in the shape of a book. Pleased with the boy's assiduity, he supplied him with a small collection of books. The perusal of these increased his desire for knowledge, and he importuned his father to afford him the opportunity of acquiring an education. Schools were rare in that region of the State, at that time; the inhabitants were impoverished by the recent war, and the father, encumbered with a family of ten children, (five of whom were daughters,) and, undervaluing a liberal education, thought himself unable to spare the services of his son from the farm. This difference of opinion appearing irreconcilable, the son eventually took his fortunes into his own hands, and privately left the parental roof. With but a change of clothing in a small bundle, and without a sixpence in his pocket, he proceeded on foot to Granby, some sixty miles from Ninety-Six, where he was fortunate enough to obtain employment, as clerk in a country store. Thus, at fourteen years of age, he was fairly embarked upon the sea of life, "lord of himself," at a time when others, more happy, have scarcely slipped their leading-strings.

Our young clerk remained at Granby but a twelve-month, when he made his way to Charleston, with a view of expending his small earnings of the past year in putting himself at school. There he again met with his early friend, Mr. Harper, who, pleased with his earnest exertions to better his fortunes, took them under his own charge, and ever remained his firm friend through life. An arrangement was effected between them, by which young Hagood was taken into Mr. Harper's office, at a salary, to perform such duties as he was qualified for. These duties were light; and he had access to an excellent library, his patron directing his reading. In addition, with the proceeds of his salary, he put himself at a night-school, where he acquired a fair acquaintance with the classics, and some knowledge of French. The ardent aspirations of his childhood were at length realized. The means of knowledge were within his reach, and he availed himself of them with a zeal corresponding with the difficulties he had had to overcome in obtaining them. His improvement was rapid, and, by the advice of his patron, he commenced the study of the law, and was admitted to the Bar, at Charleston, in 1793. In the same year, he commenced the practice, in partnership with Mr. Harper. This partnership continued until Mr. Harper entered Congress, a few years afterwards, when the latter abandoned the practice, and never resumed it again in South Carolina. When he retired from political life, and settled in Maryland, he resumed the practice there, and obtained a high position at the Bar of that State.

Mr. Hagood, upon the dissolution of their partnership, had purchased Mr. Harper's fine library, and, left in charge of a full practice, felt that now success depended upon himself alone. He applied himself closely to his business, attending, in addition to the City Courts, those of the circuit, embracing Beaufort, (Coosawhatchie,) Colleton, Orangeburgh, Barnwell, and Lexington. By method and order, as well as assiduity in his business, and by devoting himself more to the acquisition of a sound knowledge of the law, than to mere forensic display, he acquired the reputation of a safe and successful lawyer; and with it came the lucrative practice, which is apt to be its attendant.

In 1794, Mr. Hagood was married to Ann Gordon O'Hear, a young lady whose family had long been settled in Charleston. They were of Irish extraction, having first migrated to France, and subsequently from thence to Charleston, where the head of the family engaged in commercial pursuits. This alliance was, in every respect, a happy one.

Mr. Hagood continued the practice of the law, in Charleston, till 1806, when he removed to Barnwell, where he purchased lands, and made extensive improvements. He still, however, continued his attendance upon the country Courts, enjoying a fine business, until 1810, when he began to withdraw from the practice, and in 1812 or 1813, he abandoned it entirely.

During the remainder of his life, he devoted himself to planting, and the improvement of his property, with the same energy and success which had characterized him at the Bar. He lived, however, but a few years after his retirement from the profession. In 1816, while on a visit to Charleston, he died, in the prime of his life, being then in his forty-fifth year, and was buried at the Second Presbyterian Church of that city.

Mr. Hagood was a self-made man—the architect of his own fortunes—and had all the mental traits which characterize such men. Bold, self-reliant, and persevering, his mind was eminently practical. Though by no means devoid of a taste for literature, his leisure hours were more frequently amused with works of political and philosophical speculation, than with those which appealed rather to the taste and the imagination. He was fond of the mathematics, and the study of the natural sciences. He was much interested in the studies of electricity and galvanism, which then possessed much of novelty, and procured from London an excellent and complete apparatus for re-producing the experiments of the philosophers of that day.

Mr. Hagood was a man of marked social traits. A benefactor of the poor—no one, indeed, ever applied to him in vain. In employing private tutors for his children, he invariably stipulated for the privilege of adding two or three of the children of his poorer neighbors, free of charge, to them. He manifested the deepest interest in the welfare of his father's family, as he advanced in life—educating his younger brothers and sisters, and showing an affectionate interest in their settlement. Sanguine and unsuspicious in temper, with a strong relish for the pleasures of life, hospitality was almost a passion with him; and so well was this trait known, that few strangers visited his neighborhood without calling on him. At Term time, in Barnwell, his house was always the home of the Judge, and of as many of the Bar as it could contain. Such a man was well calculated to attract friends.

In the profession, he had many. Among these, many especially be mentioned Judge Bay and Judge Grimké—the latter of whom, upon his death, wrote a feeling letter of condolence to his widow, in which he spoke of him in the warmest language of friendship, both as a man and as a lawyer.

Mr. Hagood left seven children surviving him. The eldest son died in early manhood; the remaining three sons are residents in Barnwell District. His eldest daughter married Mr. Frederick Witsell, of Colleton; the second married Mr. —— Fraser, of Colleton, and, at his death, Mr. John F. Schmidt, of Barnwell; the youngest daughter married Mr. W. H. Oakman, of Georgia.

JOHN TAYLOR.

He was the son of that good and gallant old gentleman, Col. Thomas Taylor, the patriarch of Columbia and the soldier of '76, whose fire at Fishdam defeated Major Wemys in his night attack upon Sumter.

He was born in May, 1770. He, therefore, began life just before the Revolutionary struggle surrounded his father's fire-side. He caught, as a fine stirring boy, much of the enthusiasm, which, after 1780, sent his father into active service.

In 1785, he was sent to school, at Camden, and began his Latin Grammar at the Academy kept by Capt. John Reid, late an officer in Col. Hampton's Regiment of State troops in the Revolutiary war.

When that school was given up, John Taylor, with his cousins, John and Simon Taylor, and William Tucker, were transferred to Mount Zion College, Winnsboro', which was then (1786) kept by the Rev. Mr. McCall.

Col. Chesnut, of Camden, says: "I followed the next year, and lodged in the house with John Taylor. The accommodations were very deficient. The scholars occupied lofts in different boarding-houses. There were eight of us in that part of the house we lived in. I recollect, well, that William C. Pinckney, who was Speaker of the House of Representatives, in 1804, with his friend, Benjamin Ferguson, occupied the loft of a recitation building, a log-house, about twenty-four by twenty feet."

This statement is worth an attentive perusal by our young men, who frequently find some fault with their College fare. It shows to what straitened circumstances the great men of South Carolina were forced to submit, to obtain that education which fitted them for their parts in the world opening before them.

In June, 1788, John Taylor, Jesse Taylor, and James Chesnut, Sen., (since, for more than half a century, advantageously known as Col. Chesnut,) sailed from Charleston bound for Philadelphia, but ultimately destined for Princeton. John Taylor entered the sophomore class, in Princeton College, and graduated with that class in 1790. The first honor was divided between him and Judge William Johnson. "His conduct," says Col. Chesnut, "was correct at all the schools, and during his collegiate term he was uniformly studious, diligent, and lived without reproach." What a beautiful commendation of a youthful life, from the lips of a companion, now a venerable man, who has been spared, in health and unusual vigor, beyond four score.

He entered as a student at law, the office of Gen. Charles Cotesworth Pinckney, in Charleston, in January, 1791, and was admitted to the Bar, in Charleston, 1st June, 1793. He had been married, in 1792, to Miss Sallie Chesnut, the daughter of Col. John Chesnut, of Camden, and the sister of Col. James Chesnut, Sen. He settled in Columbia, where his well-known residence, on Taylor's Hill, stands. He practiced law a few years, but was more particularly devoted to planting, in which he was very successful. He was early elected to the House of Representatives, in the General Assembly of this State, and was continued as a Member for several terms.

He was elected, in 1806, a Member of the Board of Trustees of the South Carolina College, and again in 1809. After a lapse of four years, from 1813 to 1817, he was again elected a member of the board, and in 1821 was re-elected.

In 1818, he was elected a Member of the House of Representatives, in Congress, from the united Districts of Beaufort, Colleton, Barnwell, Orangeburgh, Lexington, and Richland. At the succeeding election, William Lowndes, having received a greater number of votes, became his successor.

In December, 1810, he was elected to the Senate of the United States, but did not serve out the whole term. In 1822, he was elected to the Senate of the State of South Carolina. At the election of October, 1826, Col. Wade Hampton, Jr., was elected over him; but in December, 1826, he was elected Governor and Commander-in-chief.

At the Spring Term, of 1829, Governor Taylor presented

the interesting example of waiving his privilege of exemption, as a lawyer, by serving as foreman of one of the juries of Richland District.

In the latter part of 1829, or the beginning of 1830, he joined the Presbyterian Church, of Columbia—the Church of his father. His mother was a member of the Baptist Church, Columbia.

In April, 1832, he died. His venerable father and mother, his widow, and seven children, four sons and three daughters, survived him. Of these, two sons and two daughters alone remain, to wit: Gen. Wm. J. Taylor, Major A. R. Taylor, Mrs. Harriet Elmore, and Mrs. Sallie Rhett.

Gov. Taylor was a good and useful man, in his time. His talents were very respectable. He spoke well, though with no pretensions to eloquence. In the various offices which he filled, he discharged the duties with diligence and fidelity. He was a Republican in the division of parties in South Carolina; and at a later day, he was a *Radical*—that is, in favor of a strict construction of the Constitution, and against the doctrines of Internal Improvements, &c., which were the doctrines *then* advocated by Mr. Calhoun, General Hayne, Mr. McDuffie, and Gen. Hamilton.

Gov. Taylor, from his union with the Presbyterian Church, was a pious, zealous, and active member. His life was characterized by love, mercy, and good fruits. All the duties of husband, father, son, neighbor and master, he scrupulously fulfilled. He died in the triumph of a Christian. For he could say with Job, "I know my Redeemer liveth, and that he shall stand at the latter day upon the earth: and though after my skin worms destroy this body, yet in my flesh I shall see God: whom I shall see for myself, and mine eyes shall behold, and not another: though my veins be consumed within me."

BENJAMIN JAMES.

This gentleman was the third son of John James, Esq., of Stafford County, Virginia, and was born 22d April, 1768. His education was finished under the Rev. Robert Buchan, who then had charge of the highest literary institution in Virginia. He studied law, in Charleston, with that excellent lawyer and courteous gentleman, Henry W. DeSaussure, Esq., and was admitted to the Bar, and commenced the practice of the law. He married Miss Jane Stobo, the daughter of Richard Park Stobo, a grandson of Archibald Stobo, who was a Presbyterian clergyman, and had charge of the Congregational (Circular) Church, Meeting street, Charleston, from 1700 to 1704.—(2 Ramsay's History of South Carolina, 28, 29.) Mr. Stobo was a Scotchman; and it seems, he was either wrecked near Charleston, or was, on his arrival, robbed of all which he had, except the clothes which he had on him, his hymn-book, and a Bible, published in 1658, and which is still preserved by Mrs. Ballew, a daughter of Mr. James.

Mr. James remained in Charleston until the death of his father, in 1796, when he returned to the homestead, in Virginia, and there continued the practice of the law until 1808, when he removed to Laurens District, South Carolina, and settled on a fine plantation, on Little River, now the property of Hon. James H. Irby.

He practiced law for a short time, with Capt. Robert Cunningham, perhaps until 1812, when he, (Capt. Cunningham,) was commissioned a captain in the United States Army, and entered upon active service.

My acquaintance began with Mr. James in November, 1814. The fall after my admission to the Bar, I was requested, by my friend, John G. Brown, to take his place, with Mr. James, in the defence of a man for stealing a sheep. Mr. James examined the witnesses. I made a speech. He declined to address the Jury, by whose verdict our client was acquitted.

He abandoned the practice of the law, and turned his attention to farming. He was elected to the Senate, and served one or two terms. About this time he lost his wife, "from whose society," he said, (in his introduction to James' Digest,) he had never been separated "for five hours for twenty years." This domestic bereavement made it necessary that his time should be occupied. It led him to the preparation of his enlarged Digest of the Statute and Common Law of South Carolina, which he published in 1822. This work is, I think, worthy of much more attention than has been bestowed upon it. It is a very good hand-book for common use.

He died 15th November, 1825, aged fifty-seven years, six months and twenty-three days, leaving two sons, John Stobo, and Robert, and four daughters—Maria, now Mrs. Wade Anderson; Jane, now Mrs. Patillo Farrow; Louisa, now Mrs. Ballew; and Susan, now the wife of John Garlington, Esq.

Mr. James was a good lawyer, but his great modesty prevented him from taking and maintaining that stand which he ought to have done. He was an attentive legislator, and was of greater service to Laurens than any Senator who had preceded him. As the head of a family, none better understood or performed its duties. He was a clear-headed, firm, consistent, just, and good man.

ROBERT CRESWELL.

Robert Creswell was the son of the Rev. James Creswell, whose letter from Ninety-six of the 27th July, 1776, to the Hon. William Henry Drayton, may be found in the Appendix to 2d Drayton's Memoirs, 368, and which gives a graphic account of the state of things arising from the combination of the Tories and Indians, in the incursions of the latter on the settlements.

He studied law in Charleston, under Dominic Hall, Esq., who was subsequently appointed a Judge of the United States, in Louisiana. He it was who, on General Jackson's suspension of the *Habeas Corpus*, at the invasion near New Orleans, in December, 1814, by the British, undertook to counteract the General's policy by issuing a *Habeas Corpus*, which he refused to obey, and for this contempt he fined the hero, who saved the city, $1,000.

Mr. Creswell was admitted to the Bar in the City of Charleston, on the 1st of August, 1795.

He settled at Laurens, and practiced law until the abolition of the County Courts and the establishment of the Circuit Court system of 1799, when he became the Clerk of the Court at Laurens. In the meantime he had married Nancy, the daughter of Judge Hunter, of Laurens.

In a few years he became tired of the Clerk's office, resigned it, and returned to the practice of law. When I first knew him, he had considerable practice in Newberry, and a much more extensive one in Laurens.

Before 1814, he had lost his wife, by whom he had no children. He subsequently married Miss Davis, the daughter of John Davis, Esq., of Laurens.

In 1816, Mr. Creswell was elected Comptroller General, and again in 1818. The duties of this office, he discharged with great fidelity. His annual reports will show his capacity for the office, though, following as he did, Mr. Lee, whose eminent services in that office, have never been surpassed, made him appear to greater disadvantage than he otherwise would have done.

After his retirement from that office, he did not again resume the practice of the law, but lived for several years at Huntsville, Laurens District, and, for a few years subsequently, at McThee's Mills, on the Enoree River, in Spartansburgh District.

He then removed to Alabama, where he accumulated a large property by planting.

By his second wife, he was blest with a family of children. He died, as I have been informed, several years ago.

Mr. Creswell was a good lawyer. He argued his cases very well, yet he did not possess the oratorical powers of an advocate. Good sense and a knowledge of the principles of the law, with the great confidence of the people in his honesty, carried him, generally, successfully through his cases.

He was a kind, courteous gentleman, and, in all the relations of life, discharged his duties faithfully.

JOHN DUNLAP.

John Dunlap was admitted to the Bar, in Charleston, on the 26th of January, 1795.

He married, in Charleston, Miss Anne Geddes, the sister of Robert Geddes, a merchant, in King-street, and of Governor John Geddes. He lived at Ninety-Six, and had great reputation as an advocate.

He practiced in Abbeville, Edgefield, Newberry and Laurens, but his life was a short one. He died many years before my admission to the Bar, and left no children. His widow married the Rev. Benjamin R. Montgomery, a Presbyterian Minister, who was the Professor of Logic and Moral Philosophy in the South Carolina College, from 1811 to 1818, and who was also the Pastor of the Presbyterian Church in Columbia.

Major William Dunlap, of Laurens, was a brother of John Dunlap. He was one of Col. Hay's party, who, at Edgehills, was captured by the Bloody Scout, in October, 1781.

He has told me, that he was seated in the *circle of blood and death*—that his right-hand man and left-hand man, were cut down. He was, however, spared, and next morning, at Odell's Mills, on the Beaver Dam, he was discharged, covered with the blood and brains of his slain companions..

ISAAC GRIGGS

This gentleman was a native of Connecticut, and was born in 1762. Having been educated at Yale College, where he acquitted himself with distinction, he removed to Charleston, S. C., with the view of a permanent residence. The Charleston Bar, at this period, was in its most flourishing condition, and was led by men of the first order of ability. Mr. Griggs, as we may well suppose, availed himself of all the advantages within his reach. He entered the office of Robert Goodloe Harper, studied under his guidance and supervision, and was admitted to the Bar in 1795.

Very little is known of his early struggles in the profession, and of the difficulties which he must necessarily have encountered; he came to this State a stranger, nature had denied him those strong gifts of ready elocution, which, however shallow they may be in themselves, always attract the attention and admiration of the crowd.

During the long period which elapsed between his graduation and his admission to the Bar, it is probable that his means were very limited; but, with men of real merit, circumstances, which to inferior natures, seem to present insurmountable obstacles, rouse the spirit and insure success; in spite of these disadvantages, indeed, strengthened and animated by them, he won for himself a fair share of practice, and an enviable reputation for integrity of character.

Although Mr. Griggs took no part in the debates of the Forum, nor entered into the lists, in which mind struggles with mind, and where the highest and most conspicuous honors of the profession must be earned, and, therefore, never shone as an advocate: his proper sphere was the office. From the first, he devoted himself to the close study of the "Science of the Law," and prepared himself for the more responsible and important duties of the *Counsellor*.

Gifted with a sound understanding, thorough in his reading, careful and exact in all his habits, cautious in arriving at his conclusions, he was an excellent office lawyer; his practice, "the well-earned reward of diligence, punctuality and integrity,"* became established, and, at the election for Recorder of the City Court in 1811, when lawyers of acknowledged position and ability were aspirants, Mr. Griggs was named as a candidate, and, upon ballot, received but one vote less than the successful candidate, a fact whieh, alone, is enough to show the estimation in which he was held. He died of consumption, on 16th September, 1816, at the age of 54, and his remains were attended to their last resting place, in the beautiful Cemetery of the Unitarian Church, in Charleston, by a large circle of friends, all the prominent members of the "Charleston Bar," and the "Charleston Library Society," of which he was a valued member.

Of his family there now remains but one daughter, who, as a teacher of the young, has acceptably filled this responsible position for many years, and a son, Henry S. Griggs, who, inheriting his father's character and habits, has so long and so faithfully filled the responsible office of Treasurer of that admirably conducted Bank, "The Charleston Savings Institution.

---

* Chas. Fraser's Reminiscences of Charleston, page 80.

JOHN McCRADY.

John McCrady, the only son of Edward and Eliza McCrady, was born in Charleston, on the 13th June, 1775. His father, originally from Ireland, settled first in Pennsylvania, and afterwards removed to South Carolina, where he took an active and efficient part, as a Whig, during the Revolution, and was one of those citizens whom the British authorities selected from among the patriots of Charleston, to send as prisoners to St. Augustine.

John McCrady was sent, at a very early age, to Princeton College, where he graduated with distinction, and, upon his return home, commenced and finished his preparatory study for admission to the Bar, in the office of Gen. Charles Cotesworth Pinckney. He was admitted to the Bar 29th September, 1796, and entered immediately upon a large and lucrative practice. His life, although honorable and distinguished, affords little room for biography, as it was soon terminated. He died on the 12th June, 1803, at the early age of twenty-eight years. A most flattering tradition, both of his character and reputation, still, however, survives, and that there should be preserved such a remembrance of so short a career is, in itself, strong proof of the ability and success with which it was run. The following sketch of his mind and character was written, immediately after his death, by Col. William Drayton, an eminent member of the same profession, and his intimate and valued friend:

"Nature had gifted Mr. McCrady with a vigorous understanding—clear in its perceptions, solid and discriminative in its judgments. His strong and correct mind stood not in need of, and disdained all artificial resources; and they who have heard him in debate, armed with no other intellectual weapon than manliness of diction, and nervous unsophisticated argument, can testify that he was copious, without verbosity, logical, without dryness, and eloquent, without the parade of metaphor, or the pomp of rhetorical flourish. These are the prominent features of his mind. The characteristics of his heart were candor, liberality, and a nice sense of honor. To these recommendations of a higher order, were added, the minor, though perhaps not less alluring attractions of a vivacious disposition, an accommodating temper, a genuine vein of poignant humor, accompanied by unvarying good nature. For some years, Mr. McCrady had pursued the practice of the law with reputation and emolument, and although thus involved in the labyrinths of a profession too often confounding legal with moral propriety, yet was his integrity ever untarnished and unsuspected. To sum up his character, without dishonoring the dead by flattery, it may be pronounced, such was the rare combination of qualities he possessed, that though formed to enlighten the learned, and to command the respect of the good, the sweetness of his disposition, and the charms of his conversation, equally fitted him to gladden the gay circles of social merriment."

During his short professional life, Mr. McCrady was engaged in several cases, which have not yet lost their interest, and we conclude this brief sketch with his notes in a very curious case—the only one of its kind which has occurred in the legal experience of the State:

"Joseph Lewis *vs.* Thos. Bourke. } A rule to show cause why the body of the defendant should not be interred.

The defendant, although surrendered in discharge of his bail, is not in confinement under process of execution at the suit of the plaintiff; no *ca. sa.* having been lodged in the Sheriff's office since his surrender.

Where, then, is the right of the plaintiff to arrest or to detain the body?

But admit, that he was in custody under *ca. sa.*, at the suit of the plaintiff, where is the law for the detention of the defendant's corpse? There is no such law; on the contrary, the tenor of the cases is contradictory to this right of detention.—See 3d Blackstone's Com. p. 414; Coke Litt. p. 289; Cro. Jac. 356.

Besides, if it was intended that the power of the plaintiff

should extend to the detention and imprisonment of the dead body of the defendant, what construction is to be given to the Stat. 21 Jamés, chap. 24, quoted p. 37; 11 vol. of Viner's Abridgement?

But suppose, that authority can be produced from English books, to warrant this inhuman proceeding, will the Court sanction the validity of such a doctrine in this country?"

By reference to the Journal of the Court, from 1801 to 1804, we find the following:

"WEDNESDAY, 2d February, 1803.

JOSEPH LEWIS
vs.
THOS. BOURKE.

On motion of Mr. McCrady:

Ordered, That the plaintiff in this case do show cause, to-morrow morning, at ten o'clock, why the body of the said defendant (who has died in the Prison Bounds) should not be interred, he, the plaintiff, having objected to such interment."

"THURSDAY, 3d February, 1803.

Present, Judge Johnson.

"JOSEPH LEWIS
vs.
THOS. BOURKE.

Mr. McCrady moved, that the rule in this case, obtained yesterday, be made final. The Court, after hearing Mr. Cheves on the part of the plaintiff, and Mr. McCrady, in opposition to him, *Ordered*, That the said rule be made final."

Mr. McCrady married, in 1797, Jane Johnson, the daughter of Wm. Johnson, and sister of Wm. Johnson, Associate Justice of the Supreme Court of the United States, and left three children, Edward McCrady—at one time United States District Attorney, and still practicing at the Bar—Mrs. Henry Trescot, and a single daughter.

NOTE.—The impression, that a creditor had a right to detain the dead body of a debtor, until the debt was paid, seems, at one time, to have prevailed among the people.—See Tapping on Mandamus, p. 146; and it is somewhat curious, that the year after this case was tried, Lord Ellenborough, in the case of Jones *vs.* Ashburnham, 4 East. 455, referred to the same point in the following language:

"Now, an attempt to impose upon a person an *unlawful* terror (and the threatening of an unlawful suit is as bad), can never be a good consideration for a promise-to-pay; yet that ground is insisted upon by the Chief Justice. And as to the case there cited by him of a mother, who promised to pay, on forbearance of the plaintiff to arrest the dead body of her son, which she feared he was about to do, it is contrary to every principle of law and moral feeling. Such an act is revolting to humanity and illegal, and, therefore, any promise extorted by the fear of it, could never be valid in law."

As late, however, as 1830, an incident occurred in this State, showing that the idea was not obsolete. A man was sued, in Lancaster, and imprisoned under a *ca. sa.* He died in prison. The counsel for the prisoner declined to advise the Sheriff what to do; and that functionary accordingly, preserved the body in its coffin as well as he knew how, put it in the debtor's room, and there locked it securely until the next meeting of the Court, when he applied for instruction to the Court, which, it is almost needless to add, ordered its immediate burial.

KEATING LEWIS SIMONS.

My imperfect knowledge of the distinguished gentleman whose name is above, made me unwilling to assume the responsibility of sketching one of the most remarkable men who ever stood at the Charleston Bar. I had hoped that a near kinsman would have relieved me from a labor, which would have been pleasant, if I could have spoken from personal knowledge; but that aid not being furnished, I must, as well as I can, do justice to the memory of the South Carolinian, who "descended early to the grave, bedewed with the tears of his country, and covered all over with her praises."

He was born in 1775, in the City of Charleston. Mr. Crafts, in his beautiful eulogy, delivered on the 13th September, 1819, says he was born at the "commencement of our arduous Revolution. His infant eye caught the nodding plume of the soldier of liberty—he was caressed on the knees of the victorious patriot—the trumpet, and the roar of artillery, were the music of his boyhood."

He was the son of Keating Simons, Esq., and was educated in his native State. He was prepared for the Bar by one of South Carolina's purest patriots and greatest lawyers, Edward Rutledge. His letter of November, 1797, written to Keating Simons, Esq., his father, (and herewith given to the public,) says of his son, Keating Lewis, "he is a most charming youth, full of virtue, gratitude, honor, independence and industry; and, to these excellent qualities, he possesses one of the finest tempers in the world." It was regarded as the greatest, and most enviable blessing, by the ancients, "*Laudare a laudatis.*" The praise of Edward Rutledge was just such praise, and prepares us to expect great things from its recipient.

Keating Lewis Simons was admitted to the Bar 23d May, 1796.

Mr. Crafts, in his eulogy, says, "he entered the Forum,

which he was destined to elevate, to grace, and to purify—to fill with the sentiments of his lofty soul—to enrich with the treasures of his capacious mind, and decorate with the trophies of his honest triumphs. Are there any of his clients in this Assembly? Why do I ask? I am surrounded by them—of these I would inquire: Did they ever know a lawyer more distinterested, more laborious, more devoted to their interests, and more worthy of their confidence? Did he not defend the poor gratuitously? Did he not embark his whole soul in the cause of the oppressed; and, with a zeal and industry that wore him out, and wore him down, did he not faithfully serve mankind?" These inquiries convey a lawyer's highest praise.

In 1811, when I was a college boy, I remember to have listened to the outpouring of Mr. Simons' eloquence before the Senate of South Carolina, in the defence of Wm. Hasell Gibbes, Master in Chancery, on articles of impeachment. He was associated, on that occasion, with Col. William Drayton. They were in beautiful contrast. Simons was the rushing torrent, which bore away all obstacles in its course. Drayton was the deep, limpid, flowing stream, on which all delighted to float easily to the destined point. To a college boy, they were Demosthenes and Cicero revived! And, as at present informed, they were much similar in their style to the two gifted brothers of Carolina, John and Edward Rutledge.

He was often, Mr. Crafts tells us, in the Legislature of South Carolina, and that he filled a seat with much usefulness. I remember him, as Chairman of the Judiciary Committee, in 1818. He was a remarkable and conspicuous member of that body, the House of Representatives of South Carolina, in which Huger led and McDuffie spoke. Indeed, I suppose Mr. Simons, from his position, was the most experienced and reliable lawyer in it!

I see at his death, and perhaps for years before, he was the Colonel of the 29th Regiment. This situation he adorned; for never was there a man who seemed more fitted for command. In person and character, he was like Kleber, "*the good Sultan*" of the French army. Mr. Crafts says "he was a warlike man. His tall and athletic form, his manly and erect countenance, the rapid glance of his eyes, the powerful compass of his voice, and his cool self-possession, fitted him for all the exterior of command. His intrepid and refined spirit, his enthusiasm, his dignity, and, on a level with them all, his exact knowledge of military discipline, qualified him for all its dangers and all its duties."

This great and good man was cut down in his prime: he died 1st September, 1819, in the 44th year of his life.

In a letter of the 9th of October, 1819, Judge Cheves, speaking of his death, said—"The country has sustained, in his death, a great and almost irreparable loss. He would have been a great acquisition to the Bench; his solid talent and extensive learning, (for he was, undoubtedly, a more learned lawyer than any of his cotemporaries,) with his unyielding firmness, would have sustained and strengthened, while his high and punctilious honor, and even fastidious sense of propriety, would have cast a graceful blandness over the station." This view of his character from such a man as Judge Cheves, would seem to supersede the necessity of further remark.

If, however, more be necessary, it will be found in this letter of Edward Rutledge, an eulogium from the Winyaw Intelligencer, the proceedings of the officers of the Seventh Brigade, the American Revolution Society, and the Charleston Bar, herewith published.

The beautiful and touching inscription on his tomb, said to have been written by Col. Drayton, and accompanying this sketch, is a beautiful summary of his character.

A friend, Judge Porter, of Alabama, kindly furnished a sketch from his personal observation and recollection of the dead, which I append:

"KEATING L. SIMONS.

"My recollections of this gentleman are those of my early youth. When I first began to form ideas of distinguished men, and of oratory, Mr. Simons had reached a lofty position at the Bar, and his style quite superior to that of his cotemporaries, excited even my own boyish admiration. Often did the writer climb to the windows of the Court-House, in Charleston, to listen to his impassioned eloquence, charmed and captivated by the force and impetuosity of his speeches. Possessed of a most commanding person, and of a manner at once grave and manly, his method of addressing a Jury was striking and judicious. Added to these natural qualifications, was a voice remarkable for strength and beauty of tone. His enunciation was distinct, and he had a brilliant and ready flow of language. His elocution was a torrent swelled by recent floods, breaking out of its natural channels and rushing onward, sweeping all before it. He seldom, if ever, condescended to indulge in humor; and when he spoke, particularly on questions involving feelings, he rose to the most sublime and overpowering efforts. His action was, of itself, commanding and vehement. The audience sat, overwhelmed by the *ore rotundo* of his expressions, and the nervousness of his elocution; and there was an air of authority in his address, which awed the popular mind, and enabled him to sway it at will. He was a politician of much note with his party. At the head of the opposition was John L. Wilson, with whom, as rumor went, it was Col. Simons' lot to be selected to engage in a duel.

Some years after Col. Simons died. His funeral was a splendid pageant, attesting his great popularity, and the sympathy of his friends.

Among the many orators, whom it has been the fortune of the reminiscent to hear, Col. Simons stands impressed on his memory, as the finest and most perfect specimen of Demosthenian power. His delivery was bold, spirited, and popular, without being course or vulgar; and a more vehement, perfect, exciting, and eager orator, is rarely met with at any Bar, in any age. It is true, these impressions were upon the mind of a youth, of confessed inability to judge of high literary abilities, but, certainly, that elocution must have been singularly attractive and meritorious, which arrested the wayward step of a boy, and caused him to stand for hours, listening with admiration to the strong, musical voice of a speaker, pouring out a torrent of well-chosen expressions. The standard of perfection in eloquence, is its capability of influencing the learned and the ignorant, the aged and the young; and Col. Simons, when he spoke, attracted the same attention that the master-piece of a finished sculptor would—it is no sooner seen than its wonderful resemblance to nature is appreciated by the humble observer."

"*My Dear Sir*,—I thank you very sincerely for the perusal of my *much* loved friend's letter. He is a most charming youth, full of virtue, gratitude, honor, independence and industry; and to those excellent quallities, he possesses one of the finest tempers in the world. God Almighty bless him, and may he long live to shed *his* affection around *you*, and you, my dear friend, to bestow your fond paternal affection on him. If these good wishes prevail, you will see him an ornament to society, a friend to human nature, a shield to innocence, a protector to the unfortunate and a blessing to mankind. I know him *well*, and my love for him is in proportion to my knowledge. I thank you sincerely for your goodness towards me, and we will live and die in the habits of friendship.

Yours, ever,

K. Simons, Esq." ED. RUTLEDGE."

[This letter was written in November, 1797.]

"Philadelphia, 9th October, 1819.

"*My Dear Sir*,—I have received your eloquent eulogium on the character of our excellent and lamented friend, Simons. The country has sustained, in his death, a great and almost irreparable loss. He would have been a great acquisition to the Bench. His solid talent and extensive legal learning, (for he was undoubtedly a more learned lawyer than any of his cotemporaries,) with his unyielding firmness, would have sustained and strengthened, while his high and punctilious honor, and even fastidious sense of propriety, would have cast a graceful blandness over the station. You have done me very great honor in connecting my name with the memory of so inestimable a man, and in terms, (though unmerited,) so flattering and so eloquent. It is certainly very gratifying to me to discover that I am recollected by my countrymen and friends, and that I am associated in their remembrance with the good and the great.

I am, my dear sir,

with great and sincere esteem, your ob't.

LANGDON CHEVES.

Wm. Crafts, Jr. Esq."

We, with pleasure, comply with the request of a correspondent, in copying the following handsome eulogium on the late Col. Keating Lewis Simons, from the Winyaw Intelligencer:

"It has been frequently observed that republics manifested but little gratitude to those who had served them most faithfully; and it is but too natural, perhaps, that a duty which devolves upon all alike, and upon no one in particular, should be sometimes neglected. There have been circumstances of late, however, in Charleston, which seem to prove that a whole community can be operated upon by sensations which come directly from the heart, and that the public, which can so well appreciate, can also gratefully remember merit. This alludes, as it may be supposed, to the universal burst of sympathy, which took place at the death and at the funeral of the late Col. Keating Lewis Simons—a sympathy as creditable to the feelings of the public, as it was reputable to the memory of their departed fellow-citizen. The pride of power might, indeed, have ordered, and the pomp of heraldry might have marshalled, a more splendid funeral exhibition; but pride and power have nothing in common with grief, and the unstudied, self-ordered procession which took place, and those natural tears that dropped, and those allusions which have been since made, with such pathetic eloquence, to the past life of Col. S., appear to have been well-suited to the character and conduct of that much-beloved and much-lamented individual—that good and honorable man. They who knew him as a friend, and could witness those milder virtues and endearing qualities which characterized him in the circle of his acquaintance, and in the bosom of his family, can alone conceive the irreparable chasm which this sad event has made in private life. That such a man—so dear to his friends—so useful to the community, should have been snatched away, at what might have been considered as an early period of his career, is one of those instances of the inscrutable decrees of Providence, to which it is our duty to submit with resignation. But he will not have lived in vain—the good he did remains. He will have bequeathed to his infant sons the mantle of his fair fame, and the pattern of a life devoted to honorable pursuits. To the young of his own profession, he will have left the example of a distinguished name, built on the firm basis of conscientious principles. His country, too, will long remember him—they will long remember that sound integrity, that unblemished name, that independent mind, that extensive knowledge and that unwearied attention which qualified him alike for the Senate or for the Bar. In him, the virtues of the man we loved —the heart so brave and so benevolent, the mind so dutiful when duty called, and so affectionate—the manners so cheerful, so unassuming, so liberal, so kind, were most happily blended and interwoven in the public man; they became a species of public property, and augmented very essentially, by their influence and by their example, the general stock of public virtue."

[From the Charleston Courier.]

"FRIDAY, September 3d, 1819.

"A meeting of the Officers of the 7th Brigade was held yesterday, September 2d, at 1 o'clock. Col. O'Hara was called to the Chair, and Capt. Elliot appointed Secretary.

Maj. Crafts rose, and, after a feeling and eloquent address, proposed the following resolution, which was unanimously adopted:

Resolved, That a committee be appointed to make arrangements for a suitable expression of the feelings of the officers of this Brigade, at the lamented death of Col. K. L. Simons.

The following committee was appointed :

Col. O'Hara, Col. Howard, Col. Rouse, Maj. Bacot, Maj. Crafts, and Capt. D'Oyley.

The meeting adjourned to this day, at one o'clock, to receive the report of the committee.

The officers who did not attend the meeting, are notified to attend at the above-stated time."

[From the Charleston Courier, Saturday, September 4th, 1819.]

AMERICAN REVOLUTION SOCIETY.

"At a special meeting of the above society, held on Thursday, the 2d instant, the following resolutions were unanimously adopted :

WHEREAS, It hath pleased Divine Providence to remove from a scene of public usefulness and domestic affection, the late Col. Keating Lewis Simons, in the vigor of his age and the full strength of his faculties.

Resolved, That this society, in testimony of their profound respect for his steady integrity, his lofty independence, his high sense of honor, his generous and chivalrous spirit, his solid understanding and his most useful life, will wear crape on the left arm, for the space of thirty days.

Resolved, That a member of this society be requested to prepare a funeral eulogium, to be delivered at such time and place as he shall appoint, on the character of the deceased.

Resolved, That the president do transmit a copy of these resolutions to the venerable parent of the deceased.

In conformity with the second resolution, John Gadsden, Esq., was appointed to deliver the eulogium."

At a meeting of the members of the Charleston Bar, held at the Court House, on the 3d September, 1819, Mr. Thomas Parker, Sen., was called to the Chair, when the following resolutions were unanimously approved and adopted:

"Posthumous eulogy has been so frequently lavished upon the undeserving, that the admirers of departed worth with reluctance give publicity to their sentiments. The friends and intimates of those who have ceased to be, nevertheless, experience a melancholy satisfaction in the united utterance of their griefs; and when their friends and intimates know that the sound of praise is not touched without feeling the tone expressed, its vibration strikes a kindred chord within their bosoms, which even art and eloquence, upon a baseless foundation, would in vain endeavor to excite. Who can forbear to speak of those whose amiableness gladdened society, whose talents served their country, whose virtues dignified their species? Who, then, can be silent as to him whose recent death has occasioned this meeting? Those who knew him enjoyed the rare felicity of being acquainted with one whose head was the recepticle of a sound understanding, whose soul was the seat of honor, whose heart was the fountain of every moral and generous quality. In speaking of those who are sanctified by death—who are reposing upon the bosom of their Father and their God—it were unbecoming, it were indecent, to resort to the language of flattery. The deceased had his failings, for he was mortal; but without sacrificing truth to panegyric, it may be confidently pronounced that his failings sprang from sublimated virtue. He was sometimes betrayed into exhibitions of warmth—sometimes, perhaps, into ebulitions of passion; but the flame which kindled these transports was formed of no common material—it was an ethereal flame—the excitement of high-minded sensibility, which felt a shock like a wound, when it came in contact with artifice and corruption.

In that situation in which these now assembled have been peculiarly accustomed to regard the deceased, they beheld the zealous protector of right, the open foe of wrong, the powerful and ingenious advocate, the learned and skilful lawyer, the sound and candid reasoner, adorned by the courtesy of the gentleman and ennobled by the principles of the hero.

To be deprived of such a man, must be deplored by all: by his country, for he was a patriot; by his friends, for his attachment to them was boundless; by his relatives, for he was amiable and affectionate; by his dependents, for he was kind, tender and humane. Cherishing these sentiments towards the deceased,

It is therefore resolved by the members of the Charleston Bar, as a testimony of their sorrow for the loss, of their respect for the talents and of their reverence for the virtues of their deceased brother, *Keating Lewis Simons,* that they will wear crape on their left arms, for the space of thirty days.

Resolved, That a copy of the above resolution be sent to Keating Simons, Esq., the father of the lamented Col. Simons, previous to the publication thereof, as a testimony of their respect and affection for his departed son.

Resolved, That the members of this Bar do attend, when the eulogy on their late brother, Col. Simons, shall be delivered by John Gadsden, Esq., a member of the 'American Revolution Society,' and of this Bar, by appointment of the said society.

Resolved, That the above resolutions be published in the gazettes of this city."

The following resolutions were received and adopted by the 7th Brigade:

"1st. *Resolved,* That the officers and members of the 7th Brigade, residing in Charleston, do cause to be erected in the city, a marble monument, with suitable inscriptions, to the memory of Col. K. L. Simons, where the brave and virtuous may read the narrative and behold the reward of valor and of virtue, and where the tears of posterity may be shed for one who deserves their remembrance.

2d. *Resolved,* That we commend to ourselves and to each other, his splendid example, and pledge ourselves to remember him always.

3d. *Resolved,* That military mourning be worn on three successive Sundays from the date hereof.

4th. *Resolved,* That the officers of the 7th Brigade will attend a public eulogium, to be delivered by an officer of their appointment, on the character and memory of the deceased.

5. *Resolved,* That Maj. Crafts be appointed to deliver the above-mentioned eulogium

6th. *Resolved,* That a committee be appointed to make arrangements for the erection of the above-mentioned monument.

7th. *Resolved,* That the Secretary transmit the above resolutions to the venerable father of the deceased.

CHARLES O'HARA,
Chairman Com. Officers, 7th Brigade."

EULOGY,

Delivered before and by request of the Members of the Charleston Bar, by John Gadsden, Esq.

"It is a pious office to 'scatter sweets' upon the tomb of a friend, but it is a still more pious office to endeavor to snatch from the grave those virtues whose memory must perish but for a faithful record, and to preserve them for our own age and for posterity, that they may be the themes of meditation and the models of imitation; that they may perpetuate themselves in the feelings and actions of others; and that thus the dead, if we may so say, may be raised again by their virtues in another race.

The duty which has been assigned to me on the present occasion, is to awaken your recollection to the life and virtues of that distinguished citizen and excellent man, Keating Lewis Simons. Happy should I have been, had this appointment devolved on one of his earlier cotemporaries, who, knowing him from his youth and having observed the rise of his fortune, the enlargement of his mind, and the growth of his virtues, could have furnished a livelier and more feeling portrait of him, for this melancholy meeting. His death is indeed a public calamity. When I consider the feelings of a community, among whom he had ceased to number an enemy—when I observe the almost universal grief which pervades our city, flowing not merely from a general sympathy with a bereaved parent and sorrowing relatives, but from a personal connection with the deceased; the tears of heart-stricken friends and grateful clients; the widow, the orphan, and the oppressed; those whose estates have been preserved, and whose reputations have been purified by his eloquence; and, when I call to mind the time of his death, in the freshness and perfection of his faculties, and at the summit of his fortune, whence he looked forward to a long life of eminent usefulness, and domestic endearment: Under the weight of this accumulation of afflicting topics, I feel myself unequal to the situation in which I am placed; and I must throw myself upon that good opinion, to which I owe the present appointment, while I endeavor to speak of our friend as he was: believing that to delineate his character fairly, will be at once to pay the justest tribute to his memory, and to perform an essential service to the community.

Keating L. Simons was born in this State, on the 11th of March, in the year 1775, and received his education in this city. He was, emphatically, the child of our own Carolina, the pupil of our beloved Charleston. Even at school, he discovered that energy and perseverance for which he was distinguished through life. He was placed under the instruction of Mr. Osborn, who then kept one of the best grammar schools that has ever been in our city. After leaving school he entered upon the study of the law in the office of the Honorable Edward Rutledge. It was probably to this connection that we owe the high character and great attainments of our excellent friend. Cowley's fondness for poetry is said to have been first excited by the perusal of Spenser's Fairie Queen; and Sir Joshua Reynolds, by the accidental reading of Richardson on painting, was first led to the study of that art, in which he attained such eminence. The fine genius, the noble nature, the amiable temper, and the exalted reputation of Mr. Rutledge, would naturally make an impression upon a generous and aspiring youth. The Romans were so sensible of the importance of high examples in education, that it was a part of their discipline to place their youth under the eye and care of some distinguished orator.

In the dialogue on the causes of the decline of the Roman Eloquence, the author thus speaks of that ancient practice: 'Our ancestors, (says he,) when they designed a young man for the profession of eloquence, having previously taken due care of his domestic education, and seasoned his mind with useful knowledge, introduced him to the most eminent orator in Rome. From that time the youth commenced his constant follower, attending him upon all occasions, whether he appeared in the public assemblies of the people, or in the courts of civil judicature. Thus he learned, if I may use the expression, the arts of oratorical conflict in the very field of battle.'

But it was not eloquence alone that our friend learnt under this master. It is the historian of the Revolution, the venerable Ramsay, who thus speaks of the professional character of Mr. Rutledge: 'In the practice of the law, Edward Rutledge was directed by the most upright and generous principles. To advance his personal interest, was a secondary object; to do good, to promote peace, to heal breaches, to advance justice, was a primary one. His powers of persuasion were not to be purchased to shield oppression, or to support iniquity. Where he thought his client had justice on his side, he would go all lengths in vindicating his claims; but would not support any man, however liberal, in prosecuting unfounded claims, or resisting those that were substantially just. He abhorred the principle, that an advocate should take all advantages for his client and gain whatever he could for him, whether right or wrong; or, on the other hand, should assist him with all the quirks and quibbles which ingenuity can contrive, or the forms of law permit, for defeating or delaying the claims of substantial justice.'

Those who are acquainted with Mr. Simons' professional course, can hardly fail to observe its resemblance to this faithful and animated record. Among other obligations which our State owes to this distinguished citizen, it ought perhaps now to add, as a fresh debt, the virtues and attainments of a

Simons. In his character it is a fine trait, that he seems to have thought that he never could be too grateful to his preceptor and his friend. Such an example is highly encouraging to that patronage of rising virtue and genius, which the best men in all ages have delighted to exercise, and of which, in our times, we have had so many fine examples in our city. Before this audience, it is hardly possible to dwell too long upon such a theme; and if we can suppose the deceased to participate at all in this tribute, the memorial of his gratitude would give the highest satisfaction to his generous spirit. Permit me then to add, that of his preceptor and friend he delighted to speak; and that in the language of eloquence and affection, in a public oration, describes Mr. Rutledge 'as the sweet model of manly grace and excellence; the early and eloquent asserter of his country; the favored son of genius, framed in the prodigality of nature, benign, wise, amiable and magnanimous; bewailed by all who loved philanthropy or delighted in elegance; by all who could admire the ornaments, or rejoice in the benefactors of their country.'

Such reverence merits the lofty praise of Juvenal:

> ——————tenuem et sine pondere terram
> Spirantesque crocos et in urna perpetuum ver
> Qui præceptorem sancti voluere parentis
> Esse loco.*

Mr. Simons, having made the choice of Hercules, having determined to attain a high and virtuous fame, was sensible that the severest and most constant labor would be necessary to carry him to the goal of his desires.

> 'Love, fame, esteem, 'tis labor must acquire,
> The smiling offspring of a rigid sire.'—*Shenstone.*

His aspiring and energetic mind gave him confidence in

---

* This, with a change of person, may be thus translated, and applied to the deceased:—

> The turf shall gently on his bosom press,
> Sweet breathing flowers his sacred urn shall dress;
> And spring eternal cheer his pious shade,
> Who filial reverence to his teacher paid.

his powers. With an Herculean robustness of understanding, and nerves not to be broken by labor, he could, like the great Montesquieu, look forward to the prize after the toils of twenty years. No defects of education, no difficulty in learning could impede his steady march; nor could the earlier success of more gifted candidates for fame dishearten him. His physical constitution enabled him to pursue, for years, and in the most sultry seasons, by night as well as by day, a course of the most rigid application. Often in our summer nights, when the heat allowed other persons to attend only to their personal comfort, has he been found in his study, engaged with the learning of Coke and of Plowden. If, like the younger Cato, his apprehension was slow, and his learning came with difficulty, what he had once learnt he long retained; for, as Plutarch observes, 'It is indeed a common case for persons of quick parts to have weak memories, but what is gained with labor and application is always retained the longest; for every hard-gained acquisition of science is a kind of annealing on the mind.' In preparing himself for the Bar, he did not confine himself to the municipal law; though he pursued only such learning as was connected in some way with law and politics; and, if we may judge from his liberal practice, his manly eloquence and his enlarged reasonings, he was not unmindful of the splendid course prescribed by the eloquent Bolingbroke, who says of the law, 'that it is a profession, in its nature, the noblest and most beneficial to mankind, in its abuse and debasement the most sordid and the most pernicious.' And after animadverting upon the pleaders of his day, adds, 'but there have been lawyers that were orators, philosophers and historians; there have been Bacons and Clarendons; there will be none such any more, till in some better age true ambition, or the love of fame prevail over avarice, and till men find leisure and encouragement for the exercise of this profession, by climbing up to the vantage ground—so my Lord Bacon calls it—of science, instead of grovelling all their lives below, a mean but gainful application to all the little arts of chicane.'

Mr. Simons did not allow his ambitious views, and his close application to his studies, to interfere with his social relations; and while preparing for the Bar, he, by his generous and amiable temper, laid the foundation of those friendships which have constituted so much the happiness of his life. It is delightful to hear the companions of his youth—ranking now among our most esteemed citizens—speak of their deceased friend. The honors of genius seem almost to fade away before such praise; for, in this short and uncertain life, is it not better to be loved than respected? Of one of the greatest geniuses of the age, it was said, by a cotemporary, 'that he was born to be loved,' a tribute more grateful than the loftiest panegyric.

On the 23d of May, 1796, the deceased was admitted to the Bar, and, in a short time after, he appeared in the Court as an advocate.

If he did not rise immediately in his profession, it must be recollected, that there were then, at the Charleston Bar, some of the most eminent men in the State; men equally distinguished for intellect and learning. He still continued to pursue the same course of laborious application, and, by the most solid acquirements, laid the foundation of that high professional eminence which he at length attained. His legal learning was extensive and exact. In his opinions his clients could place the greatest confidence, for they were the result, not merely of his general knowledge of law, however deep, but of a scrupulous investigation of the particular case. In conducting the business of his clients, he exercised the strictest justice; he considered himself as a person invested with a trust, or confidence, in whom nothing like indifference, or neglect, should be found. Yet he never suffered his clients to interfere with his professional courtesies. He was just to them without being illiberal to their adversaries. As an advocate his style of speaking was logical and manly. He thoroughly discussed the question in debate; placing it in every point of view, and fully illustrating it. In the examination of principles, he displayed an enlarged and investigating mind, and in the application of analogies on questions of mere law, he was very successful. The secret of eloquence he understood; he was always earnest, often pathetic and vehement. In the Court of Sessions he was eminently distinguished. It was there that his humane and generous feelings found a field for their exercise; and that his pathetic and vehement eloquence made an impression on the heart. The unhappy victim* of a false honor, and an erroneous piety, found in him a powerful, if not a successful advocate. In defence of those, who, in obedience to the sentiments and manners of the age, had incurred the penalty of the law, he spoke with a discretion and a spirit, with a reverence for the laws and a love of honor, which became so difficult and delicate a theme. The impeachment of an officer of high rank in our Courts, before the Senate of this State, gave birth, on the part of the defence, to an elaborate and dazzling eloquence, to which this State had long been a stranger. Those who heard the advocates† of the accused, still recall, with delight, the emotions which were then kindled. It is to be regretted that no record remains of those splendid productions. On that occasion the profound logic, and the vehement rhetoric of Mr. Simons, burst forth, like a flood that had been long confined, and had been long collecting into a mass of waters. It appeared as if the speaker had enjoyed, for the first time, an opportunity for the exercise of his extraordinary powers. Escaped from the little and daily contentions of the Forum, his mind walked forth in its strength and majesty upon the higher and wide-spread field of public delinquency.

But it was in the Court of Chancery that Mr. Simons' professional career was most useful. The principles of equity accorded better with his enlarged and liberal mind, than those of strict law. In the investigations of this Court, there is more room for original reasoning, than in those of the tribunals of the common law. The discretionary power, approaching almost to legislative authority, exercised in a Court of Equity, must give rise to discussions founded upon natural

---

*Richard Dennis, who was convicted of murder for shooting a person who abused Dennis' father, and afterwards flogged Dennis with a cowskin.

† Col. Drayton and Mr. Simons.

reason, or an analogy to other powers. Precedents, on many occasions, here, speak not all, or a language which can be only understood by enlightened minds. The ablest Chancellor, in the exercise of his discretion, may derive aid from the arguments of counsel. Lord Eldon has often made his acknowledgments to the solicitors of his Court; and sanctioned by his decrees the reasonings of a Romilly. In this aspect of the subject, the pleader not only serves his client, but his country. He becomes a political or legislative lawyer, and gives his assistance in settling the law of the Court. Such exercises must have admirably agreed with the public spirit of our excellent friend; and those who are acquainted with the proceedings of our Court of Chancery, know how largely he contributed to throw light upon some unsettled doctrines.

In his practice he was the friend of the poor, and especially of the widow and the orphan. No one ever found that his inability to make compensation, rendered Mr. Simons less patient, less active, and less fearless in the prosecution of truth and justice. Indeed, if he was more zealous for some clients than others, it was in those cases in which he expected no other reward than the approbation of his own mind. He has been known, after having been engaged during the morning in the Superior Courts, to attend, in the afternoon before a Justice to the defence of a poor negro. It is a fact well ascertained, that, for a large portion of his business, he received no pecuniary returns. Though not rich, the *sacra fames auri*—that passion which seems to be swallowing up every other in our country—had no charms for him.

His kindness and courtesy towards the younger members of the profession, will long be remembered by them. He encouraged them by his praise, and assisted them with his counsel. He regarded them with a paternal affection; and when the characters of individuals among them have been assailed, they found in him an active and a fearless defender.

Having spoken of his professional character, I shall now notice his political opinions and conduct. He gave an entire preference to republican institutions, where they could be established, over every other form of government. He considered it a happiness that he was a citizen of a free State, and that he lived under a constitution that allowed a full scope for the exercise of all the heroic and generous virtues; but he held, that the political duties of an American citizen were of a practical nature. Abstract discussions, about the forms of government, he thought had better be left to the philosophers; while every citizen should do his utmost to preserve that enlightened Constitution, which it had been our good fortune to secure. The noble virtue of patriotism found, in his generous affections, a congenial soil. He loved the Constitution of his country with a Roman reverence. He may be said to have been formed for a public man. Though from the unhappy differences of party, he was for many years kept from a public station; yet he carried his public spirit into his profession, which he seemed to exercise rather for others than himself. The causes, in which he took the deepest interest, were those which had some connection with the general welfare, which touched the rights of the citizen, or led to an investigation of the principles of the Constitution; or those which concerned a lesser public, and affected the condition, the feelings, or the honor of his friends. When restored to the Legislature of our State, in which he had held a seat many years ago, can we forget the almost youthful ardor with which he embarked in the public service? His unwearied diligence, his incessant activity, his sound judgment, his vehement eloquence, his urbanity and generosity won every heart; and I have heard it asserted, by a political opponent, that he was, perhaps, the most popular man on the floor. With what grief will the event, which we this day deplore, be recalled by that respectable body. Methinks I see those who parted from him, in admiration of his generosity and eloquence, looking with eyes suffused with tears, at his vacant seat, endeavoring to recall his last accents, and to portray, in imagination, that noble form which is now mouldering in the dust.

He was the decided friend of the Federal Constitution. Valuing that instrument as the chart of the General and State powers, it was the aim of his politics to preserve to the federal head its constitutional authority, and he dreaded an encroachment of the States much more than a national usurpation. He thought it the duty of the Federal Government to exercise its prerogatives fearlessly; and to consult the interest, rather than the wishes of the people: being satisfied that what was really for their good, they would eventually approve. He considered all differences of opinion between the parties of the country as of no importance, when compared to the preservation of the Union—the liberties and the glory of these States. Obedience to the government, when acting within its sphere, he judged to be the primary duty of the citizen; and in the late contest with Great Britain, whatever might have been his opinion as to the propriety of declaring war at that crisis, he decidedly thought that when the government had placed the nation in a state of war, every heart and hand should unite in the glorious prosecution of it. He, with the rest of his fellow-citizens, labored personally on your lines of defence; and he united himself, as their commander, to a volunteer company of militia. With his characteristic ardor and perseverance he applied himself to the military art. That he excelled in it, the reputation with which he sustained the high rank to which he was advanced, and the testimonies of respect which his brother officers have rendered to his memory, are the highest proofs.

Though resolute and fervent in the maintenance of his political opinions, he never allowed them to interfere with his friendships or the courtesies of life. He looked upon them as truths connected with the welfare of his country, and as doctrines, by which his conduct as a citizen was to be guided: and he therefore held them with a firm grasp; but he never felt any enmity towards a sincere opposition, or met it with bitterness of spirit and expression.

In his friendships, he was warm and constant. These he seems to have owed as much to nature as to virtue. There was in him a constitutional warmth which fitted him for this connection; and his inflexible disposition preserved the flame to the last. His earliest regards continued through life; and there were no labors, no fatigues, no dangers, which he would not undergo to maintain them. There was something romantic in his attachment. It was a sacred passion approaching almost to the sanctities of religion. It extended itself to the connections and the offspring of the person beloved; and cherished the memory of departed worth.

No man was more free than he was from the taint of vanity and affectation. What Tacitus says of Agricola, may be applied to him:

"Nihil appetere jactatione."

His sincerity and self-respect, gave to his manners, at a first view, an appearance of coldness. He had not the talent of saying pretty things, or of expressing a great deal when he meant nothing; but as far as politeness consists in a delicate observation of the feelings and circumstances of others, and in a lesser benevolence, he was no stranger to that art.

In his social relations, he appeared to be very much under the influence of high sentiment. He not only knew, he felt his duty.

Honor—"the noble mind's distinguishing perfection"—was the lamp of his life. He revolted at anything mean, and little, and base. He reverenced the man within his breast, and dreaded nothing so much as to lower and degrade himself in his own eyes. It was by "this sensibility of principle, this chastity of honor, which felt a stain as a wound,"* that he preserved a scrupulous regard to those moral distinctions, which the practice of the law is said to have a tendency to confound in the mind. I have understood that he resolutely refused, at the last session of the Legislature, to be considered as a candidate for the office of Judge, because an additional seat on the Bench had been appointed while he was a member of the House, and partly by his exertions; and such was his regard to his public station, that he declined being employed in the Court of Appeals at Columbia, and rejected a large fee, lest it should interfere with his duties in the Legislature. The sentiments of a Sidney and a Bayard, however

---

* Burke.

neglected in a calculating and an intriguing age, had found an asylum in his bosom.

In the domestic circle, he was a sincere and tender relative. Sacred be the sorrows of his house: the hearts of the community incline towards it; and would to Heaven that their sympathy could bring any relief to the agonized, widowed bosom!

Of the extent of their loss his unhappy children cannot now be sensible. His parental affection, his judicious superintendence, his careful discipline, cannot be supplied; and it is only by recalling his virtues, when they begin to feel the privation of them, that his sons can be furnished with a faint image of that living model after which they might have formed themselves, had it pleased the Divine Disposer of events to spare him to his family. However early his fate, he has lived long enough to leave them the patrimony of his high and endeared name; and it will be the delight of his friends to remember him, in their kindness to his offspring.

As a son, it was not in vain that he endeavored to pay a debt of gratitude, imposed by nature and strengthened by affection. His aged parent seemed to live again in the merit and hopes of his son. How happy and how miserable a father! That father had attained a state of felicity, rare in any country, and particularly in this inclement clime: that father found himself crowned with a double reverence, and felt in the respect of his fellow-citizens, not only the testimony to his virtues, but to those of his excellent son: that father who, in the prosperity of a numerous and virtuous progeny, and in the high reputation of his first-born, felt a satisfaction which would almost have authorized the prayer to depart in peace, now finds himself, to borrow the language of an eloquent orator,* on a like melancholy occasion, "stripped of his honors, torn up by the roots, and laid prostrate on the earth."

Would it be an exaggeration for the father of such a son to say, as the Duke of Ormond did of the gallant Ossory, "I would not exchange my dead son for any living son in Christendom."

* Burke.

I have said nothing of the failings of the deceased, not because I wished to exhibit a faultless monster, but because it is a subject of great delicacy—one which it is difficult to handle with propriety, and which would ill become me, or this occasion; and especially because, such as they were, his failings were open and known; whatever may have been his errors, there was nothing like dissimulation or hypocrisy in him. Perhaps, also, some apology may be due for the manner in which I have spoken of his virtues; if any thing, in my account of him, may be thought to savor of exaggeration, I trust it will be ascribed to the warmth of friendship, and to the excitement of the occasion; for much as I reverence the deseased, I trust I reverence truth more. We are now drawing, my friends, towards the most painful part of this discourse; but there is a sentiment which he uttered, not long before his death, which ought first to be especially noticed. A friend having spoken to him, on the prospect of his being invited by his fellow-citizens, to fill a judicial office, he spoke upon the subject in a manner which ought ever to endear him to the people. "I have (said he) endeavored, through life, to deserve the good opinion of my fellow-citizens, and if, as a mark of their favor, I should be elected to the bench, I shall with gratitude remember it as one of the happiest events of my life."

The last scene of his life harmonized with the rest of it. When he thought he must die, he communicated this opinion only to his friend, and having made up his mind to meet his fate, he lay without murmuring or complaint. Severe bodily pain did not restrain his kindness, or even his politeness. His thoughts appeared to be employed upon others rather than himself. The affliction of his father for his death he dreaded more than death itself. Under great sufferings, and the expectation of approaching dissolution, his benevolence, even to his dependents, did not forsake him; and some of his last expressions of kindness were addressed to a servant—the nurse of his children. Would it be unreasonable to ascribe his composure of mind, and his affectionate regard to others, in his last hours, to the influence of that Christian philosophy which sustained the spirit of a Hamilton—that philosophy, whose Divine origin, I am authorized to say, Mr. Simons admitted, and whose moral precepts he reverenced?

After making, with the utmost calmness, the most considerate arrangements for his family, he expired,* to use the appropriate description of a friend, with the fortitude of Cato and the serenity of Addison.

To the history of such a life, and such a death, may we not apply the philosophy of Solon?—

"Futurity (says that sage) carries for every man many various and uncertain events in its bosom. He, therefore, whom Heaven blesses with success to the last, is, in our estimation, the happy man. But the happiness of him who still lives, and has the dangers of life to encounter, appears to us no better than that of a champion before the combat is determined, and while the crown is uncertain."—*Plutarch's Life of Solon.*

---

* On the 1st of September, 1819.

UNDERNEATH

THIS STONE WAS BURIED THE MORTAL BODY

OF

COLONEL KEATING LEWIS SIMONS,

WHO DIED IN CHARLESTON, ON THE

FIRST SEPTEMBER,

1819,

AGED 44 YEARS;

"LAMENTED

"BY HIS COUNTRY, FOR HE WAS A PATRIOT:

"BY HIS FRIENDS, FOR HIS ATTACHMENT TO THEM WAS BOUNDLESS:

"BY HIS RELATIONS, FOR HE WAS AMIABLE AND AFFECTIONATE:

"BY HIS DEPENDENTS, FOR HE WAS KIND, TENDER AND HUMANE."

THIS MEMORIAL OF A BELOVED SON,

IS ERECTED BY A FATHER WHO HAS FOUND

SOLACE FOR HIS OWN SORROW IN THE

AFFECTIONATE SYMPATHY OF

A BEREAVED AND MOURNING

COUNTRY.

GEORGE BOWIE.

George Bowie was once an eminent and leading lawyer on the Western Circuit: he resided at Abbeville. His father, Maj. John Bowie, was "one of Abbeville's noblest sons, whose sword was unsheathed at the beginning, and returned not to the scabbard until the close of the Revolution." He was born about 1771, and was, therefore, literally cradled in the bursting storm of the Revolution. How, or when he was educated, does not appear. He studied law with Ramsay and Goodwyn, at Ninety-Six, was admitted to the Bar, as his brother, Chancellor Bowie says, about '97 or '8—possibly a little earlier. The early admissions, even after the establishment of the Constitutional Court, were, most usually, in the Circuit Courts; and, hence, in Columbia, we had no Rolls reaching back further than 1800. I suppose Mr. George Bowie was admitted in the Circuit Court for Ninety-Six.

His brother says he was the first lawyer who resided at Abbeville. The County Court for that district began in 1785, when Abbeville was established as one of the six counties laid off as Ninety-Six District, (P. L. 358,) and the Justices of the County Court were authorized to erect the Court House and gaol in the most convenient part of the county. Tradition is, that the Court House, at Abbeville, was first established at General Pickens' Big Spring, and there it now is!

He married about the year 1800 Margaret, the third daughter of Gen. Andrew Pickens, late of Pendleton.

He had a full share of practice, and I have often heard this anecdote: "In a case, before Judge Bay, of assault and battery, Mr. Bowie was for the defence. He pleaded *molliter manus imposuit.* The proof turned out that his client knocked down the plaintiff with *a fence-rail.* The Judge, in his excitement said, in his stammering way, putting the accent on the first syllable of Mr. Bowie's name, "Mr. Bowie, Mr. Bowie, do you call that *molliter manus imposuit,* to knock a man down with a fence-rail, like a bullock?"

My acquaintance was slight and casual. In the spring of 1817, Judge Bay sustained some injury in one of his legs at Abbeville, which incapacited him from walking. Under the Circuit Court Act of '99, which provided, if a Judge be taken sick, &c., that the Governor might appoint and commission some proper person to sit as Judge in his place, Mr. George Bowie was appointed and commissioned, and rode the whole circuit for the afflicted Judge. I met the acting Judge and Bar, at Laurens. It seemed to me that Mr. Bowie discharged the duties very well. Perhaps he could not control the members of the Bar, for I remember to have heard it said, that my old friend B. H. Saxon, the Solicitor, interrupted Tyler Whitfield, Esq., in the midst of one of his speeches, by rising and saying, in one of his sternest tones, "sit down." Mr. Bowie said what is the matter? Mr. Saxon replied—"Why, may it please your Honor, the gentleman *is ranting!*" If that was a valid objection, how often might it not be urged now?

The Act of which I have spoken, (2 Faust, 325,) was soon after adjudged to be unconstitutional, and no more such appointments have since been made. Mr. Bowie, at that time, had retired from practice, which had made him not only comfortable, but rich. In a few years after, he removed to Pensacola, Florida; after a residence there of one year, he removed to Conecut County, Alabama, and thence to Dallas, where, in November, 1858, he was still living, in his 87th year.

He is the worthy son of a noble sire, and South Carolina mourns the withdrawal of many such from her soil.

JOHN GEDDES.

Gov. Geddes, as Mr. Thomas, in his reminiscences of his "Life and Times," says, was the son of a merchant in Charleston, who, by "frugality, was enabled to educate his son at the college in that city."

He studied law and was admitted to the Bar on the 3d day of October, 1797, in the City of Charleston.

He came from the mercantile class, and was much encouraged and pressed forward by the merchants and mechanics of the city. In addition to this his manners were popular, and his attention to business close and particular. He was, too, a Republican in politics, when many of the leading men of Charleston were Federalists. These incidents made him very popular.

He was soon elected to the House of Representatives of South Carolina, and, in 1810, he was chosen Speaker, and again in 1812. In the elections of 1814 and 1816, he was defeated as Speaker by Thomas Bennett, afterwards Governor.

While Gov. Geddes was Speaker, it was his habit to address every member by some military title. This often led to ludicrous mistakes. Capt. John Henderson, a member from Newberry, alluding to this, said, "the Speaker calls James Williams, Colonel, when," said he, "he was never anything but major, and a sorry one at that! I am," said he, "Major Henderson, and never was anything but a poor captain; brother Kenner," said he, "is called Captain Kenner; he never was anything but a sergeant, and he was broke at the first muster!"

This bad habit was corrected by a rule of the House, moved by Benjamin C. Yancey, in 1816, by which it was provided that a member should be addressed by the title Mr., and by none other.

Mr. Thomas says "the rapid rise of Gov. Geddes, was the cause of great mortification to the *aristocracy*, who hated him—he was in their way."

I have often heard this assertion from various quarters. The existence of an aristocracy in South Carolina, at any time, is an absurd idea. The old families of Charleston are, I suppose, alluded to. I have had occasion to mingle much in their society—the kindest, most gentlemanly, most hospitable in the State, are to be found among them.

I was in college a part of the period while Gov. Geddes was Speaker; at that time the students were permitted to visit the State House, with a view to acquire information. Gov. Geddes seemed to me a good Speaker, a pleasant and courteous officer.

In 1818, he was elected Governor, and during his term President Monroe visited Charleston. He entertained him most magnificently at his splendid mansion on Broad-street, lately known as the "Carolina Hotel." Long after his death, the Legislature refunded to his heirs a large portion of the sum expended by him in the entertainment of the President. He was, at a time anterior to his election as Governor, the Intendant of the city, the duties of which office he admirably performed.

About 1808, he was elected Major of cavalry; and, after his service as Governor, he was, as I remember, Brigadier General of what is now the Fourth Brigade. Mr. Thomas says he was afterwards a Major-General. He married Miss Chalmers, (the daughter of a wealthy mechanic,) by whom he had two sons and a daughter, all of whom, I believe, are now deceased.

Gov. Geddes has been dead many years. His profuse hospitality very much injured his ample means.

"He was not," says Mr. Thomas, "a very talented man, but his close attention to business, and his great tact and system, rendered him an excellent executive officer, and fully supplied the want of literary culture. He was very public spirited and enterprising, a good husband, a good father, and a warm friend."

ABRAHAM GILES DOZIER.

Abraham Giles Dozier lived at Cambridge, in Ninety-Six. He was a lawyer, much older than myself or Chancellor Bowie, having been admitted to the Bar, in Charleston, 6th February, 1798.

I first remember Mr. Dozier, at Edgefield, in the spring of 1815. He had then an immense practice in that Court, in which he seemed to me to be eminently successful. He indulged very much in being sworn as a witness in his cases. This bad custom, (*malus usus abolendus est*,) has very much ceased. It is, as it ought to be, discountenanced by the Bench, and frowned upon by the Bar. Mr. Dozier was so often sworn and so often gained his cases, that the lawyers sportively said: "the Jury think every word uttered by Dozier is on oath, and must be believed."

Chancellor Bowie, who also knew him, says of Mr. Dozier: "He was a good lawyer, more remarkable for patient and thorough investigation of his cases, than for profundity, as a lawyer. I remember," says Chancellor Bowie, "an instance of thorough investigation, evincing considerable acuteness and learning, which was highly creditable to him. It was in reference to the celebrated 'Laurens land cases,' tried at Abbeville." A motion for non-suit was granted, on the ground that the use created by the will of Col. Laurens was executed, and therefore the trustees could not maintain the action. The Constitutional Court sustained the ruling below.—2d McC., 252. The action had been brought in conformity to the advice of the celebrated Mr. Hunter, of Rhode Island, distinguished counsel in England, and the ablest lawyers in Charleston, (except Robert J. Turnbull, who thought the action ought to be in the name of the *cesturi que use.*) The will had been submitted by the defendants to Mr. Dozier, and he gave a written opinion to the same effect, as the judgment of the Constitutional Court. This was several years before the case was tried in 1822. For Mr. Dozier, I think, died in the great epidemic of 1815–'16, which, like the angel of the Lord, sent to punish the disobedience of King David, in undertaking to number the Children of Israel, whom God had declared should be innumerable, went through the land, and smote off the people of the Districts of Newberry, Laurens, Edgefield and Abbeville, fully one-tenth, and like him, was only stayed by the mercy of God. He left a widow, who afterwards married John Mayrick, of Ninety-Six, and a daughter, who is the wife of the Hon. John McGee, of Florida, and perhaps other children.

WILLIAM HASELL GIBBES.

William Hasell Gibbes was born in Charleston, on 16th March, 1754. He was the great-grandson of Robert Gibbes, who was Chief Justice in 1708. His father, William Gibbes, was one of the Secret Committee of Five of the Council of Safety, when the Revolution commenced, in Charleston—(Charles C. Pinckney, William Henry Drayton, Arthur Middleton, William Gibbes and Edward Wayman.) He studied law with John Rutledge, and went to London in 1774, in company with Thomas Pinckney, and other South Carolinians, and with them, entered as students in the Inner Temple. He was one of the signers of the petition to the King of "the native Americans residing in London," against the bills in Parliament, which were the last of the series of Acts which were the immediate cause of the Revolution. Garden, in his second volume of Anecdotes, gives the petition, and among the thirty signers, we notice Benjamin Franklin, Arthur Lee, and others, with sixteen South Carolinians. Mr. Gibbes had scarcely finished his law education at the Temple, when the contest began, and passports being denied, he, with other Carolinians, managed to escape to Bermuda, and there procured a schooner, in which they reached Philadelphia. He hastened to Charleston and joined the Ancient Battalion of Artillery, of which he was Captain-Lieutenant—Thomas Lamball being Major, and Edward Rutledge, Captain. He was at the battle of Beaufort, under Gen. Moultrie, and at the siege of Savannah, under Lincoln, and was the last survivor but one of his corps. He was admitted to the Bar before 1783, and was appointed "Master in Chancery," by Governor Guerard, on the 22d May, 1783; and at the meeting of the Legislature, on the 13th August, 1784, he was elected to that office, which he held until December, 1825, when he resigned after serving a term of forty-two years. He lived several years after this. In the year 1831, he closed his long life of usefulness. Of a large family which he left, Dr. R. W. Gibbes, of Columbia, and a sister residing at the North, are the only survivors.

Mr. Gibbes' position as Master in Equity, prevented him from practicing law. But his long service in that office, shows how important and valuable were his services in that department. He began with the three first Chancellors, John Rutledge, Richard Hutson and John Mathews. He witnessed all its changes for near forty-two years. In that time it grew from a little tribunal of few cases, to be one of great power, and many cases.

The first time I ever had the pleasure of hearing Colonels Drayton and Simons, was in December, 1811, on the trial of William Hasell Gibbes, Master in Equity, before the Senate, on Articles of Impeachment preferred by Thomas Lehre, Sen., and voted by two-thirds of the House of Representatives. *He was acquitted.*

JOHN S. COGDELL.

The following sketch of this accomplished gentleman, lawyer and *artist*, is from the pen of his nephew, Robert C. Gilchrist, Esq. My acquaintance began with Mr. Cogdell in 1816, when I was first a Member of the House of Representatives of South Carolina.

I knew him intimately, from that time to his death; and of him, it is no undue praise to say he was without spot or blemish. I never had occasion to know him, as a lawyer, but, as a Member of the Legislature and Comptroller-General, he was within my observation; and I always thought he discharged his duties in these respects, admirably well.

Some of his works of art I have seen. His portraits of Governor Williams, in the South Carolina College Library, and of Judge William Johnson, in the Library of the Court of Appeals, and his bust of Chancellor DeSaussure, also in the same Library, are life-like, and are excellent memorials of three great men.

His brother, Richard S. Cogdell, speaking of his trip to Europe, on account of ill-health, mentioned in the memoir by his nephew, says, "he made a voyage up the Mediterranean, with old Captain Pratt. I accompanied him. We were some months in Italy, owing to the French invasion, which gave him the opportunity of visiting Florence, Rome, &c. On his return home, he pursued his profession for some years. His partner, Mr. McCrady, dying, he was alone in his profession for years. Mr. William Lowndes, (the great Member of Congress,) desired to join him in business—was received—the firm was Cogdell & Lowndes, and continued for a short time" until Mr. Lowndes was elected to Congress.

John Stephano Cogdell, the son of George and M. A. Elizabeth Cogdell, was born in St. Michael's Alley, in the City of Charleston, on the 19th of September, 1778. Being at a period in our country's history, when it was exceedingly difficult to get an education, his early opportunities were very limited, and he was indebted almost entirely to his mother—who was a woman of remarkably strong and vigorous intellect—for the groundwork of a thorough English education His father was a meritorious officer in the Continental army, and during his necessary absence from his family, and in the unsettled state of affairs, his wife and her three sons, had, at times, to contend even with want. He has frequently detailed to me, (his nephew,) his early struggles—how he made use of that taste for the fine arts—for which he was afterwards so distinguished—to help his mother in her efforts to maintain her family.

He completed his education at the Charleston College, then under the presidency of Bishop Smith. I believe they did not, at that time, teach the classics, and the institution was hardly more than a grammar school.

He studied law in Judge William Johnson's office, and was admitted to practice in the year 1799, being then just twenty-one years of age, and was almost immediately after appointed City Attorney. His health failing him, however, he was advised to visit Europe, and in the year 1800, he crossed the ocean for the first time. Traveling through the picturesque scenery of Switzerland, and viewing the immortal works of the old masters in the galleries of the Vattican and Louvre, kindled anew his passion for the fine arts, and he returned to his home to devote every spare moment to the cultivation of his taste. While in Rome, he made the acquaintance of Pope "Pio Septimo," and other high dignitaries of the Papal Church, and brought away with him, several marks of their favor. This, added to an almost filial affection and veneration for his early preceptor and friend, Dr. Gallagher, may somewhat account for the regard he always manifested for that church. The handsome colossal representation of the crucifixion, which he twice painted and presented to St. Mary's Church, of which the venerable Doctor was the pastor, was only one of the many marks of favor which he exhibited.

His first partner at the Bar, was John McCready, (the father of Edward McCready, Esq.,) and, after his death, he was, for a short time, connected in business, with Wm. Lowndes. I have frequently heard Mr. Cogdell say that, at that time, he had the largest attorney's business at the Bar, and that there was no lawyer whose practice was more lucrative than his. Mr. Lowndes, when he asked to be taken into partnership, said, that he wished none of the emoluments of the firm, but that his object was simply to be introduced into practice through the influence of my uncle's name—that he might make it a stepping-stone to politics. The firm of McCrady & Cogdell was formed in the year 1800, and dissolved by the death of the senior partner in the early part of the year 1804. I am unable to find the date of the second co-partnership, but believe it was of short duration. In the year 1819, he took his brother-in-law, Robert B. Gilchrist, (afterwards United States District Judge,) into co-partnership.

In the year 1806, he married Maria, the only daughter of Adam Gilchrist, who was then a wealthy and influential merchant. He was, for several terms, a Member of our State Legislature. In 1819, he was elected Comptroller-General of the State, and, although re-elected to the office, he only served out half of the second term—leaving that office for the post of Naval Officer in the Custom-House, to which he was appointed by President Monroe, in the year 1821.

In the year 1832, he was elected President of the Bank of South Carolina—which office he filled until within a few months of his death, which took place on the 25th February, 1847, in the sixty-ninth year of his age.

In the midst of his most pressing business engagements, he always found time to devote to the pencil or the chisel, of which he was no mean disciple. He would often be up at the first streak of dawn, waiting, with pallette and brush in hand, for light sufficient to go to work; and scores of paintings (historical, portrait, landscape and fancy,) attest the versatility and proficiency of his genius, as well as his industry. The busts of Judges Bay and DeSaussure, Bishop England, and others of our noted citizens, (executed after their death,) show his skill in the other branch of art. He was also a firm patron of the arts—Washington Allston, Vanderlyn, Powers, and Sully, were his warm friends—and many a poor, but deserving artist, has had reason to bless the day that he crossed my uncle's path. I should add, that he was entirely self-taught.

All the benevolent enterprises of the day found him a willing advocate. He was one of the oldest and most active Commissioners of the Orphan House. I have several addresses written by him for the children of that institution, which show the humble, child-like piety for which he was always distinguished. (He was a member and vestryman of St. Michael's Church.)

JOSEPH GIST.

Joseph Gist was born the 12th January, 1775, near the mouth of Fairforest River, in Union District. He was thirteen years of age when he removed to Charleston, where he went to school. He finally graduated in the Charleston College, of which Bishop Smith was then the president. He studied law with that eminent attorney, Robert Goodloe Harper.

After his admission to the Bar, in 1799, he came into the country, and was married in the year 1800, to Sarah S. McDaniel, and located himself at Pinckneyville, which was originally a point designated for the Circuit Court of Pinckney District, consisting then of Union, Spartanburgh, York, and Chester; and although the Court was soon abolished, and Courts appointed for each of the counties, which were afterwards called Districts, yet the central character of the location made it a very desirable one for the practice of the law.

Col. Gist served, as the Representative of Union, eighteen years, in the House. He participated largely in the passage of the general Suffrage Bill. He was the leading Member of the upper country. Indeed, when I first saw the House of Representatives, in 1811, I think, he and Caleb Clarke, Esq., were the only lawyers who were Members above Columbia. I remember his speech for Judge Grimké, and his vote against the impeachment. This was an unpopular vote in the upper country, and especially in Union, but I never heard that it had the slightest effect against Col. Gist. How he got the title of Colonel I am not apprised. I presume it was as an Aid to one of the Governors, when such an appointment *was some distinction.*

In December, 1809, he was elected a Member of the Board of Trustees of the South Carolina College, and was continued, by successive elections, until he either declined, in 1821, or had been elected to Congress. My recollection is, he was elected to that body in 1820, and took his seat in 1821. If this be so, he was a Member of the House of Representatives from 1802.

He was six years in Congress, and in consequence of ill-health declined any further service. He died on the 8th of May, 1836, in the sixty-first year of his age, leaving his widow and an only son, John, surviving him. His son William died before him. His son John, after a short life of benevolence and usefulness, also died suddenly, leaving no children. His widow, Sarah, and his mother, still survived him.

Joseph Gist, as a lawyer, had the singular good fortune to have a large practice, almost from his beginning, and to retain it to the last. His services were so much desired that they were often sought by both parties. An incident of two men of wealth and standing, in adjoining districts—after a hard run, meeting at his gate, to employ him—in an important case is remembered by his brother.

This is not wonderful, for he was, indeed, *the lawyer* of the four districts in which he practiced. His influence with the juries was almost irresistible, and was very great with the Judges. He was a good lawyer, and understood the few books of his day, and applied them well. His style of argument was plain and clear.

In the House of Representatives he was listened to with great attention. His speeches were short and to the point. He was a man of business, and discharged a great deal of duty on the different committees. In 1815, he could have been elected a Judge, but declined the office, and placed in nomination a gentleman, then little known, David Johnson, and by his influence elected him. This was evidence of his high and just appreciation of an associate. For no man in the State ever filled the judicial office with more honor to himself, and benefit to the people, than David Johnson.

Col. Gist took pleasure in advancing the interests of young lawyers. Of those who studied with him (and they were many) all experienced, in a greater or less degree, his kindness. Many of them were his partners. Of that number was Nathaniel R. Eaves, Esq., of Chester. I had occasion, more than once, to experience his favorable notice. In 1819, he caused me to be employed in the great Equity case of Reid *vs.* Moorman; and in 1820, induced his friend, Col. Chalmers, to employ me in the contested election for St. Andrews, between Colonel Cattell and himself. It was a fine trait in his character, that he envied no one in the legal race for eminence.

He was a member of the Baptist Church, for several years before his death; and adorned his profession by a walk and conversation, which showed to all men that "he had passed from death unto life."

I regret that this notice of a good and great lawyer, and of an useful, good man, should be so meagre; but few memorials of the past are kept by relatives or friends. The dead are mourned for a time, and then their lives (with a few prominent incidents excepted) are forgotten. The only records, especially in the country, are the short inscriptions on the stones placed over their graves. This is sad! but it is the fulfillment of the Scripture, that "the place which once knew them shall know them no more, forever."

EDMUND BACON.

Edmund Bacon was born in Augusta, Georgia, on the 17th of April, A. D. 1776. He was of a Virginia family, his father having removed from that State to Georgia, before the Revolutionary struggle. His education was judiciously commenced and wisely directed. At an early age, he was placed in one of the best schools of Georgia, and afterwards, at the first academy in the City of Augusta, with positive orders and instructions from his guardian—(Mr. Bacon had been early left an orphan)—that he should be schooled after the severest manner. His preference for, and progress in, the dead languages, soon became apparent in obtaining the prize for the best translation of the "Ars Poetica." Indeed, so devoted was he to the pursuit of the ancient classics, as to have exhibited an utter repugnance to the idea of choosing a profession. General Glascock, brother-in-law and guardian of Mr Bacon, who was, naturally, inclined to the same pursuits, encouraged his ward in this regard. The difference, however, between the guardian and ward, as Mr. Bacon afterwards said, was, that the one, being a gentleman of great wealth and literary tastes, could afford to indulge his inclinations, while the latter, not so fortunate in his inheritance, could only hope to do so. Circumstances did for Mr. Bacon, however, that which, perhaps, neither he nor General Glascock would have agreed upon. About this time, it was announced that *General Washington* would pass through *Augusta*, and the city collected "her beauty and her chivalry" to welcome and fête him. Among other ceremonies, Mr. Bacon was chosen by the academy, of which he was a member, to receive the hero in an appropriate manner. This delicate and honorable task he accomplished, in an address so fortunate as to have attracted, not only the attention of that great man, but to have procured from him, for the orator, a *present of several law books.* Mr. Bacon had already entertained the idea of choosing the law as his profession, but this present decided at once his future calling. Though still very young, he resolved, with the consent of his guardian, to enter the celebrated law school at Litchfield, where he applied himself with great assiduity, and was graduated with full honors. On his return, Mr. Bacon settled in Savannah, with a view to the practice of his profession. He succeeded eminently at the Bar of that city, and before the Circuit Courts of Georgia. His health, however, began to fail, and he was advised to seek another and higher climate. This advice he had already made arrangements to follow, when he was urgently solicited to assist in the settlement and management of the estate of the celebrated *General Greene.* The labor consequent upon his accepting this offer, was exceedingly onerous, and the dispatch and application with which the business was effected, left him in a state of health still more impaired, but fortunately, with sufficient means to enable him to retire from his profession. With this view, he purchased a plantation in Beech Island, on Savannah River, where he hoped to renew his health and cultivate his tastes for the classics and belles lettres. He soon awoke, however, from this pleasant dream, to find his house destroyed by fire, his farming interests entirely neglected, and his overseer the only gainer. Shortly after this, Mr. Bacon visited Edgefield village, where he was hospitably entertained by Mr. George Butler. It was during the session of Court, and the eloquence, professional skill and learning displayed in the forensic encounters of that Bar, by such men as Wilde, Harper and Gantt, McDuffie and Petigru, Simkins and Butler, together with their accomplished and fascinating deportment, impressed Mr. Bacon so forcibly as to cause him to entertain the idea of joining himself to that brilliant galaxy. Mr. Butler immediately, and with all that frankness and hospitality so peculiarly his own, urged Mr. Bacon to carry this intention into effect, and even insisted that he should take possession *instanter* of one of his (Mr. Butler's) houses, then vacant, until better arrangements could be made. Mr. Bacon did so, having first given orders for the erection of a dwelling house of his own, which was completed in a short time, and in which himself and family were scarcely lodged, when a second fire left him worth even less than the preceding one; for, on this occasion, the flames were so devouring as to have endangered the life of his infant and consumed his entire library, containing among others, the books so honorably presented by Washington, the loss of which he ever afterwards bitterly lamented.

With returning health, came returning spirits. Mr. Bacon caused to be erected, near the site of the dwelling lately destroyed, a handsome mansion, resumed the practice of his profession, and in a very short time became one of the brightest ornaments of the Edgefield Bar. He possessed the power of oratory in a high degree, spoke *ore rotundo*, with grace and ease; and it is even now traditional among the older inhabitants of the district, that his eloquent appeals in capital cases, seldom failed to move the Jury to tears. It was at the festive board, and in social, convivial intercourse, however, that Mr. Bacon shone preëminent. On such occasions he was, indeed, "the star of the goodly company;" and such occasions frequently offered themselves at that time in Edgefield, particularly at the house of Col. Edward Simkins, whose position and estate enabled him to dispense a real hospitality, and to gratify the dictates of a true and genuine taste. Here, as also at the house of Mr. Bacon himself, were wont to assemble the great names above mentioned. Even among such spirits, Mr. Bacon was the acknowledged autocrat of the table, insomuch that on a certain occasion, when the famous Dr. Maxcy, of South Carolina College, was added to the list; no sooner had Mr. Bacon left the room, than he, (Dr. M.,) enthusiastically exclaimed: "A perfect Garrick, sir, a living, breathing, acting Garrick!" On another occasion, Judge Harper invited his brother Gantt to dine with him, saying: "Come, we shall be five, and you shall not lack of good cheer." The dinner was served to three, only, Mr. Bacon making the third. Upon Judge Gantt enquiring for the absent guests, his host replied: "I said we should be five—all are here. Behold!" pointing at the same time to Mr. Bacon, "behold Messrs. Gantt and Harper sitting with Jocus, Love and Comus." Years before this, however, the extraordinary wit and humor of Mr. Bacon along the circuit of the Georgia Bar, had given birth, under the magic pen of the well-known Judge Longstreet, (now the able and beloved President of South Carolina College,) in the famous "*Georgia Scenes*," to the creation of a character, rejoicing in the sobriquet of "Ned Brace," the orignal of which conception found no equal save in the uniqueness of its action. Mr. Bacon was the *original.* Mr. Bacon was an accurate linguist, and so familiar with the ancient poets and satirists, particularly Juvenal and Horace, as to be able to finish almost any sentence one might select. During one of the Bar dinners, at that time so regularly given in Edgefield, the health of Mr. Bacon having been proposed, a famous school-master of the day, and one of the guests, added: "Yes, in a full bumper, and *occupet postremum scabies*"— "*Extremum*," cried out Mr. Bacon; "you may, perhaps, torture postremum into meaning the *posteriors*, but never the *hindmost.*" Indeed, his love for such allusions sometimes rendered him apparently pedantic. On his piano he caused to be engraved the Horatian line so universally true to nature: "*Omnibus hoc vitium est cantoribus, inter amicos ut nunquam inducant animum cantare rogate; injussi nunquam desistant.*" "Not," said he, "that I suppose the performers will understand a word of it, but inasmuch as they are generally ladies, I well know the natural curiosity of the sex will incite them to inquire the meaning." On another occasion, he is said to have met a favorite associate, from whom circumstances had estranged him, with the exclamation—"*Non amo te, Vabidi, nec possum dicere quare.*" The gentleman in question being a scholar and critic, immediately extended his hand, saying at the same time "*mutato nomine, de me fabula narratur.*" They were ever after cordial friends. His knowledge of the English classics was equally correct. It was the custom in that day to deck the dining-table with a profusion of flowers, and on a certain occasion Mr. Bacon's was almost literally covered. One of the guests expressed his surprise and admiration of the beautiful custom, when Mr. Bacon replied: "Perhaps, sir, it may be unusual with you, but 'I, who am to the manner born,' deem it well nigh indis-

15

pensable." "A most charming custom, certainly," replied the former, "but one may be to the *manor* born, and yet know nothing of it; for I think you too well acquainted with the English terms, and with Coke and Littleton, to suppose that Shakspeare used or intended the word *manner*." Mr. Bacon joined issue, saying that "his honorable friend was certainly mistaken," and adding, that "it was such a mistake as a lawyer would be apt to make." The question was mooted, and as the guests were nearly all of the legal profession, they, (with the exception of Judge Butler, then fresh from the schools, and just on the threshold of his future bright and honorable career,) unhesitatingly pronounced against Mr. Bacon. A volume of Shakspeare, however, soon decided the correctness of the Messrs. B., senior and junior. Mr. Bacon then related an anecdote of a still more striking mistake, made by one of the first and best-read men in the country: "We were seated one evening in the theatre, in breathless expectation of the celebrated Kean as Richard the Third. At length the curtain rose, the famous tragedian appeared, and in the opening soliloquy—

> 'Now is the winter of our discontent
> Made glorious summer by this son of York,'

—made a very proper and graceful gesture toward the heavens. 'My hat!' cried my friend, 'I must go; this great humbug has already marred the beauty of the play by mistaking the *son* of York for the sun of heaven.'" Mr. Bacon was as remarkable for his humor, before the populace and at the electioneering hustings, as for his wit before the Bar and at the table. Witness the woolly steed, and the various pranks of *Ned* in the "Georgia Scenes." Indeed, his proneness to the indulgence of his humor, often led him into extremes, and on more than one occasion endangered his personal security. Certainty a very remarkable coincidence in the life of Mr. Bacon was, that he should have had the honor and gratification to consult the very law books presented him by *General Washington*, in assisting in the management of the estate of his great compatriot and brother officer, *General Greene*. "The moment I opened one of those books for that purpose," said Mr. Bacon, "was certainly the proudest if not the happiest of my life."

Mr. Bacon died on the 2d February, A. D. 1826, aged fifty. His remains rest in his family burial place in Edgefield.

The foregoing is from the pen of the talented Secretary of Legation, at St. Petersburgh, John E. Bacon, the grand-son of Edmund Bacon, Esq. Having, through a friend, the promise of Judge Longstreet, to give a sketch of Mr. Bacon, I have delayed the completion of this sketch as long as I could; but it has so happened that *he* who knew Mr. Bacon best, has failed to furnish his knowledge of him on this occasion. In this sketch there are inaccuracies in some slight particulars. Mr. Bacon never knew his grandfather, and he had, therefore, to speak of him from information derived from others. Edward Bacon, Esq., from the facts obtained through his grandson James, came to South Carolina in 1809, and must, very soon afterwards, have come to Edgefield Court House, and there settled as a lawyer. I first saw Mr. Bacon at Edgefield Spring term, 1825. Judge Martin who studied law with him at Edgefield, and whom he assisted in his education at Litchfield, was then his partner, and they had a large and lucrative practice.

Major George Butler, who is stated to have entertained Mr. Bacon, and furnished to him a house when he first came to Edgefield, graduated in the South Carolina College, in the class of 1809, at Columbia. I know he was studying law in Columbia in 1811, that he entered the United States army as a captain in 1812, and that he remained in the army until the peace of 1815 was proclaimed. He finished his study of the law at Newberry, and was admitted to the Bar in November, 1815. He could not, therefore, have been the person who entertained and furnished Mr. Bacon with a house. His uncle, Stanmore Butler, who was the Clerk of Edgefield Court, where, I presume, Bacon came, might have been the man.

Neither Wilde, Petigru, Harper, McDuffie, or Butler practiced law at Edgefield, when Mr. Bacon came. Wilde came to the Edgefield Bar, from Georgia, to attend to the Augusta Bridge case, after Mr. Bacon's death. Mr. Petigru never practiced regularly at Edgefield; since Mr. Bacon's death, he has visited it occasionally. Judge Harper could not have practiced at Edgefield sooner than 1812 or 1813, and Mr. McDuffie came to Edgefield, as the partner of Col. Simkins, in December, 1814, or the beginning of 1815, when Mr. Bacon had a most commanding practice.

I make these corrections, so that there may be no error in this interesting memoir of one of the most accomplished lawyers that ever figured at the Edgefield Bar.

Mr. Bacon married Eliza Fox, at Augusta, Georgia, 29th January, 1799. This amiable and intelligent lady still survives, adorning old age by her happy and cheerful disposition, which is a blessing to all around her. He left at his death four children, John, Edmund, Sarah and Thomas, of whom Edmund, Sarah, (or now Mrs. Wigfall,) and Thomas remain.

My friend, Dr. Laborde, a Profsssor in South Carolina College, says: "Between the years 1822 and 1825, I was a law-student, in the office of Messrs. Simkins & McDuffie; and Mr. Bacon being there, in the practice of his profession, it was my fortune to witness the happiest efforts which he made during this period, at the Bar of Edgefield. It is not for me to speak of the amount of his legal learning—to compare him in this respect with others; but I am not afraid to declare, that his language was chaste and elegant, and his elocution of a very high order. His natural endowments were extraordinary. His person was commanding, his face and head uncommonly fine, his voice chorded musical, aud of wonderful power. His style of speaking was highly finished, and I think I am justified in saying that, as a model of graceful and eloquent elocution, the Edgefield Bar cannot present another entitled to equal praise. Let it not be supposed, however, that his merit was that of the *mere rhetorician*; that he won applause because of this artistic skill, which was exhibited, and exerted none of that higher influence, which appeals to the heart and commands the affections. When the occasion demanded it, no one exhibited a livelier sensibility or a deeper feeling, or was more apt to awaken a sympathetic emotion in the bosoms of others.

"I remember when quite a boy, that I was much moved by

a speech from him, in behalf of a man who was on trial for his life. His whole soul seemed melted by compassion—the tears were flowing freely down his face, and he urged the acquittal of the unfortunate man, with a natural earnestness and eloquence which touched every heart. His appeals to the sympathies of the Jury, were those of a man who was pleading for his own life; and when, after sketching most touchingly, the picture of human passion and infirmity, the sad heritage of man—he called upon every member of the Jury to adopt for himself the sentiment of the Universal Prayer:

'Teach me to feel another's woe,
To hide the fault I see,
That mercy I to others show,
That mercy show to me.'

"The effect was electric, and all could see that the prisoner was soon to be restored to his family and friends. In his *social* character, Mr. Bacon possessed extraordinary attractions. His house was distinguished for hospitality; and at the social meetings of the gentlemen of Edgefield, none contributed more to innocent pleasure and enjoyment. As the presiding officer of an old-fashioned dinner party, he was without an equal. Abounding in story and anecdote, dealing them out with most generous prodigality, and in a way, too, which none of his cotemporaries could imitate, it is not saying too much, perhaps, to add, that his presence alone was almost sufficient to mitigate every woe, and drive sorrow from every breast."

The foregoing is high, and I have no doubt, deserved praise. My acquaintance with Mr. Bacon was slight; yet, I have seen and heard him in Court, and I have no hesitation in saying, that he was one of the finest *declaimers* to whom I ever listened. His voice was equal to that of Judge Gantt, which I have always believed was never surpassed.

The following epitaph, written by Judge Longstreet and inscribed on his tomb, is in poetic lines—a just portraiture of Edmund Bacon, Esq.:

"Within this grave, wrapped in his last long sleep,
Lies one whose doom a wife and children weep,

Whose many friends with anxious sighs regret
The loss of virtues they can ne'er forget:
The loss of virtues! No, the human form,
May waste below and feed the hungry worm:
The heart that kindly felt for others' woe;
The voice of eloquence, wit's joyous flow
May fade away, or rest within the gloom
Of Death's dominion—this cold narrow tomb?
But the bright mind on wings of bliss shall rise,
To dwell immortal in its native skies."

THOMAS HENRY EGAN.

He was a native of Maryland, read law in the office of Philip Barton Key, Esq., and practiced in his native State for a few years.

He married in Maryland, but had the misfortune to see the wife of his youth sicken and die soon after his nuptials.

This sad event so distressed him, that he left Maryland, and came to South Carolina before 1800. On the 7th of February, 1800, he was admitted to the Bar in the City of Charleston.

He practiced law with eminent success in Columbia and the adjoining districts, but a misalliance, in 1807 or 1808, was a rock ahead to his promotion or happiness. He and Robert Stark, Esq., were for years the prominent lawyers of Columbia, and, I might add, of the Southern Circuit. He made money, and, as Col. Chappell says, "a good deal;" "but exorbitant prices were paid by him for anything which he needed or fancied." He was extravagant in dress, and the result was, his money took to itself wings and fled away.

Under the Circuit Court Act of '99, on the occasion of Judge Grimké's sickness, Mr. Egan was appointed a Judge, *ad interim*, by the Governor, to hold the Circuit Court at Orangeburgh. He accordingly held the Court; and, as Col. Chappell says, delivered "an eloquent and learned address to the Grand Jury;" but, entertaining doubts as to the constitutionality of that law, he refused to try any criminal cases." His doubts, it seems, were very well founded, for the law has since been adjudged to be unconstitutional.

About 1813, he removed to Charleston, where he and his partner, McCormick, did a large business for a time; but some rash remark in the Court House, uttered by Mr. Egan, so displeased McCormick, that the partnership was dissolved, and Egan returned to Columbia. His business thus failed him, and about 1817 or 1818, he died in great want, and was buried in a ground which had once belonged to him. No stone marks his place of sepulture.

Yet this man of fine manners, who had been reared and educated as a gentleman, who was proverbially polite and urbane, whose ready wit made him the delight of every company, whose legal learning and eloquence entitled him to stand at the head of his profession—was a driveller, and idled much of his time before his death. He was the boon companion of such men as Kennard and Merrett. This all came from irregular living: his habits were intemperate, and when not under the influence of spirituous liquor, he made use of opium.

He was a well-read lawyer, and of liberal education. "He possessed," says Col. Chappell, "learning and sagacity sufficient to enable him to perceive the strong and weak points of a case; but he wanted discrimination and judgment to enable him to sieze and rely upon them, hence you found him disposed rather to skirmish than to meet at once the merits of a case. He was given to technicalities, and liked to take exceptions to proceedings, though not laborious enough to indulge much in special pleading. To non-suit his adversary, seemed to afford him as much pleasure as to obtain a verdict."

He was dignified in person, and had one of the most clear and musical voices which I ever heard. He either felt or affected great sensibility for all who were in difficulty or distress. In one of my cases, at Newberry, Spring Term, 1816, he insisted on the plaintiff, a widow, in the case of Julian *vs.* Caldwell, (2 Con. Rep. by Mill. 294,) to cry, saying to her, as I was concluding her case to the Jury, "do, my dear madam, do cry, you can't tell how much good it will do!"

He will be remembered by all who ever saw him by his high receding forehead.

Col. Chappell says, "he was charitable to the full extent of his abilities. In many things he was an imprudent man, hence he lived and died poor. Nevertheless, he had many excellent traits of character." He provided amply, even in his poverty, for an adopted daughter, who was strangly spirited away from Columbia; and, many years after his death, she returned and received a part, if not all, of the negroes which by deed he had secured to her.

JOHN DICK WITHERSPOON.

John Dick Witherspoon, Esq., was born 17th March, 1778, in Williamsburgh District. He was the son of Garvin and Elizabeth Witherspoon, who were Scotch-Irish Presbyterians, having migrated from Ireland to Williamsburgh District in 1734.

His father, Garvin Witherspoon, was one of the fearless men, who, side by side with Marion, accomplished those daring feats of partizan warfare, which made the boldest and bravest of the English hosts turn pale, whenever Marion and his men were mentioned. He was one of that devoted band who chose the swamp for their resting place; and night after night, from Snow's Island, plunged their snorting steeds into the waste of waters, swam to land, and before the morning light, had struck a gallant blow for liberty, and were again in the covert of Snow's Island. His mother was Elizabeth Dick, of Sumter District.

At nine years of age, John D. was sent to school to Thomas Reese, of Sumter District, a Presbyterian preacher, and a scholar of some celebrity. He remained at this school five years, and thence went to Long Bluff, (now Society Hill,) to Thomas Park, (afterwards Dr. Park,) Professor of Latin and Greek, in the South Carolina College.* In 1795, he entered

---

*Thomas Park, L. L. D., mentioned above, was, I think, a graduate of Brown University, and a native of Rhode Island. He was the intimate friend of Dr. Maxcy; and, after teaching many years at St. David's Academy, Society Hill, South Carolina, he was elected, in 1806, Professor of the Latin and Greek languages in the South Carolina College, and was so continued until the necessity of reform was apparent, in 1834; and when the College started again, with a new aspect, he, in 1835, was made adjunct Professor of Greek and Roman Literature. With his office of Professor of Greek and Latin, he was made Librarian, in 1806; this place he held until 1823. In 1834, it, with increased pay, was conferred upon him; and, in 1839, he became Treasurer and Librarian, and continued till 1844, when he soon after died. For more than forty years he was intimately connected with the College. He saw it grow up, flourish, and decay, and then again spring

Brown University, Rhode Island. He graduated in 1797. In November, 1797, he entered Mr. Rothmaler's office, as a law student, at Georgetown, South Carolina. In December, 1800, he was examined and admitted to the Bar, at Columbia, in a class with Abram Blanding, James Ervin, and Charles Motte Lide.

After his admission, he lived in Marion District, for four years, at the residence of his father, (who, after the war, lived in the District, called in honor of his chief,) and practiced law. He removed to Society Hill, in 1805, and on the 5th May, 1808, married Elizabeth, daughter of Samuel Boykin, of Camden, by whom he has had six children, two sons and four daughters.

From 1805 to 1820, he pursued his profession with great diligence and success, in the Districts of Marion, Darlington, Chesterfield, Marlborough, and Kershaw.

In 1809, he was one of the able counsel, who in vain endeavored to turn aside the sword of justice from Hey and Rochelle for the murder of Minter. (2 Brev. 338.)

In 1818, he was elected to the House of Representatives and, after a lapse of four years, was again elected in 1824. In 1825, he performed the troublesome duty of reducing into one Act, all the Acts, and clauses of Acts, relating to the powers and duties of the Commissioners of Roads. He was elected to the Senate in 1828.

He was the intimate friend and associate of that great and good man, Judge Wilde, and succeeded him in his practice after his election to the Bench. His known ability, and honesty, and his impulsive, generous disposition, which made him throw his whole soul into his cases, rendered him a very successful advocate and Jury lawyer.

He inherits that stern integrity which distinguishes the Scotch-Irish Presbyterian; and, by his character and conduct in Court, won the enviable title of the Honest Lawyer. Honest

---

up to usefulness. In all the stages of its existence, no man contributed more to its honor and stability. His gray hairs and virtues were looked to with honor and respect by all who ever had a place *there*. When he was more than seventy years of age he followed his Saviour, in baptism, and rose to newness of life.

Jack Witherspoon, was the soubriquet by which he was known during his professional career.

When I was admitted, Mr. Witherspoon examined me in Equity. He so managed my examination as to place me in the most favorable light before their Honors, the Chancellors, and to cause my admission, as it were, by acclamation. This kindness, I always have, and still do, remember. I met him from 1814 to 1820, at the Court of Appeals, in Columbia, and afterwards in the Legislature, and I always found him, as a professional man and gentleman, entitled to the most profound respect. In 1820, he retired from the Bar; and after serving his term in the Senate he abandoned public life, and as a country gentleman filled all those kind offices of hospitality and social intercourse, for which he was so well fitted.

He was born in 1778, and his infancy was therefore in the midst of that partizan warfare which his gallant father, with Marion and his men, by night and day, waged against the enemies of their country. His memory is filled with the hair-breadth escapes and daring attacks which his father used to pour into his youthful ears. These, combined with his accurate knowledge of the political and social history of the country, render him a most interesting companion.

His father's house was burned, and his mother, while he was yet a mere infant, driven into the woods, by Major Wemys, in his memorable campaign. Such an incident was not likely to be forgotten by any child, and his heart burned with that same inextinguishable hatred of tyranny and cruelty which sent his father into the swamps of the Pee Dee in defence of liberty.

Mr. Witherspoon, as husband, parent, master, and friend, has won the respect and love of all who knew him. He still lives, in his eighty-second year, and long may he be spared the honored patriarch of Society Hill.

ABRAM BLANDING.

Col. Abram Blanding is a name which carries with it the recollection of the person of an able lawyer, a virtuous man, an ardent citizen in whatever would advance his country's interests, and a philanthropist "whose works do follow him."

He was born in the village of Rehoboth, Massachusetts, on the 18th of November, 1776, and was descended, both on the part of his father and mother, from the Pilgrims, who landed from the Mayflower, at Plymouth Rock. His mother was an Ormsbee. He entered Brown University at Providence, Rhode Island, in 1796,* and remained there three years until he obtained the degree of A. B. He taught, during his collegiate course, at night, a mathematical class, to assist in defraying his expenses. Dr. Maxcy was then President of Brown University. His classmates were Fisher Ames, who took the first honor; Obadiah Jones, (an eccentric pedestrian,) afterwards a Judge in Ohio; Wm. Grant, Esq.; David R. Williams, of Society Hill, S. C., afterwards a Representative in Congress, a General in the United States army, and Governor of South Carolina, was his room-mate. He it was who induced him to seek his fortune, and make his home in South Carolina. It is thought that Col. Blanding took the second honor of his class; it may be, that there is some mistake in this; it is certain, however, that he took a high distinction. Virgil Maxcy and Dr. Benjamin Simons, of Charleston, were also his associates.

Immediately after his graduation, in '97, he removed to South Carolina, and fixed his location first at Columbia. He

---

* The statement furnished by his son, Col. James Blanding, made his entry at College in '96. This could not have been, as he remained there three years before graduation, which would have carried him to '99; he studied law, according to the Act then existing, for three years; he was admitted in 1800. This comparison of dates has induced me to fix his entry into College at '94, and his graduation at '97.

there taught school two years, and studied law with John Taylor, Esq., afterwards Governor of the State. Some of his pupils, Col. John J. Chappell, Col. James Gregg, and Col. Wade Hampton, are remembered. Col. Chappell says, the first time he ever heard of "parsing," was when Col. Blanding taught one of Major Clifton's scholars, at the Academy, to parse a sentence. He removed to Camden the latter part of 1799, and studied law under the direction of Judge Brevard. He was admitted to the Bar, after thus studying law three years, in 1802, and instantly entered upon a large and lucrative practice.

In a memoir furnished by his son, Col. James Blanding, of Sumter, it is stated, that Col. Blanding was elected a Representative to the South Carolina Legislature, from Kershaw, in 1805, and served seven years. It is certain that he was a member in 1806 and 1807; for with him originated the amendments of the third, seventh and ninth sections of the First Article of the Constitution, (1 Stat. 193,) and which placed representation in the House of Representatives on the basis of taxation and population combined. In 1809, he, with Col. Chappell, and others, voted against the amendment of the fourth section of the First Article of the Constitution, commonly called the General Suffrage Bill. Notwithstanding the unpopularity of this vote, the confidence of the people of Kershaw, in the talents and integrity of Col. Blanding were such, that they returned him again in 1810, and he again repeated his vote against that measure.

He educated his brother William, who became a distinguished physician, settled at Camden, and afterwards removed to Indiana.

On the 14th of April, 1805, one David Clinton was murdered in Kershaw District. It turned out that he was shot by one Jenkins, who fled the State, that Jesse Key was present and aided and abetted the murder, and that Lovick Rochelle was an accessory before the fact. Col. Blanding was employed to bring the offenders to justice; this, after four years delay, he accomplished. The indictment was the first precedent of that kind in which the principal, in the first degree, was stated to have shot the deceased; that Key, the principal in the second degree, was also charged as having committed the murder, and that Rochelle was an accessory before the fact. The prisoners Key and Rochelle, were tried, convicted and executed. The indictment and Col. Blanding's able argument, at April Term, 1809, of the Constitutional Court, at Columbia, will be found in 2d Brev. Rep. 238. The precedent of that case has been followed in subsequent cases.

Col. Blanding was a Federalist, and opposed to the war of 1812; but that did not turn him aside from the path of duty. He was, at the commencement of the war, the Captain of a fine troop of cavalry; he volunteered, with his troop, for the defence of Charleston; they were never called for; he rose before 1814 to the rank of Major; for in that rank he was one of the Court organized, as is stated in the memoir of Robert Stark, for the trial of Col. Tucker. He afterwards became the the Colonel of the cavalry regiment, which was once commanded by Col. Hutchinson. It seems his popularity, in Kershaw, received a severe check from the bitterness of his constant sarcasms against Mr. Madison and his Cabinet, for running away from Washington, when the British were approaching to capture it, and his derisive commentaries upon the affair of Bladensburgh! A letter from him to his future brother-in-law, Wm. F. DeSaussure, Esq., dated 21st August, 1815, will be found appended, and will show the bitterness of his feelings towards the fallen French Emperor, the Democrats, and Mr. Jefferson.

He married in December, 1815, Caroline, the daughter of Chancellor DeSaussure. In that year, he was elected a Trustee of the South Carolina College, and, in 1817, he was re-elected by the Legislature for four years. In 1837, he was elected a Trustee for the term of four years.

He was the mover of the Public Library at Camden, and aided the Orphan School in that town; he removed to Columbia in 1819.

In 1817, the internal improvement scheme, which looked primarily to the improvement of the navigation of the rivers began.

An Act was passed to create the office of Civil and Military Engineer, and John Wilson was appointed to that office, and $50,000 was directed to be annually appropriated for the internal improvement of the State: he was, by resolution, "to commence opening as early as circumstances will permit, Broad and Saluda Rivers, and to remove all such obstructions as may have been accumulated in the Congaree River." By the appropriation Act of that year, $50,000 was appropriated, and the work began by making a canal around Beard's Falls, on Saluda River. Public opinion, by the fall of 1818, in favor of internal improvement, had become overwhelming, and the Legislature, as is too often the case, plunged wildly into the scheme, and appropriated, or rather pledged the State to appropriate, $250,000 annually for four years, to be laid out and expended in improving the navigation of the rivers, and other water courses of the State, in opening and constructing turnpike roads, in cutting canals, and in such other works as will facilitate the transportation of the productions of the soil to market; and the appropriation of $250,000 was made, and then began that shameful waste of the public money, which gave contractors *a premium* on all which they could expend. The next year, (1819,) was passed an Act which created a Board of Public Works, to consist of five Commissioners, to be elected by the Legislature, and to continue in office one year; two of their body were to be appointed as acting Commissioners, and the office of Civil and Military Engineer was abolished. The Board consisted of Gen. Davies, Joel R. Poinsett, Abram Blanding, and two others. Mr. Poinsett and Col. Blanding were appointed the acting Commissioners, and the work of internal improvement commenced on the Catawba, at Lunsford; at Rocky Mount, on Broad River; at Lockhart's Shoals, on Saluda River; and at Beard's Falls, the Saluda Mountain Road, and the State Road from Columbia to Charleston. Mr. Poinsett was mainly instrumental in constructing the Saluda Mountain Road in 1820, and the spring called Poinsett's Spring, in the heart of the mountain, constructed at his private expense, will, like Absalom's pillar, be to him in the place of sons and daughters; and, each traveler, as he drinks from the gushing fountain, will, I hope, remember Joel R. Poinsett, as one of the purest and best sons of Carolina. I think Mr. Poinsett did not act after 1820, Col. Blanding was an acting Commissioner for 1820, 1821 and 1822, and did every thing which a man could do to carry out successfully the work of internal improvement. In 1822, the Board of Public Works was abolished, and Col. Blanding appointed Superintendant of Public Works, and continued as such until 1827, when he ceased to act and returned to the Bar.

In the period from 1819 to 1827, he faithfully and ably directed those public works: the State Road, Elliott and Wappoo Cuts, the works on the Santee, Congaree, Wateree, Catawba and Broad Rivers. If all had been finished, they would have been enduring monuments of his skill, industry and perseverance. The works on the rivers have been generally abandoned, and are now in ruins; the Saluda Mountain Road, the State Road, now superseded by the Rail-road, and some minor works, are all which remain of any value to the State for the immense sums lavished for internal improvements. But Col. Blanding is not to be blamed for this expenditure: he came into the work after it had been begun, and directed it with consummate skill towards the end intended. From 1822 to 1827, the writer, as a member of the Legislature, witnessed with admiration the patience and intelligence with which he explained to the Committees on Internal Improvement of the General Assembly, the progress of the public work, and obviated the objections put forward by ignorance, or subserviency to popularity. But all was in vain, the scheme at last failed, and the well-meant labors of Col. Blanding, for eight years, were almost profitless to the State and himself.

The Lunatic Asylum, at Columbia, is indebted to him for the trees which surround it; so also Blanding-street, in Columbia, rejoices in the beautiful trees planted in its centre by Col. Blanding.

In 1824 he commenced, and, after years of toil and experience, he successfully completed the water-works for the town of Columbia, at an expense from his private funds of $75,000.

This proved an unfortunate investment for him, but a great blessing to the town. After many years, (in 1835,) he sold out to the Town Council for less than one-third of the original cost, $24,000 in stock, bearing interest at five per cent., redeemable at the pleasure of the Town Council.

The City of Columbia owes to Col. Blanding's widow and children a debt of gratitude, which is badly paid by refusing to redeem the water-works' stock.

The Presbyterian Theological Seminary, in Columbia, is indebted to Col. Blanding for its foundation in 1830.

In December, 1830, he, with B. F. Dunkin and Job Johnston, were candidates for the office of Chancellor. The latter was elected.

In 1831, the Commercial Bank, Columbia, was organized, and Col. Blanding was elected the first President, and put it in motion, and gave it that character for safety, profit, and usefulness, which it has ever since maintained.

In 1836 began the project of the Louisville, Cincinnati and Charleston Rail-road. E. S. Thomas and Dr. Drake were those who first suggested it. The suggestion was received with almost universal favor by South Carolina, Georgia, Tennessee, Kentucky, Ohio, Western Virginia, and North Carolina. In July of that year, was witnessed the assemblage of this Convention at Knoxville, from all the States which I have mentioned. Col. Blanding, Gen. Hayne, Mr. Poinsett, and Chancellor Dunkin, with many others from South Carolina, attended. The dispute between E. S. Thomas and Dr. Drake, as to the paternity of the measure, was often intruded on the Convention. Gen. Coombs, of Kentucky, after listening to one of their contests, said to one of his companions, "take notice, I suggest the building of a Rail-road to the Pacific Ocean, and I shall, hereafter, claim the paternity of that measure. He little dreamed, that before his head was under the clods of the valley, in less than forty years, that which was jest then, would be reality. But marvellous has been the growth of our country, and still more marvellous the enterprize of her citizens. Although the Louisville, Cincinnati and Charleston Rail-road failed, from the magnificence of the

16

attempted execution, and dwindled down into the branch road from Branchville to Columbia, on the purchase of the Hamburgh road, which, consolidated, became the South Carolina Rail-road Company; yet Col. Blanding and Gen. Hayne did all which men could do to give it effect. Gen. Hayne closed his valuable life in its service.

"In December, 1838, Col. Blanding was elected President of the South-Western Rail-road Bank, which was a part of the scheme for the building of the Louisville, Cincinnati and Charleston Rail-road, and as such he felt it to be his duty to accept. He accordingly gave up his office as President of the Commercial Bank, and removed to Charleston. That winter, he made explorations of the neighboring country and streams, for the purpose of supplying the City of Charleston with water, and reported in favor of a supply from the Edisto River. He organized the Bank, and put it in successful motion; but, sad to say, although having used the precaution of a summer retreat on Sullivan's Island, he was attacked with yellow fever, and died on the 20th day of September, 1839. Speaking of this to his sister, the Honorable Wm. F. DeSaussure says, with an eloquence and feeling which ought to be preserved, "the fatal result and the date you too well know. I was for many years associated with him in business, and had for him the devoted affection of a younger brother. I loved him for his devotedness to duty, his perfect integrity, his generous heart, his pure patriotism, his knowledge, his clear intellect: my unhidden tears flow while I write."

It remains that we should turn back over his life, and consider him as a lawyer. He was conceded to be first in his profession for fully twenty years. He is one of the few men who, after devoting themselves to other distracting pursuits, could and did return to a successful pursuit of the law.

Col. Blanding was remarkable for his careful preparation for the argument of his cases, and for the clear, logical, and learned presentation of his views. His arguments were never long or wearisome; what he said was to the point, and he added nothing superfluous. It is impossible to refer to the many arguments, which from 1830 to 1838, it was my privilege to hear. I select two cases only. His argument in 1834, in the State (*ex relatione* McCrady *vs.* Hunt, 2 Hill, p. 1,) is, I think, as fine a specimen of forensic argument as can be found. It commences at page 150, and extends to 189. If Col. Blanding had never made any other argument, this would have given him immortality; it literally annihilated all which was or could be said on the other side.

His argument in Murray *vs.* The South Carolina Rail-road Company, (1 McM., 388,) is a most ingenious and interesting discussion of the liability of a Rail-road Company for injuries to one of their employés.

Col. Blanding, at his death, left his widow and five sons: two of them, William and James, followed their country's standard through all the bloody fields of Mexico. (The first-named, as Captain of the Charleston company.)

Of Col. Blanding, little more need be said. As a lawyer, a man and citizen, his memoir testifies to his great, his excelling worth. Few men, in a life of 53 years, accomplished so much, or earned such a deserved reputation.

In all the relations of life, public and private, he is entitled to have it said, "well done thou good and faithful servant."

We append this letter, which may prove interesting to the reader :—

October 7, 1805.

Sir,—Nor have I the pleasure of knowing you. But as a witness, material to Gen. Harrington's defence, I have taken the liberty of sending you a subpœna. Although there may be no authority, but the Legislature, which the Constitution authorizes to question executive proceedings, yet permit me to presume, that an ex-Governor may sometimes know facts which a Court of Justice may think proper, and may possibly possess the power to compel him to disclose. It is not to investigate your official proceedings, but to testify facts, that your presence is wanting at Court, and I know of no exemption from the discharge of this duty, which every citizen owes the public justice of his country. Although it may be the first time that a person connected with the executive station has been questioned respecting a matter of office, yet the novelty of the thing will hardly convince me that, if he knows a part material to a defence, he will find in our Court of Justice an exemption from giving testimony. The source from whence he has drawn his knowledge will hardly exclude the party from the benefit of it.

I have not, in the humble station I hold at the Bar, been in the habit of calling witnesses unnecessarily into Court, much less of delaying the course of justice by resorting to the pitiful expedient you attribute to me as General Harrington's attorney. Nor should I now have called on you, could other testimony have supplied the want of your evidence, or could your examination by commission have been in the regular course of proceedings taken.

As far as your heavy censure has fallen on the conduct of General Harrington, I request you will do him the justice to believe, that his counsel have directed him in the selection of such witnesses as may be necessary to his defence. His conduct has been the result of acquiescence in their directions; and if they have erred, let him not bear the weight of your displeasure, or sink in your esteem.

To convince you how little I am disposed to give you unnecessary trouble, I now assure you, that should not the cause be tried at the next Court, I will use my best exertions to procure the plaintiff's consent to your examination by commission. But at the same time, I must beg you to believe that, should I fail in this endeavor, I shall not neglect the duty I owe my client, of compelling the attendance of such witnesses as his defence may require.

I am, respectfully, your obedient servant,

ABRAM BLANDING.

Hon. JOHN DRAYTON, Charleston, S. C.

CAMDEN, August 21, 1815.

Dear Sir,—I may be compelled to visit Lancaster this summer. This necessity I should consider a real misfortune, but that it will bring me into your neighborhood, and enable me to compensate myself for the disagreeable ride, by the pleasure I shall receive in spending a day or two with you.

The fall of the French Emperor has been more sudden than was expected, and proves very satisfactorily, that his late elevation was the work of the army; and that his power did not rest on the affections of the people. Indeed, it is strange, that a people, who have suffered so much from his ambition, should entertain any other than sentiments of detestation for him. The Democrats here are quite at a loss how to dispose of him, or how to fill the vacant throne. They seem to wish it in their power to do both. They would, no doubt, invite their fallen favorite to "this asylum of oppressed humanity." If he comes, I hope he may be quartered on his good friend, Jefferson, and both be set to writing the history of their own times. I guess they could give a tolerable account of the continental system and embargo. The young Duke of Orleans seems to be the favorite candidate for the throne. It seems our Democrats have some confidence in hereditary virtue. The son being known only by the merits of the father would, no doubt, be elected, if the choice depended on them. They want no better reason for making the one a king than that the other was a regicide.

I have understood that you visit Columbia in September. If you do, I hope you may not be prevented from passing through Camden. We shall be much pleased, if you can spend a day with us; and I will then accompany you across the sand hills to our friends in Columbia.

The much-to-be lamented death of Mr. Hooker will make some change in the course of business on your circuit; and I doubt not that you will receive your share of what must now pass into other hands. I have almost concluded to attend the Court of Common Pleas, at Columbia, in future. This I can do with ease, by dropping a Pee Dee Court. With the prospect before me, the temptation to make this change is so much increased, that I shall not be able to resist it, although a change of circuit, generally, is not advisable.

Do make my best respects to Mrs. D. I hope we may soon meet again, in that charming circle, where we first formed our acquaintance.

I am, dear sir, very sincerely, yours,

A. BLANDING.

Wm. F. DeSaussure, Esq., Landsford, Chester, S. C.

JOHN HOOKER.

How soon does the memory of great virtues and great acquirements vanish from the memory of the sons of earth? Who now has any remembrance of John Hooker, even in the city where he last lived and died? To rescue, in some degree, the memory of the Bench and Bar from this oblivion, is the end of the work to which I am devoting so much time and attention.

John Hooker was the eldest son of Col. Noadiah and Mrs. Rebecca Hooker, of Farmington, Connecticut. He was born in the year 1774, and graduated at Yale College about 1800. He studied law, and was admitted to the Bar, in Connecticut in 1802, and came to South Carolina in the following year.

He was first employed by General Wade Hampton as the tutor of his sons for one or two years, and was admitted to the Bar, and in Columbia commenced the practice, as the partner of John Henry Egan. In about four years, he removed to Yorkville and remained there three years.

Through the influence of his early friend, General Hampton, and other friends, in Columbia, he returned to that town. On the 8th of October, 1808, he was married to Miss Mary Ann Chapman, the eldest daughter of Mr. Gersham Chapman, of Columbia. He was elected a Trustee of the South Carolina College in December, 1813, and successfully practiced his profession in this city to his death.

This said event took place on the 28th July, 1815. He was then forty-one years old, and, of course, he was cut off in his prime, and in the midst of his usefulness.

Mr. Hooker was one of the committee who examined me in May, 1814, for admission to the Bar. Whether I ever saw him before or afterwards, I do not remember, and, of course, therefore, I cannot speak of him as he ought to be.

From my much-esteemed friend, Dr. George W. Glenn and his lady, the widow of Mr. Hooker, I am indebted for the means of giving this short sketch.

Dr. Glenn says: "I never heard Mr. Hooker but once at the Bar of South Carolina, and that was in Columbia, when I was a student of the South Carolina College." (Dr. Glenn graduated in the second class, December, 1806.) "Mr. Hooker spoke in behalf of a poor person, who had been slandered by a rich man. He insisted on a verdict of heavy damages, and said it would learn the defendant two important lessons, first, to be more careful about speaking evil of his neighbors, and second, the necessity of keeping his tongue within proper bounds."

He was, it seems, very cautious about the institution or defence of cases where the justice was doubtful, and, when fully satisfied that a case or defence was founded in injustice, no fee could induce him to undertake it.

The following, written by one of South Carolina's most eminent and loved sons, Chancellor DeSaussure, and inscribed upon Mr. Hooker's tomb, is the best sketch of his character, as a man and a lawyer, which can now be given.

"Possessed of an acute, logical mind, and a sound judgment, guided by the purest integrity, he became a very eminent member of the Bar of South Carolina. The public respected him for his virtues; the Court esteemed him for his talents and learning; his brethren loved him for his amenity and kindness. In private life, his unassuming deportment, his active benevolence, and the purity of his affections, endeared him to a large circle of friends, but above all, to the beloved partner of his life and her family."

From the life of Mr. Hooker, one matter deserving the imitation of the Bar of the present day, ought to be noticed, to wit: his refusal to subserve "the cause of injustice." I am well aware that lawyers, by employment, can, generally, only see justice on the side of their clients. Yet cases, and especially criminal cases, are often so obvious, that the "injustice" cannot fail to be perceived. Yet lawyers leave no means unresorted to, which may avail a client. The sickly sentimentality of the present day, which is catered to by some at the Bar, is to save criminals from capital or disgraceful punishment. The safety of society is totally disregarded, and the preservation of the guilty Cain, though covered by the blood of the righteous Abel, is regarded as a first duty, both by Bar and Jury.

Well might my pure and experienced friend, Dr. Glenn, say, "the lawyers make Herculean efforts, and compass 'sea and land,' to clear the notoriously guilty;" and I would add, are too often successful by the weakness or wrong-headedness of Jurors. "Murder," adds my friend, "is rife in our midst, and I apprehend our State will be compelled to adopt the penitentiary system to enable her, in some measure, to punish the guilty. When you and I were Members of the Legislature, many years ago, the policy of that system was brought before that body and ably argued, but no definite action taken at that time. A committee was, however, appointed to collect information and report at the next session, Daniel E. Huger was the chairman, and made an able report against the policy of adopting the system at that time. You recollect, no doubt, the main argument relied on in that report, which was from the best authority obtained in Europe and this country, that *when* it was established, crime, in proportion to population, was on the increase, while in South Carolina where there was no penitentiary, crime, in proportion to population, was on the decrease. Now the tables are turning, if not already turned."

True, most true, my good friend. We have lived to have the experience of more than forty years since that period; and of late, together, we have mourned over the blood which has stained the once pure vestments of our native Newberry. We have both learned the necessity of a penitentiary system to punish the guilty, which we once thought unnecessary; and I hope the public mind has made *that* "a fixed fact," with a certainty unknown to the origin of the term.

To the members of the Bar, it may be said: Brethren, be like Mr. Hooker—spurn the wages of injustice as you would those of *sin*. Be like him, pure and spotless, and the communities in which you live will be so too.

JOHN JOEL CHAPPELL.

It is not the general purpose of the author to give sketches of the living members of the South Carolina Bar; but of such as have retired or removed, where he could obtain suitable autobiographies, he has thought it desirable to preserve such memorials by placing the substance in this work.

The gentleman, whose name is above, is the oldest living lawyer in South Carolina. He has long been most advantageously known to the public; hence I propose that his name should live among his brethren before he is called to his last home.

He was born in Fairfield District, on Little River, on the 19th of January, 1782, but his parents, when he was an infant, removed to Richland District, on the Congaree River, where he was raised, and where he still lives. His education was, as usual, first in the common schools of the neighborhood. In 1794, or '95, he was sent to Columbia, but the small pox, which prevailed in the young town, soon broke up the school and sent him home, until the next year, when he returned, and progressed in the acquirement of an academical education under the teaching of Major William C. C. Clifton, the Rev. David E. Dunlap, the Rev. Mr. Reid, and Colonel Abram Blanding.

In the spring of 1800, he devoted himself to the study of the law for four years, (the term then required for non-graduates,) in the office of Thomas Henry Egan, Esq.

The South Carolina College had not, at that time, been founded. In the winter of that year, the Act, establishing it, was passed. The first students entered its walls in the winter of 1804, after Colonel Chappell was admitted to the Bar. He was licensed, as an attorney-at-law, at the Spring Term of the Constitutional Court, at Columbia, in 1805, and settled, as a resident lawyer, in Columbia. He says, "I rode the circuits with the Judges and lawyers whether I had cases or not, and attended at Orangeburgh, Barnwell, Edgefield, Newberry, Richland, and Lexington, after it was established as a judicial district.

The course pursued by Colonel Chappell deserves to be commended to the young lawyers of the present day. Instead of lounging about their own Court-Houses, if they would strike out and ride on horseback the circuit in which they live, and make arguments, "without money and without price," whenever they could get the chance, they would learn more law, and get more practice in a year, than they do now in ten. I recollect seeing, at Newberry, attending the Courts as far back as 1807, Robert Stark, from Columbia, Richard Gantt, from Edgefield, William Nibbs, from Ninety-Six, Eldridge Simkins, from Edgefield, John C. Calhoun, from Abbeville, Robert Creswell, from Laurens, Samuel Farrow, from Spartanburgh, George Warren Cross, from Charleston, and Colonel John Joel Chappell, from Columbia. All seemed to have business. After I was a Judge, Robert Stark and Colonel Chappell, who were lawyers of some distinction, when, as a school-boy, I looked on and wondered at their dignity as lawyers, rode a part of my first circuit with me in the spring of 1829.

In a year or two after Colonel Chappell's admission to the Bar of the Law Courts, he was licensed as a Solicitor in Equity.

Like most young lawyers, *then* and *now*, Colonel Chappell sought and found promotion in the ranks of the militia. In 1801 or '2, he was appointed Adjutant of the Thirty-third Regiment, which commission he retained until 1805, or 1806, when he was elected Captain of the Beat Company, which then included the whole town of Columbia. In 1808, or 1809, he was elected Colonel of the Thirty-third Regiment.

In October, 1808, he was elected from Richland District a Member of the House of Representatives, of South Carolina, and took his seat the fourth Monday in November following. At that session was ratified the amendments of the Constitution, which provided for the apportionment of Representatives upon the basis of population and taxation combined, by allowing one Representative for every sixty-second part of the white inhabitants, and one Representative for every sixty-second part of the whole taxes. This wise provision, which harmonized the upper and lower country, and ended all the disputes which had divided the two sections on the subject of representation, originated, as Colonel Chappell says, with Colonel Blanding, who was then a Member from Kirshaw District.

In an autobiography, now before me, Colonel Chappell says: "I had never ascribed, nor heard any other person ascribe the honor of originating this new principle of representation to any other person than Colonel Blanding, until a few years ago, meeting with Governor R. F. W. Allston, in Columbia, he requested me to give him my recollections about the matter, stating that he wished to collect facts for some work, which he designed publishing, and said he had recently seen Judge Cheves on the same subject, and mentioned that his (Governor Allston's) impression was that Mr. Lowndes had suggested the idea of such a plan of representation a year or two before the time referred to, and whilst Mr. Lowndes was a Member of the Legislature. *Of this*, I have no knowledge or recollection, but I am strengthened in my impression of Colonel Blanding being the originator, from the fact, that soon after it was published, I saw a letter from the late Governor Taylor, from Washington City, published in some newspaper, in which Colonel B. was highly complicated for having conceived so novel, just, and wise a plan for governing our State, and for harmonizing the disquietude of our people. The honor is great to whichever of these gentlemen it belongs, and if it could be divided it is sufficient to ennoble each of them."

In the session of 1808, was passed, "the Act for the better arrangement of the sitting of the Courts of Equity, and the establishment of Courts of Appeal for the same, and for other purposes therein mentioned." By this Act two additional Judges of Equity were provided to be elected, and accordingly Theodore Gaillard, (the Speaker,) and Henry William DeSaussure, were chosen to fill those highly responsible offices; in the Act and the election Colonel Chappell concurred.

In 1808, was passed the "Act to authorize the citizens of

this State, in the several Circuit Districts within the same, to elect by ballot, the Sheriffs within their several respective districts."

Of this, Colonel Chappell says: "I sanctioned, though I did not like the change, the giving the election of Sheriffs to the people. I thought it of doubtful policy, but as it could be done without altering the Constitution, and if found impolitic, the Legislature could resume the power, I approved it." This change was, it is true, very doubtful; and in fifty years it has, in many instances, operated to put bad men into the office; yet, in the main, I think it has done as well, if not better, than if the Legislature had retained the power. My friend, Colonel Chappell was mistaken in supposing the Legislature "could resume the power." Power once yielded to the people can never be resumed.

In 1809, Colonel Chappell was elected a member of the Board of Trustees of the South Carolina College. He, with Benjamin Haile, and John Murphy, a graduate, in the class of 1808, were appointed on the Executive Committee, charged very much with the government of the college during the recess of the Board. They had a very delicate duty to perform in attending to the demerits of the students, steward and faculty. These duties they seem to have performed very well. Colonel Chappell was Chairman, and says: "I don't know that my position was ever more embarrassing, than when, as Chairman, it became my duty to catechize and lecture the parties, and especially its venerated President. But it had to be done and a report made to the Board at the succeeding meeting. This was done verbally." "Our conduct," says Col. Chappell, "was approved." One of the Board (Richard Gantt, Esq., afterwards Judge Gantt), was quite complimentary to me.

Colonel Chappell says, that to induce a closer observation of the college, on the part of the Legislature, he introduced a resolution, "That both Houses would attend the College Commencement." "It was adopted," he says, "and each House, preceded by its officers, marched to the college and witnessed the ceremonies, which custom, I think, has been observed ever since, and is a good one." I have sought, in vain, for the resolution; no trace of it can be found, and had it not been for the statement of Colonel Chappell we never should have known whence came the custom for the Legislature to attend the Annual Commencement on the invitation of the Board.

In 1809, originated the amendment of the Fourth Section of the First Article of the Constitution of South Carolina, called the General Suffrage Bill, and which, in 1810, became a part of the Constitution. In 1809, Colonel Chappell voted against this popular measure with thirty-three other members. From this it seems that the measure passed by a bare constitutional majority. In 1810, he was again returned for Richland District by an increased and flattering majority; and again, with a diminished minority of thirteen other members, voted against the amendment of the Constitution (the general suffrage). The wisdom of the change is from a property qualification, a free-hold of fifty acres of land, or a town lot, or not having such, the payment of three shillings sterling tax, to mere residence of six months by a free white man of the age of twenty-one years, was then, and still is, of very doubtful policy. Its working for more than fifty years, and its universal application throughout our great and growing republic, has not, it seems, resolved the doubts of the venerable gentleman of whom we are speaking. Indeed, in the great cities New York, Philadelphia, Baltimore, Charleston, and New Orleans, its operation has been most mischievous. In the extra session of August, 1812, he was Chairman of the Committee who prepared the "Act prescribing, on the part of this State, the time, place and manner of holding elections for Representatives in the Congress of the United States."

In 1811, Colonel Chappell associated with him Mr. William Harper, in the practice of the law. The partnership was of short duration, as Mr. Harper dissolved it while the Colonel was attending to his duties as a Member of Congress.

In May, 1811, Colonel Chappell was married to Sophia Maria, the daughter of Colonel John Greene, of Georgia, who, in the Revolutionary war, was an active Whig, but who had the misfortune to be severely wounded, by having both his arms broken, and thus rendered so stiff that he could not tie his cravat. Mrs. Chappell lived until September, 1834, when she died, leaving seven children surviving her. Six died before her, all very young, except the oldest daughter, who died after her marriage with A. P. Calhoun. Colonel Chappell has testified his great respect for his deceased wife by remaining a widower.

In 1812, soon after the declaration of war, Colonel Chappell was appointed, by Governor Middleton, to the command of the militia regiment, which was ordered to be organized for the defence of the seaboard. Majors Savage Smith, of Georgetown, and Banoni Robertson, of Fairfield, had command of the battalions. The whole regiment was never called into service, and of course Colonel Chappell never rendered any service.

In October, 1812, he was elected a Member of Congress, from Orangeburgh, Barnwell, Lexington and Richland; and in May, 1813, took his seat at an extra session called by President Madison, to provide the ways and means of carrying on the war declared in the previous June, but for which Colonel Chappell says, "no adequate means had been provided." In 1814, he was the President of the Court Martial which tried Colonel Starling Tucker, a full account of which is given in the memoir of Mr. Stark.

He attended five sessions of Congress, having been elected a second time in 1814. He was, he says, "of the then Republican party, as opposed to the Federalists, and gave his support to the administration of Mr. Madison." "I have since been," says he, "Democrat, though not ultra. I have been in favor of States Rights, and of Nullification, and of Secession, though with co-operation. But all these have lost their ascendancy with me."

Col. Chappell was a good Member of Congress, and was much respected on account of his consistent course. He says he committed two great errors while in Congress. The first was in attending the first great Congressional Caucus to nominate a candidate for President. This may, or may not, have been an error; but surely it was a very venial one. The great objection to a Congressional Caucus was, that those who were never intended to guide the people in that matter, in this way, usurped the power of making the President. This destroyed the Congressional Caucus, and instead of it have sprung up the Conventions appointed by the people to nominate the Presidential candidates. It is but another name for the same thing. And I confess I don't see the just objection to either. It is but a part of the machinery which consolidates the power of the different parties into which the people suffer themselves to be divided. It is true, if we could go back to the times when merit placed a man in power, I should say, let all caucuses and conventions perish; but *now* they are necessary evils.

The second error of which Colonel Chappell accuses himself was, in advocating the establishment of the United States Bank. He says: "I then deemed it necessary to aid in the fiscal concerns of the Government, not then being, as I afterwards became satisfied, that there was no authority given to Congress to establish such an institution." If the Colonel erred in this matter, he erred in very good and great company, such as his friends Mr. Calhoun and Mr. Clay.

So too, it seems, he thinks he committed a third error in voting for the Tariff of 1815, to protect domestic manufactures. This was, however, a popular Southern measure, intended to sustain the factories, which had grown up during the war. It is true, it laid the foundation for the Tariffs of protection, which ended in producing Nullification, and the abortive attempts at secession. But the Colonel here again had the companionship of Mr. Calhoun.

The Compensation Bill passed in 1815, which provided a salary of $1500 per annum to each Member of Congress, instead of a per diem allowance, induced Colonel Chappell's constituents, in 1816, to refuse to return him. This misfortune was by no means singular, for every Member who voted for it, with the exception of Henry Clay and Richard M. Johnson, of Kentucky, and John C. Calhoun of South Carolina, was refused a re-election. In not quite forty years afterwards, the policy which gave rise to the Act of 1816, gave occasion to the Act which fixed the compensation of Members at $3,000, and not a solitary objection has been made by the people. They were at last convinced that those *who worked by the day* worked much more slowly than those who worked by the job.

Mr. (afterwards Judge Harper) having dissolved his partnership with Colonel Chappell, soon after he entered Congress, and the latter finding he could give little attention to his legal business, transferred the whole of his practice to the late Colonel James Gregg.

After failing in 1816 and 1818, to be returned to Congress, Colonel Chappell, unwilling to remain idle, and also, desiring to make his services available to the support of his young and increasing family, presented himself to the Legislature as a candidate for Secretary of State. He was disappointed in his candidacy; and after due reflection, in 1821 or '2, returned to the Bar, and resumed practice in Orangeburgh, Richland, Fairfield, and Lexington, which he continued until the last ten years. He continued longer than he intended, that he might introduce his son into practice, but at his death his motive to continue at the Bar ended.

Colonel Chappell, at the instance of Judge Colcock, in 1830, or '31, accepted the office of a Director of the Branch Bank, at Columbia, and has ever since retained it until very recently. He has never held any office of emolument under the State although he has, ever since he attained his majority, been in her service. He is now in his seventy-eighth year, and when I last saw him, with the frost of many winters on his head he presented the same erect and manly person of six feet which I had seen for half a century, and the same plain, though courteous and kind manners.

Colonel Chappell had an easy, fluent, though not impressive elocution. He was a good lawyer, and certainly has been always regarded as an honest man.

GEORGE WARREN CROSS.

George Warren Cross was born in Charleston, South Carolina, the 12th June, 1783. He was the only son of Captain George Cross, who was a zealous patriot in the war of the Revolution, and as a naval officer, rendered important service in the harbor of Charleston.

Col. Cross was educated at one of the best grammar schools in his native city, and at an early age commenced the study of the law, under the advice and direction of his uncle, Judge Lewis Trezevant, then one of the associate Judges of this State. The Judge was very conspicuous as a severe special pleader and thorough disciplinarian. With such an instructor to fit him for his work, Mr. Cross was admitted to the Bar 17th December, 1804. He diligently applied himself to his profession, and in a few years enjoyed a handsome and increasing income. He had the advantage, in his youth, of learning to read and speak fluently, the French language, which he acquired at home, and by this he obtained many clients from the French citizens of Charleston and of other States, who were among the most liberal of his patrons. He was elected First Lieutenant of the Washington Light Infantry, at its formation in 1807, when William Loundes was elected its captain, and William Crafts ensign. He succeeded to the command of the company in 1809, and held it until 1816, with the most flattering success, contributing much to its permanent establishment.

In 1816, he received the appointment of Colonel of the 16th Regiment of infantry, which he retained for many years. He, also, was several times chosen to represent his native city as a Member of the House of Representatives of South Carolina. In all these offices, he exhibited the highest integrity, fidelity and patriotism. He was an accomplished gentleman and a most affectionate son, husband and parent. He died in Charleston, after a very short illness, with symptoms of the prevailing cholera, on the 26th October, 1836.

Mr. Cross, as far back as 1808, rode the Southern Circuit. I have often seen him at Newberry. He was often employed, and had the reputation of a good lawyer.

WILLIAM LOWNDES.

This distinguished and truly great and good man, was the son of Rawlins Lowndes, the first Governor of South Carolina, under the Constitution of '78, by his third wife. William Lowndes was born in Charleston, the 7th February, 1782.

At the age of seven, he went with his mother to England, where he had the benefit of an English grammar school, for three years. He then returned to Charleston, and received instruction from that eminent scholar, Dr. Simon Felix Gallagher, a Roman Catholic Priest. This gentleman said of Lowndes' facility to learn, that "his mind drank up knowledge as the dry earth did the rain from heaven."

Mr. Lowndes studied law with Chancellor DeSaussure, then a resident lawyer in Charleston, and was admitted to the Bar on the 9th January, 1804. He had previously, in September, 1802, married Elizabeth, the daughter of General Thomas Pinckney.

In 1804, he sought an association with John S. Cogdell, Esq., in the practice of the law. The proposal was gladly accepted, and, for a short time, they practiced as partners.

In consequence of the injury done to his plantation by the great equinoxial storm of 1804, Mr. Lowndes abandoned the law, and gave himself up to the care of his planting interests.

In 1806, he was elected to the House of Representatives, in the General Assembly of South Carolina, and was again elected in 1808. His great talents, and the beautiful simplicity of his character, were seen and properly appreciated in his legislative services.

At the time of the outrage committed by the Leopard on the Chesapeake, in June, 1807, the indignation of the country roused its military spirit. Many companies were formed—among them the Washington Light Infantry, of which Mr. Lowndes was the first captain. This company has continued, ever since, one of the most popular, high-spirited and well-regulated corps of South Carolina. The Rev. Mr. Gilman, one of the most exemplary of men, for many years chaplain of the company, was accustomed to ascribe much of its high tone to the influence and example of its first commander.

In October, 1810, he was elected to the House of Representatives in the Congress of the United States, to which he was successively elected, until 1822; at that time, on account of ill health, he resigned his seat.

He had a character there for wisdom and purity of purpose, which has seldom, if ever, been attained by any other member of Congress. He seldom participated in the debates, but when he did, all were anxious to hear every word he uttered; for his speeches were truly as "apples of gold in net-work of silver." He was nominated by the Legislature of South Carolina, in 1820 or 1821, for the office of President of the United States.

Speaking of this nomination, he said: "*It is an office neither to be sought nor declined.*" Would that this sentiment was universal in our country! Then, indeed, we might expect wise and patriotic men to be our rulers!

He had visited England in 1818 or 1819, where his company was much sought after by the wisest, most learned and best men of that country.

After his resignation he again embarked, with his wife and daughter, to cross the ocean, with a hope to restore his health. But the hope was vain; he died on the passage, in the forty-first year of his life.

This was a sad event for our country. If he had lived, he probably would have been elected President of the United States, and his wisdom, moderation and purity might have saved us from the national divisions to which we have been subjected.

But God orders all things for the best, and it may be that he was taken away, to be spared from witnessing the estrangement of many of his old friends, by differences in political views.

Mr. Lowndes possessed, in an eminent degree, the happy combination of gentleness of temper, firmness of principle and force of mind, which constitute the highest type of character. His manners had an easy, natural courtesy, and quiet dignity, which refinement, associated with purity and integrity, can alone impart, and whose charm none were able to resist. All who approached him, loved and admired his fine qualities In the military company, of which he was once the captain, and in the nation whose councils he adorned, his memory is alike cherished. On all sides he commanded the confidence which he never sought. He seemed to stand above the atmosphere of party passion, and to be exempt from its influences. If he had opponents, he had no enemies. Had he lived, he would have united, in all probability, the suffrages of the whole country, for its highest office, more nearly, than any man since the death of Washington.

His mind was of the highest order, his taste exact, his intellect clear, capacious and vigorous. It was carefullly and thoroughly cultivated. His library was one of the best in the Southern States. He was a scholar and statesman. His attention was not restricted to the legal or constitutional questions which engage and engross mere politicians and leaders of parties. He delighted in the pursuit of letters and general knowledge.

In person, Mr. Lowndes was tall, slender and erect. His limbs were long and loosely put together; his face without color, the cheek hollow, the nose straight, the eye gray and full of expression.

His manner of speaking was calm, pursuasive and impressive. His style clear, precise and forcible. His eloquence, however, owed its power, in popular assemblies, to something more than mere intellectual strength, or the charms of delivery. It was imbued with the influences of a life and character, on which Providence had bestowed the distinguished privilege of mingling with men and participating in public affairs, not only without a stain, but without fear and without reproach.

JAMES McKIBBEN.

This gentleman was born on the 4th day of July, 1783, at the place where the village of Union is located. His father, it is presumed, died when he was very young, as his mother was, for many years, a widow. He was educated by John Dunlap, Esq., a childless lawyer, of some eminence, who resided at Cambridge in old Ninety-Six. He placed him under the tuition of Dr. Abner Pyles, of Laurens District, who was then the most celebrated teacher in the upper country. Benjamin C. Yancey and John Caldwell were two of his fellow-students.

On leaving school, he studied law with his patron, John Dunlap, Esq., until his death; he then perhaps studied for a short time, at Union Court House. In 1804, the writer recollects to have seen him with P. E. Pearson and William F. Pearson as students-at-law with Samuel Thee, Esq., at Newberry Court House. In that year, Mr. McKibben was admitted to the Bar, and succeeded to the practice of Mr. Thee, who then removed to Louisiana. He was the only lawyer at Newberry for several years, and thus monopolized the entire business, which was large and lucrative. In 1806, he, with George Herbert, Esq., and Dr. Jacob Baille, was elected to the House of Representatives in the General Assembly of South Carolina; and, in 1808, was a second time elected, with Samuel E. Thomas and James Dyson. At this election, he was returned the third and last member. Spring Hill was then one of the election precincts; in counting the votes of that box, three votes were found for S. Griffin; Charles Griffin, Esq., was a candidate; if those votes were counted for him, he would be elected; the managers decided, that they could not be so counted, and the result was, that, by a majority of two votes, McKibben was elected. This was displeasing to many, and increased the unfounded prejudice against *a lawyer*, which had been, with difficulty, overcome by Mr.

McKibben. He offered himself as a candidate no more in Newberry District. He was, however, universally admitted to be the most useful Member which Newberry had *then* had. During his service, he and Judge Huger, then a Member from St. Andrews, had a passage on the subject of a name. Young John Harrington, either as a candidate for the Clerk's office, or in some other way, was presented, by Mr. Kibben, before the House. Judge Huger, entirely unused to the name, wished to correct Mr. McKibben, and insisted it should be John Harrington, Junior. This, McKibben indignantly repelled, affirming that he ought to know the name of his friend better than a stranger.

Mr. McKibben never liked the law as a profession: he was fond of general literature, and the social enjoyments of his friends. The latter was often extended, in Newberry, at that time, greatly beyond prudence. He and Dr. Joseph Warren Waldo were great friends. They often indulged in a frolic at the Black Jack Tavern, two miles from Newberry; and when a little excited, they became fearless riders, and a run into the village was a piece of crack fun. On one occasion, the run came near a tragical termination. Mr. Harrington, for some purpose, had a log kitchen just below his store-house, where Julius Smith's celebrated Tupper House stands. The street to McKibben's stable was between the store and the kitchen; McKibben's horse, instead of halting, was bent on his own stable, and turning the corner suddenly, he pitched his master head-foremost against the end of the kitchen; stunned only for a moment, as he arose, he inquired, "*whose still-house is this?*"

The consequence of his dislike of his profession, and the enjoyment of his friends, (in the, then, Newberry sense of the word,) was that he neglected the preparation of his cases. A young lawyer from Fairfield, David T. Milling Esq., settled at Newberry, and, although he could not make a speech at the Bar, yet he had been well trained to office work, and understood sharp practice. By diligent attention to his business, and a careful observance of every flaw, in his opponent's practice, he was soon enabled to obtain the leading position, and, by non-suiting McKibben, again and again, to turn the attention of suitors from him.

During his practice at Newberry, occurred a matter which subsequently caused him great mortification. In a case on the Summary Process Docket, Judge Grimké, who presided, gave a decree for McKibben's client; on his way to his plantation, Belmont, in Union District, the same day, perhaps, but after the adjournment of the Court, the Judge met with the other party, who gave him such a statement as induced him to think he had decided wrong. He wrote to McKibben, stating his error, and desired him not to enter up his judgment. This letter was borne by the party to McKibben, who refused compliance with the Judge's request, and used harsh words. All was reported to the Judge. He put McKibben under a rule to show cause, at the next term of the Court of Appeals, why he should not be struck from the roll of attorneys. The cause was shown. The Court directed him to be reprimanded by the kindest and most benevolent magistrate in the State, Judge Waties. It was done, and, I presume, kindly and forbearingly done. But the sense of injustice so rankled in his mind and heart, that he scarcely ever after spoke to Judge Waties. That he was legally right in disregarding Judge Grimké's directions out of Court, is true; and yet he ought to have yielded to his written request, as a matter of respect, and if wrong, the Appeal Court, on bringing the matter fairly before it, would have redressed him.

The admission of John Caldwell and Anderson Crenshaw to the Bar, in the fall of 1809, and their settlement at Newberry, together with his diminished business, from the triumphs of Milling, determined McKibben to return to the place of his nativity. When he removed to Union is not precisely ascertained. It probably was in 1810 or 1811.

He served a tour of six months in the Union Artillery company, under the command of Colonel Means and Major Dawkins, at Haddrell's Point, in the war of 1812. Brigadier-General Thomas Moore was in command, under Major-General Butler. On the retirement of the Hon. Samuel Farrow from Congress, Mr. McKibben was a candidate, and was defeated by Colonel Wilson Nesbitt, of Spartanburgh, who, as Mr. McKibben thought, was ungenerously brought forward and sustained by General Moore, whom he thought, as his commander, should have supported him. But he was much consoled on account of this disappointment by the manner in which he was elected by the Legislature, Major in the Brigade of State troops directed to be raised in December 1814, and to the command of which Judge Huger was appointed. To be associated with him, Colonel James R. Pringle, and Major Maner, was a high honor to any man. Owing to the close of the war, in the beginning of 1815, the Brigade was never mustered; but I feel sure if it had been, the fortune of Major McKibben to raise his battalion, and to meet with the enemy, no braver or better officer would have been found.

In 1816, he was elected to the State Senate from Union District; and, in 1822, he was again returned. *Here* again, in the Legislature, his duties were faithfully performed. In July, 1828, he closed his life in a most sudden manner: he had eaten his breakfast at the house of his brother-in-law, John Gage, Jr.; he afterwards walked into the piazza, and sat down on a bench, immediately behind him; hearing a gurgling noise, his relative turned and caught his falling body; before he could ease him down, he was dead. This, his sudden death, was probably the result of suffocation.

It is probable that a disappointment in a projected matrimonial engagement contributed much to the inert, neglectful character, which somewhat diminished his usefulness. Mr. McKibben settled down, a bachelor, and became, as Dr. Fraklin said, "like half of a pair of scissors, fit only to *scrape a trencher.*" His life, when not employed in public, was very much that of a solitary; he spent most of his time in his office, and employed himself in occasional instruction to the children of his sister, the wife of John Gage, Jr. He was much attached to her; and her death, in 1826 or '7, seemed to rend the last link which bound him to earth.

His nephew, Colonel Robert Gage, of Union District, has drawn his character in a few apt words: "His unselfishness in everything, his tender devotion to his friends, his perfect honesty, his kindness of heart, his gentleness, and yet in matters of principle, his firmness and virtues, were conceded to him by all who knew him." The author knew him from 1804 to his death, (twenty-four years,) most of the time intimately; and can endorse all which his nephew ascribed to him. He was kind and generous in all his intercourse with men. To the youth, poverty, and inexperience of the author both at school and at the Bar, he afforded the opportunity to be heard and known. The first speech which he ever made in Union was in the fall of 1814, in a case of malicious prosecution brought by Mr. McKibben against James Duncan, son of Alexander Duncan. His kind invitation to assist in that case gave the opportunity to the author, so desirable to a young lawyer, of making a speech and gaining a cause.

The Bar at Union, when Mr. McKibben returned, was principally occupied by Colonel Joseph Gist and Judge David Johnson, then the Solicitor of the Circuit. The latter, in 1815, was elected a Judge, and the former, in 1822, was elected to Congress. They were succeeded by A. W. Thomson, Z. P. Herndon, John W. Farrow, R. G. H. Fair, John H. Fernandez, Joseph S. Sims as resident lawyers, and by Thomas Williams, Jr., Robert Clendenin, John E. Gunning, John Caldwell, John B. O'Neall, Job Johnston and Robert Dunlap, from York, Chester, and Newberry. Before this array, Major McKibben's business grew less and less; and he seemed to care very little about it.

The usage of the Bar before 1828, on the circuits of the upper country, abounded in conviviality. The *argenti armorum* lucubrations of Sir John Fortescue were rarely practiced. The bottle and cards were oftener studied than Blackstone. To the latter of these vices, Major McKibben never yielded. He was, however, the child of fun in all his life; a joke was his delight, and he practiced upon his friends, and they on him, both at Newberry and Union. His friend, John Caldwell, as an attorney had issued a *subpœna* for a witness in Union, who took it into his head that the attorney was liable for his attendance; this notion McKibben pretended to believe was right, and he persuaded the man to see Caldwell before a Justice of the Peace; this was done, the summons treated with contempt, and the first thing Caldwell knew, his sulkey horse was seized in execution, and dragged up before the Court-House door for sale. It is needless to add that the whole matter was set aside, but the joke was rich food of enjoyment for McKibben.

When he was admitted as a Solicitor in Equity, Judges James and Thompson rode the circuit together; to them, petitions for admission as Solicitors in Equity were presented, and by them granted. To them, McKibben presented his petition. Tradition says, Judge Thompson examined him, and asked a solitary question: "If employed to file a bill in Equity, how much, Mac, would you charge?" "Fifty dollars," was the answer. "That will do," said the facetious Judge, and the license was signed.

At Union, as Judge Johnson, in the year 1823, was calling the Common Pleas docket, he called a case in which McKibben was the plaintiff's attorney. He stated his case to be for three hundred dollars—a wager on a horse-race. The Judge, in his quiet way, said, "Mr. McKibben, such a case cannot be sustained; it is contrary to law." He very naively replied, "Well, may it please your Honor, I thought I would name it to your honor," and quietly took his seat, and submitted to the non-suit which followed.

As I have already said, he was fond of a joke, and it mattered little where it was, whether at the Bar or in the Legislature. When the author was Speaker of the House of Representatives, and McKibben was Senator, one of his jokes occurred, to which reference will be made, after a preparatory statement of another matter. Strangers had so much intruded on the Members of the House of Representatives, that complaints were made to the Speaker, who strictly charged the door-keeper, a good old Methodist, James Jenkins, to permit no such thing in future. The Duke of Saxe-Weimar was making the tour of the United States, and was then on a visit to Columbia. That good man and dignified magistrate, Chancellor DeSaussure, ever attentive to strangers, was conducting the Duke to the House of Representatives. The door-keeper, to whom the Chancellor was known, suffered him to pass into the hall, but when the Duke attempted to enter, he was stopped; the Chancellor fell back, and said to Mr. Jenkins, "he is the Duke of Saxe-Weimar." "Duke or no Duke, he don't enter here without the permission of the Speaker," was the firm reply. The Duke was only relieved by a Member, who perceived the difficulty, and directed the door-keeper to admit him. Major McKibben, as a Senator, was entitled, as of course, to *the entry.* He was unknown to the door-keeper, and attempted to enter, and was excluded. To humor the joke, and enjoy the fun, he parleyed and begged for admission, but in vain. He retired, but soon returned, and insisted upon entering, that he might "show his new red plush vest to the man who wore the blue robe." "Go away, the Speaker has other fish to fry, than to be plagued with such fools as you are," was the door-keeper's reply. In this way, he tantalized the old man, who was firm in his duty, as he conceived it to be, for a day or two, until some one told him who the man "with the red plush jacket" was.

Major McKibben was a well-informed man. He spoke French and Spanish, and had a well-selected library, and read a good deal. His elocution was easy, though not impressive. He was about five feet, eight inches high, very corpulent; his face was pitted by small-pox; his forehead was a fine one, and promised more of eminence than he ever permitted himself to attain. That he had faults, all who knew him will admit; but they were such as injured himself alone; he never knowingly harmed a living being.

WILLIAM C. C. CLIFTON.

This gentleman was a Virginian by birth; he migrated to South Carolina about 1790. My friend, Colonel Chappell, says, "when I first saw him, he was engaged as a teacher of vocal music, and soon after had charge of a school in the neighborhood of my homestead, in South Carolina, where I was one of his pupils." Before 1795, he removed to Columbia, and put up a wooden house on the site of Kinster's brick building, and kept school, and boarded some of his scholars, "of whom," says Colonel Chappell, "I was one. He was then unmarried, and his sister, Mrs. Patrick, the mother of Mrs. Andrew Wallace, kept house for him." His sister, Mrs. Patrick, married Major John McLimose, and he and Major Clifton formed a commercial co-partnership, and the latter abandoned his business as a teacher. Their business proved profitable, and, in a few years, they invested their capital in a plantation and negroes, which they continued as a joint investment for several years, when they divided the same.

About 1800, he married Miss Cooper, of Georgia, and about the same time commenced the study of the law, in the office of Thomas Henry Egan, Esq., where there were many students, viz: Charles Martin and Samuel Hammond, of Edgefield, Martin Mead, of Augusta, Georgia, Philip Edward and William F. Pearson, of Fairfield, Uriah and John Goodwyn, and Colonel John Joel Chappell, of Richland, Caleb Clarke, then of Charleston, (where he had studied law with Mr. Bailey,) and John Hooker. Major Clifton was admitted to the Bar at the Spring Term, 1805, though his name does not appear on the roll of attorneys admitted in Columbia. He was a successful practitioner and realized much money. He was, however, not a well-read lawyer. His infirmity (club-feet) created much sympathy in his favor, and he, partly on that account, received a greater share of business. He was a quick, ready man, but he wanted application, and did not seek the results of authority, and the consequence was that he was often tripped up by some other better, informed adversary. Colonel Chappell says: "A special plea or demurrer was an object of abhorrence with the Major, as much so as with our friend, Judge Gantt. He liked the practice to be *ore tenus*, which was a favorite course with him, as also a favorite expression." The only time I remember to have seen the Major in Court, was in Denton and Wife *vs.* English, 2 N. & McC. 581. I see he is not noticed in the Report. He certainly argued it. For on that occasion, an incident occurred, which fixes it in my memory. He was for the motion, and argued first in such a way as to excite much the displeasure of Judge Colcock, who tried the cause on the circuit. The Court declined to hear the other side. Mr. Gregg came in afterwards, and begged to be heard; he was accordingly permitted to argue the case, which he did, so effectually, that notwithstanding all which Colonel Blanding (who was on the other side) could say, the motion was granted.

Before Major Clifton was admitted to the Bar, he was elected Captain of the Beat company in Columbia. Subsequently, he was promoted to the rank of Major. In 1806, he was elected, with Isaac Tucker, a Member of the House of Representatives of South Carolina, from Richland District. This term of two years he served, but he was never afterwards elected.

It seems, Major Clifton was a lover of the turf; but his celebrated horse, *Dare-devil*, though often started, was unsuccessful.

He became a Methodist, probably about 1811. For I recollect he was a Methodist and a preacher, when I entered college, in February of that year. He realized a fine estate by his various pursuits, and died between 1826 and 1828, leaving his wife and two sons surviving, all of whom are since dead. His only representatives now are several grandchildren.

JOHN BLOUNT MILLER.

This gentleman was the son of Andrew and Elizabeth Miller, and was born in Charleston, South Carolina, 16th September, 1782.

He was brought up to the business of a retail merchant, in which occupation he resided at Savannah, Georgia, from December '96 to 1801.

In October of that year, he commenced the study of the law with Samuel Mathis, Esq., his brother-in-law, in the town of Camden; he studied a few months with Henry Bailey, Esq., of the City of Charleston, the father of the late Attorney-General. He was admitted to the Bar as an attorney-at-law, November, 1805—two years after, he was licensed as a Solicitor in the Court of Equity. He settled in Sumterville 30th December, 1805, and was the first person ever appointed Notary Public for Sumter District. He was married at Statesburg, on the 17th July, 1808, to Mary C., the daughter of William Murrell, Esq.

His correct and faithful deportment, the attention to his business, and the order of his papers, soon attracted attention, and obtained for him a large practice. He was an admirable collection lawyer.

He was early impressed with the duty which he owed to God; his mind became more and more enlightened by His grace, until at last he felt that he had passed from death unto life; and, on a profession of his faith in the Saviour, he was baptized by the Rev. John M. Roberts, at the church on the High Hills of Santee, on the 16th August, 1812; to this church his wife was also attached; they both remained members of it until October, 1820, when they became members of the church organized at Sumterville, of which he was a deacon. He was a life-member of the American Bible and of the Home Mission, and General Tract, Societies. Wherever a good work was to be done, his hand and heart were in it!

In 1812, he was elected Captain of a Company of Light Infantry, afterwards Major of the regiment, then Lieutenant-Colonel. Hence his title of Colonel, by which he was designated and known for near forty years.

In January, 1817, at the organization of the Court of Equity for Sumter District, he was appointed, by the Governor, Commissioner and Register in Equity, for Sumter District. At the succeeding winter, he was elected by the Legislature, to serve for four years. He was continued in that office by successive elections until his death. He was elected the ninth, and last time, in November, 1849; it was on this occasion *alone* that he was opposed.

He was a model Commissioner in every respect, and was always in his place to attend to the duties of his office; he kept the records with wonderful neatness and care. His long possession of his office, without question, was evidence enough in itself to show how well he did his duty.

In 1837, he removed from Sumterville to his plantation, ten miles below that place, and, at his request, was dismissed from the Sumterville church, and, in 1839, he placed himself under the watchful care of the Bethel Church. In 1842, he became a member of that church.

In 1838, after faithfully and diligently practicing law for thirty-two years, he retired from the active duties of the profession.

In 1840, he became a life-member of the American and Foreign Bible Society. A split had previously taken place between the Baptists and the other members of the American Bible Society, which forced them to withdraw, and to constitute the American and Foreign Bible Society, to be supported by Baptists, and to carry out their purposes in the spread of the Gospel. Col. Miller felt it to be his duty to act with his denomination, and wherever his duty pointed there he always went.

He died peacefully in the faith of a Christian, on the 21st of October, 1851, in the 70th year of his age, and was interred in his burial ground, at Bethel Church, on the succeeding day. The preceding statement was prepared from one furnished to me by his excellent and venerable widow.

Col. Miller's life was a beautiful example, in "whatsoever things are true, whatsoever things are honest, whatsoever things are just, whatsoever things are pure, whatsoever things are lovely, whatsoever things are of good report." What more need I say to embalm his memory, and to make all who read this short memoir, reverence his name!

We make the following extracts from a letter of his neighbor and friend, Col. F. J. Moses:

"On the establishment of a separate Court of Equity, for Sumter District, in 1817, he was elected Commissioner in Equity, which place he held by successive elections to his death.

"In his official position, he exhibited the same traits of character which distinguished him in private life. Firm and impartial in the administration of the duties of his office, power could not awe, or partiality influence him to an act against the dictates of his judgment or his conscience. His course, as Commissioner, elicited the highest commendation of the Chancellors, and there was not one of them who witnessed the manner in which he performed the duties of his office, that was not attached to him as a beloved friend. It may be that he carried his pertinacity to such an extreme, that if the purity of his heart and intentions had not been so well known and recognized, it may have been blameable.

"As an instance: in the case of Keels and Boyd—a case which was pending in his district, and in which a matter of account was involved—the Court of Appeals set aside his report, and ordered the account to be taken on principles fixed in its decree, and for this purpose it was again referred to him. He refused to state the account in the manner ordered, believing and averring that, to do so, would be to force a liability on one of the parties to an amount so large that he considered it unjust; and, although but an officer of the Court and subject to its power, he could not carry out a judgment which he believed was unjust and against conscience, preferring, rather than to do it, to resign his office. The Judges who composed the appellate tribunal at that time, knowing that he intended no disrespect or contempt in declining to obey their order, and referring his omission to a sensitiveness of propriety, which, though excessive, sprang from good intentions, passed over the default and made a final decree for the amount, based on the principles on which they had directed him to state the accounts."

"In his early life he had been fond of the military, in which he had attained position, and published, in 1817, the first collection of the Militia Laws of the United States and South Carolina, with the Patrol Laws of the State. The work shows great diligence and method, and, until a change in the system, was regarded as authority."

"Col. Miller was loved by the Bar of his district, among whom he stood as a father. A meeting was held at Sumterville, on the occasion of his death, at which Col. F. J. Moses, who for years had stood in the relation to him of an intimate friend, offered a tribute to his memory, which was published in the papers of the day.

"The Bar passed resolutions of regard and sympathy, and, as a further manifestation of their feelings, directed that his portrait should be obtained, to be executed by his son-in-law, Mr. W. H. Scarborough, of Columbia, and to be placed in the Commissioner's office. This was a high and delicate compliment.

"The picture, a faithful delineation of the well-remembered placid features of the original, now adorns the office. May that smiling face beaming from the picture, inspire those who succeed him to imitate his bright example."

ELDRED SIMKINS.

Eldred Simkins was the son of Arthur Simkins, one of the earliest settlers in Edgefield District.

Arthur Simkins was of the most respectable class from the eastern shore of Virginia, and emigrated early in life to this part of South Carolina. He came first to the region of the Santee, but being soon dissatisfied with that locality, pressed onward to the more distant and less frequented forests on the Savannah side of the State. After several years of observation, he ultimately settled a fine body of land on the waters of Log Creek, in Edgefield—a plantation, still remembered by many as "the Cedar fields." Here he lived and died. He was County Court Judge under the old system, and was looked up to, as a standard of worth and probity, by all who lived within the sphere of his influence. When the Revolution broke out, he, of course, sided for the independence of the colonies, and at an early period of the war the Tories burned down his dwelling house, then one of the principal large houses of the country-side. He was a member of the General Assembly of South Carolina after the war, and also of the Convention which adopted the Constitution. He voted against the adoption of the Constitution, as did nearly all of the delegates from the Ninety-Six District. The test vote was first made in the Legislature upon the calling of a Convention for the adoption of the Federal Constitution, and it was nearly defeated. General Sumter, and General Pickens, were both opposed to its adoption, upon the ground that it took too much power from the separate States and consolidated too much in the General Government; and both their sections of the State voted almost unanimously against the call of a Convention to ratify the Constitution. Arthur Simkins was not an exception to this statement. Sound in principles, and conscientious in politics, he remained a Member of the General Assembly for many (perhaps twenty) consecutive years, and was universally loved and respected for the simplicity, truthfulness, and sagacity of his life and character. He died, in 1826, leaving a large property. He was a Baptist in his religion, and was seldom missing from his place in the house of God, even in the years of his extreme old age.

Eldred Simkins, Sen., was his youngest son, and from the delicacy of his constitution, as also his great sprightliness of temperament and quickness of mind, became the favorite of his father. He was born during the Revolutionary war, on the 29th of August, 1779. At an early age he was sent to the famous Academy, conducted by Dr. Waddel, at Willington, in Abbeville District. There, he was thoroughly taught in all the fundamental branches of education, and became quite a proficient in studies of a higher grade, especially in the Latin. He was afterwards sent to the (then) celebrated law school at Litchfield, Connecticut, and remained there more than three years. Afterwards he prepared himself in the local laws of South Carolina, under the accomplished Chancellor DeSaussure, in Charleston, and was admitted to the Bar in the City of Charleston, 7th May, 1805. He and Chancellor DeSaussure were from that time the warmest friends through life.

In 1802, Colonel Simkins commenced his professional life at Edgefield Court House. From the outset his practice was large and valuable. In accuracy of business and strict accountability, no man was ever his superior. He studied his cases and prepared his papers with great care. He spoke rapidly and fluently, and addressed himself to points at issue with successful effect. He married Eliza Hannah Smith, at Millford, Georgia, in April, 1807. She was the daughter of Benajah Smith, and the grand daughter of General Elijah Clark, of Georgia Revolutionary memory. She was, as Col. Pickens justly said, "A beautiful woman, the sweetest and most entertaining lady I ever saw in any society." She was a most accomplished person, of great piety; a Christian of devoted zeal and of the most untiring aspirations.

Of her children, F. W. Pickens married Eliza, A. P. Butler married Susan Ann, and J. Edward Calhoun married Maria Edgeworth. These are now no more. Mrs. Pickens alone left children.

There are now but three sons left, of whom Arthur Simkins is the eldest; the others are John and Clarke.

He was repeatedly sent to the Legislature by his native district; and in 1816, when Mr. Calhoun went into Mr. Monroe's Cabinet, Colonel Simkins was elected to Congress. In this contest he had for competitors Mr. Edmund Bacon, a very popular and eloquent man, and General William Butler, who had served throughout the War of Independence, first as Lieutenant and afterwards as Captain, with high distinction; the latter had also formerly represented the Edgefield Congressional District in Congress.

Colonel Simkins remained in Congress four years, and, among other speeches, made one on the Missouri Compromise, of marked ability and high tone. He declined a re-election, after serving two terms; voluntarily retiring in favor of his law-partner and friend, Hon. George McDuffie. Mr. McDuffie had begun the practice of the law, some years before this, at Old Pendleton; and, after being unsuccessful there, had run for Solicitor before the Legislature, and was beaten by Benj. Saxon, Esq., of Abbeville. He was spoken of by Mr. Calhoun and others, as a young man of uncommon talents; and Colonel Simkins, then a Member of the Legislature, saw him, and offered him a partnership in his office on limited terms. Mr. McDuffie accepted, and settled in Edgefield accordingly. After Colonel Simkins retired from Congress, he resumed his profession, but divided his time between that and his planting interests. His health was extremely feeble from his youth; and as he grew older, he could not endure the close labors of the profession. He was fond of its duties, but unable to encounter its toils. His anecdote, his humor, his kind hospitality and unbounded social qualities, made him beloved by the Bar. He always, too, practiced his profession upon the most gentlemanly and liberal principles.

After Mr. McDuffie was withdrawn from the practice by his Congressional duties, Colonel Simkins took into partnership Mr. Edward Ford, a gentleman of fine heart and great intelligence. Mr. Ford was a near relative of Chancellor DeSaussure, and it was through the latter that Colonel Simkins became acquainted with him. Mr. Ford is now the eminently beloved pastor of the First Episcopal Church, in Augusta, Georgia.

In 1830, Colonel Simkins took into partnership, his son-in-law, F. W. Pickens, Esq., and did not, after that time, attend closely to the profession. His health had been failing for years before, and continued gradually sinking until he died in 1832, having lived a life as full of benevolence as ever any man was permitted to exhibit. There was no proposition of charity, no useful enterprize within his reach and influence, which did not enlist his active sympathies. He was, in truth, the light of the society in which he lived—ardent, kind, devoted in all the relations of life. He died lamented by all who knew him. Leaning, at last, upon the merits of his Redeemer, he went down to the grave, and was gathered to his fathers.

I may add, that Colonel Simkins was early employed in all the "Jews-land cases" of Abbeville, in the famous bridge cases between the Bank of Augusta and Henry Shultz, and in most of the heavy cases of his day.

From 1820 to 1832, no interior Bar of South Carolina presented abler counsellors than there appeared often in the Edgefield Courts. McDuffie and Bacon, Glasscock and Goodwin, George and Pickens Butler, Waddy Thompson, Brooks and Griffin, Bauskett and Wardlaw, were amongst the resident lawyers. Then, as circuit lawyers, Harper and Blanding, Preston and Richard Wild, Longstreet, Petigru and D. L. Wardlaw were often attendants in great cases. These were men of the highest rank—men rarely equalled at any Bar in any country. They were models of legal learning and forensic eloquence. No man could be prominent among such men without real worth and high abilities.

In addition to the preceding sketch by his son, I would add, that Mr. Simkins, as far back as 1808, rode the circuit, in company with George Warren Cross, Esq., of Charleston, Richard Gantt, Esq., of Edgefield, John C. Calhoun, Esq., of Abbeville, Solicitor Stark and John J. Chappell, Esq., of Columbia, Samuel Farrow, Esq., of Spartanburgh, and Robert Creswell, Esq., of Laurens. I have seen them at Newberry.

He was one of the many counsel employed for Dr. Reid in the great slander case *vs.* Captain John Henderson, and in which a verdict for five hundred dollars was recovered, and which Captain Henderson insisted on paying, and did pay, notwithstanding the advice of his eminent counsel, Messrs. Stark and Calhoun to appeal, and their assurance that on an appeal they could defeat them.

In 1812, he was elected Lieutenant-Governor. How he acquired the title of Colonel, I do not know, but he was so called as far back as 1815. I presume he was the Aid of some one of the Generals of Brigade. At the Spring Term of 1815, I first attended at Edgefield; Mr. Simkins then had an immense practice; having associated with him, Mr. George McDuffie in the December previous, as a co-partner.

In 1824, he was a Member of the General Assembly of the State; and, in 1825, was the author of the Act to give jurisdiction to the Judges of the Courts of Ordinary throughout the State, to order the sale or division of the real estate of intestates, not exceeding the value of one thousand dollars.—Acts of 1825, p. 25. This Act was prepared by Colonel Simkins, and passed as presented; showing what care and diligence he bestowed upon it.

His widow survived him several years. She was a member of the Baptist Church, Edgefield, and was as remarkable for her pious life, as for her beauty, various accomplishments, and her sweet and lovely disposition.

Colonel Simkins was one of the kindest men whom I ever knew. His house was open to the largest hospitality. He was a respectable lawyer, a useful public man, as Member of Congress and a legislator. He did much to give character to Edgefield; for he presented an example of polished hospitality and kindness, and of good morals. He was a good citizen, a kind husband, father, son, neighbor and master. I know no man who has so much to entitle him to the honor and respect of his fellow-men.

CHAPMAN LEVY.

This gentleman was a Hebrew by birth, and was a native of the ancient town of Camden; he was born on the 4th of July, 1787, studied law, and was admitted to the Bar, in Columbia, in 1806. He practiced with eminent success in his native town and district, as well as in Lancaster and Kershaw, and possibly in Sumter. He was occasionally employed in Columbia, and at Lexington Court House. He was one of ths shrewdest advocates with whom I was acquainted. I recollect only one case in which I had an opportunity to judge of his powers. I allude to the case of Cantey *vs.* McWillie, involving a question of water privilege. His management and argument in that case, about the year 1837, was surpassingly excellent. In 1814, he volunteered for active service, with the fine rifle company of which he was captain, in the regiment of drafted militia, commanded by Colonel Adam McWillie, and served at Haddrel's Point, near Charleston, until March, 1815.

Chapman Levy was usually called Colonel Levy, from being the Aid of one of the Governors, I suppose. He was several times a Member of the Legislature, and was, I know a Representative in the sessions of 1828 and 1829; he was the Chairman of the Committee on Retrenchment, which laid an unsparing hand on the salaries of many of the public officers. As a Member of the Legislature, he was active and untiring in the discharge of his duties. In the unfortunate political contest in this state, which gave rise to Nullification, and which has been the parent, in a greater or less degree, of all our subsequent political dissensions, Colonel Levy was an ardent and consistent Union man, and did more than any one else to keep Kershaw, Chesterfield and Lancaster in their proper places.

He removed to Mississippi, and died there in December, 1850, in the sixty-fourth year of his age. I regret that I have not the means of doing him fuller justice; but meagre as this sketch is it will place his name in company with his brethren of the Bar; and South Carolinians will remember him, and, I trust, will add much more to his fame than I have been able to do.

JOHN CALDWELL CALHOUN.

The great man whose name is above, belongs to the history of the United States. Still, he was of the Bar of South Carolina, and without some sketch of his life and character, the work to which I have devoted so much time and labor, would be incomplete. I am fully conscious of the difficulty of abridging such a life, and at the same time of doing justice to so distinguished a man; yet the task must be assumed and the duty performed.

John C. Calhoun was a native of Abbeville District, South Carolina. He was born 18th March, 1782, and was the son of Patrick Calhoun, and Martha Caldwell, his wife. His father was no common man—one of the early settlers of Abbeville District, he was distinguished for his energy and fearless intrepidity of character. He was an eminent surveyor of the back-woods of South Carolina; was often a member of the Legislature of South Carolina, after the Revolution. An anecdote is related, of how he defeated the first attempt made to change the name Ninety-Six to Cambridge. He made in large figures 96, and holding it up, said: " Turn it which way you will, it is still Ninety-Six." His argument, thus placed before the eyes of the members, was irresistable, and for the time saved the name consecrated by the Revolution.

The infant son of Patrick Calhoun and his wife, was called John Caldwell, after his uncle, Major John Caldwell, who was murdered at his own house, November, 1781, by the " bloody scout."

Mr. Calhoun received his academic education from his brother-in-law, the Rev. Moses Waddell, afterwards justly celebrated as the great teacher of an academy at Wellington, Abeville District, and subsequently the President of Franklin College, Athens, Georgia. He entered the Junior Class of Yale College in 1802, and graduated in 1804. An English oration was assigned to him, he selected for his subject: "The qualifications necessary to constitute a perfect statesman," and prepared his oration, but was prevented by severe indisposition from delivering it.

He immediately commenced the study of the law. He spent eighteen months at Gould & Reeves' celebrated law-school, at Litchfield, Connecticut; the residue of the time of study, required for admission to the Bar, three years, he spent in the law-offices of Henry W. DeSaussure, Esq., in Charleston, and of George Bowie, Esq., at Abbeville.

He was admitted to the Bar in 1807, and opened his office at Abbeville; he practiced there, and at Newberry, and I presume in the other adjoining districts. My recollection of Mr. Calhoun as a lawyer, is from hearing him, when I was a school-boy at Newberry, and of course my judgement was then very imperfect. His reputation was extraordinary for so young a man. He was conceded, as early as 1809, to be the most promising young lawyer in the upper country. Chancellor Bowie of Alabama, who lived at Abbeville, and had a fine opportunity of knowing Mr. Calhoun's early reputation, as a lawyer, says: "With the members of the Bar, as well as with the people, he stood very high in his profession. Perhaps no lawyer in the State ever acquired so high a reputation from his first appearance at the Bar, as he did. With his towering intellect and untiring energy, he could not long remain second to any man in any station. With a mind like his, so logical, so profoundly metaphysical, so powerful to analyze, and so clear in its conceptions, he could not be less than a thorough and successful lawyer. When at the Bar, the business of the Court was nearly equally divided between himself, Mr. Yancey and my brother George."

At Newberry, he had also a large practice. Newberry District was the home of his mother's relations, and by their influence he would have received practice under any circumstances, but his acknowledged legal abilities were enough to make him, in that district, a leading lawyer, where the resident lawyers, until 1810, presented no claim to learning or eloquence.

Mr. Calhoun was elected to the House of Representatives

in the General Assembly of South Carolina, in October, 1808, and took his seat on the fourth Monday in November. In that body he took a very prominent stand. In 1809, he was elected by the Legislature, a member of the third Board of Trustees of the South Carolina College. This was then, and ever since, has been regarded as a high compliment to any man.

Mr. Calhoun served in the State Legislature, the sessions of 1808 and 1809.

In October, 1810, he was elected to Congress from the district composed then of Abbeville, Laurens and Newberry. He married, in 1811, Miss Florida Colhoun, the daughter of John Erwin Colhoun, Esq., who was admitted to the Bar 24th March, 1789, and who practiced law with great reputation in Charleston and at Ninety-Six. He was a Commissioner of Confiscated Estates, and was often a member of the General Assembly of South Carolina. Towards the close of his life, he spent his summers within two miles of Fort Hill. He died there a Senator in Congress from South Carolina, in 1801.

The war feeling in 1810, was beginning to extensively pervade the United States. The message of President Madison, at the opening of Congress, was decidedly warlike. The response to it by the Committee of Foreign Relations, was of the same character. Mr. Calhoun's reply to Mr. Randolph, who spoke in opposition to the report, was universally regarded by the Republican party, as a triumphant refutation of his arguments, and a vindication of the necessity of war. At the second session, Mr. Calhoun unexpectedly found himself at the head of the Committee on Foreign Relations, Mr. Porter, the Chairman, having withdrawn from Congress. In June, 1812, he reported and carried through Congress, the bill declaring war against Great Britain.

Mr. Calhoun, until December, 1817, was actively employed in Congress, and won just distinction as a man of business and an able debater. His speeches are acceptable to all, and will be read with pride and pleasure by every South Carolinian.

In December, 1817, he entered on the arduous duties of

Secretary of War, under President Monroe. Mr. Calhoun had no previous military training, yet he showed, in a very short time, that he had the administrative genius of a great officer. He gave order, regularity and energy to the Department, which he found in great confusion. Gen. Bertrand, the Chief of the Board of Engineers, and even an officer of the great Emperor of the French, compared Mr. Calhoun's administrative talents, as Secretary of War, to his former great master. No one, certainly, ever left an office with as much reputation as Mr. Calhoun did, when he ceased to be Secretary of War, and was elected Vice President, and entered on the duties of that office on the 4th March, 1825.

In it he had little power, beyond a casting vote, and that of presiding over the deliberations of the Senate. The latter is sometimes a trying duty. It requires in general, great promptness in decision, perfect impartiality, never-failing good humor, and unshaken firmness. These qualities Mr. Calhoun possessed and exercised.

He was a second time elected Vice President, on the ticket with General Jackson as President. Unfortunately, the President and Vice-President became irreconcilably opposed to each other. The causes of this difference do not properly lie before me, and I do not undartake to say where the fault was. No doubt it was unfortunate for the country, and particularly for South Carolina, who had sustained both, with unfaultering and unanimous devotion.

The dispute between South Carolina and the United States, on the Tariff, was assuming even a threatening aspect, in 1828, when Mr. Calhoun drew the celebrated "South Carolina Exposition and Protest, on the subject of the Tariff." Nullification, of which Mr. Calhoun is said to be the father, (but which I have often heard Chancellor Harper claim to be his own progeny,) followed with all the consequences of party division, to South Carolina, to which she had been many years a stranger.

In 1832, on the resignation of Senator Hayne, to assume the duties of Governor, Mr. Calhoun was elected a Senator in Congress, and resigned the great office of Vice President.

In February, 1833, he and Mr. Clay agreed on a compromise, which led to a satisfactory adjustment of the Tariff, and to a rescinding of the Ordinance of Nullification, which restored peace and harmony to South Carolina.

Mr. Calhoun remained in the Senate of the United States, until the close of the session of 1843, when he resigned his seat, and proposed to seek the quiet and repose of private life for the balance of his life, but this he was not allowed to do. In 1844, he was appointed Secretary of State, by President Tyler, and was happily able to bring about the annexation of Texas.

In 1846, he was again elected by South Carolina, to the Senate of the United States, and felt it to be his duty to obey her call. On the 4th March, 1850, he made his last speech to the Senate of the United States. It was on the slavery question; and of him, on that occasion, Judge Butler, after his death, eloquently said: "We saw him a few days ago, in the seat near me, which he had so long and honorably occupied. We saw the struggle of a giant mind exerting itself to overcome the weakness and infirmity of a sinking body. It was the exhibition of a wounded eagle, with his eyes turned to the heavens, in which he had soared, but into which his wings would never carry him again."

He died 29th March, 1850, at the City of Washington, in the sixty-ninth year of his age.

All parties, in and out of Washington, united in the greatest testimonials of respect to his memory. *Everywhere the nation mourned his death.* His great compeers and opponents, Clay and Webster, mingled their tears with his friends, over his remains, and testified to his great and exalted worth.

On the 25th of April, 1850, his body, in the charge of the committees of Congress, accompanied by the committees from Wilmington, North Carolina, and Charleston, reached the city, and Mr. Mason, the Chairman of the Committee of the Senate, placed the body in the care of the Governor of South Carolina, Whitemarsh B. Seabrook, by whom it was committed to the Mayor, T. Leger Hutchison. On this day the funeral obsequies took place. Every place of business in Charleston was closed—the houses on the principal streets were clothed with emblems of mourning, and the grandest and most imposing pageant that ever took place in this ancient city, was witnessed by thousands and thousands of spectators. The City Hall was draped in mourning, to receive the remains, and it was there visited by thousands of the citizens, to pay their respects to the illustrious dead. On the 26th of April, his remains were conveyed to a tomb in St. Phillip's Church-yard, where they still remain. A massive monument is to be erected to his memory by the ladies of South Carolina, for which purpose $40,000 have been raised.

The short sketch of Mr. Calhoun given by Mr. Clay is, I think, most felicitous. He said that "he possessed an elevated genius of the highest order; that in felicity of generalization of the subjects of which his mind treated, I have seen him surpassed by no one; and the charm and captivating influence of his colloquial powers, have been felt by all who have conversed with him."

In poetic lines the late Rev. S. Gilman happily sketched the great man of whom we have been speaking:

"Rarest gifts in thee we saw:
Thought that probed each latent law—
Presence like a felt control,
Speech that moved a nation's soul!
Giant mind with heart of child,
Nobly roused or reconciled—
Braving but forgiving foes—
Stirred that millions might repose.
Thou wert loyal, trusting, free,
Like thy State's own chivalry
Moral stain could'st not endure,
Like thy own State's daughters pure.
Thundering through the Federal dome,
Studious at thy happy home.
Followed, feared, condemned, approved
Still thou wert revered and loved.
Falling at thy voice of Fame,
There with ripe and world-wide name,
Need'st no more from life—but we
Darkling here, have need of thee."

In August, 1850, I delivered an oration on "public speaking," I alluded to Mr. Calhoun in the following words, with which I close this sketch:

"It is only necessary to point to Fort Hill, near Pendleton, South Carolina, and in imagination, we behold the great leader of South Carolina, in all her political warfare, start from his farm, holding the Constitution of the United States high above his head, point to its violated pages, and hear him in indignant honesty, speak a people's wrongs, with all the brilliancy and clearness of Fox, and the deep and graceful reasoning of Burke!

"Honesty, morality, genius, love of country, and devoted service for forty years, will entitle him to the universal wail of sorrow, with which his death was but recently announced."

A MEMOIR OF HON. JOHN C. CALHOUN, BY JUDGE B. F. PORTER, OF ALABAMA.

"The death of this illustrious citizen, long identified with the public service, and mourned with a depth of sorrow more general, more solemn, and more impressive, than has ever distinguished any statesman since the decease of Washington, renders the tribute of praise, at once an appropriate and first duty. The deference which men of all classes pay to great abilities and incorruptible integrity, is a tribute due to a sense of the immortality of the soul and to the eminent superiority of virtue. When a life is found to be full of exhibitions of an exalted mind, and of devotion to principles of honor and morality, men, irrespective of mere difference of opinion, award it, involuntarily, the highest homage of their good opinion. Envy itself, which always accompanies the steps of the good man, and detracts from his fame and misconstrues his motives, worn out in the contest, perishes on his grave; and cotemporaries, who are ever distrustful of success, and invidious in concessions to merit, are the first to hang willows over the bier of one no longer capable of exciting jealousy, or of triumphing in the race of life.

It has been remarked, not unfrequently, with less of surprise than of disparagement, that Mr. Calhoun had a hold on the affections of the people of South Carolina, unequalled in the history of public men. This veneration for his person and opinions, has often been attributed to the predominance of a popular leader over the dependent, yielding mind of the public. This supposition is untrue. If asked to state the reason which, more than any other, caused the extraordinary popularity of this statesman, we would say, it was his stainless honor and incorruptible good faith. Out of these virtues, incomparable as they were, grew his self-denial, amidst the promptings of ambition; his firmness in the cause of right!

We will not say that, in every instance, Mr. Calhoun saw the future with a perfectly true glance; or that the objects at which he looked, invariably sent back into his orb of vision, a reflection entirely correct, not sometimes broken by the media intervening—not occasionally obscured by rather hastily formed conjectures. But this we believe, he ever looked at things with honest intent—with an anxious wish to ascertain the truth, and to avoid evil; and he both honestly and boldly spoke out what he conceived of the mischiefs or advantages presented to his mind.

Mr. Calhoun was not ambitious in the sense in which that term has been used with reference to his motives and acts. He was desirous, ardently desirous, of being known as the advocate of the solid truths of politics. For the vanities of the position of a statesman he never longed; and, therefore, to obtain them, never conciliated or bargained. He fixed his mind on justice, on principle, on the essence of the mutual obligations arising between governments and the people; and to assert these he poured forth from the copious fountains of his intellect and his heart, the most brilliant offerings, and most profound devotion. We are confident that for station and dignity, independently of the right and glory of the means by which attained, he cared nothing. 'Sir,' said he to the writer, while in Charleston, on the last journey he made to Washington, 'The Presidency has not been in my thoughts for ten years. I would not take public office at the sacrifice of what is due to my own independence, or to my own opinions, still less by waiving the most immaterial right to which my fellow-countrymen are entitled.' Mr. Calhoun's whole life attests the sincerity and truth of this declaration. Like the great Halifax, so powerfully described by Macaulay, his public career shows the prominent fact, that, if ever he did vary his opinions, the change was never from the weaker to the stronger side. Public sentiment may, as is often said, be a fair vindication of what is proper to be done in a majority of instances; but it is not always right; and certainly he who withstands it, if he furnishes no evidence of his superiority in judgment, gives incontestable proof of his candor and firmness. From the mass of politicians delineated by history, posterity delights to distinguish those, who, amidst great imputed defects of character, and many errors of mind, have still preserved their sentiments inviolate—who, though mingled with all the slanders of the times in which they lived; and, notwithstanding, the temptations of place; the corruptions of party, and the persecutions of opponents, have nobly maintained the truth, and resolutely spoken for the right. On the contrary, however successful they may have been for the period of elevation, and during the exercise of the power of patronage, mankind with one accord, the impious seductions of the age removed, condemn the dishonorable acts of the Machiavels and Woolseys of every time and country. The world is constantly deploring, and yet, while the thing is passing before it, constantly sustaining, the weaknesses and illusions of politics. Every revolution is based on a necessity for checking the corruptions of the dynasty preceding; and yet, the succession falls into the debaucheries of the power existing before. A mild and virtuous leader, raised up for the occasion, possessed of faculties to command the public voice and concentrate its suffrage, scarcely finds himself successful, before he discovers that he must be unjust. All that is violent in partizanship must succeed to whatever is sacred in principle; ability and honesty must be sacrificed to expediency, and the fortunate politician must practice guilt as if it were public virtue, and condemn integrity as if it were depravity. The country in which we live presents, it is true, exceptions; but such have never been successful politicians. Public honours have fled from the statesman most worthy to wear them, and swelled the triumphs of those who have been dissolute in their public lives.

When we assert that Mr. Calhoun was not one of this latter class, we intend to raise no issue whatever with respect to the correctness of his views, considered as mere abstract political sentiment. Such a course would not only be disrespectful to these generous men who have entertained opposite opinions, and who have opened bosoms, long mailed in the armor of vigorous conflicts, and poured out from them magnanimous streams of eulogium and eloquence; but would be unsuited to the solemnity of the occasion of this memoir. As the evil he has done, if any, must be buried with him, so should all recollection of the violent controversies of his day be alike consigned to the tomb. The storms and agitations of the various political questions in which he engaged, have, we hope, passed away; and friends and enemies alike sorrowing—alike relieved of prejudices and disarmed of resentments, amidst the departing rays of the sun of his last day, may stand in harmony around his grave, and multiply the records of his memorable devotion to the public service.

We do not intend to seek out for approbation or condemnation, any of those leading topics which, during Mr. Calhoun's public life, produced so much controversy, and in respect to which the people of the United States have been so divided. We seek to give a history of, rather than a criticism on, Mr. Calhoun's participation in public events. We will not hold a scale by which to determine his consistency or his fluctuations, if guilty of any. The Tariff, the Bank of the United States, State Rights—on all of these, whatever his views, they were invariably entertained in good faith and frankly expressed. His most inveterate enemy—and who has not such, however pure!—will admit this. In political fame, it is not the character of the man's opinions which is to be considered; it is the honesty, the truthfulness of his conceptions and of his advocacy of them. We may not dwell too minutely on the nature of a measure proposed. The human mind is forced to view things through such various media, that we may well distrust its judgment. We are compelled as often to blush at following precedents, as at condemning sentiments. But, on questions involving clear principles, we may generally express ourselves without reserve. In measures embracing interests and holding in issue the highest obligations, moral and political, we can decide without inflicting pain or exciting animosities. Of this nature shall be the incidents of Mr. Calhoun's life, on which we shall hazard approbatory reflections.

The circumstance which first brought Mr. Calhoun's name before the country, was an Address and Resolutions made to the people of Abbeville District, South Carolina, on the occasion of the attack on the Chesapeake by the Leopard. That brutal violation of the laws of nations and of humanity kindled a flame in every part of the Union. His speech in support of war was a fearless exposition of the privileges of American seamen, and an indignant denunciation of the cowardly attack which had violated them. It placed him at once so high in public confidence that he was soon after voted into the State Legislature. There his brief service was distinguished by a masterly defence and sagacious arrangement of the affairs of the Republican party. He reviewed the prospects of the country, and predicted the difficulties in which Europe and the United States would soon be involved. He denounced the restrictive system proposed for the redress of our grievances, and pointed to a war with England as both expedient and inevitable. In order to prevent distraction in the Republican party, he proposed the name of Mr. John Langdon, of New Hampshire, for the Vice-Presidency, under Mr. Madison.

In 1810, Mr. Calhoun took his seat in the House of Representatives of the United States. The period was pregnant with portentous prospects. War raged over Europe. The Berlin and Milan decrees of France, and the British orders of council had divided the commerce of the world between these nations. The policy, so earnestly pressed on the consideration of the people of the Union, of Peace and Non-interference, it was not possible for the government to pursue, without abandoning every right dear to the citizen, and forfeiting every claim to the respect of foreign States. The navy of Great Britain swept the ocean. Flushed with victories, and arrogant under the acknowledged title of mistress of the seas, she boldly boarded our vessels, and manned her ships from our crews. Apprehensions that our trade and commerce would sink under resistance, paralyzed for a time the resolution of our people. Embargoes and Non-importation Acts were the favorite measures of resistance. At this juncture, Mr. Calhoun entered the arena. He took a prominent part in the efforts to enforce the necessity of immediate preparations for war. The defence of a Report from the Committee on Foreign Relations devolved on him. He met John Randolph, and Philip Barton Key, in the discussion, and placed the question of the propriety of war beyond controversy. His speech wrung laudatory approval from the cautious and capable Mr. Ritchie. He was compared to Hercules with his club; he was likened in his moral sentiments to Fox; and when South Carolina was congratulated, it was said that Virginia, full as she was of glorious intellect, was not so rich but that she might wish him her son. The following extract from Mr. Calhoun's speech on the occasion is valuable, as disclosing striking truths, clothed in apt phrase:

'We are next told of the expenses of the war, and that the people will not pay taxes. Why not? Is it a want of means? What, with 1,000,000 tons of shipping; a commerce of $100,000,000 annually; manufactures yielding a yearly profit of $150,000,000, and agriculture thrice that amount; shall we, with such great resources, be told that the country wants ability to raise and support 10,000 or 15,000 additional regulars? No: it has the ability, that is admitted; but will it not have the disposition? Is not our course just and necessary? Shall we, then, utter this libel on the people? Where will proof be found of a fact so disgraceful? It is said, in the history of the country twelve or fifteen years ago. The case is not parallel. The ability of the country is greatly increased since. The whiskey tax was unpopular. But, as well as my memory serves me, the objection was not so much to the tax or its amount as the mode of collecting it. The people were startled by the host of officers, and their love of liberty shocked with the multiplicity of regulations. We, in the spirit of imitation, copied from the most oppressive part of the European laws on the subject of taxes, and imposed on a young and virtuous people the severe provisions made necessary by corruption and the long practice of evasion. If taxes should become necessary, I do not hesitate to say the people will pay cheerfully. It is for their government and their cause, and it would be their interest and duty to pay. But it may be, and I believe was said, that the people will not pay taxes, because the rights violated are not worth defending, or that the defence will cost more than the gain. Sir, I here enter my solemn protest against this low and "calculating avarice" entering this hall of legislation. It is only fit for shops and counting-houses, and ought not to disgrace the seat of power by its squalid aspect. Whenever it touches sovereign power, the nation is ruined. It is too short-sighted to defend itself. It is a compromising spirit, always ready to yield a part to save the residue. It is too timid to have in itself the laws of self-preservation. It is never safe but under the shield of honor. There is, sir, one principle necessary to make us a great people—to produce, not the form, but real spirit of union, and that is to protect every citizen in the lawful pursuit of his business. He will then feel that he is backed by the government, that its arm is his arm. He then will rejoice in its increased strength and prosperity. Protection and patriotism are reciprocal. This is the way which has led nations to greatness. Sir, I am not versed in this calculating policy, and will not, therefore, pretend to estimate in dollars and cents the value of national independence. I cannot measure in shillings and pence the misery, the stripes, and the slavery of our impressed seamen; nor even the value of our shipping, commercial and agricultural losses, under the orders in council and the British system of blockade. In thus expressing myself, I do not intend to condemn any prudent estimate of the means of a country before it enters on a war. That is wisdom, the other folly. The gentleman from Virginia has not failed to touch on the calamity of war, that fruitful source of declamation, by which humanity is made the advocate of submission. If he desires to repress the gallant ardor of our countrymen by such topics, let me inform him that true courage regards only the cause; that it is just and necessary, and that it contemns the sufferings and dangers of war. If he really wishes well to the cause of humanity, let his eloquence be addressed to the British ministry, and not the American Congress. Tell them that, if they persist in such daring insult and outrages to a neutral nation, however inclined to peace, it will be bound by honor and safety to resist; that their patience and endurance, however great, will be exhausted; that the calamity of war will ensue, and that they, and not we, in the opinion of the world, will be answerable for all its devastation and misery. Let a regard to the interest of humanity stay the hand of injustice, and my life on it, the gentleman will not find it difficult to dissuade his countrymen from rushing into the bloody scenes of war.'

Though the first tones of Mr. Calhoun's voice, in public life, were for war, yet they were justified, we humbly believe, in the eyes of the truest advocate of peace. They were spoken to rouse the country to a declaration of hostilities, for frightful outrages on humanity. The people of the United States have no resentment to indulge, no revenge to gratify. The judgment of Providence has given them the guardianship of that religion and those laws which have so often been the boast and admiration of England herself. Our government is a trustee for those rights, not for itself, not for our citizens alone; but for all nations, and for all objects dear to civilization and to man. War is the instrument of God, to punish nations. Communities, as such, cannot be avenged in their individuals, for crimes of their rules. The crimes which might condemn the government, may exempt the citizen; and if war were not a means in the power of Heaven, the flame of public liberty might be extinguished, and the wrongs of men, as nations, remain forever unredressed. Inexorable tyrants might, with impunity, overrun the peaceful territories of freedom, and millions of suffering human beings be subjected to the most severe political oppressions. When the United States made war on England, these principles were at stake. Had our Government failed to vindicate the aggressions perpetrated, the injuries inflicted on us would have become perpetual exercises of power over the whole civilized world. The United States, in losing her sense of right, would have lost the respect of the world. What we cease to respect, we cease to fear. The nation, now the asylum of the oppressed of all the earth, the centre of free commerce, and the locality of the altars of unrestrained religion, would have been, if not a feeble colony of Great Britain, at all events, a miserable and weak republic. M. Calhoun saw the consequences, and did not hesitate to give his powers to the justification of the principles involved. He sent forth, in trumpet tones, appeals which animated the patriotism of the American people, and stirred up the slumbering energies of a previous revolution. He dissipated the selfish views and doubtful policy of the few who considered, or were alarmed by the probable results of a war with that powerful country; and substituted, for these thoughts, a patriotic regard for the honor, the rights, and glory of the republic. In the crisis, he not only bore away victory from all his opponents, but achieved a triumph over himself, the greatest of all conquests. Had Mr. Calhoun been a mere time-serving politician, had his soul been capable of a selfish thought, now was the time for ascendency. Full as he was of honors, crowded at every step with evidences of the approbation of the public, he might have secured any place in the gift of the people. But he had no self-love inconsistent with the purity and integrity of his motives; and, having accomplished the high end for which he had labored, he looked about to see where his country might be next attacked. He saw the weak point in our internal arrangements. He saw a proclivity in the general government to concentrate power, at the expense of the authority of the States; and from that moment to the time of his death, this danger absorbed his thoughts, and directed his course. It was in vain that men looked, and turned away contemptuously, because they did not see what he did. With eyes fixed on the future, he turned neither to the right nor the left. He pointed to the dim speck on the horizon, and foretold the coming storm. It was the sole image on his mind's eye. He anticipated terrible calamities; and, to avert them, determined on new, bold, and to many men, alarming preventives. He left the ranks of a well-organized, prosperous and conquering party—a party on whose eagles victory seemed to have perched with strength all-powerful—to take an isolated position, where all said he was fighting with a phantom. He made all the sacrifices which are thought dear to the human breast. He forebore the pomp and advantage of a majority, to array himself, with little hope of success, or promise of reward, in the ranks of a small and unpopular minority. May we not, without either approving or condemning the opinions of this great man, yet give him the just award of possessing a resolute, a conscientious soul? One which justified right, and contested for truth, in the midst of every disadvantage, and upheld what seemed the right amid the severest opposition.

At the same session in which he defended the war, Mr. Calhoun, against the pre-conceived opinions of the body of the Republicans, gave his enthusiastic support to measures for the increase of the Navy. To him, to Mr. Lowndes, Mr. Cheves and Mr. Clay, are due all praise for fostering in its infancy, a branch of the national defence which has won immortal glory for the American name.

On the retirement of Mr. Porter from the position of Chairman of the Committee on Foreign Relations, the duties of that committee, all exceedingly arduous, fell on Mr. Calhoun. He discharged them with an *ability* and *industry* which elicited universal approval.

At the session of Congress ensuing, Mr. Calhoun rendered a signal service to the commercial interests of the country. A forfeiture of millions of the capital of the country, vested abroad, and, under the shape of merchandize imported into the country, to avoid loss under the Non-importation Act, had been prayed to be remitted. This the Secretary of the Treasury had recommended to be done, on the condition that the amount were loaned to the government. Mr. Calhoun, with characteristic honesty, supported the prayer of the petition, but denounced the condition. His efforts relieved our merchants of this onerous penalty.

The advocacy of the Loan Bill as rendered necessary by the exigencies of the war, gave Mr. Calhoun an opportunity for new displays of eloquence and reasoning. His speech on that occasion is a brilliant effort; the power and effect of which, in rousing the mind to a just conception of the duty of sustaining the war, transcended the immediate occasion of its delivery.

On the great question of a Bank of the United States, in 1814—a measure of the administration—Mr. Calhoun differed from his party. He opposed the bill which sought to carry out this measure, and rejected various propositions of his friends to adapt its provisions to his views.

It would be profitless, perhaps invidious, to survey the particulars of the contest on the Tariff of 1816. A denial of the charge, that it was the origin of the Protective system, or the assertion, that Mr. Calhoun's opinions respecting it have been misrepresented, would awaken sleeping feuds, in which party predilections would be substituted for arguments. While, on the one hand, Mr. Calhoun is said to be the author of the system, it is, on the other, asserted, that circumstances connected with our foreign relations, and not the idea of home protection, justified the support he gave the measure. Both positions have able and honest advocates. Both are, however, under the influence of long-favored attachments. These sensibly affect the judgment; and, like prejudices growing up with infancy and long cherished in manhood, are not easily dissipated, even by the rays of reason.

Of the like character is the dispute on Mr. Calhoun's position with respect to setting apart the *bonus* of the United States Bank, for internal improvements. Mr. Calhoun is no longer here to defend his consistency, or to furnish the explanations so necessary to enable men to arrive at truth. Enemies and friends alike err—the former in making too little, the latter too much allowance. Let the contrast, so far as his memory is concerned, be withdrawn. The gallant Saladin, and the chivalrous Richard of the Lion's Heart, did not think it unworthy of their magnanimity or courage to decline a combat long maintained without success to either.

The conduct of the war department, as Secretary under Mr. Monroe, gave Mr. Calhoun a very high character for close investigation and high administrative talent. The confused and long unsettled accounts of that office engaged his attention, with unremitted industry, for seven years. From an office difficult of management, it became one of ease for his successors. He reformed it in many particulars, cleared its affairs of all embarrassments, and literally brought order out of chaos.

In the contest for the Presidency, in which M. Adams, General Jackson, Mr. Crawford, and Mr. Clay, were the rival candidates, Mr. Calhoun, with rare self-denial, having withdrawn from the field, had the justice awarded him of being placed on nearly all the tickets for the Vice-Presidency. Having been elected to this office, he took his seat as President of the Senate in 1825; and, by the exercise of much dignity and firmness, brought the position into very great distinction. It was characteristic of Mr. Calhoun, that in all his public acts, he leaned against power. This was never more prominently displayed than in his decision of an important point arising in the debate on the celebrated Panama mission. Mr. Randolph had made on this question a most scathing attack on the administration. In reference to it, Mr. Calhoun, as presiding officer of the Senate, decided, that he had no power to restrain a Senator in respect to words spoken in debate. Out of that decision, arose a controversy engaging all the powers and prejudices of friends and opponents of the administration. No one ever doubted Mr. Calhoun's honesty of purpose in this decision, or the superiority of his defence, under the signature of 'Onslow.'

Mingling in the conflicts arising on the Tariff of 1828, and in connection with the efforts to defeat Mr. Adams on a second election, Mr. Calhoun was placed in a position to display, in strong light, his extraordinary resistance to party ties in the performance of duty. The contest in respect to the Tariff had nearly equally divided the Senate. To avoid the consequences of a tie-vote, Mr. Calhoun, who was on the ticket with General Jackson for the Vice-Presidency, was advised to withdraw from his seat. He indignantly refused; determined, as he declared, to risk all hope of advancement for himself, rather than shrink from his duty. In order to avoid, however, the possibility of injuring the prospects of General Jackson, he declared his willingness to take his name from the ticket.

We pass over various particulars in the history of Mr. Calhoun's distinguished services in the cabinet of Mr. Monroe, in the Vice-Presidency and in the Senate, all exhibiting the superiority of his judgment, and the sincerity of his attachment to the Constitution and the Union. We will pause to consider that period, when, having done so much to elevate General Jackson, he was treacherously superseded in his confidence. We will not examine into the causes of that event; we will not gather up the nearly extinguished sparks from the ashes of that disgraceful and scandalous quarrel, in which the only decency and moderation were displayed by its victim.

Two acts of Mr. Calhoun in the sessions of 1814, 1815, and 1816, have been the subject of frequent animadversion and defence. It will be understood we refer to the bill reported by him to set apart and pledge the *bonus* of the United States Bank, as a fund for internal improvement, and his assent to the policy of the Bank, recommended by Madison. It is enough to say here, in regard to these measures, that, with respect to the first, Mr. Calhoun, as we understand, has never denied that it was his early impression that the constitutional power of Congress over internal improvement was comprehended under the money power. The error, as he believed, of this view, was soon developed, and the promptest confession of it made. In reference to the Bank, Mr. Calhoun has ever insisted that he yielded to the necessity for its establishment, in view of the peculiar position of the country and its finances at the time, and not of its general policy or constitutionality.

We come to the exciting topic of State interposition. Out of the opposition of the South to the Tariff of 1828, this doctrine began to be developed. From the long fallow-ground of the Virginia and Kentucky resolutions the seeds of this principle were gathered, and scattered in a new soil. They grew and flourished luxuriantly in the South, and received the early and warm encouragement of Mr. Calhoun. The 'South Carolina exposition and Protest on the Tariff,' adopted by the Legislature of that State, was understood to have been proposed by Mr. Calhoun. The following extract from a document by Mr. Calhoun, embraces the leading features of this doctrine:

'The great and leading principle is, that the General Government emanated from the several States, forming distinct political communities, and acting in their separate and sovereign capacity, and not from all of the people forming one aggregate political community; that the Constitution of the United States, is, in fact, a compact, to which each State is a party, in the character already described; and that the several States or parties have a right to judge of its infractions, and, in case of a deliberate, palpable, dangerous exercise of power not delegated, they have the right, in the last resort, to use the language of the Virginia resolutions, "*to interpose for arresting the progress of the evil, and for maintaining within their respective limits the authorities, rights, and liberties, appertaining to them.*" This right of interposition, thus solemnly asserted by the State of Virginia, be it called what it may, State-right, veto, nullification, or by any other name, I conceive to be the fundamental principle of our system, resting on facts historically as certain as our Revolution itself, and deductions as simple and demonstrative as that of any political or moral truth whatever; and I firmly believe, that on its recognition depends the stability and safety of our political institutions.

'I am not ignorant that those opposed to the doctrine have always, now and formerly, regarded it in a very different light, as anarchical and revolutionary. Could I believe such, in fact, to be its tendency, to me it would be no recommendation. I yield to none, I trust, in a deep and sincere attachment to our political institutions, and the union of these

States. I never breathed an opposite sentiment; but, on the contrary, I have ever considered them the great instrument of preserving our liberties, and promoting the happiness of ourselves and our posterity; and, next to these, I have ever held them most dear. Nearly half my life has passed in the service of the Union, and whatever public reputation I have acquired is indissolubly identified with it. To be too national has, indeed, been considered by many, even of my friends, to be my greatest political fault. With these strong feelings of attachment, I have examined, with the utmost care, the bearing of the doctrine in question; and so far from anarchical or revolutionary, I solemnly believe it to be the only solid foundation of our system, and of the Union itself, and that the opposite doctrine, which denies to the States the right of protecting their several powers, and which would vest in the General Government (it matters not through what department) the right of determining, exclusively and finally, the powers delegated to it, is incompatible with the sovereignty of the States and of the Constitution itself, considered as the basis of a Federal Union. As strong as this language is, it is not stronger than that used by the illustrious Jefferson, who said, to give the General Government the final and exclusive right to judge of its powers, is to make "*its discretion, and not the Constitution, the measure of its powers*," and that "*in all cases of compact between parties having no common judge for itself, as well of the infraction as of the mode and measure of redress.*" Language cannot be more explicit, nor can higher authority be adduced.'

But how shall we treat this important period in Mr. Calhoun's life? How speak of his views without giving offence? How shall we mention the arguments, and relate the incidents of Nullification, without awakening the prejudices and heart-burnings of the times! How shall we do justice to Mr. Calhoun's sentiments, without wronging the sentiments of others? The cause that produced this fearful controversy was removed. The quarrel which shook the faith of men in the stability of our government was adjusted. Great God! bless the noble spirits who substituted peace for war! Immortal be the memory of the statesmen who looked beyond the animosities of a moment—who, in the midst of the excesses of the times, animated by holy emotions of patriotism, resolved, by honorable concession and compromise, to preserve and perpetuate the union of these States!

During the pendency of this question, the most momentous that ever agitated the country, Mr. Calhoun engaged in an intellectual conflict with Mr. Daniel Webster. Never had the world listened to finer exhibitions of mind. The rolling words of the great New Englander came like the swelling bosom of the great father of waters, exciting terrible apprehensions of danger to the Union. The keen logic, the clear conceptions of his opponent, filled the whole horizon with effulgence.

While the giants were contesting the field, victory now inclining to the one, now to the other, the issue uncertain—dreaded by all men—the great chieftain of compromises stepped into the arena, and threw up the weapons of the combatants. He, whose life was ever superior to the advantage of the moment. He, who revives, in our time, the most glorious conceptions of Cicero. He, who, when others strove for the triumphs of party, snatched from destiny the victories of conciliation; introduced his celebrated bill of compromise, and dispelled the storm. Mr. Calhoun was not behind Henry Clay in magnanimity and love of country. If not the first to propose the compromise, he was the first to accept it. If, as most falsely charged, he was ambitious of a Southern Presidency, he would never have gone forth so readily to accept, on the part of the South, the proffered olive branch. He stood first in the Northern States. Never had the people of these States been so united in opposition, never so warm in their confidence in Mr. Calhoun. Had their Union been dissolved, he would have been the first spirit in the South; and this he knew. But no one rejoiced more than he did, that the day of tranquillity had returned; that the conflict was at an end, and the Union saved. In the most inclement season, he hurried to South Carolina, where resistance had assumed a most decided aspect, and, by his influence, induced the State to yield to peaceful interference. No man in the United States could have produced the result but Mr. Calhoun; and the anxiety with which he pressed this compromise attests, beyond question, his love for the Union. Dissimulation has never found a place in Mr. Calhoun's heart. Had he desired a dissolution of the confederacy, he would have avowed the wish fearlessly, and without equivocation. But he believed, that the dangers of a consolidation were upon us; and if, out of his intense study of a means to avert them, he came to conclusions, and pressed abstractions, the truth of which did not strike other men, it does not follow that he was not entirely honest in his belief of their efficacy and veracity.

Shall we probe further the wounds of this controversy? Shall we draw aside the pall covering the relics of a strife, at rest, we trust, for all future time? Shall we, like opposing fanatics, as was done in the case of William the Norman, engage in repeated exhumations, in order to indulge in the ostentation of repeated funeral services? Who would be benefitted, who convinced? Let the storm rest! The winds are still! The surface of the sea is calm and undisturbed. The clouds are receding from the overhanging canopy, and men breathe freely. Out of the east, a new sun, the successor of that which yesterday declined in clouds, is beginning to rise, and pour its healthful rays over the land. Brethren of the same household are rejoicing in its splendor. May it warm and light them forever! May no dismal shadows intervene, and obscure its beams; but, full of luxuriance, may the land teem with life, all busy in the ark of peace, all faithful in devotion to the Union!

On the adjustment of the Tariff question, Mr. Calhoun gave himself, with great energy, to his labors as a Senator, in the more general measures in which the country was interested. Attached as he had been, from principle, to the party of General Jackson; desirable as it evidently was on the part of his friends to bring about a reconciliation, and to aid the administration with his talents and influence, he did no act, he said no word, indicating a desire to reconcile past differences, or to avail himself of support. He felt he had nothing to atone for, and therefore had none of the successes of compliance.

He displayed his independence of party ties prominently, in the memorable debate on the Removal of the Deposites; he condemned the dismissal of Mr. Duane, as an abuse of power; and, though he exposed such defects of a national banking system, he did not hesitate to deny the right of the Secretary to withhold the deposits, while the Bank performed its obligations faithfully. He predicted, in a speech of extraordinary ability, various errors in the management of the currency. He denounced, with temperate but decided expression, the reception of the celebrated protest of the President; and placed the powers of the several departments of the Government under the Constitution in a novel and satisfactory light. He raised, by motion, a Committee of Inquiry into the abuses of Executive patronage; the able report of which committee, prepared and submitted by himself, astounded the country as to the extent of that corrupt system, and produced a more powerful and just reaction against the administration than any effort of its avowed opponents. With a mind settled in its convictions as to the powers of a national bank, and of State banking institutions, as vehicles for the dispensing of the money patronage of the Government, he conceived and advocated the adopting the principle of that scheme, since carried into effect under the name of the Sub-Treasury. The Specie Circular next occupied his attention. He denied the authority of the President to issue the order on which it was based; but regarding the mischiefs of the step as beyond remedy, declined voting on the question of its revision.

It was at this juncture, that the political sky began to overcast with the approaching Abolition storm. The immediate fears on this subject was removed by the firmness of Mr. Calhoun, who, foreseeing the danger of receiving petitions on this topic, which began to overload the tables of Congress, by his arguments and influence, procured the settlement of a precedent against their reception. On the question of the admission of Michigan, the danger spread again. Mr. Calhoun was opposed to admitting a State on the authority of a mere informal meeting of the people inhabiting a territory. His views are presented in the following brief extract:

"My opinion was, and still is, that the movement of the people of Michigan, in forming for themselves a State constitution, without waiting for the assent of Congress, was revolutionary, as it threw off the authority of the United States over the territory; and that we were left at liberty to treat the proceedings as revolutionary, and to remand her to her territorial condition, or to wave the irregularity, and to recognize what was done as rightfully done, as our authority was alone concerned.

"A territory cannot be admitted till she becomes a State; and in this I stand on the authority of the Constitution itself, which expressly limits the power of Congress to admit new States into the Union. But, if the Constitution had been silent, he would indeed be ignorant of the character of our political system, who did not see that states, sovereign and independent communities, and not territories, can only be admitted. Ours is *a union of States—a Federal* Republic. States, and not territories, form its component parts, bound together by a solemn league, in the form of a constitutional compact. In coming into the Union, the State pledges its faith to this sacred compact; an act which none but a sovereign and independent community is competent to perform; and, of course, a territory must first be raised to that condition, before she can take her stand among the confederated states of our Union. How can a territory pledge its faith to the Constitution? It has no will of its own. You give it all its powers, and you can at pleasure overrule all her actions. If she enters as a territory, the act *is yours, not hers. Her consent is nothing without your authority and sanction.* Can you, can Congress become a party to the constitutional compact? How absurd."

This view of the subject was novel then—it is novel now. The question has been since raised on the admission of California, but the grounds on which Mr. Calhoun placed it, have been entirely overlooked.

Our limits will not allow us to follow Mr. Calhoun's brilliant career through the minor phases of his public life. We pass to two great and wonderful exhibitions of his mind and integrity. We leave out of view his able speeches on the McLoud matter; Mr. Crittenden's resolutions to permit the interference of executive officers in elections; the veto power; the Bankrupt Bill; and look to his services on the Oregon question. In this controversy Mr. Calhoun saw but the great interests of the nation, and the justice of her position. He became the great, the leading advocate of peace. He threw his influence into the scale at the very moment when that influence was most needed and could be most powerfully felt. He performed an act which both God and man approved. He rose superior to the excitements of the occasion. He repelled from his breast the national feelings, which so frequently rule the judgment. He rejected the prejudices which grow up in the American heart against English power; and in the act, anticipated the happiness of millions. Few can estimate the value of Mr. Calhoun's services in the adjustment of this international difficulty. Had Mr. Calhoun no other claim to the favor of his countrymen, that were enough to secure for his name immortality. We are disgusted with the idea of the crime and guilt which would have followed a war with Great Britain on the Oregon question; and in proportion to our detestation of an unjust war, rises our respect for Mr. Calhoun's noble effort to avert it. We almost tremble when we survey the consequences which would have ensued. We blush to view the pretexts set up for a resort to arms. Is our nation—one boasting its foundation on principles of pacification and good order, to go to war only for success? Are human beings, proud of their residence in a land of liberty and laws, to contest as wild beasts, vaunting of their strength and struggling only for spoils? Is the commerce of all civilized countries to be wrecked, the peaceful fields of agriculture to be rendered desolate; are men to be butchered, and widows and orphans to be left mourning, merely to gratify the ambition of party leaders, and to minister to the vain externals of politics? Who—what advocate of that war ever promised himself, or his country, or the cause of humanity, a single advantage which it were not a crime to boast? Who, in seeing that chivalrous spirit who interposed his magnanimous efforts to remove all cause of difficulty, did not feel honor, truth, justice, were all vindicated in their own temple, and the cause of universal peace among men subserved?

It is scarcely necessary for us to say that there are many things in the course of Great Britain we do not approve. But, we also declare, there are some things we venerate and respect. Our memory dwells with pleasure on the fact that, we have sprung from her; that we have been taught the purity of our language, amidst the glorious remains of her literature, and to appreciate the beauties of art and philosophy in her splendid monuments of genius. We take delight in the recollection that we were instructed by her in our religion and laws, and in our first rudiments of civil freedom. That her Magna Charta extends its rays to our institutions, and that the blood of Russell and Sydney sprinkled the door-posts of our dwellings, and exempted us from political death. To us with these emotions, the settlement of the cause of this last dispute brought the noblest reflections, and to the memory of him, who, more than any patriot and statesman, was the instrument, nay, the conqueror of peace, we would give the best and highest rewards which a grateful country can bestow.

Scarcely had this affair been settled, before another cloud rose on the horizon. The long-agitated question of interference with slavery in the District of Columbia, and the new territories, was opened to wide and intemperate debate. Ever jealous of the slightest invasion of the Constitution—ever believing the South, in respect to this institution, in peril, Mr. Calhoun, in feeble health, hurried to his post.

It were fruitless to open the book of this controversy over Mr. Calhoun's beir. The South knows the wrong done her in regard to this topic; she knows the moral and political influences that crowd around the question; but the whole world knows her arguments of right, and her means of repelling attack. She will make no boast of her chivalry, and hesitate long to anticipate the judgment of posterity as to her patriotism. If these have not been attested in many well-fought fields in the Revolutionary and late wars, she claims no privilege of being further heard. On the facts of her slave institutions she makes no explanation, and requires no apology. She will arbitrate mere differences of opinion with any power, but will yield no right in which the integrity of the Constitution and the principles of political liberty are at issue. For the protection of those, she places herself on the moral force of natural laws, and will never resort to physical means of defence, till all peaceful agencies are exhausted.

Will it be said—"this is Disunion?" Not so. Much as we revere the institutions of our State—far as we would commit ourselves for their preservation—we cannot doubt, we never have doubted, we never will doubt the virtue of loving the Union, and guarding its inviolability. It is true, as was said by Mr. Calhoun, declarations will not preserve it. But it is equally true that sentiments give direction to actions. Though the greatest security of it will be found in the most faithful observance of the obligations of the Constitution; this fact does not forbid our contemplating with alarm, the consequences of a dissolution. This great confederacy of States, considered irrespective of a centralizing power—which might be used as a means of destruction to the authority of the States severally, viewed in connection with the history of its origin, with the characters of the immortal men who originated and have sustained the Union—certainly is beyond all value. No speculation can be indulged as to its worth to posterity and to us, in these respects; no standard of appreciation can be formed, to designate its relative price. It is a sacred heir-loom of a family, having higher claims to respect than its age or its parents; its value consists in the memory of the ancestry which first achieved it; in the honorable recollections of the triumphs amidst which it was won and worn. Its worth is at once moral and traditionary. It is full of past glory, of present respect, of future hope. It is the title, the dignity, the birth-record of Freedom; the evidence of all that is noble in the history of her noblest contests. Adorning and enriching the story of our country, it comes to us pregnant with proofs of struggles and successes which were national at first, are national now, and should be national to the last. How can this relic be divided? Who shall take Bunker Hill, Eutaw, Saratoga, or the Palmetto Fort, in the partition of those glories? How, when we come to make up the list of the sacrifices and the victims of the Revolution, shall we divide them? Long be the period removed, when posterity shall throng about the resting places of the illustrious dead, and prepare to divide the sacred inheritance!

We approach the close of Mr. Calhoun's life. The human mind must necessarily pass through a trial, when in great calamity it is called to recognize the superior wisdom of God's judgment, and to practice resignation amidst its griefs. The vivid intellect was declining at a time of great danger to the principles he had so long defended, and which had so long filled his thoughts. On one occasion he said, he desired to be heard as one asking nothing for himself, but whose only wish was to see his country free, prosperous and happy. The same sentiment was on his lips when he died. The man who conquers the cruel terrors of death—who looks in the trying moment of dissolution, not on his own immortality on earth, but to the immortality of his country—who, anxious for her liberty, overcomes the shock of disease, the spectacle of a mourning wife and children—whose last words attest his devotion to the perpetuity of the Constitution—is surely a patriot. The confessions of one whose whole life we have distrusted, force themselves on the belief, when they come forth in the instant of dissolution. How much more solemn and impressive the admonitions of one whose long life, exhibiting the utmost purity of private character, and the firmest displays of patriotic self-denial, dying with a prayer for his country on his lips! Such was the life, such the death of Mr. Colhoun. On his cenotaph let that be written, to which his life was a martyr—Sincerity. Long in his native State—long in the history of his nation—will his memory illustrate the character of the true statesman, and furnish uncommon inducements to a life of virtue. The implacable hatred which pursued him—the secret envy that misrepresented him—are dead! A State, ever the rewarder of faithful services in the cause of public virtue, mourning her eldest son; a nation, lamenting the extinguishment of an intellect long enlightening her progress, stand about his grave, and record the incontestable triumph of The Honest Man.

Few men can withstand the influence of that love of public approbation, which, for wise purposes, is planted in the human breast. Few have the firmness to reject honors for the sake of virtue;—few, in the moment of popular *favor*, can put back the rewards offered;—few can display, amidst temptation, the immutability of conscience. Lord Camden, in English history, Mr. Calhoun in American, are conspicuous examples of these unusual gifts. Alike they were intellectual, alike unchangeably incorruptible. Always important to parties, always unaffected by their corruptions, they were alike victims to whatever was just. For them office had no allurement, and political power no terror. They declared belief of right as frankly as they denounced wrong; and, as was said by St. Jerome, of religion, if in error, it was a glorious privilege to be deceived with such guides.

CHARLES FRASER.

This distinguished and venerable gentleman was born on the 20th August, 1782, in the City of Charleston, where he was educated and has always resided. When at school he was a favorite of our great Chief Justice, the Honorable John Rutledge—the guiding star of our State during the darkest days of the Revolution. The youth looked up with veneration to the sage, and learned from his lips much of the history of our country. The Chief Justice and his father married sisters. He was reared under the happiest influences in the society to which he belonged—the best in our State—and there he learned that refinement and urbanity which characterise the Carolina gentleman. Mr. Fraser early showed a desire to become a painter; but, his father having died when he was but nine years of age, the friend who had the charge of his education would not yield to his wish, but directed his education to the law. He remained in a lawyer's office for three years, then deserted it, and pursued, for a short time, his favorite art—painting. In 1804, he resumed the study of the law in the office of the Honorable John Julius Pringle—so long the very able and highly distinguished Attorney-General of the State. With his capacities and habits of application, under the auspices of so great a master he could not fail to make much progress in his legal studies. He was admitted to the Bar on the 10th February, 1807, in the City of Charleston. Soon after his admission, he delivered an oration before the Cincinnati and Revolution Societies, on the fourth of July, 1808, which was universally admired, and furnished the strongest evidence of his fitness for his profession. His master in the law, full of years and of honors, began, about this time, to wind up his affairs at the Bar, and soon retired from the Attorney-Generalship. He well knew Mr. Fraser's integrity and ability; to him he entrusted much of his unfinished legal business, recommended him to his clients, and, by his countenance and commendation, promoted the progress of his young friend. At a future day, on the death of his venerable and venerated preceptor, that young friend showed his deep respect and regard in an obituary that did honor to the illustrious dead and to the mindful living.

In the fall of 1810, Mr. Fraser was one of the first to unite with several gentlemen of similar literary taste and pursuits in founding the Conversation Club, which has so long existed in Charleston, and has been to them and the friends who have often honored them with their company, a source of much improvement and rational enjoyment. For this Club, Mr. Fraser wrote his admirable Reminiscences of Charleston. They will remain an enduring monument to his memory, and an authentic record of an interesting portion of our history. About the same time, he contributed to a series of religious essays, which appeared every Saturday in the Charleston Courier, and which were so highly esteemed that they were collected and published in a handsome octavo volume, which, some years after, was re-published in England.

He continued to practice law for about eleven years. In that time he had secured a competency; he then abandoned the law, and devoted himself to the pursuit of the profession he loved most—painting—to the indulgence of his literary tastes, and to promoting every enterprise and institution connected with the improvement and refinement of the community. In 1817, he was elected a Trustee of the College of Charleston. Soon after, he was appointed to the Treasurership of the Board of Trustees of that institution, and for many years most faithfully performed its troublesome duties. His exertions and labors, together with those of his friend Judge King, and others, have done much to sustain the college, and place it in its present condition. At the laying of the corner-stone of the present new building, he delivered an excellent oration, which was published at the request of the Board of Trustees. On several public occasions, he has been specially solicited to address his fellow-citizens, and has uniformly acquitted himself with distinguished success. His style is remarkable for its chaste and classic purity and beauty. In

1850, on the dedication of Magnolia Cemetery—that City of the Dead, which lies on the outskirts of Charleston—he was invited to deliver the address. It was the last public discourse which he pronounced, and its opening refers thus touchingly and gracefully to himself:

" *Gentlemen,*—You have not unappropriately selected one to address you on the dedication of Magnolia Cemetery, to whom the most of life is in retrospect, and whose future is bounded by no distant horizon. The occasion is solemn and impressive, and the reflections it excites well becomes him whose early friendships have almost passed away like a dream, and whose most cherished recollections are identified with the grave."

Few men have touched life at so many points as Mr. Fraser—to few has nature been so bountiful in her gifts; as a jurist and an artist, as an orator and an essayist, he has been equally successful. His influence to humanize and refine has been widely and decidedly felt. Admiration for his virtues and accomplishments induced the Hon. Mitchell King, Daniel Ravenel, Esq., Rev. Dr. Gilman, Dr. S. H. Dickson, Messrs. G. S. Bryan, F. A. Porcher, G. W. Flagg, John A. Alston, J. H. Taylor, and others of his friends, in February, 1857, to collect as many of his paintings and miniatures as could be gathered, in a public exhibition. Three hundred and thirteen miniatures, and one hundred and thirty-nine landscapes and other paintings, were collected, and continued on public exhibition for many weeks—the whole forming a striking monument of his skill and industry.

Having thus adorned society by the graces of his accomplishments, and honored his State by the productions of his pen and pencil, Mr. Fraser now lives in the calm retirement of a venerated old age—the repose of his declining years secured, no doubt, by reflections such as are expressed in the following impressive lines, written by him in 1847:

"Keep thy heart with all diligence."—PROV. iv., 23.

Trust not that one unguarded thought,
Which idly wantons in the mind,
Shall vanish as it entered there,
And leave no trace behind.

Think not that unremembered words,
In anger or resentment said,
Because forgotten shall not live
By truth immortal made.

Nor hope a single reckless act,
Whose folly wayward youth beseems,
Shall yield to time's oblivious hour
With youth's departed dreams.

A page by angel pen inscribed
Records what ne'er can be effaced,
And all you think, or do, or say
Is there forever traced.

Then o'er the heart its hidden source
Thy vigils keep with ceaseless care ;
Let every purpose be thy best,
Offence thy only fear.

And, oh ! what higher, holier hope
Was e'er to man in mercy given,
Than angel pen in lines of light
Should write thy name in heaven.

ENOCH HANFORD.

Enoch Hanford, Esq., was born in Norwalk, Connecticut, in the year 1777. He graduated at Yale College, on the 10th September, 1800. After studying law with Roger M. Sherman, Esq., he came to Fayetteville, N. C., where, in 1803, he became acquainted with Colonel William DeWitt, a gentleman residing at Society Hill, who employed him as a private tutor for his son, Charles M. DeWitt, a young gentleman of fine talents, who was advantageously mentioned by that distinguished gentleman, James L. Petigru, Esq., in his semi-centennial address, delivered in the S. C. College Hall, December, 1855, as a member of the class of 1808. In the course of his first year's employment, he married his employer's daughter, Miss Margaret DeWitt; and, in 1804, he conducted St. David's Academy, at Society Hill.

He was elected in 1804, Professor of Languages in the South Carolina College, and, with Dr. Maxcy, President of the College, opened it on the 10th of January, 1805. This was rather a gloomy beginning, for a college—a president and one professor, but they boldly met the contingency, and commenced the collegiate education of the young men of South Carolina, from which so much good has since been realized. A grateful people ought to remember, with honor and affection, the names of Maxcy and Hanford.

On the 28th of November, 1806, Professor Hanford resigned, and, in April, 1807, he was admitted to the Bar of the Law Courts; and, on the 26th of April, 1809, he was licensed to practice in the Court of Equity.

He practiced law at Society Hill, I presume, till his death, which occurred on the 9th of September, 1817, leaving two daughters and one son, who died when young.

He is described by Dr. Laborde, in his history of the college, p. 37–38, as "a gentleman of good personal appearance, and somewhat above the common size. His attainments in scolarship were respectable, though not of that high order which would now be expected. They were the attainments of a well-educated gentleman, who did not pursue literature as a means of advancement in life; and, it is believed that he resorted to teaching, as a temporary employment, until he could establish himself advantageously in his chosen profession."

During his connexion with the college, he was much respected by the students; and he rendered truly valuable services to the institution, at this early but trying period of its existence. As a lawyer, his attainments were good. His mind was well stored with the elementary principles of his profession. His arguments in court were sound, but his manner of speaking was slow and hesitating.

Dr. Laborde's description of his person and character as a scholar and lawyer, was, I have no doubt, derived from Mr. Hanford's brother-in-law, my much-respected friend and brother Judge, Evans, and therefore I adopt it as the best which can he had.

JOHN LYDE WILSON.

This extraordinary man was born in Marlborough District, South Carolina, on the 24th of May, 1784. He received a good academic education, and studied law with Judge Chase, in the City of Baltimore, for more than three, and probably for four years, as that was the term of study required at the period of his admission to the Bar, which took place at Columbia, in 1807.

He settled in Georgetown, and married the daughter of Col. William Alston, and the sister of Gov. Joseph Alston, by whom he had two children, daughters. His wife died early; her children were raised by her sister, Lady Nesbitt. He was first returned to the House of Representatives in the General Assembly of South Carolina, from Prince George Winyaw, in 1808.

I first saw him, so that I remembered him, in November, 1812. He was then Chairman of the Committee of Privileges and Elections in the House. The seat of Thomas Rothmaler Mitchell, Esq.—returned as a Member from Prince George Winyaw—was contested by Benjamin Huger, Esq. I heard the contest. Mr. Huger stated one of his objections to be, that three votes were found in the box, in several instances, cut apart and rolled up in one; these he called "*sows and pigs.*" This singular expression fixed the matter upon my mind. The protest was sustained, and the seat of the sitting member vacated. From that period I knew Mr. Wilson as a Member of the House of Representatives, and afterwards as Senator from Prince George Winyaw. In 1822, he was elected President of the Senate, and in the course of the session he was elected Governor and Commander-in-chief.

In 1822, before his election as Governor, he had published a severe review of the Court of Appeals, and a harsh criticism on Chancellor Waties' elaborate decree, in the case of Carr and Wife *vs.* Greene. This production, I have no doubt, contributed greatly to the overthrow of the Court of Appeals in Equity, in 1824.

In 1822, I was invited to attend a friendly legal conference the house of my friend Col. Gregg, which was attended by at Gov. Wilson, Gov. Miller, Judge Evans, Judge Butler, and many other eminent lawyers. The project of a separate Court of Appeals as a necessary remedy for the supposed abuses and errors in Equity, was discussed, and my objections met and removed, for from 1816, up to that time, I had been opposed to the proposed change. In 1824, I concurred fully, in the separate Court of Appeals, and I have ever since believed that it was and is better adapted to the proper administration of justice, than any other system, which ever has been tried, or can be suggested.

After Governor Wilson went out of office, he married a Miss Eden, of New York, (who was said to have been a ward of Colonel Burr,) by whom he had two children—daughters. His second wife preceded him to the tomb.

He was a member of the celebrated Nullification Convention of 1832, and in the session of 1832 and 1833, advocated the most violent measures which were proposed.

I see it is stated in the annunciation of Major General Schnierle, that he was elected several times to the Legislature, after the close of his term as Governor. I only recollect him as a Member of the Senate, at the trial of Judge James, in 1827–1828.

In 1838, he published "The Code of Honor," which he affirmed to be the means of saving life. If so, it deserves credit; but if it be only rules for the regulation of private combats, called "duelling," then I cannot consider it of any value. For, as a friend who had been engaged in more than one duel, once said to me: "Duelling is now deliberate murder, It is," said he, "no longer an affair of chivalry, in which there is an appeal to the god of battles, for victory to the right; but *now*, the parties prepare to kill each other by superior skill in the use of the instrument of death. I will," said he, "have no more to do with it"—*and he never did.* Those were the sentiments of Matthew Irvine Keith, whose name is authority on such a subject, as that to which I have alluded.

Governor Wilson's intellect was a fine one. His speeches, political and legal, were always compiled with wonderful arrangement and care. He possessed the art of putting his thoughts, in an extemporary speech, in the *lucido ordine*, so much commended by the ancients. His voice and manner were fine and graceful. If he had cultivated the great talents with which God had endowed him, he must have been among the greatest men of South Carolina.

General John Schnierle tells us, in the article to which I have already alluded: "his nature was above disguise, and his resentments, terrible in their outbreak, were ever under the control of a gentle and kindly nature." He had often the misfortune to be engaged in bitter feuds, which, more than once, were settled by an appeal to the field of honor, as it is falsely called.

There his coolness never deserted him, and he uniformly was the victor in such scenes.

Governor Wilson died in Charleston, on the 12th of February, 1849. Appropriate military honors were paid to his body, which was interred alongside of his second wife, in St. Paul's Church-yard. The evening of Governor Wilson's life, was a dark and gloomy one; it was, however, very much brightened by the attention of a brother lawyer, who never saw suffering without attempting to alleviate it.

BENJAMIN C. YANCEY.

Of this eminent gentleman, I have sought for information, and have not been fortunate enough to obtain much aid beyond my own memory.

He was the son of James Yancey, Esq., who, as I think, lived in Laurens District, and was a County Court Lawyer, and possibly the County Attorney. One of my informants thinks he was born in Boston, another that he was born in Charleston. It is certain that his mother was a Cudworth, a lady of the lower country; and that he was educated at the school of Dr. Pyles, Laurens District. James McKibbin, and John Caldwell were his schoolmates.

He was a midshipman on board the Constellation, under Commodore Truxton, and was present and bore a part in the engagement between her and the French frigates, L'Insurgente and La Vengeance—the former was captured, the latter escaped in the night after having struck her colors.

After peace with France, he resigned, studied law with Robert Goodloe Harper, Esq., in Baltimore, Maryland, and then came to Laurens and finished his studies with B. H. Saxon, Esq., and was admitted to the Bar, but when, I cannot say, for his name does not appear on the Charleston or Columbia Roll.

On the 8th December, 1808, he married Miss Caroline Bird, of Georgia, a daughter of Colonel William Bird, and the sister of Mrs. Captain Robert Cunningham; he then settled at Abbeville. When I first saw Mr. Yancey, he was a Member of the Legislature, from Abbeville District, I think, in 1812. He was then remarkable for his talent, as a ready debater, and became the aid of Governor Alston, with the rank of Colonel.

Mr. Yancey was one of the Committee of Two, who examined Mr. McDuffie and myself in the Court of Equity, at the Spring Term of 1814.

In the summer and fall of 1814, I met Mr. Yancey, at Abbeville and Laurens as a Solicitor in Equity and an Attorney-at-law. From that time forward to his death I had frequent opportunities of knowing him.

In October, 1816, I was returned to the House of Representatives, and there met Mr. Yancey as a Representative from Charleston. He had been a Member from Abbeville in 1810, '11, '12 and '13. He failed to be returned from Abbeville, in 1814, owing, it is said, to the ascendancy of the Calhoun and Noble parties, and, as I have heard, to some unpopularity connected with the cases arising out of Patrick Duncan's right to the large tract of land granted to Livingston and his associates, and of which Francis Salvador, at his death, was the owner, commonly called the Jews'-land cases.* He removed to Charleston, was the partner of Judge Huger, and was rising rapidly to eminence at the Charleston Bar. He was the Chairman of the Judiciary Committee in 1816. In the business and debates of that Session in the House of Representatives he bore an active and useful part. In the summer of 1817, at the house of his friend, Col. Chistopher Breithaupt, in Edgefield District, on his way from Charleston, with his family, to visit his brother-in-law, Captain Cunningham, he sickened and died with yellow fever. He was about thirty-five years of age at his death. Mr. Yancey was eminent for his talents, legal acquirements, and unyielding firmness. He prepared his cases with great care; he was anxious, and even timid, about his preparation, but when in Court, he seemed as if he never knew the word *fear*. His arguments were clear, forcible, and sometimes eloquent. Most generally he relied on argument, not eloquence. He sometimes indulged in a little sarcasm. Cases, which were considered almost desperate, were confided to his care, and he was often successful where failure was anticipated.

In the Jews'-land cases he visited Washington, and, before

---

*This gentleman was killed in an ambuscade of the Cherokees, whereby Williamson was surprised in his attack about 2 A. M., of the 1st of August.—See second Drayton's Memoirs 345, '6, '7, '8, '9.

the Supreme Court, succeeded in defeating the Philadelphia Land Company, (perhaps called the North American Land Company,) which had succeeded on the circuit in recovering the land. He was the leading counsel in the case against Mitchupon for murder, which I stated in the sketch of Judge Brevard. He was concerned, at his death, for the plaintiff, in the case of "Duncan *vs.* The occupants of the Jews-land ;" and his executors, in the defence of a case brought by Duncan against them, were allowed, on a discount, a large fee for his services.—Duncan *vs.* the executors of Yancey, 1 McC. 449. This, although richly merited by Mr. Yancey, was a bad precedent in a Court of Justice. It was the first instance of a fee recovered on a *quantum* non-suit, and has since led to the association of many such claims, often exorbitant, and which have very much detracted from the standing of my brethren who, like Cæsar's wife, ought to be above suspicion.

Mr. Yancey, I have already said, was a ready debater in the Legislature. He was not only that, but he was a most laborious and useful member. In 1816, the office of Chairman of the Judiciary Committee was a post requiring unceasing vigilance and labor. It was his duty to see that the laws proposed were aptly prepared and judiciously conceived. He presided each night over the labors of his Committee, and next day presented the result of their labors in the various reports. Everything was pressed forward then to expedite the business of the usual short sessions of our Legislature. Mr. Yancey was never known to be behind, and he was always ready to run a tilt, or break a lance with any opponent to his views or reports.

Mr. Yancey was remarkable for his courage. He showed it in early youth, in the affair with the French frigate, and in all after-life. He was courteous, as brave; I never saw him rude in Court or in the Legislature. He died, as it were, in the morning of life, and the tears of the State were shed upon his early grave. He was mourned by his widow, and two sons, William L. Yancey, Esq., now of Montgomery, Alabama, and Benjamin C. Yancey, Esq., now the U. S. Minister to the Argentine Republic.

JOHN M. FELDER.

This gentleman was born about 1780 or 1781. He was a native of Orangeburgh District, South Carolina, and the eldest son of Samuel Felder, deceased. His grandfather came from Zurich, Switzerland, about 1720 or 1730, and settled in Orangeburgh District, on a plantation still in the possession of the family.

This gentleman was a very active partizan in the Revolution. He brought his love of liberty from his native canton, and, like Tell, of his fatherland, he was willing to peril all, rather than submit to tyranny. He guided General Sumter in his approach to Orangeburgh, and bore a part in the capture of that post.

At or about the close of the war, the Tories surrounded his house: the gallant Swiss, by the aid of his wife and servants, who loaded his guns while he fired, killed more than twenty of his foes. His house was at last fired, and he was thus forced to fly. In attempting to escape, he was shot, and killed.

Much of his ancestor's love of liberty and determined purpose of character descended to the subject of this sketch.

He graduated with distinction in 1804, at Yale College, with John C. Calhoun and Bishop Gadsden, and was regarded as the best mathematician of his class. He read hard, under the direction of Judge Gould, and attended the lectures of Morris and Gould, in their celebrated Law-School, at Litchfield, Connecticut.

He was admitted to the Bar at Columbia, in 1808. He was a Member of the House of Representatives of South Carolina in 1812. My recollection of Major Felder inclines me to think he was a Member in 1810 and 1811. He was, I see, a member of the Board of Trustees of the South Carolina College in 1812, and was not elected at the Quadrennial Election in 1813. This would not (I should think) have occurred, if he had then been a Member of the House; but I see, from General Quattlebaum's remarks in the Senate, on moving resolutions in relation to his death, that he was placed on an important Special Committee in the House of Representatives, "to consider the propriety of chartering a Bank of the State," in 1812. This, I presume, might have been, at the August Extra Session of 1812.

The Major, when a Member, was a young man who dressed well, and wore broadcloth, which was not then very common above tide-water. My recollection is, he spoke often in the House of Representatives, and not very acceptably. On one occasion he harangued the House at some length, on a subject which I don't remember. It had the effect to empty the seats of many of the members. After making his speech he went into the lobby, where he met Henry Hampton, who was much of a wag. Felder said to him, "Henry, did you hear my speech?" "Oh, yes, Major," was the reply. "What did you think of it?" "I thought," said Henry, "it was the most moving speech I ever heard?"

He was, at this time, I presume from his title, a major in the line of the militia; at the close of the War of 1812, when the news of peace reached South Carolina, in Feb., 1815, he was on his way, at the head of a battalion from Orangeburgh, to assist in the defence of the seaboard.

Major Felder was, I presume, several times, between 1812 and 1830, a Member of the House of Representatives, though I have no recolletion of him as a Member but once, probably from 1822 to 1824.

In 1830 he was elected to Congress in the place of Judge Martin. For four years he was a Member. He then declined a re-election, and lived in retirement until 1840, when he was chosen Senator for Orange Parish, and continued in that office by successive elections until his death. A contributor to one of the papers in South Carolina, over the signature of "A Looker On," possibly in 1840, thus speaks of Major Felder, who had then lately come into the Senate. "He is a great acquisition to it. His manner is original in every respect; he possesses a well-stored mind, but his mode of conveying his information is so perfectly unique, that his rising to speak is always a signal for something fresh and entertaining. It matters not how many have spoken on the subject, every one still wishes to hear Mr. Felder, because no one can say the samething, and look so earnestly as he. His reasoning is generally correct, but it matters not how serious he is, he is always sure to convulse the Senate with laughter some dry expression or odd maxim he utters. As a politician, he is, perhaps, too distrustful of men. He looks suspiciously on all legislation, and at present his chief political considerations are centered in the cause of agriculture. He seems to consider few men great or good who do not till the earth. With Cowley, he sees that God made Adam a gardener, Abel a grazier or shepherd, and Cain a ploughman; and it was not until Cain became an artizan, or builder of cities, that he became a murderer. Mr. Felder sees a deep moral lesson in this piece of history, and upon it he seems to build his system of political economy.

"He is one of the strictest constructionists in the Senate. The Constitution is his polar star. To step one inch beyond it is to incur his severest censure—it matters not whether it be State or General Government. Though any one can see that Mr. Felder has much enriched his mind by books, he professes to despise them. He maintains that reading one's self and nature, and the shifts and roguery of men, is all the reading God ever intended men to pursue. He attaches much weight to individual experience, and he would not give a glance of his own observation for the telescopic view of all the rest of the world put together. He cares not about the rhetoric of his speeches—'tis not the flesh and nerves of his argument he aims at—'tis the bone and muscle: hence he frequently throws out his ideas naked as they were born, without a rag to cover them."—*Mr. Billinger's Scrap Book.*

Major Felder was a thriving successful lawyer from his admission to the Bar in 1808, until 1828 or '30.

He filed the bill in Equity in Orangeburgh District, in the case of Butler *vs.* Haskell.—4 Eq. Rep. 651. It involved a vast amount of property and money. It was brought to a hearing before Chanceller Thompson, February, 1816 ; and although the Major was aided by the great talents and learning of Wm. Harper, he failed in obtaining a decree. An appeal, as of course, followed, which was heard in Columbia, in May and in December. A majority of the Court of Appeals (De Saussure, Waties and James,) reversed the Circuit Decree. This success placed the Major on the topmost round of the professional ladder in Orangeburgh. He practiced for several years after—how long I cannot say. When he retired, he became a successful planter and mill-owner. By these means he acquired an estate, valued at more than half a million of dollars. When I was holding the Circuit Court in Orangeburgh, in 1847, he very politely invited me to ride with him over his vast domain below Orangeburgh; while making that ride, he stated his annual income at $20,000. I took the liberty of hinting to him, in a friendly way, as he was childless, what an amount of good he could do by educating some meritorious poor young people. He replied, that he had educated his nephews and nieces, and was then paying the way, at Carlisle College, Pennsylvania, of a young man (the son of Mr. Bonsell, deceased, formerly of Barnwell), and a grandson or a great-grandson of Mr. Jennings, the tavern-keeper of the village of Orangeburgh, in 1805.

The Major never was married; but for many years before his death, he discharged a father's part in rearing and educating the children of his deceased brother, Samuel Felder, the nephews and nieces to whom he alludes in the conversation mentioned in the paragraph above.

In August, 1831, he carried out a cherished purpose, in visiting his half-sister, Mrs. Pou, the wife of Lewis Pou, Esq., who resided in Georgia. On his return, at Union Point, on the Georgia Rail-road, on the 1st of September, 1831, he was suddenly taken ill with bilious cholic, and as a stranger, in a hut by the wayside, breathed his last. Who he was, was not known, until memoranda in his possession disclosed that the dead stranger was the Hon. John M. Felder, Senator from Orange Parish; the owner and possessor of an estate of, at least, half a million.

Death, at all times, is contemplated with awe; but death

among strangers, with none to smooth the dying pillow, or close, with the sigh of sympathy, the dying eyes, is, indeed, more than awful. It was, however, the fate of him, who had dedicated his life to gain and politics, and who had never known the blessed influences of wife and children. His great estate did not pursue the line of descent, which, if he had been permitted, he would have designated. According to the decision of the Court of Errors, it descended to his half-brother and sister, and the children of his deceased full brother, *per stripis*, in equal shares.

Major Felder was a Democrat; and in all the phases of politics he uniformly occupied that side, and always trusted and believed that that party would save the Union.

There is no doubt, he was an honest representative in every department of legislation, in the State or Federal government. His course was generally peculiar, and his remarks eccentric. His opposition to banks, and *rag money*, always styled bank bills, was unceasing and inveterate.

As a lawyer, he was more marked by success in the Circuit Court, than by general reputation. After his retirement from the Bar, he did not rely upon books; he studied men, and looked out upon nature, for all the illustrations which he needed in his public speeches.

The speech of General Quattlebaum, on moving the resolutions in the Senate, on the occasion of his death, and an obituary, understood to have been prepared by Gov. Hammond, are appended, and will supply whatever is omitted in the preceding memoir:

THE LATE HON. JOHN M. FELDER.

The Hon. John M. Felder, Senator from Orange, died at Union Point, on the Georgia Rail-road, after a very short illness, on the 1st of September, 1851, when on his return home from an excursion into the uppear parts of Georgia. He was born on the 7th of July, 1782, in Orangeburg District, in which was his permanent residence through the whole of his long life, and for the soil of which he cherished an attachment as deep and passionate as that of the Venetian of other days for his City of the Sea.

Major Felder was educated at Yale College, and graduated there with distinction in 1804, in the same class with the Hon. John C. Calhoun—both being about the same age. He was soon after admitted to the Bar, and practiced for some twenty years at Orangeburg and in the adjoining districts, with eminent success; when the cares of a large fortune which he had accumulated by his talent and enterprise, and the exigencies of his political career, induced him to withdraw from that avocation.

For about forty years Major Felder was actively engaged in politics, filled many high posts as a Representative of the people—never any other, and occupied no inconsiderable space in the public eye.

He was elected a member of the House of Representatives in 1812, and till his death, with but a short interval, continued to be a representative of the people, either in Congress or in the General Assembly of his native State.

He supported with zeal the war of 1812, in the House of Representatives, and, on the eve of peace, he was on the march at the head of a battalion from Orangeburg District, to assist in the defence of the seaboard of the State.

In 1830 he was elected a Member of Congress, and filled that then important station with much credit to himself and great satisfaction to his constituents for the succeeding four years, when he declined being a candidate for re-election.

He was, however, soon after, in 1840, chosen State Senator for Orange, and continued to represent his beloved parish in that body without intermission until his death.

Major Felder was a Democrat, from first to last, throughout his political career; and if politicians can be said, like poets, to be born, not made, he was undoubtedly born a Democrat, and never could have been anything else. The supporter of popular rights and interests, against aristocratic pretensions and governmental invasions, in all forms and on every occasion; he carried on through life an uncompromising warfare against the attempts of every clique that grasped at power, and against every combination to monopolise the earnings of the people, whether on a grand sectional scale by tariffs, or within the State by local corporations. He was warmly opposed to the charter of the Bank of the State in 1812, and voted and spoke against it; and he was uniformly and vehemently hostile to it to the last. Indeed, the thing he had most at heart in State affairs, and to which he devoted most of his attention for the last ten years, was the overthrow of that Bank. And so inimical was he, on the same principles, to the United States Bank, that, strict constructionist as he was, he always applauded the removal of the deposits by General Jackson. He called it "the battle of the 22d of December"—alluding to the first check given by Jackson to the British on their landing at New Orleans.

The democratic instincts of Maj. Felder were so strong, that he never, to the last, gave up entirely his ancient faith in the great Democratic party of the Union; and, if, in discussing and embracing measures of resistance to the encroachments of the Federal Government, he appeared cooler, and did not go quite so far as some others, it was not that his temper was more phlegmatic, or his sense of injury less, or that any man living surpassed him in deotiovn to the South, and to South Carolina, and, above all, to Orange, but because he long believed, and to the last had some trust and hope, that the Democratic party, if not the whole of it, at least the Southern wing, would yet work out our salvation.

The mind of Major Felder was of a high order, though not of that caste that furnishes the most brilliant themes for eulogistic analysis and criticism. Endowed with close observation, a rapid generalization and a retentive memory, he acquired much, and applied his knowledge with great success to useful purposes.

In his latter years he had but little intercourse with books. "He read men," he said; and few could do it more rapidly or thoroughly. He was not what is called a metaphysician, nor a logician, nor a rhetorician. That is, he unfolded in his discourse no subtle analysis, made no formal array of syllogisms, and more adorned them with firm flourishes. Yet his conclusions, which were usually as profoundly true as they were pithily and effectively expressed, proved that he had penetrated by some process to the bottom of his subject, and brought back by the shortest route the most precious ore deposited there. He was an enterprising, and in all things, a practical man. But his practice was founded, like true faith, on accurate knowledge and deep reflection, and did not blindly grope after undefined and half-conceived results.

In short, Major Felder was an excellent specimen of that admirable and most valuable class of intellects, in which cultivation incessantly generates energy and enterprise, but over which, what for want of a better designation, we call common sense, holds unremitted and complete supremacy, cutting short at once all fantastic tendencies, and tearing the tempting veil from every delusive anticipation. This nicely adjusted balance, which in him was so well preserved through life, was dear, perhaps, more than will be allowed in this age, to a sound natural constitution, and the almost unintermitted health which he enjoyed.

In his seventieth year, his body was as erect, his step as elastic, his thinking as close and rapid, his speech as quick, his action as prompt, and his endurance as great as with most men at forty-five.

This long preservation he owed, in no small degree, to the moderation and simplicity of his habits. Major Felder was never married; but he was the head and centre of a large and most respectable family, who looked up to him with affectionate veneration, and to them he has left a very large fortune, acquired chiefly by his own exertions.

In his social intercourse with them, and with his neighbors around his different plantations, as well as with his constituents and the world at large, his manners were uniformly kind, affable and courteous. To the lowly and deserving, to the distressed and injured he was ever ready to lend a helping hand, and render the efficient support of his advice and countenance.

And his death, while it deprives the State of one of its most useful citizens, and one of its very best public servants, leaves a gap in his domestic circle which never can be filled.

PROCEEDINGS IN THE STATE SENATE OF SOUTH CAROLINA.

Mr. Quattlebaum rose and said :

Mr. President,—Since we last assembled in this Chamber, death has invaded our ranks, and bereft us of the counsels of one of the oldest and most vigilant Members of the Senate. The seat so long filled by the Hon. John M. Felder, the late Senator from Orange, must hereafter be occupied by another. In view of this dispensation of an All-wise Providence, it becomes us, his late associates, to bear living testimony to the faithful manner in which he discharged his trust as a representative of the people.

It was my good fortune, sir, to have made his acquaintance long before I met him on this floor—when I was yet a boy—and, as I merged into manhood, a free, friendly correspondence and social intercourse with him imparted to me much practical information, of which he had a mind abundantly stored ; and for his acts of kindness to one so humble in life, I shall ever hold his name in grateful remembrance.

My personal knowledge, however, of his political career does not extend beyond the period at which he entered the Congress of the United States, as the successor of the late Judge Martin, some twenty years ago. But from then till the close of our last session, the last time he appeared in the public service, I feel assured that the closest scrutiny could not detect one single act of *his*, assimilating a dereliction of public duty. Of all those with whom I have been associated, since I have been honored with a seat in the Legislature, I can say with all the sincerity of my heart that I have found no one more wholly devoted to the promotion of what he conceived to be the true interests of the people. He was one who never lost sight of the responsibility to his constituents—one rarely found absent from his post. It was a governing principle of his life, to be there, if possible, as he often assured me, until the hammer fell.

The physical, as well as the mental struggle which carried us through the trying scene of the last night of the last session, must be durably impressed upon the mind of every Senator who nerved himself equal to the crisis. Trying as the scene was—as much physical exertion as it required to hold up under the fatigue, caused by our continuous session, throughout the entire night, after several previous protracted sittings—our venerable and departed friend furnished an example which many younger Senators could not follow. With him, the governing principle of his life was never more predominant than on that occasion. The people had sent him here to watch—to take care of their interests. It was no exemption from responsibility that he was worn down with fatigue; it was not for him to admit, that because three-score and ten years had wrought upon his once vigorous constitution, he had at last become unequal to the contest—unequal to the demands made upon him. He had once more to battle in their (the people's) cause. He expected that the Treasury would be assailed. He went, as usual, to his post, to defend it; participated largely in the business of the Senate, and retired, sir, when your hammer fell, announcing an adjournment, *sine die.* Thus ended his public career. Of its commencement, I can speak only from record.

As early as 1812, we find him placed on an important Special Committee in the other House, to consider the propriety of chartering a Bank of the State. At the inception of that great question—a question which has at times engaged much of the public mind—he took the side of the minority in opposing the measure, as unsound in policy, and at variance with the true spirit of our republican institutions. There was no question that received more of his attention; and, as a financial measure, he probed it to the bottom. The Bank can hardly feel under any special obligations to his never-ceasing vigilance concerning its administration; but, sir, I cannot but believe that his constant warfare upon it restrained abuses that would have sunk it into disrepute.

Our lamented friend was no ordinary man. Far from it. If he had not command of all the graces of eloquence, his reasoning was yet terse, pointed and logical. As a parliamentary debater, he was always ready; it was seldom that his adversary was able to take him by surprise.

In early life he had to struggle against adversity. Although descended of a very respectable family—a family which periled life and fortune for the independence of the State—a family, of whose noble deeds of daring and patriotism he might well have been proud, yet his patrimony was barely sufficient to carry him through Yale College, where he graduated with honor, in the same year and class with Mr. Calhoun. It was during their collegiate course that they cultivated a feeling of devoted friendship for each other, which was terminated only by death. It was rare that they differed even in their political opinions; and while the one chose the broad field of Federal politics, in which to display his genius, the other, after four years' service in the National Congress, found the purer air of his native State more congenial to his feelings. Here, sir, Mr. Felder exercised a similar influence to that wielded by Mr. Calhoun, in the Federal Councils. Both of them, in my humble opinion, were nearly always right; but both of them were often opposed by powerful cliques, to which they were never known to give aid, countenance or comfort. Each performed an important part; and each in that particular sphere best adapted to his particular turn of mind.

Mr. Felder, when a young man, aspired to military honors; but the war of 1812, which he had supported as a Member of the Legislature, terminated before he was able to reach the scene of action, with a battalion placed at his command.

But Major Felder won his way to distinction mostly as an advocate; and for twenty years enjoyed a lucrative practice at the Bar, from which he retired in the prime of his life, when he might have continued in the profession of the law, under the most favorable auspices. But he chose to abandon it, that he might devote his time and attention to politics and his own domestic affairs.

The part which he performed on the political stage is too well known to the Senate and to the country to make it necessary that I should say more on that subject. But, sir, if delicacy did not restrain me, I would dwell with satisfaction upon his private character, and his achievements as a citizen and benefactor. It was in a domestic capacity that he did as much, perhaps, as any man now living or dead, to develop the resources of our beloved State. He accumulated an immense fortune by frugality and industry alone; and, although he never married, he left a large, respectable family of near relatives, upon whom he had devoted parental care, and to whom will descend his vast estate.

Immediately preceding the death of our lamented friend, a longing desire to once more visit an only sister, residing in Georgia, allured him from his home. He accomplished the object nearest his heart; visited that sister; was returning to his own native Carolina; and, while on the Georgia Railroad, was suddenly taken ill with billious cholic, which shortly after terminated his long and useful life, on the first of September, of the present year, at Union Point, in the midst of strangers, without a friend or acquaintance near him to receive his dying bequest. There was not a paper to be found about his person to reveal his name. His memorandum-book approximated it more than any other. Upon it were found the initials, "J. M. F.," but no one present could decipher the meaning of these letters. Further on, in this little book, was his cash account, with a credit endorsed by his own benevolent hand—"Given to my sister, Mrs. Pou, one thousand dollars.—Deposited in the Bank of   , to the credit of my sister, three hundred dollars." This unveiled the mystery—brought to light the identity of the dead stranger. It was the Hon. John M. Felder, who, before, while living, never knew the want of a friend; now, in his last, his dying moments, had not one near him to say farewell, good old faithful public servant and useful citizen.—Let thy soul depart in peace to God, who gave it; its mortal tenement shall soon return to thine own loved and loving Orange, there to mingle with the dust of thy parents.

I now move, sir, the adoption of the following preamble and resolutions:

Whereas, this Senate has heard with profound regret, that since the last meeting of the General Assembly, the late Senator from Orange has departed this life: Therefore,

Resolved, That in the death of the Hon. John M. Felder, the Senate has lost one of its oldest, most efficient, able and useful members, the people of Orange a faithful representative, and the State a valuable and valued citizen—distinguished alike for purity of motive, loftiness of purpose, clearness in design, and energy in execution.

Resolved, That as a testimony of respect for the memory of the deceased, the members and officers of the Senate will wear the usual badge of mourning during the session.

The preamble and resolutions, seconded by Mr. Gramling, were unanimously agreed to; and,

On motion of Mr. Moses, in further testimony of respect to the memory of the deceased Senator, the Senate immediately adjourned, at 20 minutes past 1 o'clock, P. M.

The following papers illustrating one phase of the life and manners of the time, may well accompany this sketch of Major Felder, whose name is identified with that of Orangeburg. They may both instruct and amuse the reader, and were furnished to me by the industry of my excellent young friend, Colonel Thomas Jamison Glover, the eldest son of my long esteemed friend, and now my legal brother, Judge Thomas Worth Glover.

[A County Court Capias.]

SOUTH CAROLINA,
WINTON COUNTY.

To the Sheriff of Winton County, greeting:

We command you that you take the body of John Buford, if to be found in your county, and him safely keep, so that you have his body before the Justices of our County Court, of Winton, aforesaid, at the house of James Mitchell, on Cedar Creek, on the first Monday in November next, to answer John Cone, in a plea of trespass, on the case * * to the damage of the said John Cone, twenty pounds, and have then there this writ. Witness: Aaron Smith, Clerk of our said Court, this fifth day of August, and the thirteenth year of the Independence of America.

(Copy,) A. SMITH, C. W. C.

[A Unique Bond.]

SOUTH CAROLINA,
WINTON COUNTY. }

Know all men by these presents, that we, William Willis and John Mitchell, are holden and firmly bound unto Aaron Smith, Esq., Ordinary for Winton County or precinct, in the full and just sum of two thousand pounds sterling, to be paid to the said Aaron Smith, or to his successors, Ordinaries of this district, to which payment, well and truly to be made, we bind ourselves and every of us, our and every of our heirs, executors and administrators, and either of them, in the whole and for the whole, jointly and severally, firmly by these presents, sealed with our seals, and dated the second day of June, in the year of our Lord, one thousand seven hundred and eighty-nine, and in the thirteenth year of the Independence of North America.

The condition of the above obligation is such, that whereas, the said Aaron Smith, hath this day, under his hand and seal, licensed any Justice of the Peace for said county, or any licensed Minister, to join in the holy state of matrimony, the above bounden William Willis, of the said State and county, school-master, and Susanah Torry, of said county, &c.

Now, if there be no lawful cause to obstruct the said marriage, and that the said William Willis and John Mitchell, or either of them, or either of their heirs, executors or administrators, or any of them, do well and truly, save harmless the said Aaron Smith, and all other persons whatsoever, as well in executing as granting the said license, against all other persons whatsoever, then this obligation to be void, or else to remain in full force and virtue.

WILLIAM WILLIS.
JOHN MITCHELL.

Sealed and delivered in presence of
THOMAS WYLD. }

[Orangeburg as it was.]

ORDERS IN THE GENERAL SESSIONS.

November 15, 1783.

Presentment of Grand Jury:

We present as a great grievance the want of a Minister of the Gospel, and earnestly recommend to the Legislature to devise ways and means of establishing the preaching of the Gospel in our district, at the next Session of the Assembly; also, the want of a Seminary of learning in said district, and the little attention paid to the cultivation of youth.

RECORDS OF THE COUNTY COURT.

Journal of Fourth Monday of April, 1786.

Present their worships—Henry Felder, Wittenhall Warner, Jacob Rumph, Samuel Felder, Stephen Curry and James S. Richards. Christian Rumph was elected Sheriff, and James Carmichael, Clerk, by their worships.

October 22, 1787.

Mr. Robert Stark appeared in Court, and moved that he might be admitted as an Attorney of this Court. The Court, therefore, admitted him as such, on condition that he should produce his credentials, obtained agreeably to law, next Court.

The Court then proceeded to the appointment of an Attorney, to attend and prosecute on the part of the State, pursuant to the County Court law, when Thomas P. Carnes was duly appointed.

October 27, 1789.

Ordered, that the Sheriff do immediately cause a pair of stocks, a pillory and whipping post, to be erected on the public square, on the place where Sanders, the vagrant was sold, and that the same be made of the best light-wood.

IN THE SESSIONS.

THE STATE,
vs.
JOHN CASWELL, } Receiving stolen goods.

On motion of Mr. Goodwyn, Attorney for defendant, ordered that the prisoner be brought up to be discharged, which was done accordingly.

Ordered, that he be discharged on proclamation, on Mr. Attorney Goodwyn assuming to pay the fees due the officers of the Court, as soon as he receives the money due on a certain note of hand, due by a certain Mr. Collins, and endorsed by the aforesaid Caswell to Mr. Attorney Goodwyn.

April, 1785.

BEFORE JUDGE PENDLETON.

THE STATE,
vs.
FREDERICK HOWELL, } Larceny.

On motion of Mr. Attorney-General, ordered that the prisoner be brought to the Bar to receive sentence.

Ordered, that he be remanded to the gaol, there to continue until the third day of May, when he is to be brought out and branded on the ball of the left thumb with the letter T.

THE STATE,
vs.
JOHN MURPHY, } Horse Stealing.

Ordered, that he be brought to the Bar; no evidence appearing, ordered that he be discharged by proclamation, having first made oath that he was not able to pay the fees due to the officers of this Court.

November, 1786.

MR. JUSTICE HEYWARD.

On motion of Mr. Sheriff, ordered that Capt. Jacob Rumph do immediately send six men, out of his company, to guard the gaol for the space of seven days; and that, after the expiration of seven days, ordered that Capt. Henry Felder do relieve the aforesaid six men with six men from his company, to continue seven days; and that, after said term, Capt. Rumph shall again send the same compliment of men to relieve Capt. Felder's men, and so each to relieve the other alternately, until the prisoners now confined in gaol, and under sentence of death, be executed according to sentence, or otherwise disposed of.

November, 1784.

THE STATE,
vs.
MICHEL SMOKE,
MARY STROMAN, } Bastardy.

Mary Stroman having made oath, in Court, that she is with child, and that it is likely to be born a bastard, and Michel Smoke is the father thereof, ordered that the said Smoke and Mary Stroman, be *each* fined in the sum of five pound proclamation money, and that the said Smoke shall give security to keep the Parish free from any charges whatever till the said child shall arrive at the age of ten years.

November, 1800.

MR. JUSTICE JOHNSON.

THE STATE,
vs.
ANTHONY DUESTO, } Murder.

The prisoner being brought to the Bar, was addressed by the Court in the following words:

Prisoner, on the 11th November, in the year 1794, in this District of Orangeburg, a certain Anthony Duesto was convicted of the crime of murder, committed on the body of Stephen Touchstone. On the 1st December, 1794, sentence of death was passed on the said Anthony Duesto, to be executed on the tenth day of the same month. This sentence was respited by the Governor until the twenty-fourth of the same month. Wm. R. Thomson, then Deputy Sheriff, has returned that on the twenty-third of the same month, the same Anthony Duesto was forcibly rescued from the gaol of the said district. You, prisoner, are now brought to the Bar of this Court to receive the sentence of death, as being the same Anthony Duesto, convicted as aforesaid, how say you? Are you the same Anthony Duesto? The prisoner answered he was not. The Solicitor, in behalf of the State, replied that he was the same, and that he was ready to verify.

Anthony Duesto was identified by three different evidences.

April Term, 1803.

MR. JUSTICE TREZEVANT.

THE STATE,
vs.
JACOB COONER,
JAMES MAY, } Cheating.

Sentenced to pay a fine of twenty dollars, refund to the prosecutor, Thomas Newell, four dollars, and be committed till these sums and costs of prosecution are paid.

January 30, 1789.

Thomas Waties was elected Associate Judge in the place of Judge Pendleton.

State of Poll.

Thomas Waties	101
Wm. Drayton	87
Scattering	2

WILLIAM FALCONER.

For an account of this gentleman, I am mainly indebted to my venerable friend, John D. Witherspoon, Esq., of Society Hill.

William Falconer was born in Scotland, and educated in or near Glasgow; he came to this State about 1785, as an amanuensis for a blind gentleman, by the name of Dr. Black. Where he studied law, or when he was admitted to the Bar, is unknown. He settled in Chesterfield District, which was then part of the District of Cheraw. In the year 1793, when Mr. Witherspoon was a school-boy, at Society Hill, Mr. Falconer visited the school, at regular examinations, very much to the terror of the students. He was a good Latin scholar, and, at that time, was the only lawyer located in Cheraw District.

The members of the Bar from Charleston usually attended the Cheraw Circuit Court, and Mr. Falconer met them frequently there; he was generally successful in his cases. His practice caused him to attend the Courts at Georgetown and Camden, where he was favorably known. His course at the Bar was strict practice. Liberality was no part of his character. He frequently tripped up a young practitioner on some technicality, or some defect in special pleading. He was selfish, and never associated with any of the Bar. He was a good lawyer; astute, and would, in these days, be called cunning. He was sarcastic and bitter in all his speeches; and kept all the young lawyers in dread of him, and compelled them to club against him.

He lived about four miles from Society Hill. He was a Member of the Legislature in '98 and '99, and was one of the most active Members in abolishing the County Courts. The Acts of '98 and '99, abolishing the County Courts, and establishing in their stead the Circuit Court system, were introduced by him. He was a Federalist, and fell with his party in the struggle for power in the contest of 1800. Hs was elected a Member of the first Board of Trustees of the South Carolina College in 1801, which shows that he was not only a man of note, but also distinguished for his literary attainments.

In May, 1805, he was engaged as counsel for Lovick Rochelle, in the case of the State *vs.* Henry Rochelle, indicted for murder at Camden. He rode from home to Camden, visited and counselled Rochelle in the gaol, and returned home on the same day. Thus making, on the same day, a journey on horseback of nearly a hundred miles. Soon after, he was attacked with fever, and died. Thus perished one of the early luminaries of the law. He left none to inherit his name or vindicate his fame. To a stranger, the duty has been left to gather some memorials of his life, and give him a place among his cotemporaries of the Bar of South Carolina.

WILLIAM CRAFTS, JR.

This gentleman, the son of William Crafts (who emigrated from Boston, Massachusetts, and married a lady of fine understanding, in Charleston), was born 24th January, 1787, in the City of Charleston. He gave early evidence of an aptness to learn, and was educated by various teachers in the city, until he was committed to Dr. Gardiner, of Boston, before he commenced his collegiate course.

In the autumn of 1802, he entered the Sophomore Class of Harvard College. No young man, or rather lad, ever gave evidence of finer attainments in his college course, and none certainly ever in his nineteenth year, graduated with as high distinction as he did, at Harvard.

He returned to Charleston, and at the age of nineteen began the study of the law, in the office of Messrs. DeSaussure & Ford. "When only twenty years of age, he was unanimously elected Ensign of the Washington Light Infantry—a new military corps, which had recently been enrolled in Charleston, composed of the most respectable young men of the city. Its first commander, whose name is his own eulogy, was the late Hon. William Lowndes, and Mr. Crafts bore the infant standard of the company. In the frequent deliberations and debates incident to the formation of such a body, he enjoyed a good opportunity, even while a student at law, to exercise himself in the art of extemporaneous speaking. Here his fine powers instinctively felt their way in a friendly collision with several congenial minds, and prepared for him adherents, admirers, and a reputation, with which to start in the outset of his approaching professional career."

He was admitted to the Bar on the 9th January, 1809. His reputation for talents, learning, and oratorical powers in college, and during his study of the law, prepared the people to take him by the hand and assist him in his ascent at the Bar.

"Few young men," says Mr. Courtenay, "ever entered on the practice with more flattering success. He enjoyed the friendship of some of the most eminent gentlemen of the Charleston Bar, who kindly allowed him to appear with them in any of the important cases entrusted to their care, and thus aided him by their learning and experience."

Mr. Crafts committed the same mistake which I and many other young men fell into, and are still committing; he sought a seat in the Legislature, *before he was ripened by experience.* I recollect to have seen him, in the House of Representative, in 1811; he must, therefore, have been elected in October, 1810, in a little over a year from his admission to the Bar. From early experience, (for I was elected first to the Legislature, in October, 1816, a little more than a year from my admission to the Bar,) and from an observation of more than forty years since, I can say that no lawyer ought to be a representative sooner than twenty-five years of age. He will have little experience to build upon, *even then,* but he will be better prepared to do justice to himself and his constituents, than when he has just fledged his wings for the trials of the Forum.

Mr. Crafts experienced a fate similar to mine; he was not returned at the succeeding election (1812); but in 1813 he returned to the State House. How long he remained a member, I cannot say; possibly only for that term, though it is possible he was elected again in 1814; for I see he was engaged in the debate on the proposition to suspend rather than discontinue the Free Schools, and that, according to my recollection, was in 1814.

In 1816 and 1817, he was not in the Legislature. Between 1818 and 1822, he was elected a Senator from Charleston; and it was, in that period, that the Lunatic Asylum was projected by Mr. Farrow, of Spartanburgh, and which he united with Mr. Crafts' project of the School for the Deaf and Dumb, and thus the first appropriation of $50,000 for the Lunatic Asylum, and a School for the Deaf and Dumb, was carried by their united efforts.

After a quarantine of four years, very much to my benefit,

I returned to the Legislature. Mr. Crafts was then in the Senate He prepared the petition of Peter Horriss, the Catawba Indian, which I transcribe from 2d Lossing's Pictorial History, p. 655, note 1, as follows: "I am one of the lingering survivors of an almost extinguished race. Our graves will soon be our only habitations. I am one of the few stalks which still remain in the field when the tempest of the Revolution has passed. I fought against the British for your sake. The British have disappeared, and you are free; yet from me have the British taken nothing; nor have I gained anything by their defeat. I pursued the deer for subsistence; the deer are disappearing, and I must starve. God ordained me for the forest, and my ambition is the shade. But the strength of my arm decays, and my feet fail me in the chase. The hand which fought for your liberties, is now open for your relief. In my youth I bled in battle that you might be independent; let not my heart in my old age bleed for the want of your commisseration." A pension of $60 was the result.

It is certainly as appropriately in character with the petitioner, as anything which was ever written. On the 19th of June, 1828, Mr. Crafts was married in Boston to a cousin, on his paternal side. This connection was a great blessing to his after-life.

Mr. Crafts, before and after this, delivered many beautiful and characteristic orations, wrote many pieces of poetry and essays, chaste and admirable in sentiment and execution. They cannot, however, be referred to in detail *here;* they will be found in a volume, now, I presume, generally out of print, entitled "Crafts' Works." How much better for the young would it be, that such a work should be in the hands of our children, instead of the trash in poetry and prose which is now flooding the land.

I have no recollection of Mr. Crafts in the State House after 1823.

He died at Lebanon Springs, N. Y., 23rd September, 1826, in the fortieth year of his age. Thus early was this child of genius called away from earth.

His life, short as it was, had not been spent in vain. In

every walk of life which he had tried, he had been found useful, as well as brilliant. I have little doubt, if instead of seeking political distinction, he had brought the powers of his noble mind to the severer duties of the law, he would have stood, if not first, among the very first, at the Charleston Bar. His unrivalled powers of oratory, combined with his poetic imagination, chastened by the stern usages of legal argument, would have won for him any distinction, and broken down the barriers of party, which often barred his advancement. For Mr. Crafts was a Federalist, and in opposition to the war measures, and this often stood in his way.

Few, if any, of the times in which he lived, were entitled to precedence over Mr. Crafts, in the graces of oratory. He was called to the Bar before the year 1820, when the writer of this sketch first remembers him; and at once took rank as an eloquent and accomplished speaker. In person, he was tall and slim, and of erect and dignified stature. His features were delicate, but prominent, and his hair thin and glossy black. His eyes were remarkable, being deeply set in his head, where they shone, dark as jet, with intense brilliancy. Mr. Crafts possessed not only the finest oratorical action, but a voice whose tones and depth gave him much power over an audience. His eloquence was not so overpowering and vehement, as distinguished for the *suada* of Ennius, the Ιειθις of the Greeks, which enabled him to appropriate more exclusively than any of his cotemporaries the fame of the orator who was said to be

"*Suadaque medulla.*"

It was his habit to write out portions of his speeches at the Bar, on small scraps of paper, a practice pursued by Mr. Webster, and by which he became accustomed to the use of the most beautiful and choice language, and to the most graceful arrangement of it. His speeches in the Courts, and his orations on public occasions, were full to repletion, with the finest language and sentiment, and yet in simplicity and clearness strictly consistent with nature. He was a perfect Latin and Greek scholar; and from the fertile fields of these schools drew the amplest embellishments of his own oratory.

He was, too, a poet of no inferior ability, though confining his efforts in this branch of literature to songs, monodies and burlesques, which he threw off without much regard for permanent fame. About the time of the advent of the sea-serpent, he wrote a *jeu d'esprit*, in dramatic verse, upon this topic, which had at the time considerable celebrity.

Mr. Crafts was a favorite in cases requiring appeals to the passions, and fine displays of wit. He possessed the happy faculty of adapting his language and sentiments, rich as they were in literary illustration and learned quotation, to the capacities and taste of his audience; who heard his orations with invariable delight, for they were ever full of the dignity of elocution, of pathos, wit, and pleasantry. In the Court of Chancery, which is no very exciting school of oratory; and where a single Judge, one or two Solicitors deeply emersed in Equity demurrers, and a yawning Master, form the entire audience, his speeches were exceedingly interesting and exciting; for no one more clearly understood the principles of Equity, or could define them with more clear reasoning, or more classic or apt illustration. We remember to have heard him before Chancellor Thompson, in that Court, on a question of alimony, in a case where the husband was distinguised for the variety of his conquests under the banners of Venus; in which he introduced, with fine effect, a verse from Virgil's Æneid:

"Freed from his keepers, thus with broken reins,
The wanton courser prances over the plains;
Or, in the pride of youth, o'erleaps the mounds,
And snuffs the females in forbidden grounds."

Though capable of exerting the powers of the most severe irony, Mr. Crafts was too kind to use this weapon, except to reprove crime or give a pleasant turn to his arguments. He had great distinction as a criminal lawyer; for though among his cotemporaries he did not have the credit of being a student, his speeches had the effect of all that labor could produce: they carried the audience. He had quite a retentive memory, and a manner so easy as to dispel suspicion of artifice and preparation; and yet few men arranged their speeches with more thoughtfulness. He made a most powerful and eloquent speech in the case of Tooey, who was tried, convicted, and executed for the murder of Mr. Gadsden—an affair which caused very great excitement in Charleston. The circumstances of this affair were of a character to make a brief recital of them a pardonable digression. As was usual on St. Patrick's Day, a volunteer company, the "Irish Volunteers," of which Tooey was a member, had a dinner. At night, Mr. Gadsden, passing the door of the house where the celebration took place, just at the moment when a crowd emerged from it, was fatally stabbed with a bayonet by Tooey. Tooey escaped, and afterwards was taken, tried, and executed.

In private life, Mr. Crafts was noted for his social virtues. His house was the centre of attraction to literary persons, who loved to share a hospitality, dispensed with judicious liberality, and seasoned with the most fluent and elegant conversation. He married Miss Holmes, of Boston; in which place, or near which, he died, while on a visit with his lady, about 1826 or '7. He was not successful as a politician; for though holding possession of the popular affections, he was never able to control party influences, so necessary to success. From the fact of having edited the Courier, he was accused of favoring the anti-war party of 1812; an odium which many patriotic and noble South Carolinians have incurred, because too judicious to suffer themselves to be swept under the vortex of revolutionary folly. Mr. Crafts was, *par excellence*, a conservatist; ardently attached to the Union of the States, and to the institutions our ancestors had so intimately blended with the glory and prosperity of the nation. In the last canvass in which he was engaged before his death, he contested the Senatorship for Charleston District with General Geddes. After an exciting canvass, the validity of the election was settled in favor of Mr. Crafts, by vote of the State Senate.

Mr. Crafts was one of the most eloquent speakers ever known in South Carolina. His style of oratory was rare, because rarely in one person is found so many of the accomplishments of an orator. "An audience," says Cicero, in his Brutus, "is either flushed with joy, or overwhelmed with grief. It smiles or weeps, it loves or hates, it scorns or envies;

and, in short, is alternately seized with the various emotions of pity, shame, remorse, resentment, wonder, hope and fear; as it is influenced by the language, the sentiments, and the action of the speaker." Such was the power of Mr. Crafts over every audience he addressed; whether in his less studied forensic efforts, or in those beautiful orations which he spoke upon the festival days of his country's history.

Mr. Crafts was the son of a highly respected merchant. He left no child. A brother, Thomas, died before him, and his wife and two sisters were all who remained of his family.

The late Rev. Samuel Gilman, in his memoir of Mr. Crafts, makes some selections from his published works, which we here append:

"His 'Eulogy on the Rev. James Dewar Simons,' is, to this day, alluded to much more frequently than any of his other orations, and is regarded indeed as a kind of landmark to his reputation—a proof of how much deeper are the impressions made upon the heart, than those upon the merely intellectual faculties. On repeatedly perusing this celebrated eulogy, we have missed discerning in it that peculiar stamp of originality and literary excellence, which we have generally held in view, as a standard in the compilation of the present volume. For much of the effect with which it was received and remembered, it must, we think, have been indebted to the nature of the occasion, to the imposing night-solemnities of the surrounding funeral scenery, and to the fond and glowing, but undoubtedly correct delineations, presented by so engaging a speaker, of a most amiable, and extensively beloved and admired young clergyman. The reflections are, on the whole, very obvious, and the principal interest belonging to the production is not at all of a general description. We have deemed it proper to state these reasons for omitting the performance in question, as an apology to many readers, who, we believe, were expecting its insertion. Yet in justice to them, to the author, to the subject, and to our own feelings, we cannot resist transcribing one or two impressive and characteristic extracts. This is the exordium:

"Death has been among us, my friends, and has left a

melancholy chasm. He has torn his victim from the heart of society, and from the altar of the living God. He has triumphed over the blushing honors of youth, the towering flight of genius, and the sacred ardor of devotion. Virtue, philanthropy, religion, are bereaved, and in tears. Death, terrible and insatiate, hath been among us, and we are met to pay him tribute.

"O, thou destroyer of human hope and happiness! was there no head, frosted by time, and bowed with cares, to which thy marble pillow could have yielded rest? Was there no heart-broken sufferer to seek refuge from his woes in thy cheerless habitation? Was there no insulated being, whose crimes or miseries would have made thee welcome! who had lived without a friend, and could die without a mourner?

"These, alas, could give no celebrity to thy conquests, for they fall, unheeded as the zephyr. Thy trophies are the gathered glories of learning, the withered hopes of usefulness, the tears of sorrowing innocence, the soul-appalling cries of the widow and the orphan. Thou delightest to break our happiness into fragments, and to tear our hearts asunder. We know that thou art dreadful, and unsparing, and relentless—else our departed friend would have continued with us. His tomb would have been where our hopes had placed it—far distant in the vale of years. Still would his manly and generous affections warm and delight the social circle—still would his pure and spotless manners invite the praise and imitation of our youth—still would he fill that sacred desk, with its appropriate virtues—still would his impressive eloquence illustrate the sacred truths of Christianity, with the countenance of an angel and the fervency of a saint—still would he be the assiduous servant of religion—the golden cord of connubial affection would gain strength and beauty from time—and still his children would call him father. Vain and deceitful illusion!

'For him no more the blazing hearth shall burn,
Or busy housewife ply her evening care;
No children run to lisp their sire's return,
Nor climb his knee the envied kiss to share.'"

Towards the conclusion, occurs the following passage, gliding with a certain Attic rapidity, and closely crowded with rhetorical beauties.

"If some ingenious youth, marking the gloom which pervades our city, should inquire what dread calamity has damped the public feeling—why our churches are clad in mourning, 'and woman's eye is wet, man's cheek is pale'—tell him that these are the sorrows which embalm the virtuous. These are the sensibilities which honor the living and the dead; these are the signs which speak the bleeding heart. And if he ask what aged benefactor of the land has fallen into the grave? What time-struck, venerable head has bowed beneath the scythe of death? Tell him, the object of our mourning was a youth, like himself, who, by the excellence of his disposition, and the purity of his life, had conciliated universal esteem, and had rendered essential services to the cause of religion; that his days, though short, had been full of charitable actions; that his perpetual aim was to enlighten, and reform, and save mankind; that we mourn not for him, but for ourselves. We know that he was innocent; we believe that he is happy. We weep for the community. Tell him, this is the godlike influence of virtue; and if he would thus live, and thus die—and, if he would be thus canonized in the affections of men—let him follow the bright example of our friend—let him keep himself unspotted from the world—let him devote his talents to the service of God—let him cling around, and support the tottering edifice of religion, and the prayers of the pious shall ascend for him; he shall live in honor, and if, (which, Heaven avert!) he should be thus early called from this mortal scene, the gracious drops of pity shall bedew his urn, and he, too, shall be welcomed by the angels to the mansions of eternal joy."

In the year 1817, he delivered the annual address before the Phi Beta Kappa Society in Harvard College. It is true, an awful weight was imposed upon him, not only by public expectation, but also by his succession to the rostrum, from which Buckminster, Dehon, and others of the same mint, had stretched out a fostering, forming, and guiding hand over the young literature of our country. The subject selected by Mr. Crafts was, *The influence of moral causes over national character.* Whether it was too abstract for his image-loving mind to cope with, or he was too impatient to give it that deliberate consideration which such a subject required, it must be confessed, that he did not entirely *come round it.* There are, certainly, about the composition, many marks of effort, and of a consciousness on the part of the author that he had much to accomplish. The paragraphs are all brilliant, and the sentences all pointed. No common talent could have been employed in its production. It was delivered in the speaker's best style. But as he proceeded, the audience continued rather to be expecting than receiving the whole of their anticipated gratification. Neither was his subject precisely announced, nor was it clearly developed in the course of discussion. Bead after bead dropped glittering, yet unthreaded from his hand. With much elegant common-place were mingled many valuable and beautiful reflections; yet no stranger to William Crafts, then present, would have known of what he was capable, had it not been for his affecting, his unrivalled peroration.

Tidings had just been received from Charleston, announcing the premature decease of Bishop Dehon, by the fever of the climate. Few names were so dear as his to the Phi Beta Kappa Society, or even to the country at large. And it was an affecting coincidence of events, which brought Mr. Crafts, his townsman, his parishioner, his friend, his associate in some of the higher gifts of genius, to proclaim the account of his death, on the spot, where but a few years before, the deceased himself had impressed every hearer with feelings of profound admiration. How vividly Mr. Crafts felt the whole interest of his position, and how happily he discharged the duty it involved, will be manifest from the following extract, which is inserted with the greater pleasure, as for reasons above suggested, the entire oration is omitted from our selection.

"*Gentlemen of the Phi Beta Kappa Society,*—When, in connection with the pleasure of revisiting, after a long interval, the scenes of my boyhood, and the land of my ancestors, I contemplated the danger and difficulty of addressing this fraternity of scholars and critics, I shrunk intuitively from a feast, where the sword of Damocles was suspended over me. Political pursuits had estranged me from the path of letters; and, to recall me, was only to show how far I had wandered. But I knew that I could rely on the hospitality of Massachusetts—I thought that I could rely on the hospitality of letters—and, rescuing something from indolence and something from ambition, I came, with the feelings of the Prodigal Son, to ask forgiveness of the Muses.

"And I wish that I had not been afflicted with a more melancholy errand. It was my misfortune to apprise his relatives of the death of one of our brethren,* who, not many years since, in this place, so much more appropriate for himself than me, addressed and delighted you. I need not name him, who was distinguished in yonder seminary for his early talents and virtues; and who employed the learning he there acquired, in the service of religion, in reclaiming the sinful, in confirming the pious, in convincing the sceptical, and in soothing the mourner. I need not name that pure and spotless man, whose example illustrated all the precepts he so eloquently uttered. Cut down in the midst of his days from the object of universal love, he has become, alas! the object of universal lamentation.

"He sleeps, by his own request, under the altar, where he ministered—in life, as in death, adhering to the church. The sun shines not on his grave, nor is it wet with the morning or the evening dew. But innocence kneels upon it—purity bathes it in tears—and the recollections of the sleeping saint mingle with the praises of the living God. Oh! how dangerous it is to be eminent. The oak, whose roots descend to the world below, while its summit towers to the world above, falls with its giant branches, the victim of the storm. The osier shakes, and bends, and totters, and rises and triumphs

---

* The Right Rev. Theodore Dehon, Bishop of the Diocese of South Carolina.

in obscurity, And yet, who of you would owe his safety to his insignificance?

"Beneath that living osier not an insect can escape the sun. Beneath that fallen oak the vegetable world was wont to flourish—the ivy clung around its trunk—the birds built their nests among its branches, and from its summit saw and welcomed the morning sun—the beasts fled to it for refuge from the tempest—and man himself was refreshed in its shade, and learned from its fruit the laws of nature. Oh! how delightful it is to be eminent! To win the race of usefulness—to live in the beams of well-earned praise—and walk in the zodiac among the stars.

"Fame, with its perils and delights, my brothers, must be ours. Welcome its rocky precipice! Welcome its amaranthine garlands! We must wear them on our brow—we must leave them on our grave. We must, we will, fill our lives with acts of usefulness, and crown them with deeds of honor; and, when we die, there will be tears on the cheek of innocence, and sighs from the bosom of virtue, and the young will wish to resemble, and the aged will lament to lose us."

No person present on that occasion can ever forget the electrical emotions produced by the delivery of these passages, particularly of the last, in which the orator's voice arose to the highest pitch of enthusiasm, while exclaiming—"We must, we will, fill our lives with acts of usefulness, and crown them with deeds of honor"—and then again sank from one musical, sweet, and melancholy cadence to another, until it reached a murmur, which the deepening silence alone of the multitude rendered audible, as he uttered—" and when we die, there will be tears on the cheek of innocence, and sighs from the bosom of virtue, and the young will wish to resemble, and the aged will lament to lose us."

In conclusion, we add the beautiful eulogy pronounced by the late Edward S. Courtenay, by invitation of the "Palmetto Society:"

Eulogy on the Honorable William Crafts, delivered before the Palmetto Society, in the Second Independent Church, by E. S. Courtenay, Esq. Published at their Request. 1826.

To dwell upon and to perpetuate the memory of departed worth is softly pleasing, though it saddens the soul. Such was the theme of Ossian as he struck the harp, in praise of departed merit. But the feeling which prompted this sentiment is not peculiar to the venerable bard. It is the voice of nature, which is heard and obeyed by both savage and civilized man! In every age, and in every clime the same disposition has prevailed, to preserve the memory of the illustrious dead. In the manner of effecting this purpose only have mankind differed. In the early stages of society the grass tufted mound, or rude stone, served to mark the spot which contained the remains of the sage, the bard or the warrior, and to keep alive the flame of gratitude, which their exploits while living had elicited. In later days, superstition lent its aid to enthusiasm, and the ideal heaven of the Greeks and Romans, became peopled with the departed sages, and patriots of their respective countries. Happy are we, who live an age, blessed by the lights of Revelation, by a faith which, while it forbids religious homage to any but the *one true God*, informs us that, though the body of man returns to the dust, and is seen no more, the spirit which animated it once, liveth forever. A faith which, by the example of its Founder, teaches us, that it is not improper to mourn over the tombs of departed friends: "Jesus wept at the grave of Lazarus." Death is at all times terrible, and his conquests painful to men, whether his victim is selected from the aged, who have outlived all the charms and attractions of life, or from the wretched, who have known naught but sorrow on the earth. The yet open grave of even the vilest felon, cannot be viewed with indifference; it excites sensations which philosophy in vain attempts to conquer, which religion alone enables us to support. But most dreadful is death when his victim is taken from among those highly gifted few, whose intellects have shone forth the beacon lights of society, who were intended by Providence as a blessing to their species; who possessed the power to protect the oppressed, and punish the oppressor. Then it is, that we are reminded how transitory are human hopes; how uncertain is human happiness! Then it is, that nature, true to herself, gives a triumph to the better feelings of the heart; charity casts the veil of oblivion over the faults of the departed, and calls to mind only the virtues and talents, which benefitted mankind. The feeling is as honorable to human nature, as it is profitable to society, for, as it is the lot of man to die, so it is the duty of man to preserve the recollection of those services, which may have rendered the dead useful while on earth, that those who succeed them, may profit by their example, and the memory of the good and the great, be embalmed in the recollection of their deeds. Influenced by feelings thus sanctioned alike by Nature and Revelation, we have met to deplore with the community at large, the premature death of one, who, while yet a boy, called forth the admiration of all who knew him, not less by the brilliancy of his genius than the goodness of his heart; who, when he had but just entered the threshold of manhood, delighted his companions with his wit, and elicited the plaudits of all, by the splendor of his eloquence.

William Crafts, the subject of our eulogy, was born in Charleston, on 24th January, 1787. At an early age, he gave proof of the possession of a superior intellect, which received all the cultivation that the mind of a discerning father could suggest. His early studies were conducted by the late Rev. Dr. Buist, then at the head of one of the best grammar schools, in Charleston. His progress in the languages was uncommonly rapid, and after spending a short time under the care of the Rev. Dr. Gardiner, of Boston, he entered the Sophomore Class of Harvard University. His conduct while there, was all that the fondest father could have wished; his talents and assiduity enabled him to defy competition, and at the early age of eighteen he graduated Bachelor of Arts, receiving the first honors of that venerable university. He shortly after returned to Charleston, and commenced the study of the law. His fame had preceded him; his company was sought by the grave and the gay; learning and beauty crowded around the youthful bard to offer homage to his genius. This was, indeed, a season of pleasure unmixed with sorrow. Few men of even mature minds, could have withstood the temptations by which he was surrounded; what could have been expected from one of his age, and in such a situation? Was it wonderful, that the solitude of the study, should have been frequently abandoned for the gaiety of the saloon? that the minstrel who had so frequently struck the harp in praise of beauty, should have loved to bask in the sunshine of woman's smiles? To our friend, was not given power to resist temptations so attractive. He was surrounded by all that was bright and beautiful, and cheering to the eye of youth; he saw nothing of that misery and affliction, which, in this cold world, so often chase joy from the heart and smiles from the cheek. The rose of life was presented to him, he inhaled its fragrance; but saw not the thorns which lay concealed beneath its leaves. Mr. Crafts was admitted to the Bar at the age of one-and-twenty. Few young men ever entered on the practice of a profession with more flattering prospects. He enjoyed the friendship of some of the most eminent gentlemen of the Charleston Bar, who kindly allowed him to appear with them in important cases entrusted to their care, aided by their learning and experience. With these advantages, he quickly acquired a distinguished reputation as an advocate. His business increased with a rapidity before unknown at our Bar. Fortune smiled upon him, and his friends fondly hoped to see him at the head of his profession. In this country the duties of Counsellor, Attorney, Solicitor and Advocate, are required of the same individual. Hence it may be conceived that he, who would possess even a moderate share of knowledge of a profession, so complicated, must bestow upon it his undivided attention. It must be admitted that our friend possessed not this qualification for eminence in the law. The want of it, rendered his success as transitory as it was brilliant.

He had early offered sacrifices at the shrine of the Muses. In after years, he struggled in vain to free himself from the allegiance he had proffered them when a boy. The quaint and antique pages of Coke and Littleton were too often laid aside for the more fascinating productions of Homer and Virgil. If the opinion of Lord Coke be true, that it requires the lucubrations of twenty years to make a good lawyer, it will not be surprising that Mr. Crafts was far from being profound in several branches of his profession, or that he should have been in many instances unsuccessful in its practice; confident in his own abilities, he relied on them to supply his want of attention to those technicalities and forms, a knowledge of which, however unimportant in itself, is absolutely necessary to success at the Bar. The consequences resulting from this error might easily have been foretold: he was frequently foiled and compelled to yield the palm to men his inferiors in everything but attention and application. Yet was he not always unsuccessful as an advocate; he possessed the power of moulding the passions of men to his own purposes in a surprising degree. As the criminal Courts afforded the best field for the display of his peculiar talents, so was it the field of his forensic triumphs. In the defence of the life or liberty of a fellow-citizen, Mr. Crafts had few equals, and no superior; often have jurors yielded verdicts of acquittal to his eloquence, which their cooler judgments could scarcely have justified. Chagrin and disappointment had done much to wean his affections from a profession, which had been chosen less for its own sake, than as an introduction to public life, and whose highest honors are bestowed on those only, who are willing to submit to severe and unremitted labor for, at least, one-third of the ordinary term of life. For some time previous to his death he seldom appeared at the Bar, and he may be said to have abandoned a profession which had ceased to yield any addition to either his fame or his fortune. As an advocate, Mr. Crafts always conducted himself in the most dignified manner; there was no trick or artifice about him; none of that affected gravity, so often mistaken by the vulgar, as the indication of wisdom, and so often assumed by the pettifogger, as a mask for the concealment of his ignorance. No lawyer could be more honorable and candid towards his brethren, than our friend; none more courteous more generous, or less disposed to profit by the errors in point of form, to which inexperienced members of the profession are liable. Though he had superiors in legal learning, he certainly was inferior to none in honorable principles and gentlemanly deportment.

Shortly after his admission to the Bar, Mr. Crafts turned his attention to public life. Two great political parties then divided the country, under the names of Federalist and Republican; both loving that country, and equally anxious for its prosperity and happiness. Taking their rise from a difference of opinion in relation to the Federal Constitution, they disagreed as to the sum of power granted by the individual States to the General Government, and, of course, as to the best means of effecting a common purpose. Our friend identified himself with the former of these parties, and adhered to their principles to the day of his death, with the constancy of a martyr. It is not my intention, nor is it necessary, on this occasion, to justify or condemn the tenets of either party. That there were pure and spotless patriots, highly gifted and honorable men, among the adherents of both, will not at the present day be denied. No good men can think, without pain, of the violence and animosity which once existed between them; nor but with pleasure on the change that in this respect has taken place. The disciples of Adams and Jefferson, like those great leaders, have long since forgotten the party feuds that once divided them, and, at length, learned, that an honest difference of opinion does not of necessity prevent the interchange of those civilities, which constitute so much of human happiness.

It is to be lamented as one of the great evils of violent party spirit, that it calls into action some of the worst passions of our nature. The most uncharitable construction is put upon the conduct of opponents; actions, innocent in themselves, are tortured into crimes, and too often an error in opinion is considered as a derelection from principle, and deprives the individual of a participation in those social pleasures and enjoyments which should always exist in a civilized community. None ever suffered more from party promises and party feuds; none deserved to suffer less than Mr. Crafts. There was an exhibition of generous feeling in the part he took in politics, as disinterested as it was magnanimous. The witchery of his eloquence had endeared him to the people, and had he attached himself to the popular party, there is no doubt that he could have commanded any office or honor in their gift. How many young men, anxious for distinction, would have resisted temptation so alluring? What good worldly reasons might have been given for his choice; but he was not the man to hesitate for a moment as to the course he should pursue. He took that part in politics which was to have been expected from his connexions and education, and sacrificing self on the altar of patriotism, he united himself with a party, which, though already in the minority, and without any prospect of regaining their power, supported principles, which he deemed essential to the honor and prosperity of the republic. It was his misfortune, in the language of one of his friends, "to have been praised too early and abandoned too soon." He was flattered, and taught to expect the highest honors which his party could command. He was, in a measure, neglected by that party, ere he had an opportunity of exhibiting the powers of his mind, benefitted as they must have been by the lights of experience. No man in public life ever displayed more purity of purpose, or more consistency of conduct. Satisfied of the soundness of the views entertained by the Federal party in relation to the Constitution, he adhered to them with firmness, and the last act of his political life, was a vote given in the Senate against certain resolutions introduced by a distinguished gentleman of the Republican party, which he thought had a tendency to weaken, if not to destroy certain powers of the General Government. If his political creed was erroneous, he had the satisfaction of knowing that he erred with some of the best and most enlightened men his country had produced: with Washington, Hamilton and Cotesworth Pinckney, of the last generation, with Calhoun and McDuffie of the present.

Notwithstanding the unpopularity of his political opinions,

he was several times elected to a seat in the General Assembly of his native State. In this situation, he rendered important services to his constituents. He was early distinguished for his love of letters, and omitted no opportunity of disseminating a love of learning among the people. He felt, to use his own language, that "knowledge was the life's blood of republics and free governments;" that the eagle was the bird of light, as well as of liberty. In the Legislature, he always advocated every measure which had for its object the encouragement of scientific and literary institutions. At a period, when a short-sighted policy, aided by a parsimonious spirit, would have abolished the Free School system of the State, and left the children of the poor to all those innumerable miseries and crimes, which are the almost certain consequences of ignorance, Mr. Crafts undertook its defence, and in a speech, replete with eloquence and good sense, depicted in glowing terms, the blessings of knowledge to a State, and the curses entailed upon it by the ignorance of its citizens. He was successful; humanity and good sense triumphed over a narrow-minded policy, which would have weighed the true wealth of the State, the intellect and moral character of the rising generation, against the gold and silver which fills its coffers.

His friends might rest his character for usefulness as a legislator on this one act, for if in ancient days, he who saved the life of a single citizen, was deemed worthy of the civic wreath, to what is he not entitled, who by his eloquence and zeal preserved to thousands that means of moral life, without which man is little better than the brute on which he banquets; the prey of appetites and passions that degrade him in the scale of creation; which unfit him for usefulness, and make him a burden to himself, and too often a curse to the State. If gratitude be not an imaginary virtue, while the free schools remain in existence, they will be identified with the name of Crafts; his memory will long be cherished by the thousands who have, and the tens of thousands who shall hereafter participate in the blessings they impart. Mr. Crafts was a philanthropist in the most extensive sense of that term;

he possessed a heart full of the milk of human kindness; the sorrows of his friend, were felt as his own, and relieved, if in his power; but his good feelings were confined in the operation to no narrow circle; to no creed; to no party; whenever the voice of misery was heard, it was attended to with promptness: his professional aid was never solicited in vain, by the poor or the oppressed. These feelings so honoroble to him in private life, were carried with him to the Legislative Halls of the State. The establishment of an asylum in a central part of the State for those unfortunate beings, who, afflicted by the hand of Providence with loss of intellect, suffered in private all the miseries attendant on a situation so dreadful, added to those which proceed from poverty and want, was with him a favorite object. Though a difference of opinion may exist as to the practicability of the measure, there can be none as to the good feeling which prompted the undertaking; for, if the deprivation of reason, "the ruins of a noble mind," the wreck of that intellect which forms the connecting link between man and his Maker, be a sight at which humanity shudders, and even angels might weep, anything which has a tendency to mitigate the sufferings of its victims must afford satisfaction to the friends of humanity. In pursuance of a bill introduced by Mr. Crafts for that purpose, and passed by both branches of the Legislature, a building was *commenced*, it remains unfinished, at once a standing evidence of his humanity and of the *economical* spirit of those who guide and govern the destinies of the State. May the time soon arrive, when the legislators of our country shall recognize the claims of this suffering class of our people—claims founded alike on religion and humanity—claims which cannot be neglected without reflecting on the philanthrophy of the State.

The glory arising from deeds of arms, is as common to barbarians as to civilized man—it is evanescent in its nature, and frequently perishes with the warriors who achieved it; but edifices designed to perpetuate the discoveries of science, or to aid the cause of benevolence and charity, constitute the proudest and most durable monuments of a nation's glory;

monuments which not unfrequently outlive the national independence of the people who erected them, and redeem the honors of war by the nobler triumphs of letters and humanity.

Mr. Crafts was instrumental in obtaining the repeal of the law, which refused to auctioneers the benefit of the Insolvent Debtor's Act—a law as unjust as it was inhuman, which converted misfortune into crime, and freemen into slaves, by depriving the debtor of the means of performing his contracts, and then punishing him for his disobedience with perpetual imprisonment. Our friend held a seat in the Legislature for eight or ten years, yet never solicited an office of profit. When it is recollected how many patriots of modern times commence their career, with speeches "loud and long" in support of the people's rights, and continue this course most zealously until they obtain an office with a good salary annexed, a better proof of disinterestedness cannot be offered.

Our friend was advantageously known as an essayist, both in this country and Europe. His compositions, published in the *Charleston Courier*, were copied into the principal newspapers throughout the United States and Great Britain, and were everywhere read and admired. As a writer he was chaste and concise; his productions abounded with classical allusions, his comparisons, drawn from the works of nature, evinced a correct taste and an imagination alive to the beauties of creation, that a good Providence had everywhere scattered around him. It is to be hoped that the orations delivered by him on various occasions, with a selection from the essays, printed in the journals of the day, will be collected and published; they would form a volume, which would be a valuable addition to the library of the man of taste, and constitute a durable and appropriate monument to his memory. In the private walks of life, no one was more amiable than our friend—possessed of a lively fancy, a social disposition, and attractive manners, he was the idol of his friends and companions. The goodness of his heart was never called in question, it was perceptible in every action of his life, it tempered his wit in such a manner, that though all acknowledged its brilliancy, none complained of its point. He was an affectionate son and brother, a fond and faithful husband; all the duties resulting from these relations, were performed in the most exemplary manner. May a merciful God, enable his afflicted relatives to sustain their loss with fortitude; may he comfort and sustain them during their earthly pilgrimage, and in due time enable them to meet him, whom they loved on the earth, in that world were the sorrows of the good and virtuous cease, "where tears are wiped from all eyes." It was the misfortune of Mr. Crafts to possess a sensibility the most acute, hence no one ever suffered more intensely from the aspersions which as a politician he was subject to, than he did. There is a sensitiveness in genius which shrinks from the assaults of the rude, the vulgar, and the violent; there is a delicacy of feeling in every honorable man, which makes the bare suspicion of improper conduct more painful to him, than is the actual commission of crime, to the worthless and abandoned. Our friend possessed too much of this feeling for his own happiness; the slanders of which party spirit is so prolific a mother, and which men of coarser minds could either pass unnoticed, or retort upon their authors, stung him to the quick; and did much to embitter the last years of his life. It is melancholy to reflect on the instability of all human honor and distinction; true it is that no man can hope for unalloyed happiness on the earth. This world is at best the scene of much sorrow and little pleasure. The visions of happiness and future bliss, which hope pictures to us in youth soon give place to the sober certainty of disappointment and woe. Such was the fate of him we mourn—he, whose genius burst upon us in the morn of life, with the brilliancy of a meteor—he, whose noon was clouded with sorrow—has sunk beneath the horizon of life! That voice which was once heard in the forum, defending the rights of the widow and the orphan, or on the rostrum, telling the praises of departed worth, or in the legislative halls of his native land, advocating the cause of humanity and science, shall be heard no more—death has set his seal upon his lips and that voice is mute forever. The sod lies on that bosom, which once beat with every manly feeling. Yet shall his fame live after him. Time, that effects the best cure of wounds inflicted by malice and falsehood, shall leave no traces of the slanders heaped on him during his public career, and while genius has admirers or eloquence votaries, so long will his memory be cherished. It is true that he was ambitious, but his was the ambition of virtue, springing from a love of country the most pure and exalted: may that country never be cursed by an ambition less pure, less honorable. His talents were an honor to his country, his country will do honor to itself, by doing justice to them. His faults were the faults of genius, they were obscured by his many virtues. There are spots on the orb of day, yet do they not deprive man of the blessings of light and heat:

> But should there be to whom the fatal light,
> Of falling wisdom yields a base delight,
> Men who exult when minds of heavenly tone,
> Jar in the music that was born their own,
> Still let them pause; ah little do they know,
> That what to them seemed vice, might be but woe.
> Hard is his fate, on whom the public gaze
> Is fixed forever to detract or praise;
> Repose denies her requiem to his name,
> And folly loves the martyrdom of fame.

JOHN CALDWELL.

John Caldwell, Esq., the eldest son of William Caldwell, of Revolutionary memory, (Annals of Newberry, 277,) was born 9th of September, 1785. He had a good academical education, mainly under the tuition of Dr. Pyles of Laurens, and Elisha Hammond, at Mount Bethel, Newberry. He had also a thorough training as a merchant's clerk, under Wiley Glover, at Ninety-Six, and Robert Geddes, of Charleston. From Mount Bethel, he went to the South Carolina College, and was one among the earliest pupils, and graduated in the second class of four, in 1807, and received the second honor. He visited Boston, either while in College, or very soon after, with his instructor of Mount Bethel, Elisha Hammond, who was a professor in the South Carolina College in 1805 and 1806. He studied law with Samuel Farrow, Esq., and kept an office and did business for him, at Newberry, previous to his admission to the Bar in 1809. He commanded a fine troop of cavalry, which usually mustered at Davenport's, on Little River.

He was married to Elizabeth, the daughter of John Hunter, Esq., of Huntsville, Laurens, on the 14th of December, 1808.* By this lady he had two children, William T. and Sarah, now the wife of Dr. Foster, of Alabama, both of whom still survive. Mrs. Caldwell was a most amiable and excellent woman.

In October, 1812, Mr. Caldwell was elected to the House of Representatives, in the General Assembly of South Carolina. In December of that year, originated the Bank of the State of South Carolina. Mr. Caldwell was one of its most active friends, and was elected a director, and to his astonishment,

*This gentleman was distinguished in his day. He was an Irishman by birth, and must have been an early emigrant to South Carolina, for he was a County Court Judge in Laurens. He was a Member of the Legislature, in early times, and I have often heard my friend, Judge DeSaussure, contrast him and General Anderson, as public speakers. "Mr. Hunter," he said, "was gentle, flowing and silvery;" the other was "rushing and impetuous as a mountain torrent." Mr. Hunter, commonly called Judge Hunter, was Senator in Congress at his death.

at the extra session of 1813, found he had vacated his seat in the House, by accepting a directorship in the Bank. He was elected Cashier in the Branch of that Bank in Columbia, and removed there in the Spring of 1814. In May, 1814, Judge O'Neall, who had studied law with him, was admitted to the Bar, and settled at Newberry, as the partner of Mr. Caldwell, and together they did a large and profitable business. He was elected a Trustee of the South Carolina College in 1813.

In January, 1816, Mrs. Caldwell died, and I am sorry to say that no marble tells where she lies, or perpetuates her memory as a wife and mother. Her remains are in the grave-yard of the Presbyterian Church at Columbia.

This unfortunate event determined Mr. Caldwell to remove from Columbia. He resigned his cashiership, which was far, very far from being profitable to him; indeed, he sustained a heavy loss in settling his accounts. He sold to Dr. Briggs, his fine patrimonial estate on Mill Creek, in Newberry, and all his negroes. This was thought, at the time, to be a wonderfully fine sale, yet, in the end, it was vexation and loss to him. He returned to the town of Newberry, and on the 17th of October 1816, he was married to Abigail, eldest daughter of Hugh O'Neall, and sister of Judge O'Neall.

The partnership between him and Judge O'Neall, closed about the period of his first wife's death. In 1816, he ran for Congress, and was defeated by Colonel Starling Tucker. I thought then, and still think, that Tucker ought not to have offered. As the mutual friend of both, I had received and communicated to Mr. Caldwell, his assurance he would not be a candidate. But friendship often overlooks what ought to be sacred—such an assurance, and Colonel Tucker's friends, very much against his will, forced him to be a candidate. From 1818, Mr. Caldwell began to resume business, as a lawyer at Newberry and Lexington.

In 1824–'26 and '28, he was returned as a member of the House of Representatives of South Carolina.

From 1830, his affairs became more and more embarrassed, until at length he disposed, by public or private sale, of the most of his property. His practice, as an attorney, grew less and less, until he gave it up. He received a serious injury in his hip by a fall, and he was subsequently paralyzed both in his limbs and tongue.

He had two children by his last marriage, Dr. John C. Caldwell, and Elizabeth Hunter Eigleburger, both of whom, with his wife, survived him. He died 15th January, 1856, in his seventy-first year.

John Caldwell, when young, was possessed of more physical powers than usually fall to the lot of a man. He was remarkably active, and could jump farther than any young man of his acquaintance. He rode well, indeed, he was regarded as an extraordinary horseman. Intellectually, he was no common man. If he had had industry, he ought to have compared very well with his great kinsman, John C. Calhoun. He was an excellent accountant and surveyor.

As a lawyer, he did not pretend to learning; as an advocate, and in the management of a case, he possessed unrivalled talents. His quick, clear perception of everything, made him ready for any turn of his case. Before a Jury, his powers as an advocate, very often gave him success. Indeed, in Lexington, he had unrivalled sway.

As a man, he was generous and honest; as a citizen he was patriotic; as a husband and father, he was kind and affectionate.

An unfortunate habit, (which has always been too common among men,) and to which he was a slave, wasted his means, laid in ruin his intellect, and stripped him of his powers as a man. But in the weakness and suffering of many years, and when he saw his Bacchanalian friends fly from his side, and when none, except his wife and children, and one to whom in youth he had been a friend, stood by his arm, to sustain and console him, he no doubt sorely repented of the follies of youth and manhood, and very probably obtained the sure mercy of his indulgent Creator, which was manifested to him, in being permitted to pass from the world as if he had fallen asleep.

ANDERSON CRENSHAW.

Anderson Crenshaw was a native of Newberry District, South Carolina. His primary education was at the school, around the Long Lane, where his father, Charles Crenshaw, the Tax Collector for many years of Newberry District, ilved and died; and where his mother and only sister died in 1815.

His academic education was at Mount Bethel. He was the first graduate of the South Carolina College in 1806. He was the Secretary of the Board of Trustees of the College from 1806 to 1808. He studied law with Judge Nott, and was admitted to the Bar in 1809.

He settled at Newberry, and there practiced law, and was remarkable, at that early day, for his knowledge of his profession. He was a good special pleader, and prepared his cases with great care, although I always thought his judgment not to be relied on.

In 1812, he was elected to the House of Representatives from Newberry, but failed to be returned in the succeeding election. In the fall of 1815, he was married to Miss Mary Chiles, of Abbeville, and removed to Alabama in 1819 or 1820.

Judge Porter, of Sydney, Alabama, furnishes the following sketch:

I became acquainted with the name of Anderson Crenshaw in South Carolina, where he had considerable reputation as a lawyer. In 1832, I saw him in person, having gone before him to obtain a license to practice law in Alabama, to which State Judge Crenshaw had previously removed. He was, at that time, holding the Circuit Court of Monroe County, at Claiborne.

Judge Crenshaw was very tall and slim in person, and noted for a stooping gait. His complexion was very dark, and his enunciation slow and hesitating. He did not remain at the Bar, in Alabama, long enough to establish much reputation as an advocate, having been elected to a Circuit Judgeship as early as 1821. He had, however, much celebrity as a sound lawyer; and it is certain, that he had filled his mind with a vast amount of knowledge of the principles of jurisprudence. He was slow in arriving at conclusions, but when he did, was generally correct, and the impression on his mind permanent. He was a disciple of the ancient system of law, and, during his whole life, opposed, earnestly and justly, the efforts of a young generation to innovate upon the establishment of my Lord Coke.

In manners, Judge Crenshaw was, at first interview, neither attractive nor forward. When the moment of formal intercourse, however, wore off, he was free in conversation, and surprised his hearers with apt quotations from the antiquities of the profession, and from classic literature. He delighted in the character and readings of Shakspeare, and, what was singular in a person of his apparent sternness, had an especial liking for Sir John Falstaff, whose calls for sack he repeated when asking for refreshment. It is told of him, that upon one occasion, at a newly settled county site, he requested a negro, unused to dramatic literature, to bring him some sack, and was astonished by being brought quite a different and ludicrous article at a moment when his room was crowded with the Bar.

A man of more amiable and kind disposition did not live than Judge Crenshaw. He was eminently just, honest, and benevolent; and the tenor of his life never was stained by the slightest moral reproach. On the organization of a separate Chancery Court, he was elected one of the Chancellors—a position in which he displayed unusual and remarkable knowledge of the principles of Equity and the pleading and practice of that Court. Previously, the Chancery jurisdiction had been connected with the Circuit Court; and from the difficulty of getting cases heard, the Bar had become quite indifferent to the system. The learning of that Court was, consequently, extremely low. When Chancellor Crenshaw took part in it, however, he gave, by his learning, a new and important impulse to it. Libraries increased, and the Bar had to make themselves good Equity lawyers, or have their bills summarily dismissed.

When Judge Crenshaw was first elected to the Circuit Bench, the Judges heard, collectively, appeals on writs of error. As one of these, Judge Crenshaw delivered many opinions, distinguished by most clear and logical enunciations of the principles of law; and which stand, in the reports, opposing and truthful monuments of judicial learning, compared with the diffusive, but weak and sickly opinions which have too often, in later times, been suffered to grow like funguses upon the once flourishing trunk of English law. These opinions will be found in the Alabama Reports of Minor, Stewart, and Stewart and Porter.

Chancellor Crenshaw, while presiding over the Equity forum, by his keen sense of justice, and his power of discrimination, gave great popularity to that Court. Few lawyers, fresh from the contests of a law Court, are enabled to exert their abilities in a manner to avoid grafting upon Equity jurisdiction, technicalities which it is the great purpose of this Court to defeat. Under Chancellor Crenshaw's administration, the Court reached and maintained a dignity and elevation which it never before, and rarely since, has had in Alabama. It was, indeed, under his control, the forum of the reason and spirit of the law—the *Ars boni et æqui* of Cicero—the doctrine of all that was equitable and good.

Chancellor Crenshaw died in the year 1847, having been twenty-six years in a judicial position. The Bench and Bar, generally, attested their sense of his loss by most honorable funeral demonstrations.

JAMES R. ERVIN.

The subject of this sketch was descended, by both father and mother's side, from some of the Scotch-Irish families who were among the first settlers of what is now Williamsburg District. James R. was the son of Col. John Ervin, and Jane, his first wife. He was born on the Pee Dee, in the year 1788, in the lower part of Marion District.

Having been deprived of a mother's care in infancy, he was consigned to the charge of an aunt, Mrs. Witherspoon, for some years after. His education commenced at a common school in the neighborhood, and could the incidents of that period of his life be recovered, there would doubtless be found many indications of those original powers of mind, and that remarkable versatility of talent, which were so strikingly exhibited in his subsequent career.

When about eleven or twelve years old, he was sent to the noted grammar school, then under the charge of the Rev. John M. Roberts, near Statesburg, an institution which maintained for many years the first rank in the north-eastern part of the State. Here he remained two or three years, and, associating there with some of those who were to rise to eminence in the different walks of life and the service of the State, was probably induced to turn his thoughts to the study of the law, as the most successful mode of rising to usefulness and distinction!

For the law he was eminently fitted by nature, as well as for political life, to which his tastes and peculiar gifts caused him to turn at an early period.

Soon after leaving the school at Statesburg, he was placed under the care of John D. Witherspoon, then the only resident lawyer in the old Cheraw District, comprising the present Districts of Chesterfield, Marlboro', and Darlington. He entered the office of Mr. Witherspoon, as a law student, in January, 1805, and not being a graduate of any college, it was necessary that he should devote four years to the study of the law, before he could be admitted to practice!

Mr. Witherspoon, though he had not himself been very long at the Bar, had acquired a considerable practice, particularly in the way of collecting.

Young Ervin was a ready writer, and had, therefore, the benefit of a large amount of office work; as such, rendering him familiar with, *what* is so often to young lawyers, the most difficult part of the practice.

In 1809, he was admitted to the Bar in Columbia, and settled immediately after in Marlboro' District, where an inviting field opened before him. His rise to popular favor was rapid, and based upon those qualities which are always attractive to the people, secured for him their hearts and lasting confidence and regard. Soon after settling in Marlboro', he was returned a Member of the House of Representatives, which position he continued to fill, until his removal from the district.

In the year 1814, he married Elizabeth, daughter of Gen. Erasmus Powe, of Chesterfield—a lady of most lovely disposition, and who, by her devotion, contributed largely to his happiness.

Soon after his marriage, he removed to Marion District, and there acquired a highly respectable practice; but, becoming dissatisfied, returned to Marlboro'. From that district, he was again returned to the Legislature, but in the higher capacity of Senator, which position he continued to fill, until the expiration of his term.

Influenced probably by the relations with which his marriage had brought him, he was induced to leave his first field of public labor again, and to settle in the town of Cheraw. Here, also, after a brief residence, the appreciative regards of the people made him their Senator.

During his residence in Cheraw, he was left a widower, with six children. This season of trial passed, he intermarried with Mrs. Vereen, of Marion, by whom he had one child, a daughter.

About this time his health began to fail, and while on his way to the Rocky River Springs, in North Carolina, an accident, which led to a profuse hemorrhage, put an end to his life in a few moments. Few men were possessed, to so remarkable a degree, of the confidence and love of the people. The tidings of his untimely end were received with unusual marks of sorrow.

In person, Col. Ervin was attractive and commanding; about 5 feet 11 inches in height, and well-proportioned, with a countenance singularly open, and beaming with intelligence and good nature, he inspired respect as he went, and captivated all with whom he came in contact. His talents were of a high order—placing him, in point of natural genius, in the opinion of competent judges, among the very first of those who have been reared on the Pee Dee; and had his application been equal to his endowments, he would probably have fallen behind no competitor in the way to fame!

As a speaker he was fluent and forcible; ready to take advantage of any turn and change of circumstance—abounding in anecdotes and repartee. His quickness and versatility made him, as was often confessed by the most learned and eminent advocates, an adversary always to be watched and dreaded.

Baffled at one point, which seemed to have been his stronghold, or driven from a position maintained against formidable odds, he would in a moment take other ground, with so much ingenuity, and such a show of reason or law, as often to confound his opponent, and not unfrequently to gain his case. In the celebrated trial of Mason Lee'will, in Marlboro', in which some of the most distinguished lawyers of the State were employed—the late Col. Blanding and Chancellor Harper being associated with Col. Ervin, and Judge Evans and Col. Preston opposed to him—this striking trait was remarkably displayed. He is said to have conducted his part in that singular case, with the most consummate tact. But, unfortunately, for his reputation and success, his convivial temperament and aversion to steady labor, caused him to take a position behind those who might otherwise have been distanced in the race.

His habit was to appear without anything like thorough

preparation, relying, as he did, mainly upon the weakness of his adversary, or his own ingenuity, to give strength to his cause; or upon his general knowledge of the law, and his power so to present the facts of the case, as to carry the jury with him, which he seldom failed to do. As a jury lawyer, he scarcely had an equal. And so, before the people he may be said to have been almost irresistible. Attached to them by sympathy, at ease in any company, with remarkable conversational talent, and though making no studied effort, master, notwithstanding, of those arts which are ordinarily used to gain their esteem, he was their favorite through life. His rich vein of humor and inexhaustible fund of anecdotes, made him the very soul of social life at the Bar. Here he had no equal. In 1832, he was the acknowledged leader of the Union party in his section of the State.

Singularly cool, and as fearless as he was cool; as able in counsel as he was efficient in action, to him the eyes of his fellow-citizens were invariably turned in times of emergency, nor were their hopes likely to be disappointed. He was prompt to respond to any appeal, and the confidence so implicitly reposed in him was never abused.

As a friend, he was constant and self-sacrificing to a remarkable degree; and in every relation of life, *all* that a noble affection could prompt, or a generous impulse move him to be—a true man and faithful!

His life, however, rich as it was in incident, and singular in all those elements of power which made it up, was one of those, the most difficult to be written, and not often lived—known only, as tradition may hand down some remains of it to posterity.

THOMAS SMITH GRIMKÉ.

The great man whose name has just been read is identified with every good and excellent recollection, in which a South Carolinian and a friend can indulge. To speak of him as he deserves, is the task which is before me. I approach it with feelings both anxious and fearful: anxiety as to the work, and fearfulness that it may not be done well, are present, and will dwell upon my care-worn pen, until I can say, *it is finished.*

Thomas Smith Grimké was born in Charleston, South Carolina, 26th September, 1786. He was cradled in the bright, blushing morn of peace, blessed peace, which followed the dark and bloody night of the Revolution. One who now knows the subsequent life of the infant then born, would say, that he came the messenger of that peace, and that which is better, the peace which goes beyond this world. He was the son of Judge John Faucheraud Grimké and Mary Smith, his wife, the daughter of Thomas Smith. His youthful mind had the benefit of the judicious training of his eminent father. Obedience to and love for his parents began with him in childhood, and only ceased with their death. He had the benefit of the best schools of the State. At the age of seventeen, he left home for Yale College, then under the care of that eminent scholar and Christian, President Dwight. Young Grimké had the full benefit of his teaching and parental care, and returned home, in 1807, with all the honors of the college clustering upon him. He wished to study for the ministry, but his father desired that he should study law. He yielded his wishes to those of his parent, and set about the preparation which made him the light of his profession, and the Christian sage of his own city.

I have followed a statement found in the "Calumet," of January and February, 1855, said to be furnished by his family, but from the date of his admission to the Bar, 30th

May, 1809, and the fact that the law then required from a graduate three years study before he could be admitted, I am convinced Mr. Grimké must have graduated in the fall of 1805, or early in 1806. For he was too conscientious to have claimed admission a day earlier than he was entitled. He was married to Sarah D. Drayton, on 25th January, 1810.

His first public effort was a Fourth-of-July oration, which I remember to have read and admired many years ago; tradition is, that he was unequal to the delivery, that he fainted, either from the heat of the day, or his own excitement, and his venerable father finished his task by reading the balance of his oration.

I happened to have preserved his admirable discourse before the Bar Association on the "Practicability and expediency of reducing the whole body of the law to the simplicity and order of a code," delivered 17th March, 1827. He said then, that "a work such as that proposed, is worthy of the most cultivated judgment, the best talents, and the soundest learning, which adorn our State." How appropriate the thought and the expression to the work which the Legislature of the last year directed to be begun. The discourse ought to be read by every thinking man in the State; it contains wisdom and truth in every line. On the 9th of May, in the same year, he delivered before the Literary and Philosophical Society his address on science, which, indeed, is one of the purest and best offerings ever laid on the altar of literature. These are a part, a small part, it is true, of his matchless productions by which he sought to benefit his fellow-men.

Mr. Grimké was remarkable for his accuracy as a lawyer. He sifted thoroughly every case, and came into Court armed at every point. He was in Court, as everywhere else, a gentleman, kind and courteous; but he was firm as he was courteous. He felt in Court he was the minister of *truth;* he never sought to mislead a Judge or a Jury. His arguments, some notes of which are to be found in our law books, principally in 1 & 2 Bailey, Bailey's Equity, 1 & 2 Hill, were full and exhausting on every subject. In the State *ex rel.*, Berney *vs.* the Tax Collector, 2 Bail. 654, his argument against the constitutionality of the Act, imposing a tax on the dividends of United States Bank stock, will be found. It is true, his argument failed to carry the Court with him, yet it presented the most ingenious and plausible views. But his last, greatest, and best legacy to the Bar and his country, is his argument, in March, 1834, on the great Test Oath question, in the State *ex relatione* McCready *vs.* Hunt, 2 Hill, 14. The sickness and death of two of my children carried me from the Court to their bed-sides; I was, therefore, prevented from hearing this matchless argument in its delivery, which, at the time, confirmed friends in their opposition to that measure, and which made Nullifiers acknòwledge in the Court House, "*thou almost persuadest me.*" It will be read and admired as long as the law and the Constitution have a home in the hearts of the people.

Mr. Grimké was not only a lawyer. St. Philip's and St. Michael's did themselves honor, by claiming the benefit of his talents as a Senator, from 1826 to 1830. His services in that department were of great value. I do not know that he originated or framed any laws; but I do know that he was always at his post, and ever vigilant in ascertaining, and ever faithful in securing the right. He was one of that august Court, in January, 1828, which tried Judge James on articles preferred by the House of Representatives. He was one of those pure and fearless Judges, whom neither sophistry nor eloquence could turn aside, and who, with tears, wrote "guilty," and pronounced the judgment of removal.

Mr. Grimké was, in fact, the father of the Temperance reform. He stood almost alone in that good work: "his name being at the head of the subscribers to the original Temperance Society, which he was mainly instrumental in forming, and whose constitution was drawn up by his own hand." In February, 1831, when I first visited Charleston as a Judge of the Court of Appeals, it was at the end of a great snowstorm; the sailors, to ridicule temperance and Mr. Grimké, made a man of ice, placed him upon the deck of one of the vessels, with a cocked hat on his head, with this label placed upon it: "The President of the Temperance Society." They little dreamed, that *that* which they thus ridiculed would enter their ranks with the olive branch of peace and love, and claim of them, in less than thirty years, more than seven thousand followers in the Mariner's Washington Total Abstinence Society. Yet so it is. Mr. Grimké heeded neither the ridicule of ignorance, nor the intelligence of enemies nor of friends. He was a temperance man both by precept and example. Often have I regretted, in the triumphal ovations of temperance, that the kind, benevolent face of Grimké was not to be seen. Before the day of jubilee, God had called him to his everlasting reward.

He left Charleston for Ohio, in September, 1834, with the double purpose of visiting his brother, Judge Frederick Grimké, and to attend the Annual Convention of Teachers, and to address the Evodelphian Society of Miami University. These two last objects he accomplished. The last speech which he was permitted to deliver, was in a temperance meeting, in Cincinnati, on Wednesday, 8th of October, 1834. He left Cincinnati for Chilicothe, to visit his brother, who was to meet him at Columbus. On Saturday night, in the stage, he was attacked with Asiatic cholera, and was obliged to stop at Gwynn's farm, twenty-two miles from Columbus, and just as the rays of the sun of the Lord's day, 12th October, 1834, streamed through the casement of his chamber, the pure spirit of Thomas Smith Grimké, took its flight from earth to heaven! His brother had reached him in time to minister to him, and hoped that the skilful physician, who accompanied him, might have been instrumental in saving him, but in vain—he was only permitted to see him roused for a few minutes, and then to die.

Having just completed forty-eight years, Thomas Smith Grimké might have been expected to spend many more years of usefulness here. But God said, *it is enough!* and he passed away.

Our duty is to profit by his example. It is one of rare and exceeding brightness. It may be followed. It may be imitated, but it cannot be excelled. As a scholar, jurist, legislator, follower of temperance, orator and Christian, he was unsurpassed.

It is as an orator and Christian, that something more may be said. Mr. Grimké was remarkable for his rapid delivery. He never was at a loss for a word, which he always used of the purest English, and in its proper place. He did not generally seek the highest flights of eloquence, but in the great "Test Oath Case," he sought and attained them. His closing words in that case, are beautiful exponents of his own character.—2d Hill, 69. He said, "I have come to lay my gift on the altar of God and my country: for what is an independent judiciary but my country, and what are the halls of justice but temples of the Most High! I have felt that I dared not offer my gift on such an altar, if any brother had aught against me. I have not willingly, uttered a word that could, in the slightest degree, give an instant of pain. And if, by aught that has been said, I have excited a momentary unpleasantness, or have cast even a transient shade over a single countenance, may I trust to be forgiven."

In the "Calumet" is said, beautifully, justly said, "his chief praise is inurned in the hearts of the poor, the widow, and the afflicted. He was a Christian in word and in deed. He felt and practiced that "pure religion and undefiled before God and the Father is this, to visit the fatherless and widows in their affliction, and to keep himself unspotted from the world." He connected himself early in life with the Episcopal Church. At his death his wife survived him, and still survives him as his widow. He left six sons at his death, all of whom except two, are in their graves. His son, J. Grimké Drayton, (who assumed the surname of his maternal grandfather in obedience to his will,) has been, for years, Rector of St. Andrew's Parish, and is now the chosen Rector of St. Peter's, in Charleston, South Carolina. Dr. Theodore D. Grimké, his other son, resides in England.

[Charleston Courier, Friday, Oct. 24th, 1834.]

DEATH OF THE HON. T. S. GRIMKÉ.

"Our community was yesterday filled with deep gloom and sorrow, by the melancholy and unlooked-for tidings of the decease of this excellent and truly distinguished man. We learn that the mournful event took place in the State of Ohio, whither he had gone, among other objects, to deliver a literary address; and that he fell a victim to a sudden and speedily fatal attack of Asiatic cholera. He was yet in the prime and vigor of his faculties, and full of the promise of long-continued usefulness to his country and his race, when thus struck down, at a distance from his home and his family, by the mysterious shaft of death. Although almost a stranger to public station, so well known was Mr. Grimké by means of his various literary and political performances, and his zeal and activity in the cause of religion, benevolence, and human improvement, that there were few men in the United States enjoying a more wide-spread reputation, and filling a larger and more honorable space in the public eye. He was both a politician and a statesman, after the order of Washington; in the one character, maintaining the political creed of the father of our republic, and in the other, emulating that illustrious model in a single-eyed and single-hearted devotion to his country. As a lawyer, he stood at the very head of his profession. As an advocate, he was both able and eloquent, and in his practice he set an example of scrupulous fairness and courtesy well worthy of imitation. His habits of industry, and economy of time, were really wonderful, and enabled him to accomplish labors truly Herculean. His extensive legal practice—perhaps the most extensive in the city—was, of itself, almost sufficient to overtask his physical and moral energies; yet he was ever ready to contribute the oration, the address, the essay, in compliance with the public, social, literary or religious call; and he displayed alike on every occasion a vigorous and cultivated intellect, enriched with the results of extensive reading, profound thought and unwearied research. As a speaker, he was energetic and persuasive, distinguished for an utterance wonderfully rapid, yet perfectly distinct; and even in extemporaneous harangues clothing his thoughts in language critically correct. Christianity found in him an advocate zealous and efficient. The Bible he valued above all works; whether in a literary or religious point of view; whether as containing the canons of saving faith and the rules of a righteous life, or as affording high enjoyment to a refined taste; and his pen, his tongue, and his purse, were freely dedicated to the promotion of Bible, Tract, Temperance, Missionary and Educational Societies, and every other rational and benevolent scheme for the diffusion of the Gospel, and the melioration of the human race. In all the concerns of life, public, professional, or private, he acted on the strictest principles of duty; and his integrity and honesty of purpose were proverbial. His charities were of the most liberal and diffusive character; freely dispensed at home, and extending to other and far distant lands. He was emphatically a useful citizen and an eminent man, and his decease is a heavy loss to our city, our State, and our country. Having now prematurely closed an honorable career on earth, to enjoy, we trust, the reward of a well-spent life, in another and a better world. He will long live in the memories of those who knew him as having been one of the best men in our community, one of the purest patriots of our country, and one of the most genuine philanthropists in the world."

[Charleston Mercury, Friday, October 24th, 1834.]

DEATH OF MR. GRIMKÉ.

"We yesterday received the afflicting intelligence of the death of the Hon. Thomas S. Grimké, of cholera, at Columbus, Ohio. Mr. Grimké's eminence in his profession, and his distinguished virtues, private and public, make this painful event a heavy blow to our community; and his loss is felt with deep and unaffected sorrow by all parties and all classes in our bereaved city."

TRIBUTE OF RESPECT FROM THE BAR.

[*From the Southern Patriot, Charleston, Oct.* 27, 1834.]

Pursuant to public notice, a numerous meeting of the members of the Bar was held on Saturday, at 1 o'clock, P. M., in the Federal Court Room. His Honor Judge Lee was called to the Chair, and W. P. Finley requested to act as Secretary.

The meeting was opened by an address from the Chairman, in which he announced, in a very feeling and impressive manner, the mournful object for which it was convened, and alluded in terms not more glowing than just, to the pure and exalted character which the deceased had sustained in all the relations of life.

The Attorney General, R. Barnwell Rhett, Esq., then rose, and, after a few appropriate remarks, submitted the following preamble and resolutions, which, being seconded by Charles Fraser, Esq., were unanimously adopted by the meeting:

It is the natural impulse of sympathy, upon even ordinary occasions, that those who suffer a common loss, should seek consolation under their bereavement, by commingling their regrets; but when such a man as Thomas Smith Grimké is suddenly taken from the society in which he was so distinguished an ornament and support, duty as well as sympathy call upon us to express our profound sense of the loss we have sustained.

The deceased, indeed, was no ordinary man, either in his intellectual or moral endowments. The energy—the astonishing energy—with which he pursued the objects of life, was at once the indication of superior powers, and the cause of his great success. He appeared continually to watch the dial-plate of time, that no hour of his existence should be fruitless of improvement or usefulness; and as his life advanced to its close, instead of remitting his habits of toil, his spirit seemed to burn with intenser activity. Hence his wonderful acquirements in every department of knowledge, whilst he found time to obey every call of religious, social, or domestic duty. As a lawyer, he had long stood at the head of our profession. It was here, that his vast memory, stored with the rich fruits of his industry, gathered from every side as he passed through life, was more peculiarly exemplified. His legal knowledge was accurate and profound, comprehending the minutest details and the broadest principles. So fertile and original were the resources of his mind, that if he had any fault as an advocate, it was in advancing too many arguments to support his positions. He may thus, sometimes have dazzled a weaker vision by the profusion of light he threw upon his subject; but he never lost a cause from superficial examination or shallow views. In a country, peculiarly a country of laws, he possessed a high sense of the importance and dignity of that profession through which the laws are administered; and endeavored to wield his knowledge and power, to the great purpose for which they were created—the maintenance and advancement of justice. Hence, at the Bar, and in public estimation, he long stood, and justly stood, pre-eminent among us.

It has been remarked in England, that lawyers have seldom proved able statesmen. The technical nature of the profession in that country, especially in the branch of special pleading, by habitually contracting the views to "precedent on the file," may probably account for the fact, if this observation is correct. But under our system of government and laws, judging from the results, it must be erroneous. The profession of law, at least upon the mind of the deceased, appeared not to have affected its broad and philosophical cast. As a statesman, his views were comprehensive, his knowledge extensive and accurate, and his motives above suspicion or imputation. A purer and more devoted spirit, never spoke or felt for the interests of his country. Although living in times of bitter party contention, and differing from many of us upon all the leading subjects of politics, none of us—no man in our community, we sincerely believe—ever entertained a doubt of his simple integrity and disinterestedness in the opinions he professed; or beheld with other feelings than those of admiration, the boldness with which they were avowed and maintained. His patriotism, in truth, was a part of his piety. Its essential aim was the approbation of God. Towards men, it was an impulse of duty; but it looked beyond the applause and honor of the world, from a deep sense of his accountability for the rectitude of his motives and conduct towards his country.

Nor was the information of the deceased, profound and extensive as it was, confined to the great subject of government and the laws. He was essentially a literary man. At every pause from the labors of his profession, he turned with avidity to the innocent and enchanting pursuits of literature, communing with the mighty dead, still living in the imperishable thoughts they have left behind them. In a country like ours, where capital is not yet accumulated, and to live, is necessarily the chief object of life, to be a literary man is itself a distinction. But his aim was far beyond that proficiency in literature which might adorn an accomplished gentleman.—He pushed his researches into the wide fields of ancient and modern lore, and became acquainted with all, and familiar with most of their branches. His published productions evince the accuracy and the extent of his erudition; but it was in the social circle that the affluence of his acquisitions was more amply recognized and more justly appreciated. Here, with a prodigal hand, he scattered the flowers he had gathered from every field; and while he delighted, he amazed his associates, by their wonderful variety. But it was chiefly at the Bar that we knew his attainments and felt his virtues. There are few of us who have not drank from the full fountain of his legal acquirements, and learned from the very generosity with which he imparted his information, the effect of knowledge in liberalizing the heart. Plain, yet dignified—patient and affectionate, yet immovable in firmness—offending none, and courteous to all, amidst the contentions and harassments of our difficult profession, he exhibited in his demeanor at the Bar, the rare but bright example of what a Christian advocate ought to be. The poor and the friendless, the orphan and the widow, never sought his professional assistance in vain; and it was, when pleading for them, looking upward alone for his reward, that his powers often soared highest, and his eloquence was most touching and effective.

That trait in his character, however, which the deceased most valued, and which he was most truly solicitous to perfect, was his piety. On religion he had built the whole structure of his moral character. To be worthy of his profession as a Christian, was the chief object of his existence. In early youth he had assumed the garb of piety, and continued steadfastly through life one of the brightest props and ornaments of Christianity in our land, exemplifying in his life and conversation all its ennobling principles. From being, according to his own representation, violent in temper, he became the calmest and mildest of men. He bereft himself of all those selfish principles to which we are so prone by nature, and devoted his life to God and the welfare of others; until, at length, to consider himself least, became the ordinary habit of his thoughts and conduct. To do good, indeed, to him seemed the bread of life. His charities were ever for the necessitous, and his tender sympathies for the afflicted and bruised in spirit, and even the wayfaring man, and the stranger with no claim upon him but the impress of humanity, would seek relief in his wide benevolence, and have his claim allowed:

Had he been otherwise than he was, the prayers and blessings of the poor whom he relieved, the applause of the good, and the admiration of the world, might have elevated him with pride and vanity; but his humility increased with his distinction and elevation; and he closed life as he commenced it, walking humbly with his God. In his character were combined the simplicity of the child with the moral courage of the martyr.

Shall we lift the veil of private life, and disclose the affectionate son, the devoted husband, the tender father, the faithful friend, the kind and patient master, moving in the light of his noble but simple virtues, and shedding joy and peace and happiness on all around him? The memory of his virtues, in these tender relations, belong peculiarly to the keeping of others; and *there* should we leave them, sacred from our eulogies, enshrined in the hallowed sanctuary of private affection. The days of his pilgrimage are done, and he has entered into his rest. His mild face will no longer be seen amongst us, but the monuments of his public usefulness and benevolence are still with us, and the memory of his virtues will still dwell within our hearts. None of us may expect to equal, but all of us may grow better and wiser by recollecting the great and holy man who once lived and moved amongst us.

Resolved, That in the death of Thomas Smith Grimké, the

poor and destitute have lost a friend—society a useful member—the Bar a distinguished ornament—Christianity a zealous advocate and supporter—and our country at large a learned, able and patriotic citizen.

Resolved, therefore, That the members of the Charleston Bar, in testimony of their profound sense of his virtues, and their deep regret at his decease, do wear mourning for the the space of thirty days.

On motion of Joshua W. Toomer, Esq., seconded by M. King, Esq., it was

Resolved, That the above preamble and resolutions be published in all the papers of the City, and that a copy thereof, attested by the Chairman and Secretary of the meeting, be transmitted to the family of the deceased.

On motion of H. A. Desaussure, Esq., the meeting was then adjourned.

W. PERONNEAU FINLEY,
Secretary.

PATRICK NOBLE.

Patrick Noble was born in the year 1787, in Abbeville District, South Carolina.

He was a scholar at Willington, under the justly celebrated teacher, Dr. Waddell. He entered Princeton College, New Jersey, in the fall or winter of 1804, and graduated in 1806. He studied law with John C. Calhoun, and was admitted to the Bar in 1809, when he settled in Abbeville, and practiced with John C. Calhoun, as his partner, until the election of the latter to Congress, in 1810.

He was married in September, 1816, to Elizabeth Bonneau Pickens, daughter of Ezekiel Pickens, and grand-daughter of Gen. Andrew Pickens.

He was elected a Member of the House of Representatives in the General Assembly of the State of South Carolina, in 1814, and was successively elected until 1824, when he declined being a candidate, in order to run against Joseph Black for the Senate, in which election he was defeated. In 1818 he was elected Speaker of the House of Representatives, and was continued as such by successive elections until he ceased to be a Member. As the author, in 1824, succeeded him in the Speaker's chair, it is right and proper that he should speak of the manner in which his predecessor discharged his duties. He transacted business with dispatch and ease; he had a perfect knowledge of Parliamentary rules, presiding with great dignity and with perfect good humor. He was impartial and just in his decisions, and firm in the preservation of decorum and order.

After a voluntary retirement from public life of several years, he was returned to the House of Representatives in 1832, and in 1833 was elected Speaker in the place of Henry Laurens Pinckney, of Charleston, who had been elected to Congress. In 1836 he was elected Senator from Abbeville, and, on the organization of the Senate in that year, he was elected President, in the place of the Hon. Henry Deas, who had declined to serve longer as a Senator. He remained in the Chair of the Senate until his election in December, 1838, to the office of Governor. He died 7th of April, 1840, before his term of office expired; his excellent wife died some years before him, leaving five sons and two daughters.

The preceding statement of the offices which he held is evidence of the high appreciation of Gov. Noble by the people. He was not an imposing, but a *good man.* His high moral character was exhibited and sustained in all his public offices. He was not a striking public speaker; but he spoke with ease and uniform good sense. His manner was fashioned after the strictest modes taught by the teachers of his time when at school.

He was a good lawyer, and if he had not abandoned the Legislature in 1824, it is very likely he would have been placed upon the Bench. As it was, his younger friends took precedence.

Chancellor Alexander Bowie, gives the following amusing account of a foot-race, in which Mr. Noble and others were concerned:

While Mr. Calhoun was a practicing lawyer, at Abbeville, there was a number of young men, students of law, in the offices of Calhoun & Noble, B. C. Yancey and George Bowie, viz: Nathaniel Alcock Ware and Robert Cunningham in the first, Charles Yancey and Tyler Whitfield in the second, and the late Chief Justice Lipscombe, of Alabama, and myself in the last. In the summer evenings we were accustomed to assemble in Mr. Calhoun's piazza for conversation, Mr. Calhoun and Mr. Yancey leading the conversation, of course. To the young men, these were rare occasions for improvement. The street in front of us presented an inviting spot for a foot race, being smooth and level.

On a certain evening, (I don't know from whom the suggestion came,) it was agreed we should pair off, and have a succession of foot-races. All were then for the sport. Yancey was pitted against Calhoun, Ware against Noble, Lipscombe against Whitfield, and Charles Yancey against myself.

None of us doubted that Mr. Yancey, being more accustomed to athletic exercises than Mr. Calhoun, would distance him in the race. To our surprise it resulted differently: Mr. Calhoun came out ahead. I do not remember how the race resulted between Whitfield and Lipscombe; but I well remember that I was beaten by Charles Yancey. The most amusing contest of the evening was that between Ware and Noble. Both were exceedingly clumsy; each did his very best; there was much grunting and puffing; their progress was so slow that there was a general burst of laughter when they came out "*an incontestible tie.*"

His friend, Gov. McDuffie, inscribed upon his tomb the following just description of his character: "As a public man, he was distinguished by moderation, resulting from a mild and even temperament; and by firmness of purpose proceeding from a high sense of duty, and a sound judgment, drawing its conclusions from careful and dispassionate examination. In all the relations of private life he was singularly exemplary, and in public and private, such was the unblemished purity of his character, that both friends and opponents would concur in inscribing on his tomb, 'Here lie the bones of an honest man.'"

One of his distinguished cotemporaries, Chancellor Bowie, of Alabama, says: "His mind was rather more practical than brilliant. He had little imagination, but a retentive memory. He was a well-read lawyer, and, without brilliant parts, he was a safe counsellor. He was one of the most amiable men I have ever known. There was no unkindness in his nature. He was a pleasant and interesting companion. With a strong perception of the ludicrous, he described with much zest and accuracy of detail such incidents and scenes as were of that character. In his life he was one of the most uniform men I have ever known. What he was one day you were sure to find him on the next. I never saw him out of humor, and he was my intimate friend and associate from our boyhood to near the close of his life. With the people he was always popular, and the steadiness and uniformity of his principles and character made that popularity fixed and durable. *His moral character was without a blot.*"

These descriptions of his character and virtues by such men

as Governer McDuffie and Chancellor Bowie, supersede any additional remarks from the author, unless it be to say, that with a knowledge of him for thirty years, he fully subscribes to all which they have said.

He had a fine engaging person, and was about five feet ten inches high, perfectly straight, hair dark, his eyes blue, his teeth perfectly white, and his countenance kind and benevolent.

HENRY DANA WARD.

The gentleman whose name is above, was once a lawyer of reputation in this State. He practiced for years, with great success, at Orangeburgh, and married a lady of wealth in that district.

He afterwards removed to Columbia, and lived in the house lately purchased by John Waties, Esq., at the north-west corner from the Episcopal Church. I recollect seeing him frequently—a tall, fine-looking, gray-haired, and dignified gentleman. He was a trustee of the college when I graduated in 1812, and at the quadrennial election of 1813, he was elected by the Legislature for four years.

He, as a trustee, superintended, in 1815, the planting of the beautiful elms, which are now so much an ornament to the College Campus. He was a native of Shrewsberry, Massachusetts, and from the inscription on his tombstone, erected to his memory, in Pottersfield, Columbia, I learn that "he died of typhus fever, while on a visit to his friends in Middletown, Connecticut, on the 23d of August, 1817." Alongside of his tomb repose the remains of his second wife and two of his children.

His son and only child who survived him, was, I think, a child of his first wife, who was a northern lady. Not long after his father's death he removed to one of the north-eastern States.

Mr. Ward was a man of education; and if the old Latin adage be true, "*nosciter societas*," then Mr. Ward was a high-minded, gentlemanly, upright man. For I know he was in the society of such men as Judge Nott, Chancellor DeSaussure, Mr. Hooker, Col. Chappell, Mr. Stark, and Dr. Maxcy.

But it is mournful to think, that before half a century has come and gone, his memory, beyond the record of Pottersfield, and the recollection of one who merely remembered him by having seen him in Columbia, has entirely perished in the city where he last lived.

ROBERT CUNINGHAM.

The name above is less known as a lawyer, than as an officer of the war of 1812, and a successful agriculturist afterwards. He was descended from Patrick Cuningham, the brother of General Robert Cuningham, of the British Army, and cousin of John Cuningham, who, after the Revolution, lived and died in Charleston, a successful merchant, and who there realized a large fortune. The brothers were Loyalists. Robert was the eldest, and took an active part in the Revolution. Patrick, the second brother, took part in the attempt to rescue his brother, who was seized and sent to Charleston in the first outbreak of the Revolution; in the seizure of the powder about the 1st of November, 1775, sent by the Committee of Safety for the Cherokees, the siege of Ninety-Six, the snow camps, and the final dispersion of the Loyalists, in arms, at the Cane Brake, on Reedy River, on the 22d December, 1775. This closed his military services. He, after the British captured Charleston, resided in the city. When the British forces evacuated Charleston, he and his brother, Robert, applied for leave to remain, which was refused. He then went to Florida, where he employed his slaves in cutting live oak timber until January, 1785, when he returned, and, on the 13th of March, he presented his petition to the Governor, which was backed by all the influential men and his neighbors of the upper country, for leave to remain in South Carolina. His sentence of banishment and the confiscation of his estate were rescinded and repealed on his paying twelve per cent. on the value of his estate, and being deprived of the rights of citizenship, such as voting and holding office, for seven years. These hard terms he accepted, paid the amercement, and submitted to the disqualification. Tradition is, he swore that he would not vote for seven years after his disqualification expired. This was in 1785. In 1790, our present Constitution was adopted by a Convention of the people; this placed all citizens of the State on the same footing, and Patrick Cuningham was returned to the first General Assembly by the people of Laurens. He served two terms, but believing that he was overlooked in the duties of the House by the malignity of those who governed, he refused to serve any longer. In 1793, he was appointed a Deputy Surveyor, and in that capacity, surveyed much of the land in the upper country. His fine homestead, on the Saluda, near the mouth of Reedy River, he, perhaps, acquired soon after his return from Florida, though it is possible he owned it before the Revolution. His third son, Robert, the subject of this memoir, was there born, on the 18th of October, 1786. His father died in 1794 or 1795, his mother in 1796; his brother, William, and sister, Pamela, died young. His brother, John, lived till 1817, then died unmarried. The whole large patrimonial estate, thus became the property of Robert. His primary instruction was received in Charleston.

Dr. Abner Pyles taught in the vicinity of Milton, Laurens District, during the youth of Robert. To him, who was a rigid disciplinarian and good teacher, he was indebted for a a good classical education. At that school, he met Benjamin C. Yancey, John Caldwell and James McKibbin. After the establishment of Mount Bethel Academy, in Newberry, about 1803 or 1804, he was, for a short time, a student there, under the direction of Elisha Hammond, the father of Governor Hammond, or his successor, Mr. Smith. At these schools he was prepared for the Junior Class of Yale College, for which he started to obtain admission; but in passing through Virginia, he met with friends, at whose instance, especially of a Mr. Preston, he was induced to enter the college at Lexington, in that State, where he graduated. His graduation address so pleased his family and friends, that it was published in a Charleston paper, which, after a few years, was discontinued or merged in some other journal.

He, although with the hopes, views and expectations of a planter, for a time devoted his mind to the acquisition of legal knowledge, as a fit and suitable preparation to discharge well the duties of an agriculturist and citizen. For a short time, he read law in the office of Mr. Cheves, then the leading lawyer of the City of Charleston. Tiring of the city, or fearing for his health, he returned home and pursued his legal studies, in the office of Mr. John C. Calhoun, at Abbeville. To him he became *personally* devotedly attached, and so continued during his life. He completed his legal education by attending, for a season, the *legal lectures* of Reeves and Gould, at Litchfield, Connecticut. In December, 1810, he was admitted to the Bar in Columbia.

He opened his office as an Attorney at Law, at Laurens Court House, but never resided at the village. He resided at the *paternal mansion*. He was the partner of Benjamin James, Esq., and as such practiced law until June, 1812, and managed or aided in a few cases, with what success I am unable to say, but I have very little doubt, he did full justice to them. For, he was a well-read lawyer, and the character of his mind was to do well whatever he undertook.

In June, 1812, the second war of independence, that which was waged for the protection of our flag and of our seamen on the high seas against the lawless invasion of the British ships, was declared. Young Cuningham, goaded by the taunts of malice, on account of the association of his name with the leader of the "Bloody Scout," and burning with the desire to wipe out forever the popular stigma, and to win for himself and his future family (if ever he should have one) a glorious immortality, as the soldier of liberty and his country, applied for, and, through Mr. Calhoun, obtained a captain's commission. He filled the ranks of his company in a marvelously short period of time and at great expense.

In August, 1812, he marched his company, consisting of the young men of his neighborhood, to Columbia; on the same day, Captain Robinson, from North Carolina, with another company of recruits, reached Columbia. Together they took possession of the lot and building once occupied as the Rope Walks; afterwards owned by Judge Nott, and latterly by Mr. Richardson, as their barracks and quarters. I recollect that Bishop Gale, of Cambridge, Abbeville District, was the first lieutenant of Captain Cuningham's company. They, after a short time, under the command of Lieut. Col. Andrew Pickens, marched for Charleston and Fort Moultrie. My recollection is, that Colonel Wellborn, of North Carolina, had the command of the regiment. After reaching Fort Moultrie, Capt. Cuningham was attached to the 18th Regiment, under the command of Colonel Drayton, who commanded the troops at the fort; and his company of recruits, who had only enlisted for eighteen months, were distributed to various volunteer regiments. He was soon transferred to the 8th Regiment of the regular army, commanded by Colonel Jack. Of this regiment, Lawrence Manning, brother of the elder Governor Manning, of this State, was lieutenant-colonel. In it, also, were Captains Twiggs, (now general in the army,) M. I. Keith and Edward Tatnall; and in it, or in Colonel Newnan's command, was Major William Cumming, of Georgia. As aid was to be despatched from this regiment to Colonel Newnan in his expedition against the Indians in Florida and southern Georgia, Captains Cuningham and Keith offered their companies to constitute it, and were accepted. They saw much sharp and exposed service. This service consisted in several partisan affairs, and in traversing swamps and dislodging the lurking enemy from their hidden recesses. In one of these severe contests, Lieutenant Smith, of Tennessee, was killed, as two companies, under Captain Cuningham, were charging into and through a hammock.

The constant exposure of Captain Cuningham, in this harrassing service, prostrated him with a violent attack of fever at Point Petre, on the Georgia coast. On his recovery from it, he found that a shattered constitution was the only reward of his active military exertions. He resigned his commission in January, 1814, and sought the restoration of his health on his paternal acres. On the 22d of February, 1814, he married an accomplished lady, Miss Louisa Bird, the daughter of Col. William Bird, formerly of Virginia, and then resident on the Ogeechee, Georgia; and with her and the society of his elder brother, who was still alive, he sat down to enjoy, at the paternal home, now and henceforward called Rosemont—the blessings of "*Home, sweet home.*" His son states he resigned when he was about being promoted to the rank of Major.

In 1820, his friends and neighbors of Laurens put him in nomination for the House of Representatives, in the General Assembly. He was elected by an overwhelming vote, and took his seat in November, 1820. During his term, John Cunningham, Esq., a lawyer of Laurens, was a candidate for the office of Treasurer of the Upper Division. Some malignant whispered the falsehood that he was of the Tory family of Cuningham, of Laurens. The slander came to the ears of Capt. Cuningham; he arose in his place, and denounced it as an unmitigated falsehood. He said—"I, not the candidate, belong to the Tory family of Cuningham, of Laurens." The slanderers, whoever they were, shrunk into obscurity and insignificance; John Cunningham was elected, and Capt. Cuningham acquired additional honor from his manly avowal. Many remembered that the frail man before them was one of the heroes of the war of 1812, and that he had not only perilled life in the service of his country, but that he had impaired his health, in the privations and hardships of an inglorious Indian service, which she had demanded from him.

But this matter, so ungenerously brought before the public, so affected his sensitive nature, that he determined never more to hold public office; and this determination he maintained to the close of life. In the retirement of his farm, in the enjoyment of his wife, children, and friends, in doing good all around him, and in his devotion to religion and its duties, most of his subsequent life was spent.

In the Nullification contest, although his friend, Calhoun, was the reputed father of the scheme of Nullification, he never hesitated for a moment. He was a Union man first and last. He could not bear to think of destroying that glorious flag under which, in 1812, he had offered up health and perilled life.

Before and during 1850–51, the ill health of his noble and gifted daughter, Miss Ann Pamela Cuningham, (whose name will live in honor and glory as long as Mount Vernon and

Washington are remembered,) caused him to travel much in the Middle and Eastern States. The hostility continually exhibited to Southern slave-owners, and the bitter denunciations of slavery constantly poured into his ears, made him think the hour had come when disunion should take place. He was, therefore, a Secessionist in 1851; and has since thought a Southern Confederacy necessary. This was, however, I know, a reluctant conclusion of a devoted friend of his country; and I rejoice that what he thought necessary did not occur, and, hope, never will. In the Union, and under the Constitution, we are safe. Deprived of these safeguards, anarchy, civil war, and ruin, will be our portion.

Captain Cuningham became a member of the Presbyterian Church in '28 or '29; he was set apart as an elder in 1831. His Christian and religious principles were opposed to duelling; yet an ungenerous fling at him as connected with the leader of the "Bloody Scout," in a newspaper publication of a speech made in the Court House, Columbia, by Colonel Wm. C. Preston, during our Nullification excitement, so exasperated him, that he thought he was justified in calling him to the field of honor. Friends interfered, and prevented the sad catastrophe of shedding the blood of one or both of two noble-minded gentlemen. It is due now to the memory of the dead and the living, that it should be said Colonel Preston did not utter the charge as published; it was the embellishment of the fruitful imagination of the proprietor.

Captain Cuningham, during his services in the army, made himself very well acquainted with surgery and medicine. His knowledge he successfully applied in his family, among his slaves, and to his neighbors.

To his slaves, reared by himself, his brother and his father, he was especially kind and attentive. He took great pains to have them properly instructed in the truths of Christianity; yet his discipline was strict and firm, to maintain honesty, fidelity and obedience.

He died at his paternal mansion and seat, called Rosemont, below the confluence of Reedy and Saluda Rivers, in Laurens District, on Thursday, the 7th day of July, 1859, in the seventy-third year of his age, after a protracted illness of four months, from dropsy. He leaves his excellent wife and two children, Colonel John and Ann Pamela Cuningham, to deplore their great loss.

Thus has ended the day of trial of a good and virtuous man. As a lawyer, he was not sufficiently tried to have acquired that reputation which his talents, honesty and firmness might have won for him. As an officer, he served and suffered for his country more than occurs generally to the short term in which he was in active service. He was beloved by his soldiers, for whom he made many sacrifices. As a citizen, man and neighbor, his works do follow him, and entitle him to the plaudit of "well done." As a master, his slaves will long mourn the absence of his kind face and mild rule; as a husband and father, none can know their loss but the wife and children. He lived to see most of his compeers in the army—Twiggs, Cumming, Hamilton, Huger, Manning, Bond I'On, Keith, Ferguson, Tatnall—enjoying the laurels of worth, valor, and old age, or gathered to their fathers in distinction. His latter days were even and quiet as he looked forward to the closing evening.

BENJAMIN ELLIOTT.

Amongst the men who flourished in South Carolina within the last half century, there were few more conspicuous than Benjamin Elliott. He was born in Charleston in the year 1786, and departed this life in 1836, being, at the time of his decease, fifty years old. He was the eldest child of Thomas Odingsell Elliott and Mary Pinckney, who was a sister of the late Honorable Charles Pinckney. He was related, on the paternal side, to the Odingsells and Elliotts, and on the maternal side to the Pinckneys and the Brewtons—all of whom were amongst the very oldest families in South Carolina. He was educated at Princeton College, where he graduated with distinction. In his early boyhood he exhibited a remarkable inquisitiveness of mind, and a strong disposition for the attainment of knowledge. These qualities pervaded his life. He was ever curious, and diligent in research upon literary and scientific subjects, and always endeavoring, by every means in his power, to add to his stock, not only of useful information, but of mental embellishment. He was not a mere reader, but an ardent and devoted student. He employed all the time that could be spared from professional or official duties, in the improvement of his mind, and the extension of his learning; and the natural consequence of all this industrious application was, that, having an excellent understanding, thus highly cultivated and enriched by study, he became a vigorous, thoughtful, and elegant writer, as he was also an accomplished speaker.

He was a student in the law office of Mr. Thomas Parker, and was admitted to the Bar in 1810. Soon after, he married Catharine O. Savage, by whom he had six children—three sons and three daughters. Of all his numerous family and progeny but one survives, and the family is represented by his grandson.

Mr. Elliott entered immediately upon the practice of the

law. He began his career as a lawyer in co-partnership with the late lamented Robert Y. Hayne, with whom he had long been upon terms of the most intimate friendship. His legal learning was extensive, and accurate, and profound. It used to be said of him that he was a walking library, as well of law as of other kinds of knowledge. He continued in partnership with Mr. Hayne until the latter was compelled, by political avocations, to abandon practice. Soon after that, Mr. Elliot was elected Commissioner in Equity, and, subsequently to that, he was elected Register in Equity, which latter office he retained to the time of his decease. He was several times elected a Member of the City Council of Charleston, and of the Legislature of the State.

Mr. Elliott was the author of numerous literary, historical, and political productions. There are still extant, "Reports of the Historical Committee of the Charleston Library Society," prepared by him, which contain a large body of valuable information, not only as to the United States, but especially as relates to the early history of South Carolina. This was a species of labor in which he delighted, for he had a remarkable fondness for exploring and illustrating the antiquities of his native State. There is, also, amongst his works, "A Refutation of the Calumnies circulated against the Southern and Western States, respecting the Institution and Existence of Slavery," being a pamphlet of very nearly one hundred pages. This was written as far back as 1822—the memorable year of an attempted insurrection, and was designed to repel the aspersions that were cast by the North upon the South in consequence of that event. It is a production of great research and eminent ability. It traces the history of slavery from its origin—shows that it is sanctioned by Divine authority—shows the agency, both of England and the Northern States, in its introduction and establishment in the slave-holding States—exhibits the true character of the institution, in its mild and patriarchal form of government—and illustrates the superior condition and comparative happiness of the negro, in the light labor he undergoes and the liberal indulgences he enjoys, as contrasted with the severe labor and physical and pecuniary suffering and privation of the Northern hireling. As this is not only one of the first, but, perhaps, the very first production that appeared in print, in relation to the Northern assaults upon our domestic institutions, so it is, unquestionably, one of the most historical, one of the fullest, ablest, and most complete defences of the South, and retaliations on the North that has issued from the press during the whole of the excited and eventful controversy that has been carried on between these two different sections of the Union. Indeed, certainly to Mr. E. belongs the high honor of having been a distinguished pioneer in the sacred cause of Southern defence and resistance against Northern calumny and aggression. In his political sentiments and feelings, he was a very decided and unyielding disciple of the Jeffersonian school. High evidence of this is found in an oration which he delivered before the '76 Association, in 1813, upon "The Inauguration of the Federal Constitution," which contains a masterly analysis of the true principles and structure of our government, showing it to be federative and not national—a compact between equals and sovereigns and not consolidated, elucidating the relative powers and duties of the General Government and the States, insisting on the maintenance and exercise of the reserved powers of the States, and demonstrating the absolute necessity, to the continuance of the Union and the peace and prosperity of the country, of a strict adherence, on the part of Congress, to the limitations of the Constitution, and a firm determination never to assume or exercise any ungranted, or merely constructive and doubtful power. In this oration there are passages of a high order of eloquence, especially those in which he contrasts a republic with monarchy, and in those in which he alludes to the sufferings of the Whigs, and the barbarous atrocities of the Tories, during the Revolutionary war in South Carolina. War was then raging between the United States and England; and this oration, able and patriotic as it is, was succeeded, early in 1814, by "A Sketch of the Means and Benefits of Prosecuting this War against Britain," in which Mr. Elliot again displayed his high ability as a writer, and his deep devotion to the honor and welfare of his country. In this essay he undertook to demonstrate the ample capabilities of the nation to sustain the war, by drawing a comparison between her resources in 1812 and the condition in which she conducted the war of Independence, showing the immense superiority of the former over the latter, and then exhibited the happy results by which success would be crowned, in the permanent establishment of a navy, the expulsion afar from us of a dangerous foe, by the acquisition of the British Provinces in America, commercial independence, and the strengthening of the Union by those ties of interest and friendship, by which the States would be interwoven, as it were, into one nation. In 1817, Mr. Elliott delivered another oration before the '76 Association, full of eloquence and patriotic ardor and enthusiasm. His conceptions were always strong, his diction terse and elegant, his delivery manly and impressive. Under the authority of an Act, passed in 1833, "To provide for the Military Organization of the State," he prepared and published "The Militia System of South Carolina," being a Digest of all the Acts of Congress and of this State concerning the militia. It was, and probably still continues to be, the Military Code of the State; at all events, it must still be very useful as a book of reference. We are also indebted to him for rescuing from oblivion, and preserving and publishing, the Debates in our Legislature, in '88, by which a Convention was called to consider the Constitution of the United States, then submitted to the States, by the Federal Convention, for their adoption or rejection; and also the Debates in the State Convention, by which the Federal Constitution was adopted and ratified, as far as they could possibly be procured. These debates are incomplete, especially those in the State Convention; but, imperfect as they are, they constitute a precious political relic, and, no doubt, every man who possesses them thanks Mr. Elliott for the labor and research by which he was enabled to preserve them.

Mr. Elliott was the author of other works, not now in possession of the writer, and therefore not so well remembered. He was a classical scholar, thoroughly instructed in, and deeply imbued with, the spirit of the ancient literature of the Greeks and Romans. Amongst other things of a purely literary character, he wrote a beautiful criticism, or commentary, upon a translation, by the Hon. John L. Wilson, of the interesting allegory of "Cupid and Psyche," from "The Metamorphoses of the Golden Alps," of Apuleius.

In November, 1835, he delivered a very beautiful and interesting address before the congregation of St. Philip's Church, upon the occasion of laying the corner-stone of their new edifice—their former building having been destroyed by fire. That building was one of the oldest, most beautiful, and most imposing in America. It was filled with monuments of exquisite sculpture, all of which were hallowed by the dearest associations and the most sacred memories. When their "beautiful house was burned by fire," the congregation of St. Philip's were clothed in mourning. It was whilst their sorrow was still fresh, and their tears still flowing, that Mr. Elliott delivered his address. He had a fine theme, and he made admirable use of it. Like all his other speeches, the whole of it was eloquent; but at those parts of it in which he described the ancient and venerable temple, and alluded to the speaking images by which it was adorned, and which never failed to solemnize the minds, and improve the hearts of all who beheld them—the whole of the vast assemblage was bathed in tears. That address, and the interesting circumstances under which it was pronounced, will never be obliterated from the minds of any of that old and highly respectable congregation who were partakers or spectators of the scene.

The legal learning of Mr. Elliott was extensive and profound. He was much attached to the study of political or constitutional law. His political writings abundantly manifest his familiarity with it. They are full of able discussions of constitutional questions. But though he wrote a great deal, he wrote principally for his own gratification, or for the purpose of taking part in matters of great public moment, in which, as a patriot, he felt an interest.

In his political principles, he was a decided Republican of the Jeffersonian school, and an ardent supporter of our last war with Britain. Subsequently, when difficulties arose between South Carolina and the General Government, in relation to the Tariff and other usurpations and oppressions by that government, he early adopted the Carolina doctrines, steadily maintained them through the whole of the Nullification contest, and was always ready, at all times and under all circumstances, to assert the rights and uphold the sovereignty of his native State, at any hazard and to the last extremity.

In the family and social circle, he shone with distinguished lustre. Of him it may truly be said, he was most loved by those who knew him best. He was very popular and highly esteemed in the literary and scientific associations, of which he was a member. As a citizen, he was remarkable for high-toned sentiment, elevated principles, ardent enthusiasm, and a generous disinterestedness, and self-sacrificing disposition, almost amounting to a fault. As a man, certainly no juster description can be given of him than in those beautiful words of Horace, "*Integer vitæ, scelerisque purus*;" and with equal truth may it be said of him, as a writer, "*Nullum tetigit, quod non ornavit.*"

JOHN S. GLASCOCK.

John Sellard Glascock was born near Augusta, Georgia, on the 18th of April, 1788. His parents were from Virginia. He studied law at Edgefield Court-House under Edmund Bacon, Esq., and was admitted to the Bar at Columbia in 1811. Previous to his admission, (on the 18th of August, 1810,) he married Eliza Simkins, the daughter of John Simkins.

He resided, and practiced law, at Edgefield Court-House, and was more successful as an advocate than as a lawyer. He was an exceedingly popular man, and was elected to the House of Representatives in 1820, and again in 1822. In the military he was promoted to the highest grade, that of Major-General of the First Division of Militia.

In December, 1822, after his return from the session of the House of Representatives of that year, he was wounded in his hand, by the accidental discharge of a gun while hunting game. This produced tetanus, or lock-jaw, which caused his death.

He left a widow and four children, Thomas, Sarah, Eliza and Edmund.

Dr. Laborde, speaking of General Glascock, says: It is certain, however, that he attained distinction in the Courts of Edgefield, and that he was a popular lawyer. I am ignorant of the extent of his legal learning. He was a man of pleasing manners, a good talker, of a most genial nature, and had the rare talent of making himself agreeable to all. I think, of all men I have ever known, he enjoyed the most uniform popularity. He represented the people of Edgefield for a long period in the State Legislature, and was their Senator at the time of his death.

All who knew him will say, that any notice of him would be inexcusable, if allusion were not made to his fondness for field sports, and particularly for the fox chase. He was an uncommonly fine shot, and often betook himself to this manly exercise. But who will describe him as a *fox-hunter!* He rode the noblest horse in the upper country, and his large pack of fox-dogs would excite the envy of an English nobleman. How often have I been aroused from my slumbers, on a freezing December night, by his " echoing horn," and the excited cry of his anxious pack, as he passed my father's house, on his way to his hunting grounds; and how often have I seen him making his triumphal entry into the village, with the fox suspended to his saddle, and his faithful dogs following, and listened to the story of his chase until my *little heart* caught the inspiration, and beat with an exultant feeling, almost equal to his own.

He was in the prime of life when removed from this mortal scene, and it so happened that I saw him breathe his last. I was present, as one of his youthful friends, and engaged in dispensing those attentions which his situation demanded. The picture is now before me. He had accidentally inflicted a gun-shot wound upon one of his hands, and was dying of lock-jaw; and his lovely wife was near by, in the last stage of consumption. Their weeping " little ones" were around them, and it was apparent that in a few short days, or fleeting hours, both parents were to be committed to the tomb, and their happy home made desolate. And so it was. They died within the same week, and their bodies were buried in the Baptist church-yard of the village. The house passed into the hands of strangers, the children were distributed among their relations, and he who, but a short time before, filled so large a space in the community of that intelligent district, like the whole family of the dead, (with fewest exceptions,) soon ceased to be remembered.

STEPHEN D. MILLER.

Stephen Decatur Miller, the son of William Miller and his wife, Margaret White, was born in May, 1787, in the Waxhaw settlement,* of Lancaster District. The original white settlers of that section, among whom were Mr. Miller's paternal and maternal ancestors, were rigid Presbyterians, from the north of Ireland. When they migrated to this State, they brought their pastor with them, and had, therefore, the benefit of constant religious instruction for themselves and their children. They "trained up their children in the way in which they should go," according to the strictest principles of Presbyterian faith and practice. *They loved liberty*, and, like Cromwell's Ironsides, they were ready to pray, and if need be, to fight for its preservation. Their descendants were like their ancestors, a brave, energetic, and a determined people. This was shown throughout the Revolution, for *they were Whigs*, and toiled, and suffered, and bled for liberty until it was attained. His father died when he was young. He was raised, as he says in a letter written to his daughter, principally among his "mother's relations, and, like all children, thought my mother and her kin most worthy of my affection and the cleverest people in the world." His maternal grandmother, Margaret White, is mentioned in Ramsay's History as an instance of longevity.

Mr. Miller was of the same family with the Crawfords, and, possibly, this family connection created the first beginning of his attachment, in mature life, to the great Georgian, William H. Crawford.

He received in early youth, what was, in that time and country, called a classical education. The Rev. Mr. Conser, of the neighborhood, who was a strict disciplinarian, and well

* The Waxhaw settlement lies upon the Waxhaw Creek, the Catawba River, and the North Carolina line, in Lancaster District. It is even now, the finest body of land with which I am acquainted, in South Carolina. The Waxhaw tribe of Indians, now totally extinct, originally occupied it.

qualified to teach, was his preceptor. He was not only instructed in classical literature, but he was thoroughly imbued with a knowledge of the Scriptures. He could repeat with wonderful rapidity and accuracy, almost any portion. His quotations were frequently drawn from this source, while at the Bar, and were always pointed and telling. He was a bright, energetic, and daring boy, and though not large of stature, possessing unusual strength and activity.

In the athletic sports, which greatly obtained in that day, he had few equals and no superiors. In fact, he delighted to indulge in them after he had arrived at mature age, and reached the highest positions in the State.

In the letter to his daughter, (23d July, 1835,) in speaking of his maternal relations, he says, that the second daughter of his aunt, Jane Crawford, then Mrs. Dunlap, is the oldest of my relations. She was a *little girl* when General Jackson lived with her father, and is said to have rejected him." Perhaps there was little in the hard-featured and obscure youth to attract the attention of a young and beautiful girl.

Stephen D. Miller graduated in the South Carolina College, in the talented class of 1808, and soon afterwards entered the office of John S. Richardson, Esq., at Sumter, as a student at law.

In 1811, he was admitted to the Bar, in Columbia, and settled in Sumter District, to practice law, succeeding to the practice of his instructor, Mr. Richardson, who had been elected Attorney General, in December, 1810, and had removed to Charleston. Mr. Miller resided at Statesburg. He had an office there, and also at Sumterville. The Clerk of the Court, Mr. Horan, *then* lived at Statesburg, and *there* kept the Records of Sumter District.

In 1814 or 1815, he intermarried with Miss Dick, of Sumter District.

In 1818, Judge Richardson was elected to Congress from the Congressional Election District composed by Sumter, Kershaw, Lancaster, and Chesterfield. For reasons stated in the sketch of this eminent gentleman, he declined the distinction, and Stephen D. Miller, his pupil and friend, was elected in his place. Before the close of his first session, he was compelled to hasten home to close the eyes of his wife in death. She died in 1819, leaving three children, Elias Dick, John Richardson, and William Smith. Mr. Miller may have returned to Congress in 1819 and served until March, 1820. During his service in Congress, he became much attached to the Secretary of the Treasury, under Mr. Monroe, the Hon. William H. Crawford, and espoused his principles, and with Judge Smith, the Senator in Congress, was in opposition to Mr. Calhoun's doctrines of that day. They belonged to the Radical school of politics, as it was termed in South Carolina. He resumed his practice on his return from Congress, and pursued it most successfully, in Sumter, Kershaw, and Lancaster, and, possibly, in other Districts. In May, 1821, he married his second wife, Miss Mary Boykin, of Kershaw. In 1822, he was elected Senator in the State Legislature, from Claremont, Sumter District, and so continued to serve until 1828, when he was elected Governor of the State. In 1830, he was elected Senator in Congress, over his old friend, Judge William Smith. He served only two years and then resigned on account of ill-health. He was a member of the great Nullification Convention of 1830, the action of which, whether for good or evil, as an opponent, it does not behoove me to say. In 1832, when it re-assembled to rescind the ordinance of Nullification, the contest about allegiance began. The members of the Union party felt, as the contest with the United States Government was happily ended, that nothing further ought to be done. The Nullifiers prepared the ordinance to nullify the Force Bill, and further proposed to declare, that the primary and paramount allegiance of the citizen was due to the State of South Carolina. This, the members who were of the Union party, strongly opposed, and insisted that the only allegiance known in the United States, was obedience to the Constitutions of the United States and the State, and the governments thereby constituted; and that the constitutional oath existing, was quite sufficient. Pending the debate, a recess took place, and the Nullification party went into caucus, professedly with a view of modifying the measure proposed.

Governor Miller and myself lodged at the same hotel. When he returned from the caucus, I asked him what was done? He replied, "*they have made it a d——d sight worse than it was before.*"

On the re-assembling of the Convention, the measure proposed was the definition of allegiance, as it stands now in the ordinance. Governor Miller moved to strike it out, and said that, "the Nullification party were charged with a secret intent to dissolve the Union." "If," said he, "this measure passes, it will make the charge true." His motion was overruled by a very small vote. If the members, who were Union men, had been present, as they ought to have been, his motion would have prevailed, and South Carolina would have been saved from the bitter strife of 1833 and 1834, and its consequences in 1835.

His children by his first wife, except his eldest son, Elias Dick Miller, died very young. Elias Dick Miller is said to have been "a youth of rare and noble qualities. Those who were in college with him are now chiefly on the stage of public action, and while the mention of his name cannot fail to call up recollections, the tenderest love and admiration for the unusual combination of excellencies in his character, they will renew their sighs for his early withdrawal from a world he seemed so well fitted to benefit and adorn." He died in 1832, in his sophomore year, in the South Carolina College. From the terrible shock occasioned by the death of this noble boy, the ardent and devoted nature of his father was never able to recover.

In 1835, Governor Miller having bought land in Mississippi, removed thither with a large number of slaves, and settled a large and valuable plantation. He was then, and sometime before, in bad health. He bore up against it with his usual buoyancy, but in vain. On the 8th of March, 1838, at the house of his nephew, Major Charles M. Hart, in the town of Raymond, Mississippi, he closed his eventful life in the fifty-first year of his age. His family he had left in South Carolina. They had, therefore, not the consolation of smoothing his dying pillow, nor of dropping upon his marble features the tears of affection. He was there buried, and there his remains still repose.

He left surviving him his excellent wife, Mrs. Mary Miller, and four children, (one son and three daughters,) his son Stephen D., is a planter living in Albama, his eldest daughter, Mary B., is the wife of James Chesnut, Jr., one of the Senators of South Carolina in Congress; his second daughter, Kate B., is the wife of David R. Williams, the grandson of Gen. Williams, of Society Hill, and his third daughter is the wife of Thomas E. Boykin, of Dallas County, Alabama.

The means of Governor Miller in the beginning of life, were very small. He inherited two or three slaves, which he sold to enable him to complete his education, and start fairly on the way of life. Thus, like most of the great men of the nineteenth century, in Carolina, he began poor; but by those greater endowments of head and heart, which God had provided for him, he, in the short period of life assigned to him, obtained "wealth, fame and power."

When I first came to know Governor Miller intimately, (about 1820,) he was a lawyer in full and successful practice. His voice was not a pleasant one, and, in his speeches, fell rather harshly on the ear. His flow of words was easy and abundant. He was entirely argumentative. Nothing of fancy entered into his speeches. He was an excellent lawyer. He was a leading Member in the Senate of South Carolina, being Chairman of the Judiciary Committee, and of course most of the Acts, making important changes of the law, passed through his hands. The Act to make the stealing of corn or other grain from the freehold, owed its origin to him—he framed *it as it now is.*

Of his course in Congress, I know little; he was a respectable Member of the House, but had little opportunity to distinguish himself. In the Senate, he was, with the other South Carolina Senators, in opposition to most of the measures of President Jackson.

As Governor of South Carolina, he administered her affairs

with prudent discretion, and aided much in arousing the people to the work of Nullification. Whether that ought to be praised or censured, is not for me to determine.

I have no reason to believe that Governor Miller did not think he was pursuing the means which would contribute to the honor and glory of South Carolina. That he was mistaken, I did not then, nor do I now entertain a doubt.

Governor Miller, by nature, was "a bold and vigorous man, he had high ambition and lofty purposes. He loved his friends, and they returned his love with ardent and devoted affection." "He was a man of great power in his day and generation, in society, at the Bar, and in the councils of his country."

In all the relations of private life, he was true, devoted and faithful. His mourning widow and his young orphan children, felt the early blight which fell upon them in his death, as the bitterest stroke which God could inflict upon them. But, like good old Job, they bowed submissive to the chastisement, and felt with him, "the Lord gave, and the Lord hath taken away, blessed be the name of the Lord."

JOHN MURPHY.

Governor John Murphy was a native of South Carolina, and graduated with the second honor of the class of 1808, at the South Carolina College. Senator Evans and Chancellor Harper were among his class-mates.

He married the daughter of Robert Hails, and was very soon noticed by the people of the State. He was elected a Trustee of his *Alma Mater* in 1809, and re-elected in 1813; he was the first graduate who had that honor. He was elected Clerk of the Senate in November, 1810, and continued by successive elections till the close of 1817, when, I presume, he removed to Alabama. He was not admitted to the Bar in South Carolina. Judge Porter, of Alabama, gives the following sketch:

Mr. Murphy removed to Alabama at a very early period in the history of the State. He entered the political arena so soon after his emigration, that he was scarcely known as a lawyer. He was made Governor about the year 1828, and remained in that post for four years; after which, he made several unsuccessful efforts to get into Congress, from the Montgomery District over Dixon H. Lewis. The contest, at that time, turned upon State-rights; and Governor Murphy was a full-length Union, or coercive-doctrine man. Dixon H. Lewis was a Nullifier; and the canvass between them was marked by extraordinary excitement. The question was regarded as one between South Carolina and the Northern States—between Federalism and State-rights—tariffs and free trade; and the speeches of these gentlemen elicited whatever the history of these phases of politics could generate. Dixon H. Lewis was well adapted, in the character of his mind and in manners, to the curious task of exciting the enthusiasm of the masses. He had a graceful and captivating delivery, and possessed a high order of talents; added to which, he controlled the sympathies of the people, who cared little for, and understood less of, the abstract principles then at issue. Mr. Murphy, while noted for order and precision, was not regarded as either a graceful or an accomplished orator. He was a plain and matter-of-fact speaker, cold and uninspiring. He was, too, in the decline of life, while Mr. Lewis was in the out-set of his career, energetic, and bold in the assurance of victory. The canvass between these two gentlemen was animated, and tended to impart a vast amount of political knowledge. The writer was present upon one occasion when Governor Murphy was placed in quite a mortifying position. To turn aside the invective of Lewis against the waste of public money for internal improvements, the Governor gave a long and warm account of rail-roads, then an almost unheard-of improvement. In the midst of his discussion of their merits, he was interrupted by the voice of an ignorant, but influential Democrat, who inquired, if the roads the Governor was advocating, were "real good roads, or roads made out'en rails?"

In every position of a public nature held by Mr. Murphy, and as a private citizen, he was regarded with very great respect. He was faithful to his party; as a man and member of society, he was eminently honorable and just. In person, he was unwieldy; of light, sandy complexion; his pronunciation strongly marked with Scottish accent.

Governor Murphy was a Member of Congress in, I presume, '34 and '35; he was present when General Blair rashly ended his own life. Removed from the public eye, in his retirement to private life, he spent the remainder of his days, after 1835, in the performance of the duties of a neighbor, in the circle of his acquaintance. He died about the year 1839–'40, in the bosom of his family, full of years, and consoled by the reflections of a life graced by public honors. His education was good; being understood to be an *alumnus* of the South Carolina College.

WILLIAM LOMAX.

William Lomax was a native of Abbeville District. He graduated at Dartmouth College, about the year 1808, and returned to his native district, studied law, and was admitted to the Bar, in 1812. He was elected to the Legislature in 1830, as a Union man.

He was the partner of Mr. Yancey for a short time, and had considerable practice both in law and equity. He wrote a wretched hand, and on one occasion, in term time, he wrote an affidavit which he could not read, so as to be understood. Col. Noble undertook to read it, but was unable to do so. Judge Bay ordered it to be handed up to him, and when he saw it he declared the Justice who wrote it, ought to be struck from the rolls. "Wh-what mag-magistrate wrote it?" was the Judge's impatient inquiry. Col. Noble said, brother Lomax wrote it! The Judge, turning to him, said: "Br-brother Lo-Lomax, wh-what schoo-schoolmaster t-taught you to write?"

Mr. Lomax's utterance was so rapid and vehement, as to confuse his own mind and that of his hearers. On one occasion, he had committed a mistake in the grammatical construction of a sentence. If he had let it pass, it would have escaped notice, when even Mr. Calhoun indulged in *mala grammatica.* Mr. Lomax, however, undertook to correct his error, and made it worse at each trial. He said: "May it please your Honor! the state of the pleadings *are these—are this.*"

Notwithstanding things like these, which are only the bubbles on the stream of life, Mr. Lomax deserved much of his native district. He was a good lawyer and an honest man. "He married a most excellent lady, the daughter of William Tennent, Esq., whose ancestors were alike distinguished for their piety and their patriotism." Mr. Lomax died early. About 1833 or 1834, in his usual good health, while walking his piazza, he fell and expired. The shortness and uncertainty of life was thus fearfully illustrated. Chancellor Bowie, who knew him well, and who is very well qualified to judge, says: "I have known few men whose minds I would find it so difficult to characterize as his. He had capacity enough to acquire knowledge, and he had evidently been a student not wanting in diligence, and yet he never became a *successful* lawyer. I think his main defects were want of discrimination, a want of self-confidence, and a total want of tact in the conduct of a case. An adroit opponent could easily draw him off from the strong points of his case, and cause him to exhaust his powers on immaterial issues. He was a fearless man, without self-possession; but with many noble traits of character—a true friend, a moral and upright citizen, and a most exemplary husband and father."

ALEXANDER BOWIE.

Alexander Bowie was a son of that eminent revolutionary patriot, Major John Bowie, of Abbeville, and was born and raised, and lived a large part of his life in that district. He has not even told me when he was born. I know, however, from another source, that he was born 14th December, 1789.

He graduated, in the fourth class of the South Carolina College in 1809, with the second honor, alongside of his friend and room-mate James L. Petigru, to whom was assigned the first. It is gratifying to know, that eight out of that distinguished class of eighteen, after a lapse of fifty years, are still spared to honor and bless their country.

Alexander Bowie studied law with his brother George, was admitted to the Bar in April, 1813, and entered immediately into a pretty extensive practice, as the partner of his brother, till 1817, and afterwards either alone, or as the partner of some junior member of the Bar. Mr. Bowie was a man of fine talents and excellent elocution, and, as he says of himself, "if he had not been a lazy dog," he might have stood, always as he did at his graduation, only second to James Louis Petigru, in the noble profession which they both pursued.

In 1818, he was a Member of the House of Representatives, of South Carolina; in 1822, he, and Baylis John Earle, were competitors for the Solicitor's office of the Western Circuit. Earle was successful. In 1828, my impression is Mr. Bowie was again a Member from Abbeville. The storm of Nullification was threatening in the sky of South Carolina; in 1830, under the name of Convention, Mr. Bowie sided with that party; whether he was then a candidate or not, I do not know.

The whole of the candidates of that party were excluded in October, 1830. Subsequently, however, Nullification had held the ascendancy in Abbeville; and if Mr. Bowie desired it, I have no doubt he was returned again to the Legislature.

He removed to Alabama in the fall of 1835, and in December, 1839, was elected Chancellor of the Northern Division of Alabama. He held the office for six years, and then retired to private life, which he still adorns, and which he will long grace, if my good wishes will in any way contribute to that end.

I append a sketch of Chancellor Bowie, by my friend Judge Porter, of Sydney, Alabama:

It is to be regretted that, from the habitual retirement of this gentleman, but few memorials of his public character are known. He was born in Abbeville District, South Carolina, on the 14th December, 1789, and was admitted to the Bar, in 1813. After occasional displays in the Forum, and on public occasions, in his native State, in which he gave promise of very high distinction as an orator, he removed to Alabama, and settled in Talladega County, in November, 1835. Here he practiced law until the 16th December, 1839, when he was elected one of the Chancellors of the State. He held this office for six years, much to the satisfaction of the Bar; when, retiring, he devoted himself to his planting interests, at his beautiful farm, Ben Lomond, where he now resides; less anxious for public employment, than for that quiet independence which characterizes his household.

Chancellor Bowie served some years as Trustee of the University of Alabama; a position in which he took great pride, and to which he carried very high enthusiasm in the cause of education. His labors, indeed, contributed much to elevate the University; and had the State always possessed trustees and professors of equally sound judgment, independent minds, and classical attainments, it would doubtless have maintained a quite respectable attitude, as an institution of letters. Chancellor Bowie is distinguished for remarkable graces of elocution. He possesses a finely-toned, well-modulated voice, and a sensibility which gives considerable effect to his enunciation. His powers of entertainment in the social circle, are extensive, and always regulated by modesty and good sense. He is not at all given to affection; but is courteous and affable, without pretension. Among his neighbors he is regarded as a citizen always ready to exhibit his public spirit and patriotism in whatever can advance the prosperity of the country. He resists, however, all attempts to draw him into political life, where, without being a partizan, he would be firm in the support of democracy, and where an enlightened judgment would temper an impetuous and suasive elocution, in the cause of truth and conservatism.

ROBERT CLENDENEN.

Tully, in his Orator, speaks of a middle species of oratory, which has neither the keenness of the utmost polish, nor the thunder of the most rough. Of this character was the eloquence of Mr. Clendenen. It would be readily inferred by one observing him, for the first time, that he had not, in early life, possessed very great educational advantages. At the same time, he had received from nature much quickness of intelligence, and a sound judgment, which, by judicious application in youth, he had made most effective instruments to his success in after-life at the Bar. He had also a good person and agreeable manners; was pleasant and facetious, and master of that most desirable of accomplishments for a speaker, fine action. The great basis, however, of his success in life, was his integrity and stability of character; without which, the most brilliant capacity, and most striking accomplishments will not secure permanent success: for it is the nature of men, however little they may practice virtue, and however degraded they may become in life, to render an involuntary homage to the character whose course has been marked by an uniform and determined adherence to principle. Even the most vicious members of society find it to their interest to sustain the supremacy of that incorruptible conduct which checks the career of crime. Governed by this standard, Mr. Clendenen was not long in securing the public confidence. It displayed itself in a large and lucrative practice, and in his frequent elevation to political station. As a politician, he was prudent and conservative; as an advocate, cool, sagacious, and scrupulously exact. In person, he was inclined to be portly, his face, round and florid, and his eyes intensely black. In style of oratory, he had more care for ideas than for words; but his enunciation was agreeable, and in choice of words, he was judicious and correct. In criminal cases, he could be warm and impetuous, and exercise considerable influence over the passions, and yet be perspicuous, natural, and weighty. Mr. Clendenen's success did not cause him to relax his application: for he had opposed to him at the Bar, Thomas Williams, who possessed great powers of popular oratory; Robert G. Mills, a man of wonderful industry and energy; Job Johnson, who stood high in popularity, and had much ability; and others, who would soon have obscured any cotemporary, whose talents and diligence had not been of very high order.

Mr. Clendenen's place of residence was Yorkville; and he practiced at Union, Chester, Fairfield and Lancaster. By economy and good management in early life, he acquired a considerable fortune; and up to the time of his death, which occurred about 1832–3, he regularly rode the circuit, more to enjoy the conversation of his associates than for profit. He possessed one qualification, which, more than any other, shows the accomplished lawyer and true gentleman. He was the kind and indulgent protector of the younger members of the Bar, especially of those who, like himself, had had their opportunities circumscribed by poverty, and the absence of influential patronage.

Mr. Clendenen's career illustrated the necessity of industry and attention to business, and of an undeviating adherence to the substance not the mere name of honor. By such a course, he reached a position in life, which his talents alone could not have secured him. Had he lived, he might have risen to the highest dignities of the State. As it was, he gradually advanced in public estimation, and died warmly esteemed by all who knew him. It was admitted, with regret, that his habits were rather convivial; and that, led by his love of company, he too often worshiped the god

"*Cingentam tempora viridi pampino.*"

Mr. Clendenen was, I think, in the beginning of life, a merchant. He studied law with Judge Smith, and was admitted to the Bar, in Charleston, on the 11th of January, 1813. Either before his admission, or soon after, a bitter quarrel took place between Judge Smith and himself, which resulted in an enmity never reconciled. Mr. Clendenen's voice very much resembled Judge Smith's, and in bitterness of sarcasm and denunciation, he was much like him. He was the Senator from York for several years; probably for two or three terms. He married the eldest daughter of Colonel David Myers. Surrounded by affluence, and blest with a family, and attended by great popularity, one would have thought, that he had cause to live without any appeal to extraneous circumstances; but he was devoted to idle company, and acquired bad habits, which led to his death about the time mentioned. His widow and two daughters survived him.

JAMES DELLET.

This gentleman was born in Ireland, and, though young when his parents migrated to South Carolina, could not have been very youthful when he connected himself with the South Carolina College, in which institution he graduated with the first honor of the class of 1810, and was assistant librarian to Prof. Park. He studied law in Columbia, and was admitted to the Bar in 1813. He was also Commissioner in Equity. In Columbia, he married Miss Willison, the niece of Robert Stark—a lady of fine mind and attractive person, who, by a very close attention to the duties of a wife and mother, contributed greatly to his prosperity and happiness. As early as 1817 he removed to Alabama, and settled in Claiborne, Monroe County—at that period a very promising town, and of considerable commercial importance. There Mr. Dellet commenced the practice of law, and such was his industry, perseverance and attention to business, that he soon took the lead of the Bar, which he maintained with constantly increasing reputation till his death. Having the advantage of an early removal to a new country, he selected a body of valuable land, on the Alabama River, which, increasing in worth as the country became settled, was the foundation of a considerable fortune. He accumulated, too, a vast amount of money by his profession; for such was his punctuality and diligence, that he secured the principal part of the then large collecting business of that section of country. His talents so soon developed his capacity for political station, that he was, at an early period, invited to accept office, which he did, on important occasions, to the extent of a seat in the Legislature. There he was distinguished as an effective and eloquent debater, and as a man of unbending resolution and integrity; the ardent supporter of public improvement; the firm opposer of all demagoguism, and of all mere electioneering policy. He usually filled the post of

Chairman of the Judiciary Committee, and, by his good sense and speaking ability, did much to keep in check that flood of ignorant innovation which usually overflows the legislation of a new country.

Though a man of fine judgment and brilliant imagination, Mr. Dellet did not rely upon these as a lawyer. He studied books effectively, and became as familiar with cases as he was with principles. Like most eminent speakers, he was not always equally happy as an orator. Sometimes, but very rarely, he was an indifferent, at other times, a most powerful and effective elocutionist.

In 1835, he met with a calamity in his family circle, from which he never recovered. Three, out of four children, the eldest, died of malignant fever, in the space of a few weeks. This event was followed by the death of his wife, and his own sudden decline in health.

Towards the close of his life, he was elected to Congress from the district previously represented by Dixon H. Lewis. He was opposed by the late Judge Henry Goldthwaite, a man of fine abilities, and great astuteness as a politician. The canvass was a contest between the Whigs and Democrats, and was one as brilliant as ever distinguished the history of party. In this position, though in declining health, he more than sustained his reputation. Few men had been more consistent. In the contest between Mr. Adams and General Jackson, he was a warm supporter of the former. His veneration for Mr. Clay was unlimited, and the elevation of that great statesman to the Presidency was the most ardent wish of his life. In the Nullification and Union controversy, he sided with the latter, taking the field with alacrity, and canvassing with all his ability against the theory of Nullification. He was the advocate of a Tariff and of internal improvement, but a not very moderate opposer of the measures of Jackson, which he took every opportunity of assailing. The principles of the Proclamation and Force Bill, and Jackson's course in the Florida war, especially met his disapproval.

During the administration of Mr. Adams, a Judge for the Federal Court for Alabama had to be appointed. The names of Mr. Dellet and Judge Crawford were before the Cabinet, and the latter received the appointment, on the ground that Crawford was the most likely of the two to remain firm against the torrent of Jackson's popularity. Crawford, however, went over to Jackson as soon as he got his commission in his pocket, and Dellet remained firm to the day of his death. In 1844, Mr. Clay told the writer of this sketch, that Mr. Adams and himself had never been more grossly deceived, and for once, at least, had been mistaken in their friends.

In person, Mr. Dellet was stout, thick-set, and rather ungainly in form. To strangers he was taciturn, and to the masses anything but dependent or conciliating. His own ideas of independence and sincerity forbade every species of deception; and he scorned to solicit the good opinion of men, except by honorable actions openly performed. To those, however, with whom he could not be suspected of making court for merely interested purposes, and especially to ladies, he was one of the most elegant and engaging of men. His face was round and florid, his features small and well shaped, and his eyes remarkably keen and sparkling.

On the circuit, Mr. Dellet was the soul of the Bar. Possessed of fine conversational powers, of extensive stores from reading, of a vast fund of anecdote, and of a humor truly Irish, he was a most agreeable companion.

In style of oratory Mr. Dellet had, in his time, few equals. His language was pure, and his diction elevated and natural, though occasionally florid and ornamental. His voice was finely toned, and he had the power of controlling it by the most agreeable modulations. He always spoke with vehemence, and with an action at once correct, lively, and graceful. He possessed striking powers of sarcasm, which, however, he never exerted, except to lash vice, or to oppose the factious madness of abandoned demagogues. So generally acknowledged was the strength and dignity of his language, his wit, and the elegance of his address, that when he spoke the forum was filled with hearers, either spell-bound by his pathos, or hurried into successive bursts of laughter.

Mr. Dellet loved to expose every attempt to minister to the

passions of the mob, by exciting prejudices against official persons. On one occasion he was associated in the Legislature of Alabama with a very ignorant man, the result of excitement on the county-site question. The latter, to render himself famous, on the principle of burning down the temple, introduced a bill to lessen the salaries of the Judges. He supported this measure by a speech, in which he said, "that there were many good men who would perform the duties of Judges for a much smaller salary than two thousand dollars. That he (the speaker) would be willing to take the office for five hundred dollars a year." Here Mr. Dellet interrupted him with some vehemence of manner, and said: "If the Member desires to control the question by that kind of argument, I can furnish him my overseer, who is as capable as the gentleman of playing an incumbent of the woolsack, and who will do it for one hundred dollars a year." This killed off all attempts upon the Judiciary that session.

But Mr. Dellet's ability as a lawyer, the uncommon merit of his elocution, the pleasant mixture of wit and pathos, his clear and distinct reasoning, were not his chief claims to reputation. The great foundation of his fame was his incorruptible integrity, his unflinching firmness in the cause of right. He was peculiarly one of the few "who would not have flattered Neptune for his trident." Without the affectation of liberality, he was charitable whenever charity could be well bestowed without parade and publicity. He was the friend and supporter of young men when they deserved patronage. But he possessed nice discrimination as to men's characters and abilities, and was reserved and discouraging to all who had not fully exhibited their self-denial and self-reliance. Of him it could, with great justice, be said, with Horace of Quintilius, when will purity, and the sister of justice, uncorrupted faith, and naked truth, find any equal to him?

JAMES GREGG.

The distinguished man, whose name is above, was born on the 4th of July, 1787, in that part of Marion District which lies west of the great Pee Dee River.

He received the most of his academic education from Dr. Thomas Park, at St. David's Academy, Long Bluff, afterwards Society Hill. At the commencement of 1806, Mr. Gregg entered the Junior Class of the South Carolina College. His name in the catalogue of the Clariosophic Society of 1806, is put down as James Gregg, in the class of 1808, at their graduation, as James R. Gregg. The "R." it seems, he adopted to distinguish him from some other of the same name. He dropped it when it ceased to serve that purpose.

He graduated on the first Monday of December, 1808, in a class of thirty-one members with the first honor. Among his classmates are some justly celebrated names, Rev. Dr. William Brantly, Judge Josiah J. Evans, Chancellor William Harper, Governor Stephen D. Miller, Governor John Murphy, Charles Stevens, Esq., Rev. Charles Strong, Judge Nathaniel A. Ware. To be ranked first, among such men, at his graduation, evidenced what might be expected of the future man, and he fully met that expectation. He was a tutor in the South Carolina College, when I entered it in February, 1811, and he most probably was elected to that office immediately after his graduation. In the spring of 1811, Paul H. Perault, Professor of Mathematics, ceased to be such, and Mr. Gregg filled his chair *pro tem.*, until November, 1811, when Professor Blackburn was elected. Mr. Gregg remained a tutor until 1813, when he resigned.

In January, 1813, he married Cornelia Maxcy, the eldest daughter of President Maxcy.

He was admitted to the Bar, in Columbia, as an attorney-at-law, 22d April, 1813, and as Solicitor in Equity, 27th April, 1814, and as attorney, solicitor, and proctor, in the Circuit

Court of the United States, 22d April, 1822. Mr. Gregg, soon after his admission, rode the Western Circuit. He attended Newberry, then on the Southern Circuit, for several terms. Business came slowly, year after year; he was to be seen, daily in his office, on Richardson street, just below Faust's corner, with few cases; but patience and persevering industry overcame all obstacles. He succeeded in a great land case between Colonel Myers and Lieut. Gov. John Hopkins, and business flowed in apace. He was soon among the first, and after a few years he was the acknowledged leader of the Columbia Bar.

The case of Denton and Wife *vs.* English—2 N. and McC., 581—November Term, 1820, was a striking evidence of his power as a lawyer. On referring to the case it will be seen that the verdict was against him, with the full concurrence of the presiding Judge, Mr. Justice Colcock. "The defence was, that the bill of sale was founded on a consideration, "*contra bonds mores.*" Major Clifton's argument had failed to produce any impression on the Judges; they had declined to hear the opposite attorney, Colonel Blanding. Mr. Gregg, who was accidentally absent at the argument, asked to be heard. He was accordingly heard. Colonel Blanding was directed to answer him, and a majority of the Judges granted the motion for a new trial. This was unusual honor and success.

It is impossible to refer to the numerous cases argued in the Constitutional Court, or Court of Appeals, by Mr. Gregg. I propose to notice a few. Before I do so I will remark, that he prepared his cases with great care, both on the circuit and in the Appeal Court. He reduced every matter of law to writing, and came into Court armed at every point with his authorities. His arguments, both on law and fact, were remarkable for their plain, straightforward truthfulness. Judge Huger once remarked to me, before I was on the Bench, "whatever Gregg states, whether it relates to law or fact, I can always rely on, for I know he would state nothing untruly." This was high praise from such a man as Judge Huger, who highly appreciated truth.

The case of Myers *vs.* Myers, decided first by the Court of Appeals in Equity, in 1827, 2 McC. C. R. 214, and again in 1830, Bail. Eq. 23, and Hall *vs.* Hall, 2 McC. C. R. 269, furnished fine opportunities for the display of Mr. Gregg's legal learning and forensic powers. His arguments will be found, 2 McC. C. R. 241, '2, '3, '4, '5, '6; and 283, '4, '5, '6, '7, '8, '9.

In the Court of Law the following cases may be referred to, in some of which some traces of Mr. Gregg's arguments may be found; but in general they are so slight that no judgment can be formed. In all of them, I very well know, that he argued the cases well, and I regret that I have no means of giving his arguments. The cases are as follow: Nixon *vs.* Bynum, 1 Bail. 148; Guphill *vs.* Isbell, 1 Bail. 250, 2 Bail. 349; Jones *vs.* McNeill, 1 Bail. 235, 2 Id. 466, 1 Hill 84; Westbrook *vs.* McMillan, 1 Bail. 259, 1 Hill 317; Richardson *vs.* Croft, 1 Bail. 264; Hall *vs.* Moye, 2 Bail. 9; Johnson *vs.* Lemons, Id. 393; Treasury *vs.* Taylor, Id. 524; Anonymous, 1 Hill 251; Lee *vs.* Ward, Id. 313; McDaniel *vs.* Cornwall, Id. 428; Moore *vs.* Aiken, 2 Hill 403; Carey *vs.* Lyles, Id. 404; Cleverly *vs.* McCullough, Id. 445; Brown *vs.* Hilligas, Id. 447; The State *vs.* Chatward, Id. 459; Means *vs.* Brickill, Id. 657. Many other cases in succeeding years have occurred, but it is useless to refer to them. Like the preceding, they will furnish little more than that Mr. Gregg was concerned in them.

On the 3d of April, 1816, Mr. Gregg was elected Intendant of the town of Columbia for that year.

In 1822 or 1823, Mr. Gregg was waited on by a military company, of light infantry, called the Columbia Volunteers, of which he was not a member, to inform him that they had elected him their captain. Such an honor he could not, and did not decline. He held this commission until his election, 14th November, 1823, to the command of the Upper Battalion, Twenty-third Regiment, South Carolina Militia, with the rank of Lieutenant-Colonel. In March, 1825, he was part of the brigade, under my command, which received Gen. LaFayette, on his visit to Columbia. He became Colonel of the Twenty-third Regiment, 18th November, 1829. When the military commissions throughout the State were vacated, by that *unwise Act* of December, 1833, he was re-elected and held his commission until the spring or summer of 1835, when he resigned.

Mr. Gregg was elected to the House of Representatives, in the General Assembly of this State, in 1822, and served in that House until 1830. In 1824, when I first took the Speaker's Chair, Mr. Gregg became the Chairman of the Committee of Elections. In 1826, he was the Chairman of the Judiciary Committee. From 1822, until 1828, I can speak from my personal notice and observation, and I have no hesitation in saying that Mr. Gregg discharged every duty devolving upon him, as a legislator, admirably well.

In 1830, he was elected to the Senate, and continued a member for 16 years. In 1846, his deafness, he thought, made it proper that he should decline being a candidate. For the unusual period of 24 years, he was in the Legislature of South Carolina, representing the District (Richland) in which the Capitol is situated, and therefore, constantly under the eyes of his constituents; and yet, he was always returned without difficulty, and often without opposition. Such facts show his capability and virtue, and the great confidence of the people.

In December, 1821, Mr. Gregg was elected one of the Trustees of his Alma Mater, the South Carolina College, and was continued as such by successive elections, until 1849, when he declined further service in that capacity.

On the 24th day of October, 1852, this good and great man closed his useful life. He left surviving him his excellent and amiable wife, and four children, to wit: Col. Maxcy Gregg, Edward F., Julia de B. and Cornelia M.

This sketch of the life of James Gregg, shows with what unerring propriety he must have lived. For our people are unusually jealous of their public functionaries, and any man who is a legislator for 24 years, without interruption, must be *very wise and very good*, or *very fortunate*. Mr. Gregg held many public appointments as long as he chose.

He very well merited these evidences of confidence, for he

intended to do right; and if he was in error, as I have no doubt he sometimes was, sure am I, it was the error of the head, and not of the heart.

In 1852, immediately after his death, I gave the following sketch of his character. I do not think I can improve upon it, and therefore make it a part of this sketch:

"As a speaker, Colonel Gregg relied not upon ornament. His mind, like his body, was plain, straight, strong and unyielding. His arguments, whether in the Legislature, or at the Bar, were remarkable for being clear, plain, and direct to the subject in hand. He was always listened to with the feeling that truth was before him, and that he was searching for it with all the light which he could obtain. Few lawyers did more business, or met more success than he had.

Colonel Gregg delighted in order; his books, papers, and every matter of which he had charge, were in their proper places. His business was always ready at the moment when it should be done. His life was regulated by rule; he took exercise and diet according to established laws which he had made for himself.

His life was one of undeviating honesty and purity. To society and his friends, he brought all the powers of his mind and body to do good. To his relations he was kindness, in every sense of the word. To his father-in-law, the great and good Dr. Maxcy, he was more than a son: *he was a friend always.* To Dr. Park, his early preceptor and friend, he showed an attachment, pure as it was just, on all occasions.

Husband, father, master, were relations in which Colonel Gregg was without fault. He will live in the sacred circle of home as long as its inhabitants remain.

Col. Gregg was not, as the writer believes, the member of any religious sect; but he knows that he was a Christian, and that he could have said, with great truth: "I know that my Redeemer liveth." He was in principle a tetotaller; and the last dinner which he gave to his friends, the Judges, was without wine. Cold water was the only beverage drank.

Colonel Gregg was more than six feet high; he was straight as an arrow, scrupulously exact in his dress. No one ever saw him otherwise than neat. His features were plain, but regular, and betokened great firmness; his eyes were blue, and his hair dark; his nose and mouth large, and his teeth good. Never shall we look upon a more faultless and proper man."

> "His youth and age, his life and death, combined,
> As in some great and regular design,
> All of a piece, throughout, and all divine;
> Still nearer Heaven his virtues shone more bright,
> Like rising flames, expanding in the night."

BENJAMIN FANEUIL HUNT.

Col. Hunt, as shown from a sketch in Livingston's Biographical Magazine, was born 20th February, 1792, at Watertown, Massachusetts. His father died in 1804. He completed his education at Harvard University, his mother defraying the expenses of his education, both at the Academy and the University.

He graduated in 1810. His attending physician, on account of the delicacy of his health, recommended a removal to a Southern climate. Accordingly, he left the soil of his nativity, and selected South Carolina as his future home. He arrived in Charleston 1st November, 1810, and entered the office of Keating Lewis Simons, Esq., as a student of law, and on the 6th May, 1813, was admitted to the Bar, and soon distinguished himself as a young man of talents, and gave assurance of becoming a prominent lawyer.

In 1812, he aided in forming a company which was called into the United States' service, and, as an officer, he served for, I presume, six months, at Fort Moultrie, Sullivan's Island.

Mr. Hunt's talents attracted attention and favor, and the result was, that in 1818, he was elected to the House of Representatives, in the General Assembly of this State. Here, he probably served for several years. He was much distinguished for business habits, and ability as a debater.

He was not, I think, returned at the general election for St. Philip's and St. Michael's, in October, 1824. In 1825, he was elected to fill a vacancy, and was continued in the successive elections, every two years, until he was overborne in the storm of Nullification, I presume, in 1832.

It ought to be remembered to Col. Hunt's honor, that while others yielded to the flood-tide of popularity in favor of that measure, he remained firm in his devotion to the union. He perhaps did as much as any man, in sustaining the Union party of Charleston through all the trials of '30, '31, '32, '33, and '34.

He rose through the successive grades of military command to that of Colonel of the 16th Regiment, which he attained in 1818, and which he retained for many years, discharging the duties remarkably well.

In the great case of The State, *ex relatione* McCrady *vs.* Hunt, the question was made and decided in May, 1834, and by the Court of Appeals, that the new oath of allegiance required by the Act of 1833 (commonly called the Test Oath), was unconstitutional.—2d Hill's Report, 1. Thus, Col. Hunt's name is indissolubly connected with one of the chapters of Nullification.

After the angry feelings arising from that party contest died out, Col. Hunt was returned to the House of Representatives in the General Assembly of the State, and was there continued by successive elections, for many years. His service was generally distinguished by talents and usefulness.

He was, I believe, the author of the Act, extending the bounds of the gaols to the limits of the respective districts. He, too, is entitled to the credit of remodelling the Representative Hall in the old State House. So, too, is due to him the honor of leading the Legislature imperceptibly into the scheme of building a new State House. Whether this was a wise measure or not, it will, certainly, sooner or later, by a large expenditure of money, give to the State the most magnificent State House in the Union; and Col. Hunt's name, as the projector, ought to bo placed on the front portico.

Col. Hunt, for more than forty years, had an extensive practice at the Bar. Many of the most difficult cases in Charleston and Georgetown passed through his hands, both in law and equity, in the Circuit and Appeal Courts. That he was adroit and confident, in every case, is generally believed; that he often found fault with decisions against him, is also well known; but with an experience of nearly thirty years on the Bench of the Court of Appeals, I am not aware of any case in which he had not a full measure of justice. Before Juries he had, when young, great influence, and it may be, that *there* his success, in doubtful cases, in the early part of his life, led him, in his latter years, when his success was not so uniform, to think he had to contend against prejudices.

That he gained many difficult cases, and for large amounts, both before the Juries, and also the Law and Equity Courts, is true; but the author of the biographical notice in Livingston's Magazine, has ascribed to him more honor than I think ought to be ascribed to any lawyer; for I believe the day, when Justice was blinded or hoodwinked by the art or talent of lawyers, has long passed away. I never yet have seen a case decided contrary to right, when the facts were properly brought out.

Col. Hunt's biographer manifestly thinks that prejudice, on the part of the Court, often decided against him. That *that* was his own feeling, I have, on more than one occasion, believed. But my knowledge of the Courts, and the cases in which he was concerned, makes me give a most positive denial to any such assumption.

The criticism on Pell and Ball, (1 Rich., Chan. Reports, 361—419,) and the sweeping denunciation of two such distinguished Judges and good men as Johnson and Harper, will be found, on examining the case, to be as unjust as it was unmanly. On reading the case at 361, and the subsequent pages, it will be seen that it was before, successively, Chancellors Dunkin, Johnston, Johnson and Harper. Chancellor Job Johnston first threw out the expression, that an appeal did not supersede a decree. *That* for the purposes of the case, as then before him, was *a mere obiter;* for he decided that the circuit decree, ordering a sale, was, according to the power given by the Court of Appeals; and, of course, an appeal could not supersede such a decree. Chancellor David Johnson, subsequently simply concurred in Chancellor Johnston's view. Chancellor Harper, when the case came before him, ruled that according to the ancient and settled practice of the Court of Equity, land, whether belonging to infants or adults, might even against the will of the parties be ordered to be sold, in a proper case in partition, or otherwise.

The case at 419, before the Court of Errors, was heard on

a motion to strike the case from the docket, as improperly docketted. This motion the Court granted, and laid down rules for the future government of the clerk, and the parties concerned in docketting cases in that Court.

The annotator on Col. Hunt's life, in Livingston's Magazine, No. 2, vol. iii., p. 416, could not have read the case.

In 1842, we are told Col. Hunt retired from the Committee on Federal Relations, in the House of Representatives of the State, and became Chairman of the Judiciary Committee, which, with the exception of a single term, he retained as long as he continued a member.

That this position was due to his age and experience, is true; that he rendered good and faithful service, is also true; for no one who knew him could question either his ability or attention. That he was often misled, by visionary notions of amending the Judiciary system; that he often indulged in them, and pursued mischievous amendments with all his usual zeal and pertinacity, is also true; that it required all the ability and watchful care of his colleague, Col. Memminger, to counteract these efforts, is well known in South Carolina.

In the year 1853 Colonel Hunt lost his wife, the daughter of William Mathews, Esq. The father of his wife was a wealthy man, who, whether unjustly or not, thought proper to place his estates, as "far as Colonel Hunt's wife and children were concerned," in such a way that he had no control of it. This involved him in an angry litigation with the gentleman to whom Mr. Mathews chose to confide the management of his estate as executor.

The excitement to which Colonel Hunt gave way in this matter operating upon his constitution, already much weakened by lapse of time and other circumstances, cut short the term of life. I last saw Colonel Hunt in 1855 or 1856, in Broad-street, Charleston, on the eve of his departure for New York. It was to me most manifest that he would no more return; and with that belief on his own mind he bade me farewell. He was the mere wreck of what he once was. I felt that to him the time had come, when the strong man was bowed down, when the "grasshopper was a burden;" and if a sincere sympathy with him, as a dying man, could have been any benefit to him, he had it, on my part. He never did return, but died in a few months after, in New York, (5th of December, 1854.) His three sons and a daughter survived him.

Colonel Hunt was an able advocate. I never regarded him as a safe legal adviser. He seemed to me to be rash and over-confident in his legal conclusions; yet I have often heard him argue a legal point remarkably well.

He possessed a fine elocution—often have I been struck with his powers of declamation; he was often eloquent. His person, in early manhood, was a fine one—this, associated with great fluency, force of expression, and boldness of assertion, gave great weight to his political speeches, and his arguments before Juries.

A friend, who had ample opportunities to know Colonel Hunt as a lawyer, says: "He, so far as my knowledge extends, never availed himself of any quibble, inadvertence, or omission in mere matters of form, or pleading, to defeat a suit, or injure an opposing lawyer. In this respect he was liberal. He was bold, daring, unceremonious and aggressive—but it was manly and open—often presumptuous, reckless aggression. He never seemed to me to employ trickery or cunning, or to take petty little advantages of his antagonist. Perhaps he was indulgent to others in his practice because he was exceedingly loose and irregular in his own."

On the whole, it may be said with truth, that Colonel Hunt, if there was right in his cases, was sure to bring it out; for he exhausted every possible remedy before he yielded. He relied more upon perseverance than an early ascertainment of the means of justice.

ANGUS PATTERSON.

This gentleman was the son of Alexander and Elizabeth Patterson, who were of Scotch extraction. They belonged to a colony of Highlanders, who emigrated to North Carolina, before the Revolution, and settled in the Counties of Cumberland, Moore, Richmond, and Robeson. Angus was born in the latter, on the 5th day of December, 1790. His parents were as well educated as the times and the then state of the country admitted; they were, in common with most of their neighbors and countrymen, poor, but moral, religions, contented, industrious, economical, and anxious for the education and advancement of their children. They could, though they did not, generally speak the Gaelic language, which at that time was the common dialect of the elder inhabitants of the Scotch settlement. They were, as were all their countrymen, rigid Presbyterians, and a branch of the Kirk of Scotland. No clergyman was allowed to preach, permanently at least, in their churches, who was not sent out and recommended by the Kirk—the ability to preach in Gaelic, being an indispensable qualification. His paternal grand-parents were Daniel and Mary Patterson; the maiden-name of the latter was McMillan; they emigrated twelve or fifteen years before the Revolution, and first settled in Cumberland, but soon removed to the Raft Swamp, in Robeson County, where a few of their descendants still reside. His maternal grand-parents were John and Isabel Patterson. They lived and died at a very advanced age, in Moore County, near the head of Rockfish, a tributary of the Cape Fear. John Patterson was sixteen years of age, when he came to America, and must have been among the first emigrants, as he had acquired considerable property, and had several children grown at the commencement of the Revolutionary war. His maternal grandmother, whose maiden name was McDuffie, spoke Gaelic imperfectly, and was born in America; her family, or rather her brother,

Archibald McDuffie, the only portion of her family we ever heard of, lived in Cumberland, near Fayetteville. The family is now extinct, or removed to parts unknown. His father was too young to take part in the Revolutionary war, and both his grandfathers were, as were most native Scotchmen, neutral. A brother of his mother, served in the American Army at Guilford, and probably in other engagements. His father's and mother's maiden-name were pronounced alike, but the families were not connected, and, besides, they spelled the names differently—one with one *t* and the other with two. His grand-parents, on both sides, left a numerous offspring, who have generally removed to the west, south, and south-west, and are to be found in every State, from the Cape Fear to the Rio Grande. His father, as far back as he can recollect, worked with one or two slaves on his farm, in summer; and for two years, in winter, taught a small school, a little more than a mile from his residence. To this school our subject was carried, sometimes by his father, and sometimes by a servant. He must have been young, and could have learned but little.

About 1803, or 1804, several young Scotchmen, having acquired a classical education, became Presbyterian ministers, and opened several academies in the Scotch settlement. To one of these, located at Solemn Grove, in Moore County, in charge of the Rev. Murdoch McMillan, Mr. Patterson was sent, where he remained nearly two years, boarding gratuitously in the family of a maternal uncle, who lived in the neighborhood. There he made some progress in Latin, and reviewed English Grammar.

About this time he became sensible that he would have to shift for himself; that for further progress in obtaining an education, he would have to rely on his own exertions. Though his father had increased his property a little, he had a number of children, by three marriages, of whom Angus was the oldest. He saw that he could expect no material pecuniary aid from him. When he left Solemn Grove, he was invited by his kinsman, Kenneth Black, to act as his assistant in the Lumberton Academy, of which he had charge. Mr. Patterson instructed the lower classes, during school hours, for which he received a small salary, scarcely sufficient to pay for board and clothing, and had the privilege of joining a class. Mr. Black was a pretty accurate classical scholar, and afforded his pupils every facility he could. Mr. Patterson read portions of Ovid, Virgil, Horace, and Cicero's Orations, and managed to keep up with his class, but it may be supposed he did not indulge in much sleep. He could understand Horace best, and he was his favorite author. He made a little, and but little, progress in Greek. Here Mr. Patterson resolved to direct all his efforts to the acquisition of a collegiate education. His plan was to obtain the necessary funds by teaching school; and, accordingly, in December, 1808, failing to get employment nearer home, he came to South Carolina, and succeeded in obtaining a school in Colleton District, near Patterson's Bridge. He had Virgil and Horace, and spent most of his time when not in school, in reading them. Not liking the manners of the neighborhood, he gave up his school at the end of the first quarter, and obtained employment as a private tutor, in the family of Mr. John Witsell, in the same district, near Jacksonborough, then the seat of justice of Colleton District. There he remained a year, in charge of three boys, who improved but little under his instruction. He attended the Court of Common Pleas, as a spectator, and became acquainted with one or two lawyers, who suggested the idea of giving up going to college, and to read law. Having conceived a fondness for forensic proceedings, he readily adopted this suggestion, and borrowing a copy of Blackstone's Commentaries, read it through, and portions several times, while living in the family of Mr. Witsell. Near the end of his engagement with Mr. Witsell, he received an offer from the late Johnson Hagood, Esq., of Barnwell District, to understand the nature of which, it is necessary to premise, that Mr. Hagood had been a lawyer of considerable practice, but having become a planter, was withdrawing from the profession. He had a good library, both law and miscellaneous. The proposal was to instruct a few children certain hours, for a small pecuniary compensation, and the use of the library and office. This situation was well adapted to his views. Mr. Hagood still had some professional business, which he soon left almost entirely to Mr. Patterson's management, visiting the office occasionally, when Mr. Patterson requested his advice. He issued writs, drew declarations, and prepared cases for trial, by noting the facts and looking up the law. He had ample time, and took no step without consulting every book in the office, treating of the matter under investigation. In this way he became pretty well acquainted with the rules of pleading and evidence. Special pleading, in those days, was countenanced, if not encouraged, by the Bench and the Bar, though it is quite different now: the declaration is seldom looked into, and a special demurrer is regarded with little favor. Besides books of practice, he read Burlamaqui on Natural Law, Montesquieu's Spirit of Laws, Vattel on International Law, Fearne on Contingent Remainders, Foublanque's Equity, and some history, biography, and poetry.

He was advised by most persons whom he consulted, as to the proper course of reading, to study Coke on Littleton attentively. He accordingly commenced the task several times, but never could get more than half through the book. He began with Mr. Hagood in July, 1810, and in November, 1812, he went to Charleston and entered the office of the late John S. Richardson, then Attorney-General of the State, and for many years subsequently, a Judge of the Court of Common Pleas. He now bid adieu to the business of school-master, having succeeded in it but poorly. To him it was a labor of necessity, and not of love. His principal employment in the office of Mr. Richardson was drawing indictments and declarations, but he made shift to look into many of the then modern cases, such as are reported in Burrows, Douglas, &c. For the principles established in the old reports he relied on Comyn's Digest, and Viner's and Bacon's Abridgments. Here he first resorted to the practice of acquiring a general knowledge of the contents of a book without reading it, which proved of much advantage to him when pressed for time, in subsequent life. While in Charleston, he attended a session of the Circuit and Appeal Courts, and was complimented by the late Judge

Colcock for his attention. From that time that able Judge, and amiable man, as long as he lived, was his personal friend. In May, 1813, he was admitted, by the Court of Appeals, in Columbia, to practice in the Courts of law. He forthwith opened an office in the village of Barnwell, and Mr. Hagood having died, in the mean time, he purchased his law library, and fell heir to some of his cases and clients. Mr. Patterson had but little local competition. The late Hon. William D. Martin had studied law in Barnwell, where he had respectable connections, and was, deservedly, personally popular. He had been admitted some months, perhaps a year, before Mr. Patterson, and settled in the adjoining District of Beaufort, but, through a partnership, had an extensive and increasing practice in Barnwell. With that gentleman Mr. Patterson practiced long and pleasantly. The transient Bar was numerous, considering the quantity of business, and formidable for talents. The principal members were—Robert Stark, Solicitor of the Circuit, Richard Gantt, afterwards Judge Gantt, Edmund Bacon, John Joel Chappell, Eldred Simpkins, and John M. Felder. The three last named have since been Members of Congress and of the State Legislature. By these gentlemen he was treated with marked kindness, particularly by Mr. Stark, who not only gave Mr. Patterson his countenance and advice, but aid. All these gentlemen, except Colonel Chappell, have "shuffled off this mortal coil."

There is nothing a young man remembers so long or so gratefully as the courtesies of his senior brethren. Mr. P. came to the Bar a stranger—an inexperienced youth, without money, and with no friends except a few whose confidence he had gained in the office of Mr. Hagood. These adhered to him as long as they lived, and he has had the pleasure of rendering important professional service to some of their descendants. Before his admission he lived very retired, avoiding rather than seeking society; and was bashful to an unreasonable degree. Conscious of having made all the preparation he could, he did not lack confidence in himself; yet he was so timid, excitable and nervous, that, after an argument, he could scarcely recollect a word uttered. Nothing but necessity enabled him to overcome this timidity. His business increased rapidly, and by 1818 he was in full practice. From 1820, as long as he continued an active member of the Bar, he had as much, and sometimes more, business than he could do justice to. In 1818, he first appeared as counsel in the Court of Appeals.

He early commenced investing a portion of his income. He first became a farmer. In 1827 he began to plant with a moderate capital, which was increased from time to time. In common with most professional men, at least of the South, he was passionately fond of agricultural pursuits, but never permitted them to interfere with his professional engagements, and, therefore, had to divide the proceeds of his planting interest with agents and managers.

In 1818, he was elected to the House of Representatives, re-elected in 1820, and after serving four years in that House, was elected to the Senate in 1822, and re-elected every four years until he retired in 1850. The sessions of the Legislature of South Carolina are so short—never more than twenty days—that a seat in it does not interfere with professional duty. While on the floor of the Senate he acted as chairman of one of the working committees, at the same time serving as a member on several others. At the session of 1832 he was appointed Chairman of the Special Committee, to which the ordinance of nullification was referred, and of which the Hon. A. P. Butler and the Hon. James Gregg were members. A similar committee was raised in the House of Representatives, of which the Hon. B. F. Dunkin, now Chancellor Dunkin, was chairman, and the Hon. Wm. C. Preston, and other gentlemen since distinguished, were members. In the nullification contest, party spirit ran high, and was, in some instances, bitter. Though his political course was decided, he retained throughout the contest, many personal friends in the ranks of political opponents. While in the Senate, he had the happiness to be associated with many of the most distinguished men who appeared on the political stage in the State during the present century. They have now, with a few exceptions, passed away. In December, 1838, he was elected President of the Senate, and being re-elected every two years, occupied that office while he continued a member of that body. On the adjournment of the session of 1849, he became engaged in preparing for the Court of Chancery, which was to sit early in February. About the middle of January his health suddenly gave way. In a few days he became so feeble as to be scarcely able to walk, had a troublesome cough, and lost his voice almost entirely. As advised, he went directly to East Florida. By this movement he escaped the cold of February, March and April, and his health improved a little, more probably from the repose enjoyed, and which he stood much in need of, than from any other cause. It is doubted whether the climate was favorable to his case. On returning home he purchased a residence in the town of Aiken, which he made his principal place of abode. His health gradually improved, his voice was, in some measure, restored, but the disease—consumption—still maintained its hold upon him. From that time, 1850, he may be said to have retired from his profession, except occasionally, he was seldom seen in the Court House. He died 24th May, 1854.

In 1819, he married a daughter of the late Francis Trotti. His wife is of Italian, Greek and Irish descent. Their union was one of uninterrupted happiness. Of eleven children, two died in early infancy. A third, his second daughter, married Dr. Adolphus Nott, of New Orleans, and died, leaving a son, Angus, now a promising boy. The remaining eight children, three sons and five daughters, survive him.

Mr. Patterson was not an eloquent, but he was a remarkably sound lawyer. I knew him well, as a lawyer, from 1829 to 1854; he managed and argued his cases well, being generally eminently successful before a Barnwell Jury. The people thought he knew the law, and that he was honest. He, therefore, generally had the ear of the Jury; and, though the style of his speaking was slow, halting and repeating, yet, like Sergeant Scarlet, he hammered his ideas into the heads of the Jury. He was, however, by no means a tedious speaker. I think I never listened to him impatiently.

I have been, when in the separate Court of Appeals, often

instructed by his arguments. His argument in Stallings *vs.* Foreman, (2 Hill's Chan. Rep., 401,) brought the whole Court to the conclusion, that an administratrix, selling under the order of the Ordinary, if he sold fairly and paid the full value, might purchase at his own sale. His argument has not been preserved, but his leading views are very much followed, and enforced in the opinion delivered by myself. (Idem 405.)

That was one of the vexed questions which very much divided the Bench and Bar; one of the Judges, who, after 1836, sat in the Court of Appeals in Equity, said to Mr. Patterson, "the case of Stallings *vs.* Foreman will be reversed." He replied, "*if it is, the good sense of the case will never be reversed.*" The Act of 1839, (11 Stat. 62,) affirmed the rule of Stallings *vs.* Foreman, and established certain guards to prevent possible loss.

In Calhoun *vs.* Calhoun, (Rich. Eq. cases, 36,) his argument was also a fine one; it has not been preserved, but the opinion very much embodies his legal argument.

His argument before the Court of Errors in Kottman and wife, *vs.* Ayer, reported, (1st Strob., 559—569,) is a specimen of his legal reasoning.

As a legislator, he was faithful and untiring: being always at his post, he acquired that knowledge of parliamentary rules which enabled him so long to preside over the Senate.

As a citizen, husband, father and master, the proceedings of the citizens of Barnwell, 5th July, 1854, after his death, give the highest and best testimonial of his worth. They were his neighbors, and knew him early and late. Their proceedings, speeches and resolutions, are hereto annexed.

Happening not only to know Mr. Patterson as a lawyer and legislator, but also as a man, it cannot be amiss that I should add my good word, and say that he was plain and artless as a child, sincere and devoted as a friend, firm and resolute in every duty, affectionate and trusting as a husband and father, and, as a master, kind, but insisting on and enforcing obedience. Take him all in all, we shall seldom find one so humble in his pretensions, yet deserving so much; so afflicted and yet so patient; so prosperous and happy in his affairs and domestic relations, and yet making so little show; so much honored, and yet demanding so little observance.

He was a good and virtuous man; his life of 64 years was spent for good and valuable purposes; he has left to his posterity that most valuable of all inheritances, the "*Recordatio actœ vitœ bene est jucundissima.*"

TRIBUTE OF RESPECT.

The following were the proceedings of a meeting of the Barnwell Bar, held on the 5th of July, 1854, in relation to the death of the Hon. Angus Patterson.

The Hon. S. W. Trotti was called to the chair, and John A. Bellinger appointed Secretary.

After explaining the object of the meeting, the Chairman spoke as follows:

It is the humble privilege of the living to recall the virtues of the dead, and hold them up for our own, and the encouragement of others; and it is a noble impulse of the heart which prompts us to strew the grave of departed friends with the cypress and the willow. Time after time have we been assembled in this hall to pay our last tribute of respect to some professional brother, struck down in the pursuit of his profession, full of promise and full of hope. But to-day we feel as children gathered around the grave of an honored parent. Angus Patterson, whose loss we all so much deplore, might well have been called the Father of the Barnwell Bar. Many of us studied law in his office, and under his direction, and none of us can remember the time when he was not a prominent member of the profession. Here, at this place, and a this Bar, more than forty years ago, he commenced that professional career, which, after many trials and struggles, led to fame and fortune. Mr. Patterson, like almost all men who have ever risen to eminence, placed but little reliance upor what is called genius. Integrity, strict attention to business, and constant mental application, were the steps by which he attained success. Mr. Patterson was a native of North Carolina, but emigrated to this State at an early age, and studied law while engaged in teaching a school. Admitted to the Bar, he established himself in this place, and by the strength of his mind and the integrity of his character, gradually acquired an extensive practice. Nor let it be supposed that there was any lack of talent at the Bar at that period, for there were then "giants in the land." The late Chancellor Harper, then a distinguished practicing lawyer, frequently attended this Court, as did also the late Judge Colcock. Edmund Bacon, whose brilliancy might well have entitled him to the appellation of the Murat of the profession, likewise practiced at this Court. And the Hon. James L. Pettigru, to whom, with one accord, has been assigned the position of head of the profession in South Carolina, and who, as a lawyer, has no superior in the Union, and the late Judge Wm. D. Martin, a name that we "would not willingly let die," were constant attendants at the Barnwell Court. And these were the intellectual giants with which Mr. Patterson had to measure strength; and not one of them ever encountered him in legal argument, that did not find in him "a foeman worthy of his steel;" and yet Mr. Patterson was neither a fluent nor a handsome speaker; but he was more, he was a profound thinker and reasoner. He spoke not so much to please the fancy as to convince the understanding, and whenever he spoke there was sure to be one man in the Court-House whose attention was entirely and altogether engaged, and that was the Judge himself. He would grapple the most difficult questions, and solve them with the accuracy of mathematical demonstration.

His efforts in the Court of Appeals, more especially on the Equity side of that Court, are among the ablest that have ever been made before that body.

Mr. Patterson's high position at the Bar, and his stern integrity, made it desirable to the people of the District that he should represent them in the Legislature; and for over thirty years consecutively, he represented the people of Barnwell District, first in the House of Representatives, and then in the Senate, of which latter body he was, for a number of years, President, until his failing health rendered it necessary for him to decline a re-election to the Senate. Such fidelity on the part of the representative, and such entire and continued confidence on the part of his constituents, is, perhaps, without a parallel in the legislative history of South Carolina. His district not only confided in him, but was proud of him, and he repaid her confidence with the love and affection of a son.

It was during his service in the Senate that the great Nullification contest of 1832 occurred; and he was one of the counsellors whose wisdom and firmness conducted our ship of State in safety through that dark and stormy period.

In his intercourse with the members of the profession, Mr. Patterson was extremely kind and courteous, and all yielded to him the most unbounded deference and respect, and which was the more readily yielded on account of his gentle, modest and unostentatious bearing. As was very properly said of him, a few days ago, by a member of this Bar, Mr. Patterson, in his palmiest days, when professional fame and fortune had crowned his efforts with success, exhibited the same modesty and unpresuming manner as when a young man, struggling for the means of support. For several years past, the declining health of Mr. Patterson admonished us all that his earthly career was drawing to a close. He was, himself, fully aware of the fact. By the advice of friends and physician, he several times tried a change of climate, hoping that that might benefit his health, but it was all of no avail; and Providence kindly permitted that when the messenger of death did come, he should find him at home, and prepared for the summons; and here, at home, surrounded by every member of his family, who eagerly sought to do for him everything that affection could suggest or contribute, he left this world in peace with all men, and in peace with his God.

I have thus briefly alluded to some of the incidents connected with the life and character of Mr. Patterson, which will be readily recognized by others. As to my own private relations with the deceased, I may not be permitted to speak. I will not unveil the friendship which was extended to me by him from my earliest entrance on the threshold of manhood up to the last hours of his existence: of this it is proper that I should say nothing.

> "But I'll remember thee, Glencairn,
> And all thou hast done for me."

Colonel W. A. Owens then rose, and made the following remarks:

Mr. Chairman,—The cause of our assembling, which you have announued in such appropriate terms, is truly one of mournful interest. Death has again obtruded himself in our midst, and borne away one on whom we were all accustomed to look with veneration and respect, and who was connected with most of us by the tenderest ties. As a man, as a preceptor, and as the Father of our Bar, Mr. Patterson had united in himself the warmest regard, not only of his professional brethren, but all with whom, in social life or political pursuits, he came in contact; and in meeting, as we do, to pay the last tribute of respect to one so regarded, it is gratuitous to say we perform not a mere empty ceremony. His life and character are eminently suggestive; and now, when the grave has closed upon him, we feel that we can find much profit and interest in the inquiry as to how he filled up the measure of his days. He was the son of Alexander and Elizabeth Patterson, who were of Scotch extraction, and were natives of North Carolina, where he was born, in the County of Robeson, on the 5th day of December, 1790. From various teachers in that State he received a good academical education, of which, to a respectable extent, the ancient classics formed a part. At this early period in life he manifested that quiet earnestness and laborious zeal which were ever his distinguishing characteristics. Desiring to complete his education, and being unable to obtain adequate means in his own State, he came to South Carolina, in 1808, and obtained a school near Patterson's Bridge, in Colleton District. While engaged in teaching, he devoted all his leisure time to the improvement of his own mind. Soon after this, having determined to embrace the profession of the law, he accepted an invitation from the late

Johnson Hagood, Esq., of this District, who was a member of the Bar, to become a private tutor in his family. His preparation for the Bar was completed under the direction of the late Judge Richardson, in Charleston, who was, at that time, the Attorney General of the State.

In May, 1813, he was admitted to the Bar, and, Mr. Hagood having died, Mr. Patterson settled in Barnwell, and succeeded to most of his business. Since that period, his name and fortunes have been identified with nearly every matter of interest connected with his adopted district. His success, from his first entrance into the law, was rapid and permanent; and for forty years suffered no abatement. Without aspiring to the higher powers of an advocate, he had within him an earnestness and perspicuity often more successful than that attained by the most brilliant parts. He was always at his post, prepared for the professional conflicts in which he engaged; and being keenly alive to the interest of his clients, it is questioned whether any member of the Bar of the State enjoyed, for so long a period, such uninterrupted success. Mr. Patterson's judgment in all matters on which he professed to be informed, was of the highest order; and his powers of discrimination in the departments of the law and of politics, were such as would, to one more pretending, have secured a far wider fame. But from the time he passed the threshold of manhood, until he passed away, upon all occasions, and under all circumstances, he was accompanied by a modesty and an unaffected simplicity of character, that elevated to an inappreciable degree his worth, to those who knew him intimately. He would have much preferred the imputation of ignorance than that of arrogance.

He rose by the strength of his own merits, and fought the battle of life with a calm determination that never flagged. In 1818, he was elected a Representative from this district, which office he held for four years, and was then transferred by his constituents to the Senate, where he remained for twenty-eight consecutive years; the last twelve of which he was the presiding officer of that body. The fact, that for thirty-two years he maintained the confidence of his fellow-citizens in these high positions, and never once sustained a defeat, when it is added, that, during the period, our State passed through some of the severest struggles that she has ever known, is, in itself, a sufficient eulogy. His constituents always felt, that their political bark was safe, while his hand was at the helm. His position was obtained and kept without other exertion on his part, than the performance of duty; he never trimmed his sails to catch the popular gale, but rested his claims on the merits of his acts.

As President of the Senate of South Carolina, as chairman of many of the most important committees in that body, he received the highest respect and regard of those over whom he presided, and with whom he was associated. Their confidence ever rose in proportion as their knowledge of him extended; having commenced by regarding as a compeer and an officer, they soon learned to venerate and love. He was impartial, able, dignified and just; and the even tenor that marked his official course, is the highest evidence of his fitness for the elevation he enjoyed. He entered the Legislature known to but few; he left it, after a connection of a third of a century, possessed of its highest honors, and without an enemy.

But it was in his domestic relations that Mr. Patterson's excellence shone with a peculiar lustre. In the sequestered walks of life, parallels may frequently be found to that which is claimed for him in this regard; but rare, indeed, are examples to be met such as he afforded when accompanied by conflicts, in which to triumph, taxes and absorbs the best energies of our nature. He was simple as a child, confiding as a woman, and the word of unkindness to his household never passed his lips. In his home, all his affections were garnered up, and even in his dying hour, shed a sweet fragrance around him. Under a somewhat cold and reserved exterior, the fire of feeling burnt intensely. All his struggles for position and fortune, both of which he obtained in an eminent degree, were more for his, than himself, and his chief delight in success was, as the sharer of the joys of others. In the decline which set in upon him, and which was protracted to an unusual severity, he bore himself with all "the native hue resolution," which had accompanied him through life. His patience, resignation, and calm fortitude failed him not in his dying hour; and as he sank to his last slumber, surrounded by those he had lived to bless with honors and with fortune, he could not but be solaced with the reflection, that he had done his duty well.

He came to our district a poor, unfriended stranger; he lived to become the most distinguished and wealthy citizen she possessed, and died in a home only unhappy because he had left it. I move you for the adoption of the following resolutions:

Resolved, That, in the death of the Hon. Angus Patterson, the State has sustained the loss of one of her most distinguished and patriotic citizens, who, in every station he was called on to fill, discharged his duty with a zeal, ability and fidelity, that endeared him to the hearts of all with whom he was associated.

Resolved, That our district recognizes in the deceased not only a faithful and tried public servant, but a citizen who was closely identified with, and who constituted much to advance all her varied and increasing interests; and who, as her Representative and Senator for more than thirty years, never faltered in the discharge of his duty, and in whom her confidence was never shaken.

Resolved, That as the senior member of our Bar, and a bright ornament to our profession, he was eminently entitled to our highest regard and veneration; and while we are unable to recall all the acts of kindness which we have received at his hands, we are equally unable to bring to our minds one act of unkindness that he ever did.

Resolved, That we deeply sympathize with his afflicted family in their sad bereavement, and tender to them the only consolation that we can offer, in an earnest recognition of the great deprivation they have sustained.

Resolved, That, as a manifestation of our regard for the deceased, the members of this Bar will wear the usual badge of mourning for thirty days.

Resolved, That a copy of these resolutions be communicated, by the secretary of this meeting, to the family of the deceased.

Col. A. P. Aldrich arose to second the resolution, and said,

"Mr. Chairman, as I hold the oldest commission at this Bar, perhaps it will not be considered obtrusive or inappropriate, if I offer a few remarks on this mournful occasion. My relations with Mr. Patterson while living, do not preclude me from paying a tribute of respect to his memory, now that he is dead.

"This has been a season of trial and affliction to our small community. If death has not entered into each family, he hath so cast his darts, that the sympathies and affections of us all have been aroused; not one of us but feels that he has had cause to mourn. The death of Mr. Patterson has been expected—his brethren at the Bar have for many Courts missed his venerable form in its accustomed place, and we have long known that he would never again raise his voice in this hall. When last he was here, his emaciated form and his sunken voice, were sure tokens that his race was run, that he had fought his last battle, tried his last cause, and now that he is dead, it is fit that we pay appropriate honors to his memory.

"The history of Mr. Patterson is full of profitable instruction. I do not propose to enter at large into a narrative of his life; it is sufficient for my purpose to say, that he was not blessed by nature either with the graces that become an orator, or the ready delivery of an accomplished advocate; but he had that which overcame all difficulties: he had the will to succeed, and the industry to accomplish. Hence, by laborious preparation, we find him gradually rising, step by step, until he established himself as the leader of the Bar, which post he kept undisputed until disease drove him from the field of his labors. And this is no small praise, when we remember that such men as Martin, Elmore, Preston and McDuffie, contended on the same field where he won his highest honors. The sound logic of Martin and Elmore, and the brilliant eloquence of Preston and McDuffie, never deterred Patterson from pressing with earnest zeal the cause that was committed to his care. He won the confidence and affection of his fellow-citizens, and retained to his death the respect of the Bench and the Bar. It is true, he did not attain the highest honors of the profession, so far as office was concerned, but his rewards were ample. For years he was returned to the Senate of the State without opposition, and he presided over that body for a longer period than any other who has preceded him. In his illness and death, he illustrated his life. For long weary months he bore the pains of disease with the patience and fortitude which had been taught him in the struggles of life; his mind was made up to meet death, and when death came, he received him with the calm philosophy of one who perfectly understood and justly comprehended, the ordeal through which he had to pass. He had prepared to meet his God, and, to use his own language, 'he went out as a flickering candle.'

"My brethren of the Bar, this death speaks to us in strong, very strong language. You who are just commencing your professional career, are admonished not to be deterred by difficulties; patient industry, earnest effort, will overcome them all. When you feel disheartened and your spirits flag, remember, that your old leader, by determined will, conquered as great, if not greater, opposition, than that which now obstructs your path. He rose to eminence and to opulence. Labor as he did, work as he did, and eminence and opulence await you in the distance. Be not disheartened: the true, brave heart, will conquer ere it die. All of us are admonished to live as he lived; be modest, be faithful, and let us all try so to live, that when we come to die, we may pass from time to eternity, with the hope of a glorious immortality.

"I second the Resolutions."

At the conclusion of Col. Aldrich's remarks, the resolutions were unanimously adopted.

On motion of I. M. Hutson, Esq., it was

Resolved, That the Chairman of this meeting present the above resolutions to the presiding Judge of the Court of Common Pleas, at the next term, with the request, in behalf of the Barnwell Bar, that they be entered on the minutes of the Court; and that they also be presented to the presiding Chancellor at the next term of the Court of Equity, with the request that they be also entered on the minutes of that Court.

Resolved, That the proceedings of this meeting be published in the Barnwell Sentinel, with the request that the Charleston and Columbia papers publish the same.

On motion, the meeting then adjourned.

HON. S. W. TROTTI, Chairman.

J. A. BELLINGER, Secretary.

THOMAS WILLIAMS.

Colonel Thomas Williams was born in Williamsburg District, on the 8th of June, 1789, and from that time to the 25th of August, 1858, sixty-nine years, he remarked, in a letter to the author: "During the whole of this time, God, in his merciful Providence, has blessed me with the most remarkable health, never having had but one attack of fever in my life, and that was in 1815."

He studied law in the office of William Grant, Esq., of Georgetown. Matthew Irving Keith, late of Charleston, was one of his fellow-students. Of him he said, in his letter to me: "A more noble man never lived—no man ever sustained loss by his friendship. He was my near and dear friend. May God grant protection to his family left behind."

Colonel Williams says: "I am the last out of nine young men, who read law at the same time" in Mr. Grant's office.

He was admitted to the Bar in Charleston, January, 1811, as he informed me by his letter, but his name does not appear on the roll of attorneys furnished to me by my excellent and obliging friend, Daniel Horlbeck, Esq.

Colonel Williams' modesty has prevented him from furnishing to me a full autobiography, as I hoped he would have done. I know, from reputation, he settled at Lancaster, and there practiced law. When he lived there, Lancaster possessed many bold, and, some very, ungovernable spirits. Among them Colonel Williams was forced to bear his part, which he did with that strong arm and bold spirit with which he was endowed by nature.

In the same way, I have been informed, he was induced by his friend, Judge Smith, to leave Lancaster, and settle at York, where he lived and practiced law in that and the adjoining Districts of Union, Chester and Lancaster, with eminent and signal success, until his removal in 1835.

I first saw Colonel Williams at Union Court-House, at an

extra term of the Court, held by Judge Johnson, in August, 1818; and there I first had the pleasure of hearing one of his forensic efforts. He then seemed to me to be worthy of the position which he long held in our Courts, as one of our ablest jury lawyers. I did not then attend Union Court. I was merely passing as a traveler to the Pacolett Springs.

In 1820, I became a regularly practicing lawyer at Union Court, and often had occasion to test the powers of Colonel Williams, and I always found him a prompt and ready lawyer, prepared to bear his part, whether in guerilla or regular warfare.

Colonel Williams came into the House of Representatives in the General Assembly, in 1820. He was a Member until 1834, and nobly sustained his patron and friend, Judge Smith, in all the storms and difficulties of Nullification. When early friends deserted the brave old man, he uniformly found his friend Williams by his side.

In December, 1830, Colonel Williams ran for the office of a Circuit Law Judge, and was only defeated by a single vote, by that admirable Judge, William D. Martin. In 1831, I think, he attended, as a delegate from York, with Judge Smith, the great Philadelphia Anti-Tariff Convention. That it ended in nothing was no fault of him or his colleague.

There were master spirits at work to bring about the unfortunate estrangement of South Carolina from the Union, and for more than a quarter of a century we have felt its fatal effects, and are now just recovering.

Colonel Williams bore a part in all the controversies between the Nullification and Union parties from 1830 to 1834, when, in December, fortunately, the strife ceased. Colonel Williams, in the fall of 1835, removed to Mobile, Alabama, and remained there three or four years, when he removed, from the belief that the yellow fever would then prevail. In 1841, he settled in Montgomery, where he now resides. He was a Member of the House of Representatives from 1820 to 1834; and my knowledge of him as a legislator enables me to say that he was a good and useful one. His modesty kept him back from assuming and maintaining, as a *debater*, that stand to which his eminent abilities entitled him. He spoke rarely in the House of Representatives, and often with evident embarrassment.

He was concerned in the great cases of the State *ex relatione* McCrady *vs.* Hunt, and the State *ex relatione* McDaniel *vs.* McMeckin, (12 Hill, page 1,) in which the constitutionality of the oath of allegiance prescribed by the Act of 1833, and required to be taken by the militia officers of the State, was drawn in question, and which, in May, 1834, was decided by a majority of the Court of Appeals, (Johnson and O'Neall,) to be unconstitutional. Mr. Williams' able argument will be found in 2 Hill, p. 133.

In speaking of this matter, my mind recurs to the great excitement which followed that decision—the threats with which the majority of the Court were pursued—the overwhelming of the most useful branch of jurisprudence, (the separate Court of Appeals,) which has ever existed in the State; and the final compromise, which, by the resolution of 1834, deprived the new oath of allegiance of its odious meaning, and, in point of fact, made it no more than the former constitutional oath. One of the great errors of my public life was committed in not resigning in December, 1835, when the Court of Appeals was destroyed. Then I could have returned successfully to the Bar, and enjoyed my home and attended to my private affairs; from both of which I have been almost ever since a stranger. But that which has been loss and grief to me may have been for the good of South Carolina—my own, my native home—and, if so, I ought to bow submissively, as I hope I do.

Colonel Williams, in a Court-House, and before a Jury, was one of the most plausible, forcible, and successful advocates whom I ever heard. He never pretended to be a learned lawyer. I recollect his saying to me, relative to the case of Howard *vs.* Williams, 1st Bail., 575: "I always understand the law better when ruled in one of my own cases."

When I speak of him as a jury-lawyer, I do not mean to detract from him in other respects. I have heard him make many, very many, fine arguments, in the Circuit Court of Equity and in the Court of Appeals.

Colonel Williams, when I last saw him, was a firm specimen of a Carolina gentleman, fully six feet high, of athletic frame and proportion, complexion and hair dark, with a remarkably intelligent face, manners courtly and polished. Time, I know, has, ere this, blanched his raven locks, dimmed the lustre of his eyes, and shaken that frame which was once unyielding. Still I know that, although he may soon see three-score and ten, he, like my venerable friend, Governor Johnson, said of himself, he has "a young heart," and one which beats true to wife, children, friends, and country.

GEORGE McDUFFIE.

This extraordinary man and myself were intimately associated in early life. We were in the South Carolina College together; I in the Senior, while he was in the Junior Class. We were members of the same society—the Clariosophic—and debated many a question together. He was regarded, then, as a young man of extraordinary talents, but he had not that passionate and eloquent declamation which he afterwards displayed in Congress. His speeches were more argumentative than eloquent. In his junior year, about June, he left college, by the permission of the Faculty, to accept a place as private tutor in the family of Colonel Haskell, of St. Matthews; this being necessary to give him the means to complete his education. He returned in October, 1812, and graduated with the first honor, in the Class of that year.

George McDuffie, it is said, was born in Columbia County, Georgia, about the year 1788. He was a clerk in the mercantile establishment of James Calhoun, in Augusta, Georgia. This gentleman mentioned him to his brother, William Calhoun, as a lad of great talents, but having no means to procure an education. Mr. William Calhoun, with his characteristic generosity, proposed to board and educate him, at Dr. Waddell's school, Willington, in the neighborhood of which he lived.

He accordingly took him into his own family, and sent him to the school at Willington. A lady stated to me, that Mr. McDuffie was then so poor that he had nothing but a little blue box, in which his scanty supply of clothing was contained. He soon distanced all competition, and in a very short time was prepared for College; and at the Commencement in December, 1811, he entered the Junior Class, and was soon acknowledged as the first man in it. His graduating speech on the "Permanence of the Union," was printed, at the request of the students. It is a little remarkable, that his opening speech on the threshold of life, should have set before the country his belief in the permanency of that Union which many of his speeches, in and out of Congress, subsequently, so much jeopardized.

He studied, and in the short period from December, 1813, to May, 1814, he prepared himself for admission in Law and Equity. We were admitted in the same class, in May, 1814. He settled at Pendleton, and literally did nothing. In December, following, he was a candidate for Solicitor of the Western Circuit. He received a respectable vote, considering that he was only a few months old at the Bar. Benjamin H. Saxon, of Abbeville, and William F. Downs, Esq., of Laurens, were also candidates, and Mr. Saxon was elected. This defeat, which seemed to him, at the time, to be his greatest misfortune, was, I have no doubt, the turning point of his life, which enabled him to seize wealth, fame and power, as rapidly as he could desire.

He became, about that time, the partner of Colonel Eldred Simkins, of Edgefield, who had a full practice and a fine library. These were the means which Mr. McDuffie needed to place him among the first lawyers of the State. Colonel Simkins' kindness introduced him into the best society.

His rise was rapid, beyond parallel, arguing successfully and ably, both on the Circuit and in the Court of Appeals, many of the most abstruse and difficult points of law. He practiced on the entire Western Circuit, as well as at Edgefield. There, too, in his own name, he obtained a large practice. At Abbeville, he managed successfully Patrick Duncan's cases (commonly called the Jew's-land cases), for the recovery of 50,000 acres of land and upwards. His fee on that matter was, in itself, a moderate fortune. Business from all quarters, and at all Courts—Civil and Criminal, poured in upon him. His speech for General Hampton, in the case of Taylor *vs.* Hampton, upon a question at that time novel in our Courts, was said to have been a fine one; but his eloquence could neither sway the Jury nor the Court. His argument for Mr. Stark, in the Constitutional Court, in favor of his view, *i. e.*, that his Commission as Solicitor, was "for good behavior," and consequently, that Mr. Jeter could not supersede him by his election by the General Assembly, I heard, and it satisfied me thoroughly, that he was right. The Court, however, thought otherwise, and their decision, and not my opinion, became the law of the land.

In October, 1818, Mr. McDuffie was elected to the House of Representatives of South Carolina from Edgefield District. His speeches *there*, and his business habits, won him great celebrity.

In 1818, he was elected by the Board, a Trustee of the South Carolina College. In October, 1820, he was elected from Edgefield and Abbeville to Congress, as the successor of his early friend and patron, Col. Simkins.

About this time he was involved in the unfortunate duel with Colonel Cumming, which was brought about by the indiscreet zeal of his friends, and which inflicted upon him a wound, which certainly changed the whole character of his disposition, embittered his life, and finally sent him, shattered and a wreck, to his tomb. When I make these observations, I do so from a perfect knowledge of Mr. McDuffie. In his youth and until he was wounded, he exhibited no irritability. Indeed, I should have said, as his sister did, that his temper was a good one. All who knew him afterwards are obliged to admit his great irritability. He certainly exhibited great uneasiness from the nervous irritation arising from his spinal wound. And would that I could forget, now and forever, the condition in which I last saw him, in October, 1850. He was no longer the man who once delighted Senates, and governed men by his eloquence. He then needed the hand of friendship to sustain him, and the mind of more than a friend—a father—to guide him.

In December 1821, Mr. McDuffie entered Congress, the advocate of a liberal construction of the Constitution, and the friend of Mr. Calhoun. When he changed his views as to the construction of the Constitution, I do not know. That he did so, I do not doubt, and I have as little doubt that the change was the result of an honest conviction. But I presume it was shortly after Judge Smith had changed the politics of the State, in 1824.

The Tariff controversy began soon after, and Mr. McDuffie threw himself into the front rank of the opponents of that measure. Many of his propositions were novel and extravagant, as for instance his forty-bale theory, which he maintained with great earnestness. Yet, in the main he was right. That measure was unjust and oppressive; and, certainly while it had the letter of the Constitution in its favor, it violated its spirit, in favoring one class of industry at the expense of another. He sustained President Jackson, in the canvass which preceded his election in 1828; but after 1829, he ceased to stand alongside of the Hero of the Hermitage. In 1829, Mr. McDuffie married an accomplished and wealthy young lady, the daughter of Colonel Richard Singleton; but he had scarcely touched the cup of bliss when it was dashed from his lips—she died in 1830, leaving an only child, now the interesting wife of Colonel Wade Hampton. In 1830, the Nullification movement was rushing to a head. From a conversation had with him in December of that year, I know that he had no faith in "Nullification, as a peaceable and Constitutional measure." He believed in revolution as the only measure of redress, and went for Nullification as the nearest approach to that which he could obtain.

He certainly was the strongest and boldest member of his party, in the celebrated Nullification Convention. He assented most reluctantly to the compromise made by Clay and Calhoun, of the Tariff, and, consequently, to the recision of the Ordinance of Nullification. It was then, and now, a source of unmingled joy, that more moderate councils prevailed, and that our country has, in spite of his belief to the contrary, continued for more than a quarter of a century, to promote the liberty, wealth and happiness of our citizens.

In 1824, (April 3d and 4th,) he delivered one of his strongest speeches against the removal of the deposits from the Bank of the United States by President Jackson, which he characterized "as an act of usurpation, under circumstances of injustice and oppression, which warranted him in saying that the rights of widows and orphans had been trampled in the dust by the foot of a tyrant." This grave charge he proceeded to maintain in a speech of twenty-four pages, the result of his indignant feelings. But what has been the result of time? Now many are satisfied that the President was right, and Mr. McDuffie mistaken.

In December, 1834, he was elected to the office of Major-General, and he became instantly enamored of a military life, which, when I held the same distinction in another part of the State, he had ridiculed as mere pomp and parade. He became, as he believed, capable of anything in the military world, which the greatest commanders ever had achieved; and if the country had been involved in the horrors of a civil war, I think it very likely that Gen. McDuffie would have been the successful leader in many a bloody field. But here I again rejoice, that his vaulting ambition was disappointed.

In December, 1834, he was elected Governor and Commander-in-Chief in and over the State of South Carolina. In that capacity as President of the Board of Trustees of his Alma Mater, in 1835, he contributed much to raise her up from her fallen and perishing condition, by the re-organization of the Faculty. At the expiration of this office, which had only been signalized by the organization of the regiment of mounted volunteers, under Col. Robt. H. Goodwyn, who were dispatched by the Governor, under the requisition of the war department, against the Seminole Indians, he retired to private life for about six years, with the exception that, in 1836, he was elected by the Board a Trustee of the South Carolina College, and the Legislature in 1837 conferred on him the same distinction; but these offices did not interfere with his retirement. In 1842, he obeyed the call of the State to represent her in the Senate of the United States. His want of health would very well have excused him from this duty, but he would not refuse as long as he had strength enough to carry him to the Senate Chamber. He took a prominent part in the passage of the Sub-Treasury Bill and the annexation of Texas. Both of these measures had met with his denunciation formerly. He had, however, lived to see his errors, and honestly came forward to correct, and did correct them. He aided, too, in the Tariff of 1846, which, in some degree, yielded principles against which he had formerly contended.

At the close of the session of 1846 he resigned, and, until the spring of 1851, he lingered, a dying man. Then he closed a life which had been remarkable for genius, honesty and eloquence.

Mr. McDuffie was in youth, manhood and old age, a remarkable man for his taciturnity and reserve. He literally seemed to commune with himself; yet there were occasions, when he met old friends and companions, in which he seemed to enjoy life with as much zest as any man.

He was very abstemious, seldom touching wine and never strong drink (within my knowledge). It was this feature of his life, which in a wasting and suffering body, enabled him to accomplish so much.

Mr. McDuffie was, I believe, a true patriot; it is true I often thought him wrong, yet I believed he thought the oppressions of the majority sanctified his course.

In 1851, the fall after his death, at Davison College, in my address on public speaking, I gave, what I believe, a just description of him as an orator and a man, in a few words. "With a thousand times more honesty, McDuffie has surpassed the most brilliant efforts of France's greatest orator, Mirabeau. McDuffie, with a head as clear as a sun-beam, with a heart as pure as honesty itself, and with a purpose as firm as a rock, never spoke unaccompanied with a passionate conviction of right, which made his arguments as irresistible as the rushing flood of his own Savannah."

ROBERT ANDREW TAYLOR.

Robert Andrew Taylor, the son of John and Margaret Taylor, was born in the City of London, on the 9th of February, 1792.

When but a few weeks old, he was brought by his parents to Georgetown, in the State of South Carolina; and, within the first year of his life, he had a malignant attack of confluent small pox, from which he recovered, as if by a miracle, after his case had been abandoned by his physicians as utterly hopeless. The indelible marks of that peculiar disease, although thus early impressed, he carried with him to his grave.

His early school days were passed at Georgetown, until he had reached his thirteenth year, and then, for two years, he was at a classical academy at Newark, in New Jersey. His studies preparatory to his entering the South Carolina College, were directed by Mr. Roberts, the teacher of a once famous school at Statesburg, in the District of Sumter. When just ready to apply for admission to the privileges of his college, at the Commencement in December, 1808, he was suddenly summoned to the death-bed of his mother! It was that mother to whose unslumbering watchfulness he had been indebted, under God, for his continuance in life, and to whose tender lessons of virtue and wisdom, he owed those qualities of heart and of character, which rendered his life a blessing to himself and to society.

Up to this period of his days, young Taylor had been remarkable for a steadiness of character, and unyielding consistency of conduct, very unusual in one of his years. In January, 1809, he joined the Sophomore Class at College, and from the first to the last of his college career, he was amongst the most diligent, and stainless, and accomplished of his fellows. He graduated with distinction in the class of 1811, and immediately afterwards entered upon the study of law at Charleston, in the office of the then Attorney-General, and afterwards one of the Judges of the State, the Hon. John S. Richardson.

In the summer of 1813, Mr. Taylor came to Newberry and studied law with Anderson Crenshaw, Esq., afterwards Judge Crenshaw, of Alabama. His class-mate, John G. Brown, of Newberry, and John Waties, of Sumter, were also students at the same time with Mr. Crenshaw. Judge O'Neall, who had been in college with Mr. Taylor, but who graduated in the class of 1812, was also a student at Newberry, but studied with John Caldwell, Esq.

Messrs. Taylor and Brown, were admitted to the Bar in Charleston in January, 1814.

Judge O'Neall remarks, "that he knew Mr. Taylor while in college, from February, 1811, to December, 1812, and afterwards while studying law with Judge Crenshaw, and he concurs fully in all said of him."

In due season he was admitted to the Bar, and commenced his professional life at Georgetown. The law business with which he was entrusted, was, from the very first, extensive and lucrative, and few young lawyers ever rose more rapidly in the estimation of the profession, and in the confidence of the community. For eight years after entering on the practice of law, he devoted his time and all his energies, with unrelaxing industry, to his profession. Unseduced by the glitter of military life, and standing strong against the temptations to political advancement, he gave himself entirely to the interests of his clients.

At the election for Members of the Legislature in October, 1822, he, for the first time, yielded to the wishes of his friends, and was chosen a Representative from the election District of Prince George, Winyaw. After serving for the two sessions of 1822 and 1823, he was again returned as a Member of the Legislature of the State in 1824,* and served in the session

---

* At the close of the session of 1824, occurred one of those saturnalia, which was the cause of much mirth.

In the course of the session, a worthy lady from Georgetown, Mrs. R. S. M. Hardwicke, had been elected Register Mesne Conveyances. Saturday night,

of that year, and for the year 1825. In the year following, he was again a candidate for the suffrages of the people, but a few weeks before the time for the election, he was seized with a bilious fever, which terminated his brief but highly useful life, on the *22d day of September*, 1826.

In 1824, Mr. Taylor was appointed the aid of his class-mate, Gov. Manning, and thus had the title of Col. Taylor. He was a part of that brilliant cortege who accompanied the Governor in March, 1825, in his reception of Gen. La Fayette.

During the four years that Col. Taylor was a Member of the House of Representatives, Judge O'Neal was also a Member; and from 1824 to 1826, was Speaker. He had a perfect opportunity of observing and knowing Col. Taylor, and he has no hesitation in saying that he was not only one of the most upright, but also one of the most useful members. His early death was deplored by every one who knew him, and certainly his constituents had great cause to lament the sad event which deprived them forever of his services.

---

the House was waiting upon the engrossing of the Acts. To enable the members to enjoy the contemplated fun, the Speaker was desired to appoint some one in his place, and retire to take his tea. Accordingly, the late Tandy Walker, Esq., of Greenville, was called to the Chair. Samuel Dixon, Esq., of Pendleton, who was a man of considerable power of language, but who was constantly more or less under the influence of wine, was selected as the leader of the frolic. John G. Brown, of Newberry, who loved fun as he did a feast, drew up a resolution to this effect:

"*Resolved*, That a Committee be raised to inquire whether R. S. M. Hardwicke, lately elected Register of Mesne Conveyances, for Georgetown District, is a free white man within the meaning of the Constitution."

Mr. Dixon moved the resolution and Mr Brown seconded it; when I returned to the House, Mr. Dixon was in the full blast of an oratorical display. He deplored the effect of electing a female to office. One of the consequences, said he, will be that we shall have petticoats strutting in the lobby of the State House. Sir, said he, "the honorable gentleman from Prince George, Winyaw, (meaning Col. Taylor,) intends to commit a fraud on the Constitution. He knows he cannot hold two offices at the same time: he intends to go home and marry the lady, and thus evade the Constitution." Hugh S. Legaré, who was busily writing at his place, and who had not observed what was going on, and who supposed the Speaker was in his place, sprung to his feet and said, "order, Mr. Speaker, order!"

Mr. Dixon crossed the floor near to Mr. Legaré, and making a low bow, said—"Mr. Speaker, I always yield the floor to the celebrated orator from the City of Charlestown." The House exploded in laughter, the Speaker took his seat and the frolic was ended!

Mr. Taylor was never married, and at his death he left behind him an aged father, and an only brother,* much younger than he was, and who thus found himself the sole survivor of a family of eleven children.

Mr. Taylor was not only a lawyer and legislator, from his school-days he had cultivated a taste for elegant literature, and was always distinguished for the purity and touching felicity with which he wrote the English language. In his hours of relaxation from severer studies, he amused himself with preparing articles for the newspapers and magazines of the day; and to the friends who well knew the contributions thus made to the ephemeral literature of the times, it has ever since been a source of curious interest to mark how frequently, and in how many ever-varying shapes, his articles have been served up, as new things, by the petty and pilfering caterers for the press.

---

* The Rev. Thomas House Taylor, D. D., of "the South Carolina College," class of 1819. At this time, (June, 1859,) and for more than twenty-five years past, the Rector of Grace Church, in the City of New York.

WHITFIELD BROOKS.

This gentleman was the son of Col. Zachariah Smith Brooks, and Elizabeth, the youngest daughter of Captain James Butler, who was killed in the foray of the "bloody scout," in October, 1781, at Turner's Station, on Cloud's Creek, Edgefield District. She was about seven years old at her father's death, and is better known as the youngest sister of General William Butler. Whitfield Brooks was born in Newberry District; but his father afterwards removed to Big Creek, Edgefield District, where he lived, and died beyond the age of three-score and ten. Whitfield Brooks received his academic eduaation mainly at Mount Bethel, in Newberry District. He graduated in the South Carolina College, in the class of 1812, and was one of four (Preston, O'Hara, Brooks and Massey), who were appointed to deliver orations at Commencement. Some of his classmates—Pinckney and O'Neall—who received the first and second honors, and Preston, who was the first of the four to whom orations were assigned, are not unknown, and are still spared by the mercy of God.

He studied law at Edgefield, with Col. Simkins, and was admitted to the Bar, in Columbia, in 1815. The Court of Equity for Edgefield, was established in 1814, and immediately thereafter, Whitfield Brooks received the *pro tem.* appointment of Commissioner in Equity for Edgefield, from the Governor. He was, subsequently, in December, 1815, elected by the Legislature to the same office, which he held for eighteen years, and until he was forced to resign, on account of ill health. He married, on the 16th of June, 1818, Miss Mary P. Carroll, of the City of Charleston. He served in the House of Representatives, from Edgefield District, one or more terms.

He removed from his pleasant home, in the village of Edgefield, to his Roseland Plantation, in the spring of 1849, leaving his eldest son, Preston S. Brooks, and his family, in possession of his village residence.

His son, Whitfield Butler Brooks, was one of the volunteers in the Palmetto Regiment, in the company commanded by his brother, Preston S. Brooks. He received a mortal wound in the battle of Cherubusco, on the 20th August, 1847, and died in the City of Mexico, on the 2d October following, in the twenty-second year of his age. "This," Mrs. Brooks says, "was the first great sorrow of our lives, and from it his poor father never recovered. His health, which was not good at the time, continued to decline, until he sunk to his peaceful grave, on the 28th December, 1851, in the sixty-second year of his life." He left surving him his accomplished lady, Mrs. Mary P. Brooks, and four children, Col. Preston S. Brooks, James C. Brooks, Ellen, the wife Gen. R. G. M. Dunovant, and John Hampden Brooks, Esq.

Since his death, his eldest son, Col. Preston S. Brooks, a Member of Congress, died suddenly in the City of Washington. His death was as much mourned in the State of his birth, as any other which perhaps ever occurred.

Mr. Brooks, in college and in after-life, exhibited a high order of talent. As a lawyer, he was well informed, and his practice was accurate. He possessed a ready, pliant, and easy elocution.

As a Commissioner in Equity, he was remarkable for his industry, order, and accuracy. The business done in his Court, during his Commissionership, was immense. He never was complained of, as being in default, in a single particular. His reports presented the points involved in the accounts with great clearness and precision; in every respect, a model Commissioner.

Mr. Brooks was a high-minded, chivalric, and generous gentleman. If he had a fault, it was that he was too impulsive; but his impulses were generally right. If sometimes he may have acted rashly, he never, to my knowledge, injured a human being. As his classmate and friend for forty years, I had the opportunity of knowing him intimately; and my belief is, that he was as pure and sincere a man as I ever knew.

In all the relations of husband and father, he was kindness

itself. As a son, his aged parent always leant upon his arm with perfect confidence; as a brother, he was to his sisters in all their trials, a brother indeed; as a friend, he was never false to his pretensions; as a citizen, he was always ready to discharge his duty.

In fine, Whitfield Brooks lived a useful life, and died with the love and respect of all who knew him. "He now rests from his labors, and his works do follow him."

GEORGE BUTLER.

Major George Butler, the second son of Major-General William Butler and his wife, Behethelon Foote, was born at their residence, Big Creek, Edgefield District, on the 24th day of September, 1786.

His academic education was, mainly, received at the Mount Bethel Academy, in Newberry. He graduated at the South Carolina College—with a respectable distinction—third in the Class of 1809, in which James Louis Petigru had the first distinction, and Alexander Bowie the second. He commenced the study of the law in Columbia, but before he had completed his term of three years, then required, the war of 1812 was declared. He solicited and obtained a Captain's Commission, recruited, and marched his company to Fort Moultrie, where he remained on garrison duty, till the war closed. In the mean time, he had been promoted to the rank of Major.

At the cessation of hostilities, he again directed his attention to the Bar. He studied for a short time, in 1815, under Anderson Crenshaw, Esq., at Newberry, and was admitted to the Bar in November, of that year, and immediately commenced the practice of the law at Edgefield, where he resided, and at Newberry and Lexington, in which he was very successful. But life was to be to him, a short period of probation. He died the 19th day of September, 1821.

Major George Butler was a young man of fine principles and talents. If he had been spared to live long, he would have been a distinguished lawyer and an eminent man. His death carried unutterable sorrow into the bosom of his family. His father was crushed by this sad event, and soon followed his favorite son to the grave.

The wife and mother, however, bore with uncomplaining fortitude, this, heaviest blow to her woman's heart. She lived on to a great age, and saw her numerous family go down to the grave with one exception, Judge Butler, having survived her a short time.

BENJAMIN F. PEPOON.

This gentleman was born 2d January, 1794, and graduated in the Class of 1812, at the South Carolina College, with Henry L. Pinckney, Judge O'Neall, W. C. Preston and Ebenezer Thayer. He was regarded as a good scholar, but received no distinction. His mind was rather speculative and metaphysical than solid or showy. He was admitted to the Bar 3d January, 1815, and was the partner of Judge Huger, and when he was placed upon the Bench, he gave him much lucrative business, and authorized him to sell for him the property on Charleston Neck, in Morris street, which reverted to him by the extinction of a society of Baptists, to whom his ancestors had conveyed it.

He was, subsequently, the partner of the late Recorder, G. B. Eckhard, and of Edward S. Courtenay. He was a well-read and acute lawyer; his arguments in Hilson *vs.* Blair—2 Bail, 168, and in Sebring *vs.* Keith, Id., 192—although not preserved, I well remember; and in the last case, in delivering the opinion, I took occasion to compliment him and Mr. Rice on their knowledge of pleading, which their arguments had shown, by saying, "the learned counsel concerned in this case, have, however, shown themselves to be too well versed in its rules and principles, not to appreciate its value, and wield it with advantage."

Mr. Pepoon certainly was not one having the highest order of intellect, yet he was above mediocrity. This is true, as evidenced when in college, and in all his after-life.

He took an active part in city affairs when he was a young man, and was chiefly instrumental in extending Broad and Rutledge streets, so as to make them meet. And so deep were the feelings of interest in the improvement of his native city, and so proud of his exertions in having mainly effected it, that he would have been gratified had his name been attached to the new street. He has often said, but for rivalry this extension would have been called Pepoon street.

In the latter years of his life, at one time, he was the Clerk of Sheriff Yates, and at another, the Surrogate, or Clerk of Ordinary Lehre. These offices he filled with great fidelity and exactness. The office hours, from 9 A. M. to 2 P. M., and from 3 P. M. to sundown, he kept with great precision. He closed at the hour, and if one came to transact business after the expiration of the hours of business, he had to come again. While acting as the deputy of the Sheriff, he threw out from under the stair-case, in the lobby of the Court House, to make room for coal, an immense mass of old papers, appertaining to the administration of criminal justice in Charleston, orders of discharge under writs of *habeas corpus*, &c., &c. They were so scattered by the autumnal gale over the streets, that the City Guard collected and burned them. A leading member of the Bar condemned the act, and remarked, that "Pepoon, though a conservative, is too destructive a creature to have charge of ancient records." Pepoon, however, maintained he had done good service *in destroying disagreeable reminiscences of the past.*

This, unintentional destruction, I very much regret, although the place where the papers were deposited, was not a very proper one. For, if they had remained, I am persuaded they would have furnished much judicial information as to the early members of the Charleston Bar, in their administration of criminal justice, presentments of Grand Juries, and orders of Court, in times of the Revolution. But regrets are useless; they have perished, and sooner or later must perish the best works of life.

Mr. Pepoon, in the unfortunate political divisions beginning in 1830, was an uncompromising Union man; and to the closing hours of his life, he remained unchanged. In 1850, when secession began to be the prevailing element of a new agitation of the political atmosphere, and when, as a friend said to me, it was as universal as "break-bone fever," a friend once said to him, "the true course was a Southern confederacy, a cheerful and spontaneous action of the Southern States, and not the hazardous attempt of single State action, to force the other Southern States into line, which might prove abortive and destructive of the interests of the South; and this course only to be resorted to, after solemn appeal to the sister States of the North, to desist from hostile action." He replied, "that is nonsense, and worse than nonsense; we have important chartered rights secured under the Constitution, a glorious inheritance from our illustrious ancestors. I am not for basely surrendering this noble bequest of a brave ancestry. I am for remaining in the Union, and compelling the Abolitionists, forgetful of the precepts of their ancestors into an observance of our noble Constitution."

Some of his pleasantries ought to be preserved in connection with his fidelity to the Union. He and the late Major Charles Parker were intimate friends, but of different politics. "Ah," said Parker to him, "if they had let me alone, I would have thrown shells, and cracked the skulls of the army; for I knew the exact distance between Charleston and Castle Pinckney." "Well," replied Pepoon, "Major, they would not then be worse off than you, Nullifiers." "How?" said the Major. "Why," said Pepoon, "all your skulls have been cracked since before '32."

At another time, meeting another Nullifier who was continually talking about State Sovereignty, Mr. Pepoon asked him where this boasted Sovereignty resided. He replied, "in the people of the State to be sure;" but, said Pepoon, "the people are divided into two parties—which side has it?" "The majority, to be sure," said his friend. "But, suppose the parties to be equally divided, where is it then?" "Sir," said the Nullifier, "I will not admit so foolish a supposition."

Pepoon was "indomitable and unyielding," when he thought he was right; yet he was very far from being indiscreet. After he had lost his sight, it occurred to him, seeing the public mind was calm, to set the people to thinking as to their peculiar form of State Government. He procured the services of a friend to write out his views. In this way, though laboring under great physical infirmities, his great interest in his native State caused him to dictate several numbers, which were signed "Warwick," in which he thought he demonstrated that one-fifth of the white population of the

State, elected one-half of the Senators. These numbers were published in the Greenville Mountaineer. He urged in them equality of taxation and representation. It was his opinion, a check against the over-balanced majority of the Democracy was to be found in the veto power of the Executive.

Mr. Pepoon was, unfortunately, sceptical in his religious views; yet he sought to unsettle no one's faith, or to give a wrong direction to the young or the weak. He said "he never would converse about religion to a child, or to a female, as he was *sceptical*." He regularly had the Bible near to him. He considered it, as he often said, the most ancient book now extant; that it was the collected wisdom of ages gone by, and more was to be learned from it than all other books.

Though he was a bachelor, yet he had a high appreciation of woman. This was shown when making his will; he gave legacies to some female friends "out of gratitude. He made these legacies, because, as he said, in his early life, he made money and spent it freely, and would now be poor but for the kindly advice given by the mother and grandmother of these legatees."

He gave $500 to the South Carolina Society, (the largest charitable society in the city.) I have heard it remarked to a friend "he gave this legacy, as the Society had given that amount to him as a fee, and he thought the best thing he could do was to give it back." He gave $1,000 to the *Roper Hospital*, saying he considered it the noblest institution in the city; that Colonel Roper was a noble benefactor in establishing an hospital without regard to religion or color.

The rest of his property he gave to his nieces in Boston, with the exception of $500, which he gave to each of his three nephews. This interesting account of his will shows his benevolent mind. Mr. Pepoon's gift to the Roper Hospital is one which must always redound to his honor. The Roper Hospital, in the City of Charleston, was founded, and is governed by the Medical Society, in consequence of the very liberal devise of Colonel Thomas Roper of his whole real estates upon the death of his son without issue, to the Medical

Society, "to erect, maintain, and regulate an hospital of such dimensions, as they, in their better judgment, may direct, for the permanent reception, or occasional relief, of all such sick, maimed, and diseased paupers as need surgical or medical aid, and whom, without regard to complexion, religion, or nationality, I would they should admit therein. The site of the said hospital, or infirmary, to be in or near Charleston."

This institution, like the Angel of Mercy, has ministered, in the darkest hours of pestilence, to the poor and the stranger, to the white and also to the black, to the Protestant and the Catholic, and, indeed, to all of every religion, and to those of no religion. Such an institution commended itself to Pepoon's large and liberal heart, and his bequest says to all, who are situated like him, "Go thou and do likewise."

Mr. Pepoon, from his youth, had been compelled to wear glasses on account of near-sightedness. As age began to grow upon him, "the windows were darkened," until, in total blindness, in his sixty-first year, he approached his end. He died on the 21st of October, 1854.

Thus life, without the endearments of wife or children, closed upon a clear-headed, well-educated man, with some eccentricities of manner, but of a genial, confiding nature, that will be long remembered by his friends.

ZACHARIAH P. HERNDON.

This gentleman was the son of Colonel Benjamin Herndon, of Duncan's Creek, Newberry District. In the Revolution, Colonel Benjamin Herndon resided in Wilkes County, North Carolina. He was Captain of a company of sixty men in the regiment commanded by Colonel Cleveland, in the battle of King's Mountain, and soon after emigrated to Newberry. Colonel Zachariah P. Herndon, his youngest son by his first wife, was born 19th April, 1795. His academic education was received at Mt. Bethel, Newberry. He entered the South Carolina College, in the Junior Class, at Commencement, 1811. He remained only until vacation, July, 1812; after spending some time at home, he went to Pinckney, Union District, and studied law with Colonel Joseph Gist. He was admitted to the Bar of the Court of Law, 25th April, 1816, and settled at Union, as the partner of Colonel Gist. He was elected Commissioner in Equity, 15th December, 1818, and continued in that office until 1822. He was admitted to practice in Equity 6th April of this year, and to the practice of the United States Court in 1824. He was appointed by Governor Manning one of his aids, and accompanied him in the review of the regiments in Spartanburg and Union, in September, 1825. He entered political life about 1830, and connected himself with the Nullification party, which had largely the ascendency in Union District. He was chosen a delegate, in 1831, to the Anti-Tariff Convention, at Philadelphia; whether he served or not I don't know. In 1832, he was elected a Member of the House of Representatives in the General Assembly of this State. On the 8th January, 1834, he was elected Colonel of the Thirty-fourth Regiment, Ninth Brigade, Fifth Division of South Carolina Militia. He had the singular good fortune, on the 8th March, 1842, in the forty-fifth year of his age, to marry an accomplished young lady of the village where he lived, Miss Eliza L. Pratt. He was perhaps more than once or twice elected to the House of Representatives, and was a diligent and faithful Member in the discharge of his duties.

For many years, Colonel Herndon had a large, lucrative, and laborious practice at Union and the adjoining districts, by which, and prudent management, he amassed a large fortune. For several years, his health had been failing. In March, 1859, he removed to Columbia. It then continued to decline, until there was little prospect of his recovery. He, however, in the hope of amendment, visited Glenn's Springs, Spartanburg District, where he died, 12th July, 1859, in the sixty-fifth year of his age, leaving his widow and several children surviving him.

Colonel Herndon was a good lawyer, understanding and managing his cases well. Perseverance in the conduct of his cases was a remarkable trait in his character. He exhausted every remedy before he surrendered. His mind was not quick; but he had great good sense, and, when undisturbed by passion, uniformly applied it. His legal arguments were well prepared. He sifted every case to the bottom; and never failed to be understood. The best argument which I ever heard him make was at York, in April, 1858, in the case of The State *vs.* Bell. He was for the State; and, unquestionably, his argument put every possible view of the case in array against the prisoner. It was a powerful argument, worthy of his best days.

Colonel Herndon was rather a rough and impulsive man in a Court House; but in private and domestic life, he was a kind, hospitable, polite gentleman. As a husband and father, he was devoted; as a master, he was kind and indulgent to his slaves. He was a follower of temperance, both in theory and practice. On the whole, there were few men in his section who had more virtues and fewer faults. The proceedings of the Union Bar, on the occasion of his death, are appended:

"According to adjournment, the members of the Bar at this place met on Tuesday, 26th July, at ten o'clock, A. M.

Dr. Goudelock, Esq., chairman, resumed his seat, and J. B. Steedman acted as secretary.

The chairman, after a few remarks, stated that the object of the meeting was to receive the report of the committee appointed at the last meeting, to prepare a preamble and resolutions, relative to the death of Colonel Z. P. Herndon.

B. F. Arthur, Esq., rose, and said:

Mr. Chairman,—Having been appointed chairman of this committee, in the absence of those better qualified than myself, I feel some embarrassment. There are those here, who have been associated with him daily, for many years—those who have been his colleagues and adversaries in many a forensic encounter. I have known him for nearly ten years, during most of which period we were as intimate as the great difference in our ages would warrant, and I may, therefore, be excused for a few remarks.

Colonel Z. P. Herndon was the son of Colonel Benjamin Herndon, who resided in Wilkes County, North Carolina, at the time of the Revolutionary war; and who commanded a company of sixty men, in Cleveland's Regiment, at the battle of King's Mountain, and soon after emigrated to Newberry District, South Carolina, where Colonel Z. P. Herndon was born, on the nineteenth day of April, 1795. He was, therefore, in his sixty-fifth year, at the time of his death. He was admitted to the Bar in 1810, and located at this place, where he continued to reside until his removal to Columbia, in March last. He entered political life in 1830, and connected himself with the Nullification party. He was chosen a delegate to the Anti-Tariff Convention, which met at Philadelphia, and in 1832 was elected a Member of the House of Representatives. From the commencement of his political career, down to the close of his life, he was a consistent member of the States-Rights party. He was several times elected a Member of the Legislature, where he displayed fine powers of debate, and great talent for legislation.

However distinguished his political career, it was as a lawyer we knew him best; as a lawyer we most appreciated him, and as a lawyer I shall speak of him. For many years past, he has been at the very head of this Bar, and enjoyed a more extensive reputation than any lawyer in the upper country.

He did not have, perhaps, great quickness of apprehension, or vivacity of intellect; but he had a strong mind, capable of great effort, great powers of observation, and a remarkable memory for legal principles. In preparing his cases, he acquired slowly but surely. He had great power of expression, and a remarkable command of simple yet forcible language. Few excelled him in clearness and vigor of style; none in his powers of argumentation. He was one of those rare examples of the highest intellectual qualities, united with sound, practical, sturdy common sense. He never studied the graces of oratory, or that petty *mannerism*, which is becoming so common, and which is so offensive to good taste. There was nothing in his nature that could court favor or conciliate opinion; but his character was resolute, self-reliant and independent. He relied rather upon the strength of his case, than the factitious aid derived from empty rhetoric or fine address. His speeches were generally simple, unaffected, and without pretension or anything like an effort at display. He always showed a nice appreciation of the difficulties of his case, and great facility in surmounting them. Instead of attempting to conceal weak points, by a brilliant display of empty declamation, he met them and mastered them with a force of logic rarely surpassed. His powers of discrimination and analysis were very fine; and the most complicated question of law and fact took shape, and form, and life, under his touch.

As chairman of the committee, I beg leave to present the following preamble and resolutions:

The melancholy duty has been assigned us, of paying a tribute of respect to the memory of one, who, for a long period, has occupied a prominent position at this Bar, and who has just passed away from our midst.

Profound as is the regret inspired in this community by the intelligence of the death of Colonel Herndon, it cannot but affect with a deeper sense of loss, the members of that profession with which he was so long and so honorably connected. For a great many years, he has dignified and enriched the profession with the exertions of his cultivated and vigorous intellect. As an advocate, he has long enjoyed the respect and confidence of his fellow-citizens, and how well he has justified their high opinion, we, who have labored at his side, will bear ample and willing testimony. In all that was entrusted to his care, he was earnest, zealous and faithful, and devoted himself with indefatigable assiduity to the wearisome duties of his profession. Throughout life, an earnest, consistent and uncompromising States-Rights Republican, he never swerved from the line of duty; but, under the most trying circumstances, ardently supported the principles of his youth and manhood.

Be it, therefore,

Resolved, That, in the death of Colonel Z. P. Herndon, the State has lost a distinguished citizen, and the legal profession one of their most eminent and useful members.

Resolved, That we sympathize with his family in their great affliction, and that the Secretary of this meeting be requested to transmit a copy of these resolutions to them.

Resolved, That the chairman of this meeting present these resolutions to the presiding Judge, at the next Court, with the request, that the same be entered on the minutes.

Resolved, That these proceedings be published in the Unionville Times.

The preamble and resolutions were seconded briefly by A. W. Thomson, Esq., and unanimously adopted.

The meeting then adjourned.

D. GOUDELOCK, *Chairman*.

JAS. B. STEEDMAN, *Secretary*."

JOHN McCRAVEN.

John McCraven, Esq., was a native of Abbeville District, and was admitted to the Bar in 1817. Chancellor Bowie says of him: "He was rather a remarkable man, and was without any preparatory instruction, except a good common English education, embracing only reading, writing and arithmetic."

I remember to have heard Mr. McCraven argue Duncan *vs.* Hodges, 4th McC. 239. A short note of his argument will be there found. I was much impressed with the clearness and neatness with which his views were stated.

He had an extensive practice, and was rising to eminence and distinction among such men as Noble, Bowie, Wardlaw, and Burt. "He was a man of indomitable energy. As a proof of this, while diligently attending to a very respectable practice, he acquired, by his own unaided industry, some knowledge of Latin, and such a knowledge of French, as to be able to read the language with facility."

He died early, in 1828 or '9; for I know that at the first term at which I presided, at Abbeville, November, 1829, he was not present, and doubtless must have died some time just previous.

The value of Mr. McCraven's example, is very great to our young men. By industry, he triumphed over all the difficulties which presented themselves to his early advancement. If our young lawyers would do as he did—set themselves down in their offices, make their books their companions, and seek improvement wherever it could be found, we should have few, very few, instances of ignorance at the Bar.

EDWARD PETER SIMONS.

To recall the character and virtues of one who impressed his name upon his times, and who, departing, left behind a high and honorable fame, is ever a pleasing task; but, especially, when to the gift of mind has been added integrity of character and chivalrous principles. We believe there is no State more sensitive than South Carolina to the moral traits of those who, by their talents, claim her regard. She has often preferred to honor those but moderately endowed by nature, in whose principles she could place implicit confidence, rather than those, who, though as "suns" in intellect, have yet been deficient in high moral sentiment—and justly so, for talent but confers power; but whether to be exerted for the injury or prosperity of a people, depends upon the spring of action of its possessor—the motives by which he is governed; "*non tam percunctatur,*" says an old Latin adage, "*quid fiat ut quo animo fiat.*" He who in life sets out with the determination to abandon everything like policy as a guide to his actions, and to be governed alone by earnest conviction and duty, must meet with that which is far more valuable than the trappings of office, or the affixing of titles to the name. He will retain and preserve his self-respect; he will possess the consciousness of having faithfully striven after right and truth, and will enjoy the confidence and esteem of those among whom he lives. The "well done" of conscience, and of the true and good of the community, is far more to be desired than the temporary applause of the fickle multitude. Strive, then, for duty; make effort, then, for right, and in the end there will be full and rich success.

The mother, when she beholds the babe of her affections cold and still under the icy touch of death, feels keen and poignant sorrow. The father, the son of whose hopes and high expectations has been laid low in the cold and dark tomb, is bowed down under the burden of his grief. The

State, from whose bosom has been snatched, by a sudden and untimely end, one in the first vigor and prime of manhood—one who, by his mental and moral qualifications, filled a large place in her esteem and regard—one, whose attainments, high and honorable as they were, were but the presage of higher and more honorable renown—drops over his grave the tear of affection, and remembers him as one of "her jewels."

Edward Peter Simons, the subject of this notice, was born at Rice Hope, in Georgetown District, on the 15th September, 1794. He was the lineal descendant of Benjamin Simons, who, at the Revocation of the Edict of Nantz, removed, in company with the Duprëe family, to the then wilderness of South Carolina, and united in marriage with one of the daughters of Mr. Duprëe, by the name of Mary Esther. He died on the 18th August, 1717, having been the parent of fourteen children, from whom are descended the numerous family of his name in this State. The immediate ancestors of Edward Peter Simons, were Maurice Simons, Esq., of Georgetown, who intermarried with his first cousin, Elizabeth, the daughter of Peter Simons, Esq.

Before he arrived at the age of eight years, it was his misfortune to lose both of his parents, and he was at this early age left without the kind guardianship of a mother, and the judicious counsels of a father. To add to his misfortune, he was shortly after deprived of a second parent, in the person of his uncle, Thomas Simons, on whom all his hopes had rested for proper care and control. In this situation, he was left entirely undirected, both in studies and morals, except by the school tutor, and the occasional advice of a good old lady, with whom he boarded. After remaining some time at the Charleston College, under the tuition of Rev. Dr. Buist, its able and learned head, he was removed to Georgetown, and placed under the tuition of Mr. John Waldo, who at that time enjoyed a high reputation as an excellent instructor of youth, by whom he was prepared for an entrance to college.

In him he found an able and affectionate preceptor, one who, with kind and judicious counsels, directed his studies and guided his steps. He was ever remembered by Simons with the kindest feelings of esteem and regard.

Simons was always conspicuous. From the hours of infancy to manhood, he was ever prominent. As an instance of his youthful aspirations, it is said, "while at school there was a juvenile company formed, at the head of which he marched, on the fourth of July, and delivered to them an oration of his own composing, having then scarcely exceeded the age of twelve years." He displayed early in life those traits of character, for which he was afterwards distinguished—a spirit, high-toned in its principles, and emulous of honorable distinction; a mind above the ordinary mould, ardent in its pursuits, and eager in the attainment of knowledge; a soul open as the day, candid in the expression of its views, and scorning everything mean and low. He possessed great facility in the acquirement of the Greek and Latin tongues, and though among "the first scholars in his class at school, he was at the same time always a leader in the active exercises of recreation."

In 1810, he was sent to Connecticut, to finish his education, but on arriving at New Haven, so great was his ambition, that he feared he might not pass the examination with eclat, and desired and was granted some months' preparation, under the Rev. Dr. Bacchus, afterwards President of Hamilton University.

He then applied and was admitted to the Freshman Class of Yale College, in 1810. This institution was, at that time, under the superintendence of the Rev. Dr. Dwight. We are told that during the first year of his collegiate course, he was so impressed by a remark in Bissett's Life of Burke, "that that great man was not conspicuous, at the University, for his attention to the course of studies prescribed for the students, but leaving ordinary geniuses to pursue the beaten track, marked out a road for himself," that he resolved to devote his time to classical and *belles-lettres* studies, in opposition to the sciences, for which the college at New Haven is remarkable, and for a short period actually persevered; but early perceiving his mistake, and finding that the University honors were not to be obtained without a suitable attention to the mathematics, he relinquished his plan, and with uncommon diligence, aided by vigor of intellect, not only recovered his standing in the class, but when the honors were distributed, was rewarded with one of the most distinguished. Yet he found time to cultivate his favorite studies, and in the debates before the society was almost foremost. He was decidedly the boldest speaker in his class, and on one occasion, undertook, in the college chapel, before all the students and faculty, and in the most heated and excited times of New England politics, to repeat Mr. Clay's phillipic, delivered in Congress, just after the declaration of war. Perhaps no circumstance ever exhibited the energy of his character, in a more decided view.

"The southern students were few in number, in comparison with the northern; the government of the college were known to be in favor of the line of policy then pursued by Massachusetts and Connecticut; and in the chapel itself, the excitement among the students was so great, that repeated efforts were made to stop him; he paused until the turmoil was over, and then proceeded, refusing, until the whole speech was delivered, to leave the rostrum."

It was the custom of President Dwight, during the senior year, to give various subjects for written disputations. Two of the efforts of Simons yet remain to us. The one "on the comparative excellencies of the Constitutions of Great Britain and the United States;" the other, "whether human nature is advancing to a state of perfection?" They are both well-written productions, and exhibit a matured and reflective mind.

As a mark of the deep impression he left at college, we would mention an anecdote, connected with a relative of his, who, not many years since, was an inmate of the classic shades of Yale. One day, at the close of a recitation, Professor Kingsley, the able and much-loved professor of Latin, (in 1813, tutor,) called him up and expressed a desire to see him. Having been talking a good deal during recitation, he approached the professor's desk with some anxiety, expecting a reprimand for having expressed his thoughts too freely, during recitation hours, when, to his great astonishment and relief, the professor inquired: "Did you ever, sir, have a relative in this institution?" Without reflecting, he answered, "No sir;" but after a little while, remembering the subject of this memoir, answered, "Yes, sir—one Edward Peter Simons," responded the professor. "Well, sir, you are somewhat like him; your eyes are very similar;" and a conversation then ensued, with regard to his subsequent career. Here had thirty-three years elapsed since his graduation, and yet is it not strange, that among the thousands who had, in the meantime, passed before the professor's eye, he should have remembered and called to mind the features and memory of Simons?

His bearing was such as to impress every one with whom he mingled, that he was a gifted man—one who would do honor to his name, and reflect credit on the State of his birth. After graduating at Yale College, in 1814, he returned to Charleston, and immediately commenced the study of the law, with his friend and relative, Col. Keating Lewis Simons, a gentleman eminent in his profession. He remained in his office for the space of twelve months, when finding that the large business in which Col. Simons was engaged, prevented his receiving those advantages of instruction which his well-matured mind and rich experience, would have otherwise afforded, young Simons, with the approbation of his relative, repaired to Litchfield, Connecticut, the seat of a flourishing law school, and there attended the lectures. Delighting in the law, as the profession of his choice, admiring its principles, he diligently applied himself, not that he might "see through a glass darkly," further than which, alas, but few aspire; but that he might possess a grand, comprehensive and enlightened view of its structure and applicability to the wants and necessities of society.

While here he was selected by his fellow-students to deliver an oration on the approaching anniversary of American Independence. It was just after the close of the war of 1812, when the contests between the Federalists and Republicans waxed fierce, when party dissension ran high, and many feared for the perpetuity of the Union. The weakness and instability of our government was at that time the constant theme of declamation. The gloomy genius of false prophecy had predicted the swift approach of our final doom. The departed spirits of ancient republics were invoked to indicate the political grave to which we were descending, and the finger in triumph was pointed to the lofty columns of Grecian architecture—those splendid specimens of human ingenuity, crumbled into dust—to the descendants of those heroes who fell at the heights of Thermopylæ, and bled on the plains of Marathon and Platœa, under the dominion of galling and oppressive tyrants—to the proud trophies and triumphant monuments of republican Rome, mingling with the dust around in undistinguishable ruin. Therefore, after eloquently depicting the immense sacrifices of feeling, wealth, toil and precious blood with which this nation had wrought her freedom, he portrayed its value and blessings by a comparison with the constitution and laws of the other nations on the globe. Believing the government to be composed of materials as durable as human imperfection will allow, he inferred its lasting duration as a legitimate deduction from its nature and form, strengthened by local situation, the benign influences of Christianity and the growing spirit of patriotism. Looking upon the Constitution as a fixed and unalterable charter, (except in the manner prescribed by its very terms,) formed by the people immediately through their representatives containing and defining the rights and duties of the citizens and the corresponding rights and duties of the rulers, he regarded the Union alone as safe, when the Constitution was preserved by a strict adherence to its principles. We have, with much pleasure, read the oration in question, many parts of which are, alas, but too applicable to the present condition of affairs, especially where he calls upon his countrymen to rouse all the latent energies of soul, and, singing the requiem of party spirit, to rally as one man in defence of the imperiled Constitution, and thus, with vestal vigilance, maintain the laws and preserve true liberty.

Upon his return to Charleston he was admitted to the Bar, and immediately entered with great success on the practice of the law. The distressed prisoner found in him a warm and zealous advocate. He soon acquired a reputation for eloquence and legal knowledge, and his services were engaged in many cases of importance.

In the latter part of 1819, the community were called upon to mourn the loss of Col. K. L. Simons, his legal preceptor and much-honored friend, of whom there can be no more appropriate epitaph than that placed by Crafts at the head of his eloquent eulogy,—

——"He kept
The whiteness of his soul, and thus men o'er him wept."

On his decease, the whole of his large and profitable business was transferred to the care of young Simons. "Though young, when such a weight of responsibility was imposed upon him he shrunk not from the task, and so successful were his efforts, that he not only retained the confidence of his clients, but what was intimately more dear to him, the fullest approbation of those who transferred their papers into his possession." He enjoyed great popularity, and was, at the first vacancy, elected a Member of the House of Representatives, in the State Legislature, from the City of Charleston, and was regularly returned at each election, with a handsome support. He was also elected a warden of the city, and continued as such to the day of his death. In 1823, the most animated election ever known, up to that date, for Members of the Corporation, took place. Though well known to be thoroughly opposed to the successful candidate for Intendant, yet such was the opinion entertained by the people, of his talents and integrity, that he was triumphantly elected at the head of his ward. "One military company, that high-spirited and patriotic corps, the Washington Light Infantry, which knew and estimated his worth, promoted him to a lieutenancy, and, in a short period afterwards, he was unanimously invited to the command of another, the United Blues, the members of which were zealously attached to him, and most sincerely deplored his loss." While he was thus eminently distinguished for his attachment to the interest of his constituents by his industry and talents as a warden, and by the many and excellent qualities of his private and public life, the edict of death had already been pronounced, and the summoning angel was winging the air on his fatal and deadly mission.

"However ardent and diligent he may have been in the pursuits of honorable renown—for he thought with Tacitus '*contemptu famæ contemni virtutem*'—yet the basis of his happiness was laid in the domestic circle. United to an amiable woman, and the father of two children, he cheerfully retired from the cares and perplexities of business into the bosom of his family, and from that centre of affection and usefulness, diffused comfort and joy around him. Hospitable and generous, and open, there was not a husband, brother, master and friend, more fondly regarded in the several relations of life—no young man in this community looked out upon brighter and bolder prospects than himself—at the Bar, in the Council, and in the Senate, public office awaited him. In the more sequestered walks of private life, esteem, gratitude, friendship and respect, shone mildly around him. At one and the same time, attentive to the prosperity and grandeur of his country, and to the interests and welfare of his immediate friends, and sensibly alive to honor, and dreading the very semblance of shame, he was in a manner *compelled* to hazard office, prosperity and life upon a single cast"—like Hamilton, forced contrary to his best convictions to the duelling field, he fell a martyr to the code of honor—

"Let the dead past bury its dead."

On the 7th October, 1823, at the early age of 29 years, his spirit passed from time to eternity. His death was universally lamented. He was intered on the 8th, at the Second Independent Church with military honors, attended by the City Council of Charleston, and a large number of respectable citizens. He left surviving him an affectionate family, two brothers, Maurice Simons, for many years Register of Mesne Conveyance for Charleston District, and the late Dr. Thomas Y. Simons, former Professor of the Theory and Practice of Physic in the Medical College of South Carolina. Thus ended the life of Edward Peter Simons, after a short but active exertion for the good of his fellow-citizens. The following tributes to his memory will show that this pen has neither exaggerated his public worth nor his private virtues.

At a meeting of the Charleston Bar, called for the purpose of expressing their sentiments of regret, for his loss, the Attorney-General, James L. Petigru, Esq., was called to the chair. The meeting was addressed by John Gadsden, Esq., who submitted the following preamble and the customary resolutions, which were unanimously adopted:

"Though our friend should not be conscious of the tribute which we have met to offer; though his shade may not be refreshed by our sympathies, let us gather up those virtues which time may soon dissipate, and redeem them if possible from oblivion, for ourselves and posterity. The love of fame, the instinct of noble minds, sends a ray even from the grave, and seeks in the fond remembrance of congenial spirits, an immortal existence. The violent transition from life to death, from the hopes, the activity, the offices and the affections of our nature, to the extinction, the silence, the torpor and the dampness of the tomb, awakens all our sensibility and excites the deepest compassion for the person who has been doomed to realize the horrid contrast. It was almost yesterday that, vigorous in intellect, high in expectation and ardent in pursuit, our friend Simons mingled with us in the labors of the forum or sought the public weal in the deliberations of the council; and now his manly form, the earthly tenement of thought and action, 'lies festering in its shroud.'

'O fallacem hominum spem, fragilem fortunam et inanes nostres contentiones!'

"How long shall we deplore the unnatural divorce of laws and manners, of religion and honor? Must the youth of our country fall by each other's hands, and shall the spring of our years suffer a blight?

"They, who untimely perish, leave us only the promise of virtue, unless like our departed friend, they have early and diligently improved the advantages of nature, and secured a reputation over which even death has no power. Though cut off in the midst of his unfinished labors, he has left us materials to treasure up for the instruction of those who choose to profit by his example. At school, at college, at the Bar, in the City Council, in the Legislature, we find in him a love of distinction, an ardor of character, a vigor of intellect, a generosity of temper, an openness of conduct, and an intrepidity of spirit, which promised extensive usefulness to the public, and a lasting reputation to the individual.

"As a member of our profession, we have seen him more closely, and may expatiate with more propriety and justice upon his merits. Few persons came better prepared to the Bar. His education had been systematic, but decidedly practical. His general attainments were considerable, and his stores of legal knowledge extensive and recondite. Yet whatever he possessed appeared to be always within his reach and at his command. He had no lumber of learning to oppress his mind; occupying the place of valuable acquisitions, and fostering vanity instead of supplying invention. In a ready apprehension, a just discrimination, a copious expression, and a happy elocution he was rarely excelled. In extempore speaking he was prompt, facile, lively and bold.

"A fearless assertion of right, a superiority to mere personal influence, and the artificial distinctions of society where they interfered with the claims of justice, fairness in conducting a cause, candor to his opponents, zeal for an honest client, and a contempt for fraud and baseness; these were the virtues of his professional life. They were sufficient to preponderate over many errors, if his feelings had even had any other source than an impetuous temper, which time and reason would have gradually chastened. Would to God that he had been spared until his understanding had broken entirely through the passions which occasionally darkened it; and that we could have seen him moving steadily along under its light and influence, in the path of public and private usefulness! But he has been taken from us ere the autumn of life, and we can only weep over the half-ripened fruits that lie scattered around us, while we record our grief, and testify our respect."

At a meeting of the Charleston Delegation, held in the City Hall, the following preamble and resolutions were submitted by their Chairman, the Hon. H. L. Pinckney, and unanimously adopted:

"Whereas tributes of honor to the memory of departed worth, operate as incentives to imitation on the part of the survivors, while they afford a mournful gratification to their afflicted feelings: And whereas, our late lamented colleague, Edward P. Simons, was eminently distinguished by the possession and display of a superior order of intellect and eloquence, by the undeviating consistency of his political career, and by the irreproachable purity and correctness of his principles, in all the various relations by which he was connected with society: And whereas, we regard the chasm which his death has caused, not only in this delegation, but in the Legislature of the State, as a severe and public loss, which may not easily be repaired, and which, therefore, calls strongly upon us to express our sense of his character and merits, and our sincere participation of the sorrow of his relatives, and of the community in general. Therefore be it Resolved, unanimously,

"1st. That we deeply deplore the death of our lamented colleague, Edward P. Simons, as a loss to the State, of an able, eloquent, upright, and independent representative.

"2d. That we sincerely sympathize with his afflicted relatives and mourning widow."

We know not that we can better close this tribute to the memory of the dead, than with the ensuing extract from the chaste, pathetic and eloquent funeral address, delivered by the late lamented Rev. Samuel Gilman, D. D., upon the melancholy occasion of the decease of the lamented Simons:

"We will weep for the dead! His sun is extinguished when scarcely advanced beyond its morning prime. The labors, the sacrifices, the studies of his youth are bereft of their reward, and the life which was short in years, though long in achievements, is forbidden to accomplish its flattering promise. The cup of sweet and delicious expectations has been suddenly filled with bitterness and dust. Smiling prospects of usefulness, of activity, of glory, and of happiness, have been fatally overcast. Fond schemes and projects for the public good, are irretrievably frustrated; an ardent career of congenial, intellectual, and energetic pursuits, is forever terminated; visions of future bright and hard-earned eminence have fled; and more; more than all this, the enjoyment of domestic happiness, which formed the central spring of all other efforts, plans, and wishes, has been thus early intercepted. Yes, for him whose eyes have been forced to close on the scenes of tender and faithful conjugal endearments; for him who can no more watch the opening bloom and increasing loveliness of that infancy to which he had given being, and which was fastened, like a flower, to his bosom; for him who will no longer exchange the frankness and confidence of fraternal affection; for him, who must henceforth cease to pay with unremitting, yet, pleasing assiduity, the claims of filial duty; for him who will never again grasp the warm hand of friendship, nor mingle in the social walks of living men; (especially, when we imagine the mental struggles with which this rare combination of felicity must have been resigned,) for him we will let our tears flow forth—we will weep for the dead!

"We will weep for the disconsolate living. For her, whose woe is still like an unreal dream—but a dream, oh, how troubled, and how soon to settle down to the repose of intolerable reality! For her, who has now nothing to lean upon, this side of heaven, but the energy of harrowed and despairing affections! For her, who, as she reaches out her widowed hand for support, finds that she grasps at shadows, and that she must tread the toilsome pilgrimage of life alone. We will weep for those infant orphans, whose memories will retain, but for a few days, the image of their departed father; and when they have done wondering and mourning for his absence, will shortly know not how to pronounce his name. Yet in advancing years, too soon will they be reminded, of the loss they shall have borne; when they shall find a vacancy in their hearts which nature cannot fill, when they shall feel the need of paternal support, affection, example, society, protection, and advice, they will learn with frequent pangs, to utter the sacred but ineffectual name of father. We will weep for those, who, born beneath the same roof with the deceased, have, under every aspect and vicissitude of life, saluted him with fond and proud affection by the title of brother. We will weep for those afar, whom the ocean now severs from his last embrace, but who, if Providence shall speed their way, are on the eve of coming, though they know it not, to plant one of the greenest and saddest turfs upon his tomb, and one of whom will be ready to exclaim, with the patriarch of old, 'I will go down to my son mourning, and my gray heirs, shall be brought with sorrow to the grave.' We will weep for the disconsolate living.

"We will weep for ourselves and the public around us. A promising member of the commonwealth lies like a motionless branch beneath its parent-tree. He who sat in the council halls of his native city, and devoted the energies of his prime to her defence in danger, and to her improvement and prosperity, when at quiet, will no longer 'go out and in before his people.' He, who mounted at an early age the still higher seats of legislation, and sent the influence of his talents and exertions through an extended civil sphere, will not again think, speak, or labor, for the welfare of his State. He whose voice resounded within the walls of justice, will no more be heard vindicating the injured rights of the humble, the ignorant, the helpless, the oppressed. He, to whose fidelity and integrity were entrusted the interests of the widow and the orphan, will no longer devote to them his incessant and guardian attention. He, to whom his fellow-citizens resorted on every occasion with unshakened confidence and untiring alacrity, whether the objects in view were civil, martial, municipal or social, has laid aside his gown, resigned his sword, has put away the badges of office, and has gone down to commune in darkness and in silence with the mouldering congregation of the dead. We will mourn for the loss which will be felt through so many and so various public relations of life—we will weep that we are here."

BENJAMIN T. ELMORE.

This gentleman, the eldest son of General John A. Elmore and Sarah Saxon, his wife, was born in Laurens District. His father, as is mentioned in the sketch of the Hon. Franklin H. Elmore, was a Revolutionary soldier. I think he came to South Carolina with General Greene. His mother was of that old Revolutionary stock of Laurens, the Saxons.

He, Benjamin T., graduated in the Class of 1810, in the South Carolina College, of which James Dellet had the first honor, William Lowry the second, and Chancellor Job Johnston, (then very young,) the third.

At the commencement of the war of 1812, he received a First Lieutenant's Commission, served at Fort Moultrie, and before the close of the war, was promoted to the rank of Captain.

"When war's wild blast was blown
And gentle peace returning,"

he left the army, and studied law, at Newberry, with Anderson Crenshaw, Esq., and in November, 1815, at Columbia, was admitted to the Bar.

I think he opened an office at Laurens, but practiced little, for in 1817, he presented himself as a candidate for Treasurer of the Upper Division of South Carolina, and was elected in December, to serve for four years.

He was elected twice as Comptroller-General, and served during the years '23, '24, '25 and '26, filling these various offices remarkably well.

He married Sarah Aurora, the youngest child of Judge Brevard.

He was elected Captain of the Company of Rifles of the town of Columbia, and served several years in that capacity. He volunteered and commanded that company in the expedition to Florida against the Seminole Indians, in 1835 and 1836.

Captain Elmore was a pleasant companion. His military and office habits did not fit him for success in any active occupation in life. He, therefore, never made any reputation as a lawyer. After his marriage, he had no necessity to pursue his profession. He had very considerable financial capacity, as will be seen by his annual reports as Comptroller-General.

He was a kind-hearted man, who was always popular with the people of Columbia. I have little doubt that his early death is very much to be ascribed to his habits of conviviality, and his enjoyment of social life.

I knew him well, and can say, as I do, with pleasure, that he was a patriotic citizen and an honest man, a good husband and kind father.

His death occurred at the Limestone Springs, in 1840; his amiable and accomplished widow, and several children, still survive him.

PATILLO FARROW.

This gentleman was the son of Thomas Farrow, Esq., a native of North Carolina, and afterwards of Spartanburg District, by his second wife, who was the daughter of the Rev. Henry Patillo, a Presbyterian clergyman of North Carolina; he was born on the 2d of September, 1796. He was a boy of much promise, acquired an education at the usual country schools and academies, with rapidity.

He graduated in the Class of 1815 in the South Carolina College. I see the names of some of his classmates, whom I happen to know as useful and distinguished men, who are still living, viz.: Dr. Henry Boylston, Nathaniel R. Eaves, Esq., John Farley, Esq., Gov. John Gayle, of Alabama, William H. Inglesby, Esq., the Rev. Maurice Harvey Lance, Rev. Albert A. Muller, Dr. Thomas E. Scriven and Dr. John A. Scott. Mr. Farrow had a high distinction in his class.

He studied law at Laurens Court-House with Robert Creswell, Esq., and was admitted to the Bar in December, 1818. He had a good practice from the outset, both in Law and Equity, at Laurens and Spartanburg. His sensitiveness and extreme modesty were always in his way. He possessed fine speaking powers, and, if he could have been induced to address a Jury, as he was able to do without fear, he would have been a most eminent lawyer. Of the many cases in which he was concerned, I recollect the following, which found their way into our reports, viz.: Felts *vs.* Simpson, 1 McC. C. R., 217; Warden *vs.* Burtz, 2 McC. C. R., 73; Fowler *vs.* Stuart, Harp. Eq.; Garrett *vs.* Stuart, 1 McC. C., 514; Fowler *vs.* the same, 1 McC., 504; Stuart *vs.* Fowler, Harp. 403; Cleveland *vs.* Darr, Harp. 407; Boyce *vs.* Barkdale, 4 McC. 401; Byrd *vs.* Boyd, *id.* 246; Byrd *vs.* Ward, *id.* 228; Commissioners of the Poor *vs.* Dooling, 1 Bail. 23; Sinclair & Kiddle *vs.* The Administrators of Price, 1 Hill's Eq., 431.

On the 2d of January, 1826, he married Jane Strother,

daughter of Benjamin James, Esq. He was an Union man in the stormy period of Nullification, and was placed by the Union party of Laurens District as a candidate for the Senate. He refused to electioneer, and set that best of all examples that he would not treat to a drop of intoxicating drink, and would not ride to a single muster to obtain votes. The consequence was that the free and enlightened men of Laurens refused the services of one of her best and most enlightened citizens, for he never was a candidate for office on any other occasion. He retired from the Bar in 1837, and joined the Presbyterian Church, at Laurens, in 1841, devoting himself very much to every good word and work, both in temperance and religion. He was soon elected and set apart as a Ruling Elder. He was taken sick with typhoid fever on the 8th of August, 1849, and lingered to the 18th of October, when he died in the fifty-fourth year of his age, at his dwelling in Laurens, giving, in his last illness, evidence of a consciousness of his approaching dissolution, and gratifying evidence of his readiness and willingness to go. He left, at his death surviving him, his excellent wife, and the following children, who are now alive: James Farrow, Esq., Anna P., wife of J. Wistar Simpson, Esq., Susan W., wife of Major John Witherspoon, of Laurens, T. Stobo Farrow, Commissioner in Equity for Spartanburg, and Henry Patillo Farrow, Esq., of Cartersville, Georgia.

He enjoyed his home and family so much, that he was reluctant to forego such comforts for the glories of the world; and hence he preferred private life, its quiet and ease. There is no doubt he thus enjoyed more happiness. But a man's country has a right to his services, according to his ability.

Mr. Farrow was a good and virtuous man, and the citizens of Laurens ought to cherish his memory as that of one of their brightest jewels.

WILLIAM McWILLIE.

To this gentleman, who is yet alive, and who, I hope, is to be spared for many years to come, I would gladly pay a tribute equal to his worth. But I fear I shall fall very far short in the attempt. Yet his great example belongs to the Bar of South Carolina, and, so far as I am able, I desire to place it before my brethren now and for all time to come. He was born in Kershaw District, on the 17th of November, 1795. He received his common-school education in the neighborhood of his birth, and his academic education in Camden.

The regiment of militia drafted for the United States service, under the command of his father, Col. Adam McWillie, was mustered into service in October, 1814; of that regiment, William McWillie was the Adjutant; the duties of that office he performed to the entire satisfaction of his superiors, at Haddrel's Point, near Charleston, until the regiment was discharged in March, 1815. In October of that year, he entered the South Carolina College, and graduated (receiving one of the higher distinctions of his class) in December, 1817. He studied law, I presume, with Chapman Levy, Esq., was admitted to the Bar in 1818, and was married on the 13th of December, of the same year, to Miss Cunningham, the daughter of Joseph Cunningham, a wealthy planter in the neighborhood of Liberty Hill, Kershaw District. Mr. McWillie settled in Camden, and successfully practiced law in Kershaw and Lancaster Districts.

In April, 1827, he sustained the great loss of his young and lovely wife—leaving him seven young children. On the 17th of March, 1831, he married Miss Anderson, the daughter of Dr. Edward H. Anderson, of Camden, a worthy and accomplished lady. He continued the practice of law until the 1st of October, 1836, when he was elected President of the Bank of Camden. The intervening eighteen years spent by Mr. McWillie at the Bar were not passed in vain; he had made money and acquired reputation. Necessity, however, had not forced him to acquire that transcendant reputation to which his known abilities pointed. He was a rich man from his beginning, and, therefore, made the law more a pastime than a profession.

At the Spring Term, 1834, Mr. McWillie argued, before the Court of Appeals, in Columbia, the great Test Oath question; his argument against that measure entitles him to stand alongside of Williams, Blanding, Petigru, and Grimké; and if their arguments, compared with those of their opponents, be not as the sun is to the moon in clear effulgence and power, I must be much more mistaken than I usually am. For Mr. McWillie's argument, I refer to 2 Hill, 123.

Colonel McWillie was a member of the Senate of South Carolina (I presume from 1836 to 1840). The following is taken from Mr. Bellinger's scrap-book; it is written by an anonymous contributor to one of the South Carolina papers: "Mr. McWillie has a high reputation, and but for his modest and retiring habits, would long since have occupied a more conspicuous station in the country. His mind is one of superior cast. It is bold to originate, and is yet cautious; and few men possess more niceness or exactness of judgment. As a speaker, he is fluent, and always uses the *proper* words in the *most proper* places. His elocution is pleasant and his gesture graceful. The arrangement of his speeches is always logical, and he eminently succeeds in compressing into the narrowest compass, all the best arguments appertaining to the subject before him. Though his style is seldom ever other than argumentative, he yet declaims, at times, in language of the most impassioned kind. Upon such occasions, few men can inspire the hearer with more fervency of feeling. He possesses great flexibility of voice, and his tones, though usually soft and insinuating, when excited, become high and commanding; and every word he utters is listened to as the language of one who speaks for the cause of truth, and commands to be heard for her sake. Though Mr. McWillie was of the unpopular party in this State, some years since, yet no one is more universally respected or esteemed. His great integrity of purpose, his general intelligence as a statesman, and amiable and lofty character as a man, render him one of the first men in the Senate, and one of the most estimable citizens of which our State can boast."

Subsequent to 1836, my circuit duty now and then enabled me to hear and admire Mr. McWillie (then commonly called Colonel McWillie, from, I suppose, an aidship to one of the Governors). In the State *vs.* Ingram and others, a great assault and battery case, for lynching a man named Love, tried at Lancaster in the fall of 1842, he succeeded in saving several worthy men from conviction. His speech was an admirable one, and showed how much better he was suited to the Bar than to be cooped up in the walls of a banking house.

Mr. McWillie, like myself, was a thorough-going temperance man. In this particular, he was the life and soul of total abstinence in the ancient town of Camden, alike dear to both of us; to me, by descent, and to him by early and long associations. As a total-abstinence man, I have often heard and admired Mr. McWillie. As the President of the Camden Bank, till '45, (nine years,) he discharged admirably well its various duties; he gave to it that character for general usefulness and prosperity to which it has ever since shown itself so well entitled.

On the 25th of September, 1845, Colonel McWillie abandoned the soil of his birth, and sought a home in the Southwest. The removal of no citizen created more universal regret. For I hazard nothing in saying, that he was a favorite son of an honored mother; and if he had thought fit to remain, she would have given him honor and office to any extent he might have desired. But I am delighted to know, that the State of his adoption (Mississippi) has not been slow to perceive and reward his worth. She elected him a Member of the Thirty-first Congress, in November, 1849, and Governor in October, 1857. He is now enjoying that greatest dignity in a republican State, and wearing its honors with that modest, dignified usefulness, which has always so distinguished him.

He remarks, in a letter to the author: "I have been, throughout my life, a planter; and fortune has been kind to me, for which I am most thankful. I have raised a numerous family, and with the conduct of my children, and their success in life, I have every reason to be satisfied. Last, though not least, I am a member of the Episcopal Church, to which communion I have been attached for many years."

So much for the past life of Governor McWillie. He will soon complete his sixty-fourth year, and yet his fine constitution and temperate habits promise to add many more years of usefulness to his life, which has been a bright example of talents of love, purity, and fidelity, coupled with an useful and a religious walk and conversation. Long may he live, honored, respected and loved; serene and happy may his evening be, and bright and everlasting the dawn of the morning of a future life.

DAVID J. McCORD.

David J. McCord was a native of St. Matthew's Parish. He was a student of the South Carolina College, in the class which graduated in 1814, but for some cause, he left the college in his Senior year. He studied law, and was admitted to the Bar, in Columbia, in 1818. He married, very young, Miss Wagner, a beautiful young lady in, or near Charleston. He and Henry J. Nott, were associated together as partners, in the practice of the law, in Columbia. Their practice was not very large, but quite enough for young men. They were both under ordinary size. A Polander was employed as an engineer on the canal around Beard's Falls, on Saluda River. He frequently thumped the operatives under his command, and they employed, as he termed them, "little Messrs. Nott & McCord," as attorneys to sue him. His principal was also sued by them, about something connected with the work. He appealed to the Polander, and asked him what he should do. "Burn the —— papers," was his prompt advice. They, (Messrs. Nott & McCord,) under a contract with Mr. Faust, the State Printer, published 1st and 2d Nott & McCord, containing the decisions of the Constitutional Court, in 1818, 1819 and 1820.

In 1821, his partner, H. J. Nott, left for Europe, and their partnership was dissolved. Mr. McCord, continued the Reports under the same arrangement with the State Printer, and published 1st and 2d McCord's Reports, containing the decisions of the Constitutional Court in 1821, '22 and '23. In 1822, he and Col. Preston became partners in the practice of the law.

In December, 1823, an appropriation of $1,000 was made for the salary of the State's Reporter, and William Harper, Esq., who had just returned from Missouri, was elected. In December, 1824, the Court of Appeals was established; and as Mr. Harper did not desire the office of Reporter, Mr. McCord was elected, and continued until the winter of 1827. He reported the law decisions of the Court of Appeals, for 1825, 1826 and 1827, in 3d and 4th McCord's

Reports, and the Equity Decisions for 1825, 1826 and 1827, in 1st and 2d McCord's C. R. These last Reports, (3d and 4th McCord, and 1st and 2d McCord's C. R.,) are very creditable to the industry of Mr. McCord. In March 1825, Mr. McCord was the Intendant of Columbia, who received and welcomed General Lafayette, on his visit to that town.

About this time, 1828, I think Mr. McCord visited Europe. He was present in Paris, at the Revolution of three days, which sent the Bourbons from France, and placed Louis Philippe on the throne. He returned full of the incidents of that period, which he took great pleasure in narrating.

He soon became a violent politician—wrote largely and spoke vehemently in favor of Nullification. He was a Member of the House of Representatives several times, between 1832 and 1840. He was very much identified with Dr. Cooper, while he was President of the South Carolina College.

In 1829, 1833 and 1837, he was elected a Trustee of the South Carolina College

He lost his first wife, who left a large family of children. Some time afterwards, he had the good fortune to find a "help-mate" in the person of a most intelligent lady, Miss Louisa Cheves, the daughter of Judge Cheves.

He became, by the election of the parent Bank in Charleston, President of the Branch Bank, Columbia.

Mr. McCord was a Whig in 1840; his politics little suited the atmosphere of South Carolina; he was consequently removed, and Colonel R. H. Goodwyn, the present excellent president, was placed in his stead.

Mr. McCord retired to private life; he lived in Columbia, and managed his wife's estate in St. Matthew's.

He died about 1855, or 1856, leaving his wife, and several children by his first and last marriages, surviving him.

Mr. McCord was a sprightly, lively, entertaining companion; he was about the bitterest politician with whom I was acquainted. He was a good lawyer, and argued his cases with great legal ingenuity; but he wanted that degree of force and point, which is necessary to make an impression on a Jury, and sometimes became tedious in his legal arguments.

This is a fault, which I know it is hard to avoid; for lawyers desire to show their legal knowledge, and very often forget that the Judges to whom they are speaking, do know, at least, the alphabet of their profession.

On the whole, Mr. McCord may be stated to have been a good lawyer, ardent in pursuit of success, violent in his politics—honest, though mistaken—a friend "who sticketh closer than a brother," a devoted husband and father, a good citizen and officer—one who drained to its dregs the cup of persecution, which, in the day of his power, he most violently presented to his political opponents.

HENRY JUNIUS NOTT.

Henry Junius Nott, the second son of Judge Nott and Angelica Michell, his wife, was born in Union District, on the Pacolett River, on the 4th November, 1797. His father is well known as an eminent Judge; his mother was an extraordinary woman, remarkable for her pleasant, cheerful disposition, her great intelligence, and for an unfailing and uncomplaining fortitude, which carried her through the great privations to which her later years were subjected, in the death of her husband and many of her children.

His father removed to Columbia in 1804; his education he received in the Columbia Academy, until he entered the Sophomore Class of the South Carolina College, in December, 1810; he graduated in 1812, in the highly cultivated and intellectual class of which Hon. Hugh S. Legaré had the first honor.

H. J. Nott, about 1816, visited Europe in company with Ainsley Hall and wife. His tour was a short one; he returned the same year and studied law with Wm. Harper, afterwards Chancellor Harper, and was admitted to the Bar in 1818. He and David J. McCord were associated together as partners; their practice was not extensive. They published two volumes of Reports, covering the cases decided by the Constitutional Court in 1818, 1819 and 1820. These reports are little more than the decisions, with suitable heads and indexes; yet they were, and are now, of great value to the profession.

His health failed, and he abandoned his profession, and, in 1821, he sailed for Europe, and spent most of his time in France and Holland, in the pursuit and acquisition of knowledge.

On the 7th of December, 1824, before he reached home, he was elected Professor of the Elements of Criticism, Logic and the Philosophy of Languages, in the South Carolina College. While in Europe, he was married to a French lady.

He was for thirteen years connected with the South Carolina College, and was an excellent teacher and professor. He had a great fund of knowledge and incident, which he communicated with marked facility to his classes.

He wrote several learned and valuable contributions to the Southern Review. He wrote a lively little novelette, called Thomas Singularity. Although this was a sprightly tale, well written, yet there was much in it which was displeasing to the religious community.

On the 13th of October, 1837, he and his wife were lost at sea, off the coast of North Carolina, in the unfortunate steamer "Home." It is believed he could have escaped, if he had abandoned his wife. Rather than do this, he chose to perish with her. They left an only child, Amelia, now the wife of William McKenzie Parker, Esq.

Mr. Nott was small—under the common size. He was of a lively, cheerful disposition, fond of anecdote, and a companionable man.

At the Bar he was more remarkable for his knowledge of the law, than for his power of impressing that knowledge to the Court or Jury.

He spoke fluently, but without that point and force which is so necessary to make an impression.

It is possible if he had continued longer at the Bar, he might have risen to distinction as a lawyer.

PLEASANT H. MAY.

This gentleman was admitted to the Bar in 1819; moved to Charleston from Chesterfield District, in the year 1824, where he practiced law until 1834–5, when he emigrated to Alabama.

He soon drew public attention, by his fluency as a speaker, and by his early attention to politics. In 1828, he entered warmly upon the political canvass between Mr. Adams and General Jackson, taking side with the former. The writer of this memoir heard him make quite a stirring speech from the steps of the stairs in the Hall of the Court House in Charleston, to a small crowd of Mr. Adams' supporters. This step was unsuccessful, and probably retarded his advancement; not being taken at what might have been a more happy juncture, when the full tide of Jackson's popularity had rolled back, and left his reputation tainted with the Proclamation and Bloody Bill.

Mr. May surprised the audiences of Charleston by a species of elocution, to which, until then, they had not been accustomed. He was a loud, florid, but not unpleasant speaker, though eccentric in his manner of expressing himself, and given to more declamation than was the practice of the city advocates. He had a graceful address, and an agreeable person, fine large eyes, and a voice of much power and beauty of tone. In stature, he was tall, erect, and slim; his face handsome, his forehead broad and intellectual.

In 1834 or '5, he removed to Alabama, and settled at Tuscaloosa, the then capital of the State. He immediately attached himself to the Democratic party, and for several years edited "*The Flag of the Union*," the leading party paper, with ability. In this post, though an ultra State-Rights man, he maintained the Union doctrines, as they were then styled; which were, in other words, the principles of the Jackson party. He was subsequently elected to the Legislature, by the casting vote of the Sheriff; and it was remarked as a singular coincidence, that on several occasions, prominent men in that county had owed their seats to a similar accident. In this office, Mr. May acquitted himself with honor, and bade fair to reach an elevated nich in his party honors, when the opposition, or Whigs, obtained an ascendancy, which the Democrats were never able to reverse. Soon after this event, Mr. May removed to Sumpter, where he had a brother residing, and where he practiced law until his death, which occurred about 1846. He met the melancholy fate of being drowned in the Tombigbee River; having, by accident, fallen from the deck of a steamer.

Mr. May, in the qualities of his heart, was kind and benevolent. Indeed, he was liberal to a fault; for, like too many of the most brilliant minds, he neglected that attention to pecuniary matters, which is so necessary to secure the confidence of mankind. He had great command of language, and was an orator of quite uncommon qualifications. He was not, however, regarded as very stable in opinions. Depending alone upon his natural advantages, he did not pay that attention to books, without which, the most splendid talents cannot be maintained. He was inordinately ambitious of political distinction; and had his genius and capacity for popular oratory been regulated by more discretion, he might have reached, had he lived, the highest rank in his party. His heart, however, was warm, and his disposition social; and those who were most in contest with him in politics, and in times of great bitterness in party issues, never failed to recognize him as a companion, or suffered the pleasantness of intercourse to be interrupted.

His wife was Miss Randolph, of Columbia, South Carolina, who died before he removed from that State. One son was the sole inheritor of his name, who, it is believed, yet lives in Alabama.

JOHN STOBO JAMES.

John Stobo James, Esq., the son of Benjamin James, was born in Stafford County, Virginia, on the 19th of March, 1799. He received the benefit of a good education, and was graduated in the South Carolina College in the Class of 1818. He studied law at Newberry with Judge O'Neall, and was admitted to the Bar in the spring of 1820. He settled at Laurens, and had a good practice from the beginning. In January, 1823, he married Elizabeth, the third daughter of Captain Sampson Pope, of Edgefield. In 1824, he became the partner of his brother-in-law, John B. O'Neall. In December of that year, he was elected Commissioner in Equity for Laurens District, and held that office much to his advantage and credit until 1832, when he declined to be a candidate, and soon after removed from the village of Laurens and settled at his mills on Rabun's Creek.

He lost his wife in August, 1830; four small children, Benjamin S., Sarah, George S., and Helen Maria, were left to his widowed care. One of these, Sarah, in a short time, followed her mother to the grave; the others still survive. After several years of widowhood, he married a second time, and found in Emma Eliza Young, the daughter of James Young, a worthy successor to his first wife. He began the mercantile business at the mills on Rabun's Creek, in Laurens, and failed in 1843 or 1844. He removed to Columbia, and by the aid of his brothers-in-law, John Garlington and John B. O'Neall, he resumed the mercantile business, which he pursued until 1850, when he again failed, much to the injury of his friends. He removed to Charleston, and died in April, 1851, leaving, by his second marriage, his widow and two children, Jane and Belton O'Neall, besides those already mentioned of his first marriage, surviving him.

Mr. James was a good lawyer, spoke well, and might have very well succeeded and realized a fortune in his office, and at the Bar, if he had been content to let "well enough alone;" but, like many another, he grasped at the shadow and lost the substance. His report in Simpson *vs.* Feltz, 1 McC. C. R., 214, is evidence of his knowledge of the law, and of his ability as a Commissioner. Before his death he joined the Presbyterian Church, and died in the hope of a Christian.

Mr. James was a worthy, good man, unfortunate in his life, but entitled to the respect of all who knew him.

LAURENCE E. DAWSON.

This gentleman, the son of John Dawson and Mary Huger, and a native of Charleston, South Carolina, was born in 1799, admitted to the Bar 12th January, 1821, and died in Dallas County, Alabama, in February, 1848, very soon after a removal from his native State, and just when rising to considerable distinction as a lawyer, in that of his adoption.

When the writer of this sketch first saw Mr. Dawson, the latter had been at the Bar about seven years. In person, he bore a remarkable likeness to Keating Lewis Simons; and the circumstance which impressed this resemblance forcibly upon the mind of the reminiscent, was a trial, in which Mr. Dawson greatly distinguished himself. About the year 1828, if the reminiscent does not err, at a Court of Sessions in Charleston, Mr. Petigru, the then Attorney General, was represented by Mr. Dawson. He was conducting a prosecution against a person for excessive cruelty to a slave; and his effort was truly a master-piece of eloquence, distinguished for richness of language, weight and solidity of argument, and a solemnity and vehemence of style, very like that for which Col. Simons, who had so long thundered in the Forum, was noted. The speech made a deep impression at the time, and the reminiscent has never forgotten the effect upon his own feelings, he being then quite a youth.

On the fourth of July of the same year, 1828, Mr. Dawson was the orator of the Revolution Society. His oration was a chaste and dignified composition, full of zeal for the Union, and of advocacy of General Jackson; but warm in the support of those theories in politics which afterwards became fully developed in the doctrine of Nullification. He administered, in the course of his oration, the most just and salutary rebuke to the press, for its general proneness to villify private character for party purposes; and invoked the spirit of the Revolution, to the task of keeping the government pure as it came from the hands of its original architects.

Aside from the representation of Prince William's Parish, in the Legislature, from 1832 to 1835, and from being prominently before the country as the proposed successor of Mr. Grayson for Congress, a nomination for which position Mr. Dawson declined, he was little in political life; having the good sense to see the futility of a service so dependent upon the voice of a changeable mob; so unsatisfactory in its honors and emoluments, and so directly in opposition to the ease and happiness of domestic life; besides which, he preferred the profession in which he had been reared, a success in which can never be obtained, when connected with political strategy.

In 1830, Mr. Dawson left Charleston, and removed to Prince William's Parish. This was not the result of a doubt as to his success in the city; but in the pious wish to gratify his wife with a residence near her parents, who were Dr. Rhodes and Mary, the daughter of Gov. Paul Hamilton. A heavy practice in his new location, particularly in the Court of Chancery, to which Mr. Dawson was much attached, prostrated his health; and, on the advice of his physicians, he abandoned his profession, and sought a more genial residence in St. John's, Berkeley.* In 1842, he removed to Dallas County, Alabama. Mr. Dawson was a pupil of the celebrated Dr. Waddell, in a school which has trained the brightest intellects of South Carolina. He read law successively under Col. William Drayton and Mr. Petigru, then the associate in business of his relative, Gen. James Hamilton.

Mr. Dawson was gifted with a fine manly person. He was tall and well-formed, and possessed of features exceedingly striking and attractive. His manners were at once so graceful, and his general appearance so dignified, that no one could

---

* In Means *vs.* Henry, 2d Hill, 328, Mr. Dawson made the only argument which I ever heard. A short note of it will be found at 329, 330. It was a well-considered effort on a difficult subject, the construction of the will of Thomas Bell, deceased. It carried the Court with him; and, although the decision was subjected to the opposition and witticism of such lawyers as Judge Frost and Mr. Petigru, it was, on a review of the whole subject, in the case of Henry and Talbird *vs.* Archer, Bail, Eq., 534, in the Court of Errors, sustained by a majority of seven, consisting of DeSaussure, Johnson and Harper, Chancellors; and Gantt, Richardson, O'Neall, and Butler, Judges at Law; and has ever since been acquiesced in as settled law.

see him without feeling that he was in the presence of a finished gentleman, in the true sense of the term. When he first appeared before the Supreme Court of Alabama, the Bench and Bar were struck forcibly by his person and address, and the remark was general, "there stands a perfect model of the high-toned, elevated, and accomplished advocate of South Carolina, upon whom seems to have fallen the mantle of Hale and Mansfield."

The language of Mr. Dawson at the Bar, was energetic and lofty; his voice sonorous and manly; his action appropriate and full of authority. He had the rare gift of combining elegance of diction and a flow of melodious and well-rounded periods, the ornaments of speech, with convincing, clear, and perspicuous reasoning.

The school of Bar eloquence, in which Mr. Dawson studied, stands in striking contrast with the thing called oratory in the present time. It may be, that the decline is in the audience, not the orator; for we have the authority of Cicero for saying, that the taste of an audience governs that of the speaker; "for those," says he, "who wish applause, consult the characters and inclinations of those who are to hear them; and accommodate themselves to their several humors and dispositions. However this may be, the difference is quite evident to one who has had the advantage of hearing speakers in both periods; and with what patience, may we again say with Tully, can a Mysian or Phrygian be heard at Athens, where even a Demosthenes, when he condescended to jest, was reproached as a nuisance? Then the orator was on his guard against the slightest indelicacy of expression, against every faulty and distasteful word. The commencement of a speech was ever modest and temperate; the body of it, full of clear, powerful reasoning, addressed to the good sense, not to the prejudices of the hearers. It was in a style, pure and correct; and embellished with those glowing ornaments which, without clouding, give grace, dignity, and eloquence to an oration. Now, orators are generally triflers, full of the antics of the clowns of a circus, whose power consists in thundering forth a volume of corpulent sentences, pregnant with trash and detestable words, uttered in grave tones, unenlighted by a single idea; interspersed with low abuse, or vulgar ribaldry, designed solely to make the common herd laugh. How different from the flimsy whinings of this class, was the energy, pathos, and decorum of the orators, who, as was said by Aristophanes, used to "Thunder and lighten, and throw all Greece into a ferment."

These reflections flow from a recollection of the resemblance of Mr. Dawson's elocution to that of a perfect orator. It is to be regretted that so early in life, before the State of his adoption could be benefited by his talents and example, he was called on to yield to unconquerable death. But in vain do we murmur:

"*Not your family, oh Torquatus, not your eloquence, not your piety, shall restore you. For neither Diana delivers chaste Hyppolitus from infernal darkness, nor is Theseus able to break off the lethean chains from his dear Pirithous.*" —Horace, Book iv., Ode 7.

It is only necessary to add, that Mr. Dawson was long an exemplary member of the Protestant Episcopal Church. That he was an upright, just and public-spirited citizen, and that, as the head of a family, he was at once the light and oracle of a wife and children, who at last are those upon whom falls the heaviest blow. Public honors and public regrets may, for a brief moment, illustrate the obsequies of so wise and virtuous a man; but they cannot assuage the griefs of the survivors at the domestic hearth, to whom time and civic demonstration give no consolation, because they bring no restoration.

JAMES EDWARD HENRY.

James Edward Henry was born in Providence, Rhode Island, on the 8th November, 1796; he lost both his parents when quite young; his father having been killed, while commanding, as captain of an American merchant vessel, in capturing an English vessel, during or preceding the war of 1812. Captain Henry succeeded in making the capture, but lost his life in the engagement.

James Edward Henry migrated to Spartanburg District, South Carolina, in 1816, being then nineteen years of age. Before he left Providence, he came into the possession of his patrimony, and spent it. This I have learned from some of his friends. From others of his friends, I have been told, he lost his patrimony by the insolvency of his father's executor; which is most probable. When he found himself obliged to work, he went into one of the cotton factories of Rhode Island, where he remained but a short time, till he was induced to come to Spartanburg by the Messrs. Weaver, two gentlemen of Rhode Island, who were about erecting a cotton factory in Spartanburg District. He came to Spartanburg at their solicitation, and began business for them; but he was not there long—more than a few weeks—before the neighbors prevailed on him to take charge of a school in the neighborhood. He taught two or three years, then went to school a year (1819) to Mr. Chaney Stone, near Sandy Spring, in Laurens District. Then he taught again one year (1820) near Cross Keys, in Union District, at the same time studying law.

He began the study of law by reading books kindly furnished him by William Hunt, Esq., still living, and at that time practicing law at Spartanburg Court House. After beginning the study of law, and while he was still teaching, he formed the acquaintance of Colonel James Brannon, then residing at Spartanburg, and enjoying a large practice, who was so pleased with Mr. Henry, that he urged him to come to

Spartanburg, to live in his family, and study in his office; which kind offer Mr. Henry accepted, on the termination of his school engagement. From the end of that year (1820) till April following, *i. e.*, to April, 1821—about three months—he was a student in Colonel Brannon's office. He was admitted to the Bar, in April 1821.

Upon his admission, he was associated in partnership, at Spartanburg Court House, with Colonel Patillo Farrow, of Laurens, and with him practiced about four years, when he began to practice by himself. Previous to his admission to the Bar, Mr. Henry, being treated in a way that roused his indignation, gave expression thereto by an open insult to the offender. He was sued for damages, and engaged Colonel Farrow as his counsel; and in the intimate and unreserved relations of counsel and client, Colonel Farrow observed those high traits of character, which not only made him a friend *then*, but in all after-life. And no man was more pleased at Mr. Henry's brightening prospects than his counsel and senior partner, who has often said, that he never knew any lawyer who surpassed Mr. Henry in grasping and clearly presenting the strong points of his case. The friendship thus early formed between Mr. Henry and his senior partner continued on the part of both through life.

In 1821, Mr. Henry was appointed Notary Public by Governor Bennett. In April, 1823, he was licensed to practice in Equity. On 30th January, 1826, he was appointed aid to Major-General J. B. O'Neall; and in same year was an unsuccessful candidate for the Legislature. In 1828, he was again a candidate for Legislature, and was elected.

He was married June 25th, 1828, to Miss Ann Eliza Jones, daughter of General Edmund Jones, of Wilkes County, North Carolina, and had six children: Edmund Jones Henry, Caroline P., wife of James Farrow, Laura Ann, wife of T. Stobo Farrow, James Edward Henry, Eliza Freelove Henry, and Patrick Lenoir Henry. Of these, only the two last named survive; Mrs. Henry having died in 1855.

Mr. Henry, in 1839, joined the Methodist Church, at Spartanburg Court House, with the purpose of connecting himself with the Episcopal Church, in which he had been brought up, should a society of that denomination ever be organized in Spartanburg village; this he did some years afterwards.

In 1846, Mr. Henry, having been for several successive years a Member of the Legislature, announced his purpose of not being a candidate again. He persistently refused all solicitations to change his purpose. But notwithstanding this, and notwithstanding there was no lack of candidates struggling for seats, the people voted in such numbers for Mr. Henry, *nolens volens*, as to elect him the second or third Member out of a delegation of five Representatives. He was so impressed by this generous manifestation of confidence, that he then declared, he would serve as long as the people would elect him. He was again elected in 1848. He died January 28th, 1850, just having finished his second term under the election of 1848, and at the age of fifty-three years.

To the close of his life, he never forgot the kindness of those who had extended to him a generous hand during his various steps in life. For many of the people around the neighborhood where he first located in Spartanburg, he felt, to the close of his life, a strength of attachment, which usually is awarded only to kindred. Towards Landen Miles, Esq., Major William H. Miles, and Miss Polly C. Miles—each of whom in his early life, had shown him marked kindness—he cherished to the last the warmest regard.

Mr. Henry was admitted to the Bar in 1821, and settled down at Spartanburg to practice law. He soon found his deficiency, and read most diligently to remove his defects. He has told me, that he read every case in the sixteen volumes of Johnson's Reports then published. He soon made an impression at the Spartanburg Bar. Between '21 and '25, he wrote a pretty, little novelette, called "Myra Cunningham." This was published by Patrick Carey, at Yorkville, first in his paper, and afterwards in book form. It attracted great attention.

In 1824, I first made the acquaintance of James Edward Henry, and was struck by his lively disposition and his general knowledge. In 1825, I was elected Major-General of the

Fifth Division, and appointed Mr. Henry one of my aids, with the rank of Major. He accompanied me, fall of 1826, in my first review of the division, at York; Colonel Roger's Regiment, at Union; Colonel Beatty's Regiment, near the line of Spartanburg and Union; at McCarter's, Colonel Collins's Regiment; and in Spartanburg District, at Timmons's Old Field, Colonel Brannon's Regiment. Major Henry had no military talent; he had acquired all the benefit which he desired from his appointment. He soon afterwards resigned.

He rose rapidly to eminence and distinction. He was first elected a Member of the House of Representatives in 1828. In 1832, he was a Member, and stood in that glorious minority of Union Members, who withstood all the abuse, which was lavished upon them by the unbridled licentiousness of the press of that day. He, however, knew well the noble, gallant yeomanry upon whom he could fall back at home. He was elected again and again; and, I believe, longer than he chose to offer. In the failure of the Bivingsville Cotton Factory, he sustained a heavy loss His income and estate were diminished, but still he was independent. The rapid growth of Spartanburg village, and the appreciation in value of his property, fully covered his losses. In the course of time, between '36 and '44, he wrote the "Tales of the Pacolet," which were published in, I think, the "Magnolia;" they were full of humor, and calculated to please the readers of light literature.

Major Henry was a most delightful companion; his conviviality was, perhaps, the cause of his greatest misfortune.

He was an excellent lawyer. He has often stood before me, both on the Circuit and in the Court of Appeals; and there were few, very few, who managed or argued their cases better. Indeed, before a Jury of Spartanburg, it required all the weight of a Judge in whom they had confidence, to keep the scales of justice fairly balanced. He was a speaker of great force and effect. His rapidity of utterance never was checked by his want of ideas. He poured an incessant stream of words, conveying knowledge in every sentence, until he exhausted his subject. I have often listened with delight, and, at the same time, in amazement, at his matchless efforts. My amazement arose from my knowledge of his early history. He stood before me, the child of genius, who had broken the net of poverty, and who was soaring, like the lark, higher and higher, towards the sun-light of glory. Oh, that he could have lived, and had never known that which makes the strong man weak; then, indeed, he would have been the first among Carolina's sons. But the wish is vain; he lies in the Spartanburg village cemetery, surrounded by his wife and children, cut down soon, alas! too soon, by the fell destroyer. His early death was and is mourned, by all who knew him, and by no one more than by him who was his friend in early life, who again and again pointed him to the dangers with which he was beset, and who to-day drops a tear, and plucks a laurel to lay upon his tomb.

"Major Henry was a great lover of books, a hard student, and, consequently, a man of extensive reading, not only in reference to his profession, but generally. His library was well furnished with the best religious, historical, political and miscellaneous works, to which he devoted the whole of his time when not engaged in the active duties of his profession. Major Henry seemed from his youth to have had fixed habits of study. He gave his attention exclusively to books, having no avocation but his profession for a living. For many years, when engaged in the work of rearing and educating a young and interesting family, he was rarely to be seen but in his office or in the domestic circle, never on the side-walks, and in the long piazzas amid the loafers and blackguards who infest these common places of daily meeting. Major Henry deserved, among the literary men of his day, a high rank; in his own district he stood at the head of the list; he wrote much for the newspapers of his day; his "Tales of the Pacolet," founded in fiction, and published some thirty years since, were much admired. He was a constant and thorough reader of the Bible for many years before he made profession of religion, and often enriched his conversation and pleadings at the Bar, and other public addresses, with beautiful and appropriate quotations from its sacred pages. I knew him for more than twenty-five years; formed his acquaintance when he was a young man, young in years, young in his profession; wedded but a few short years before to a young but cultivated wife. Two "little ones," the fruits of his youthful marriage, then enlivened his domestic circle, and stimulated his energies to extensive usefulness and future greatness. I first met him at church, where I continued to meet him constantly to the day of his death.

As an intellectual man, Major Henry ranked foremost in his district, and among the first in the State. He was a close-thinker, a forcible reasoner, and remarkable for the ingenuity and dexterity with which he managed his subject. He possessed a supple ready mind. I should think he might have been justly styled a *genius*. With his splendid imagination, and his sparkling witicisms, he never failed to interest his auditory in his public addresses, and to delight his friends in the social circle.

Major Henry's political career was brilliant at times, but always stormy, and attended oftentimes with very unpleasant annoyances to him. He commenced public political life in the exciting days of Nullification, took a prominent stand on the Union side of the question, and confronted his opponents everywhere successfully, but amidst a shower of personal abuse. Being a native of the New England States, he was everywhere, by his bitter political enemies, denounced as a "Yankee" often to his face. This to one of his refined and sensitive feelings was a source of constant irritation, and led to hostility and bitterness between himself and certain leading men of the opposite party, which time could never wholly erase. The Smiths and himself were never reconciled. They could never stand before him in argument and fair discussion, and consequently took revenge in denouncing him as a Yankee.

These political differences, springing up from time to time, contributed much to embitter his feelings, and, doubtless, laid the foundation of habits of intemperance, so much deplored by his friends, in the after part of his life. Although the people were always on his side, and sustained him often with heavy majorities, and once elected him at the head of the ticket without his announcing himself a candidate, and without his knowledge of such intention till a day or two before the election came off. Still it would have been better for him if, like his friend, Mr. Bobo, he had never known politics. Had he confined himself to the cultivation of his literary taste, and to his profession, he would have proved himself a better and a greater man.

His services in the Legislature were valuable, and his career a brilliant one. I might rehearse some incidents in his political life, but they were generally of an unpleasant nature, and would involve names that prudence would suppress.

In the year 1839, during a protracted meeting of fourteen days' continuance, Major Henry professed religion, and united with the Methodist Church, declaring that he yielded to the preference of his wife, who, at the same time, connected herself with this church. He continued steadfast as a Christian, and remained a Methodist for some years; during which time he read the Scriptures, and theological works, extensively; expressing to his friends, privately, his growing dislike to the government of the Methodist Church. This led to a coolness between him and its members; and finally ended in his withdrawal from the church.

After this period, which was but a few years, not exceeding three or four, I suppose, before his death, the habit of which we have spoken, seemed to grow on him; and his friends became anxious for his safety; still, all the time, he professed to be a religious man, and to live under religious restraints. A disease of the bronchial organs, which had seated itself in the mean time, (which may have been aggravated, too, by the habits of which we have spoken,) continued to grow and afflict him more and more, till the close of the session of the Legislature, I think, in 1851 or '2; he returned home from this session but to spend a few brief days in the midst of his family. His disease spread rapidly; and soon his friends were summoned to his bed-side to witness his sufferings and his manly battle with the monster, death. His servant came to me with a note from Mrs. Henry, stating that her husband desired to see me at my earliest convenience; residing some miles in the country, I reached his house late the same night, and inquired for his health and wishes; it was clearly to be seen that he was on his death-bed. He said, that he had sent for me—that our friendship extended back for many years—that he had made me his confidant—that he was dying—could never rise again—that he had a request to make of me. That was: that I should say to his friends, and all that might wish to know, that I had seen him in the dying hour, and that he departed this life in the faith of the Son of God. Said he, be kind enough to mention this from the pulpit: that you saw Major Henry die in the faith of the Son of God. This I determined not to do, unless I should be able, from subsequent conversations with him, to satisfy my own mind, that he had an intelligent understanding of his condition. I immediately inquired of him as to his enemies; his feelings toward them, and his contrition for his sins, his love to Christ, &c.; and found him, as I think, to be a true penitent at the foot of the Cross; forgiving all his enemies, and expressing his deep regret and sorrow for his sins, and firm confidence of his acceptance through the blood of Christ. I have complied often with his dying request, both in the pulpit and to his many inquiring friends.

Major Henry was a true friend to his friends; bitter to his enemies, but never wantonly provoked enmity; was a gentleman, in a strict sense of the word; would have had but few occasions for strife or enmity, if others had been in this respect like himself.

Spartanburg District owes much to Major Henry, for its present high state of prosperity in manufactories and education. He was an early and able advocate for both; and furnished much valuable information to those engaged in the making of iron and nails, and to the various establishments for making cotton yarn and cloth. He contributed from the first, and to the end of his life, his whole influence to the support and upbuilding of the Limestone Springs High

School. Two of his daughters graduated in this school with the first distinction.

He died, leaving a comfortable living to his wife and six children, which he acquired by an assiduous application to his profession. A few brief years have laid by his side, in death, his faithful wife and four of their children; two only survive them—Freelove and Patrick, a lovely daughter and son.

He began life poor; procured a good English, and limited classical education, near Cross-Aukre, Spartanburg District South Carolina.

Major Henry came to the South when a boy, was an orphan; his mother, a widow and a member of the Baptist Church, died before he left the North; was a self-made man; sought and carved out his fortune in a strange land, without any means, save those furnished by the Great Father of the fatherless, and those which his own energy and industry brought to his aid."

(The foregoing, beginning with "Major Henry was a great lover of books," is from the pen of the Rev. John G. Landrum, of Spartanburg District, South Carolina, his intimate friend and confidant.)

WILLIAM CAMPBELL PRESTON.

Owing to the circumstance that his father was in attendance as a Member of the Congress of 1794, Wm. Campbell Preston was born in the City of Philadelphia, on the 27th of December of that year.

"His paternal grandfather was the Lieutenant-Colonel Commanding in Augusta County, Virginia, during the Revolution, and afterwards of the militia from the Blue Ridge to the Ohio River. His mother was the only child of Colonel Campbell, of King's Mountain celebrity; her mother was the sister of Patrick Henry."

This is a statement of a noble ancestry, and from it we should expect heroic bearing and unrivalled eloquence. The expectation is fully verified in the youth, manhood and old age of the subject of this sketch. His early education seems to have been under very competent teachers.

It seems that his matriculation in the South Carolina College was purely accidental. Owing to anticipations of diseased lungs, he was started with a trusty servant to Florida. Reaching Columbia, he was induced, by the persuasion of young men with whom he then became acquainted, and with the consent of his attendant, to enter that institution. Accordingly, on the 25th of September, 1809, then in his fifteenth year, he entered the Sophomore Class. In February, 1811, I entered the Junior Class, of which Colonel Preston was a member, and our acquaintance, then commenced, has ever since continued.

Colonel Preston was then remarkable for his powers as an extemporaneous speaker. I have heard him in college, at the Bar, in the State Legislature, and on many other occasions during his public life, and I confess, as to mere oratory, I think he was, in college boyhood, as perfect a speaker as he was in after life. He afterwards acquired more knowledge, more powers of argumentation, but he never exceeded himself in his youthful displays of eloquent declamation. He was an orator by nature; the subsequent additions of art did not add to his brilliancy; they often marred his otherwise matchless declamation.

He graduated in December, 1812, and received the third distinction of his class, in company with Whitfield Brooks, James R. Massey and Arthur H. O'Hara.

In the spring of 1813, he entered the office of William Wirt, of Richmond, as a student at law. His father, at the approach of summer, dispatched him, on horse-back, to the "far West." He made, in a tour of seven months, four thousand miles through Tennessee, Kentucky, Ohio, Indiana, Illinois and Missouri, and thus acquired physical strength, and stored his mind with incidents and imagery, useful in after-life.

After the close of the war of 1812, probably about 1817, Colonel Preston visited Europe to complete his education. In the course of his sojourn *there*, he met his college acquaintance, Hugh S. Legaré, of South Carolina, and made the acqaintance of many other eminent men. He stored his mind with knowledge, both by observation of all which was remarkable in the Old World, and also by the books and the literary men of that day.

He returned to the United States in 1819, and was soon afterwards married, in Missouri, to that beautiful and excellent lady, Miss Maria Coalter, to whom he had become attached while in College. He was admitted to the Bar in Virginia in 1820; but he and his wife, both preferring Columbia, South Carolina, as a residence, he removed to that city in 1822, and was in that year admitted to the Bar in Columbia. In the fall of that year he was elected a Trustee of the South Carolina College. In 1829 and in 1843, he was also elected. In 1851, after he ceased to be president, he was elected a Member of the Board of Trustees. He was, in 1853, re-elected by the Legislature. In 1857 he declined an election, and thus dissolved his connection with the College.

In 1822, he became the partner of D. J. McCord. Esq., then the Law Reporter of South Carolina, and who had considerable practice. This introduced him at once to the notice and knowledge of the people; and, when once heard, he needed no helping-hand to carry him forward.

His speech in the Senate, in the case of the contested election of Crafts by General Geddes, I do not remember.

In 1823, Harper and Preston were heard before the House of Representatives against the unfavorable report of the Committee on Claims on the petition of Asa Delozier. His speech, although producing no result in favor of the claim, was remarkable for its eloquence and argument.

In January, 1828, he defended Judge James before the Senate on the articles of impeachment voted against him by the House of Representatives. His speech was a great effort to save the poor old man; but truth and justice were mightier than eloquence or pity. The Judge was convicted and removed from office. Mr. Preston wrote the beautiful address of Judge James when called to the Bar of the Senate for sentence. It will be found in the sketch of Judge James. It is a perfect gem, radiant with eloquence, and full of claims for sympathy in behalf of the venerable sufferer.

For over forty years I have been in the Courts of Appeal as a lawyer or a Judge. I have heard all the great advocates of South Carolina, and I am sure I have heard as fine legal arguments from Colonel Preston as from any other. His argument in Myers *vs.* Myers, 2d McC. C. R., 219, will serve as a specimen, which can be consulted. His argument for McLemore, 2d Hill, 680, is not reported, except by the citation of his authorities. They will show his research; but his speech was unrivalled in argument and eloquence.

His circuit speeches, especially in criminal cases, were unsurpassed. His defence of Fleming, for the murder of Barkley, Sheriff, of Fairfield, both in tact, ability, and eloquence, deserves all praise. He selected, contrary to all that was or is usual, the most intelligent men on the panel for his jury. It was a plain case of *murder;* yet, notwithstanding, a capital argument by Solicitor Player, and the weight of my authority as the presiding Judge, he obtained a verdict of manslaughter. In 1829, he was elected to the House of Representatives of the State. In 1829, he lost his excellent wife, who left an only child, a daughter.

In 1830 and 1832, he was returned to the House of Representatives. In 1830 or 1831, he fortunately replaced the wife of his youth by the amiable, beautiful, well-informed and accomplished lady, Miss Penelope Davis, the second daughter of Dr. James Davis, of Columbia.

In 1836, he was elected to the Senate of the United States, where he further distinguished himself as an orator and statesman. Differing from the State, as to her support of Mr. Van Buren's policy as President of the United States, he resigned his place as Senator in Congress in 1839 or 1840, and returned to the Bar.

Shortly afterwards he lost his only child, Miss Sally Preston, a beautiful and accomplished girl, just budding into womanhood. This was a crushing blow to my old friend and class-mate. I sympathized with him deeply, and our difference in political views was thereby completely blotted out. In 1845, I nominated him for the Presidency of his Alma Mater, the South Carolina College, and had the pleasure to see him elected with great unanimity.

He entered upon the duties of his office in January, 1846, with great eclat and universal confidence. The College sprang forward from its lethargy; its walls were crowded with students. The president was known to be an extraordinary man. All who could receive the benefit of his instruction were eager to do so. Many a young man, as in the days of Dr. Maxcy, caught the enthusiasm of their gifted instructor. Eloquence was no longer regarded as not worthy of note or pursuit. The young learned to speak from the daily example of the first of orators. That he was able and capable to teach clearly and satisfactorily the subjects committed to his chair, is fully shown in Dr. Laborde's History of the college.

His failing health compelled him to resign, which he did in November, 1851. Never was a resignation received with more regret by the Board of Trustees.

Soon after he lost his admirable wife. It seemed as if

he, too, must cease to be numbered among the sons of men. But God in his mercy spared him, and gave him a portion of health, which still enables him to do good.

He established the Columbia Athenæum, and made a donation of his library of about three thousand volumes.

This admirable institution, of which he is the head as President, is calculated to afford information by lectures and by the opportunity of consulting its library.

Thus this benevolent and great man, as a closing benefit to Columbia, opened to her people the rich resources of knowledge.

It is their duty to honor his name and reverence his person while he yet lives, and to make his evening happy as his morning and mid-day were glorious.

EDWARD S. COURTENAY.

The subject of this brief notice was born at Charleston, South Carolina, July 11th, 1795; admitted to the Law Bar, May 14th, 1823; to the Equity Bar, November 23d, 1825; and died at the residence of his son, in Charleston, October 5th, 1857. He was of Protestant Irish descent, from a family of consideration and respectability in the North of Ireland.

His father, Edward Courtenay, was the son of Edward Courtenay, Esq., of Newry, County Armagh, Province of Ulster, who intermarried with Miss Carlisle, of the same place. They were the parents of a large family, two of whom, Edward and John, came to America in 1789.

Edward settled in Charleston, where, in 1793, he married Miss Lydia Smith, of Newburyport, Massachusetts. He died at Savannah, August 4th, 1807, while on a visit to that place, in the thirty-fourth year of his age, leaving a widow and six children, the eldest of whom, Edward Smith, had just completed his twelfth year.

They were left in narrow circumstances, at a period of our history, when the opportunity for acquiring education, except to the wealthy, was far more restricted than at present. We find, however, that the eldest son had, at the age of nineteen years, so successfully struggled with the pressure of adversity, that he was elected to the mastership of one of the public schools of the city—a position which he continued to hold with great credit to himself and usefulness to the public, until he was admitted to the Bar in 1823.

As a teacher many still remember him with gratitude, who, in their own persons, bear testimony to his fidelity and success, in that honorable and responsible vocation.

He had previously, in 1821, intermarried with Miss Elizabeth S. Wade, a native of New York, who, with four sons, still survive him.

While his livelihood was thus secured by his labors as a

teacher, his own education was not neglected; his preparation for the Bar was prosecuted under the direction of B. F. Pepoon, Esq., and accomplished in the twenty-eighth year of his age.

Immediately on his admission to the Bar, he entered upon the practice of his profession, but continued to devote several hours each day to teaching in McCullough's then flourishing grammar school.

Mr. Courtenay continued at the Bar about ten years, and with every prospect of a successful career, during the first seven years of his devotion to it. He was commissioned and acted as one of the Magistracy in Charleston, under the old system, and his professional labors were mostly devoted to magisterial duties, to office business, and to practice in the criminal courts. If we may judge of him as an advocate in the defence of criminal causes, by his forensic efforts outside the profession, which are alone preserved to us, the traditions of his success are well sustained.

About 1827, commenced the great political contest in South Carolina, which culminated in 1832 and 1833, and which, for earnestness and intensity, has never since the Revolution been exceeded in this country. Mr. Courtenay's warm and earnest temperament did not permit him to remain neutral. Indeed, neutrality, where there was intelligence, or position, or spirit, was unknown. There was no neutrality. Every man took his stand on one side or the other. Mr. Courtenay's natural position seemed to be with the Union party, and there he found himself — though others, whose political faith had previously been entirely in harmony with his own, identified themselves with the dominant party in favor of the Nullification doctrine.

This contest, and the great public depression and changes it was working, seems to have called back Mr. Courtenay's attention to his early and happier pursuits. He again became a teacher, and for a time with great success, at the head of a large and flourishing private school. But it was not a time when the school-room, any more than the forum, could shut out political influences; and the necessity of a fixed and certain income to provide for the education of a rising family, at length induced him to accept an office under the Federal Government, in the Custom-House, which he held till within a short time of his death, when a stroke of paralysis confined him to his chamber.

In political faith, Mr. Courtenay was a Federalist of the truest stamp. He never for a moment swerved from his faith or its avowal, no matter what the consequence, or what others might think. From 1807, when he was a boy of twelve years, to 1815, was just the period when political discussion would make its enduring impression upon an ingenuous and youthful mind. It was, too, the most remarkable juncture in the history of our own country since the Revolution—the times of the Embargo and of the War of 1812; in the history of the Old World, it was the period of the zenith and the fall of the French Empire—of the great and wonderful genius, its founder.

The great men who had made for themselves great names in the American Revolution, adhered in those days mostly to the Federalist side. It is not to be wondered at, that a youth like young Courtenay, impulsive, and full of glowing sentiment, should not only adopt the doctrines of such men, but should also embalm them and their teachings in his memory, with all the idolatry of a first love.

But among the men of that day, no one seems more to have fixed his admiration, than William Crafts, Jr. Mr. Crafts was his senior by about ten years. They were members of the same profession, and of the same political faith and party. Upon the occasion of his death, in 1826, Mr. Courtenay was selected to speak his eulogy. The manner in which he performed this labor of love, is on record. It is almost the only, if not the only evidence of his style as a forensic speaker, which has been preserved, and it is well worthy of preservation. If the space were allowable, we would insert it entire, for the sake of the memories of Mr. Courtenay, whom we knew and loved, and of Mr. Crafts, whom we did not know, but of whom tradition has impressed the generation that succeeded him with a wonderful love and admiration. We venture upon an extract, which at this time is especially attractive, in consequence of the great good that has lately been accomplished by the zeal and devotion of a few men, to the very cause in which the orator portrays his friend as a laborer and pioneer.

"Notwithstanding," says the eulogist, "the unpopularity of his political opinions, he was several times elected to a seat in the General Assembly of his native State. In this situation he rendered important services to his constituents. He was early distinguished for his love of letters, and omitted no opportunity of disseminating a love of learning among the people. He felt, to use his own language, that 'knowledge was the life's blood of republics and free governments.' That the eagle was the bird of light as well as of liberty. In the Legislature, he always advocated every measure which had for its object the encouragement of scientific and literary institutions. At a period when a short-sighted policy, aided by a parsimonious spirit, would have abolished the free-school system of the State, and left the children of the poor to all those innumerable miseries and crimes, which are the almost certain consequences of ignorance, Mr. Crafts undertook the defence, and in a speech replete with eloquence and good sense, depicted in glowing terms the blessings of knowledge to a State, and the curses entailed upon it by the ignorance of its citizens. He was successful: humanity and good sense triumphed over a narrow-minded policy, which would have weighed the true wealth of the State—the intellect and moral character of the rising generation—with the gold and silver which fill its coffers.

His friends might rest his character for usefulness as a legislator on this one fact; for if, in ancient days, he who saved the life of a single citizen, was deemed worthy of the civic wreath, to what is he not entitled, who, by his eloquence and zeal, preserved to thousands that means of moral life, without which man is little better than the brute on which he banquets; the prey of appetites and passions that degrade him in the scale of, creation, which unfit him for usefulness, and make him a burden to himself, and, too often, a curse to the State. If gratitude be not an imaginary virtue, while the free schools remain in existence, they will be identified with the name of Crafts: his memory will long be cherished by the thousands who have, and the tens of thousands who shall hereafter participate in the blessings they impart."

The man who spoke thus was gifted with the power of just and elevated thinking, and with a scope and grace of language to express his thoughts, sufficient to have insured high professional and forensic position. The whole production is equal to, and, in some parts, rises above this specimen of his powers of thought and language.

Mr. Courtenay's religious opinions settled down in an adherence to the doctrines and discipline of the "Methodist Episcopal Church," in the full communion of which he lived and died. But there was no sectarianism in the ample folds of his noble and flowing Christian heart. The charity of his soul was only circumscribed by the numbers of the human race. He was an active and devoted servant of the Master he loved, at Trinity Church, Hasel-street, Charleston, where his mortal remains are buried. The teachers and pupils of the Sunday school where he labored, asked and obtained from his family permission to erect a monument to his memory. There it stands, a simple and truthful witness to the affection he had inspired by his efforts and usefulness, where the precepts of the Gospel were most likely to influence a true judgment of his character.

In his personal figure, he was above the middle stature, and his bearing was commanding and courteous. Genial in his feelings, full of kindness in his manner to all who approached him, he bore the trials of life, which were neither few nor light, with patience and resignation—leaving a memory most cherished by those who knew him best. His name survives, and is worthily represented by his sons. One of his brothers, the late Professor James Carlisle Courtenay, of the Charleston College, died, unmarried, several years since, greatly lamented for his private virtues, and for his devotion to the cause of science, having been one of the earliest advocates for the establishment of the present "National Observatory." Another brother, of remarkable promise, died young. The Hon. Edward Courtenay Bullock, of Eufaula, Barbour County, Ala., is the son of one sister. Col. Charles Courtenay Tew, of the Hillsboro', North Carolina, Military Institute, is the son of another.

The writer of this humble attempt to rescue Mr. Courtenay's name from the mists and oblivion with which the unceasing work of time enshrouds all things, performs a grateful duty to the memory of a friend, gone before, who loved and served him with a zeal that would not cease when he ceased to live, but descended, with his last blessing, to those who received his dying sigh and inherited his name.

HENRY GRIMKÉ.

He was the youngest son of Judge John Faucheraud Grimké and Mary Smith, his wife; he was born 3d January, 1801, in the City of Charleston, and was educated there until he entered the South Carolina College, where he graduated in December, 1818. (He is entered in the college catalogue as Henry W. Grimké.)

He studied law in the office of his distinguished brother, Thomas Smith Grimké, and was admitted to the bar, in Charleston, on the 10th of January, 1823.

He was the partner of his brother, Thomas Smith Grimké, until his death, in 1834. In 1829 he married Selma T. Simons, of St. Paul's Parish, who died in 1843.

Mr. Grimké, both before and after his brother's death, enjoyed an extensive and lucrative practice in the city, together with some in the country.

In 1847, he retired from the practice in order to manage his agricultural interests in St. Paul's Parish. On the 28th September, 1852, he fell a victim to country fever. Three children, a son and two daughters, survived him.

Mr. Grimké was as firm a man as ever I saw at the bar. He was often opposed to Colonel Hunt, and very often compelled him to yield some arrogant assertion to the firm, unyielding manner which he (Mr. Grimké) presented.

Mr. Grimké was a man of uniform good humor. He was a good lawyer, and managed some very important insurance cases with great ability.

In the cases of Joseph Cohen, Jr., *vs.* The Fire and Marine Insurance Company, Desaussure, 147; Oliver Simpson, *vs.* The Same, Desaussure, 239; he conducted the defence with distinguished ability against his friend, the greatest lawyer in the city, James L. Petigru, Esq.

Mr. Grimké was a virtuous man and good citizen. He made no effort at distinction, though, I think, he was a Major in the militia, and had great reputation in his military capacity. In the State *vs.* Henry Grimké, 3d Hill, 17, it was decided, that his service, as a militia officer for seven years, did not exempt him, under the Act of '94, from further service.

A life of fifty-one years, spent generally in private life, presents very few points on which remarks can be made. But notwithstanding the paucity of illustrations, such a life cannot be permitted to rest in the silence of the grave. For virtue, though unadorned by brilliancy, must be remembered by all those who lived with or after him, both with respect and veneration.

THOMAS HARRISON.

This gentleman was a native either of Greenville, or of Pendleton, before its division. After diligent inquiry, I have been unable to ascertain his birth-place, or anything about his early life. He must have had a good education at the academies in the upper districts. He studied law and was admitted to the Bar; but when, does not appear; his name is not on the roll of attorneys. He married a daughter of Gen. John B. Earle, and was a Member of the House of Representatives, in the General Assembly of South Carolina, in 1822 and 1823, where he was remarkable for his quick perception of a subject, and his able exposition of it.

About this time he argued in the Constitutional Court, Means *vs.* Moore, *et al,* (Harper's Rep., 314; 3d McC., 282.) The questions arose upon the will of Gen. Moore, of Spartanburg. The main one was, whether erasures and interlineations with a pencil, with the view of having prepared for execution another will, was a revocation? Two Juries, at successive terms, found for the revocation, and against the will. The Court set the verdicts aside, thus deciding in favor of Mr. Harrison. In Maverick *vs.* Lewis & Gibbes, (3d McC. R., 211,) he discussed learnedly the question, what is a lease? His argument at (p. 214) is very well reported, and will show his powers as a lawyer.

His difficulty of hearing, which was approaching deafness, made him soon withdraw from professional business, and seek other employment.

He was elected Treasurer of the Upper Division in, I believe, 1826, and served for four years. When elected to this office, against the remonstrance of his friends, he determined to perform the duties in person. The duties of that office had been, and since have been, often performed by deputies. He thought this a violation of the Constitution; he said to his friends, "I must go to Columbia, and personally conduct the office, or I will resign." His friends ceased to urge him in the matter; whether he removed his family or not, I do not remember, but he certainly conducted his official duties in person.

He was Comptroller-General, as appears by his reports in 1830, 1831 and 1832. They evince great capability for that office.

He was elected Cashier of the Branch Bank at Columbia, and performed the duties for a short period, when he resigned and sought the enjoyments of his home in Anderson District.

There he closed his life by his own hand. This was the result of mental alienation. He survived several days, was able to discourse sensibly, and stated the mental delusion under which he was laboring, and which led to the sad act. He probably would have recovered, but his malady recurred, and he refused to suffer a particle of nourishment to enter his body; he died, as I have understood, from voluntary starvation.

Thus perished, in the meridian of his days, an eminent lawyer, a perfectly pure and amiable man.

He was sober and temperate in all things; was a firm, conscientious man, a good officer and citizen, a faithful and devoted husband, an affectionate father, and, in all the other relations of life, above exception.

N. L. GRIFFIN.

Nathan Lipscomb Griffin, the son of Richard and Mary Griffin, was born in the neighborhood of White Hall, Abbeville District, on the 9th of February, 1803. He had the benefit of a good academical education, principally obtained at Church Hill, in the lower part of his native district.

He began the study of the law in the office of Judge Whitner, at Cambridge, (formerly old Ninety-Six.) In the year 1823, he removed to Edgefield, and placed himself in the office of A. P. Butler, Esq. In February, 1824, he was admitted to the Bar, and established himself, as a practicing lawyer, at Edgefield. On the 18th of May, 1824, he was married to Miss Anna Butler, a daughter of Stanmore Butler, Esq. About the year 1826, he entered into co-partnership with his legal instructor, Mr. Butler, and so continued until the elevation of the latter to the Bench of South Carolina. He subsequently formed a partnership with Armstead Burt, Esq., which continued until Mr. Burt became a Member of the House of Representatives, in Congress. Mr. Griffin then did what he ought to have done before, relied on his own powers, and showed that he was not only an office lawyer, but capable of managing and arguing his cases in Court. His friend, who pens this memoir, heard him first, with great delight, in a capital case, which he had much at heart, and in which he saved his client from a conviction of murder, by a verdict of manslaughter. Ever after that he maintained a standing, fully equal to that of the first, at the Edgefield Bar: success generally attending him.

In August, 1831, he joined the Baptist Church, at Edgefield, and was soon after set apart as one of the deacons. His walk and conversation, as a Baptist, was of the most exemplary character.

He joined, also, the ranks of the Tetotallers, and as a temperance man, illustrated the example of total abstinence favorably before the people.

In 1838, he was first elected to the House of Representatives, in the General Assembly. His course, as a legislator, was one which challenged the respect of every other member.

In 1846, he was elected Senator, from Edgefield, and in 1850 he was re-elected. In this high legislative position he was an uniformly active and useful member.

As a church member, he made himself particularly useful, by taking charge of the negroes, for which purpose the church, at his suggestion, was opened every Sunday afternoon. This duty he cheerfully, nay, even gladly performed. For he often said, that he experienced more pleasure from it than from any other duty which devolved upon him.

Thus honored and useful, his life drew early to its close. On the 16th of February, 1853, having, by a few days, completed his fiftieth year, he died, leaving a widow and eight children. The annunciation of this sad event created more general and heartfelt sorrow than is usual. High and low, rich and poor, bond and free, united in the universal wail. For he was loved and honored by all who knew him.

After a lapse of six years, and turning back over his life, little can be found to blame, and much, very much to praise. As a lawyer he triumphed, by untiring industry, over a defective education, and by a punctuality, which was unwavering, and a devotion to business, which was unceasing, he obtained, and held to the day of his death, the confidence of a larger number of clients than any member of the Edgefield Bar.

As a man, he had the respect of all who knew him. For his word was truth, and his life honesty itself. As a citizen, he might have been carried forward by a party to the adoption of mistakes in politics, but yet his forbearance made him not even obnoxious to violent party condemnation. No one ever doubted the purity of his principles, and the patriotic devotion of his heart.

As a husband, father, and master, none but those who knew him in that sacred circle of home can form a just estimate. It may, however, be said, that, weighed in the balances, he was not found wanting in any of these respects. His noble, high, and spiritually-minded widow, still lives, and cherishes his memory with that enduring affection which looks forward, evermore, to that blissful re-union beyond the grave, to which he pointed on his dying bed.

In fine, as a friend and brother, I would say of Nathan L. Griffin, few men deserved more of the affection of men *here;* and few could look forward beyond the grave with a more certain hope of everlasting happiness.

B. F. PORTER.

This gentlemen was born in the City of Charleston, South Carolina, in September, 1808, two doors north of Market-Street, on the west side of Meeting-Street, where, in 1850, Miller's bakery was standing. He was a weak and sickly child from his birth, and grew up without any education, except such as his mother could give.

He was the son of Benjamin R. Porter and his wife, Elizabeth Fickling. His father was born in Bermuda, and at the age of ten years, ran away from his grandfather, Benjamin Richardson, of Hamilton, Bermuda, and hid himself, with a stock of bread and cheese, under the yawl of a Yankee vessel bound for Charleston. He made the voyage successfully, and on his arrival, found a friend in Mr. Marshall, a cabinet maker, to whom he bound himself as an apprentice, and served out his full time.

Judge Porter's paternal grandfather, Colonel John Porter, married Alice, the daughter of Mr. Benjamin Richardson. He was an Irishman, and removed from Pennsylvania to Poughkeepsie, New York, thence to Charleston. After the death of his first wife, he was married a second time to Miss Cox, and with her he lived at Mar's Bluff, till his migration to the west. One of his daughters married Dr. Haynesworth, of Sumter; and a son, John, was killed at the battle of New Orleans.

Judge Porter states he was admitted to the Bar, in Charleston, in 1826, through the influence of the Hon. William Crafts, Jr. On referring to the rolls, in Charleston, I find that B. F. G. Porter, whom I suppose to be the same person as Judge Porter, was admitted to the Bar, 22d November, 1825. He was then only in his eighteenth year, but he states he was under the belief that he was of full age. His mother had concealed his age from him.

In the year 1826, he lost his father, and to support himself, his mother and sisters, he wrote in the office of George B. Eckhard, Esq., till the fall of 1828, when he took his budget on his back, and started for Chesterville. "Years," he says, "will not efface that first parting from home, humble as it was, when my dear pious old mother concealed, in broken accents, her grief; and my two sisters, (one of whom I was destined to see no more,) seized my hair, and cut two locks from it to remind them of the absent only son of the household."

In Chester, he became the partner of Robert Clendenin, Esq., and practiced there till the fall of 1830, when he removed to Monroe County, Alabama. Just before his removal, he married, Eliza, the daughter of Captain John Kydd, of Beckhamsville, in Chester District.

On his removal to Alabama, he had, he says, "fifty cents in his pocket. He had previously studied medicine, under Dr. Thomas Legaré, of Charleston," and finding this the only means of obtaining a living for his family, he obtained a license as an M. D., and practiced for a year.

In 1831, finding a South Carolinian indicted for murder, at Claiborne, he volunteered for his defence. James Dellett, Esq., an eminent lawyer, heard Mr. Porter's speech, and at its close, came to him and said: "Throw your pill-boxes to the devil, and come into my office." He did so, and continued with him until he removed to Tuscaloosa, in 1835, after his election as Reporter of the Supreme Court.

In 1832, he was elected to the Legislature, from Monroe County, and served as such until his election as reporter, in 1835. In 1840, he was again a member, I presume from Tuscaloosa, when he was elected a Judge. He only retained this office until the end of the year, when he resigned in consequence of "some doubts," as he says, "of the constitutionality of his election, he being, at the time of his election, a Member." He was a Whig, and the objection was less for the integrity of the Constitution, than his politics. "After my resignation," he says, "a subservient Supreme Court overruled its own decision, and declared my election void. It was a sacrifice to the rancor of political rage."

Judge Porter says, that in 1838, he had saved ten thousand

dollars, which he invested in the Planter's and Merchant's Bank of Mobile, and lost it all. In 1848, on his way to Washington, he had his leg badly broken, and in consequence of that injury, remained at Cave Spring, Georgia, until 1850. He was advised by his friends to return to Charleston, which he did. In May, 1850, I came to know Judge Porter. He was one of those concerned in the defence of Davenport, charged with the murder of a lady, by the administration of ergot to produce abortion. He made the second speech for the prisoner, and it seemed to me to be fully equal to what might have been expected, from his great reputation. The evidence was wholly insufficient to convict the prisoner, and after a tedious trial, he was acquitted. At the same term, and subsequently, at the January term, 1851, of the Court of Appeals, Judge Porter, with his friend, Mr. Yeadon, argued the case of the State *ex relatione*, Ravenel, Brothers & Co., James Welsman, James Chapman, Gourdin, Matthiessen & Co., *vs.* the City Council, 4 Richardson, 286. Here, again, both on the circuit and in the Court of Appeals, his arguments were everything which could be said, in a case, where the law was plainly against him.

I believe these two cases were the only occasions in which I ever had the opportunity of hearing and knowing Judge Porter, of whom I then formed a high opinion, both as a lawyer and gentleman. I then hoped he might find it to be his interest to make Charleston his permanent home, but it seems that his friends had promised more than they could effect. The business promised and expected did not come. His means were not sufficient to justify him in remaining in the city of his birth, and he returned to Alabama, where he has since been successfully pursuing his profession.

"The fourteen volumes of Alabama Reports," which he says, he "prepared in manuscript himself," are a work of which any man may be proud.

The Judge is very much a self-made man. He says, "in the intervals of professional employment, I have studied every branch of the sciences and philosophy. I have become a fair Latin, and a good French scholar. Taking a fancy to this

Civil Law, I have explored it from the earliest fragments, through Paul, Ulpian, the Institutes, Panderts, Novels, and Code, to the Spanish and French law, and in it found the true source of the principles of jurisprudence."

"By temperance and industry, I have found time to spend many hours to the advocacy of education, and every means of improving this country: to write occasionally for the papers and magazines, and to prepare works on the law, &c., which may one day find their way to the press. I have prepared a translation of 'Heinnecius Elements of the Institutes.'"

"In 1834," the Judge says, "he removed his mother and sister, with her children, and one child of a deceased sister, Mrs. Jenkins, to Alabama. All, with the exception of a niece, the wife of the Rev. Richard Furman, and a nephew, are dead."

Of his own family, he says, "I have nine children, who have received, and are receiving, a fair education. At fifty-one years of age, I feel as energetic as I did at twenty, and can labor with any young man in the country. I attribute my youthful energy to extreme temperance in eating and drinking, to regular hours and cold water." True, most true, my experience of sixty-six years fully coincides with Judge Porter. Although I have reached that period of life, when "the windows are darkened," "when the almond tree flourishes," and when usually "the grasshopper is a burden," yet have I found that a life of twenty-five years of total abstinence has enabled me to do and bear more than younger men can.

The Judge says, "of my disposition and capacity I will not speak. I am satisfied, so far as success in life is concerned; I have two great defects of character—too much openness of conduct, and too little care of money. I have the satisfaction of feeling that I have never ground the face of the poor, nor refused the defence of the oppressed, nor taken a fee to prosecute against truth and justice."

Judge Porter's life shows that his disposition is kind. He has fulfilled to the utmost the duties of a son and brother.

His capacity, who can doubt, after what he has achieved. He is, indeed, now to be ranked amongst the first in literature and law. All this he has achieved by untiring industry.

In every department of life—as a man, a citizen, a husband and a father—none better deserves the plaudit, "well done." It is to be hoped that his country will yet amply reward him, and crown him with the honors to which he is eminently entitled.

We append an interesting extract from one of Judge Porter's letters, and an extract from the "Law Reporter."

"When I went to Mobile, as Judge of the Tenth Circuit, there were six thousand cases on the docket, and it had not been cleared in two years. The jail was full, and as the yellow fever was approaching, I resolved to clear the prisons. The Sheriff was required by me to furnish a list of every person in jail. I held Court till June. On the evening of the last day of Court, I had gone to my hotel, worn out. A company of sea-captains were abusing the law of Alabama, and several who had been in the jail, to look after their men, put in under a law of Congress, for fear of desertion, spoke of the prisoners in jail. The Sheriff, that day, had declared, in open Court, that no prisoners were in jail. It was then dark; I went, without eating my supper, to the State's Advocate, and getting the Sheriff, went to the jail. There I found the dungeons full of sailors, and State's witnesses, who had not been able to give surety. In one dungeon, I found a woman, with a dozen men, about giving birth to a child. In another, I found a mother, with a child in rags, in a raging fever. I turned them all out of jail; giving the women and sick money, and providing a carriage for those unable to walk.

"On one occasion, I was requested to watch over the case of two fine young negroes, indicted for burglary. The Attorney-General requested me to submit the case, as there was no hope of saving them. I refused; insisting on a regular trial. The evidence took till night. It was positive. I went home; could not sleep. Got up at midnight, and went to my office, where I sat up till day-light. The idea struck me, which is stated in the within note, published in the "Boston Law Reporter." I went into Court. The Jury turned their backs to me, as did the Judge, as I rose to speak. They were vexed at my taking the time of the Court when there was so much to do. As I opened the point, the Judge turned towards me, and as he saw the point, told me he would direct an acquittal. The negroes fell on my neck, and cried aloud."

"Larkin and Henry, two negroes belonging to Mr. Marr, were charged with having broken into a dwelling-house, not then inhabited, and stolen goods to the amount of more than twenty dollars, during one Saturday night. The goods were found in their possession, and they had fully confessed the facts charged. Indeed, the case was considered so clear, that it was proposed to submit the facts proved without argument. This, however, was declined by Judge Porter, who took the following ground: That, by the laws of the State of Alabama, as they now stand, supposing the facts to be all proved, the prisoners had not committed the crime of burglary. It seems, that burglary is adopted by its generic name into the Alabama penal code. Not attempting to define it, it must be held to be the offence defined under that name by the common law, (State *vs.* Absence, Porter's Reports, 401,) namely: 'breaking into a dwelling-house, in the night-time, *with intent to commit a felony.*' The question now arises, therefore, what is a *felony* by the laws of the State of Alabama. This the State code has not left to the common law definition, but has undertaken to define as follows: 'The term felony, when used in any statute, shall be construed to mean any offence, for which the offender, on conviction, shall be liable by law, to be punished by death, or for which imprisonment in the penitentiary is made the appropriate punishment.'—Ala. Digest, Penal Code, chap. viii. sect. 8. If, therefore, the above facts had been proved against any white person, or free person of color, it would have been a case of burglary; as stealing from a dwelling house, above the value of twenty dollars, is a penitentiary offence, and, therefore, a felony. But, by the laws of this State, this offence is only punishable, in slaves, by whipping. Hence, he contended, that the offenders did not intend to commit a felony according to the law, as it now stands in the

State, and, therefore, could not be convicted of burglary. The case excited more interest, as no capital conviction had occurred in the county for several years; and the confessions of the prisoners had made it apparently clear against them, and there was little doubt that, if convicted, they would be executed. Several convictions of negroes for burglary have taken place under the law, as it now stands, in other parts of the State. Judge Porter, however, being strongly opposed to all capital punishments, in such cases, exerts himself to the utmost. This point was argued with great ability. Judge Phelan, on the Bench, charged the Jury at length in accordance with the argument of Judge Porter, declaring that, with the law as it at present stands, he could not lay his head peacefully upon his pillow, if he charged otherwise; and the prisoners were acquitted."

THOMAS H. POPE.

Thomas Herbert Pope was the eldest son of Capt. Sampson Pope, of Edgefield, and Sarah Strother, his wife. He was born 12th of November, 1803, was educated in the best schools and academies within his father's reach, and had the benefit of a clerkship in his father's store. He was, for a short time, in Yale College. He studied law in the office of his brother-in-law, Judge O'Neall, and acquired a knowledge of the profession with more ease and facility than any of the twenty-one who first and last studied in the same office.

He was admitted to the Bar in 1825, and settled at Edgefield Court House. He was married on the 19th January, 1830, to Miss Harriett Neville Pope, the second daughter of Young John Harrington, Esq., and his wife, Nancy Calmes, of Newberry. He removed to Newberry about 1832, and entered upon a large and lucrative practice, which he pursued with uncommon success. He was elected Commissioner in Equity for Newberry in 1836, and served until 1840, when he resigned.

He was elected a member of the House of Representatives in the General Assembly of the State in 1840, and served two years. How he was then regarded may be seen by what was said of him by a contributor to one of the South Carolina papers: "Mr. Pope, of Newberry, is a lawyer, and a most worthy and estimable man. He is a new member, and has, on several occasions, spoken with great effect. His speech on increasing the taxes was a most argumentative and practical one. He is in favor of strict economy, and has shown himself the advocate of morals and temperance. He is a business man, and possesses a most discriminating mind. I have no doubt he will be found a useful and valuable member."

He was opposed to the Bank of the State of South Carolina, and this gave rise to much unhappiness on his part, and, perhaps, persecution on the part of those who ought to have been his friends.

He was a warm and ardent friend of the Greenville and Columbia Railroad, and did much to secure the charter. He threw himself into the ranks of those from Abbeville and Anderson, who desired to effect the location through Abbeville District *via* Anderson, and was very influential in carrying that point against the open and active opposition of the President, and many of the largest and most influential stockholders. That it was a great mistake has been shown by the continual difficulties through which the road has had to struggle. Much, however, was done at Abbeville, in 1849, to remedy that mistake, by making the extension from Belton to Greenville instead of from Anderson.

Mr. Pope was taken sick with typhoid pneumonia in December, 1850, and lingered until the 4th of February, 1851, when he died, leaving his excellent and intelligent wife and six sons and one daughter surviving him. One of his sons, Neville, has since died.

Mr. Pope was not, by any means, an orator; yet he spoke easily, plainly, and forcibly. His legal arguments were remarkable for their applicability and clearness. He managed his cases with great success, and very much to the satisfaction of the Court. He never committed those greatest of blunders, of tedious, unnecessary examinations and cross-examinations of witnesses, and of long prosy speeches. What he did or said was to the point.

His reports, while Commissioner in Equity, were lucid, lawyer-like expositions. He was a good accountant; his novitiate, in his father's store, gave him great facility in this respect.

Mr. Pope was an honest, good legislator; and Newberry, though somewhat celebrated for her capricious changes of her legislators, never committed a greater blunder than when she rejected Mr. Pope. Whether she agreed with him or not on the Bank question, she ought to have been assured that she would have the services of a clear-headed, upright, industrious, firm, honest, good man, and no demagogue.

But he is in his grave, and with his faults and virtues he must there rest until God shall bid his dust arise.

ISAAC DONNOM WITHERSPOON.

Isaac Donnom Witherspoon, the son of Col. J. H. Witherspoon, and the grandson of Isaac Donnam, of Lancaster, was born at Lancasterville, December 3d, 1803; he came to Yorkville in the year 1824, to study law with Col. Thos. Williams, and was admitted to the Bar, in Columbia, in January, 1826.

He entered into partnership with Col. Thomas Williams, who was the leading lawyer, not only at York, but also on the Middle, now the Northern Circuit. On the 18th July, 1826, he married Ann T. Reid, daughter of Joseph Reid, once of Union District, and Senator from that district, but who was then residing in York.

He was elected to the House of Representatives in the General Assembly in 1836, and served two terms.

In 1840 he was elected Senator, and by successive elections continued until 1856.

He was elected Lieutenant-Governor in 1842, but never qualified; he, therefore, retained his place in the Senate of the State.

In 1845, he was elected a Trustee of the South Carolina College in 1849, and in 1853 he was re-elected. He was the aid of one of the Governors, and thus acquired the title of Colonel. In 1857, he was struck with apoplexy or paralysis, at his plantation in Lancaster, and never entirely recovered. In the hope of improving his health, he visited the White Sulphur Springs, Virginia, in the summer of 1858, but the hope was vain. He died there on the 20th July; his body was brought on to Yorkville, and buried in the Presbyterian Church-yard, in the presence of his family, and a large body of the citizens of Yorkville and of the district.

Col. Witherspoon left surviving him his amiable lady and several children. He was a good man, was raised in the bosom of the Presbyterian Church, and was, I think, a member for years before his death.

He was a very respectable lawyer, and had a large practice. The last term which I held at York, April, 1858, it was manifest to me that Col. Witherspoon was not long to be numbered among the sons of men; yet so anxious was he for one of his clients, that he ventured to speak to the Jury. It was as the pleading of the dying for the living.

He maintained an honorable standing in the Senate of the State, and rendered good service to the district, which had so long honored him with her confidence.

In all the relations of life he was much respected by all who knew him. His wife, children and servants, experienced an irreparable loss in his death; but that which to them was loss, to him was everlasting gain!

ALEXANDER DROMGOOLE SIMS

Was born in the County of Brunswick, Virginia, near Randal's Ordinary, on the 12th of June, 1803. His parents were Richard Sims and Rebecca Dromgoole, his wife; she was the daughter of Richard Edward Dromgoole.

Alexander D. Sims went to the University at Chapel Hill, North Carolina, but graduated at Union College, Schenectady, New York. He came to South Carolina about 1826, and had charge as principal of the academy at Darlington Court-House. He studied law while he thus taught, and was admitted to the Bar in 1829. He opened an office at Darlington Court-House, and there continued the practice of the law until his death. He was married on the 28th of October, 1830, to Margaret A. P. Dargan, the daughter of Timothy Dargan, Esq.

Mr. Sims was elected to the House of Representatives in the General Assembly of the United State, in October 1840, and was re-elected 1842. He was elected to Congress from the District composed of Georgetown, Williamsburgh, Horry, Marion, Marlborough, Darlington and Chesterfield, in the place of John Campbell, Esq., who died in 1844 He was then elected, in preference to the Honorable John McQueen, the present Member, and again in 1846. He was re-elected in 1848, just before his death, which took place at Kingstree, Williamsburgh District, on the 22d of November, 1849, whither he had gone to meet his constituents, and to attend the Law Court. His daughter, Gertrude L., still survives him. She lives with her uncle, Julius A. Dargan, Esq., who is her guardian, she having lost her mother on the 8th of July, 1844.

Mr. Sims was a good scholar, and had a keen, discriminating mind. His taste was eminently literary. He published a revolutionary romance, the title of which has escaped my recollection.

He was a very respectable lawyer, managed and argued his cases very well, possessing great fluency of language. All his aspirations were, however, political. In the House of Representatives in the General Assembly, he was an assiduous Member, remarkable for his business habits, and as a ready debater. His greatest ambition was, however, a seat in Congress. This he attained, and continued a Member until his death. His addresses to his constituents I frequently heard in the fall of 1846, and I considered them very fine specimens of such harangues. Indeed, I never saw any one who was so well calculated to win and retain the affections of the people.

His death, in the forty-sixth year of his age, cut short his career of usefulness as a Member of Congress.

He died possibly before a blight fell upon him; for Washington was a place not at all suited to a man of Mr. Sims' habits, and his quick, vivacious, and companionable disposition.

I append the eulogy of his friend, Dr. John P. Zimmerman, pronounced at Darlington soon after his death. It will give to every one a full, and, I presume, a just notion of Mr. Sims' excellencies:

"In all ages it has been common for the living to testify by some public act their high estimate of the worthy dead. It is a pleasing and melancholy task to assemble around their last resting place, and make some kind oblation to their memory. It seems to be a beautiful and appropriate outpouring of love and friendship as well as of gratitude for kind offices that are past, and cherished affections that are now sundered forever. In accordance with a time-honored custom of our ancient and venerable order, we have this day met at the grave of our departed brother to pay the last sad respects to his memory. He lies before us in his narrow bed, in the solemn repose of death, alike unconscious of our eulogy or regrets. Anything which we may say or do can confer no benefit on him; but the living—those of us who now surround his sepulchre—may here learn lessons which will profit us in time to come.

But a few months ago we saw him in our streets, in this sanctuary, full of life and health, buoyant and happy. Possessed of great physical strength, he seemed to be destined to many years of life and happiness. But he is gone, and the scene we are called on to witness to-day is a sad commentary on human life.

How transient—how uncertain! We are forcibly reminded that in the midst of life we are in death.

'Man that is born of a woman is of few days and full of trouble. He cometh forth like a flower and is cut down; he fleeth as a shadow and continueth not.'

His days upon earth are as a shadow, and are swifter than 'a weaver's shuttle.' 'In the morning he flourisheth and groweth up; in the evening he is cut down and withereth.'

We shall be excused if, on this mournful occasion, we briefly advert to some points in the life and character of our brother, which seem to require public notice: it is for this purpose we are assembled here to-day.

With much of the early history of our friend, we are wholly unacquainted, and, therefore, the most we may say of him, is drawn from the time he came among us. We know, however, that he was descended from a very worthy and intelligent family of Virginia, and that he was favored in early life with every opportunity to acquire an education. At the University of North Carolina (than which there is no better institution in the South), and then at Union College, Schenectady, he distinguished himself, exhibiting great industry and ardor in the pursuit of knowledge. How he profited by his collegiate studies, which are so often neglected and misimproved by the youth of the country, his learning and acquirements sufficiently testify. He was a thorough scholar. Perhaps it would be hazarding but little to assert, that he had but few equals, and no superiors in this part of our State, in the variety, extent aud accuracy of his knowledge. It was, however, in mathematical and classical learning he excelled; and all his life, even after he had retired from the pursuits which seemed to require him to keep up his knowledge of these sciences, he devoted a portion of every day to his favorite studies, and was as well acquainted with the Latin and Greek, as with his own vernacular tongue.

Here he was peculiarly fitted for the interesting and important task of training the young minds of our youth, and preparing them for stations of respectability and usefulness. In this employment he very much delighted and spent several years of his life. Many of his pupils (some of whom I have the honor now to address) remember him with gratitude, as well for the thorough instruction he imparted, as for his kindness of heart, and zeal for their improvement. No individual in this district, engaged in the interesting work of teaching, has gained for himself so enviable a reputation. Several of his pupils completed with him their academical studies, and have gone on in their professional pursuits with great success and promise of future distinction.

It is too commonly thought, that the man who follows what is usually esteemed the humble, but what is in reality the highly-honorable vocation of an instructor, is but poorly qualified for anything else. This is a great mistake. This business eminently qualifies a man for the study and practice of the learned professions. In training others the instructor trains himself; in imparting knowledge he acquires it; in teaching others to think he learns to think himself.

Our departed friend found great advantage in this way in the practice of the law, to which he devoted the remnant of his life. It was in this field he particularly exhibited his great talents and acquirements. The success which rewarded his exertions ought to encourage every young man in his efforts.

Without money, destitute of family influence or rich friends, a stranger far from the place of his nativity, depending on his own strength and courage, he commenced the practice of the law in this district. Though he had able competition in this intellectual profession, he never allowed himself to doubt of success. He determined to succeed. Possessed of a quick and retentive memory, much power of research, strong attachment to the metaphysical speculations, and great amenity of manners, he could not fail of success.

He did not seem to require the usual slow and tedious routine through which most men have to pass to eminence.

In a few years after his beginning, he was known and appreciated as a distinguished lawyer. But few of the Bar of the Eastern Circuit have ever been so generally successful in their practice. No one has ever taken so deep a hold on the affections and confidence of the masses.

At the time of his lamented death, he was thought by his colleagues to be the ablest lawyer in the Congressional representation of South Carolina.

Had he devoted himself with all the energies of his great mind to the profession, he might have aspired to its highest distinctions; and no one would have worn the judicial dignity with more suavity and usefulness.

In speaking at the Bar, he was plain, lucid, methodical, always instructive, and frequently eloquent. His last efforts at the Bar, just a few weeks before his death, were remarkable productions, far superior to what we usually hear in our Courts of Justice from the Bar or the Bench.

The benevolence of his nature enabled him to do much good in the practice of his profession, not only in prompting acts of kindness and courtesy, but in adjusting difficulties and disputes among friends and neighbors, and in giving such gratuitous advice as prevent litigation and its evils.

It might be expected, from the moral and intellectual qualities in the character of our brother, that he would be a popular man. No man in our district ever succeeded in taking deeper hold on the popular feeling. He was emphatically a people's man—not the favorite of a clique, elevated to stations of dignity and responsibility by management and family influence—but the favorite and friend of the masses, who loved him for his social qualities, and respected him for his good sense and talents. With him it was natural and easy to please. His suavity and good humor were the natural outpourings of a benevolent heart, not the trick and finesse of the demagogue.

For several years he represented the people of Darlington in the Legislature of the State, and in this relation he was faithful and diligent, the constant friend and advocate of the interests of the masses. He was also the respected representative, for several terms, of the now first Congressional district in the national Legislature; and when he fell a victim to the destroyer, he had just passed victoriously through a warm and exciting contest for a seat in the Thirty-first Congress.

How our friend and brother demeaned himself in that more elevated and larger arena, is matter of history. In his political faith he was a Jeffersonian republican—a State-right man of the strictest sort—opposed to all latitudinarian construction of the Constitution—a Democrat in sentiment and in practice.

Having a good voice, and an easy elocution, he took part in most of the debates on the floor of Congress, and spoke with good sense and effect.

On the vexed question, which divides the two great geographical sections of the Union, no man was sounder or better understood and maintained our rights. The subject, in all its vast interests and importance, early engaged his attention, and he embodied and published his thoughts on it, in an interesting essay, which, at the time, had an extensive circulation.

In all his public course he secured the approbation of the people. He consulted their interests and feelings, and they rewarded him with their confidence and friendship.

I do not know that in performing the duty which has been assigned me, I should follow our departed friend into the retirement of the domestic circle. 'Tis there, however, the true character is seen—no cloak is thrown over the shoulders around the fire-side of home. There we all throw off the restraints which the public gaze imposes, and are known in our true likeness. Our brother was a kind and affectionate husband, a doting father, and an indulgent master. As a friend, he was constant and faithful; as a neighbor, friendly, conciliating, and hospitable. That he had faults, all will admit, none can deny. But faults are the common heritage of poor human nature.

Let us throw the mantle of charity over his faults, and remember them only to avoid them ourselves. Happy is he who, seeing the deficiency of his neighbor, learns to correct and remove those of his own heart.

But the grave of our departed brother, seen in its solemn stillness, speaks to us in accents of warning. Though dead, we hear his voice filling this sepulchral grove with its deep tones of admonition. It tells us—we must die!

Listen to that voice, my brethren, and while we surround his tomb, and perform the solemn rites of our order, let us resolve to go away from this consecrated spot better and wiser men. Hearken, my countrymen! as he is, so must you be. This is the end of life, but not the end of living. It is the beginning of existence! In the beautiful liturgy of another order, 'Men appear upon, and disappear from, the stage of life, as wave meets wave and parts upon the troubled waters.' In the midst of life we are in death. He whose lips now echo these tones of solemn warning, in turn will be stilled in the cold and cheerless house of the dead, and in the Providence of God none may escape. Let us all make that preparation which will insure our happiness beyond the grave.

He only is wise who learns to live well, that, at last, he may die well."

RICHARD W. SINGLETON.

This gentleman was an universal favorite in the sections where most of his life was passed, (Coosawhatchie and Gillisonville,) and yet it has been with difficulty that mere shreds of his life could be gathered after he had slept in the silence of the grave for only nine years.

He was born in Colleton District, about 1806 or '7, and was the son of Major Richard Singleton and of his wife Eliza Postell, the daughter of Major John Postell, of Revolutionary memory. His mother died when he was about six years old. His father lived freely and died in narrow pecuniary circumstances. He was about twelve years old when his father died, leaving him a destitute orphan. His uncle William, took charge of him, but death soon deprived him of this his last near relative. But a kind and benevolent lady, of Walterboro,' Mrs. Margaret Ford, took charge of the poor orphan boy, until God raised up for him a friend and protector in Colonel John D. Edwards, who supported and educated him out of his small means. He went to school at Walterboro,' successively to the Rev. Mr. Fowler, Mr. Querton, and the Rev. Mr. Layton. When he was about sixteen he went with his friend and patron to Barnwell. Colonel Edwards sent him to school at the Boiling Springs, where he completed his education. He then taught school in the Village of Barnwell, and studied law with Colonel Edwards. In 1829 he removed to Grahamville, where he taught school. He was admitted to the Bar, in the City of Charleston, on the 27th March, 1833, and settled at Coosawhatchie, where he practiced law. He was mainly instrumental in removing the Court House from Coosawhatchie to Gillisonville. The Act for that purpose was passed on the 21st December, 1836.

During the storm of Nullification, extending from 1832 to 1835, Colonel Benjamin Alston, Richard W. Singleton, and Postell, were the only Union men in St. Luke's Parish, and nobly did they breast the storm. They never were shaken in its darkest hours. He was an aid to one of the Governors, and thus acquired the title of Colonel.

In 1849 Richard W. Singleton was elected to represent St. Luke's Parish. He died at Dr. Strobharts', in Grahamville, in the fall of 1850, in the forty-fourth year of his age, without being married. His mature life had been spent first in attending schools, which he taught with great success; and secondly, in attending to the practice of the law at Coosawhatchie, and afterwards at Gillisonville.

He made little money at either place, and what little he made he divided with a liberal hand with the poor and friendless. He was kind-hearted and benevolent almost to a fault.

He was one of the most pleasant companions and friends with whom I ever associated; his good humor made even the solitude of Gillisonville pleasant. He was a teetotaller for many years before his death. "He did not keep his spirits up by pouring spirits down."

He was a respectable lawyer, managing and arguing his cases very well.

The business at Coosawhatchie and Gillisonville was so much divided, after his admission to the Bar, that it rarely fell to any lawyer to have more than ten or twelve cases at a term. Under such circumstances "talent was literally wasted on the desert air."

I know that Colonel Singleton was a Baptist in sentiment, and I believe a Christian. His death, therefore, was not the darkness of despair, but was radiant with the hope of a happy immortality beyond the grave.

ALBERT M. RHETT.

Albert Moore Rhett (formerly Smith) was the seventh and youngest son of the late James Smith of Charleston, and Marianna Gough. He was born in the year 1809, in Brunswick County, North Carolina, during a temporary residence of the family there, and spent his early years in the country, where his father was his only teacher. His vivacity in childhood was so great, that his father found it impracticable to teach him the alphabet; and, despairing of success, gave him up to his mother's care, who, after some vain efforts, called in the aid of his eldest brother, and he at length accomplished the task. After the return of the family to Beaufort, he was for a short time a pupil of Mr. Hallonquist, a teacher of reputation at that time. In his sixteenth year, he was sent to Philips' Academy, at Andover, Massachusetts, and in fifteen months completed his preparatory studies for the Freshman Class of Yale College, which he entered in 1827. From the beginning to the end of his academic life, he had not a competitor, and there was no department of study in which his superiority was not marked. He was pre-eminent in the classical, literary and forensic exercises of his class. But it was in mathematics that his talents shone most brightly. He prepared *pari passu* with the college curriculum—a system of his own, beginning with algebra, and running through the whole range of the pure mathematics, in two manuscript volumes, which, on leaving college, he put into the hands of a friend in one of the lower classes. These volumes were, it is said, within these few years, still in the hands of the students. In this elaborate performance he improved in more respects than one on the text of the standard authors, by introducing new arrangements, by simplifying the propositions, and by multiplying sometimes the demonstrations fourfold. He was urged by a friend to revise and recast it into an original work of his own, and to publish it by way of honorable introduction into active life. But he thought too lightly of its merits to forego his habitual repugnance to appearing in print. It may be added as a circumstance worthy of the attention of young men, that while he fell short of no excellence in the exercises of his college course he improved every opportunity of cultivating himself in English composition and debate. He wrote and spoke unremittingly in the literary societies. Not a week passed in which he failed to take part in one or the other of these exercises, and he frequently engaged in both. He considered writing the first and last condition of good speaking; and on whatever subject his mind was employed, his pen was never out of his hand. The nature of this task may be imagined, when it is stated that his fingers were so weak that he wrote at all with the greatest difficulty, and only by an ingenious contrivance.

The first year after his return from college he spent at home in general studies. "Newton's Principia," the Greek Tragedians, the Political Economists, and British Classics absorbing most of his hours. He held, with Mr. Burke, that the poetry of literature lay as much in its language as in its sentiment, and he therefore memorized as he read every striking passage of his chosen authors. He knew, by heart, the whole of the first book of "Paradise Lost," and there were few of Shakspeare's "Delphic Lines" that did not come to his lips at his bidding. The prose books of Milton he read and re-read with fresh interest, agreeing with the late Mr. Legaré, that they were unequaled as examples of prose compositions by any productions of their class in our language. But the business of life was pressing (for he was without fortune), and in 1832 he entered the office of his relative, the late Thomas S. Grimké, and, after twelve months' preparation, was admitted to the Bar on the 20th February, 1834. An opening for immediate employment in the country occurring, he availed himself of it, and began the practice of his profession in Beaufort and Colleton. The first case in which his remarkable talents were displayed, in Colleton, was the case of The State *v.* Riggs, on an indictment for murder. The Solicitor was not in attendance, and the relations of the deceased employed Mr. Rhett in behalf of the prosecution. The prisoner was defended by Mr. Petigru, but was convicted. Mr. Rhett rose at once to the head of his profession. In the year 1834, he was returned to the House of Representatives from St. Helena Parish. In that body, in the Second Session of his first term, he delivered a most remarkable and able speech on the Independence of the Judiciary, and forthwith took rank amongst the ablest debaters in the State. He represented St. Helena for four years, and subsequently St. Luke's.

In 1843, he became a resident of Charleston, and in October of that year was stricken by yellow fever, and died, aged thirty-four years, in perfect and hopeful resignation to the will of God.

Mr. Rhett was a hard student. He took with him into his profession, the same method of study he had cultivated in his youth, and that was most exhausting. His synthesis was as perfect as his analysis. When he seized a principle, he pursued it from its first faint expression in the text-books to the very last judgment upon it in the Reports; throwing aside, step by step as he advanced, the perversions and errors that had gathered about it in its progress to established truth. He considered law the noblest system of reason ever wrought by the genius of man; and he loved it not less for the severity of its truths than for its large and practical philosophy. It was not with him an instrument of vulgar profit merely, or a plaything of ambition. He did not treat it as a cunning device of happy expedients for correcting men's errors, and still less as a useful engine for ventilating the bad humors of society; but as the organ of truth herself, as the justest expression of the most valuable of all metaphysics—the metaphysics of common life—and as the ripest and richest food of a refined and refining civilization. For this reason, his success as an advocate, remarkable as it was, fell short of his efforts in the Court of Equity and the Courts of Appeal. There it was that, untrammeled by the traps and sophistries of the Jury-trial, his severe intellect delighted to wrestle with the masters of legal science, and to discourse fine reason with Coke and Hardwicke, Mansfield and Eldon.

In his address, Mr. Rhett was self-possessed, grave, and earnest; but when he was warmed by debate, his invective was overwhelming. His fine voice, and tall, handsome person, added not a little to the graces of his elocution; while his choice and pregnant English reminded one, by turns, of the terseness of Tacitus and the solid periods of Milton. He was as severe in the selection of his phrases, as in the order of his logic; and whether he spoke on the spur of the occasion, or after much preparation, no link ever dropped from the chain of his argument, and his periods were filled up and rounded with all the completeness that rhetoric art could impart.

Except an address on temperance, which he delivered in Charleston, a short time before his death, Mr. Rhett published nothing over his signature. But he wrote much, anonymously, for the fugitive publications of the day; not for the sake of reputation, (for he thought little of his accomplishments as a writer,) but with a view to correct speaking. His facility in composition was, however, great; and, if he had lived longer, it is likely the favorable judgment of the public would have overcome his diffidence in this particular, and his reputation as a writer have become as great as it was for speaking.

We have referred to Mr. Rhett's system of mental training, as furnishing, by its success, some useful lessons to the young. Perhaps, it is not out of place, to add a word or so as to his interest in the young. Youth was recommendation enough for anybody to his sympathies; and any, the least, demonstration of personal merit in such, engaged his active friendship. He loved to lift up the head of the poor boy, and give heart to the desponding; and although his means were never large, yet the tidings of his early death brought tears to the eyes of more than one strong man who had found in him (when friends were few) the kindest of benefactors and the truest of counsellors.

The foregoing is from the pen of an early friend of Mr. Rhett, who was, indeed, all that he represents him to have been, and more. He was, indeed, a fine specimen of a lawyer. His style of speaking was fully equal to any which I ever heard. He had, too, a very good knowledge of legal principles, and knew well how to successfully apply his knowledge. Both at the Bar and in the State House, I observed his course with delight. He was a teetotaller, and was one of the few young lawyers of his day who never clouded his mind with wine or strong drink. If it had pleased God that he should live to old age, he would have been one of the first men of South Carolina. He married Sarah C. Taylor, the youngest daughter of Governor Taylor, who survived him with at least two, and perhaps more children.

JAMES M. WALKER.

For the hours of recreation, we find no repast more captivating and exquisite than that which memory offers in a review of the worthy who have passed away. Few men, in early life, gave higher promise of usefulness and distinction, than the subject of this notice, and few have so well fulfilled them, if we judge by the traces they have left behind.

Nil turpius est quam gravis œtate senex, qui nullum aliud habet argumentum, quo se probet diu vixisse, præter œtatem, was a favorite quotation of the late James M. Walker, and it indeed was the object of his ambition to signalize the period of life allotted to him, by such *mental* exertion, as to claim the respect and remembrance of the community. He was moved by that noble impulse, which aims to leave its mark on its day and generation. Possessed of a mind highly cultivated, and a cheerful temper, he was a delightful companion. One of his marked peculiarities, was his fondness for classical quotation. The writer remembers well, when a student, how Mr. W. was welcomed by all, at a very pleasant and usual place of rendezvous, on a winter's evening, and has in his possession a classic work, on the fly-leaf of which Mr. Walker wrote the following lines:

" *Quam cuperes votis hunc revocare diem.*"—*Ovid.*

" *Ut ager quamvis fertilis, sine culturâ fructuosus esse non potest; sic sine doctrinâ animus.*"—*Senaca.*

There comes a voice that awakes the soul. It is the voice of years that are gone; they roll before me with all their deeds. It is delightful to recall the past, and live o'er again such pleasant moments.

James Murdoch Walker was born in the City of Charleston, on the 10th day of January, 1813. He was the son of Robert Walker, of Fifeshire, Scotland, and Mary Murdoch, of Charleston, South Carolina. His early education was received at the best schools in his native city, and at the usual age he entered as a student of the South Carolina College, then under the rule of its able and distinguished President, Dr. Thomas Cooper. He occupied a fair position as a scholar, and graduated with distinction in the Class of 1830, leaving a reputation for talent and industry.

Mr. W. had determined at the time he entered college, that the law should be his profession. Knowing how jealous was his future mistress, he assiduously applied himself to obtain a solid education, and ever after, in his leisure, he devoted himself to the treasures of Clio, and turned with delight to Caliope. He was well read in literature, a good *belle-lettre* scholar; and, to a mind strong, energetic, and naturally of an inquiring turn, he added that embellishment which can only be obtained by a careful study of the ancient classics. Thus prepared, he entered the law office of the Hon. Mitchell King, and was admitted to the Bar in Columbia, in 1834. He appeared as counsel in the well-remembered case of the State *vs.* the Bank of South Carolina (1st Speers, 433), and his entire argument, which we would select as a specimen of his legal learning and ability, is given in the report of that case, by Attorney-General Bailey, and published in pamphlet form, under the order of the Legislature.

He wrote and spoke well, and was a constant contributor to the Southern Quarterly Review; his articles are filled with classic references, his style was terse and pointed; as a speaker, he was clear and fluent. Mr. W. served several terms in the State Legislature, representing the Parishes of St. Philip's and St. Michael's, and was among the useful and prominent Members of the House.

In 1850, appeared a pamphlet by Mr. W., entitled "*An Inquiry into the use and authority of Roman Jurisprudence in the law concerning Real Estate;*" letters from many distinguished gentlemen, flowing with high commendation, was his reward; the essay is dedicated to the Hon. James Louis Petigru, whose letter to the author constitutes its preface.

In 1852, his "*Theory of the Common Law*" appeared, which he inscribes to the Hon. Mitchell King, "as a tribute of the respect and regard of an 'Apprentice to the Law' to his former master." This work gave Mr. Walker a very decided position at the Bar, and was highly praised from all quarters.

In 1853, he published a trac tentitled "*On Government*," inscribed to the Hon. W. D. Porter: it was severely criticised in the Southern Quarterly, but in the reply, Mr. W. sustained himself with signal and approved ability.

During the early part of the succeeding year, it was very evident to his friends that his health was fast failing, and on the 18th September, 1854, at the age of 41 years, 8 months and 8 days, he breathed his last.

His remains were interred at the First Presbyterian Church, at Charleston, and his funeral discourse was preached by the Rev. John Forrest, the Pastor of the Church. There is no false praise in this short tribute; if it hath any recommendation, it is its truth, for

"Flattery hideth her varnished face when friendship sitteth at the board."

LETTER FROM HON. W. D. PORTER.

"My recollections of James M. Walker, go back to the time when we were both apprentices to the law. He had fixed his standard of legal attainment very high, and was a most industrious reader. His attention was particularly directed to the study of the Common Law, and it gave him great delight to explore its sources, and trace its course and history. He bestowed considerable attention also upon the Roman Law, but chiefly for the purpose of comparing and contrasting it with the English Jurisprudence. There was, perhaps, no young man of his day in our State, who pursued his profession more as a liberal science, and less as a gainful craft. He believed that no one could know the law without apprehending its reason; because law, whether universal or municipal, has its foundation in truth, and is, in fact, a regular system or science, and not a mere promiscuous collection of rules and precedents. To penetrate to this fundamental truth or reason was his aim and endeavor; and it is not surprising that with such a spirit of investigation, aided by extraordinary powers of analysis and logic, he should have become, in his early maturity, not only a well-read lawyer, but an accomplished jurist.

Mr. Walker gave to the profession as the fruits of his study, several tractates on the law. The first of these was an "Inquiry into the use and authority of Roman Jurisprudence, in the law concerning real estate." His object was to show that prior to the time of Edward I., when the common law became a separate and independent system, the principles of the civil law had been largely infused into the municipal law of England, and were to be found at the bottom of the English doctrines of real estate. He thought that the national and professional pride of the early English law writers, would not suffer them to admit what his investigations led him to regard as a historical fact. His theory was new, and he sought to establish it by tracing to their sources some of the more important rules of the feudal law, and showing the use and authority therein, of Roman Jurisprudence. He defended his theory with great ingenuity, and illustrated it with much curious learning. This essay excited the attention of the legal fraternity, and received the liberal commendations of the distinguished gentleman to whom it was dedicated—the Hon. James L. Petigru, now and for many years the leader of our Bar, and the acknowledged master of the profession in our State.

His next essay was entitled the "Theory of the Common Law." This work was on a larger scale than the preceding one, and attracted still greater attention. His purpose was to show that the common law, in all its parts, rests upon the fundamental principle of the attribution of political power to the proprietors of the soil; that notwithstanding the modifications it has undergone, in the progress of time, property is still, in England, the source of power; and, that even in the midst of great revolutions and changes of dynasties and subversions of governments, this common law has manifested a continuity of doctrines and a stability of character, that make it not merely an incident or episode in the life of the nation, but the very expression and embodiment of that life itself. His discussions of some of its leading topics are characterized by searching investigation, sound learning and bold and philosophical thought; and seem all intended to illustrate and establish his leading principle, viz: the unity and durability of that great and noble system of jurisprudence. Upon the publication of his book, Mr. Walker received a large number of complimentary letters. It was also brought to the attention of the Legislature, and the Judiciary Committees of both Houses bestowed upon it high commendation, and recommended a subscription to a number of copies for the use of the Legislative Library. Lawyers and Jurists, the most distinguished in the country, pronounced it a work of great originality and singular merit. I had, at the time, in my possession, copies of a number of these testimonials, but am at present able to lay my hands only upon the two following:

Professor Greenleaf, himself one of the most eminent law-writers in the country, addressed to him a letter, from which we make this extract:

"CAMBRIDGE, Mass., Aug. 24th, 1852.

"It has interested me extremely by the originality of the views it presents, the striking character of the observations scattered through its pages, and especially the profound thought everywhere apparent. It is eminently a suggestive treatise, and will be read by real students of the law with great avidity. I have mentioned it to Professor Mittermaier, of Heidelburg, as *the only philosophical treatise which our profession has of late produced.*"

Chancellor Job Johnson, the Presiding Judge of our Chancery Court, wrote as follows:

"NEWBERRY, S.C., Oct. 19th, 1852.

"*My dear Sir,*—Little, Brown & Co. sent me, a short time since, a small work of yours, on the Theory of the Common Law, which my business engagements did not permit me to examine at the time. I have lately had leisure, of which I avail myself, and have just finished the perusal of it; and I cannot defer for a moment the expression, to yourself, of the admiration and pleasure with which it has inspired me.

"You have, my dear Sir, at once conferred a lasting obligation on your profession by this little work, and elevated yourself to high rank among juridical writers and thinkers. You have succeeded in establishing, that private rights take their roots in, and are moulded and controlled by public law; and your illustrations of this truth are marked by extensive research, remarkable learning, and great discrimination. There is displayed throughout this noble disquisition, a philosophy which has seldom been exhibited among law writers, a philosophy which alone marks the masters of the profession, and distinguishes them from the mass of mere plodders, who rest in cases and precedents, because they can go no deeper; who stick to the shell and the letter, because they are incapable of reaching the spirit and the reason.

"No such key work has appeared for a long time. It is just such works as this that rescue the law from the opprobrium of being merely arbitrary; that elevate it into a science, and vindicate its claims to the system of justice. With unfeigned respect, I am, dear Sir,

"Your obedient servant,

"J. Johnson."

His next essay was on politics, and was entitled a "Tract on Government." His propositions were, that government is only an instrument auxiliary to the reason of society, that its proper object is *restraint*, and that as soon as it ceases to be merely an instrument of restraint, it becomes an instrument, not of conservatism, but of *progress*. That the possession by government of *progressive powers* is identically the same as if reason, which ought to restrain our passions, should incite them to increased activity. That the progressive powers cannot accomplish the ends for which they are conceded to society, and that the happiness and liberty of our people will be made more secure when the State and Federal Constitutions are purged of the progressive powers. Whatever may be thought of his theory, no one who reads his pamphlet will deny that he displayed great boldness of thought and power of logic in developing it.

Mr. Walker was the youngest of the splendid array of

counsel in the famous case of the *scire facias* against the Banks for forfeiture of charter on account of their suspension of specie payments. He was solicitor of one of the Banks, and his printed argument in the cause is not only a specimen of his forensic power, but a monument to his ability and learning as a lawyer.

But Mr. Walker was not a mere reader of law. He was fond of the Latin classics, and frequently indulged in apt classical quotations. He cultivated his mind by various reading. The effect of liberal study was manifest in his style, which was polished as well as pointed. He was a jurist, even more than a lawyer, and loved the science rather than the practice of the law. He said, in one of his essays, that "the common law had no *Sulpicius*, because philosophy has been generally regarded as incompatible with its successful pursuit."

Now that he is dead, it is no flattery to say that, with a longer lease of life, and under more favorable auspices, he might himself have become its *Servius Sulpicius*.

With respect,

W. D. PORTER.

TO HON. J. BELTON O'NEALL.

BENJAMIN ELLIOTT, JR.

Among the young men who, some twenty years ago, were admitted to the Bar in South Carolina, and who gave early promise of professional distinction, no one was more remarked by his cotemporaries than the late Benjamin Elliott, Jr. Descended from a family who had always won favor from society by the urbanity of their temper and the intelligence of their mind, he inherited their amiable qualities in an eminent degree. His father was among the most popular and respected men of his generation, and the son equally possessed all those properties of head and heart which attract affection and insure esteem.

Benjamin Elliott, Jr., was the second son (and the fourth child) of Mr. Benjamin Elliott, of Charleston, South Carolina. He was born in the old family mansion in Legaré street, on the 31st day of March, A. D., 1818. His earliest education, as a boy, was received at the school of Mr. Southworth, a gentleman of classical acquirement and reputation, and there he obtained a rudimental knowledge of those ancient authors, for whose writings he ever afterwards preserved a fondness and familiarity, and expressed a genuine and devout admiration. From the Academy he passed, in customary course, to the college. The Charleston College was at that time under the care of Rev. Dr. Jasper Adams, a man of very extensive and profound erudition in all the learning of a gentleman and a divine. He did not remain here, however, very long. His ambitious mind aspired to a wider field and a larger circle of educational advantage. The Columbia College, the much-loved and fostered institution of the State, offered to him much greater inducement, in the larger number and distinction of its professorships, and the extended compass of its range of studies. In the seventeenth year of his age he entered the Junior Class, and graduated in the year 1837. His class was a large one, consisting of forty-two members, who had graduated—and it may be mentioned to his honor that he received the first appointment from among so many competitors—several of whom have since acquired a very honorable fame and position in the State. From college, he immediately entered upon the study of the law, and was received and invited into the office of Mr. Henry A. DeSaussure. It would be needless to mention to any South Carolinian the high reputation of Mr. DeSaussure's office, and the great advantages which would be enjoyed there by an intelligent and ambitious student. Mr. Elliott knew well the advantages which he had the good fortune to possess there, and, appreciating, he availed himself of them. He soon passed the usual examination, and was admitted to the Bar on 12th February, 1839, and now entered upon the pursuit of that profession for which he had been so well prepared. The same years he delivered an oration before the Washington Light Infantry, which received high commendation from no less a judge than the Rev. Samuel Gilman. Circumstances invited him to establish himself in Georgetown, and he therefore removed his residence from Charleston, with the purpose of practicing in Georgetown and Horry Districts. He was very soon offered a partnership in his business by Gen. W. W. Harllee, and associating himself with him, he gave evidence of superior cultivation, of a high order of intellect, and of an impassioned yet winning style of eloquence. But, although adorned by nature with all those virtues and affections which secure the happiness of being loved by friends, and bountifully endowed with those intellectual powers which command esteem and honor among our fellow-men; yet Providence did not permit that he should reap any of the harvest whose seeds he had so carefully planted. His constitution seemed to have been always delicate, and the active and laborious energy of his mind tended still further to impair its resources. In the hope that a temporary change of climate might check the ravages of a pulmonary disease, he had traveled northward, and while in Philadelphia, the slow and solemn advance of death arrested him there, and there he died, away, indeed, from the peculiar comforts and tenderness of home; yet friends surrounded him with the sympathy of friendship, and softened his pillow with the kindness of affection. At the early age of twenty-two and a half years, he closed his career, beloved, regretted, and esteemed—a man of mark among his fellows—and though so young, yet already widely known and honored.

Mr. Elliott was a man of middle stature. His face was pleasing. To regular features and a fine dark eye was added that peculiar charm of expression which equally results from intelligence and amiability.

Nearly twenty years have passed away since his death, yet his memory remains distinct upon the recollection of his friends, with that deep impression which the waves of time have no power to efface, and which only true virtue and a rare excellence of mind can ever hope to make.

The following are the resolutions passed at a meeting of the Georgetown Bar:

TRIBUTE OF RESPECT.

TO THE MEMORY OF THE LATE BENJAMIN ELLIOTT, ESQ.

At the opening of the Court of Common Pleas, at Georgetown, on the 11th inst., the Hon. Judge O'Neall presiding, the Attorney-General asked leave, at the request of his brethren of the Bar, to submit the following preamble and resolutions, and to move that they might be entered on the Minutes of the Court:

"The members of the Bar attending the Eastern Circuit, have learned, with profound regret, the recent death of their young associate, the late Benjamin Elliott, Esq., whose brief career at the Bar, marked as it was by the possession of those talents, which lead to eminence in his profession, and of those virtues which secure the esteem, and attach the friendship of the community, furnished a bright promise of distinguished usefulness, and calls upon his associates for that tribute of affectionate respect to his memory, which is always the just meed of departed worth, and more especially so where, as in the present instance, it was united to a retiring modesty of character, no less than of manner. Therefore

Resolved, That whilst we deeply deplore the loss of our late lamented associate, whose early death has frustrated the well-founded hopes entertained of honor and distinction for himself, and of eminent usefulness to society, we will ever cherish his memory, with respect for his talents, esteem for his character, and a fond recollection of the amiable and persuasive virtues which endeared him to our friendship.

Resolved, That we sincerely sympathize with his surviving relatives in their afflictive bereavement, and tender to them our condolence under this severe visitation of an all-wise, but to us inscrutable Providence.

Resolved, That the foregoing preamble and resolutions be published in the gazettes of Georgetown and Charleston, and that permission be asked of the Court, now in session, to have them inscribed on its Minutes.

The motion, directed by the last resolution, was supported by the Attorney-General, who was followed in a feeling and eloquent eulogy on the deceased by William W. Harllee, Esq., whereupon the Court made the following order:

On hearing the above preamble and resolutions, and on motion of the Attorney-General, seconded by Mr. Harllee, it is ordered that they be entered on the Minutes.

JOHN BELTON O'NEALL.

November 11, 1840."

Our record is ended—our little task is done. For ourselves, but not for him, we mourn his early and unripened grave, and we leave him to that calm, mysterious repose, which sleeps within the tomb where the good lie down to rest without alarm—the retreat of virtue and the refuge of the just. He was the idol of his family in his life, and he keenly enjoyed that love from them which his own affection had excited. His remains were afterwards removed from Philadelphia to Charleston, and laid in the family burying-ground of St. Philip's Church, where they are now, surrounded by all of those who knew him best, and, therefore, loved him most.

ROBERT LAWRENCE TILLINGHAST

Was born in Effingham County, Georgia, November 2d, 1817. He was removed to Savannah at about the age of six years, when his education commenced at a free school in that city.

He was afterwards transferred by the "Union Society," to the academy at Springfield, where he remained until the winter of 1833. Here, although a small boy, he outstripped all his competitors. He then removed to Gillisonville, South Carolina, and was there instructed by the Rev. Stiles Mellechamp, until the fall of 1834, when he entered Columbia College, Washington City. He remained there not quite a year; but in that brief period he secured the friendship of that eminent man, Dr. Chapin, then at the head of the college. On his return, he commenced the study of the law with a relative, Judge Polhill, in Hawkinsville, Georgia. The Judge died in a few months, and Mr. Tillinghast discontinued his legal studies.

He married in Tallahasse, Florida, in January, 1836, returned to Gillisonville, and read law with R. J. Devont, Esq. In 1837, he took charge of the academy at Robertville; this he continued for two years. In 1839, he returned to Gillisonville, and took charge of the academy there. He was admitted to the Bar in Columbia, in 1840, and was then probably teaching the academy at Gillisonville, and may have continued it to 1844. I see he was called to the charge of the school at Grahamville, where he taught three or four years. He then returned to Gillisonville, and practiced law until his death.

He was elected to the House of Representatives from St. Luke's Parish, in 1846, '48, and '52. He was elected to the Senate from the same parish, without opposition, in 1856.

He died on the 11th of March, 1858, in the 41st year of his age, leaving his widow and eight children surviving him.

His ancestors, on his father's side, came to Rhode Island

with Roger Williams; on the part of his mother, they came from England to Georgia, with Gen. Oglethorpe.

Mr. Tillinghast was a well-educated man, and an excellent teacher, a well-informed lawyer, and was succeeding very well at Gillisonville.

He argued his cases with good sense and precision. His style of speaking showed too much his early occupation, being very much in the dictatorial style of a school-master haranguing his class. His voice was not pleasant; it sounded harshly on the ear.

In the management of his business, he seemed to have learned the value of being "prompt, ready, and eager," which is now somewhat overlooked at the Bar.

Mr. Tillinghast was much respected by his cotemporaries and neighbors. The position which he ast held withou opposition, shows how much he was regarded by the people of his parish.

WILKES THURLOW CASTON.

This young man, who died in early life, deserves to live in the memory of his brethren. He was born on the 22d March, 1822, in the District of Lancaster. He lost both of his parents at an early age. The care of his youth and education devolved on that kind-hearted, excellent man, lawyer, and citizen, Minor Clinton, Esq., of Lancaster Village. He placed him in the preparatory department of Davison College, in North Carolina, after its organization, and he continued through the different stages until he graduated, in 1843, at that interesting institution.

He began immediately the study of the law, under the care of his guardian and friend, Minor Clinton, Esq. He pursued the study, read the usual course, and was admitted to the Bar in 1845.

While studying law he became the subject of converting grace, and connected himself with the Methodist Church, at Lancasterville, then under the care of the Rev. John R. Pickett, and ever after lived a consistent Christian. His walk and conversation was uniformly creditable.

He became early a follower of total abstinence, and showed his sincerity and zeal by an ardent advocacy of this interesting subject. He removed to Camden to practice law, and there became a member of Wateree Division Sons of Temperance. He was placed at its head as W. P. In 1854, his brethren in the whole State, impressed with his useful talent, made him G. W. P. of the Grand Division of South Carolina. From 1834 till the same time in 1855, he admirably discharged the great duties of his office, and carried forward the work placed in his hands.

He married a daughter of Robert Boyce, of Columbia.

He pursued his profession in Camden, first as the partner of the Hon. James Chesnut, and afterwards alone. He, by his industry and talents, acquired a profitable practice; he also, always had business in the district of his nativity. In the village of Lancaster, at the April extra Court, 1858, I last saw him.

He was an active and efficient friend of education.

He, with his family, attended (as was his habit) the Annual Commencement of the Wafford College, at Spartanburg, in July, 1858. On Monday he was in his usual health, on Tuesday evening, the 13th, he was struck down with apoplexy, and in a few hours was in the presence of his Judge and his Master. He left a widow and three young sons. Thus, in his thirty-seventh year, was closed, suddenly and unexpectedly, the life of this excellent man and promising lawyer.

Having known Mr. Caston intimately from his admission to the Bar, I have no hesitation in saying, he was a most promising lawyer, an useful, good man and citizen, kind and affectionate in all his domestic relations, and above all, a devout Christian, exhibiting all the works of "righteousness and temperance," and looking forward to his everlasting reward in "the judgment to come."

JOHN SIEGLING, JR.

This young gentleman, who had attracted the attention of the Judges, by his correct deportment in Court, his remarkable accuracy in business, his knowledge of his profession and his beautiful elocution, when he chose to speak, which was seldom, was suddenly cut off from the society of which he was an ornament, on the 18th day of October, 1857. John Siegling, Jr., was born on the 31st of August, 1825, in Charleston, South Carolina.

He attended school at the usual age, where he applied himself to learning with great diligence, and acquitted himself with ability. The tastes which he there acquired for study, induced his parents, at his request, to send him to Europe, to pursue the higher branches of education. At fifteen, he was sent to Germany, to reside with his father's family. There, under the ablest professors, he acquired a practical education, and a thorough knowledge of book-keeping, mathematics, surveying, civil engineering and topography, and a proficiency in the German and French languages. Amid the labors of study, he found relaxation in music and drawing, in which he was a proficient, and in gymnastic exercises.

After a course of two years' severe study, he left Germany, and traveled on the Continent and in England, visiting and enjoying all the accessible curiosities of nature and art.

On his return to his native city, he conducted, as clerk with his father, for over a year, a large mercantile business, and acquired during that time, a knowledge of the Latin and Greek languages, but more especially the former, which knowledge became more thorough by study, and by directing the education of a younger brother; but evincing an inclination for the law, and having obtained the consent of his parents, he pursued the study of the law, in the office of his friend, the Clerk of the Court for Charleston District, and after indefatigable attention, and study of the details of legal proceedings, in 1845, he entered the Law University of Cambridge, and attended the lectures of Judge Story, Professor Greenleaf, Dr. Warren, and others.

In 1847, he was admitted by the Courts of Appeal in Law and Equity, at Columbia, to the practice of Law and Equity.

Industrious, careful and prudent, in all of his legal affairs, he was opposed to taking any cause, the justice of which he did not recognise, and when he found his client wrong, declined managing, unless he first made a suitable amend. As far as he could, consistently with his duty as an attorney, he would not appear in criminal cases, where he saw clear guilt. Where a person had committed a violation of the criminal law, and there were circumstances of extenuation, through ignorance, or improper seduction, he would at times take part, especially where he saw that an undue pressure was made for punishment.

Possessing a fluency of speech, yet his ability consisted more as a private adviser, and adjuster of complicated accounts and titles, than a public speaker.

So diligent, exact and correct was he in investigating titles, that where property was once bought under a conveyance which he drew, subsequent purchasers generally did not care to look further back than that conveyance, that being considered as a stand-point.

A fondness for study was his ruling passion, and he was noted for the extent of his reading, and remarkable retention of memory. Many practical men, from his knowledge of his profession, would consult him for information, which he always cheerfully gave. He did this so often, so readily and so exactly, that many of his young brother lawyers considered him a perfect adept in his profession.

Upright in his character, correct in his advice, he exhibited throughout his life, a holy veneration and regard for truth, and demonstrated in his intercourse with the world, that only justice and truth were always expedient. Influenced by this mighty principle, age frequently yielded to his better judgment.

From the pursuit of the law he had amassed a small fortune, although he had never made any great effort at the Bar, as a public speaker, to draw to him business.

He was elected a Representative to the Legislature from the Parishes of St. Phillip and St. Michael. After serving two terms, he declined being a candidate. During his term of service, he advocated the giving of the election of electors for President to the people.

Although strictly temperate and regular in his habits, he was suddenly attacked with paralysis, which in a few days terminated his life, on the 18th of October, 1857, in the thirty-third year of his age. Although possessed of every virtue calculated for happiness in domestic life, he never married. He died beloved, honored and regretted.

We append the following tribute by his brethren of the Bar, and the editorial remark of the daily paper:

"A very general attendance of the members of the Bar was held in the Equity-room, at ten o'clock yesterday morning, in order to pay a tribute of respect to the memory of their late brother-member, John Siegling, Jr.

The Attorney General, I. W. Hayne, Esq., was, on motion, called to the Chair, and stated the object of the meeting in a few affectingly appropriate remarks.

Hon. W. D. Porter, after a touching tribute to the many virtues which had distinguished the deceased, both as a lawyer and a citizen, introduced for the adoption of the meeting the following

PREAMBLE AND RESOLUTIONS.

Of late years the Bar of Charleston has been not unfrequently called together for a purpose similar to the present. The object has heretofore been to lament the departure of the middle-aged or the old; of those whose years have rendered them, in some measure, ripe for the grave, and whose services and honors have given a sort of finish to their lives. But, on the present occasion, it has been assembled to mourn the death of one who has been stricken down by an unexpected visitation, and a mysterious and inexplicable form of disease, in the prime of young manhood, and in mid-career of those honors and distinctions upon which his gaze was still steadily and ardently fixed. How have the promise of youth, and the pride of intellect, the bright dreams of ambition, and the fair and fond hopes of parents, and relatives, and friends, been suddenly blighted and buried in that untimely grave!

John Siegling, Jr., was a young man of mark, and of distinguished promise; all of his young cotemporaries so regarded him. He had the talent and the industry to achieve success; and he had also that substratum of *character*, which is the true and only foundation of solid excellence. His integrity of purpose and faithfulness to duty were beyond all impeachment. He was proud of his profession, and determined to excel in it. His system of study, and the completeness of his preparation, and his performances, showed how high his standard was. Although early honored with public trusts, he voluntarily declined a further acceptance of them, in order that he might the more earnestly and exclusively devote himself to professional attainments. Whatever he did, was done thoroughly and well. If his aim was high, so was his purpose steadfast, and his exertions unrelaxing. Men marked his course, and saw that it was destined to be a lofty and an honorable one; and the public confidence, which always waits upon well-deserving efforts, generally sustained him, and bore him onward in his career of usefulness and honor. Much was accomplished; but still more was before him, fated, alas! never to be performed.

For the purity of his principles, and the fitting examples of his life; for his integrity, which was unstained by a shadow of doubt or suspicion; for the hopeful promise of talent and virtue, which has been so sadly and suddenly extinguished in the gloom of the grave; for that early achievement of reputation which may well excite the emulation of his friendly rivals in the race of professional distinction; and for the many manly and generous qualities, which endeared him to his friends, and attracted towards him the regards and respect of the community; his brethren of the Bar will not fail to cherish his memory, and to hold his name and his character in long and affectionate remembrance. Therefore,

Resolved, That we deeply deplore the decease of John Siegling, Jr., as of a young fellow-member, who, in his brief life, adorned the profession of the law by a character of blameless integrity, and by talents and virtues, which had already elicited the high admiration, and excited the warmest hopes of the Bar and the community; and that, in token of respect for his memory, we will attend his funeral ceremonies this afternoon in a body.

Resolved, That the Attorney-General be requested to present this preamble and resolutions to the Court of Common Pleas and General Sessions, now in session, for such action as the Court, upon his motion, shall see fit to take.

The resolutions were seconded by T. Y. Simons, Esq., in a very feeling address, and after some eloquent remarks by M. P. O'Connor, Esq., they were unanimously adopted.

On motion of Mr. Buist, it was further

Resolved, That the preamble and resolutions be published in the daily papers, and a copy of the same sent to the family of the deceased.

The meeting afterwards, on motion of John Phillips, Esq., adjourned to the Court-room, where his Honor Judge Glover was then presiding. The chairman of the meeting presented to the notice of the Court the action of the Bar, and moved that the preamble and resolutions be spread upon the Minutes of Court.

I. W. HAYNE, *Chairman.*

F. J. SCHAFFER, *Secretary.*

The District Court of the United States, his Honor Judge Magrath presiding, convened yesterday morning at ten o'clock.

The District Attorney announced to the Court the death of Mr. John Siegling, Junior, a member of the Bar, and after rendering a tribute to the memory of the deceased, submitted the resolutions adopted by the Bar of Charleston, expressive of their sorrow at the loss of so esteemed an associate, and moved that they should be entered on the journals of the Court, and that the Court stand adjourned.

On the resolvtions being submitted, the Court expressed

the sorrow with which it received the announcement of the death of one whose career had been so bright, and whose future was so promising, and as an expression of the sympathy of the Court with the Bar and the community, ordered that the proceedings be entered on the journals of the Court, and that the Court stand adjourned.

H. Y. GRAY,
Clerk United States District Court.

THE DEATH OF JOHN SIEGLING, JR.

Who that knew John Siegling can refuse to drop a tear upon his early grave? He was mild and amiable, and sincere and honorable and talented. He had ambition, but it was of that high order that would attain its end only in the true and the right. He never sought to rise by pulling down another. In his intercourse in private and at the Bar, and in public life, he never failed to yield to others all that should be granted, and so he was beloved by his associates and esteemed by his opponents. He had much to live for. His life was full of promise, sustained by earnestness of performance. Though yet young, he had acquired a large practice in which he had the full confidence of his clients. He was almost the idol of his family and was the centre of many warm friends. From all these he has been taken suddenly away in his youth, and the blow is sad and heavy.

His funeral at the English Lutheran church was largely attended, and there the sad countenances of the brightest of his profession attested their sense of his worth. The reverend and venerable Dr. Bachman, his pastor and friend, in his funeral service, paid fitting tribute to his character and virtues, which, though he lies buried, cannot soon be forgotten.—*Charleston Standard.*

DEATH OF MR. JOHN SIEGLING, JR.

We have to announce the melancholy intelligence of the death of John Siegling, Jr., Esq., a prominent member of the Bar, and a useful and active citizen. Mr. Siegling has died in the very noon of manhood, having achieved great success in his walk of life, and apparently with every hope for future and higher results. From principle, honor and integrity had become a habit; with the same single-mindedness with which he maintained right and accused wrong, he pursued those studies that enabled him to receive with clean hands the meed of well-merited achievement. As Counsel to several law officers of the State, his advice has been of material assistance in tempering and enforcing the execution of justice; and the result of that experience, embodied in a well-known Manual, has regulated the entire administration of the Courts throughout the State. In his private practice—one of the most extensive at the Bar—he was liberal and accommodating; at the same time his thorough accuracy furnished frequent precedent.

Mr. Siegling had served in the Legislature, and on occasions involving his political principles, had mingled in party issues, but without ever estranging a friend or exciting enmity. He held the command of a volunteer company of this city, and was universally considered as worthy, in his rare union of talent and integrity, to advance still higher in the confidence and dignities of our community. The future had, apparently, every prospect of earthly reward; but that inscrutable decree which gathers in those ripened for eternity, has—while he seemed exuberant in the first strength of life—closed with its dark pall the vista of time.—*Charleston Mercury.*

DEATH OF JOHN SIEGLING, JR.

We regret to learn the death—after an illness of nearly three weeks—of John Siegling, Jr., Esq., one of the most prominent and promising of the younger members of the Charleston Bar. His legal studies were commenced in Charleston and finished at the Law School of Cambridge, Mass. His rise in his profession was rapid and sure, and his worth and merit were recognized by all with whom he was thrown into association. He was popular and successful as the commander of one of our companies of citizen soldiery, and as a Member of the Legislature of South Carolina, he had the approbation and respect of our community.—*Charleston Courier.*

CHIEF JUSTICES.

Names.

1698..Bohun, Edmund,
1712..Trott, Nicholas,
1718..Allien, Richard,
1730..Wright, Robert,
1739..Dale, Thomas,
Whitaker, Benjamin,
1749..Græme, James,
1752..Pinckney, Charles,

Names.

1753..Leigh, Peter,
1759..Michie, James,
1761..Simpson, William,
1762..Skinner, Charles,
1771..Gordon, Thomas Knox,
1776..Drayton, William Henry,
1795..Rutledge, John.

LAW JUDGES.

Names.

1736..Dale, Thomas,
1737..Austin, Robert,
Conseillere, Dela Benjamin,
Lamball, Thomas,
1740..Mazyck, Isaac,
Bull, William, Jr.,
Yonge, Robert,
1741..Beale, Othniel,
1744..Lining, John,
1753..Drayton, John,
1760..Simpson, William,
Pringle, Robert,
1764..Burrows, William,
Brisbane, Robert,
1766..Loundes, Rawlins,
Smith, Benjamin,
D'Oyley, Daniel,
1769..Powell, G. Gabriel,
1771..Savage, Edward,
Murray, John,
Fewtrell, John,
1772..Caslett, Mathew,
1774..Drayton, William Henry,
Gregory, William,
1776..Mathewes, John,
Bee, Thomas,
Pendleton, Henry,
1778..Burke, Ædanus,
1779..Heyward, Thomas.

Names.

1779..Grimké, John F.,
Waties, Thomas,
1789..Drayton, William,
1791..Bay, Elihu Hall,
Ramsay, Ephraim,
1800..Johnson, William, Jr.,
Trezevant, Lewis C.,
1801..Brevard, Jospeh,
1804..Lee, Thomas,
Wilds, Samuel, Jr.,
1808..Smith, William,
1810..Nott, Abraham,
1811..Colcock, C. J.,
1815..Gantt, Richard,
Johnson, David,
1816..Cheves, Langdon,
1818..Richardson, J. S.,
1819..Huger, Daniel Elliott,
1828..O'Neall, John Belton,
1829..Evans, Josiah J.,
1830..Martin, W. D.,
Earle, Baylies J.,
1833..Butler, A. P.,
1841..Wardlaw, D. L.,
1843..Frost, Edward,
1846..Withers, T. J.,
1850..Whitner, J. N.,
1852..Glover, Thomas W.,
1853..Munro, Robert.

JUDGES OF THE COURT OF EQUITY.

Names.

1784..Rutledge, John,
Hutson, Richard,
Mathewes, John,
Rutledge, Hugh,
Hunt, James Green,
1800..Burke, Ædanus,
Marshall, William,
James, W. D.,
1805..Thompson, Waddy,
1808..DeSaussure, H. W.,

Names.

1808..Gailliard, Theodore,
1811..Waties, Thomas,
1828..Harper, William,
1830..Johnson, Job,
1835..Johnson, David,
1837..Durkin, B. F.
1846..Caldwell, James J.,
1847..Dargan, G. W.,
1850..Wardlaw, F. H.

RECORDERS

OF THE CITY COURT OF CHARLESTON.

Names.	Names.
1783..Gibbes, W. Hasell,	1825..Prioleau, Samuel,
1786..Holmes, John Bee,	1836..Axson, Jacob,
1792..Marshall, William,	1842..King, Mitchell, (*pro tem.*)
1796..Edwards, Alexander,	1844..Eckhard, George B.,
1811..Holmes, John Bee,	1845..Rice, William,
1819..Drayton, William,	1856..Macbeth, Charles,
1919..King, Mitchell, (*pro tem.*)	1858..Pringle, William Allston.

ATTORNEY GENERALS

OF SOUTH CAROLINA.

Names.	Names.
1762..Græme, Adam,	1810..Richardson, J. S.,
1764..Moultrie, James,	1818..Hayne, Robert J.,
1764..Rutledge, John, (*pro tem.*)	1822..Petigru, James Louis,
1765..Leigh, Egerton,	1830..Legaré, Hugh S.,
1776..Moultrie, Alexander,	1832..Rhett, R. Barnwell,
1792..Pringle, John Julius,	1836..Bailey, Henry,
1808..Cheves, Langdon,	1848..Hayne, Isaac W.

SOLICITORS.

Names.	Names.
1794..Lee, Thomas,	1824..Pearson, P. E.,
James, W. D.,	1829..Mayrant, John,
1798..Colcock, C. J.,	1830..Thompson, Waddy,
1803..Wilds, Samuel,	1833..Withers, T. J.,
1804..Ervin, James,	1833..Player, T. T.,
Evans, David R.,	1835..Whitner, J. N.,
Thompson, Waddy,	1835..Caldwell, James J.,
Taylor, John,	1836..Edwards, J. D.,
1806..Starke, Robert,	1841..McIver, Alexander,
1811..Johnson, David,	1844..Dawkins, T. N.,
1814..Saxon, B. H.,	1846..Fair, Simeon,
1816..Clarke, Caleb,	1848..Bonham, M. L.,
1818..Davis, W. Ransom,	1850..Reid, Jacob P.,
1820..Jeter, J. Speed,	Hanna, W. J.,
1822..Earle, Baylies J.,	1853..McIver, Henry.
1822..Elmore, F. H.,	

JUDGES IN ADMIRALTY

IN SOUTH CAROLINA, PREVIOUS TO AND SINCE THE REVOLUTION.*

Names.	Names.
1716..Trott, Nicholas,	1760..Rattray, John,
1719..Blakeney, William,	1761..Leigh, Egerton,
1721..Smith, James,	1787..Drayton, William,
1727..Whitaker, Benjamin,	1789..Drayton, William,
1732..Treewin, William,	1790..Bee, Thomas,
1736..Lewis, Maurice,	1812..Drayton, John,
1742..Græme, James,	1823..Lee, Thomas,
1752..Michie, James,	1839..Gilchrist, R. B.,
1758..Leigh, Peter,	1856..Magrath, A. G.,

* The earliest record of, a Court organized, is the 13th November, 1716, Nicholas Trott presiding as Judge; from which time the records are in existence.
The first Court of the United States, organized under the Constitution in South Carolina, was held at Charleston, the 14th December, 1789, by William Drayton, as Judge; under a Commission from President Washington, dated 8th November. 1789. At the same Court John Julius Pringle took the oath of the Attorney of the United States for the District of South Carolina, under a Commission from President Washington, dated 26th September, 1789.

UNITED STATES DISTRICT ATTORNEYS

FOR SOUTH CAROLINA.

Names.

1789..Pringle, John Julius,
1792..Parker, Thomas,
1821..Gadsden, John,
1830..Frost, Edward,
1831..Gilchrist, R. B.,
1839..McCrady, Edward,
1850..Petigru, J. L.,
1853..Evans, Thomas,
1857..Conner, James.

LIST OF ATTORNEYS

ENROLLED AT CHARLESTON, SOUTH CAROLINA, FROM 1772 TO MAY, 1859, INCLUSIVE.

ARRANGED IN CHRONOLOGICAL AND ALPHABETICAL ORDER.

Names.

A.

1794..Allison, Jacob,
1798..Allen, John C.,
1799..Allston, Joseph,
1807..Anderson, Robert,
1817..Alston, Thomas P.,
Axson, Jacob, Jr.,
1818..Allston, Benjamin G.,
1829..Allen, Thomas P.,
1832..Ashby, James A.,
1834..Alston, William Ashe,
1835..Aldrich, A. P.,
1842..Atkinson, Samuel T.,
1853..Amaker, A. Perry,
1858..Allston, Robert A.

B.

1783..Bay, Elihu Hall,
Bay, John,
1784..Bagley, Peter,
1786..Beaumont, H.,
1787..Bampfield, William Hardy,
1792..Bowles, Tobias,
Brevard, Joseph,
1793..Bailey, Henry, Sr.,
Baldwin, M.,
1796..Butler, Anthony,
1799..Bailey,
1801..Bacot, Henry,
Bacot, Henry H.,
1808..Bay, Andrew,
1810..Bacot, Peter,
Bee, Barnard E.,
Bennett, Joseph,
1811..Bentham, Robert,
1813..Bennett, J. S. K.,
Bull, William A.,
1814..Bullard, Royal,
1815..Black, Charles L.,
1816..Bailey, William Edward,
1817..Bonneau, Symes,
Bricknell, William A.,
1818..Baker, W. F.,
1818..Belcher, Manning,
1820..Barker, S. G.,
1822..Bonsall, Sermon,
1823..Barnwell, Robert W.,
Boylston, N. H.,
1824..Benbow, Moses M.,
Biscell, J. Humphrey,
Brown, Lewis M.,
Brannan, William B.,
1825..Butt, Patt M.,
Bynum, Alfred,
1826..Barnes, John M.,
Beck, David,
Brenan, Richard,
Buist, George,
1827..Barnwell, William H.,
Burgoyne, Martin O. D.,
1828..Breaker, Samuel G.,
1829..Bellinger, Edward, Jr.,
1831..Brown, Alexander H.,
Bryan, George S.,
1833..Boone, William J.,
1836..Boyle, Charles R.,
1838..Burden, T. L.,
1839..Butler, T. P.,
1841..Benjamin, S.,
1842..Bobo, W. M.,
1847..Brolley, Arthur P.,
1848..Boyce, Robert,
1851..Bell, C. E.,
Buist, C. B.,
Buist, Henry,
1852..Bailey, David,

C.

1783..Calhoun, John Ewing,
1785..Carnes, Peter,
1786..Cheves, Langdon,
Carnes, W. P.,
1787..Cogdell, Charles,
1792..Caulkins, John,
Colcock, Charles Jones,
1793..Cox, George P.,

Names.

1795..Cochran, R. E.,
Creswell, Robert,
Cromwell, O.,
1797..Cheves, Langdon,
Cotte, Jean Paul,
Croft, Edward,
1799..Clement, William,
Cogdell, John S.,
1802..Condy, Jeremiah,
1803..Cart, Thomas,
1804..Cross, George Warren,
1809..Crafts, William, Jr.,
1813..Clendenen, Robert,
1814..Chesley, John R. E.,
1817..Clarke, Joseph,
Cawlkins, John,
1818..Campbell, W. S.,
Chipman, Edwin,
Condy, Thomas D.,
1819..Cart, Vernal,
1820..Chitty, Charles C.,
1822..Campbell, John,
Coit, John C.,
1823..Courtenay, Edward S.,
Cummins, William,
1824..Cruger, H. V.,
1825..Colcock, W. F.,
Coleman, G. W.,
Cruger, Lewis,
1826..Carroll, Charles R.,
Cochran, Charles B., J.,
1827..Cogdell, J. G.,
1829..Cohen, W. M.,
Corbett, Thomas, Jr.,
1830..Cheves, J. H.,
Cox, Adam Tunno,
1832..Campbell, James B.,
1833..Carnell, E.,
Carr, Thomas Graham,
Carroll, B. R.,
1834..Cooper, George W.,
1835..Carroll, Edward,
Crafts, G. J.,
Crouch, C. W.,
1837..Caldwell, W. S.,
Chesnut, James,
Clapp, John M.,
1840..Campbell, B. R.,
1841..Coleman, Henry,
1850..Crawford, Martin P.
1851..Conner, James,
1857..Cohen, J. Barnett.

D.

1784..Drayton, Jacob,
1785..DeSaussure, H. W.,
1786..Deas, William Allen,
1787..Dickinson, Richard,
1791..Dart, Isaac Motte,
Deas, Henry,
Dickinson, Francis,
1793..Darrell, Edward, Jr.,
Deas, David,
Dewitt, John, Jr.,

Names.

1795..Duffy, George D.,
Dunlap, J.,
1797..DeVeaux, Charles Henry,
Drayton, William,
1798..Dozier, Abraham,
1799..Dart, John S.,
1801..Duncan, James,
Duncan, J.,
1807..Dawson, Charles P.,
1808..Dees, James,
1809..DeLesseline, F. A.,
1810..DeSaussure, Henry A.,
1813..DeSaussure, W. F.,
1814..DeBesse, Frederick,
1815..D'Oyley, Charles W.,
1820..Deas, Henry, Jr.,
1821..Dawson, L. E.,
1823..Denisen, William,
1825..DeTreville, Richard,
1828..DeSaussure, John M.,
1838..DeTreville, Ellis,
1840..Dawson, A. V.,
DeLeon, Edwin,
1842..Dawkins, J. B.,
1844..Dunkin, A. H.,
1846..Davega, Isaac,
1854..DeTreville, W. J.

E.

1787..Edwards, Alexander,
1800..Egan, Thomas,
1810..Elliott, Benjamin,
Elliott, Charles,
1816..Eckhard, George B.,
Edwards, Edward H.,
1817..Egleston, G. W.,
1818..Edwards, J. D.,
Elliott, Thomas O.,
1820..Elfe, Robert,
1827..Elliott, Stephen, Jr.,
1836..Evans, T. C.,
1839..Elliott, Benjamin, Jr.,
1841..Elliott, J. H.,
1842..Evans, C. D.,
Evans, W. H.,
1845..Elliott, Milton,
1848..Evans, Beverly D.,
1858..Elliott, W. S.

F.

1783..Fraser, William,
1785..Fraser, Alexander,
1786..Ford, Timothy,
Fowke, Charles D.,
1793..Farrow, Samuel,
1796..Ford, Jacob,
1800..Ferguson, W. C.,
1805..Ferguson, James,
1807..Fraser, Charles,
1814..Flagg, Henry Collins,
1817..Footman, W. C.,
1819..Furman, C. M.,
1823..Frost, Edward,
1824..Finley, W. Peroneau,

Names.

1826..Ford, Frederick A.,
1827..Fiske, Thomas,
1828..Fishburn, B. C.,
1829..Faber, Joseph W.,
1837..Fuller, Thomas,
1842..Felder, P. S.,
1845..Fickling, W. B.

G.

1784..Goodwin, Charles,
1788..Gailliard, Theodore,
1795..Griggs, Isaac,
1796..Gist, J. C.,
1797..Geddes, John,
1798..Gibbes, W. Hasell,
1800..Gervais, Sinclair D.,
Grant, William,
1803..Gist, John,
1808..Gadsden, John,
1809..Grimké, T. Smith,
1813..Grimké, Frederick,
1814..Gibson, W. M.,
1815..Godfrey, John G.,
1817..Gilbert, Elijah,
1818..Gantt, Thomas J.,
Gilchrist, R. B.,
Gourdin, P. G.,
1820..Gadsden, T., Jr.,
Geddes, James,
Gibbes, M. G.,
Gourdin, S., Jr.,
1822..Greyson, W. J.,
1823..Gregorie, J. Ladson,
Grimké, Henry,
1825..Godfrey, B. F.,
Goodwin, J. G. H.,
1834..Gibbes, M. G.,
Gibson, D. C.,
1835..Gause, John P.,
Gough, T. P.,
Gourdin, R. N.,
1836..Giles, John A.,
1841..Greyson, W. J., Jr.

H.

1783..Holmes, John Bee,
1786..Hunt, J. G.,
1787..Hall, Thomas,
Harper, Robert G.,
1789..Hall, Dominic C.,
1792..Hinds, Thomas,
1793..Hay, Samuel,
Horry, Elias,
1795..Heard, Stephen,
Huger, Jacob Motte,
1796..Herdon, Joseph,
Home, James,
Hunt, Thomas,
Hunt, Warren,
1797..Heriot, Robert,
1799..Henderson, George,
Huger, Daniel Elliott,
Huger, Daniel,

Names.

1804..Hasell, W. Lorango,
1807..Heath, John Davis,
1808..Hort, Robert S.,
1809..Heyward, William, Jr.,
1812..Hayne, Robert Y.,
1813..Hunt, B. F.,
1814..Habershaw, R. W.,
1816..Hunter, J. L.,
1817..Haselhurst, R., Jr.,
Holding, Joseph,
1818..Holmes, Isaac E.,
1819..Haig, James,
Holmes, James G.,
Howard, Amasa,
1820..Heriot, Daniel T.,
1821..Hibben, James, Jr.,
1822..Holt, Benjamin,
1824..Humphrey, T. J.,
Hutchings, Elisha P.,
1826..Hogan, William,
1827..Huger, D. E., Jr.,
Hunt, T. Gailliard,
1828..Henderson, Francis, Jr.,
Hearsey, George T.,
Hunt, Randall,
1829..Horlbeck, Daniel,
1832..Henderson, D. J.,
1836..Hutson, W. M.,
Hutson, W. F.,
1839..Hay, Charles C.,
Hurlburt, S. A.,
1841..Hopkins, T. T.,
Hutson, J. M.,
1842..Holmes, George Frederick,
1846..Hunt, B. F., Jr.,
1850..Hanckel, C. F.,
1852..Hopkinson, George,
1853..Haskell, S. C.,
1857..Haynesworth, J. R.

J.

1793..Johnson, William, Jr.,
1794..James, Benjamin,
1802..Johnson, John William,
1805..Jervey, James,
Johnson, Andrew F.,
1807..Jones, Noah,
1811..Johnson, Roswell Post,
1819..Johnson, James S.,
1823..Jones, Joseph,
1825..Jones, T. L.,
1834..Jones, Joseph L.,
1835..Jones, Edwin P.,
1839..Jones, Lambert J.,
1850..Jenkins, W. E.

K.

1784..Knight, Christopher,
1796..Ker, Samuel,
1809..Kenedy, Lionel Henry,
1810..Keith, M. Irving,
1817..Keitch, John A.,
1838..Kunhardt, W. W.,
1841..King, Henry C.

Names.

L.

1774..Lining, Charles,
1783..Lance, Lambert,
1786..Lowrie, Samuel,
1789..Loundes, Thomas,
1790..Loundes, James,
1794..Leak, Isaiah,
1797..Legge, Edward B.,
Logan, William, Jr.,
1798..Lee, W., Jr.,
1799..Lourence, Robert D.,
Lightwood, Edward C.,
1802..Lee, Stephen, Jr.,
1804..Loundes, William,
1807..Logan, G. R.,
1811..Lance, William,
1813..Lining, Edward B.,
1815..Linah, James,
1818..Legaré, J. Berwick,
1820..Laurens, J. B.,
1821..Leake, Richard,
Legaré, H. S.,
Linton, B. F.,
1824..Lee, Stephen,
1825..Logan, George W.,
Lyon, Levi S. D.,
1829..Lee, T. B.,
Loundes, William P.,
1834..Limehouse, R., Jr.,
1839..Laurence, Samuel,
Lee, W. H.,
1845..Legaré, J. Berwick, Jr.,
1846..Lux, Joseph,
1858..Lining, Arthur P.

M.

1772..Moultrie, Alexander,
1792..Michie, Patt,
1793..Myers, Moses,
1794..Mathewes, James,
1796..McCready, John,
Myers, Abraham,
1797..Michie, Matt,
1805..McCall, Hext,
Mitchell, James Dean,
1808..Mitchell, Thomas R.,
Morrall, G. W.,
1809..Markley, Benjamin A.,
1810..Morris, William Elliott,
1811..McCormic, Richard,
1814..Mayrant, Charles,
Mayrant, William, Jr.,
1815..Massey, J. C.,
1816..Moultrie, Alexander,
Mitchell, J. W.,
1817..McMillan, John R.,
1819..Mawger, John G.,
1822..Mazyck, Alexander,
Middleton, Henry, Jr.,
Moise, Abraham,
Muhall, Jacob H. M.,
1823..Manigault, Joseph, Jr.,
McGhee, J. C.,
Middleton, Arthur,

Names.

1823..Mulinow, Simon C.,
Munro, Robert,
1824..McCready, Edward,
1825..McElhenney, James,
Moses, F. J.,
1826..Makay, G. C.,
McBeth, Charles,
1827..Manigault, C. D.,
Manigault, P.,
1828..McRhee, J.,
1829..Maybank, Samuel,
1830..Martin, Thomas,
1831..Mihard, Peter,
1832..Mathewes, E. W.,
1833..Malone, T. W.,
McCarthy, F. J.,
1834..Mitchell, N.,
1835..McHugh, F. Q.,
Magrath, A. G.,
1837..Martin, William E.,
1841..Morrall, Edward F.,
1842..Magrath, Edward,
May, J. W.,
Morse, A., Jr.,
1848..Moury, E. C.,
1851..Moore, William,
1852..McClenaghan, C. H. S.,
1857..Maulden, A. A.,
Meyer, H. Melville,
1858..Moses, Joseph W.

N.

1784..Nicholas, Henry,
1788..Nicholas, James,
1791..Nott, Abraham,
1792..Nibbs, William,
Norris, Andrew,
1797..Nelson, John,
1805..North, John Laurens,
1808..Northrop, Amos,
1822..Nixon, H. G.,
Neuville, John, Jr.,
1831..Nixon, C. J.,
1834..Northrop, C. B.

O.

1795..Oswald, Leonard,
1808..Osborne, Charles L.,
1810..Ogden, Robert,
1815..O'Driscall, Dennis,
1834..Oswald, Thomas M.,
1342..Owens, William A.

P.

1783..Pringle, John Julius,
1784..Parker, Thomas,
1785..Parker, John, Jr.,
1787..Perkins, Benjamin,
1791..Peyton, Richard H.,
1792..Pearce, James,
Pinckney, M. Brenton,
Pinckney, Roger,
1793..Parker, William McK.

Names.
1793..Pickens, Ezekiel,
1795..Parker, Ferguson,
1796..Parker, John,
Parker, John,
1798..Pugh, Ezra,
1805..Porteous, John,
1808..Prioleau, Samuel,
1810..Parker, John, Jr.,
1812..Peroneau, Henry William,
Petigru, James Louis,
Pinckney, C. C., Jr.,
Prioleau, Elias,
1813..Phillipps, John W.,
Price, William, Jr.,
1814..Parker, Thomas, Jr.,
1815..Pepoon, Benjamin F.,
1818..Porter, John,
1822..Postell, Edward P.,
Pringle, Edward Jenkins,
1823..Perry, Stephens,
1824..Philipps, John, Jr.,
Pow, Joseph,
1825..Porter, Benjamin F.,
1826..Prioleau, F. C.,
1827..Peroneau, Edward C.,
1828..Pouncey, John A.,
Pressley, David A.,
1829..Philipps, P.,
1830..Prince, J. B.,
1831..Postell, John,
1833..Porter, W. D.,
1834..Peters, John Henry,
Porcher, Isaac,
Prioleau, S. Hamilton,
1837..Pringle, B. Garden,
1838..Patterson, James,
1839..Preseley, B. C.,
1840..Perry, Josiah Bedon,
1842..Pinckney, H. L., Jr.,
1850..Parks, George,
1851..Price, C. A.,
1852..Pope, J. W. R.,
1856..Price, W. P.

Q.

1817..Quash, Francis D.

R.

1791..Randall, Paul R.,
Robertson, William,
Rutledge, Edward,
1793..Rutledge, Frederick,
1796..Rutledge, Henry Middleton,
1797..Roper, B. D.,
1799..Richrrdson,
Read, Jacob,
1810..Read, J. Harleston,
1816..Ramsey, David,
1818..Rogers, Henry William,
1819..Raysor, James,
Rolando, F. G.,
1822..Rice, William,
Robins, W. H.,

Names.
1825..Rogers, T. G.,
1827..Richardson, John S.,
Riley, William M.,
1828..Robinson, William,
1829..Rutledge, H. A.,
1830..Robinson, S. T.,
Roper, B. D.,
1832..Rogers, Robert,
Rutledge, N. Harleston,
1833..Reilly, Henry,
1836..Richardson, J. S. G.,
1839..Read, J. H., Jr.,
Richardson, F. D.,
1842..Renwick, W. W.,
Rhett, H. S.,
1845..Requiere, A. J.,
Rhett, C. H.,
1846..Robertson, L. F.,
1851..Rutledge, B. H.,
1853..Rowe, Andrew G.,
1854..Ramsey, David,
1855..Riley, Peter Roscoe.

S.

1784..Shaw, William,
Smith, William,
1787..Smith, James,
1792..Starke, A. Bolling,
1793..Smith, William S.,
1796..Simons, K. L.,
1797..Smith, Benjamin B.
1798..Shackelford, J. A.,
Stewart, C.,
1801..Shackelford, W. F.,
1805..Simkins, Eldred,
1806..Smith, Samuel W.,
1808..Smith, Edward,
Snowden, C. B.,
1809..Strobel, Martin,
Saxon, B. H.,
1812..Smith, Grisham,
1815..Smith, T. Loughton,
Smith, Thomas Rhett,
1817..Simons, Edward P.,
Singleton, William,
Starke, Robert, Jr.,
1819..Sargent, John H.,
Smith, William Skirving,
Smith, James H.,
1820..Smith, William S., Jr.,
1821..Smith, William H.,
Sumter, William,
1822..Shand, Peter J.,
Smith, Robert Barnwell,
Stewart, John A.,
1823..Smith, Edward,
Seymour, R. W.,
Strohecker, C. C.,
1827..Simms, W. Gilmore, Jr.,
Smith, John R.,
Stone, Thomas,
1829..Simons, B. D.,
1830..Smith, W. Wragg,
1831..Schnierle, John,

Names.

1831..Stokes, C. Lloyd,
1833..Spann, M. C.,
Singleton, R. W.,
Smith, Edward,
1834..Smith, Albert M.,
Smith, Oliver M.,
1835..Simons, James,
1836..Smith, John M.,
1838..Smith, J. J. Pringle,
Smith, John Bolton,
1839..Seibels, John J.,
1842..Spann, Henry R.,
Strobhart, James A.,
1847..Shaffer, F. J.,
1851..Smith, Walter D.,
1853..Sams, Horace H.,
1854..Screven, Thomas E.,
1855..Stirling, Samuel R.,

T.

1784..Torrans, William Hunter,
1785..Taylor, George,
1787..Tate, William,
1791..Trezevant, Lewis,
1792..Tennent, William P.,
Thompson, William,
1793..Taylor, John,
1794..Turnbull, R. J.,
1795..Troup, James,
1798..Taylor, John,
1805..Trescot, William,
1811..Toomer, Joshua,
1812..Trezevant, J. F.,
1816..Timothy, Peter,
Tohuan, Thomas,
Taylor, Simon,
1820..Trescot, Henry,
1821..Trotti, Gaspar,
1822..Tyler, Horatio N.,
1827..Thompson, J. B.,
1832..Thomas, Nestor B.,
1837..Thompson, Thomas,
1838..Trotti, S. W.,
1842..Thomas, William H.,
Tompkins, J. J.,
Tupper, James,
1845..Tate, T. D., Jr.,
1847..Tracy, Charles,
1850..Taveau, A. L.,
1851..Tison, John Allen,
1853..Torre, Thomas Dela.

U.

1851..Urner, J. Newton.

Names.

V.

1812..Verdier, John M., Jr.,
1829..Vaughan, John C.,
1830..Venable, William Edward.

W.

1785..Winstanley, Thomas,
1786..Walcones, W.,
1787..Ward, John,
1793..Waring, Daniel,
White, C. Gadsden,
1794..Weston, J. H.,
1795..Ward, Henry Dana,
Ward, James M.,
1797..Wychy, W.,
1798..Wiletz, Samuel, Jr.,
1801..Wilmer, J. R.,
1808..White, J. B.,
1809..Warly, Felix B.,
1811..White, John Philip,
1814..Ward, F. S.,
1816..White, James J. B.,
1817..Waring, D. Jennings,
1818..White, Symes,
1819..Winthrop, Augustus,
1821..Waterhouse, Benjamin,
1822..Wardlaw, F. H.,
Wright, John J.,
1826..Wheeler, E. B.,
1827..Waring, P. H.,
1829..Webb, E. J.,
1830..Webb, B. C.,
Whitaker, D. K.,
1832..Waties, Julius C.,
Wilson, J. D.,
1837..Wilson, J. H.,
1839..Whitaker, J. Smith,
Wilkinson, J. W.,
1841..Walker, H. P.,
1842..Wilson, B. H.,
1846..Whaley, B. J.,
1848..Wagner, Charles,
1851..Williamson, J. A.,
1853..Wilkins, M. L.,
1856..Waring, P. H., Jr.

Y.

1786..Yancey, James,
1798..Yeadon, William,
1824..Yeadon, R., Jr.,
1825..Yates, J. D.,
1826..Youngblood, R. S.,
Youngblood, W. F.,
1836..Youmans, Leroy F.,
1841..Yancey, B. C.

LIST OF ATTORNEYS

ENROLLED AT COLUMBIA, SOUTH CAROLINA, FROM 1800 TO MAY, 1859, INCLUSIVE.

ARRANGED IN CHRONOLOGICAL AND ALPHABETICAL ORDER.

Names.

A.

1806..Allen, George,
1810..Adams, Joel,
1818..Ayer, Zaccheus,
1823..Arnold, Sumner Wilde,
1826..Alsobrook, L. H.,
1828..Addison, John A.,
1835..Allston, P. J.,
Armstrong, Wm. M.,
Arthur, E. J.,
1836..Austin, Samuel L.,
Alston, John A.,
1839..Atkinson, Wm. R.,
1840..Alexander, E. P.,
1841..Anderson, Thos. S.,
1842..Abney, Joseph,
Aldrich, James T.,
Ayer, Lewis M., Jr.,
1843..Anderson, J. Monroe,
1845..Atkinson, W. H. H.,
Adams, W. M.,
Adams, David,
1846..Anderson, E. M.,
Aiken, J. D.,
1847..Alston, Charles, Jr.,
Anderson, Julius,
1848..Adams, F. M.,
Arthur, B. F.,
1850..Adams, James P.,
Allemong, Alexander A.,
1851..Avery, J. W.,
1852..Anderson, Edward J.,
1853..Austin, Aaron,
1854..Allston, Joseph Blyth,
Adams, H. W.,
1855..Anderson, M. G.,
Adams, Cicero,
Adams, Thomas J.,
Addison, Henry W.,
1856..Allison, R. E.,
1857..Allen, Thomas W.,
1858..Addison, John L.,
1859..Abney, W. H.

B.

1800..Blanding, Abram,
1811..Bickley, John,
1813..Bowie, Alexander,
Broyles, Cain,
Brown, John G.,
1814..Bliss, Joel,
1815..Brooks, Whitfield,
Butler, George,
1816..Butler, Frank,
Benson, Nimrod E.,

Names.

1816..Bruster, James,
1817..Bauskett, John,
Burnside, Thomas E.,
1818..Boykin, John, Jr.,
Brummitt, F. K.,
Brevard, Edward C.,
Butler, Andrew Pickens,
1820..Ballard, Charles A.,
1821..Blair, George D.,
1823..Burt, Armstead,
Bailey, Henry,
Boykin, Addiston,
1824..Bacon, Edmund S.,
Barrett, Thomas S.,
Bacon, John W.,
1825..Brownfield, Robert J.,
Bobo, Simpson,
1826..Butler, Leontine,
Brumby, Richard T.,
Brown, James,
1828..Bowie, Langdon,
Burt, Francis,
Bethea, Philip P.,
Buford, Jefferson,
Bonham, James,
1830..Baker, David D.,
Brevard, T. W.,
Banks, Winston,
Black, Joseph A.,
Brownfield, John W.,
1831..Black, William C.,
1832..Belcher, R. E.,
1833..Boozer, Lemuel,
Brewster, C. R.,
1835..Blakeney, James W.,
Backhouse, Benjamin,
1837..Brown, J. W.,
Bonham, M. L.,
1839..Burnet, A. W.,
Black, Samuel R.,
Barr, James,
Blanding, William,
1840..Barron, S. D.,
Barnwell, Robert G.,
Bryce, Campbell R.,
1840..Boyce, W. W.,
Bowers, Levi S.,
1842..Blanding, J. D.,
1843..Brooks, P. S.,
Bellinger, E. E.,
Brown, Alfred B.,
Boylston, R. B.,
Burckmyer, C. L.,
1844..Bealer, G. B.,
Baskin, J. G.,
Blocker, B. M.,

Names.

1844..Burns, J. R.,
1845..Brodie, Samuel H.,
Buchanan, John M.,
Buchanan, Andrew H.,
Beatty, W. C.,
1846..Bell, Thomas J.,
Baskin, A. G.,
1847..Broyles, G. M.,
Broyles, C. E.,
1848..Beckmann, J. F.,
Buchanan, Samuel W.,
Bratton, William M.
Bailey, Samuel J.,
Boone, James S.,
Black, James A.,
Brown, Robert C.,
Bynum, John Gray,
1849..Baxter, James M.;
1850..Brown, C. C.,
Broyles, A. T.,
Bostick, Edward,
Blanding, L. S.,
1851..Bacon, John E.,
1853..Bethea, J. T.,
Brown, J. C.,
Barker, Theodore G.,
Bailey, G.,
Barnwell, John G.,
1854..Bachman, W. K.,
Ball, B. W.,
Bellinger, J. A.,
Blake, W. K.,
Blue, John G.,
Breare, Joseph R.,
Brown, Joseph J.,
1855..Buchanan, W. C.,
Brice, Charles S.,
1856..Bowden, J. M.,
1857..Beattie, Hamlin,
Bedon, Josiah,
Brice, R. R.,
Burnet, B. S.,
Butler, M. C.,
1858..Barker, S. W., Jr.,
Brown, Joseph N.,
Bowles, P. D.,
Butler, Loudon,
1859..Bowie, Robert E.

C.

1805..Chappell, John J.,
1808..Caldwell, James,
1809..Chipman, Harry,
Caldwell, John,
Crenshaw, Anderson,
1810..Crenshaw, Walter,
Campbell, Colin,
Cunningham, Robert,
1813..Carr, Isaac,
1814..Carter, J.,
1815..Creagh, John G.,
1816..Cunningham, John,
1818..Carter, John C.,
Colcock, Thomas H.,

Names.

1819..Clinton, Minor,
Choice, William,
Coggeshall, P. C.,
1820..Caldwell, J. J.,
1822..Carr, George,
Caldwell, Patrick C.,
1823..Coggeshall, James C.,
Campbell, David C.,
Cohen, Solomon,
Clark, James L.,
Coit, David G.,
1824..Chilton, Leven P.,
1825..Cochran, Henry S.,
1826..Cole, James J.,
1827..Conover, James S.,
Carter, Alexander,
Chestney, James, Jr.,
Clifton, W. C.,
Crosby, Joseph J.,
1828..Collier, William,
Clowney, W. K.,
1829..Caughman, H. J.,
Cannon, William R.,
Calhoun, John A.,
1830..Clarke, Kenneth,
Coachman, J. W.,
Clinton, J.,
Carroll, J. P.,
Creswell, Robert,
1831..Carloss, Robertson A.,
Crook, John M.,
Crook, James, Jr.,
Cooper, T. F.,
1832..Cheves, Thomas A.,
Cain, John M.,
1833..Choice, Jefferson,
1836..Cheves, Langdon, Jr.,
Casey, Abner McK.,
1837..Campbell, R. L.,
Clawson, W. J.,
1838..Cole, James P.,
1839..Clarke, H. H.,
Cunningham, John,
1840..Chambers, Edward M.,
Currell, William,
Creswell, John H.,
Coleman, John,
Cooke, John W.,
Cantey, James, Jr.,
1842..Colcock, R. W.,
1843..Chapman, Samuel T.,
Carew, John E.,
1844..Cogdell, J. Walpole,
1845..Carlisle, W. B.,
Caston, W. Thurlow,
Cochran, James N.,
Culp, B. W. D.,
Chalmes, John McM.,
Crawford, A. S.,
1846..Crosson, James M.,
Cash, E. B. C.,
Chapman, John W.,
Crosland, D. E.,
1849..Campbell, W. H.,

Names.
1852..Calhoun, J. E.,
1853..Chambers, Z. C.,
Cuthbert, G. B.,
1854..Carlisle, John W.,
Carr, Joseph P.,
Coit, John T.,
Cothran, James S.,
1855..Caldwell, H. H.,
Chapman, John A.,
Cohen, M. M.,
Coogler, T. S.,
1856..Calhoun, James C.,
Clarke, D. M.,
Clarke, Joseph A.,
1857..Culp, W. B.,
1858..Cavis, A. T.,
Cooke, Thompson H.,
1859..Connors, W. M.

D.

1808..Durham, John H.,
1809..Duffy, William,
Daniel, C.,
1810..Downs, W. F.,
1811..Dubose, William,
1813..Dellet, James,
Dyson, Jeptha,
Davis, Thomas P.,
1814..Davis, Warren R.,
1818..Dunn, W. W.,
Dunkin, John,
1819..Dinkins, James W.,
1820..Dunlap, Robert,
1822..Dozier, A. W.,
Dunlap, Samuel F.,
Doby, James O.,
1823..Dargan, George W.,
1825..Dunlap, J. A.,
1827..Daniel, J. M.,
Davis, John R.,
Davant, R. J.,
1828..Dawkins, T. N.,
Daniels, C. F.,
Dean, H. J.,
Dawson, Drayton,
1829..Dudley, C. W.,
1830..Davis, W. K.
1831..Davis, James E.,
1832..Davis, G. L. A.,
1834..Davis, Benjamin F.,
1835..Duncan, W. H.,
1836..Dargan, Julius A.,
1839..Dukes, Joseph H.,
1840..Dickinson, James Polk,
Dewalt, G. G.,
1841..DeSaussure, W. D.,
1842..Davis, N. H.,
1843..DeSaussure, Wilmot G.,
1844..DeBow, J. D. B.,
Dozier, Richard,
1845..Davey, Chalon F.,
Denton, R. W.,
1847..Dargan, Charles A.,
Dillard, C. H.,

Names.
1847..Dyson, Richard M.,
1848..Davis, Henry C.,
Davis, Thomas G.,
1849..Dantzler, O. M.,
1852..Davis, W. C.,
Dawson, Andrew H. H.,
1853..Dingle, G. W.,
1854..Dick, W. E.,
Duryea, R. S.,
Duncan, W. P.,
1855..DeSaussure, D. B.,
Dingle, W. D. B.,
DeTreville, Robert,
Donaldson, T. Q.,
Douglass, A. S.,
1856..Dozier, James A.,
DeBruhl, S. C.,
1857..Dozier, P. C.,
DePass, W. L.,
Davis, James M.,
Drennon, R. H.,
Duncan, David R.,
Davis, J. J.,
1858..Dudley, Thomas E.,
1859..Dinkins, T. W.

E.

1800..Ervin, James,
1801..Ellison, W.,
1809..Ervin, James R.,
1811..Eastland, Joseph,
Evans, Josiah J.,
1815..Elmore, B. F.,
1816..Earle, Baylis John,
Earle, John T.,
1817..Everett, Alexander J.,
1818..Eaves, N. R.,
Earle, Andrew P.,
1820..Evans, Thomas P.,
1821..Elmore, F. H.,
1822..Ellison, Robert D.,
Edwards, Charles A.,
1826..Ellerbe, John C.,
1827..Edwards, E. W.,
Evans, Harris Smith,
1828..Edwards, John A.,
Edwards, Thomas H.,
1829..Earle, Elias D.,
Edwards, Alexander L.,
1832..Elmore, J. A., Jr.,
1838..Ervin, Erasmus P.,
Ervin, Samuel J.,
1839..Ellis, Henry,
1841..Eppes, George F.,
1842..Edmonston, B. W.,
1843..Elford, C. J.,
1845..Earle, Thompson,
Edwards, O. E.,
1848..Elliott, D. A.,
1849..Evans, Thomas,
1850..Ewart, James B.,
Easly, W. K.,
1853..Earle, Samuel G.,
1854..Edwards, B. W.,

Names.
1856..Elford, J. M.,
Euins, John H.,
1857..Edwards, Augustus F.,
Ervin, John B.,
Evans, A. L.,
1859..Edwards, W. D.,
Eichelberger, P. A.

F.

1808..Felder, John M.,
Farrar, T. W.,
Farrow, J. W.,
1815..Ford, James M.,
1817..Foster, John S. B.,
Flanagan, James,
1818..Farrow, Patillo,
Farr, Robert G. H.,
Fernandis, John H.,
1819..Foster, Simpson,
1820..Falconer, William,
1822..Ford, Edward E.,
1823..Felder, Nathaniel F.,
1824..Fair, Simeon,
Frazer, Peter W.,
Ferdon, John P.,
1825..Fuller, Richard,
1828..Farley, William R.,
1830..Foster, Henry,
1834..Fernandis, Walter,
1835..Fair, E. Young,
1838..Fickling, F. W.,
1843..Farmer, C. B.,
Ferrell, W. C.,
Fair, Robert A.,
1844..Fraser, F. W.,
1845..Felder, J. H.,
1847..Fraser, T. B.,
1848..Farrow, James,
1849..Fraser, L. L., Jr.,
Flagg, C. E. B.,
1850..Frost, Thomas,
1851..Ford, John Drayton,
1854..Fort, William,
1857..Fairlee, George M.,
1858..Ferguson, John W.,
Ferguson, J. DuGué.

G.

1809..Grant, John,
1811..Goodwyn, James T.,
Glascock, John S.,
Gill, John,
Goodwyn, William F.,
1812..Goodwyn, John J.,
1813..Gunning, John Edward,
Gregg, James,
Gee, Edmund,
Gray, Simon P.,
1816..Ghollock, Oliver H.,
Gray, James W.,
Gillespie, J., Jr.,
1818..Glover, Thomas W.,
1819..Geddes, John, Jr.,

Names.
1821..Gantt, Richard A.,
Goldthwaite, R. H.,
1822..Green, Samuel M.,
1823..Goodman, B.,
Glass, John,
1824..Griffin, Nathan L.,
Glascock, Thomas,
Gray, Matthew,
1826..Grant, William J.,
Garret, William,
1827..Graham, Alexander,
Geiget, John W.,
1828..Gill, William,
Gee, Willard F.,
1829..Gaston, Leroy B.,
1831—Godfrey, S. W.,
Glenn, Edward M.,
1834..Garden, Alester,
Gray, James T.,
1836..Goudelock, Davis,
1839..Gregg, Maxcy,
1840..Gregg, Alexander,
1841..Gist, James F.,
1843..Goodwyn, John T.,
Gadberry, J. M.,
Graham, Winchester,
Grimké, James M.,
1844..Garlington, A. C.,
Godfrey, William,
1845..Gardner, James, Jr.,
Glover, C. B.,
Goff, David,
1847..Gourdin, T. S.,
Goin, Wyatt J.,
1848..Gillespie, Thomas T.,
Green, J. T.,
1849..Grice, A. E.,
Garlinton, Robert,
1850..Gilchrist, R. C.,
1851..Gary, S. M. G.,
Glenn, John E.,
Glover, T. J.,
1853..Gist, State Right,
Galluchat, Joseph,
Gaston, J. F.,
1854..Goodlett, Spartan D.,
1855..Gary, M. W.,
Grimball, Berkeley,
1856..Gantt, F. H.,
Gillespie, Samuel J.,
Graham, Robert F.,
1857..Garlington, Creswell,
Green, F. M.,
Griffin, S. B.,
1858..Green, John S.,
Garlington, J. N.,
1859..Gay, L. B.,
Grimball, W. H.

H.

1807..Hanford, Enoch,
Hampton, John P.,
1808..Hammond, M.,
Hampton, Benjamin F.

Names.
1811..Huger, Daniel E.,
Harvey, William S.,
Hampton, H. P.,
1814..Higgings, Frank B.
1815..Huguenin, William J.,
Haynsworth, William,
1816..Herndon, Z. P.,
1817..Hunt, William,
1818..Hunter, John L.,
Hickman, Harris H.,
1819..Hunter, George R.,
1820..Herbert, John,
1821..Henry, J. E.,
Hill, W. R.,
1822..Hart, William B.,
Hoey, S. J.,
Hay, W. H.,
1824..Hemingway, Wilson,
1827..Hudson, J. W.,
1828..Heller, Silas L.,
Harrington, S. C.,
Hasell, Bentley,
Hammond, James H.,
1829..Hemphill, John,
Hanna, William J.,
1831..Hard, William J.,
Hayne, Isaac W.,
1832..Heriot, J. Ouldfield,
1833..Hammond, John D.
Harllee, W. W.,
1835..Hayne, Robert Y., Jr.,
1836..Hemphill, James,
Hall, James G.,
1837..Harrison, W. H.,
Hayden, G. B.,
Haynsworth, T. B.,
Hallonquist, L. D.,
1839..Harrison, J. W.,
1840..Harrison, Richard,
Henry, A. J. H.,
1842..Haile, Columbus,
Habersham, B. Elliott,
1843..Hay, William A.,
Harleston, Edward,
Hewie, Thomas J.,
Hayne, William Alston,
Hanckel, Thomas M.,
Henderson, W. B.,
1844..Heriot, P. Septimus,
1845..Hammet, J. B. N.,
Harllee, J. J.,
Haynsworth, W. F. B.,
1845..Holmes, Joseph C.,
1846..Hamer, L. M.,
Higgins, J. C.,
1847..Hanson, John S.,
1849..Herbemont, A., Jr.,
Harllee, D. S.,
Harris, N. S.,
1850..Hagood, Johnson,
Hay, W. M.,
1851..Henry, E. J.,
Hume, Robert W.,
Hadden, W. M.,

Names.
1852..Harris, W. C.,
Hayne, Paul H.,
1853..Hunter, James O.,
Hutchinson, M. E.,
1854..Hunter, W. M.,
1856..Hickson, William,
1857..Hoadly, F. W.,
Hudson, J. H.,
1858..Hudgins, W. L.,
Hallonquist, L. B..
1859..Hammet, W. J. N.
Heath, W. M.,
Humphreys, W. W.

I.

1817..Irby, James H.,
1840..Inglis, John A.,
1845..Isham, John,
1857..Izlar, James F.,
1859..Inglesby, Charles.

J.

1811..Jeter, John S.,
1817..Johnson, Harmon A.,
1818..Johnston, Job,
1820..James, John S.,
1822..Jones, William,
1823..James, John J.,
1825..Juhan, N. B.,
1826..Jackson, W.,
1827..Jones, James,
1831..Jervey, William,
Jamison, B. F.,
1833..Johnston, B. F.,
1835..Jones, Edward W.,
1838..Johnson, Charles K.,
1840..Jones, H. A.,
1843..Johnson, B. J.,
1844..Johnston, John W.,
1846..Jones, Thomas L.,
Johnson, W. D.,
1848..Jeter, Thomas B.,
1850..Jackson, John B.,
1851..Johnston, Silas,
Jackson, John K.,
Johnston, R. E.,
1854..Jones, D. F.,
Johnson, James H.,
1856..Jamison, David R.,
Jeter, John P.,
1858..Johnson, Daniel W.,
Johnson, Neill D.

K.

1810..King, M.,
1818..Kelsey, J. W.,
1824..Klinck, John G.,
1828..Kenner, Robert R.,
1841..Key, John C. G.,
1842..Kerr, A. H.,
1843..Kershaw, J. B.,
Keys, Thomas G.,
1844..Keitt, L. M.,

Names.

1845..Keith, E. M.,
Kincaid, James,
1846..Karr, Z. H.,
1848..Kanapaux, Charles E.,
Kennedy, W. J.,
1849..Kirkpatrick, James D.,
1850..Kennedy, W. G.,
1853..Kirkwood, W. D. H.,
1857..Keels, W. E.,
Kennedy, William, Jr.,
1858..Knotts, J. Elvin.

L.

1800..Lide, Charles Motte,
1801..Lesly, James,
1806..Levy, Chapman,
1810..Lamar, Thomas G.,
1812..Lomax, William,
1815..Lewers, Samuel B.,
Livingston, Thomas,
1816..Lansdell, Benjamin, C.,
1818..Leigh, David G.,
Lewis, Jesse P.,
1819..Lesly, David,
1822..Lenoir, W. R.,
1823..Lynch, W. E.,
1827..Ludlow, Alfred,
1828..Lockhart, Thomas B.,
Lesly, Samuel W.,
Longstreet, A. B., of Georgia,
1831..Lesesne, H. D.,
Law, E. A.,
Latta, W. A.,
1834..Lesesne, J. W.,
1836..Lowry, J. M.,
1838..Leitner, E. C.,
1842..Lawton, A. R.,
Leland, J. A.,
1843..Landrum, J. M.,
Lester, W. F.,
1844..Lewers, Charles A.,
1845..LaRoche, James,
1846..Lomax, Lucien H.,
1847..Lee, W. A.,
Lesly, John W.,
1848..Lockwood, Thomas P., Jr.,
Landrum, G. W.,
Logue, W. H.,
1850..Laborde, John B.,
1851..Lang, J. Boykin,
1852..Larey, Peter H.,
1853..Lord, Samuel, Jr.,
Leitner, W. Z.,
Lowndes, William,
1854..Lockwood, P.,
Livingston, John W.,
1855..Laurens, Henry,
Lamotte, C. O.,
Livingston, Edward,
1858..Ligon, Robert B.,
Logan, R. T.,
1859..Legg, M. B. A.

Names.

M.

1805..Miller, John B.,
1807..Milling, D. T.,
1808..Maxcy, Milton,
1811..Mayrant, John, Jr.,
Martin, William D.,
Miller, Stephen D.,
1812..McIver, John E.,
1814..McLeod, Alexander,
Massey, James R.,
1815..McComb, John,
McCall, J. B.,
Mayson, Charles E.,
1817..McCraven, J.,
McCollough, John L.,
1818..McCord, David J.,
Maxwell, Robert A.,
McWillie, William,
Marsh, Samuel B.,
1819..Martin, Joseph G.,
Murdock, J. H.,
McCord. R. P.,
May, Pleasant H.,
McDowell, David,
Mills, John,
1820..McIver, Alexander M.,
Mays, James B.,
Maxcy, E. H.,
1820..Mills, Robert G.,
1822..Moore, James,
Mayrant, J. W.,
1823..Martin, Julius M.,
McWhorter, M. S.,
McClintock, Joseph,
1824..Memminger, C. G.,
1825..Meriwether, John A.,
1826..Mathews, Wiley J.,
1827..Marshall, Henry,
Moore, Dennis F.,
1828..Mays, Samuel W.,
McQueen, John,
Maxcy, Hart S. H.,
McAliley, Samuel,
Mittag, J. F. G.,
McClanaghan, J. F. G.,
1829..Maverick, Samuel A.,
McCants, J.,
McCreary, John, Jr.,
1830..Mays, Thomas S.,
1831..Manigault, Gabriel,
Moses, Montgomery,
1833..Mitchell, W. H.,
Moore, T. J.,
1834..Miller, Charles W.,
1837..Martin, B. Y.,
Miller, William M.,
1838..McBee, L. M.,
1838..McMullan, Joseph J.,
Massey, Samuel B.,
1839..Myers, William M.,
1840..Marshall, J. Foster,
1841..IMcHenry, Daniel,
McCants, James B.

Names.

1842..McGowen, Samuel,
1843..McKenzie, James,
McMillan, J. R.,
Magrath, T. P.,
Meetze, Henry A.,
McDowell, R. M.,
McDonald, Matthew,
1844..Moragne, W. C.,
Miller, Lawrence H.,
Moragne, J. B.,
McNair, Murphy C.,
Moore, H. Judge,
Melton, C. D.,
1845..Moore, Edward,
Murphy, M. G. N.,
McFarlan, Allan,
Mabry, J. F.,
Moore, John V.,
McBee, W. P.,
1846..McGilvray, B. F.,
Mickle, J. Belton,
McDonald, B. F.,
Martin, A. M.,
Miller, D. B.,
Moore, J. A.,
1847..Matheson, Donald,
McIver, Henry,
Moore, H. T.,
1848..McKnight, A. Isaac,
Martin, John J.,
1849..Moore, W. A.,
McLure, John J.,
Maher, John J.,
McDuffie, A. Q.,
McMaster, F. W.,
Munro, R., Jr.,
McLaws, W. R., Georgia,
Miller, A. J., Georgia,
1850..Morgan, G. W.,
Miller, J. L.,
1851..Means, G. W.,
McKenzie, Lawrence,
Mazyck, Isaac,
Miles, C. Richardson,
Mabry, Samuel W.,
1852..Moore, H. S.,
1853..McLaurin, P. B.,
1854..McCall, J. N.,
Marshall, J. H.,
McCants, J. M.,
1854..Means, B. W.,
1855..McCrady, Edward, Jr.,
McInnis, John,
Middleton, J. Izard, Jr.,
Moses, M. B.,
Mars, William D.,
McLure, E. C.,
Mordecai, D. H.,
Moore, Maurice A.,
1856..Malloy, J. R.,
McGowan, A. H.,
1857..McClenaghan, J. C.,
McIver, F. M.,
Maurice, S. W.,

Names.

1857..Muse, T. H..
Melton, S. W.,
Metts, W. B.,
Miley, W. F.,
Moore, Baxter H.,
Morrison, M. M.,
1858..Macbeth, Charles A.,
Middleton, Thomas A.,
Moore, J. P.,
McIntosh, Daniel C.,
McKerall, W. J.,
1859..Montgomery, Charles W.,
Moore, John B.,
Moore, Maurice A.,
Munro, William.

N.

1809..Noble, Patrick,
1816..Noble, Joseph,
1818..Nott, Henry Junius,
1822..Nott, Richard T.,
1823..Nance, Drayton,
Nuckolls, William T.,
1826..North, John G.,
1829..Noel, Adolph W.,
1842..Norris, J. W., Jr.,
1843..Newhall, Edward R.,
1844..Nesbitt, E. D.,
1846..Noble, Edward,
Norwood, J. H.,
1847..Norris, F. M.,
Nevitt, John B.,
1856..Norton, J. J.,
1858..Nathans, Jacob N.,
1859..Nance, James D.

O.

1814..O'Neall, John Belton,
1823..O'Hanlon, James,
1830..O'Bannon, John T.,
1843..Orr, James L.,
Oswald, J. C.,
1844..O'Brien, A. L.,
1852..O'Connor, M. P.,
1855..O'Cain, W. A.,
1858..Oliver, Thomas P.

P.

1802..Puckett, D. J.,
1807..Pearson, Philip E.,
1808..Porter, Thomas,
1810..Pearson, William F.,
1812..Patrick, C. C.,
1813..Patterson, Angus,
1821..Palmer, Edward G.,
1822..Preston, William C.,
1824..Pelton, Charles B.,
1825..Pope, Thomas H.,
1826..Peyton, Edward W.,
Paul, John W.,
Potts, John T.,
1827..Perry, B. F.,
Powell, C. P.,

Names.

1827..Player, Thompson T.,
Pearson, Bird M.,
1828..Pressley, J. B.,
Perrin, Thomas C.,
Parker, Edward W.,
Pickens, F. W.,
1830..Price, Reese,
Pope, Solomon,
Pyles, Milton,
1833..Parham, John,
1837..Pope, James A.
1838..Postell, J. A.,
Pearson, John H.,
1840..Powell, Joseph,
1841..Perry, Ralph,
Patton, A. R.,
Percival, Theodore M.,
1842..Phillips, N.,
1843..Pope, Joseph Daniel,
Pringle, William Alston,
Paul, William A.,
1844..Peronneau, William H.,
Prince, W. L. T.,
Poag, William R.,
1845..Peeples, Darling G.,
Palmer, Edward G., Jr.,
Porter, Edward J.,
1846..Petigru, D.,
Porcher, A. H.,
1847..Pringle, E. J.,
Pope, J. J., Jr.,
1849..Phillips, John E.,
Parker, William H.,
Pettigrew, J. Johnston,
1853..Patterson, Giles J.,
1854..Perrin, Abner M.,
Pressley, John G.,
1856..Pulliam, Z. C.,
Perrin, J. Wardlaw.

Q.

1824..Quinn, Henry A.,
1828..Quarles, Robert G.

R.

1812..Rice, D. B.,
1814..Roddy, E.,
1816..Rembert, Alexander,
1817..Rogers, James,
1818..Reid, John,
1820..Rutledge, Benj. Huger,
1823..Ross, John M.,
1824..Rogers, John M.,
Richardson, William E.,
1826..Reese, James E.,
1831..Rice, B. H.,
1836..Rich, N. G.,
1837..Rice, Samuel F.,
Reid, B. F.,
1840..Robertson, W. R.,
1841..Red, D. J.,
Rutland, James M.,
Russell, Thomas B.,

Names.

1842..Randall, Vans,
Reed, J. P.,
1843..Rivers, John E., Jr.,
Rice, W. H.,
Ruff, J. C.,
1845..Ramage, Burr J.,
Raymond, W. W.,
1846..Rhett, William,
1848..Rice, A. G.,
1851..Rhett, R. Barnwell, Jr.,
Ross, J. W.,
1852..Rice, Ibzan J.,
1853..Richardson, John S.,
Rion, James H.,
1854..Reilly, W. L.,
1858..Ravenel, E. Prioleau,
Ready, William J.,
Robinson, Warren D.

S.

1801..Stark, Theodore,
1809..Spann, James G.,
Shields, S. B.,
Smith, Samuel, Jr.,
1812..Smith, Isaac,
1813..Silliman, A.,
Shanklin, Joseph V.,
Starke, Wyatt W.,
1819..Simpson, Richard F.,
1820..Sanford, Ezekiel,
Samuel, Beverly,
Shackelford, A. B.,
1822..Starke, John M.,
Sims, Joseph S.,
Scott, J. W.,
1823..Sims, Clough S.,
1824..Spencer, Robert H.,
1825..Simkins, Eldred, Jr.,
1828..Saxon, L. P.,
Starke, Theodore,
Spierin, Thomas S.,
1829..Smith, E. T.,
Sims, Alexander D.,
1830..Summer, Nicholas,
1831..Smith, James S.,
Speers, Robert H.,
Sumter, Thomas D.,
1833..Smith, Thomas F.,
Summer, Henry,
1835..Sullivan, C. P.,
1836..Sumter, Francis B.,
Smart, John,
1839..Seymour, Edward A.,
1840..Summer, A. G.,
1841..Saxon, Benjamin T.,
1842..Spain, Albertus C.,
Starnes, E.,
1843..Salmond, Burwell B.,
Shannon, W. M.,
Spring, A. B.,
Stokes, J. W.,
Seabrook, E. M.,
1844..Scates, C. Woodman,

Names.

1844..Screven, John H.,
1845..Scott, W. D. O.,
Stewart, R. O. P.,
Simpson, W. D.,
Secrest, John C.,
1846..Simpson, J. Wistar,
Stokes, T. Henry,
Siegling, John, Jr.,
1848..Sutherland, John B.,
Schroder, Henry W.,
Starke, W. Pinkney,
1849..Snead, John C., Georgia,
Sellers, W. W.,
Simons, Thomas Y., Jr.,
1850..Sparks, Samuel, Jr.,
Styles, C. W.,
Seibels, Emmet,
Spratt, L. W.,
1851..Simonton, Charles H.,
Stuart, Julius W.,
Suber, C. H.,
1852..Shaw, A. J.,
1853..Slider, Thomas P.,
Sloan, Joseph Berry,
1854..Simons, William,
1855..Stroman, C. J.,
1856..Salley, A. G.,
Steedman, James B.,
1857..Smith, H. J.,
1858..Shaw, J. F.,
1859..Seabrook, Henry,
Smith, B. F.

T.

1809..Threewits, Llewellin,
1814..Thomson, A. W.,
Tillinghast, Daniel H.,
1815..Trimmier, William,
1819..Thompson, Waddy,
1820..Taylor, James S.,
1821..Terry, James,
1823..Theus, W. R.,
1828..Thomson, H. H.,
Taylor, William J.,
Tompkins, Thomas B.,
1829..Tompkins, H. M.,
Tatom, M. B.,
Thompson, James W.,
Tillinghast, Samuel T.,
Townes, Samuel A.,
1832..Tradewell, J. D.,
1834..Townes, George F.,
1835..Taylor, George T.,
Taylor, James M.,
1838..Torre, P. D.,
1840..Tillinghast, Robert L.,
1842..Thornwell, Charles A.,
1843..Thompson, W. Butler,
Tobin, J. E.,
Tilman, Hiram,
Trescott, William H.,
1844..Tucker, John W.,
1847..Talley, S. Olin,
Tillman, G. D.,

Names.

1848..Trimmier, J. V.,
1849..Tracy, Clement C.,
Tobias, V. J.,
Taber, William R., Jr.,
Tobias, C. H.,
1851..Talley, William H.,
Tew, C. C.,
1853..Taylor, William R.,
Townsend, S. J.,
1854..Thomas, William M.,
1855..Thruston, H. Lee.
1856..Townsend, C. P.,
1857..Todd, R. P.,
Tompkins, R. W. S.

V.

1810..Vance, James R.,
1827..Verdries, Joseph P.,
1840..Vandiver, P. S.,
1842..Vernon, T. O. P.

W.

1800..Witherspoon, John D.,
1807..Wilson, John L.,
1808..Witherspoon, Robert L.,
1809..Williamson, C. E.,
1811..Whitefield, Joseph T.,
1812..Whitner, B. F.,
1813..Wade, William,
1814..Waties, John,
Wade, Nathan C.,
1816..Wooldridge, Thomas,
1817..Willisson, Thomas T.,
Wright, James,
1818..Whitaker, John W.,
1819..Wallis, W. B. A.,
Williams, Charles, Jr.,
Watts, Beaufort T.,
Walker, Tandy,
1820..Wardlaw, David Lewis,
Whitner, J. N.,
1821..Woods, James F.,
1822..Williams, Matthew,
1823..Wilde, Richard Henry,
Wilkins, Samuel B.,
Waties, Wilson,
1824..Warren, John D.,
1826..Witherspoon, J. D.,
Weathersbee, W. T.,
1827..Wyles, David F.,
Williams, George W.,
Williams, Thomas,
Wallace, B. A.,
1828..Wethers, Thomas J.,
Woodward, Thomas B.,
Woodward, J. A.,
Watkins, John D., of Georgia,
1829..Wright, T. J.,
1830..Wigfall, A. Thomson,
Williams, G. W.,
1831..Woodward, John J.,
Whitmore, Joshua,
1833..Wimbisk, John W.,

Names.
1834..Walker, J. Murdoch,
Witherspoon, George M. C.,
Williams, John,
1835..Watson, John,
1837..Whaley, William,
1838..Wright, John D.,
1839..Wigfall, Lewis Trezevant,
1840..Wallace, James M.,
1841..Wright, R. S.,
Wilson, James J.,
1842..Walker, William A.,
1843..Williams, O. P.,
Wilkinson, Daniel J.,
Williams, James F.,
1844..Wilson, John S.,
1845..Whilden, Charles E.,
Wording, W. E.,
Whaley, T. Baynard,
Williams, Charles H.,
Wilkes, Samuel M.,
Wilson, R. W., Charleston Dist.
Wiseman, W. C.,
1846..Wilson, M. H., Abbeville,
Wallace, William,
1847..Wilson, W. L., Charleston,
Workman, John J.,
Workman, W. H. R.,
Waller, P. M.,
1848..Wilson, W. B., York,
Wilson, Laurens E., Williamsb'g.

Names.
1848..Williman, Jacob,
Wilson, J. F., Newberry,
1849..Wallace, Thomas S.,
1850..Williams, S. T. H.,
1851..West, C. S.,
1851..Waters, Henry W.,
1852..Warley, F. F.,
Walker, J. F.,
1853..Wolfe, M. Y.,
1854..Wickliffe, Isaac,
Williams, D. T.,
1855..Wallace, John W.,
1856..Walsh, J. T.,
Witherspoon, J. D., Jr.,
Whitner, J. H.,
Wright, Henry T.,
Wylie, John D.,
Waties, John,
Wolfe, C. W.,
Whitner, B. F.,
1858..Whitner, W. H.,
1859..Winsmith, J. C.

Y.

1815..Yancey, Charles C.,
1816..Young, Henry C.,
1822..Young, John S.,
1855..Young, Henry E.,
1858..Youngblood, E. H.

ERRATA. VOL. I.

PREFACE—Page 6, read *Powe* for Power; *J. R. Ervin* for J. D. Sims.

INTRODUCTION—Page x., 21st line, read *leges* for liges; xv., 30th line, *became the preceptor. In that year and the next, Young, O'Neall, &c.;* xvi., 7th line, *mother's* for father's; xvii., 164th line, *Bond's* for Bord's; xix., 2d line, *now* for and, *Regiment* for Regiments, 39th line, *G & C* for forty-fifth; xxiii., 7th line, read *direction* for devotion; xxiv., 1st line, read *Tilly* for Tilby; 11th line, read *often* for afterwards.

4, 7th line, read, *6th & 7th Wm.* iii.; 8th line, *Brev.* for Bryce.

40, 9th line, add *contributed to his unpopularity.*

53, 17th line, read 1783 for 33; page 56, 10th line, *Eifert* for Eifer.

81, 13th line, *fiats* for facts; 15th line, 1815 for 1818.

85, 18th line, read *forum* for former.

104, read *Theus* for Thurs.

129, 29th line, read 1815 for 1818.

133, 7th line, *Farmers* for Farms.

141, last line, read, *this was high praise.*

142, 13th line, read, *defended his position with much acuteness.*

185, 14th line, read *Ware* for Ward.

191, read *Gould & Reves* for Gov. Reves.

192, read *Ravenel* for Barnwell.

193, read *Billy Martin* for Betty Martin.

198, 1st line, read 1796 for 1776.

204, 21st line, read, *on such an occasion,* for, in such a state.

276, in Note, read *Union* for Marion.

290, read *Player* for phyer.

308, Note, last line, *reversed* for received.

325, Note, read *Durant* for Surant.

327, 20th line, read *O'Neall* for Wall.

352, read *Loring* for Loung.

430, 11th line, read *deceived* for decided.

ERRATA. VOL. II.

12, Note, 4th line, read *Col. Starling Tucker;* read *Major Word* for Wood; read *David M.* for David R.

38, 14th line, read *argued* for arrayed.

65, 30th line, read *huffed* for puffed, &c.

66, 30th line, read *ridge* for bridge.

71, 14th line, read *Key* for King; 18th line, *properly* for probably; 36th line, and in other places, *Toules* for Joub.

72, last line, read, *he prepared it and made the argument.*

79, 8th line, read *should be* for shined.

84, 11th line, read 1842 for 1841.

85, 25th and 26th lines, 1836 for 1834 and 1835.

99, 8th line, read *Kerr* for Thee.

100, 8th line, read *statutes* for statistics.

101, 17th line, read *Thomas N.* for Thomas M.; 31st line, read *Sheriff* for Shiff.

102, 31st line, read *on* for over.

132, 6th line, read *covered* for carried.

136, 15th line, read *inferior* for superior.

146, 27th line, read *Cherokees* for children.

147, 5th line, read *tone* for rage.

156, 14th line, read *Kelly* for Holly.

157, 6th line, " " 16th line, *Lauders* for Saunders.

161, 26th line, read $30,000 for $70,000.

176, 17th line, read *McKees* for McThees.

227, 32d line, read *when* for where.

233, 6th line, read *Gavin* for Garvin.

234, 18th line, read *Fley* for Hay.

236, 10th line, read 1794 for 1796.

237, 10th line, read 1800 for 1802; 31st line, read *Minton* for Clinton; 33d line, read *Fley* for Key.

239, 28th line, read *Davie* for Davies; 31st line, *Lansford* for Lunsford.

246, 27th line, read *unbidden* for unhidden.

248, 4th line, 1807 for 1806.

252, 25th line, read *complimented* for complicated.

263, 15th line, read *Kerr* for Thee; 19th line, *Beillar* for Baille; 22d line, *Kenner* for Thomas.

267, 28th line, read *Viginti aunorum* for argente armorum.

280, 11th line, read *Governors* for Generals of Brigade.

324, 13th line, read *Quantum meruit* for quantun non suit; 14th line, *assertion* for association.

325, 22d line, read *law* for hard; 25th line, *Reeves* for Marris.

327, 7th line, add *at.*

329, 10th line, read *Stirpes* for Shipis; insert—*as he,* after rag money.

343, 14th line, read *three* for two; and after James, add—*and another;* 19th line, 63 for 53.

344, 6th line, *Fley & Rochelle* for Henry Rochelle.

346, 35th line, $30,000 for $50,000.

347, 2d line, read *Harris* for Horris.

394, 26th line, read *noscitur sociis.*

432, 17th line, read *Treasurer* for Treasure.

463, 15th line, read 1813 for that year.

504, read *John Wills Simpson* for John Witherspoon.